ILLUSTRATED WORLD ATLAS

The World
Table of Contents

The world – physical and political maps 8

The World
Map locator

Europe

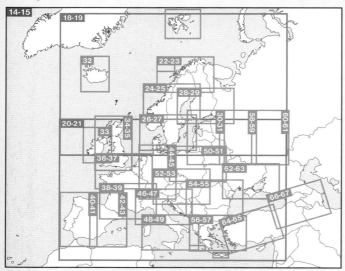

Asia

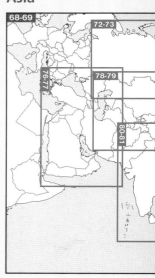

Africa

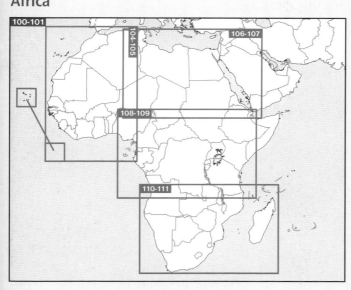

North America

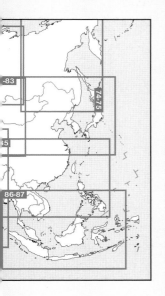

Australia/Oceania

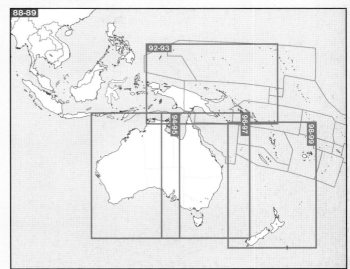

88-89
92-93
94-95
96-97
98-99

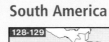

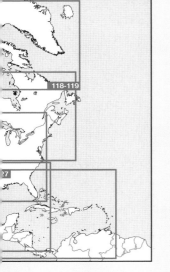

-83
74-75
45
86-87

118-119

27

South America

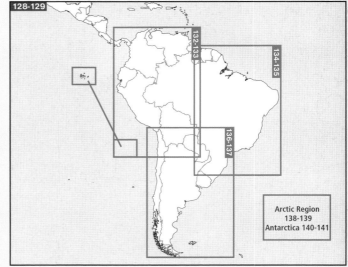

128-129
132-133
134-135
136-137

Arctic Region
138-139
Antarctica 140-141

The World
Legend

Bodies of water

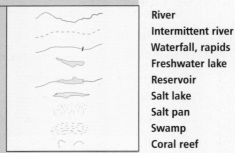

River
Intermittent river
Waterfall, rapids
Freshwater lake
Reservoir
Salt lake
Salt pan
Swamp
Coral reef

Topography

Mountains
Region/area
Glacier
Mountain height
Depression

Political and other boundaries

International boundary
National capital
Disputed international boundary
Administrative boundary
Administrative capital
National park

Special symbols

International Airport
National Airport
Elevation above/below sea level
Wall
Motorway
Primary highway
Railway
Ferry
Archeological site
Tourist attraction

Type faces

INDIAN OCEAN	Ocean
Gulf of Mexico	Gulf, bay
Java Trench	Undersea landscapes, trenches
Lake Superior Nile	Lake, river
Great Plains	Region/area
ANDES	Mountains
Acongagua	Mountain
North Cape	Cape
Greter Antilles Mauritius	Islands, Island
BRAZIL	Sovereign state
North Dakota	State/province

Classification of cities and towns

□ DALIAN	Town over 1 million inhabitants
○ Colorado Springs	Town 100,000 - 1 million inhabitants
○ Dodge City	Town 10,000 - 100,000 inhabitants
○ Brady	Town under 10,000 inhabitants
• Georg von Neumayer (D)	Research station

Place locator

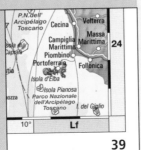

Search for the name of the sought after area/city in the alphabetically arranged map index. The place names are followed by the page numbers of relevant maps as well as a number-letter combination indicating the area's location in the map. Letters indicate the east-west position and numbers the north-south position of an area.

Example:
Follonica 39 Lf 24
Page 39
Map section Lf 24

The Earth, the so-called blue planet, is the third planet from the sun and the fifth largest planet in the solar system. Formed from a cloud of dust and gas around 4.5 billion years ago, the Earth travels in an elliptical orbit at distances between 147 to 152 million kilometers away from the sun.

The Earth is not a perfect sphere; the area around the poles being relatively flat. The polar diameter of the Earth measures 12,714 kilometers, about 42 kilometers less than the equatorial diameter of the planet. The maximum circumference of the Earth measures 40,075 kilometers. Our planet has a total area of 510 million square kilometers; 71% of the Earth's surface is wcovered by bodies of water and 29% by land.

The world
Physical map

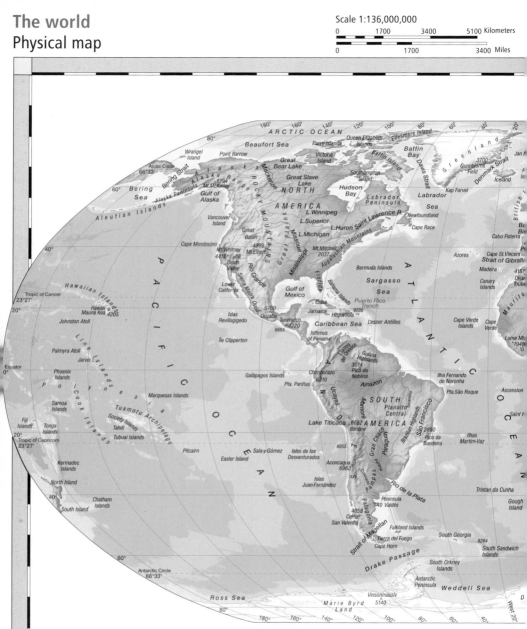

ARCTIC OCEAN

Beaufort Sea

Queen Elizabeth Islands   Ellesmere Island

Wrangel Island   Point Barrow

Baffin Bay

Greenland

Jan M

Victoria Island

Baffin Island

Gunnbjorns Field

Denmark Strait

Great Bear Lake

Arctic Circle 66°33'

Bering Strait

Southampton Island

Davis Strait

Iceland

Bering Sea

Alaska Peninsula   6194 Mt McKinley

Gulf of Alaska

Great Slave Lake

NORTH

Hudson Bay

Labrador Peninsula

Kap Farvel

British

Aleutian Islands

Vancouver Island

AMERICA

L.Winnipeg

L.Superior

L.Huron Saint Lawrence R.

Labrador Sea   Newfoundland

Be Bis

Cape Race

Cabo Fisterra

PACIFIC

Great Basin

L.Michigan

Appalachian Mountains

Azores

Cape St.Vincent

Strait of Gibralta

Cape Mendocino

Mt.Whitney 4418   86   Mt Elbert 4399

Death Valley

Rio Grande

Mt.Mitchell 2037

Madeira   4167

Canary Islands   Dahou

Hawaiian Islands

Tropic of Cancer 23°27'

20°

Lower California

Sierra Madre

Florida

Bermuda Islands

ATLANTIC

Sargasso Sea

Mauritia

Hawaii Mauna Kea 4205

Gulf of Mexico

Bahama Islands

Loma Mt 1948

Johnston Atoll

Islas Revillagigedo

5700 Orizaba

Cuba

Puerto Rico Trench 9220

Cape Verde Islands

Cape Verde

Palmyra Atoll

Jarvis

Île Clipperton

Tajumulco 4220   6883

Jamaica   Hispaniola

Caribbean Sea   Lesser Antilles

Equator 0°

Phoenix Islands

Galápagos Islands

Isthmus of Panama

Llanos del Orinoco

Guiana Highlands

3014

Ilha Fernando de Noronha

Ascension

Samoa Islands

Pta. Pariñas

Chimborazo 6310

Pico da Neblina

Amazon

Pta.São Roque

Saint P

Marquesas Islands

Tuamotu Archipelago

Tahiti

SOUTH   Planalto Central

Brazilian Highlands

São Francisco

Fiji Islands

Tonga Islands

Society Islands

Lake Titicaca 6882   AMERICA

Ilimani

2890 Pico da Bandeira

Ilhas Martim-Vaz

Tropic of Capricorn 23°27'

Tubuai Islands

Gran Chaco

Paraguai

Kermadec Islands

North Island

Pitcairn

Easter Island

Sala-y-Gómez

Islas de los Desventurados

8055

Aconcagua 6963

Pampas

Rio de la Plata

Chatham Islands

South Island

Islas Juan-Fernández

4058 Cerro San Valentin

Patagonia

Península 40 Valdés

Falkland Islands

Tristan da Cunha

Gough Island

South Georgia

Tierra del Fuego   Cape Horn

8264

South Sandwich Islands

Antarctic Circle 66°33'

Drake Passage

South Orkney Islands

Antarctic Peninsula   Weddell Sea

Ross Sea

Márie Byrd Land

Vinsonmassiv 5140

West 20°

D

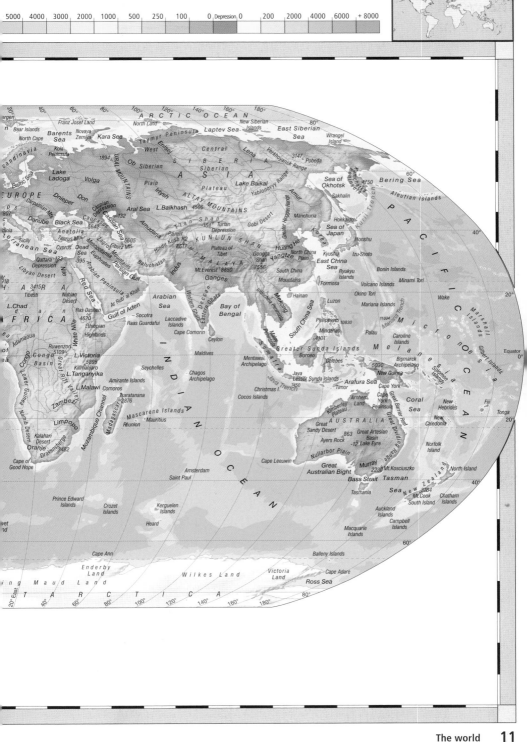

The world
Political map

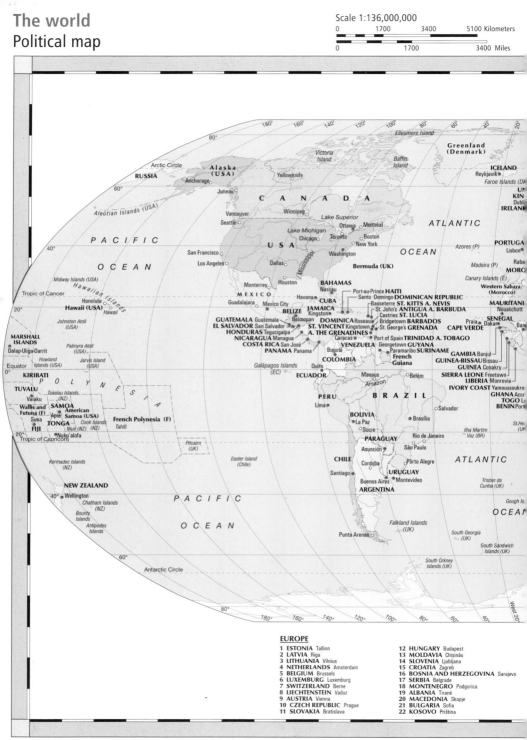

EUROPE

1 **ESTONIA** Tallinn
2 **LATVIA** Riga
3 **LITHUANIA** Vilnius
4 **NETHERLANDS** Amsterdam
5 **BELGIUM** Brussels
6 **LUXEMBURG** Luxemburg
7 **SWITZERLAND** Berne
8 **LIECHTENSTEIN** Vaduz
9 **AUSTRIA** Vienna
10 **CZECH REPUBLIC** Prague
11 **SLOVAKIA** Bratislava

12 **HUNGARY** Budapest
13 **MOLDAVIA** Chișinău
14 **SLOVENIA** Ljubljana
15 **CROATIA** Zagreb
16 **BOSNIA AND HERZEGOVINA** Sarajevo
17 **SERBIA** Belgrade
18 **MONTENEGRO** Podgorica
19 **ALBANIA** Tiranë
20 **MACEDONIA** Skopje
21 **BULGARIA** Sofia
22 **KOSOVO** Priština

AFRICA
1 BURKINA FASO Ouagadougou
2 EQUATORIAL GUINEA Malabo
3 SÃO TOMÉ AND PRINCIPE São Tomé
4 RWANDA Kigali
5 BURUNDI Bujumbura

ASIA
1 AZERBAIJAN Baku
2 ARMENIA Yerevan
3 LEBANON Beirut
4 ISRAEL Jerusalem
5 KUWAIT Kuwait
6 BAHRAIN Manama
7 QATAR Doha

Europe
Physical map

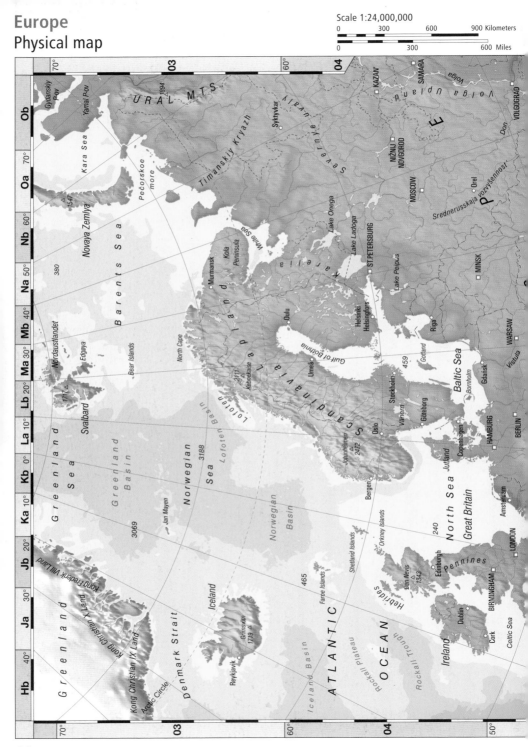

5000 4000 3000 2000 1000 500 250 100 0 Depression 0 200 2000 4000 6000 + 8000

o.El'brus
5642
CAUCASUS
Crimea
Trabzon
Pontic Mountains
Black Sea
2180
Anatolia
Tuz Gölü
ANKARA
Taurus Mts.
3524
Cyprus
ADANA
ALEPPO
DAMASCUS
2427
BEIRUT
AMMAN
Jerusalem
Port Said
El Aqaba
Sinai
2285
CAIRO
1207
Eastern Desert
Nile
Luxor
Aswân
Western Desert
Lake Nasser
ALEXANDRIA
134 Depression
Qattara Depression
A
A
Nubia
1893
Djebel Al 'Awaynat
ODESSA
Carpathian Mts.
2100
Transylvanian Alps
2544
BUCHAREST
Balkan Mts.
Danube
SOFIA
Rhodope Mts.
Varna
ISTANBUL
İZMIR
Aegean
Sea
Crete
2456
Levantine
Basin
Great Sand Sea
Libyan Desert
El Kufrah
Oasis
Erdi
A
P
L
O
I
D
I
Dinaric Alps
Dalmatia
BELGRADE
Zagreb
Tiranë
ATHENS
Peloponnesus
5054
MEDITERRANEAN SEA
Tubruq
Benghazi
882
Cyrenaica
Tripolitania
C
Ramlat Rabyanah
Sahir Tibesti
R
Tibesti
VIENNA
BUDAPEST
Olymp
2917
Phindos Mts.
Ionian
Sea
Gulf of Sirte
Sahra Surt
Al Jufra
Oasis
I
3376
A
3415 Tarso Emissi
MUNICH
A
L
P
S
3797
Mt Blanc
4807
Berne
Po
MILAN
2622
2914
Vesuvio 1281
NAPLES
ROME
Etna
3323
Palermo
Sicily
Ile de Jerba
Sfax
TRIPOLI
Tyrrhenian
Sea
1965
Awbari Sahra
Fezzan
H
A
Ténéré du
Tafassasset
Pic Toussidé
3376
Lb
E
Burgundy
Berne
Lyon
Rhône
Provence
Marseille
Corsica
2622
Sardinia
2784
Apennines
334
TUNIS
Constantine
2206
A
F
R
Tassili n'Ajjer
2158
Adrar
Tahat
2918
Tassili du Hoggar
Loire
Bordeaux
Massif
1895
Central
BARCELONA
Palma d.M.
Balearic Is.
ALGIERS
Oran
Great Eastern Erg
Hamada de Tinrhert
A
H
O
G
G
A
R
Bay of
Biscay
La Coruña
Cabo
Fisterra
Gijón
Pyrénées
3404
Pico d'Aneto
Valéncia
Ebro
Sistema Ibérico
Atlas Tellien
Atlas Saharien
Great Western Erg
El Ménia
Plateau du Tademaït
Asedjrad
Ahnet
Tropic of Cancer
Porto
MADRID
Cantabria Mountains
Cordillera Central
Sierra Morena
Sevilla
Cordillera Bética
Granada 3481
Tagus
Béchar
Hamada du Drâa
A
T
L
A
S
M
T
S
Djebel Timétrine
Tanezrouft
LISBON
Cabo de
São Vicente
Tangier
RABAT
Fâs
AR-RIF
Kb

Europe 15

Europe
Political map

Scale 1:24,000,000

0 300 600 900 Kilometers

0 300 600 Miles

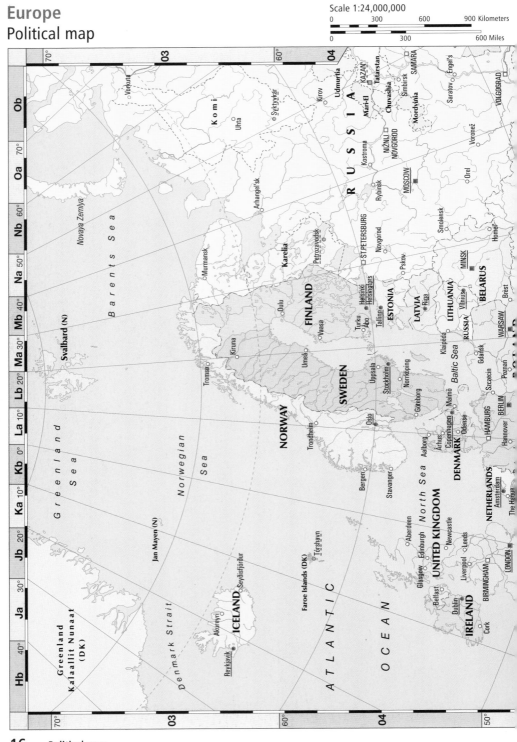

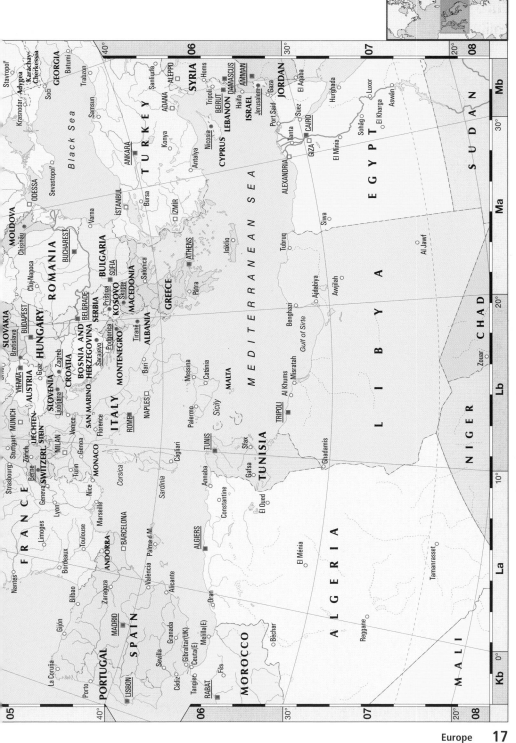

Scale 1:16,000,000

| 0 | 200 | 400 | 600 Kilometers |

| 0 | 200 | 400 Miles |

05

Denmark Strait

Icelandic

Plateau

Jan Mayen 2277
Jan Mayen (N)

Norwegian Sea

36 Hamm

65°

Hornbjarg
Ísafjörður
Breiða
fjörður
Ólafsvik
Keflavik
Hafnarfjörður
Reykjavik

Saudárkrókur
Rifstangi
Raufarhöfn
Fontur

Akureyri
Iceland
Grímsvötn
1719
Seyðisfjörður

1344

3188

2639

Tromsø

Vesterålen Harstad

2111
Kebnekaise Kiru

Narvik

Norwegian

1555

Lofoten
Vestfjorden Bodø

06

Vik Höfn

ICELAND

Iceland
Faeroe Rise

465 Faroe Islands

Faroe Islands (DK)

Tórshavn

Basin

3970

Vøring Plateau

123

Mo i Rana

96 Namsos

Storuman

S W E D E N

60°

ATLANTIC

2089

Iceland Basin

1170

90

Shetland Islands (UK)

1540

Trondheimsfj.

Trondheim

Snøhetta
2286

Røros

Steinkjer

Sylarna
1768

Umeå

Östersund

Härnösand

Sundsvall

Hudiksvall

Gulf of B

07

O C E A N

Rockall

531 St.Kilda

Hebrides

Stornoway

Lewis

Skye

Thurso

Orkney Islands (UK)

Kirkwall

Duncansby Head

Lerwick

294

Bergen

Ålesund

Dombås

Jotunheimen
2472 Lillehammer

NORWAY

Oslo

Haugesund

Drammen

Falun Gävle

Borlänge

Svealand

Västerås Uppsala

Örebro

809

55°

Rockall Trough

33

Islay

Moray Firth

Inverness
Ben Nevis
1343

Grampian Mts.

Perth

75

Kinnaird's Head

Aberdeen

Stavanger

Boknafjorden

Otra

Skien

Kristiansand

81

Göteborg

Frederikshavn

Skagen

Skagerrak

44

Fredrikstad

Karlstad

Linköping

Norrköping

Jönköping

Borås

Visby

Stockh
Södertälje
459

Gotlan

V

08

Londonderry

**IRELAND
ÉIRE**

Sligo

Galway

Galway Bay

Ireland

Limerick

Tralee

1041

Cork
Corcaigh

Belfast

Newry

Dundalk

**Dublin/
Baile Átha
Cliath**

Waterford

Rosslare

Fishguard

Man

Douglas

Irish Sea

Stranraer

Glasgow

Edinburgh

Dunfermline

Carlisle

240

Newcastle u.Tyne

Middlesbrough

Blackpool
Liverpool Leeds

Manchester
Sheffield

91

**United
Kingdom**

Great Britain

Kingston u.Hull

North

36

Jylland Århus

Götaland

Växjö

Helsingborg

Skagen

Ålborg

Kattegat

Esbjerg

DENMARK

Kalmar
Öland
9

Karlskrona

Malmö

Balt

Sea

Kl

Kalin

50°

Galway

Barnstaple

BIRMINGHAM
Swansea

Cardiff

IRELAND

Sligo

Cork

Nottingham

Leicester

Cambridge

NETHERLANDS

Ipswich

Groningen

Emmen

Osnabrück

Bielefeld

German
Bight

Cuxhaven

Flensburg

Kiel

Lübeck

HAMBURG

Bremen

Hannover

Magdeburg

BERLIN

Schwerin

Rostock

Stralsund

Rügen

50

Sassnitz

Koszalin

Szczecin

Słupsk

Gdynia

Gdańsk

Bydgoszcz

O

Bristol

Oxford

Celtic Sea

115

Devon

Cardiff

73

185

Land's End
Isles of Scilly

Brighton

Poole

Southampton

LONDON

Calais

Dover

Antwerpen

Rotterdam

The Hague

Utrecht

Düsseldorf

Bonn

COLOGNE

Dortmund

Erfurt

Leipzig

Cottbus

Dresden

Chemnitz Liberec

GERMANY

PRAGUE

Plzeň

Poznań

POLAN

Kalisz

Legnica Łódź

Wrocław

Częstochowa

Opole Ka

POL

09

English Channel

Plymouth

Channel Islands
(UK)

Cherbourg

Le Havre

Brest

Pointe du Raz

Quimper

Lannion

Dinan

Caen

Brittany

Belle-Île

St.Nazaire

163

Nantes

5294

Brighton

BRUSSELS

BELGIUM

Luxembourg
LUX.

Amiens

Rouen

Laon

Reims

Metz

Nancy

Mainz

Frankfurt a.M.

Mannheim

Nürnberg

Würzburg

Saarbrücken

Karlsruhe

Stuttgart

Augs-
burg

Fulda

CZECH REP.

Olomouc

Brno

Linz

Vienna

SLO

45°

St.Malo

Rennes

Versailles

PARIS

Troyes

Angers

Le Mans

Loire

Tours

Bourges

Orléans

F R A N C E

Niort

Poitiers

la Rochelle

Autun

Dijon

Besançon

Freiburg

Basle

Zürich

Mulhouse

Strasbourg

Ulm

Kempten

Innsbruck

Salzburg

MUNICH

Passau

Regensburg

St.Pölten

AUSTRIA

BUDAPES

Scale 1:16,000,000

0	200	400	600 Kilometers

0	200	400 Miles

Ka 20° **Kb** 15° **Kc** 5° **Kd** 0° **La** 5° **Lb** 10° **Lc**

Rockall Trough

07

155

Aberdeen
Skagerrak Göteborg Borås
Skagen Jönköping
33 1343 Grampian Mts. Frederikshavn Göt. Väx
Islay Perth Dundee 81 Ålborg Kattegat
Londonderry Glasgow Dunfermline 240 Helsingborg
IRELAND Sligo Belfast Edinburgh **UNITED** North Jylland Århus Copenhagen Malm
ÉIRE Stranraer **KINGDOM** **DENMARK**
Galway Dundalk Newry Carlisle Newcastle u.Tyne Sea Esbjerg 36 Odense Køge Rügen
Galway Bay Dublin Man Douglas Middlesbrough Great Britain Flensburg Kiel Stralsund
Ireland Baile Átha Great Britain Kingston u.Hull German Cuxhaven Lübeck Rostock
5023 Tralee Cliath Blackpool Leeds 91 Bight **HAMBURG** Schwerin Szcze
1041 Waterford Liverpool Sheffield Groningen Bremen **BERLIN**
55° Cork Rosslare Manchester Nottingham **NETHERLANDS** Emmen Osnabrück Hannover
Corcaigh Fishguard **BIRMINGHAM** Leicester Amsterdam Bielefeld Magdeburg Cott
115 Swansea Cambridge Utrecht Münster Dortmund **GERMANY** Leipzig
Celtic Sea Cardiff Oxford Ipswich The Hague Brugge **COLOGNE** Fulda Erfurt Dresde
Barnstaple Southampton **LONDON** Rotterdam **BRUSSELS** Bonn Frankfurt a.M. **PRAGUE**
73 Land's End Devon Poole Dover Antwerpen **BELGIUM** Mainz Würzburg Plze
08 4861 Isles of Scilly Plymouth Brighton Calais Düsseldorf Luxembourg Mannheim Nürnberg Regensburg
185 Channel Islands Cherbourg Le Havre Amiens Laon **LUX.** Saarbrücken Karlsruhe Augs- Passau
(UK) Lannion Caen Rouen Reims Metz Nancy Stuttgart burg **MUNICH** Salzb
Brest Dinan Normandie Versailles **PARIS** Troyes Strasbourg Ulm **AUST**
Pointe du Raz Quimper Rennes Le Mans Orléans Mulhouse Freiburg Kempten Groß- 3797
50° Belle-île St.Nazaire Angers Tours Bourges Dijon Besançon Basle Zürich Innsbruck glockner Villa
2499 163 Nantes Loire **FRANCE** Autun Lausanne Berne **SWITZERL.** Bozen **SLOVE**
5294 Niort Poitiers Clermont- Vichy Geneva Mt.Blanc Mte.Rosa Bellinzona Trento Udine Ljubljan
Pta.da Estaca la Rochelle Ferrand 4634 4807 Brescia Padova
de Bares Royan Limoges **MASSIF** Lyon Varese **MILAN** Verona Venice Rijek
560 La Coruña Avilés Gijón Périgueux **CENTRAL** Grenoble Novara Turin Parma Ferrara Po
Cabo Finisterre Santiago Oviedo Bordeaux Agen Montauban Valence Rhône Genoa Bologna Ravenna
09 Vigo Lugo León Cantabria Mountains Biarritz Toulouse Nîmes Avignon La Spezia Livorno **SAN MARIN**
Porto Braga Bilbao S.Sebastián Pau Carcassonne Aix-en-Prov. Provence Nice Florence San Marino
Vila Nova Bragança Burgos Pamplona **PYRÉNÉES** Narbonne Golfe Marseille Toulon **MC** Siena Perugia Gran Sasso
de Gaia Zamora Valladolid Logroño 3404 Andorra la Vella du Lion Monte Bastia Grosseto Terni d'Italia 291
45° **PORTUGAL** Salamanca Zaragoza **ANDORRA** Perpignan 3070 Carlo Corsica (F) 2622 Tivoli Pes
Caldas Coimbra Plasencia Lleida Manresa Girona Calvi Ajaccio Gran Sass
da Reinha Abrantes **MADRID** Guadalajara Sabadell 902 **ROME**
Peniche Cáceres Getafe **BARCELONA** Tarragona Bonifacio **ITALY**
LISBON Trujillo Toledo Cuenca Teruel Sassari Olbia **NAPLES**
Barreiro **SPAIN** Castelló 2132 Nuoro Vesuv. Sale
10 Évora Badajoz Mérida Submeseta Sur de la Plana Mallorca Oristano Arbatax 3623
Algarve Beja Zafra Ciudad Real Albacete **València** Menorca 1834 Sardinia Tyrrhenian Sea
Sines Lagos Huelva Córdoba Alcoi Eivissa Palma de Cagliari
Cabo de Jaén Linares Murcia (Ibiza) **Mallorca** Capo Palermo Mes
São Vicente Jerez de Sevilla Granada Lorca Eivissa 281 Teulada Trapani **Sicily**
Cádiz la Fra. Málaga Sierra Nevada Elx Formentera Balearic 2784 Agrigento Gela
Algeciras 3481 Alacant Islands **MALT**
40° Tangier Gibraltar(UK) Almería Cabo de Gata Cap La Galite Bizerte **TUNIS** Valletta
El-Araïch Ceuta (E) 2814 Bougaroun Isola di
RABAT Tétouan 2407 Ténès **ALGIERS** 2305 Bejaïa Annaba Pantelleria
Melilla (E) Oran Mostaganem Chlef Bilda Skikda Hammamet
CASA Kénitra Al-Hoceima **RIF** Tiaret Constantine Jendouba Golfe de
BLANCA Meknés Fès Taza Oujda Tlemcen Bou Saâda Sétif Souk Ahras El Kef Hammamet
Khouribga **ATLAS** Azrou Chott Sidi Batna Kairouan Sousse
11 **MOROCCO** Mechería Chergui Djelfa Biskra Tebessa Kasserine **TUNISIA**
Ain Sefra El Bayadh Chott Laghouat Gafsa Sfax
Tendrara Melrhir Golfe de Gabès
ATLAS Ar-Rachidia Chott El Jerid Gabès Île de Jerba
Ouarzazate Bèchar Figuig **ALGERIA** El Oued 178
Touggourt Medenine
Ghardaïa

Kc 5° **Kd** 0° **La** 5° **Lb** 10° **Lc**

Northern Scandinavia, Svalbard
Europe

Scale 1:4,000,000

0 — 50 — 100 — 150 Kilometers

0 — 50 — 100 Miles

Svalbard inset

Scale 1:8,000,000

ARCTIC OCEAN

Sjuøyane

Kvitøya

1248

Lågøya 690

Storøya

Nordøst-Svalbard naturreservat

Nordvest-Spitsbergen nasjonalpark

607

Nordøst-Svalbard

Nordaustlandet naturreservat

Hinlopenstretet

1130

Oksindane 1368

Ny Ålesund

Newtontoppen 1717

Spitsbergen

Olgastretet

Erik Eriksenstretet

Kongsøya

Svenskøya

Kong Karls Land

Nordøst-Svalbard naturreservat

Prins Karls Forland

Forlandet nasjonalpark

Barentsburg

Longyearbyen

Gustavfjellet 1235

Haasteberget 665

Barentsøya

Sørøst-Svalbard

Svalbard (Norway)

Bellsund

Barentsburg

1205

Kvalpynten 395

Edgeøya naturreservat

Sør-Spitsbergen nasjonalpark

Horrsundtind 1430

Storfjorden

155

B a r e n t s S e a

Øyrlandsodden

Hopen 103

86

10

Le 14° Lf 18° Lg 22° Lh 26° Lj 30° Lk

16° Lj 18° Lk 20°

05

80°

06

78°

07

Le Lf Lg Lh

Nord-Kvaløy Vanna Vannareid Arnøy Skjervøy

Ringvassøy Skulgam Lyngen

Kvaløya Tromsø Svensby Lyngseidet Skibotn

Vikran

L o f o t e n   B a s i n

Grylleford Senja Finnsnes Nordkjosbotn

Andenes Anderdalen n.p.

V e s t e r å l e n

Andøya Andfjorden Andfjord-landet Stonglandet Sjøvegan Øvergård

Myre Harstad Hamvik Hinnøya Grov Innset Setermoen

Langøya Sortland Bogen Bjerkvik Øvre-Divial nasjonalpark

3070

Steine Hadseløya Stokmarknes

Austvågøya

Vestvågøy Svolvær Lødingen Ulvsvåg Skarberget Narvik Abisko Tornetrask Tornet Abisko n.p.

Leknes Kabelvåg Ballangen

Ballstad Henningsvær Stamsund Skarberget Kebnekaise 2111 Jukkas

Moskenesøya

Sørvågen Åstad

L o f o t e n

68°

Værøy Nordfold Mørsvik Sitas-jaure Nikkaluokta Kiruna Ritsem Akka-jaure Stora Sjöfallets nationalpark Sjaunja naturresse

Røst Folda Rago n.p. Padjelanta nationalpark Sarektjakka Vietas L a p o n i a P

Rosvik Virihaure 2089 Sareks nationalpark

V e s t f j o r d e n

Løding Stalolukta

N o r w e g i a n

Bodø Fauske Sulitjelma 1914 Kvikkjokk Porjus

125 Innøy Vesterli

Ørnes Sulitjelma Storjord Jåkkvik A S W E D

Storjorda Saltfjellet-Svartisen nasjonalpark Stødi Hornavan Jokkmokk

Arctic Circle Vågaholmen 1594 Meltjelden

N O R W A Y

S e a

Pieljekaise nationalpark Kåbdalis

Storkvågen Mo i Rana Jåkkvik Hornavan

Tomma Hemnesberget Hemavan Uddjaure Arjeplog

Nesna 1915 Ammarnäs

66°

Dønna Korgen Bjelkvassli

Sandnessjøen Hemavan Tärnaby Storavan Arvidsjaur

Tjøtta Mosjøen Hemavan Västansjö

Forvika/Vevelstad Rossvatnet Sorsele

Gladstad Hattfjelldal Slussfors Glommersträsk

Vega Trofors

Brønnøysund Tosbotn 1703

Le 10° Lf 12° Lg 14° Lh 16° Lj 18° Lk 20°

11

12

13

2° **Mb** 24° **Mc** 26° **Md** 28° **Me** 30° **Mf** 32° **Mg** 34° **Mh**

191

260

10

North Cape

Mehamn

Berlevåg

Barents Sea

Havøysund
Honningsvåg
Kjøllefjord

Båtsfjord

Kåfjord
Hopseidet

Vardø

70°

Hammerfest
Olderfjord

Rusterfjelbma

*Varanger-
halvøya*

Kvalsund

Ifjord

Varangerbotn
Vadsø

*Varanger-
fjord*

Børselv

Tana bru

p-ov
Rybačij

Alta

Stabbursdalen
nasjonalpark

Polmak

Liinahamari

kbotn

Lekselv

Lævvajokgiedde

Kirkenes

sfjord

11

Sørstraumen

Utsjoki

Severomorsk

Karasjok
Karigasniemi

Sevettijärvi

Zapoljarnyj

Kola

F i n n m a r k s -

Nikel'

Murmansk

Reisa
nasjonalpark

Lappoluobbal

Kaamanen

Nyrud

Murmaši

v i d d a

119
Inarijärvi

Nautsi

irvi

Kautokeino

Inari

*Verhnetulomskoe
vdhr*

Verhnetulomskij

Øvre Anarjohka
nasjonalpark

Menešjärvi

Ivalo

68°

Kaaresuvanto
Kárasavvon

*Lemmenjoen
k.puisto*

Raja-
Jooseppi

Olenegorsk

Enontekiö
Enokodak

*Urho Kekkosen
k.puisto*

Moncegorsk

Karesuando

Palojoensuu

Pokka

Tankavaara

R U S S I A

Apatity

Soppero

*Pallas-
Ounastunturi
k.puisto*

Porttipahdan
tekojärvi

*Lokan
tekojärvi*

Kovdor
Ena

oz. Imandra

Muonio

D

Muodoslompolo

N

Kittilä

Sodankylä

Martti

Kandalakša

12

avaara

Torneälven

A

Kolari

Pelkosenniemi

Kelloselkä

Alakurtti

*Kovd
ozero*

Masugnsbyn

Unari

Ruokojärvi

Pajala

Kemijärvi

berget

Ullatti

F I N L A N D

Hautajärvi

*Oulangan
k.puisto*

*Paanajärvi
N.P.*

66°

vare
dus
onalpark

Pello

Raanujärvi

Vikajärvi

Rovaniemi

Kemijärvi

Vanttauskoski

*Riisitunturin
k.puisto*

Yli-Kitka

Pjaozero

N

Övertorneå
Gyllen

Mellakoski
Koivu

Posio

Kuusamo

Kärpänkylä

Sofporog

Topozero

kollerim

Vuottas

Ylitornio

Överkalix

Kemijoki

el

Luleälven

Edefors

Morjärv

Karungi

Tervola

Ranua

*Syötteen
k.puisto*

Peranka

Vojnica

Kalevala

13

Boden

Töre

Haparanda

Tornio

Simo

Asmunti

Syötekylä

Gammelstaden

Kalix

Kemi

Kuivaniemi

Metsäkylä

Kipinä

vsbyn
Luleå

*Haparanda
skärgårds n.p.*

*Perämeren
k.puisto*
Perämeri

Antnäs

Suomussalmi

Kostomukša

gträsk

Piteå

Bottenviken

Hailuoto

Oulu

Puolanka

Ma 22° **Mb** 24° **Mc** 26° **Md** 28° **Me** 30° **Mf**

Scale 1:4,000,000

| 0 | 50 | 100 | 150 Kilometers |

| 0 | 50 | 100 Miles |

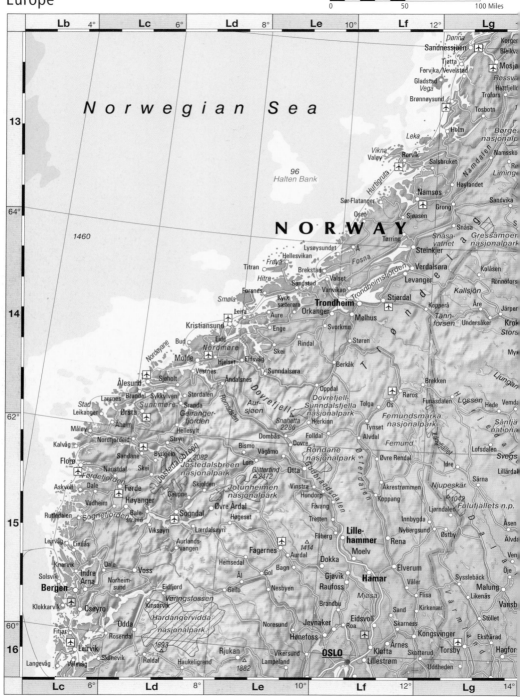

Norwegian Sea

96
Halten Bank

1460

NORWAY

Dønna
Sandnessjøen
Korgen
Bleikvasslia
Tjøtta
Førvika Vevelstad
Mosjøen
Gladstad
Vega
Brønnøysund
Rossvatnet
Hattfjelldal
Trofors
Tosbotn

Leka
Holm
Børgefjell
nasjonalpark
Namsskogan
Vikna
Valøy
Rørvik
Salsbruket
Re
Liminge

Sør-Flatanger
Namsos
Høylandet
Sandvika

Osen
Grong
Sjøasen

Snåsa
Snåsa-
vatnet
Gressåmoen
nasjonalpark

Lysøysundet
Å
Tørring
Steinkjer
Kolåsen

Hellesvikan
Fosna
Verdalsøra
Rønnöfors

Titran
Frøya
Brekstad
Valset
Levanger
Kallsjön

Hitra
Sandstad
Vanvikan
Stjørdal
Åre
Järpen

Smøla
Forsnes
Kyrk-
sæterøra
Trondheim
Kopperå
Tänn-
forsen
Undersåker
Krok
Stors

Leira
Aure
Orkanger
Melhus

Kristiansund
Enge
Svorkmo
Støren
My

Bud
Nordøyane
Eide
Rindal

Molde
Nordmøre
Hjelset
Eidsvåg
Skei
Berkåk
Brekken
Ljungan

Ålesund
Vestnes
Sunndalsøra
Oppdal
Røros
Funäsdalen
Lossen
Hede
Vemda

Sjøholt
Åndalsnes
Dovrefjell-
Sunndalsfjella
nasjonalpark
Tolga
Os
Femundsmarka
nasjonalpark
Säntjä
nationa

Larsnes
Brandal
Sykkylven
Stordalen
Stranda
Hjerkinn
Tynset
Femund
Lofsdalen

Stad
Leikanger
Ørsta
Åheim
Sunnmøre
Geiranger-
fjorden
Snøhetta
2286
Folldal
Alvdal
Svegs

Måløy
Hellesylt
Dombås
Dovre
Lillärdal

Kalvåg
Nordfjordeid
Stryn
Bismo
Vågåmo
Rondane
nasjonalpark
Øvre Rendal
Idre
Särna

Floro
Sandane
Byrkjelo
Jostedalsbreen
2082
Lom
Glittertind
2472
Otta
Njupeskär
1042
Fulufjällets n.p.

Askvoll
Naustdal
Skei
nasjonalpark
Skjolden
Jotunheimen
nasjonalpark
Vinstra
Hundorp
Fåvang
Åkrestrømmen
Koppang
Ljørndalen
Åsen

Dale
Førde
Høyanger
Gaupne
Øvre Årdal
Høgeset
Tretten
Innbygda
Nybergsund
Østby
Älvda

Rutledalen
Vadheim
Sognefjorden
Bale
strand
Sogndal
Fåberg
Lille-
hammer
Rena
Ven

Lærdalsøyri
Lillehammer
Moelv

Leirvåg
Cindås
Viksøyri
Aurlands-
vangen
Fagernes
1414
Aurdal
Dokka
Gjøvik
Elverum
Sysslebäck
Öje

Knarvik
Dale
Voss
Hemsedal
Bagn
Gol
Moelv
Raufoss
Hamar
Väler
Malung
Vansb

Solsvik
Indre
Arna
Norheim-
sund
Ål
Nesbyen
Brandbu
Sand
Flisa
Likenäs
Stöllet

Bergen
Eidfjord
Geilo
Hønefoss
Kirkenær
Vansb

Klokkarvik
Osøyro
Vøringsfossen
Noresund
Jevnaker
Roa
Eidsvoll
Skarnes
Kongsvinger
Ekshärad

Fitjar
Odda
Kinsarvik
Hardangervidda
nasjonalpark
Hønefoss
Arnes
Torsby
Hagfor

Leirvik
Rosendal
1693
Rjukan
Vikersund
Lampeland
OSLO
Kløfta
Skotterud
Uddheden

Langevåg
Valevåg
Skånevik
Røldal
Haukeligrend
1882
Lillestrøm

+ 5000 4000 3000 2000 1000 500 250 100 **0** Depression 0 200 2000 4000 6000 **+ 8000**

Arjeplog

Ammarnäs
Hemavan
Tärnaby
Uddjaure
Storavan
Vidsel
Storforsen
Boden
Kalix
Töre
Haparanda
Tornio
Simo
Kuivaniemi

stansjö
Slussfors
Sorsele
Arvidsjaur
Alvsbyn
Antnäs
Luleå
Gammelstaden
Haparànda
skärgårds n.p.
Perämeren
k.puisto
Perämeri
Kemi
Kittelfjäll
Långsjöby
Saxnäs
Storuman
Björksele
Malå
Jörn
Byske
Piteå
Bottenviken
Hailuoto
Hailuoto
Oulu
Kempele
13

S W E D E N
Lycksele
Bölen
Skellefteälven
Norsjö
Boliden
Åsträsk
Skellefteå
Skellefteshamn
Brahestad
Raahe
Vihanti
Risbäck
Vilhelmina
Vägsele
Lövånger
124
Oulainen
Ylivieska
Nivala
Norråker
Dorotea
Meselefors
Hällnäs
Burträsk
Kalajoki
64°
Tallsjö
Granö
Vindeln
Röbertsfors
Karleby
Kokkola
Toholampi
Hoting
Åsele
Bjurholm
Vännäs
Umeå
Jakobstad
Pietarsaari
Evijärvi
Strömsund
Solberg
Holmön
Ångesön
Holmsund
Fäboda
Lappajärvi
Kauhava
Kyyjärvi
Hammerdal
Häggenäs
Junsele
Hemling
Angermanland
Björna
Nordmaling
Sandön
Vaasa
Soini
14
Ramsele
Ramsjö
Forsmo
Sidensjö
Sollefteå
Bjästa
Husum
Örnsköldsvik
Dockst
Norram Kvarken
Merenkurkku
Lapua
Seinäjoki
Östersund
Brunflo
Pilgrimstad
Österforse
Skuleskogens
nationalpark
Korsnäs
F I N L A N D
Bispgården
Kramfors
Liden
Utansjö
294
Teuva
Kurikka
Alavus
Keuruu
Kälarne
Bräcke
Stavre
Ånge
Stöde
Alandsbro
Timrå
Härnösand
5
Kaskinen
Kauhajoki
Karvia
Virrat
Mänttä
Östaval
Sundsvall
Kristinestad
Kristiinankaupunki
Vilppula
62°
Ytterhogdal
Hennan
Hassela
Skottsund
Gnarp
Merikarvia
Kankaanpää
Parkano
Ljusdal
Delsbo
Dellen-
sjöarna
Jättendal
Hämeenkyrö
Ylöjärvi
Orivesi
Järvsö
Hudiksvall
12
Noormarkku
Lavia
Nokia
Tampere
Valkeakoski
Edsbyn
Vallsta
Enånger
Pori
Vammala
Huittinen
Viiala
Hämeenlinna
Skattungbyn
Furudal
Holmsveden
Söderhamn
Rauma
Eura
Humppila
15
 Orsa
ora
Bingsjö
Ockelbo
Nystadt
Uusikaupunki
Mynämäki
Loimaa
Forssa
Rättvik
Enviken
Somero
ksand
Bjursås
Falun
Sandviken
Skutskär
Åland/
Ahvenanmaa
Raisio
Nådendal
Naantali
Turku
Åbo
Salo
Lohja
Djuräs
Björbo
hammar
Borlänge
Hofors
Färnebo-
fjärdens n.p.
Tierp
Geta
Kumlinge
Pargas
Parainen
Karis
Karjaa
Smedje-
backen
Hedemora
Östhammar
Eckerö
Mariehamn
Maarianhamina
Dalsbruk
Hangö
Hanko
Erkenäs
Tammisaari
60°
idvika
ngesberget
Avesta
Sala
Heby
Bälinge
Uppland
Hallstavik
Alunda
Ålands hav
Ålands hav
Föglö
Kökar
Saaristomeren
kànsallispuisto
16
Fagersta
Uppsala

Southern Scandinavia, Denmark
Europe

NORWAY

Leirvik, Langevåg, Valevåg, Skånevik, Røldal, Haukeligrend, Rjukan, Vikersund, Kløfta, OSLO, Arnes, Skotterud, Torsby
Haugesund, Nedstrand, Sand, Amot, Sauland, Lampeland, Mjøndalen, Drammen, Siggerud, Lillestrøm, Uddheden
Åkrahamn, Kopervik, Dalen, Notodden, Kongsberg, Svelvik, Drøbak, Skjønhaug, Amotfors, Sunne, V.Åmtervik
Skudeneshavn, Tau, Hjelmeland, Kviteseid, Siljan, Horten, Oslo-fjorden, Moss, Rakkestad, Arvika, Fagerås
Stavanger, Jørpeland, Amot, Valle, Fyresdal, Ulefoss, Nissedal, Skien, Tønsberg, Sarpsborg, Årjäng, Valberg
Sandnes, Riska, Ålgård, Austad, Bygland, Drangedal, Porsgrunn, Sandefjord, Fredrikstad, Grums
Bryne, Helle-land, Åseral, Neslandsvatn, Larvik, Halden, Bengtsfors, Säffle
Sirevåg, Tonstad, Moi, Eiken, Evje, Åmli, Kragerø, Langesund, Strömstad, Ed, Amål
Egersund, Hauge, Flekkefjord, Liknes, Hægeland, Blakstad, Søndeled, Risør, Tanumshede, Bäckefors, Väner
Borhaug, Lyngdal, Moshy, Vennesla, Tvedestrand, Kungshamn, Uddevalla, Vänersborg, Mellerud, Göte
Lindesnes, Måndal, Grimstad, Arendal, Lysekil, Trollhättan, Vara, Färgelanda, Lidköpi
Kristiansand, Lillesand, Orust, Stenungsund, Fjord, Kungälv, Alingsås, Vårgårda, Falki
463, Skagen, Göteborg, Landvetter, Ulriceham
81, Hirtshals, Älbæk, Billdal, Kinna, Borås, Trane
Hjørring, Sindal, Frederikshavn, Kungsbacka, Svenljun
Brønderslev, Sæby, Frillesås, Läsø, Gislave
Hanstholm, Fjerritslev, Aabybro, Varberg, Ullared, Tvååker, Småla-sten
62, Thisted, Nibe, Aalborg, Aars, Hals, Falkenberg, Oskarström, Halmst
14, Hurup, Nykøbing M, Støvring, Anholt, Gullbrandstorp
Thyborøn, Lemvig, Skive, Hadsund, Hobro, Laholmsbukten, Laholm
NORTH, Holstebro, Viborg, Langå, Randers, Trustrup, Grenaa, Torekov, Båstad, Markar
Vemb, Herning, Silkeborg, Århus, Ebeltoft, Ängelholm, Örkelljur
Ringkøbing, Ikast, Brande, Skanderborg, Odden, Helsingør, Helsingbo
Ringkøbing Fjord, Skjern, DENMARK, Færgehavn, Frederiksværk, Nykøbing S, Landskror
Nørre Nebel, Varde, Grindsted, Vejle, Juelsminde, Kalundborg, (COPENHAGEN), Lund
SEA, Blåvands Huk, Kolding, Fredericia, Middelfart, KØBENHAVN, Malm
Esbjerg, Vejen, Odense, Slagelse, Roskilde, Køge, Svedala
Ribe, Vojens, Haderslev, Fünen, Nyborg, Ringsted, Fakse, Rødvig, Trelleb
Skærbæk, Toftlund, Aabenraa, Faaborg, Svendborg, Næstved, Vordingborg, Stege, Møns Klint
List, Westerland, Tønder, Bojden, Rudkøbing, Sakskøbing, Falster
North Frisian Islands, Sylt, Niebüll, Leck, Sønderborg, Nakskov, Lolland, Nykøbing F
German, Amrum, Föhr, Wyk, Flensburg, Kappeln, Rødbyhavn, N.P.Vorpommersche Boddenlandschaft
Bight, N.P. Schleswig-Holsteinisches Wattenmeer, Schleswig, Eckernförde, Puttgarden, Gedser, Rüge
St. Peter-Ording, Husum, Schleswig, Fehmarn, Warne-münde, Barth
Helgoland, Tönning, Rendsburg, Kiel, Plön, Oldenburg, Zingst, Darß, Ribnitz-Damgarten, Stral
54°, Büsum, Heide, Holstein, Neumünster, Bad Segeberg, Eutin, Travemünde, Rostock, Greifs
East Frisian Islands, Meldorf, Itzehoe, GERMANY, Wol
N.P. Niedersächsisches Wattenmeer, Cuxhaven, Brunsbüttel
Norderney

Telemark, Setesdal, Norskerenna, Skagerrak, Kattegat, Jutland, Sjælland, Limfjorden, Great Belt, Little Belt, Femern Bælt, The Sound

| 5000 | 4000 | 3000 | 2000 | 1000 | 500 | 250 | 100 | 0 | Depression 0 | 200 | 2000 | 4000 | 6000 | + 8000 |

Lh 16° **Lj** 18° **Lk** 20° **Ma** 22° **Mb**

Ludvika
Grängesberg
Smedje-backen
Fagersta
Sala
Avesta
Hallstavik
Heby
Bälinge
Alunda
Mariehamn
Maarianhamina
Saaristomeren
kansallispuisto
Hangö
Hanko
Kopparberg
Storvik
Skinnskatteberg
Knivsta
Rimbo
Norrtälje
Västerås
Enköping
Bålsta
Vallentuna
Täby
STOCKHOLM
Ahvenanmeri
Ålands hav
Foglö
Kökar

Kumlinge
Hällefors
Filipstad
Storfors
Nora
Lindesberg
Köping
Sträng-näs
Sollentuna
Österby
Katrineholm
Gnesta
Vingåker
Hjälmaren
Eskilstuna
Söder-
tälje
Mälaren
Västerhaninge
Ristna neem
Hiiumaa
Käina
Vormsi

Karls-
koga
Örebro
Arboga
Frövi
Kungsör
Nykvarn
Ösmo
Nynäshamn

ESTONIA
Orissaare

EDEN
Hova
Askersund
Bettna
Trosa
Nyköping
Landsortsdjupet
459
Undva neem
Vilsandi
rahvuspark
Saaremaa

Töreboda
Motala
Ljungsbro
Söderköping
Öxelösund
Gotska
Sandön
Kuressaare

Tibro
Hjo
Norrköping
Linköping
Mjölby
Atvidaberg
Valdemarsvik
Säre

Kolkasrags
Kolka

Tranås
Kisa
Gamleby
Lärbro
Fårösund
Ventspils
Leči
Talsi
Sabile

Huskvarna
Nässjö
Eksjö
Rydsnäs
Vimmerby
Västervik
Visby
Slite
Gotland
Kuldiga
Courland

Savsjö
Vetlanda
Hultsfred
Klintehamn
Ljugarn
249
Pävilosta
LATVIA
Aizpute

Oskarshamn
Högsby
Byxelkrok
Hemse
Burgsvik
Liepāja
Saldus

Alvesta
Växjö
Lenhovda
Monsteras
Borgholm
Öland
Mažeikiai
Skuodas

Liatorp
Lessebo
Nybro
Lindsdal
Färjestaden
Žemaitijos n.p.
Palanga
Kretinga
Plungė
Rietavas

Tingsryd
Kalmar
Vissefjärda
Södra Ölands
odlingslandskap
Klaipėda
Kuršiu n.p.
Gargždai
LITHUANIA

Älmhult
Ryd
Karls-
hamn
Kallinge
Rödeby
Jämjö
Ottenby
Juodkrantė
Žemaičiu
Naumiestis
Tauragė

Ronneby
Karlskrona
Sölvesborg
BALTIC SEA
13
102
Neringa-Nida
(Nidden)
Šilutė
Sovetsk
Pagėgiai

Kristianstad
Åhus
Degeberga
Courland
Lagoon
Bol'šakovo
Neman

Simrishamn
Bornholm (Denmark)
Svaneke 105
Svetlogorsk
Zelenogradsk
RUSSIA
Kaliningrad
Černjahovsk

Allinge
Hasle
Rønne
Nexø
Władysławowo
Krasnotorovka
Primorsk
Baltijsk
Južnyj
Gvardejsk
Gusev

Słowiński P.N.
Ustka
Wejherowo
Reda
Hel
Mamonovo
Braniewo
Železnodorožnyj

Darłowo
Lębork
Sopot
Gdynia
Gdańsk
Lidzbark
Warmiński
Bartoszyce
Węgorzewo

Słupsk
Kartuzy
Pruszcz Gdański
Tczew
Elbląg
Dobre Miasto
MASURIA
Giżycko

Koszalin
Sianów
Bytów
331
Kościerzyna
Malbork
Morąg
Kętrzyn
Mrągowo
Orzysz

Kołobrzeg
Kamień
Pomorski
Karlino
Białogard
Miastko
POLAND
Starogard Gdański
Biskupiec

Lh 16° **Lj** 18° **Lk** 20° **Ma** 22°

Southern Finland, Karelia
Europe

Scale 1:4,000,000

| 0 | 50 | 100 | 150 Kilometers |

| 0 | 50 | 100 Miles |

SWEDEN

FINLAND

Vuollerim · Gyljen · Överkalix · Ylitornio · Koivu · Kuusamo
Edefors · Morjärv · Karungi · Tervola · Ranua · Syötteen k.puistö
Kåbdalis · Töre · Haparanda · Tornio · Simo · Asmunti · Syötekylä · Peranka
Vidsel · Kalix · Kemi · Kuivaniemi · Metsäkylä · Vojnica · Kal
Älvsbyn · Boden · Gammelstaden · Luleå · Haparända skärgårds n.p. · Perämeren k.puistö · Perämeri · Kipinä · Suomussalmi · Koston
Antnäs · Hailuoto · Puolanka
Piteå · Bottenviken · Hailuoto · Oulu · Kempele · Utajärvi · Härmänkylä
Långträsk · Brahestadt · Raahe · Säräisniemi · Kuhmo · Kiekinkö
Glommersträsk · Jörn · Byske · Vihanti · Manamensalo · Oulujärvi · Kajaani
Norsjö · Boliden · Skellefteå · Oulainen · Pulkkila · Maanselkä
Åstrask · Skelleftehamn · Pyhäntä · Nurmes
Hällnäs · Burträsk · Lövånger · 124 · Kalajoki · Nivala · Pieline
Vindeln · Robertsfors · Karleby Kokkola · Ylivieska · Iisalmi · Rautavaara · Karjalanselkä
Umeå · Jakobstad · Pietarsaari · Toholampi · Kiuruvesi · Säyneinen · Kontiolah
Vännäs · Holmön · Ångesön · Holmsund · Fäböda · Viitasaari · Tervo · Kuopio · Outokumpu
Nordmaling · Norram Kvarken · Merenkurkku · Evijärvi · Suonenjoki · Tuusniemi · Joens
Vaasa · Lappajärvi · Kauhava · Kyyjärvi · Siilinjärvi · Lj
Lapua · Seinäjoki · Soini · Saarijärvi · Äänekoski · Leppävirta · Oni
Korsnäs · Uurainen · Varkaus · Hauki-vesi
Teuva · Kurikka · Alavus · Keuruu · Jyväskylä · Pieksämäki · Linnansaaren k.puisto
Kaskinen · Kauhajoki · Virrat · Mänttä · Korpilathi · Lievestuore · Toivakka · Haukivuori · Savonlinna
Kristinestad · Kristiinankaupunki · Karvia · Parkano · Vilppula · Kangasniemi · Juva
Jämsä · Mikkeli · Puumala · Rautj
Merikarvia · Kankaanpää · Hämeenkyrö · Ylöjärvi · Orivesi · Paijänne · Hartola · Ristiina · Ruokolahti · Saimaa
Noormarkku · Lavia · Nokia · Tampere · Mäntyharju · Savitaipale · Imatra · Sveto
Pori · Vammala · Valkeakoski · Heinola · Kuusankoski · Jaala · Luumäki · Lappeenranta · Kamennogo
Rauma · Huittinen · Viiala · Hämeenlinna · Lahti · Nastola · Kouvola · Ylämaa · Vyb
Eura · Loimaa · Humppila · Forssa · Riihimäki · Orimattila · Vaalimaa
Nystadt · Uusikaupunki · Mynämäki · Mäntsälä · Hamina · Primorsk
Åland/Ahvenanmaa · Geta · Raisio · Somero · Nurmijärvi · Järvenpää · Kotka · Itäisen Suomenlahden kansallispuisto
Eckerö · Mariehamn · Maarianhamina · Nådendal · Naantali · Turku Åbo · Salo · Uusula · Porvoo Borgå · o.Moščnyj · o.Les
Kumlinge · Pargas · Parainen · Lohja · Vantaa Vanda · Espoo Esbo · o.Gogland
Karis · Karjaa · Helsinki Helsingfors · Gulf of Finland · Ust´Luga
Erkenäs · Tammisaari · Dalsbruk

Gulf of Bothnia

Pohjanmaa (Österbotten)

Suomenselkä

Salpausselkä

Baltic States
Europe

Scale 1:4,000,000

0   50   100   150 Kilometers

0   50   100 Miles

30   Europe

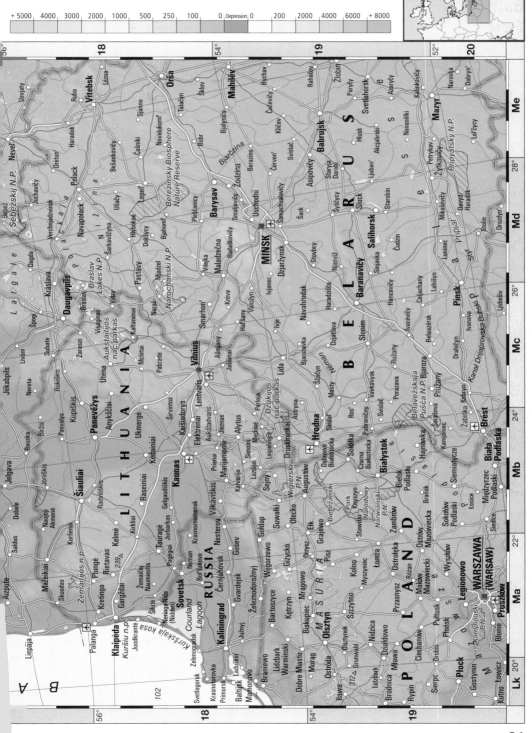

Scale 1:4,000,000

0   50   100   150 Kilometers

0   50   100 Miles

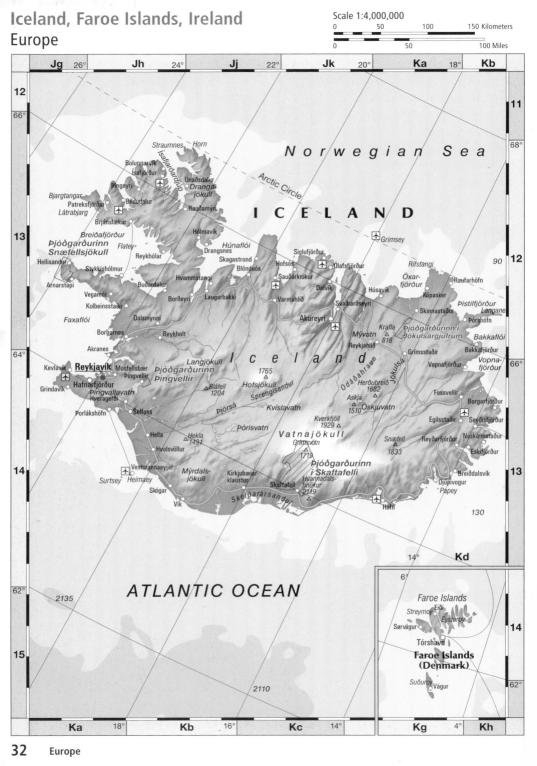

| Jg | 26° | Jh | 24° | Jj | 22° | Jk | 20° | Ka | 18° | Kb |

12   **11**

66°   68°

N o r w e g i a n   S e a

Straumnes   Horn

Bolungarvík
Ísafjörður
Ísafjarðardjúp
Unaðsdalur
Þingeyri   *Dranga-jökull*
Bíldudalur
Arctic Circle
Rauðamýri

I C E L A N D

Bjargtangar
Patreksfjörður
Látrabjarg
Brjánslækur
Hólmavík

13   **12**

Breiðafjörður
Þjóðgarðurinn
Snæfellsjökull   Flatey
Hellissandur
Reykhólar
Stykkishólmur
Húnaflói
Drangsnes
Skagaströnd
Blönduós
Hofsós
Siglufjörður
Ólafsfjörður
Grímsey
Rifstangi
90
Arnarstapi
Búðardalur
Hvammstangi
Sauðárkrókur
Öxar-fjörður
Raufarhöfn
Vegamót
Borðeyri
Laugarbakki
Varmahlíð
Dalvík
Húsavík
Kópasker
Skinnastaður
Þistilfjörður
Langane
Faxaflói
Dalsmynni
Svalbarðseyri
Þórshöfn
Borgarnes
Reykholt
Akureyri
Iceland
Mývatn
Krafla 818
Þjóðgarðurinn í Jökulsárgljúfrum
Bakkaflói
Akranes
Reykjahlíð
Grímsstaðir
Bakkafjörður

64°   **66°**

Kevlavík
Reykjavík
Mosfellsbær
Þingvellir
Langjökull
Þjóðgarðurinn
Pingvellir
1765
Hofsjökull
Ódáðahraun
Herðubreið 1682
Jökulsá
Grímsstaðir
Vopnafjörður
Vopna-fjörður
Grindavík
Hafnarfjörður
Þingvallavatn
Hveragerði
Bláfell 1204
Sprengisandur
Kvíslavatn
Askja 1510
Öskjuvatn
Fossvellir
Borgarfjörður
Þorlákshöfn
Selfoss
Þjórsá
Kverkfjöll 1929
Egilsstaðir
Seyðisfjörður
Hella
Hekla 1491
Þórisvatn
Vatnajökull
Snæfell 1833
Reyðarfjörður
Neskaupstaður
Hvolsvöllur
Grímsvötn 1719
Eskifjörður

14   **13**

Vestmannaeyjar
Mýrdals-jökull
Kirkjubæjar-klaustur
Þjóðgarðurinn í Skaftafelli
Hvannadalshnúkur 2149
Breiðdalsvík
Surtsey   Heimaey
Skógar
Skaftafell
Djúpivogur
Papey
Vík
Skeiðarársandur
Höfn
130

ATLANTIC OCEAN

62°   2135

15   2110

| Ka | 18° | Kb | 16° | Kc | 14° | Kg | 4° | Kh |

Faroe Islands

| | 6° | | Kd |

Faroe Islands
Streymoy   Eiði
Sørvágur   Eysturoy
Tórshavn
Faroe Islands (Denmark)
Suðuroy   Vágur

14

62°

+ 5000   4000   3000   2000   1000   500   250   100   0 Depression 0   200   2000   4000   6000   + 8000

ATLANTIC

OCEAN

Rockall Trough

3244

2414

88

97

18

54°

19

52°

20

50°

Belmullet

Bangor

Achill Island

Westport

△817

Clifden

Oughterard

Galway

Aran Islands

Burren
N.P.

Ennistimon

Mouth of
the Shannon

Kilrush

Ennis

Dingle

Listowel

Tralee

Cahersiveen

Carrauntoohil
△1038

Killarney

*Killarney
N.P.*

Bantry

Bandon

**Cork/
Corcaigh**

Youghal

Glencolumbkille

Killybegs

Donegal

Bundoran

Ballina

Sligo

Castlebar

Claremorris

Ballyhaunis

Tuam

Loughrea

Castlerea

Roscommon

Athlone

Dunglow

Errigal
752

Glenveagh
△ N.P.

Letterkenny

Strabane

Omagh

Enniskillen

Carrick-on-
Shannon

Castlebar

Connacht

Longford

Mullingar

Trim

Nenagh

Port Laoise

Birr

Thurles

Tipperary

Cashel

Clonmel

Mitchelstown

Mallow

Dungarvan

Waterford

New Ross

Maghera

Coleraine

**Londonderry
(Derry)**

Cookstown

Northern Ireland

Dungannon

L. Neagh

Monaghan

Cavan

Kells

Navan

Kildare

Naas

Carlow

Kilkenny

IRELAND

Munster

Roscommon

852
△
Kilkeel

Dundalk

Drogheda

Bray

Wicklow

Arklow

Enniscorthy

Wexford

Dublin/Baile Átha Cliath

Dun Laoghaire

Wicklow Mts.N.P.

Wicklow Mts.

924

Rosslare Harbour

Ballycastle

Ballymena

Antrim

Belfast

Bangor

Ards
Peninsula

Portadown

Newry

Downpatrick

Larne

Stranraer

33

Castlebay

Barra

Rum

Mallaig

Coll

Tiree

Tobermory

Isle of Mull

Fionnphort

Oban

Colonsay

Jura

Islay

Port Askaig

Kennacraig

Port Ellen

Kintyre

Arran

Campbeltown

Girvan

245

Luce
Bay

Isle of Man

Ramsey

Peel   621
△

Isle of Man (Brit.)

Douglas

Irish Sea

180

Holyhead

90

Celtic Sea

99

87

115

55

62

Saint George's Channel

**UNITED
KINGDOM**

Aberystwyth

W a l e s

*Cardigan
Bay*

892

Caernarfon

1085

Snowdonia N.P.

Bangor

Cambrian Mountains

Pembrokeshire Coast
National Park

Fishguard

Milford Haven

Pembroke

Tenby

Carmarthen

Llandovery

Brecon

Llandovery

*Brecon
Beacons N.P. 886*

Swansea

Port
Talbot

Merthyr
Tydfil

Cardiff

Bristol Channel

Ilfracombe

Exmoor N.P.

17

56°

18

54°

19

52°

20

Isle of Man

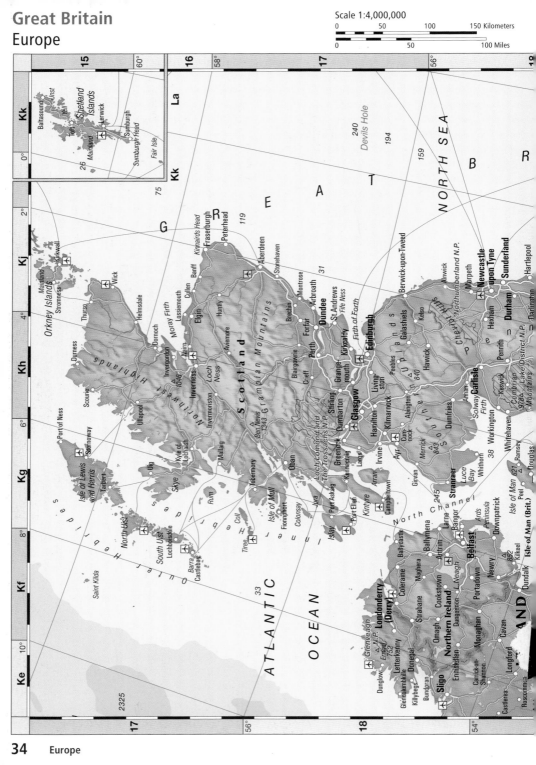

+ 5000 4000 3000 2000 1000 500 250 100 0 Depression 0 200 2000 4000 6000 + 8000

Kd 12° **Ke** 10° **Kf** 8° **Kg** 6°

Castlebay Barra
Rum
Mallaig
Coll
Tiree Tobermory
Isle of Mull

17

Rockall Trough

2414

3244

33

Fionnphort Oban
Colonsay
Jura

18

A T L A N T I C

Islay Port Askaig
Kennacraig
Port Ellen

Kintyre Arran
Campbeltown

56°

O C E A N

88

Glenveagh
N.P.
Errigal 752
Dunglow

Girvan

54°

97

Glencolumbkille
Killybegs Donegal
Letterkenny
Coleraine Ballycastle

Belmullet
Bundoran
Bangor
Strabane Maghera
Omagh

**Londonderry
(Derry)**

North Channel 245

18

Achill Island

Sligo
Ballina
Enniskillen

Northern Ireland
Cookstown Antrim
Dungannon
L.Neagh

Ballymena
Larne
Bangor

Stranraer
Luce
Bay

Westport
Castlebar
817

Claremorris
Ballyhaunis
Carrick-on-
Shannon
Monaghan
Portadown

Belfast
Ards
Peninsula

19

Clifden
Castlerea
Cavan

Newry
Downpatrick

Ramsey

Oughterard
Tuam
Roscommon
Longford
852
Kilkeel

Isle of Man 621
Peel

Galway
Athlone
Kells
Dundalk

Isle of Man (Brit.)
Douglas

54°

Aran Islands
Burren
N.P.
Loughrea
Mullingar

Trim Navan
Drogheda

Irish Sea

Ennistimon

I R E L A N D

Dublin/Baile Atha Cliath

52°

Mouth of
the Shannon
Ennis
Birr
Port Laoise
Kildare
Naas

Dun Laoghaire
Bray

180
Holyhead

Kilrush
Nenagh

924
Wicklow Mts.N.P.
90

Listowel
Thurles
Carlow
Wicklow Mts.
Wicklow

Bangor

Dingle
Tralee
Newcastle
West
Tipperary
Cashel
Kilkenny
Arklow

Caernarfon 1085

Limerick
Clonmel

Snowdonia N.P.

Killarney
Mallow
Mitchelstown
New Ross
Enniscorthy

19

Carrauntoohil
1038
Killarney
N.P.
Dungarvan

Waterford
Wexford

Cardigan
Bay
892

Cahersiveen
Bantry
Bandon
Youghal

**Cork/
Corcaigh**

Rosslare Harbour

W a l e s

Saint George's Channel
Aberystwyth

20

99

**UNITED
KINGDOM**

87
Pembrokeshire Coast
National Park
Fishguard
Carmarthen
Llandovery

52°

Milford Haven
Pembroke
Tenby

Brecon
Beacons N.P. 886

115

Swansea

C e l t i c S e a

55
Port
Talbot

Merthyr
Tydfil

62

Bristol Channel
Cardiff

Ilfracombe

Exmoor N.P.

20

Kf 8° **Kg** 6° **Kh** 4° **Kj**

Iceland, Faroe Islands, Ireland **33**

Great Britain
Europe

Scale 1:4,000,000

0   50   100   150 Kilometers

0   50   100 Miles

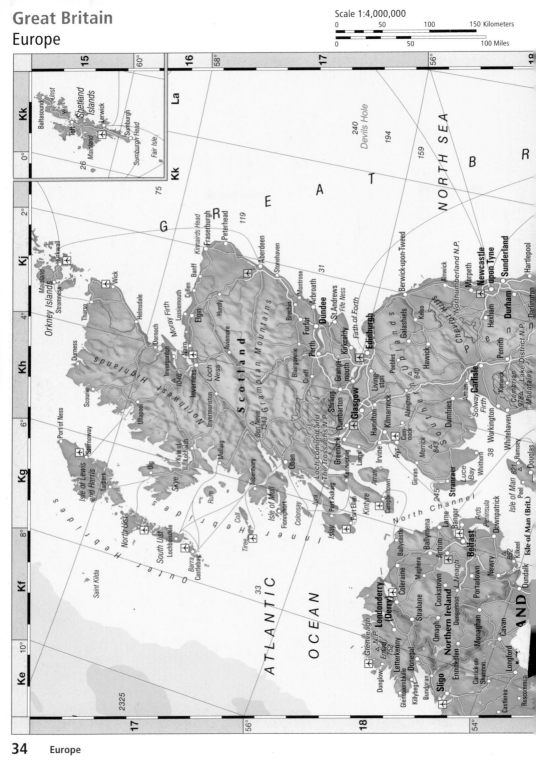

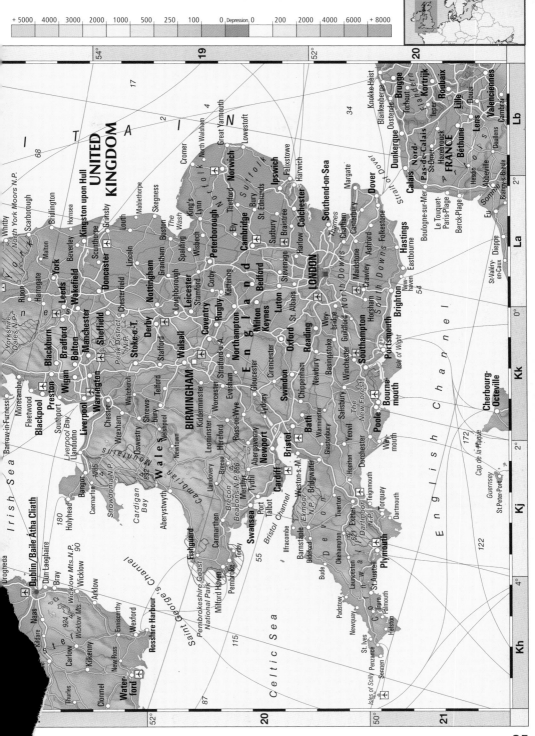

Benelux, Northern France
Europe

Scale 1:4,000,000

0   50   100   150 Kilometers
0   50   100 Miles

Aberystwyth Welshpool Telford Stafford Derby Nottingham Grantham Skegness Boston
Fishguard Newtown Shrews-bury Loughborough Spalding Wisbech King's Lynn The Was-
Saint George's Channel Cambrian Mts. Wales BIRMINGHAM Walsall Leicester Stamford Corby
Pembrokeshire Coast National Park Kidderminster Coventry Rugby Kettering Peterborough Ely
Milford Haven Carmarthen Llandovery Leominster Worcester Northampton Cambridge Bury St. Edmun.
Pembroke Tenby Brecon Hereford Evesham Milton Keynes Bedford Sudbury
Swansea Merthyr Ross-on-Wye Gloucester Stratford-u-A. England Braintree
Port Talbot Tydfil Abergavenny Luton Stevenage Harlow
Cardiff Newport Lydney Cirencester Oxford St. Albans Colchester
Ilfracombe Bristol Chippenham Swindon Reading LONDON Southend-on-Sea
Barnstaple Weston-s.-M. Bath Newbury Basingstoke Wey-bridge Thames
Bideford Exmoor N.P. Bridgwater Warminster Guildford North Downs Chatham Canterbury
Bude Devon Glastonbury Salisbury Winchester Crawley Maidstone
Padstow Okehampton Tiverton Yeovil The New Forest Southampton Horsham South Downs Ashford Folkestone
Newquay Launceston Exeter Honiton Dorchester Poole Portsmouth Brighton Hastings
Isles of Scilly St. Ives Dartmoor N.P. Teignmouth Wey-mouth Bourne-mouth Isle of Wight New-haven Eastbourne Strait
Penzance Truro St. Austell Torquay Portsmouth
Sennen Helston Falmouth Plymouth Dartmouth

UNITED KINGDOM

English Channel

Le Touquet Paris-Plage
Berck-Plage
Cap de la Hague St-Valéry-en-Caux Dieppe Eu
Guernsey Cherbourg-Octeville Valognes Fécamp Blangy-s.-Bresle Neufchâtel-en-Bray
St.Peter-Port Barneville-Carteret Ste-Mère-Église Yvetot
Kanalinseln (UK) Jersey Le Havre Rouen Haute-Normandie
St.Helier Carentan Trouville-sur-Mer Gournay-en-Bray
Ploudalmézeau Perros-Guirec Bayeux Ouistreham Pont-Audemer Magny-en-Vexin
St-Renan Roscoff Lannion Golfe de Coutances Saint-Lô Caen Lisieux Louviers Vernon
Le Conquet Lesneven Paimpol Saint Malo Granville Basse- Bernay Évreux Mantes-la-Jolie
Parc Nat.Rég. d'Armorique Brest Landerneau Morlaix Guingamp St-Malo Vire Normandie Falaise Gacé Verneuil-sur-Avre Dreux
Douarnenez St-Brieuc Dinard Avranches Normandie Flers Domfront Argentan L'Aigle Rambouillet
Audierne Carhaix-Plouguer Lamballe Dinan St-Hilaire-du-Harcouët Mayenne Alençon Bellême Chartres
Quimper Pontivy St-Méen-le-Grand Fougères Mamers La Ferté-Bernard Nogent-le-Rotrou
Penmarc'h Quimperlé Hennebont Rennes Vitré Laval Le Mans Châteaudun Bonneval
Lorient Ploërmel Guer Château-Gontier La Flèche FRANCE
Larmor-Plage Auray Redon Château-briant Segré Château-du-Loir Vendôme Orléan.
Quiberon Vannes Pontchâteau Pays de la Loire Ancenis Angers Château-Renault Blois Orl.
La Roche-Bernard Nantes Chemillé Loire Amboise Selles-
St-Nazaire Trignac Tours Beaugé s.-Ch.
Guérande Pornic Cholet Doué-la-Fontaine Saumur Chinon Touraine
Noirmoutier-en-l'Île Challans Thouars Loudun Châtellerault
Beauvoir-s.-Mer St-Jean-de-Monts Aizenay Mauléon Bressuire La Châtaigneraie
St-Gilles-Croix-de-Vie La Roche-sur-Yon
Les Sables-d'Olonne

Celtic Sea
ATLANTIC OCEAN

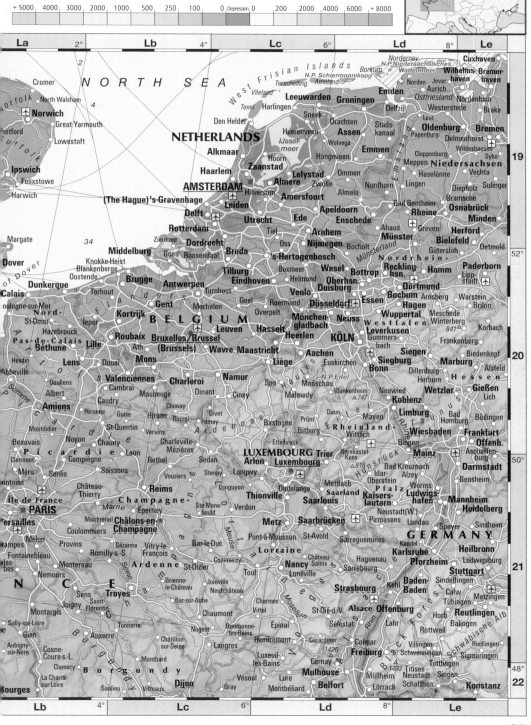

+ 5000 | 4000 | 3000 | 2000 | 1000 | 500 | 250 | 100 | 0 | Depression | 0 | 200 | 2000 | 4000 | 6000 | + 8000

N O R T H   S E A

West Frisian Islands

Cromer
North Walsham
Norwich
Great Yarmouth
Lowestoft
Ipswich
Felixstowe
Harwich
Margate
Dover
of Dover
Dunkerque
Calais
oulogne-sur-Mer
Nord-
St-Omer
Hazebrouck
Pas-de-Calais
Béthune
Lille
Roubaix
Lens
Douai
Abbeville
Doullens
Albert
Valenciennes
Cambrai
Maubeuge
Hesdin
Amiens
Péronne
Guise
Montdidier
Noyon
Chauny
Beauvais
Picardie
Clermont
Compiègne
Méru
Senlis
Château-Thierry
ntoise
Île de France
PARIS
ersailles
Soissons
Reims
Champagne-
tampes
Melun
Coulommiers
Montmirail
Châlons-en-
Champagne
Fontainebleau
Provins
Sézanne
Vitry-le-
François
Nemours
Romilly-s.-S.
Montereau
Ardenne
St-Dizier
N   C   E
Sens
Troyes
Joigny
Saint-
Florentin
Brienne-
le-Château
Montargis
Bar-sur-Aube
ℓes
Sully-sur-Loire
Gien
Aubigny-
s-Nère
Cosne-
Cours-s.-L.
Auxerre
Tonnerre
Bourges
La Charité-
sur-Loire
B u r g u n d y
Clamecy
Montbard
Châtillon-
sur-Seine
Saulieu
Dijon
Vitteaux

Norfolk
hetford
Suffolk

Texel
Den Helder
Alkmaar
Haarlem
AMSTERDAM
(The Hague)'s-Gravenhage
Delft
Rotterdam
Zierikzee
Middelburg
Knokke-Heist
Blankenberge
Oostende
Brugge
Torhout
Flanders
Ieper
Kortrijk
Gent
Mechelen
Antwerpen
Turnhout
Ath
Mons
B E L G I U M
Leuven
Bruxelles/Brussel
(Brussels)
Wavre
Charleroi
Namur
Dinant
Ciney
Chimay
Rocroi
Fumay
Givet
Hirson
Vervins
Charleville-
Mézières
Rethel
Sedan
Vouziers
Stenay
Longuyon
Vouziers
Longwy
Arlon
LUXEMBOURG
Luxembourg
Ste-Mene-
hould
Verdun
Thionville
Metz
Pont-à-Mousson
Bar-le-Duc
Commercy
Lorraine
Toul
Nancy
Lunéville
St-Avold
Sarreguemines
Sarrebourg
Haguenau
Château
Salins
Neufchâteau
Charmes
Vittel
Chaumont
Bourbonne-
les-Bains
Nogent
Épinal
St-Dié-d.-V.
Langres
Luxeuil-
les-Bains
Remiremont
Gérardmer
Sélestat
Colmar
Cernay
Mulhouse
Vesoul
Lure
Gray
Montbéliard
Belfort

Borkum
Norderney
N.P.Niedersächsisches
Wattenmeer
N.P. Schiermonnikoog
Schiermonnikoog
Ameland
Terschelling
Vlieland
Leeuwarden
Harlingen
Sneek
Groningen
Emden
Norden
Jever
Aurich
Ostfriesland
Westerstede
Wilhelms-
haven
Bremer-
haven
Cuxhaven
Nordenham
Brake
Leer
Delfzijl
Stads-
kanaal
Assen
Drachten
Heerenveen
Wolvega
Hoogeveen
Emmen
Ommen
NETHERLANDS
Hoorn
Zaanstad
IJssel-
meer
Hilversum
Leiden
Ede
Amersfoort
Almere
Lelystad
Zwolle
Almelo
Nordhorn
Lingen
Meppen
Cloppenburg
Papenburg
Oldenburg
Delmenhorst
Wildeshausen
Syke
Bremen
Niedersachsen
Vechta
Diepholz
Haselünne
Sulingen
Bramsche
Osnabrück
Minden
Rheine
Greven
Ahaus
Enschede
Apeldoorn
Arnhem
Nijmegen
Bocholt
Münster
Münsterland
Herford
Bielefeld
Gütersloh
Detmold
Bad Bentheim
Nordrhein-
Wesel
Bottrop
Recklling-
hsn.
Hamm
Lipp-
stadt
Paderborn
's-Hertogenbosch
Boxmeer
Oberhsn
Duisburg
Essen
Bochum
Dortmund
Arnsberg
Hagen
Warstein
Brilon
Venlo
Oberhsn.
Helmond
Eindhoven
Roermond
Overpelt
Geel
Mönchen-
gladbach
Neuss
Düsseldorf
Wuppertal
Meschede
Westfalen
Winterberg
Korbach
841
Hasselt
Heerlen
Maastricht
Aachen
Euskirchen
KÖLN
Leverkusen
Gummers-
bach
Siegen
Biedenkopf
Frankenberg
Liège
Spa
Malmedy
Blankenheim
Monschau
Bonn
Siegburg
Dillenburg
Herborn
Marburg
Alsfeld
Hessen
Neuwied
Wetzlar
Gießen
Lich
Givet
Bastogne
Prüm
Daun
N.P.Eifel
△747
△818
Rheinland
Mayen
Koblenz
Limburg
Bad
Homburg
Büdingen
Wittlich
Bitburg
Ettelbruck
Bernkastel-
Kues
Trier
Wiesbaden
Bingen
Mainz
Frankfurt
Offenb.
Aschaffen-
burg
Darmstadt
Bensheim
Hunsrück
Idar-
Oberstein
Bad Kreuznach
Alzey
Worms
Mettlach
Saarland
Dudelange
Saarlouis
Kaisers-
lautern
Pfalz
Ludwigs-
hafen
Mannheim
Heidelberg
Neustadt(W.)
Speyer
Sinsheim
Saarbrücken
Pirmasens
Landau
GERMANY
Kandel
Karlsruhe
Heilbronn
Pforzheim
Ludwigsburg
Stuttgart
Sindelfingen
Kehl
Baden-
Baden
Calw
Tübingen
Metzingen
Reutlingen
Balingen
Horb
Rottweil
Offenburg
Lahr
Freiburg
Villingen
Schwenningen
Tuttlingen
Riedlingen
Sigmaringen
Schwäbische Alb
Black Forest
Müllheim
Titisee-
Neustadt
Singen
Lörrach
Schaffhsn.
Konstanz
△1426
△1493
Vosges

19
52°
20
50°
21
48°
22

Scale 1:4,000,000

0   50   100   150 Kilometers

0   50   100 Miles

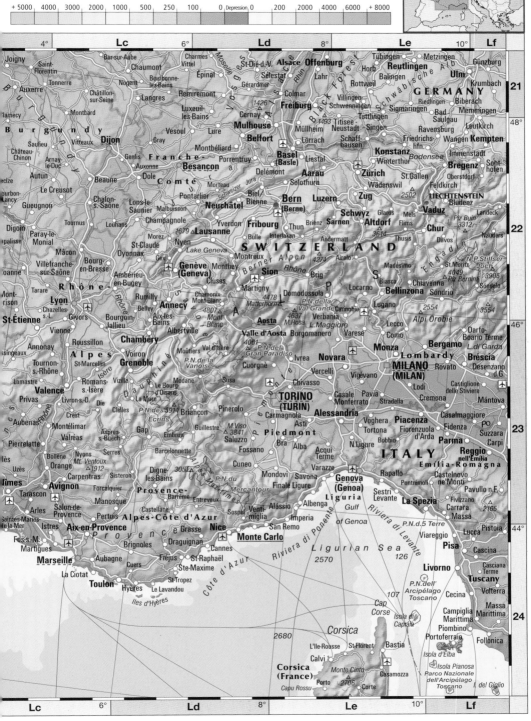

Western Spain, Portugal
Europe

Scale 1:4,000,000

0　　50　　100　　150 Kilometers
0　　　50　　　100 Miles

Eastern Spain, Balearic Islands
Europe

Eastern Spain, Balearic Islands 43

Scale 1:4,000,000

0	50	100	150 Kilometers
0		50	100 Miles

NORTH SEA

BALTIC SEA

Pomeranian Bay

SWEDEN

DENMARK

KØBENHAVN

GERMANY

BERLIN

NETHERLANDS

AMSTERDAM

HAMBURG

Bornholm (Denmark)

German Bight

West Frisian Islands

North Frisian Islands

East Frisian Islands

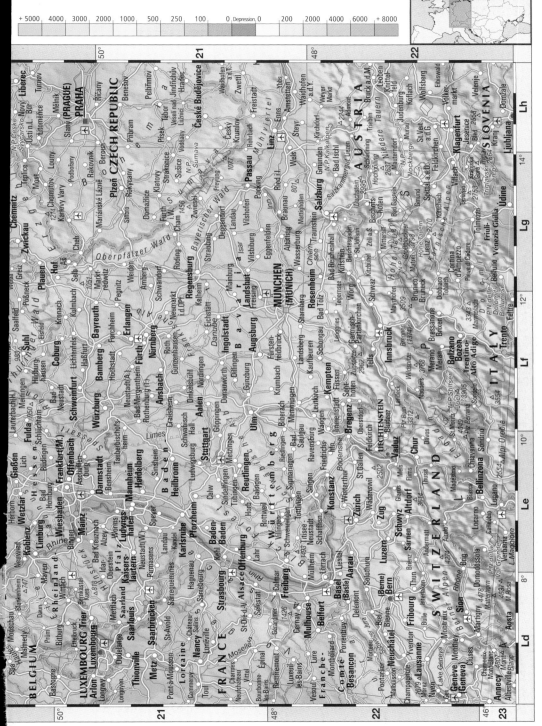

Scale 1:4,000,000

| 0 | 50 | 100 | 150 Kilometers |

| 0 | 50 | 100 Miles |

Lc 6°   Ld 8°   Le 10°   Lf 12°

SWITZERLAND

Besançon, Delémont, Aarau, Winterthur, Bregenz, Sont-hofen, Füssen, Zugspitze 2962, Garmisch-Partenkirchen, Wörgl, Kufstein, St.Jo
Franche-Comté, Morteau, Solothurn, Zürich, St.Gallen, Oberstdorf, Telfs, Schwaz, Kitzbühel, Zell a.
Pontarlier, Schweizer Jura, Biel/Bienne, Zug, Wädenswil, Feldkirch, LIECHTENSTEIN, Mittersill
Malbuisson, Neuchâtel, Bern, Luzern, Schwyz, 2502, Bludenz, Vaduz, Innsbruck, Mayrhofen, Hohe Ta
Champagnole, Yverdon, Fribourg, Thun, Brienz, Sarnen, Altdorf, Glarus, Mels, Landeck, Piz Buin 3312, Nauders, Brenner (1374), 3509, Großglockner
1679, Lausanne, Bulle, Interlaken, Andermatt, Flims, Chur, Davos, 3768, Brunico, Brunnek, Hohe Tauern, Lienz
Morez, St-Claude, Nyon, Montreux, Berner Alpen, 4274, Airolo, Thusis, Merano, Meran, Bressanone, Brixen, Dobbiaco, Toblach, Cortina d'Ampezzo
Gex, Genève (Geneva), Monthey, Sion, Rhône, Brig, Madésimo, St.Moritz, N.P.Stilfser Joch, 4049, Piz Bernina 3905, Sondalo, Bolzano, Bozen, 3343, Marmolada, Pieve di Cadore
Annecy, Cluses, Martigny, 4478, Domodóssola, Locarno, Biasca, Bellinzona, Sóndrio, Trentino-Alto Adige, P.N.delle Dolomiti Bellunesi, Belluno, Friu
Rumilly, Chamonix-Mont-Blanc, Matterhorn, 4637, P.N.della Val Grande, Cannóbio, Lugano, 2554, 3554, Riva del Garda, Feltre, Trento, Vittorio Véneto, Pordenon
Aix-les-Bains, 4807, Mont Blanc, M.Rosa, Verbania, L.Maggiore, Lecco, Como, Alpi Orobie, Darfo-Boario Terme, Rovereto, Schio, Bassano d.G., Conegliano, 376
Albertville, Valle d'Aosta, Borgomanero, Varese, Monza, Bergamo, L.di Garda, Treviso
Chambéry, Aosta, 4061, P.N.del Gran Paradiso, Ivrea, Novara, Lombardy, Brescia, Vicenza, Véneto, Mestre
Moûtiers, Val d'Isère, Cuorgnè, Vercelli, Vigevano, MILANO (MILAN), Rovato, Desenzano d.G., Verona, Villafranca di Verona, Pádova, Monsélice, Venézia (Venice)
P.N.de la Vanoise, Modane, Susa, Chivasso, Casale Monferrato, Pavia, Lodi, Castiglione delle Stiviere, Mantova, Legnago, Rovigo, Adria, Chióggia
Le Bourg-d'Oisans, 3914, Briançon, Pinerolo, TORINO (TURIN), Asti, Stradella, Piacenza, Cremona, Casal-maggiore, Suzzara, Mirándola, Carpi, Ferrara, Podélta
P.N.des Ecrins, Guillestre, 3841, Carmagnola, Alessándria, Voghera, Fiorenzuola d'Arda, Fidenza, Parma, PO, Modena, Comácchio
Embrun, M.Viso, Piedmont, Tortona, Bóbbio, Reggio nell'Emília, Emília-Romagna, Bologna, Ravenna
Gap, Saluzzo, Bra, Alba, Acqui Terme, N.Ligure, Vignola, Lugo, Imola, Forlì, Cervia
Barcelonnette, Cúneo, Fossano, Mondovi, Rapallo, Pontremoli, Castelnovo ne'Monti, Pavullo n.F., Brisighella, Cesena, Cesenático
Digne-les-Bains, 3051, P.N.du Mercantour, Finale Ligure, Genova (Genoa), Sestri Levante, Fivizzano, 2765, Borgo S.Lorenzo, P.N.Casentinesi-M.Falterona-Campigna, Rimini
Provence-Barrême, Entrevaux, Castellane, Sospel, Venti-miglia, Imperia, Albenga, Liguria, Gulf of, Riviera di Levante, Carrara, Massa, Lucca, Pistoia, Prato, SAN MARINO
Alpes-Côte d'Azur, Grasse, Nice, San Remo, Genoa, La Spezia, P.N.d.5 Terre, Viaréggio, Pisa, Firenze (Florence), Bagno di Romagna, San Marino, Urbino
Draguignan, Cannes, Monte Carlo, Riviera di Ponente, Ligurian Sea, 2570, 126, Viaréggio, Livorno, Cascina, Empoli, Poggibónsi, Arezzo, Fossombrone, Cagli
Fréjus, St-Raphaël, Ste-Maxime, St-Tropez, Le Lavandou, Iles d'Hyères, 107, Cap Corse, P.N.dell'Arcipélago Toscano, Cecina, Volterra, Siena, Cortona, Città di Castello, Perugia
2680, L'Ile-Rousse, St-Florent, Bastia, Isola di Capraia, Campiglia Maríttima, Piombino, Massa Maríttima, Pienza, Monte-pulciano, L.Trasimeno, Umbria, Foligno
Calvi, Corsica (France), Monte Cinto, Casamozza, Isola d'Elba, Portoferraio, Follónica, 1738, Acquapendente, Orvieto, Todi
Capu Rossu, Porto, 2706, Corte, Isola Pianosa, Grosseto, L.di Bolsena, Narni, Terni
Corse, 2622, Cateraggio, Orbetello, I. del Giglio, Parco Nazionale dell'Arcipélago Toscano, Tarquínia, Viterbo, Rieti, Lázio
MEDITERRANEAN SEA, Ajáccio, Zícavo, Civitavecchia, Civita Castellana, Tivoli
Capu di Muru, Auilène, VATICAN CITY, ROMA (ROME), Velletri, Latina
Propriano, Sartène, Porto Vecchio, 645, Anzio, P.N.del Circeo
Bonifacio, P.N.dell'Arcipélago de la Maddalena, Navan
Santa Teresa Gallura, La Maddalena

Southern Italy, Malta
Europe

Scale 1:4,000,000

| 0 | 50 | 100 | 150 Kilometers |
| 0 | | 50 | 100 Miles |

L'Ile-Rousse
Calvi
Corsica
(France)
Monte Cinto
Capu Rossu
△2706
Porto
△2622
Corte
St-Florent
Casamozza
Bastia
Isola d'Elba
Isola Pianosa
Grosseto
I. del Giglio
Acquapendente
Orvieto
Orbetello
L.di
Bolsena
Umbria
Narni
P.N.del Gran Sasso
e Monti della Laga
△2476
Todi
Terni
Viterbo
Rieti
L'Aquila
△2487

Ajaccio
Zicavo
Aullène
Capu di Muru
Propriano
Sartène
Porto Vecchio
Bonifacio
Cateraggio
Parco Nazionale
dell'Arcipélago
Toscano
Tarquinia
Civitavecchia
Civita Castellana
Lazio
VATICAN
CITY
ROMA
(ROME)
Tivoli
Avezzano
Anagni
Velletri
Frosinone
Latina

Bocche di Bonifacio
Santa Teresa
Gallura
P.N.dell'Asinara
Tempio
Pausánia
△1359
Porto Torres
Sassari
Algero
Thiesi
Ozieri
Bonorva
Bono
Bosa
Macomér
Núoro
Dorgali
P.N.dell'Arcipélago
de la Maddalena
la Maddalena
Costa
Smeralda
Olbia
Siniscóla
Sardinia
(Italy)
645
Anzio
P.N.del Circeo
Terracina
Gaeta
ITALY
Golfo d

P.ta Marmora
△1834
P.N.del Golfo di Orosei
e del Gennargentu
Árbatax
1740
Tyrrhenian Sea
Oristano
S a r d i n i a
Lanusei
925
San Gavino
Monréale
Guspini
Iglesias
△1236
Villacidro
Carbonia
Sant'Antioco
△1116
Quartu
Sant'Elena
Cagliari
1420
2690

Costa del Sud
161
2010
2410
3010
M E D I T E R R A N E A N   S E A
87
64
La Galite
995
11
Capo San Vito
Castellammare
del Golfo
Monréale
Palermo
Bagheria
Trapani
Isole Egadi
Alcamo
Lercara
Friddi
Marsala
Castelvetrano
Menfi
△1578
Castel-
termini
Mazara
del Vallo
Sciacca

Cap Serrat
L.Ichkeul
Sedjenane
Bizerte
Menzel Bourguiba
Mateur
Golfe
de Tunis
Zembra
Cap Bon
El Haouaria
20
Agrigento
Sicily
Annaba
Ben
Mehidi
El Kala
El Tarf
Tabarka
Nefza
Tébourba
Téboursouk
Béja
Ariana
La Marsa
Kelibia
53
El Al
Oréan
Aïn Draham
Bou Salem
Medjez
el Bab
Menzel
Termine
Korba
I.di Pantelleria (Italy)
Pantelleria
Monts de la Medjarda
△1041
Jendouba
Tunis
Soliman
Mechroha
Ghardi-
maou
Souk
Ahras
Zaghouan
Hammamet
T U N I S I A

Ld 8° Le 10° Lf 12° Lg

24
42°
25
40°
26
38°
27

2840

Poland
Europe

Scale 1:4,000,000

0   50   100   150 Kilometers

0   50   100 Miles

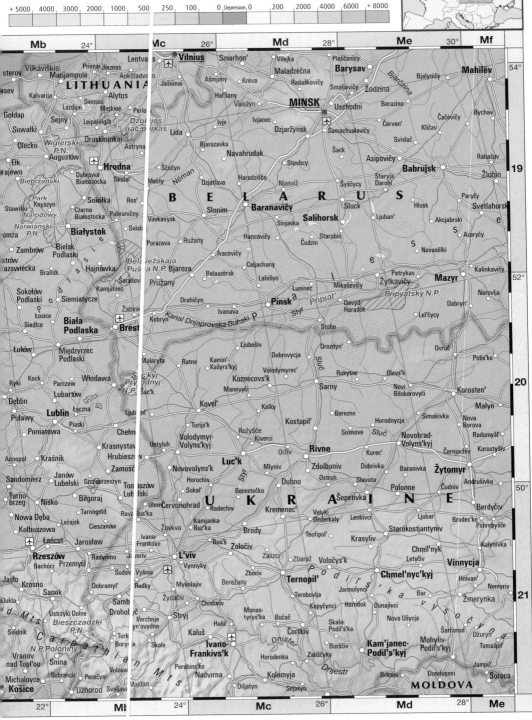

Austria, Czech Republic, Hungary
Europe

Scale 1:4,000,000

0   50   100   150 Kilometers

0   50   100 Miles

Scale 1:4,000,000

0   50   100   150 Kilometers

0   50   100 Miles

Le 10°   Lf 12°   Lg 14°   Lh 16° (Grünberg)

GERMANY

CZECH REPU

AUSTRIA

ITALY

SLOVENIA

LIECHTENSTEIN

Hann. Münden, Göttingen, Nordhausen, Lutherstadt Eislehen, Herzberg, Szprotawa, Głogów, Raw.
Kassel, Leinefelde, Sangerhsn., Halle(S.), Delitzsch, Eilenburg, Elsterwerda, Weißwasser, Polkowice, Lubin
Fritzlar, Melsungen, N.P.Hainich, Leipzig, Grimma, Meißen, Großenhain, Hoyerswerda, Niesky, Bolesławiec, Legnica
Behra, Eisenach, Erfurt, Weimar, Naumburg, Altenburg, Döbeln, Dresden, Pirna, Bautzen, Görlitz, Zgorzelec, Jelenia Góra, Świdnic
Alsfeld, Bad Hersfeld, Gotha, Thüringen, Jena, Gera, Sachsen, Freiberg, Nový Bor, Zittau, Liberec, Krkonošský N.P., Śnieżka 1602, Walbrzy
Lauterbach(H.), Meiningen, Ilmenau, Saalfeld, Greiz, Zwickau, Chemnitz, Teplice, Ústí n.L., Turnov, Náchod, Klodzko
Fulda, 950, Hildburghausen, Eisfeld, Plauen, Hof, Aš, Chomutov, Louny, Mělník, Jičín, Hradec Králové
Schlüchtern, Bad Neustadt, Coburg, Kronach, Karlovy Vary (Karlsbad), Podbořany, Slaný, (PRAGUE) PRAHA, Pardubice, Lanškroun
Aschaffenburg, Schweinfurt, Lichtenfels, Haßfurt, Kulmbach, Selb, Eger, Mariánské Lázně, Rakovník, Beroun, Říčany, Kutná Hora
Würzburg, Bamberg, Bayreuth, Marktredwitz, Plzeň, Příbram, Benešov, Zruč nad Sázavou, Hlinsko, Svitavy
Tauberbischofsheim, Höchstadt, Forchheim, Pegnitz, Sulzb-Rosenberg, Stříbro, Rokycany, Pelhřimov, Žďár nad Sázavou, Velké Meziříčí
Neustadt(A.), Erlangen, Weiden, Amberg, Domažlice, Klatovy, Písek, Tábor, Veselí nad Lužnicí, Jindřichův Hradec, Jihlava, Brno
Rothenburg(T.), Bad Mergentheim, Fürth, Nürnberg, Schwandorf, Furth i.W., Cham, Sušice, Vodňany, Telč, Třebíč
Ansbach, Roth, Neumarkt i.d.Opf., Regensburg, Zwiesel, Šumava N.P., České Budějovice, Znojmo
Crailsheim, Gunzenhausen, Kelheim, Straubing, Freyung, Český Krumlov, Waidhofen a.d.T., Laa a.d.T.
Schwäbisch Hall, Dinkelsbühl, Nördlingen, Eichstätt, Deggendorf, Landau, Zwettl, Waldviertel, Poysdorf
Aalen, Göppingen, Donauwörth, Dillingen, Ingolstadt, Mainburg, Vilshofen, Passau, Rohrbach, Freistadt, Krems, Hollabrunn, Stocker
Ulm, Günzburg, Augsburg, Landshut, Freising, Vilsbiburg, Pocking, Linz, Mühlviertel, St.Pölten, WIEN, Danube
Riedlingen, Biberach, Krumbach, Fürstenfeldbruck, MÜNCHEN (MUNICH), Eggenfelden, Ried i.l., Braunau, Wels, Enns, Ybbs, Amstetten, Bade
Bad Saulgau, Memmingen, Landsberg, Starnberg, Altötting, Wasserburg, Mattighofen, Steyr, Kirchdorf, Hainfeld, Berndorf
Ravensburg, Leutkirch, Kaufbeuren, Rosenheim, Chiemsee, Traunstein, Salzburg, Gmunden, Weyer, Waidhofen a.d.Y., Mariazell, Ternitz, Eisenstadt
Friedrichshfn., Wangen, Kempten, Füssen, Schongau, Bad Tölz, Bad Reichenhall, Bad Ischl, N.P.Kalkalpen, Liezen, Mürzzuschlag, Wiener Neustadt, Sop
Bodensee, Immenstadt, Sonthofen, Leoggries, Tegernsee, Kufstein, Berchtesgaden, St.Johann, Dachstein 2995, Schladming, 2244 Admont, Trieben, Leoben, Bruck a.d.M., Kirchschlag, Köse
Bregenz, Feldkirch, Oberstdorf, Telfs, Garmisch-Partenkirchen, Wörgl, Schwaz, Kitzbühel, Zell a.S., Bischofshofen, Hochgölling, Niedere Tauern, 2637, Judenburg, Hartberg, Fürstenfeld, Szombathe
Vaduz, Bludenz, Landeck, Piz Buin 3312, Wildspitze 2962, Innsbruck, Mayrhofen, Mittersill, Bad Gastein, Mauterndorf, Nockberge, Murau, Köflach, Graz, Feldbach, Leibnitz, Körme
Chur, Nauders, 3768, Brenner (1374), 3509, Hohe Tauern N.P., Großglockner 3798, Matrei, Gmünd, St.Veit a.d.G., Wolfsberg, Murska Sobota
Davos, Merano, Brunico, Bruneck, L. Hohe Tauern 2770, Lienz, Spittal a.d.D., Feldkirchen, Völkermarkt, Maribor, Ormož, Čakovec
St.Moritz, N.P.Stilfser Joch, 3905, Bressanone, Brixen, Dobbiaco, Toblach, Karnische Alpen, Villach, Klagenfurt, Jesenice, Bled, Velenje, Slov.Bistrica, Varaždin, Ludbr
Piz Bernina 4049, Sondalo, Bolzano Bozen, 3343, Cortina d'Ampezzo, Pieve di Cadore, Tarvisio, 2753, Kranjska Gora, Triglav 2864, Kranj, Domžale, Celje, Krapina
Sóndrio, Marmolada 3554, Trentino-Alto Adige, P.N.delle Dolomiti Bellunesi, Tolmezzo, Friuli-Venezia Giulia, Triglavski n.p. 2558, Ljubljana, Zapřešić, Zagreb
Alpi Orobie, Darfo-Boario Terme, Trento, Rovereto, Belluno, Vittorio Veneto, Pordenone, Udine, Nova Gorica, Idrija, Postojna, Novo Mesto, C R
Bergamo, L.d'Garda, Riva del Garda, Feltre, Gorizia, Latisana, SLOVENIA, Ribnica, Metlika, Karlovac
Brescia, Schio, Bassano d.G., Treviso, Porto-gruaro, Aquileia, Trieste, Ilirska Bistrica, Kočevje, Petrinja
Rovato, Desenzano d.G., Vicenza, Vedena, Portorož, Koper, Umag, N.P.Risnjak
Castiglione delle Stiviere, Verona, Padova, Mestre, Venezia (Venice)

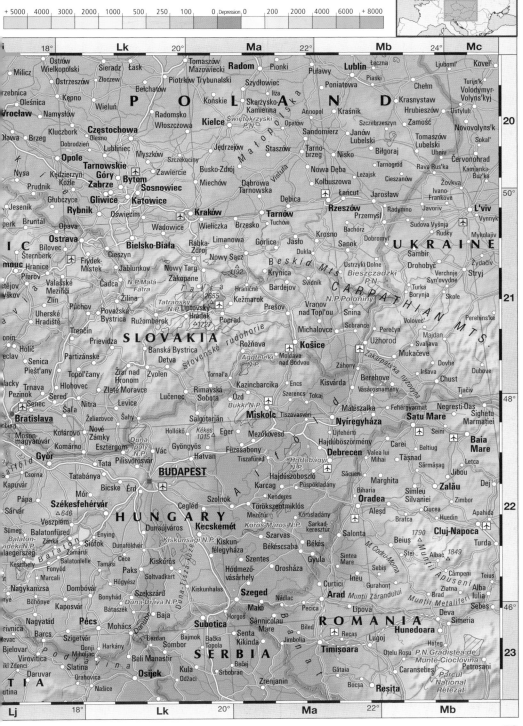

Serbia, Romania, Moldova
Europe

Scale 1:4,000,000

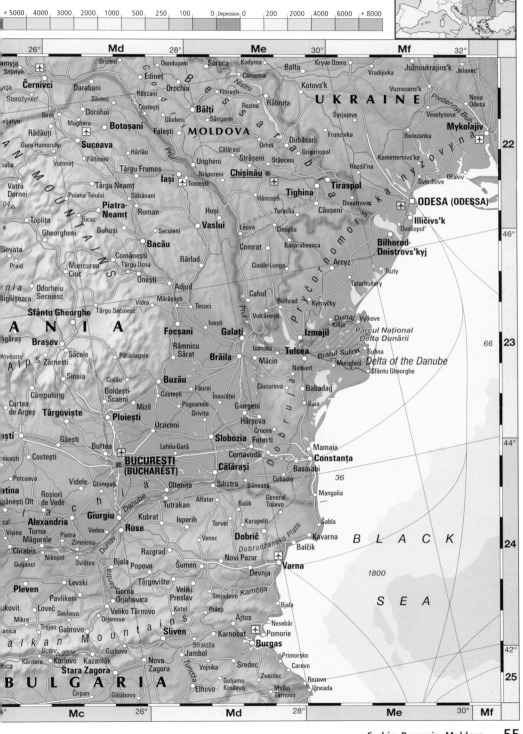

Scale 1:4,000,000

0   50   100   150 Kilometers

0   50   100 Miles

Scale bar (top): 000 4000 3000 2000 1000 500 250 100 0 Depression 0 200 2000 4000 6000 +8000

Mc 26° Md 28° Me 30° Mf

BLACK SEA

Čirpan Galábovo Elhovo Malko Rezovo İğneada
lijski Pârvomaj Dimitrovgrad Tŭrnovo Kıyıköy Pazarbaşı
Plovdiv Asenovgrad Haskovo Harmanli Lalapaşa Kırklareli Karadeniz Boğazı Burun
Lyubimets Pınarhisar Saray (Bosporus) Şile
ARIA Svilengrad Edirne Karaburun İSTANBUL Kandıra
Lâki Kârdžali Ivajlovgrad Çerkezköy Subaşı Esenyurt Beykoz Kocaeli Yarımadası
Smoljan Ardino Popsko Orestiáda Lüleburgaz Ergene ç Çatalca Yarımadası Bugaz Sangazi İZMİT Kocaeli
Madan Podkova Didymóteicho Uzunköprü Çorlu Silivri 1355 Gebze Hereke
Mountains Paranésti Ehínos Soufli Hayrabolu Gölcük
1087 Tekirdağ Sea of Marmara Yalova İznik İznik
Xánthi Íasmos Komotíni Sápai Keşan Mudanya Gölü Yenişehir
Hrissoúpoli Ágios Malkara Marmara Adası GEMLİK
rála Keramotí Charálampos Alexan- Enez Şarköy Kapıdağı BURSA
Tháossos droupoli Erdek Yarımadası Mudanya Bilecik
Thássos Samothráki Saros Körfezi Bolayır Bandırma Karacabey Uludağ İnegöl
Aliki Samothráki Gelibolu Kuşcennetil M.P. Ulubat M.P. Uludağ T.
Thrakikó Yarımadası M.P. Lâpseki Biga Kuş Gölü Gölü 2543 Bozüyük
ü Eceabat Gönen Mustafa- Orhaneli
os Pélagos 1205 Gökçeada İmroz Çan Susurluk kemalpaşa Harmancık
ranoúpoli Dardanelles Çanakkale Tavşanlı
Áthos 2033 TROY Biga Yarımadası Balıkesir Kepsut Kütahya
Akrotírio Akráthos Bayramiç Emet
Ezine Kaz Dağı İvrindi Bigadiç Çavdarhisar
ia Bozcaada 1710 M.P. Simav 2120 Gediz
1240 Ayvacık Edremit Savaştepe Demirci △ 2308 Banaz
Gülpınarı Burhaniye △1344 Sındırgı Gördes Ahide
Ágios Efstrátios Mithimna Edremit Körfezi Soma Uşak
Ayvalık PERGAMON Kırkağaç TURKEY
Arísba Dikili Bergama Yunt Dağı Akhisar Borlu Selendi
Gioúra Polihnitos Yunt Dağı 1077 Saruhanlı Kula Ulubey
anagiá Pipéri Lesbos Mytillíni Aliağa Manisa Salihli Alaşehir Eşme
Peristéra Çandarlı Körfezi Foça Menemen Turgutlu Sarıgöl
via Melá Foça Salihli
Limariá Skíros Karaburun Boz Dağları
Psará Mármaro 1218 İZMİR
Kími 82 Chíos Urla Ödemiş Sarayköy PAMUKKALE
da Alivéri Chíos Çeşme Torbalı Bayındır *
assiliko Avlóna Alaçatı Tire Denizli
Párnitha N.P. Seferihisar EPHESOS Aydın Dağları Nazilli Karacasu Serinhisar
HINA (ATHENS) Káristos Kuşadası Selçuk Söke Bozdoğan Tavas
Gávrio Ándros Körfezi Kuşadası Aydın
Vouliagméni Ándros Sámos Çine
Lávrio Kéa Giáros Sámos 1422
Saronída Kíthnos Síros Tínos Ikaría Ágios Yenihisar Milas Yatağan Muğla 2421
Kírikos Gökova Köyceğiz
Kíthnos Mýkonos Pátmos Güllük Ören Ortaca
Ermoúpoli Siros Rinía Delos Lipsí Körfezi Gökova Dalaman
Sérifos Kímolos Naxos Léros HALIKARNASSOS Marmaris Fethiye
Kíthnos Filóti Kálimnos Bodrum Gökova Körfezi Fethiye
Antíparos Páros Náxos Kéros Amorgós Kálimnos Kós Datça Körfezi
Sífnos Íos Kós Bozburun
Kímolos Pollegos Amorgós Astipálea Kéfalos Sími
Antímilos Mílos Sikínos Astipálea Níssiros Ródos
Mílos Folégandros Anáfi Tílos (Rhodes) 4338
í Maléas Thíra Sírna Háldki Afándou
Thíra Monólithos Lindos Rhodes
(Santorin) 1215
Kattavia
irtóon Sea
Saria
Kárpathos
Sea of Crete Ólympos

24° Mc 26° Md 28° Me

Western Russia, Moscow region
Europe

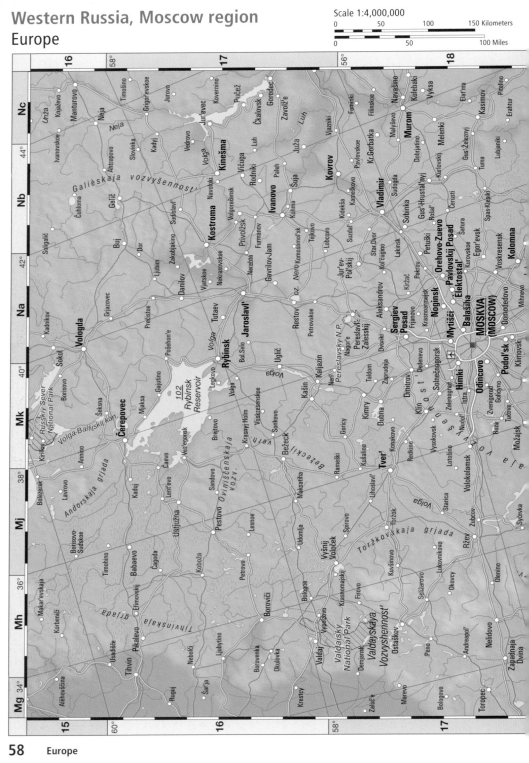

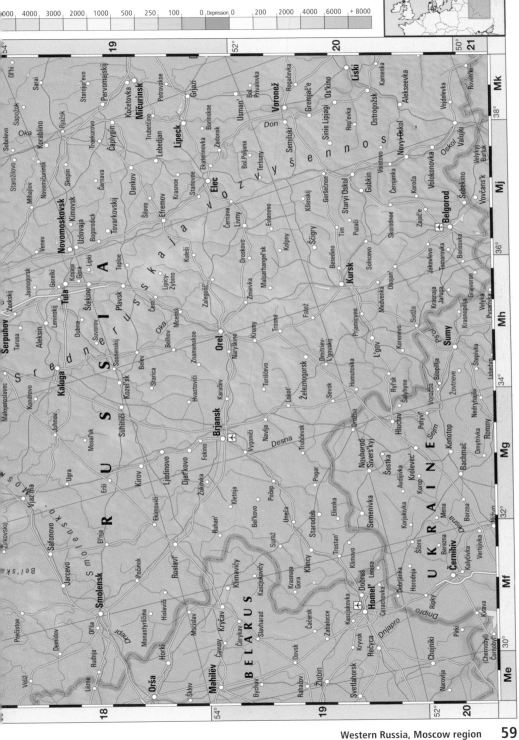

Scale 1:4,000,000

0   50   100   150 Kilometers

0   50   100 Miles

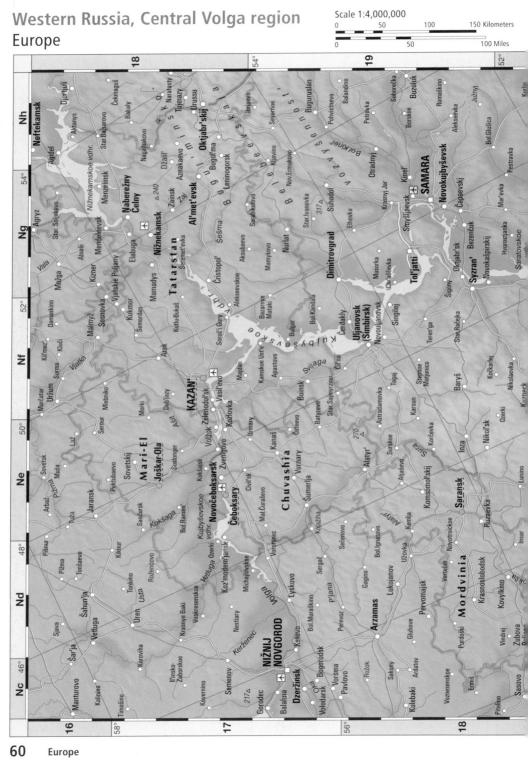

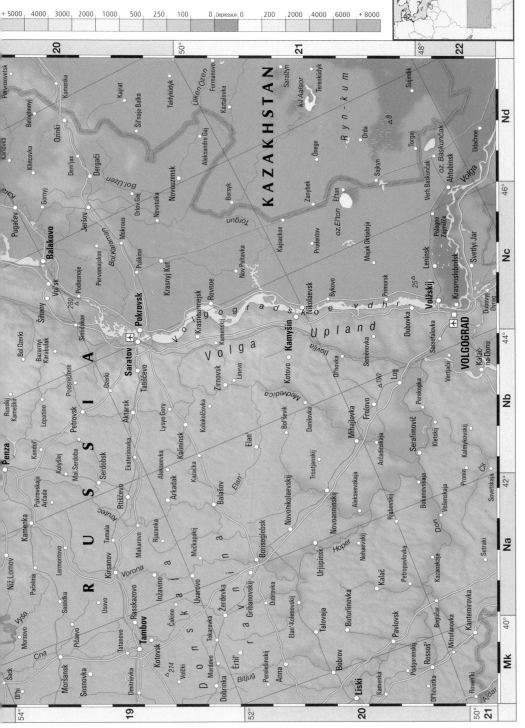

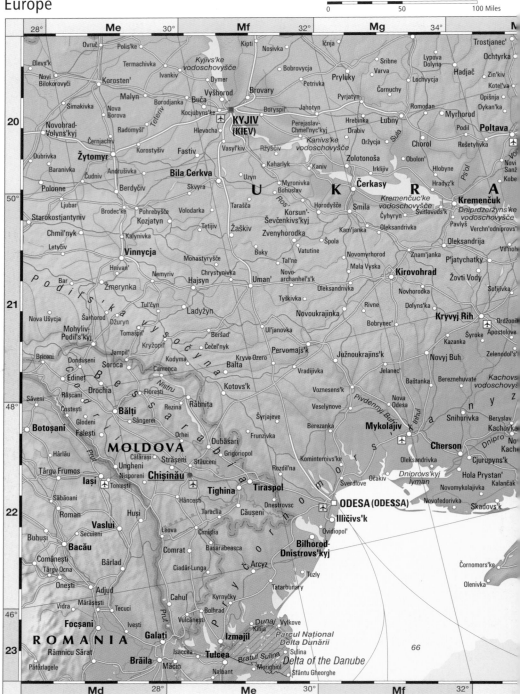

Moldova, Ukraine
Europe

Scale 1:4,000,000

0   50   100   150 Kilometers

0   50   100 Miles

Md 28° | **Me** 30° | **Mf** 32° | **Mg** 34° | **M**

20

50°

21

48°

22

23

Ovruč · Polis'ke · Kipti · Nosivka · Ičnja · Trostjanec'
Olevs'k · Termachivka · Kyjivs'ke vodoschovyšče · Bobrovycja · Sribne · Lypova Dolyna · Ochtyrka
Novi Bilokorovyči · Korosten' · Ivankiv · Dymer · Petrivka · Varva · Lochvycja · Hadjač · Zin'kiv
Simakivka · Malyn · Borodjanka · Buča · Brovary · Pryluky · Čornuchy · Romodan · Opišnja · Oykan'sk
Nova Borova · Radomyšl' · Kocjubyns'ke · **KYJIV (KIEV)** · Boryspil' · Jahotyn · Pyrjatyn · Podil · **Poltava**
Novohrad-Volyns'kyj · Hlevacha · Vyšhorod · Perejaslav-Chmel'nyc'kyj · Hrebinka · Drabiv · Myrhorod · Rešetylivka
Žytomyr · Čaniachiv · Korostyšiv · Fastiv · Vasyl'kiv · Ržyščiv · Kanivs'ke vodoschovyšče · Oržycja · Chorol · Hradyz'k · Novi Sanž
Dubrivka · Baranivka · Andrušivka · **Bila Cerkva** · Uzyn · Kaharlyk · Kaniv · Zolotonoša · Irklijiv · Obolon' · Hlobyne · Kobe
Polonne · Čudniv · Berdyčiv · Skvyra · Myronivka · Horobuslav · **Čerkasy** · Kremenčuc'ke vodoschovyšče · **Kremenčuk**
Starokostjantyniv · Ljubar · Pohrebyšče · Volodarka · Taraščá · Korsun'-Ševčenkivs'kyj · Smila · Čyhyryn · Svitlovods'k · Pavlyš · Verchn'odniprovs'k
Chmil'nyk · Brodec'ke · Kozjatyn · Tetijiv · Žaškiv · Zvenyhorodka · Kam'janka · Oleksandrivka · Oleksandrija · Vil'noh
Letyčiv · Kalynivka · Monastyryšče · Buky · Vatutine · Špola · Znam'janka · P'jatychatky · Vil'noh
Vinnycja · Hnivan' · Nemyriv · Chrystynivka · Tal'ne · Novomyrhorod · Mala Vyska · **Kirovohrad** · Žovti Vody
Bar · Žmerynka · Hajsyn · Uman' · Novoarchanhel's'k · Oleksandrivka · Novohorodka · Sofijivka
Nova Ušycja · Šarhorod · Tul'čyn · Ladyžyn · Tyškivka · Novoukrajinka · Rivne · Dolyns'k · **Kryvyj Rih** · Oržoniki
Mohyliv-Podil's'kyj · Tomašpil' · B=eršad' · Ul'janovka · Bobrynec' · Šyroke · Apostolove
Briceni · Donduşeni · Jampil' · Kryžopil' · Čečel'nyk · Kodyma · Kryve Ozero · Pervomajs'k · Jelanec' · Kazanka · Zelenodol's'k
Edineţ · Soroca · Camenca · **Balta** · Vradijivka · Južnoukrajins'k · Baštanka · Bereznehuvate · Kachovs'ke vodoschovyš
Săveni · Drochia · Florešti · **Kotovs'k** · Voznesens'k · Nova Odesa · Snihurivka · Beryslav · Kachovka
Briceni · Răscani · Rezina · Râbnița · Šyrjajeve · Veselynove · Berezanka · **Mykolajiv** · Novohorodka · **Cherson** · Kach
Botoşani · Glodeni · Bălți · Sângerei · Frunzivka · Berezanka · Sverdlove · Oleksandrivka · Cjurupyns'k
Hârlău · Fălești · Orhei · Dubăsari · Grigoriopol' · Kominternivs'ke · Očakiv · Dniprovs'kyj lyman · Hola Prystan' · Novomykolajivka · Kalančak · Skadovs'k
Târgu Frumos · Ungheni · Călărași · Străşeni · Stăuceni · Rozdil'na · Novofedorivka
Iași · Tomeşti · Nisporeni · **Chişinău** · Sverdlove · **ODESA (ODESSA)** · Novomykolajivka
Săbăoani · Huşi · Hâncești · **Tighina** · **Tiraspol** · Dnestrovsc · **Illičivs'k**
Roman · Leova · Căuşeni · Ovidiopol'
Buhuşi · Secueni · Cimişlia · Basarabeasca · **Bilhorod-Dnistrovs'kyj** · Čornomors'ke
Vaslui · Taraclia · Arcyz · Olenivka
Bacău · Comrat · Ciadâr-Lunga · Tuzly
Comăneşti · Bârlad · Tatarbunary
Târgu Ocna · Oneşti · Adjud · Cahul · Kyrnyčky · Bolhrad
Vidra · Mărăşeşti · Tecuci · Vulcăneşti · Dunaj · Vylkove
Focşani · Iveşti · **Izmajil** · Kilija
R O M A N I A · **Galaţi** · **Tulcea** · Parcul Național Delta Dunării · 66
Râmnicu Sărat · Isaccea · Bratul Sulina · Sulina · Delta of the Danube
Pătârlagele · **Brăila** · **Măcin** · Nalbant · Murighiol · Sfântu Gheorghe

U K R A
Podils'ka vysočyna
Bessarabia
Codru
MOLDOVA
Prutul
Delta of the Danube

+ 5000   4000   3000   2000   1000   500   250   100   0   Depression   0   200   2000   4000   6000   + 8000

Lypci
Derhači
Vil'šany
CHARKIV   Kup'jans'k   Pokrovs'ke   Novopskov   Markivka   Čertkovo   Kašary
duchiv   Čuhujiv   Kup'jans'k-   Bilokurakyne   Bilovods'k   Krivorože
hokuts'k   Mérefa   Vasyščeve   Ševčenkove   Vuzlovyj   Millerovo   Judin
Valky   Zmijiv   Lyman   Svatove   Starobil's'k   Bol'šinka   Černyškovskij
Nova   Balaklija   Stanyčno-   177   Morozovsk
Vodolaha   Pervomajs'k   Kun'je   Borova   Sjeverodonec'k   Luhans'ke
Krasnohrad   Hrušuvacha   Izjum   Lysyčans'k   Siv. Donec   Glubokij   Gornjackij   Šolohovskij
Krasnopavlivka   Barvinkove   Slov'jans'k   Zolote   Luhans'k   Kamensk-   Tacinskij
Lozova   Oleksandrivka   Stachanov   Lutuhyne   Šahtinskij   Belaja
Šandrivka   Kramators'k   Artemivs'k   Brjanka   Alčevs'k   Krasnodon   Kalitva
Pereščepyne   Jur'jivka   Kostjantynivka   Debal'ceve   Antracyt   Sverdlovs'k   Gukovo   Konstantinovsk
Hubynycha   Dobropillja   Horlivka   Krasnyj   Semikarakorsk
Malynivka   Oleksandrivka   Krasnoarmijs'k   Jenakijeve   Luč   Šahty
omoskovs'k   Petropavlivka   Jasynuvata   Makijivka   Novošahtinsk   Novočerkassk
Pavlohrad   Krasnohorivka   DONEC'K   Matveev   ROSTOV-   Stanica   Veselovskoe
pro-   Synel'nykovo   Havrivlivka   Kurgan   NA-DONU   Bagaevskaja   vdhr.
ržyns'k   DNIPRO-   Vasyl'kivka   Vel.Novosilka   Dokučajevs'k   Aksaj   Krasn.Manyč
PETROVS'K   Novomy-   Don   Batajsk
kolajivka   Pokrovs'ke   Tel'manove   Fēdorovka   Zernograd
vopokrovka   Zaporižžja   Vil'njans'k   Volnovacha   Azov   Egorlykskaja   Celina
Marhanec'   Orichiv   Huljajpole   Novoazovs'k   Kugej
Nikopol'   Tomakivka   Kachovs'ke   Polohy   Rozivka   Taganrog   Kuščevskaja
vodoschovyšče   Andrijivka   Mariupol'   Taganrogskij zaliv   Staromynskaja
erhodar   Dniprorudne   Vasylivka   Osypenko   Margaritove   RUSSIA
Mychajlivka   Zelenivka   Ejsk   Pavlovskaja   Novopokrovskaja
lyka   Tokmak   Prymors'k   Berdjans'k   Dolžanskaja   oz.   Kanevskaja
ytycha   Vesele   Berdjans'ka   Hanskoe   Čelbas   Tihoreck
vyna   Melitopol'   kosa   Jasenskaja   40   Berezanskaja
Nyžni   Pryazovs'ke   Primorsko-   Korenovsk
Sirohozy   Ivanivka   Obytična   Ahtarsk
Nyžni   kosa   Grivenskaja   Ust'-Labinsk
Torhaji   Kachovs'kyj kanal   Sea of Azov   Timaševsk   Krasnodarskoe
vdhr.   Adygea
Heničes'k   Slavjansk   Krasnodar   Belorečensk
na-Kubani   Paškovskij
Pivnično-Kryms'kyj kanal   Temrjuk   Majkop
Novoolejsijivka   zatoka Syvaš   Troickaja   Holmskij   Apšeronsk
mjans'k   Vejinka   Kerč   Starotitarovskaja   Gorjačij   Ključ
Džankoj   Nyžn'ohirs'kyj   Lenine   150   Kiziltašskij   Krymsk
vdzol'ne   liman   Anapa   920
selivs'k   Krasnohvardijs'ke   Kirovs'ke   Zavitne   Novorossijsk   Džubga   Sochinsky
Crimea   Feodosija   Gelendžik   Novomihajlovskij   Nacional'nyj park
evpatorija   Bilohors'k   Koktebel'   2140
Saky   Mykolajivka   Sudak   Tuapse
Simferopol'   Lazarevskoe
Bachčysaraj   Alušta
Hurzuf   2200
evastopol'   Yalta
Alupka   BLACK SEA

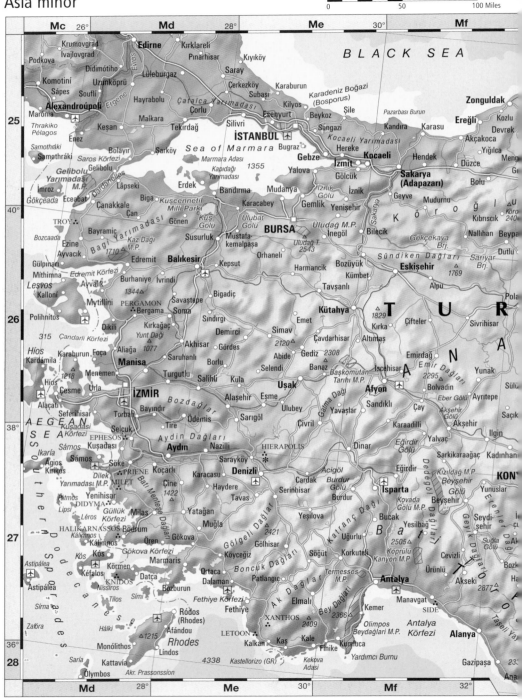

Western Turkey
Asia minor

Scale 1:4,000,000

0   50   100   150 Kilometers

0   50   100 Miles

| Mc | 26° | Md | 28° | Me | 30° | Mf |

B L A C K   S E A

Krumovgrad
Ivajlovgrad
Podkova
Didimótiho
Komotiní
Sápes
Soufli
Uzunköprü
Marónia
Thrakiko Pélagos
Enez
Imroz
Samothráki
Samothráki
Gelibolu Yarimadasi M.P.
Gökçeada
Eceabat

Edirne
Kırklareli
Pınarhisar
Lüleburgaz
Saray
Kıyıköy
Çerkezköy
Karaburun
Subaşı
Kilyos
İSTANBUL
Silivri
Esenyurt
Beykoz
Karadeniz Boğazi (Bosporus)
Şile
Pazarbaşı Burun
Zonguldak
Kozlu
Ereğli
Devrek
Akçakoca
Yığılca
Düzce
Meng

Maróni
Keşan
Malkara
Tekirdağ
Çatalca Yarimadasi
Çorlu
Hayrabolu
Bolayır
Şarköy
Sea of Marmara
Bugraz
Gebze
Hereke
İzmit
Kocaeli
Hendek
Kocaeli Yarimadasi
Sangazi
Kandıra
Karasu
Gölcük
Geyve
Mudurnu
Sakarya (Adapazarı)
Bolu

TROY
Bozcaada
Ezine
Ayvacık
Gülpınar
Mithimna
Lesvos
Kalloní
Polihnítos

Çanakkale
Çan
Bayramiç
Kaz Dağı M.P.
Biga
Kuşcennetil Mill Parki
Gönen
Kuş Gölü
Bandırma
Karacabey
Ulubat Gölü
Mustafa-kemalpaşa
BURSA
Uludağ M.P.
İnegöl
Bilecik
Gökçekaya Brj.
Nallıhan
Beypa

Erdek
Mudanya
İznik
İznik Gölü
Yenişehir
Uludağ T. 2543
Orhaneli
Bozüyük
Sündiken Dağları
Eskişehir
Sariyar Brj.
Dutlu

Edremit
Balıkesir
Kepsut
Harmancık
Kümbet
Tavşanlı
Alpu

Burhaniye
İvrindi
Savaştepe
Bigadiç
Emet
Kütahya
1829
Kırka
Çifteler
Sivrihisar

PERGAMON
Bergama
Kırkağaç
Yunt Dağı 1077
Soma
Sındırgı
Demirci
Simav
Çavdarhisar
Altıntaş
TURA

Dikili
Aliağa
Foça
Akhisar
Gördes
Abide
Gediz
Banaz
Başkomutan Tarıhı M.P.
Emirdağ
Emir Dağları 2295
Yunak

Híos
Kardámila
Karaburun
Manisa
Saruhanlı
Borlu
Selendi
İscehisar
Bolvadin
Eber Gölü
Ayrıtepe

Híos
Çeşme
Menemen
Turgutlu
Salihli
Kula
Uşak
Afyon
Çay
Akşehir Gölü
Akşehir

Alaçatı
Seferihisar
İZMİR
Bayındır
Alaşehir
Eşme
Ulubey
Yavaşlar
Sandıklı
Karaadilli
Yalvaç
Ilgın

A E G E A N   S E A
Ikaría
Sámos
Torbalı
Tire
Ödemiş
Sarıgöl
Çivril
Dinar
Eğirdir Gölü
Eğirdir
Sarkıkaraağaç
Kadınha

Selçuk
EPHESOS
Aydın
Nazilli
HIERAPOLIS
Saraköy
Denizli
Çardak
Acıgöl
Burdur Gölü

Kuşadası
Sámos
Söke
PRIENE
Koçarlı
Karacasu
Haydere
Serinhisar
Kovada Gölü M.P.
Isparta
Beyşehir
KON'

Dilek Yarımadası M.P.
MILET
Çine
1422
Tavas
Burdur
Bucak
Beyşehir Gölü
Yunuslar

DIDYMA
Milas
Yatağan
Yeşilova
Uğurlu
Seydişehir

HALIKARNASSOS Bodrum
Ören
Muğla
Gölgeli Dağları 2421
Köprülü Kanyon M.P.
Cevizli
Ürünlü
Akseki

Gökova
Gölhisar
Köyceğiz
Söğüt
Korkuteli
Termessos M.P.
Kemer
Manavgat

Marmaris
Ortaca
Dalaman
Patlangıç
Bey Dağları 2366
SIDE
Antalya Körfezi

KNIDOS
Datça
Bozburun
Fethiye Körfezi
XANTHOS
Elmalı
Olimpos Beydağları M.P.
Antalya Körfezi
Alanya

Ródos (Rhodes)
Afándou
LETOON
Fethiye
Kalkan
Kaş
Kale
Finike
Kumluca
Gazipaşa

Monólithos
Líndos
Rhodes
Kastellorizo (GR)
Kekova Adası
Yardımcı Burnu
Ana

Scale 1:4,000,000

0   50   100   150 Kilometers
0   50   100 Miles

38° Mk 40°   **Na 42°**   **Nb 44°**

23 Apšeronsk · Mostovskoj · Otradnaja · Čerkessk · Suvorovskaja · Mineral'nye Vody · Zelenokumsk · Irg
Novomihajlovskij · Sočinskij nacional'nyj park · Adygea · Psebaj · Kurdžinovo · Ust'-Džeguta · Pjatigorsk · Georgievsk · Aga-B · R U S
Tuapse · Hamyški · Zelenčukskaja · Ordžonikidzevskij · Essentuki · Svobody · Novopavlovsk · Mozc
44° Lazarevskoe · g.Čugus 3238 · Krasnaja Poljana · Kavkazskij zapovednik · Karačaevsk · Karachay-Cherkessia · Nacional'nyj park Prielbrus'e · Baksan · Prohladnyj · Majskij
Dagomys · Avadkhara · Teberda · Tyrnyauz · Nal'čik · Nartkala · Malgobek · Terek
Soči · Adler · Teberdinskij zapovednik · g.Dombaj · g.El'brus 5642 · El'brus · Kabardino-Balkaria · Sovetskoe · Ardon · Naz
Gagra · Gudauta · Dombaj 4046 · Kabardino-Balkarskij zapovednik · Digora · North · Alagir · Beslan
24 Bitčvinta · **Abkhazia** · Zemo Ažara · Mestia · g.Djdlas 5204 · per. Mamisonski (2829) · Mizur · Kazbegi · **C**
Sokhumi · Tqvarčeli · 4008 · Čazasi · Severo-Osetinskij zapovednik · g.Kazbek 5033 · North Ossetia
Očamčire · Džvari · Tsageri · Oni · Ambrolauri · Rioni · Kre
Gali · Ingur · Tsaltubo · Tqibuli · **South Ossetia** · **Tkhinvali**
Zugdidi · Senaki · **Kutaisi** · **GEORGI**
Poti · Samtredia · Zestaponi · Surami · Khašuri · Gori · Mtsk
42° Ozurgeti · Bagdati · Mta Mepistskaro 2850 · Abastumani · Bordžomi · Bakuriani · **TBIL**
Kobuleti · **Adzharia** · Šuakhevi · Akhaltsikhe · (TIBIL)
Batumi · Kemalpaşa · Posof · Akhalkalaki
Hopa · Borčka · Meydancik · Hanak · Ninotsminda
25 Arhavi · (2640) · Čıldır · g.Ačkasar 3194 · Tashir · Alav
Ardeşen · Pazar · Artvin 3348 · Ortaköy · Čıldır Gölü · 3042 · **Gyumri** · Step'anavan
Ordu · Tirebolu · Vakfıkebir · Trabzon · Rize · Çayeli · Yusufeli · Olur · Kars · Spitak
Bulanlak · Akçaabat · Aralık · İyidere · Kaçkar Dağı 3937 · Göle · Art'ik · **ARM**
Giresun · Tonya · Altındere Vadisi M.P. · Çoruh Nehri · Akşar · Senkaya · Kars · 4090 g.Arač · Ch'arents'a
Dereli · Doğankent · Oltu · Sarıkamış · Digor · Kağızman · Ashtarak
Şebinkarahisar · Torul 3331 · Gümüşhane (1900) · İspir · (2600) · Narman · Karaurgan · Akçay · Echmiadzin
Süşehri · Siran · Kaledibi · Maden · Ovacık · Pasinler · Karakurt · Horasan · Tuzluca · Iğdır · Masis
40° Refahiye · Köse · Bayburt · Aşkale · **Erzurum** · Eleşkirt · Ağrı · (2010) · Iğdır · Artaşa
Erzincan · Üzümlü · Tercan · Çakmak Dağı · Karayazı · (2040) · Ağrı Dağı (Mt. Ararat) 5165 · Doğubeyi
Sarıpınar · Çat · Tekman · Hacıömer · Tutak · Diyadin · Maku
Sincan · İliç · Kemah · Pülümür · Yedisu · Kökpınar · Göksu · Aktuzla · Patnos · Ala Dağlar 3533 · Çaldıran · Erciş
Divriği · Fırat Nehri · Munzur Dağları · Karagöl Dağları · Hınıs · Yolüstü · Malazgirt · Doğansu · Samsu · Siyah cheshn
26 Kozlupınar · 2631 · 3147 · Munzur Vadisi Milli Parkı · Kiği · Karlıova · Çaylar · 3193 · Varto · Erentepe · Bulanık · Süphan Dağı 4058 · Ahlat · Muradiye
Arapkir · Cemişgezek · **Tunceli** · Gökçek · Sancak · Şerafettin Dağları · Ovakışla · Adilcevaz · Erçek Gölü · Özalp
Hekimhan · Kara Kaya Brj. 2116 · Karakoçan · Bingöl · Solhan · Söğütlü · Aşağı Üçdam · Van Gölü · Erçek · Van
Yazıhan · **Güney Doğu Toroslar** · **Elazığ** · Palu · Kovancılar · Muş · Güroymak · Tatvan

38° Mk 40°   **Na 42°**   **Nb 44°**

+ 5000 4000 3000 2000 1000 500 250 100 0 Depression 0 200 2000 4000 6000 + 8000

Terekli-Mekteb
Komsomol'skij
ostrov Čečen
Syghyndy müyis
KAZAKHSTAN
Manghystau
Krajnovka
Aktau
Zhetibai
Kizljar
Omirzak
Munaishy
-132
Lenina
Agrahanskij
poluostrov
Kargalinskaja
Kuryk
Goragorskij
Chechenia
Sulevkent
Pesschanyi müyis
Gudermes
Hasavjurt
Rakushechnyi müyis
Goragorskij
Groznyj
Argun
Najbere
Kiziljurt
Mahačkala
Leninkent
Kaspijsk
Šali
gushetia
avkaz
Argun
Šatoj
per.
Harami
(2177)
Bujnaksk
Manaskent
C A S P I A N   S E A
Tloh
Oboda
Izberbaš
g.Addala
Šuhgel'meer
4151
Golotl'
Levasi
Kajakent
Mamedkala
Kundy
Tianeti
khmeta
Telavi
Kvareli
Kuli
Derbent
Kurah
Belidzi
Yalama
Gurdžaani
Balaken
Kasumkent
Xudat
Ahty
Saga-
redžo
Zaqatala
Samur
Rutul
Qusar
Xaçmaz
Gardabani
Alazani
Qax
Quba
rneuli
Šeki
g.Bazazbjuzi
4466
Deveç
Qazax
Qebele
Siyezen
Tovuz
Mingeçevir su
anbari
Babadag
3629
Apšeronskij poluostrov
Ijevan
Šamkir
Mingeçevir
Ismayilli
Haçi
Sumqayit
Dilijan
Gänzä
Agdas
Göyçay
Šamaxi
Zeynalabdin
Buzovna
ARMENIA
Artzvashen
Yevlax
Laki
Ahsu
Xirdalan
Artyom
IA
Toganaly
Barda
Ucar
Kürdämir
Lökbetan
Hövsan
Qarabattaq adasi
Chambarak
razdan
g.G'amys Çayli
3725
AZERBAIJAN
Qazimemmed
Qobustan
BAKI
(BAKU)
Suiti
burnu
vian
Lake Sevan
Agdžabedi
Sabirabad
Alat
REVAN
Vardenis
Kalbacar
Agdam
Saatli
Ali Bayramli
Bakinskij arhipelago
Martuni
Istisu
Tartar
**Nagornyy-
Karabakh**
Bahramtapa
Imishli
Muganskaja
ravnina
Ararat
Yeghegnadzor
**Xankendi
(Stepanakert)**
Xocavand
Beylaqan
Salyan
1025
Karki
Lacin
Šuša
Füzuli
Pars Abad
Xıllı
Banka
Bicanak asr.
(2346)
Goris
Horadiz
Moradlu
Bilesuvar
Sisian
Qubadli
Aslanduz
Celilabad
AZERBAIJAN
Kapan
3904
Khoda Afarin
Ghermi
Masalli
Naxçivan
Kadhzaran
Havali
Yardimli
Lerik
Lekeran
Culfa
Mincivan
Meghri
Kharvanaq
Salavat
Qosmeliyon
Astara
Jolfa
Almandar
Kalalaq
Qare
Ziya' Eddin
Ev Oghl
Kiyamaki Dagh
3347
I R A N
Razi
Shahrivar
Astara
Khoy
Marand
Alanjeq
Vardin
Meshgin Shahr
Ahar

Asia
Physical map

Scale 1:50,000,000

0   500   1000   1500 Kilometers

0   500   1000 Miles

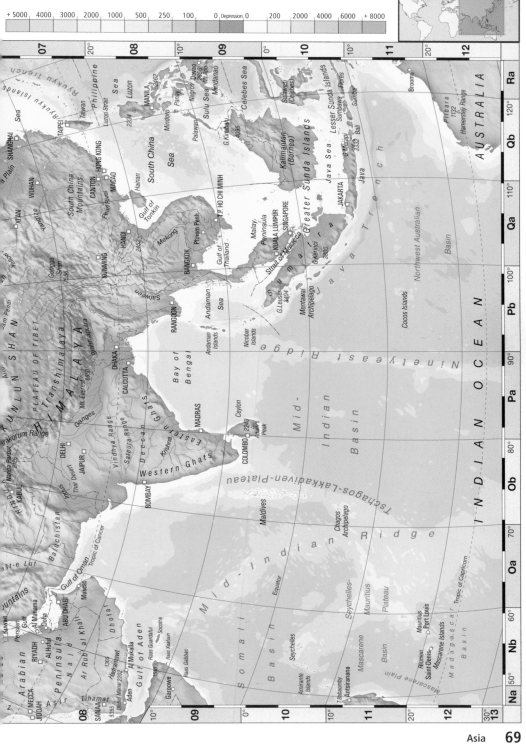

+ 5000 | 4000 | 3000 | 2000 | 1000 | 500 | 250 | 100 | 0 Depression 0 | 200 | 2000 | 4000 | 6000 | + 8000

Top scale: 07 20° 08 10° 09 0° 10 10° 11 20° 12

Right scale: Ra Qb 120° Qa 110° Pb 100° Pa 90° Ob 80° Oa 70° Nb 60° Na 50°

Bottom scale: 08 10° 09 0° 10 10° 11 20° 12 30° 13

Ryukyu Trench
Ryukyu Islands
Philippine Sea
Taiwan
TAIPEI
Luzon Strait
Luzon
MANILA
2234
Mindoro
Panay
Negros
Davao
Mt. Apo 2954
Mindanao
Sulu Sea
G.Kinabalu 4096
Celebes Sea
Sulawesi (Celebes)
Palawan
 Pertis
Sumbawa
Sumba
Lesser Sunda Islands
G.Rinjani
G.Merapi
Bali
3332
AUSTRALIA
Broome
Pilbara 1132
Hamersley Range

SHANGHAI
Plain
XI'AN
WUHAN
South China Mountains
HONG KONG
CANTON
MACAO
Pearl River
Hainan
South China Sea
Gulf of Tonkin
HANOI
2452
KUNMING
Gongga Shan 7556
Nu
Salween
Mekong
BANGKOK
Gulf of Thailand
Phnom Penh
TP. HO CHI MINH
Malay Peninsula
KUALA LUMPUR
SINGAPORE
Strait of Malacca
Kalimantan (Borneo)
Java Sea
JAKARTA
Java
Sumatra
Greater Sunda Islands
Java Trench
Northwest Australian Basin

KUNLUN SHAN
Nam Penon
Transhimalaya
PLATEAU OF TIBET
HIMALAYA
Brahmaputra
Karakorum Range
Mt. Everest 8850
DHAKA
CALCUTTA
Ganges
MADRAS
Eastern Ghats
Krishna
Bay of Bengal
Andaman Islands
Andaman Sea
Nicobar Islands
Mid- Indian Basin
Ninetyeast Ridge
Indian Basin
G.Leuser 3404
Mentawai Archipelago
G.Kerinci 3800
Cocos Islands

INDULH
DELHI
KABUL
JAIPUR
Thar Desert
Indus
Vindhya Range
Satpura Range
Deccan
Western Ghats
Ceylon
Adam's Peak 2243
COLOMBO
BOMBAY
Maldives
Tschagos-Lakkadiven-Plateau
Chagos Archipelago
Mid - Indian Ridge
INDIAN OCEAN

Baluchistan
Dasht-e Lut
Gulf of Oman
Tropic of Cancer
Muscat
Dhofar
Ar Rub' al Khali
Equator
Seychelles
Seychelles
Mauritius Plateau
Tropic of Capricorn

Kuwait
Persian Gulf
RIYADH
Al Hufuf
Doha
ABU DHABI
Al Manama
DOHA
Nejd
Arabian Peninsula
Asir
MECCA
JIDDAH
Tihamat
3355
SANAA
Aden
Gulf of Aden
Hadramawt
Al Mukalla
Jebel Marra 2002
Socotra
Raas Guardafui
Raas Xaafuun
Raas Gabbac
Garoowe
Somali Basin
Amirante Islands
T.Babaomby
Antsiranana
Mascarene Plain
Madagascar
Mascarene Basin
Mascarene Islands
Réunion
Saint-Denis
Mauritius
Port Louis
1365

Asia 69

Asia
Political map

Scale 1:50,000,000

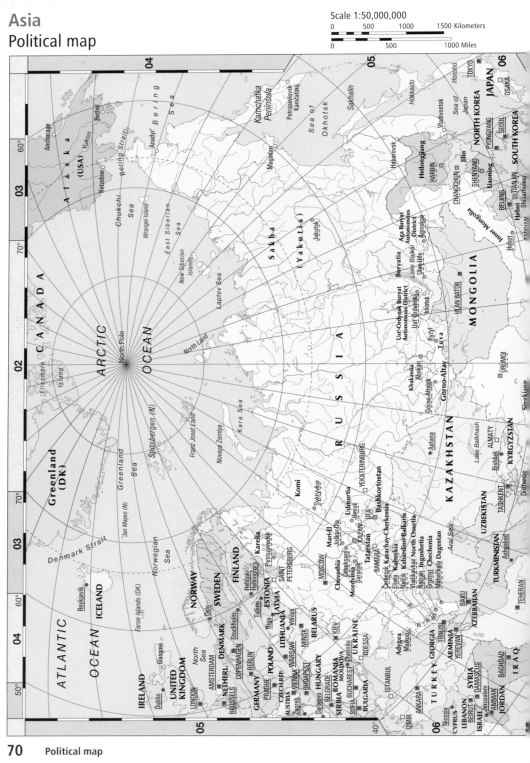

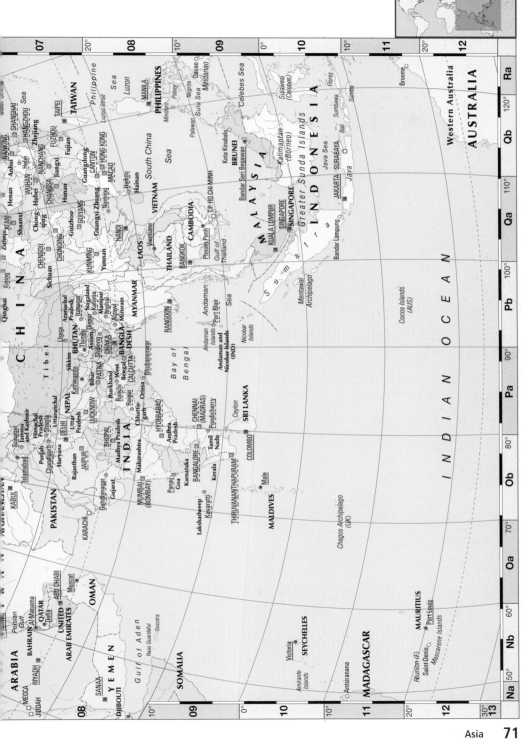

Scale 1:16,000,000

| 0 | 200 | 400 | 600 Kilometers |
| 0 | 200 | | 400 Miles |

15° 20° 25° 30° 35° 40° 45° 5°

Mo i Rana
Narvik
2111 △
Kebnekaise
Hammerfest
North Cape
Kiruna
Alta **NORWAY**
Storuman
Muonio
Inari
S W E D E N
Gällivare
L a p l a n d
Jyväskylä
Kuopio
Pielinen
Joensuu
Savonlinna
Kostomukša
Karelia
Kem'
Belomorsk
Onežskaja guba
Lappeenranta
Vyborg
Segozero
Medvež'egorsk
Kola Peninsula
Murmansk
Severomorsk
Mončegorsk
Kandalakša
Apatity
Gremiha
Ponoj
m.Kanin Nos
Varangerfjorden
Kirkenes
Inarijärvi
Rovaniemi
Sodankylä
Kemi
Oulu
Kuusamo
Vaasa
Kokkola
Hailuoto
Karlö
FINLAND
Gulf of Bothnia
Umeå
Luleå

B a r e n t s   S e a
Murmanskoye Rise
33
Pečorskoe more
p-ov Kanin
Čёšskaja guba
o.Kolgujev
Nar'jan-Mar
Nenets Autonomous District
Amderma
Jugorskij p-ov
proliv Karskie Vorota
o.Vajgač
Bajdarackaja guba
Novaya Zemlya
1547
pik Sedóva △
1115
Kara Se

60° SAINT PETERSBURG
Petrozavodsk
Lake Onega
Lake Ladoga
Borovici
Toržok
Tver'
Dubna
Rybinsk
Sergiev-Posad
MOSCOW
Orehovo-Zuevo
Vladimir
Rjazan'
Murom
Šack
Mordvinia
Saransk
Penza
Kuzneck
Syzran'
Saratov
Engel's
Kamyšin
Volgogradskoe vdhr.
Čapaev
Oral
Žambejti
Orenburg
Novotroick
Orsk
Irklinskoe vdhr.
Žetikara
Orenburg
Ural
Balakovo
Eršov
Simbirsk
Čeboksary
Chuvashia
Dimitrovgrad
Kujbyševskoe vdhr.
Tatarstan
Tol'jatti
SAMARA
Novokujbyševsk
Buguruslan
Bugulma
Malmyž
Nabereznye Celny
KAZAN'
Joškar-Ola
Mari-El
Udmurtia
Iževsk
Sarapul
Okt'jabr'skij
UFA
Bashkortostan
Sterlitamak
Kumertau
Salavat
Magnitogorsk

Kargopol'
Konoša
Vel'sk
Ust'-Varga
Vologda
Kostroma
Kinešma
Šar'ja
Kotel'nič
Veluga
Vjatka (Kirov)
Kirovo-Čepeck
NIŽNIJ NOVGOROD
Čerepovec
Rybinsk Reservoir
Onega
Severodvinsk
Arhangel'sk
Mežen'
Pinega
Kotlas
Vycegda
Syktyvkar
Severnye uvaly
Solikamsk
Berezniki
Kamskoe vdhr.
1569 △
gora Konžakovskij Kamen'
Serov
Pervoural'sk
PERM'
Nižnij Tagil
Irbit
Kamensk-Ural'skij
Šadrinsk
YEKATERINBURG
Tjumen'
Tavda
Tobol
Zavodoukovsk
Tobol'sk
Tara
Irtyš (Irtysh)
OMSK
nizmennost
Barabinskaja
Petropavl
Isil'kul'
Západnoe
Rudnyj
Kostanaj
Troick
Kopejsk
Kurgan
Išim
ČELJABINSK
Miass
Zlatoust
Troick

Kandalakšskaja g.
White Sea
Belomorsk
Timanskiy Krjaž
Pečora
Ust'-Cil'ma
Boľšezemeľskaja tundra
Komi
Uhta
Pečora
Inta
Sosnogorsk
gora Telposiz 1617 △
gora Narodnaja 1894
gora Pajer 1499
Vorkuta
Yamal Nenets Autonomous Distr
Ob
Belojarskij
Njagan
Khanty-Mansi Autonomous District
Hanty-Mansijsk
Neftejugansk
Surg
Si bi
W e s t
S i b e r i
P l a i n

06
07
08
09
55°
50°

| Nb 50° | Nc 55° | Nd 60° | Oa 65° | Ob 70° | Oc 75° | 5° |

Eastern Russia
Asia

Scale 1:16,000,000

| 0 | 200 | 400 | 600 Kilometers |
| 0 | | 200 | 400 Miles |

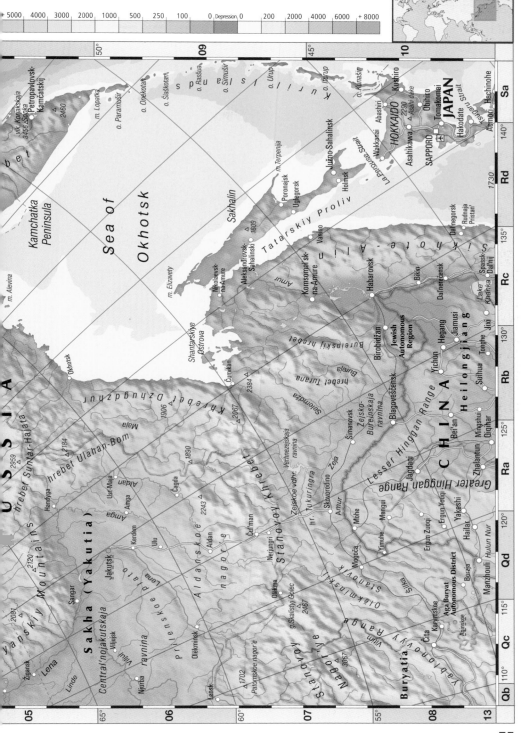

Map labels

vlk. Konjakskaja 3456
Sopka
Petropavlovsk-Kamčatskij
2460
m. Lopatka
o. Paramušir
o. Onekotan
o. Šiaškotan
p Rasšua
o. Simušir
Kuril Is lands
o. Urup
o. Iturup
o. Kunašir
Kushiro
Obihiro
Tomakomai
HOKKAIDO
2290
Asahi dake
Abashiri
Wakkanai
Asahikawa
SAPPORO
JAPAN
Hakodate
Hakodate Strait
Atmori Hachinohe
1730

Kamchatka Peninsula

b e t

m. Alevina

Sea of Okhotsk

Sakhalin

m. Terpenija
1609
Južno-Sahalinsk
Poronajsk
Uglegorsk
Holmsk

Tatárskiy Proliv
La Pérouse Strait

Sikhote-Alin'

Vanino
Dalnegorsk
Rudnaja Pristan'

Nikolaevsk-na-Amure
Aleksandrovsk-Sahalinski
Amur
Komsomol'sk-na-Amure
Habarovsk
Bikin
Spassk-Dalnij
Lake Khanka

m. Elizavety
Shantarskiye Ostrova

Okhotsk

Čumikan
2384

Khrebet Dzhugdzhur
1906
Maja
2667

Bureinskij hrebet
hrebet Turana
Bureja
Birobidžan
Jewish Autonomous Region
Hegang
Jiamusi
Jixi
Yichun
Tonghe
Suihua
Heilongjiang
CHINA

Selemdža
Zejsko-Bureinskaja ravnina
Blagoveščensk
Bei'an
Mingshui
Qiqihar

hrebet Suntar-Hajata
2184
2059

Aldan
Handyga
Ust'-Maja
Amga
1890

Verhnezejskaja ravnina
Šimanovsk
Zejsko vdhr.
Zeja
Skovorodino
Amur
Mohe
Mengui

Lesser Hinggan Range
Jagdaqi
Zhalantun
Yakeshi
Hailar

Amga
2243
Čul'man
Nerjungri

Stanovoy Khrebet
hr. Tukuringra
Mogoča
Jimuhe

Greater Hinggan Range
Ergun Youqi
Ergun Zuoqi

2120
Šangar
Jakutsk
Kerden
Ulu
Aldan
nagore

Olekminskij stanovik
Šilka
Buraja

Manzhouli
Hulun Nur

RUSSIA

Sakha (Yakutia)

Aldanskoe nagore

Central'nojakutskaja ravnina

Prilenskoe plato

Aldan
Lena

Handyga

Olëkminsk
Olëkma
g. Skalistyj Golec
2467

Vitim Range
Karymskoe
Čita
Aginskoe
Aga-Buryat Autonomous District
Buryatia

2081
Žigansk
2120

Viljujsk
Lena
Vilюj
Njurba
Linde
Lensk
1702

Stanovoye nagorye
3067

Vitimskoe ploskogorye

yanskiy Mountains

hrebet Ulahan-Bom

50°
45°
140°
135°
130°
125°
120°
115°
110°

09
10
Sa
Rd
Rc
Rb
Ra
Qd
Qc
Qb
13
05
65°
06
60°
07
55°
08

Near and Middle East
Asia

Scale 1:16,000,000

| 0 | 200 | 400 | 600 Kilometers |

| 0 | 200 | 400 Miles |

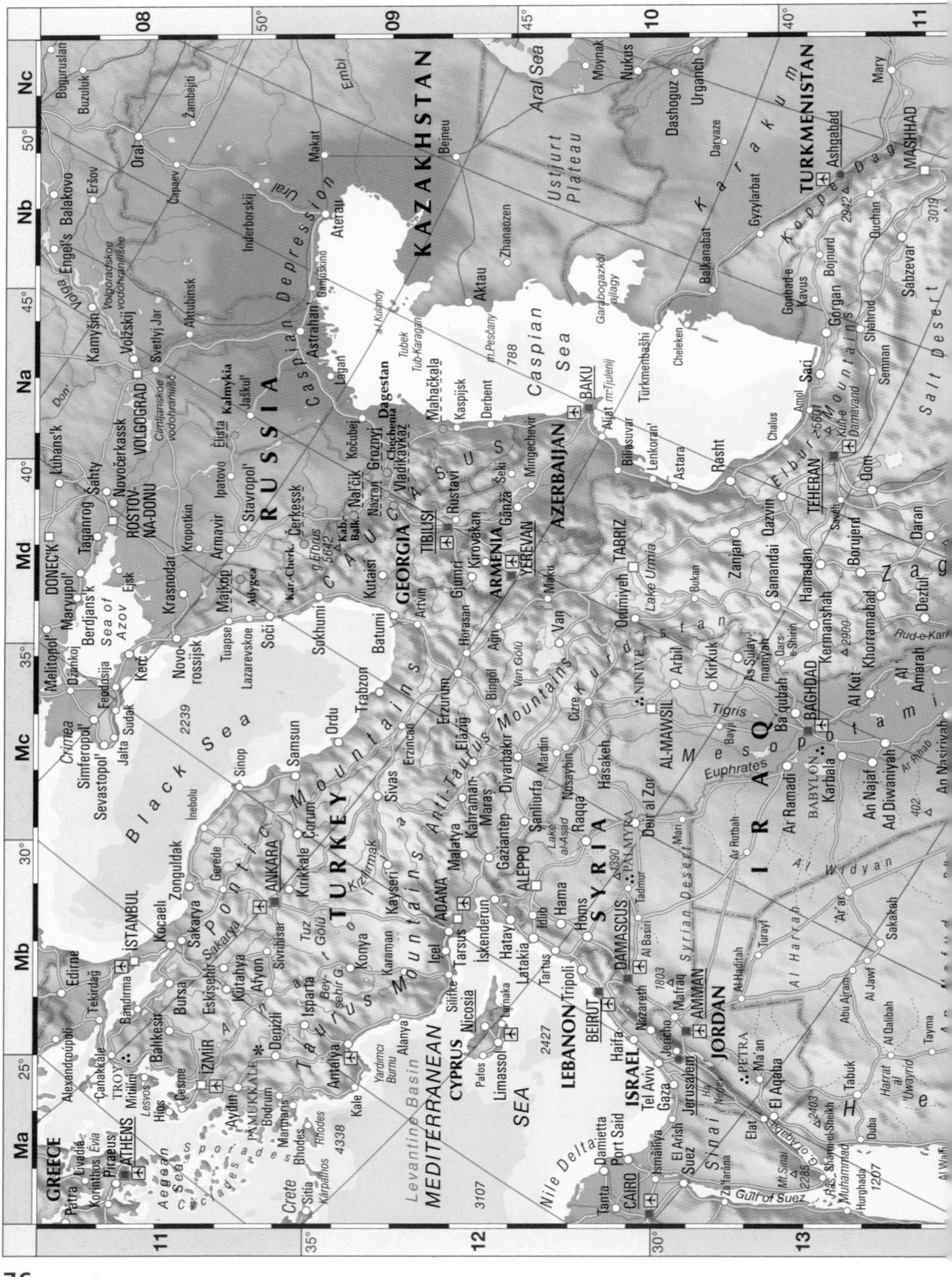

KAZAKHSTAN

TURKMENISTAN

MASHHAD

RUSSIA

Caspian Sea

Aral Sea

Ustjurt Plateau

Kara kum

Köpet Dag

Elburz Mountains

Salt Desert

VOLGOGRAD

ROSTOV-NA-DONU

DONECK

Sea of Azov

Crimea

Black Sea

GEORGIA

TBILISI

ARMENIA

YEREVAN

AZERBAIJAN

BAKU

Caucasus

Dagestan

Grozny

Vladikavkaz

TEHERAN

TABRIZ

Lake Urmia

Zagros Mountains

GREECE

ATHENS

ISTANBUL

ANKARA

TURKEY

Taurus Mountains

Anti-Taurus Mountains

Pontic Mountains

IZMIR

TROY

CYPRUS

Nicosia

LEBANON

BEIRUT

SYRIA

DAMASCUS

ALEPPO

PALMYRA

IRAQ

BAGHDAD

AL-MAWSIL

Mesopotamia

Euphrates

Tigris

BABYLON

Karbala

ISRAEL

Jerusalem

Tel Aviv

JORDAN

AMMAN

PETRA

El Aqaba

CAIRO

Sinai

Nile Delta

Gulf of Suez

MEDITERRANEAN SEA

Levantine Basin

Aegean Sea

Syrian Desert

Al Widyan

76   Asia

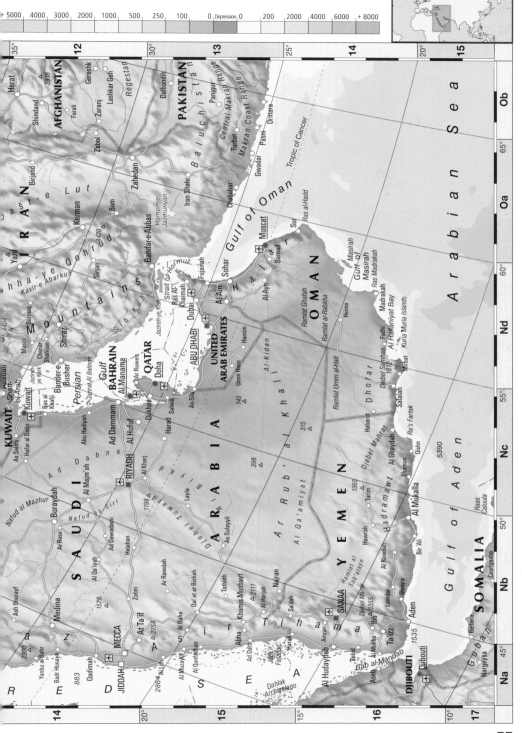

5000 4000 3000 2000 1000 500 250 100 0 Depression 0 200 2000 4000 6000 + 8000

35° **12** 30° **13** 25° **14** 20° **15**

Ob

Herat
Shindand 3916
AFGHANISTAN
Gereshk
Lashkar Gah
Regestan
Farah
Zaranj
Dalbandin

PAKISTAN

Panjgur
Central Makran Range
Makran Coast Range
Turbat
Ormara

Oa

Birjand
Kerman
Bam
Zahedan
Iran Shahr
Chahbahar
Gwadar
Pasni
Tropic of Cancer

Yazd
Kavir-e Abarkuh
hha-ye Qohrud
4404
Sirjan
Bandar-e-Abbas
Hamun-e Jazmurian
Ras al-Hadd
Sur

Nd

I R A N
Mountains
Shahjan 4420
Shiraz
Strait of Hormuz
Jazireh-ye Kish
Ras Al Khaimah
Muscat
Sohar
Samail
Masirah
Gulf of Masirah
Ras Madrakah

Chenar
Masiri
Bander-e Busher
Sibkun
Fujairah
Al 'Ain
Al Ayn
Ramlat Ghafah
Ramlat ar-Rabka
Heima
Madrakah
Al Halfaniyat Bay
Kuria Muria Islands

Nc

Auduh
Jazireh
Bander-e Busher
B A H R A I N
Al Manama
Q A T A R
Doha
ABU DHABI
Al-Kidan
Umm Husn
O M A N
Djebel Samhaan 1812
Fadhi
Mirbat

Kuwait
Ras al Khafji
Ar Ruweis
Dukhan
UNITED ARAB EMIRATES
Hamim
Dhofar
Salalah

KUWAIT
As Salihy
Hafar al Batin
Abu Hadiyah
As Sila
Salwa
145
315
Djebel Mahrat
Haruni
Ras'a Fartak

Ad Dammam
Al Hufuf
Harad
398
Ar Rub' al Khali
Ras al-Hadd
5390
Nb

S A U D I
Ad Dahna
RIYADH
Al Kharj
Layla
Al Qa'amiyat
Tarim
Thamud
Al Ghaydah
Qishn

Nafud al Mazhur
Burayduh
Nafud as Sirr
1198
As Sulayyil
1365
Y E M E N
Hawrah
Bir 'Ali
Shiqra

Ar Rass
Ad Dawadami
Djebel Tuwayq
A R A B I A
Tathlith
Najran
Ramlat al Sab'atayn
Lawdar

Al Qa'iyah
Ar Rawdah
Khamis Mushayt
Al Harjah
2111
SANAA
Djebel Nabi 3355
Ta'izz

Medina
1578
Zalim
Dal'at at Bishah
Sa'dah
Ibb
Aden
1535
Na

Badr Hunayn
883
Qadimah
At Ta'if
Al Baha
2754
Atha
Ad Dahr
Amran
Zeila
Berbera
SOMALIA

2300
Yanbu al Bahr
MECCA
JIDDAH
2864-Al Lith
Al Muzaylif
Al Qunfidhah
Harad
Jaza'ir Farasan
Al Hudaydah
Al Mukha
Bab al-Mandab
Aseb
DJIBOUTI
Djibouti
Ceelgaabo
Hargeysa

Dahlak Archipelago

R E D S E A
S i r a t
T i h a m a
Gulf of Aden
Raas Caluula

A r a b i a n S e a

Persian Gulf
Gulf of Oman

14 20° 15 15° 16 10° 17

Near and Middle East 77

Scale 1:16,000,000

Southern Asia
Asia

Scale 1:16,000,000

0 200 400 600 Kilometers

0 200 400 Miles

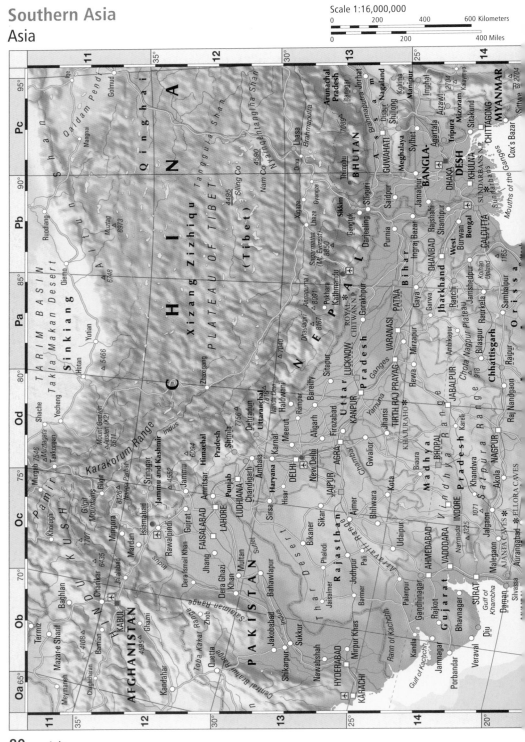

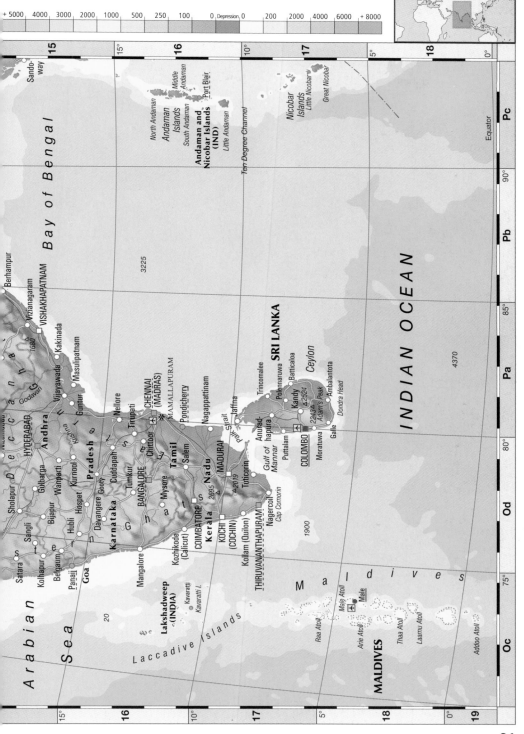

+ 5000 | 4000 | 3000 | 2000 | 1000 | 500 | 250 | 100 | 0 Depression 0 | 200 | 2000 | 4000 | 6000 | + 8000

Sando-
way

Berhampur

Vizianagaram
VISHAKHAPATNAM
Kakinada

Bay of Bengal

1680

Godavari

Masulipatnam
Vijayawada
Guntur

3225

Nellore

HYDERABAD
Andhra

Krishna

Tirupati

Sholapur
Gulbarga
Wanparti
Kurnool
Cuddapah
Chittoor
CHENNAI
(MADRAS)
MAMALLAPURAM

Bijapur
Hospet
Tumkur
Salem
Pondicherry

Hubli
BANGALORE
Mysore
Tamil
Nagapattinam

Sangli
Davangere
Gooty
Karnataka
2695
Nadu
MADURAI
2019

Belgaum
Ghats
COIMBATORE
Tuticorin

Panaji
Goa
Mangalore
Kozhikode
(Calicut)
Kerala
Nagercoil
Cap Comorin

20
Kavaratti I.
Kavaratti
KOCHI
(COCHIN)
Kollam (Quilon)
THIRUVANANTHAPURAM

*Lakshadweep
(INDIA)*

1900

Laccadive Islands

M a l d i v e s

Raa Atoll
Arie Atoll
Thaa Atoll
Laamu Atoll
Addoo Atoll

Male Atoll
Male

MALDIVES

A r a b i a n   S e a

North Andaman
Middle
Andaman
Andaman
Islands
South Andaman

**Andaman and
Nicobar Islands
(IND)**
Little Andaman

Nicobar
Islands
Little Nicobar
Great Nicobar

Ten Degree Channel

Port Blair

SRI LANKA

Ceylon

Trincomalee
Polonnaruwa
Batticaloa
Kandy
2524
Jaffna
Adam's Peak
2243
Anurad-
hapura
Ambalantota
Puttalam
COLOMBO
Dondra Head
Moratuwa
Galle
*Gulf of
Mannar*

Palk Strait

I N D I A N   O C E A N

4370

Equator

Pc
Pb
Pa
Od
Oc

Scale 1:16,000,000

0   200   400   600 Kilometers

0   200   400 Miles

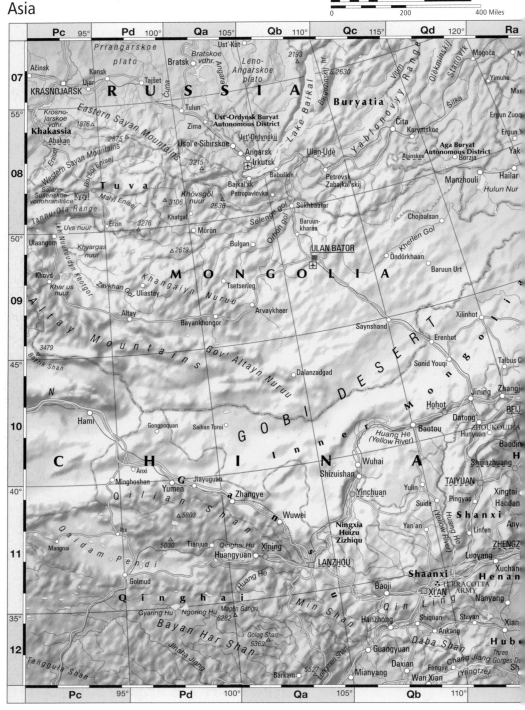

| Pc | 95° | Pd | 100° | Qa | 105° | Qb | 110° | Qc | 115° | Qd | 120° | Ra |

Ačinsk

KRASNOJARSK

Kansk

Ujar

Tajšet

Priangarskoe plato

Bratsk

Bratskoe vdhr.

Ust'-Kut

Leno-Angarskoe plato

2193

Bagdarinskij hr.

2630

Mogoča

Yimuhe

Mar

R U S S I A

Buryatia

Stanovrk

Oljókminskij

Tulun

Čuna

Angara

Khakassia

Krosno-jarskoe vdhr.

1876

55°

Zima

Ust'-Ordynsk Buryat Autonomous District

Vitim

Yablonovyy Range

Čita

Karymskoe

Šilka

Ergun Zuoqi

Ergun

Abakan

2875

Usol'e-Sibirskoe

Ust'-Ordynskij

Angarsk

Irkutsk

Aga Buryat Autonomous District

Aginskoe

Borzja

Yak

Western Sayan Mountains

3215

Babuškin

Petrovsk Zabajkal'skij

Manzhouli

Hailar

Sajano-Susenskoe vodohranilišče

Bij-Sol Enisei

Enisej

Maly Enisei

Tuva

08

Bajkal'sk

Lake Baikal

Hulun Nur

Kyzyl

Khövsgöl nuur

3106

2636

Petropavlovka

Selenge gol

Sükhbaatar

Chojbalsan

Tannu-Ola Range

Érzin

3276

Khatgal

Mörön

Oth on gol

Baruun-kharaa

Uvs nuur

Kh Nuruudyn Khotgor

Ulaangom

Khyargas nuur

2619

Bulgan

ULAN BATOR

Kherlen Gol

Öndörkhaan

50°

Khovd

Khar us nuur

K h a n g a i y n   N u r u u

Tsetserleg

Baruun Urt

A l t a y

Zavkhan Gol

Uliastay

M O N G O L I A

09

Altay

Bayankhongor

Arvaykheer

Saynshand

Xilinhot

M o u n t a i n s

3479

Gov' Altayn Nuruu

Dalanzadgad

Erenhot

Sonid Youqi

Talbus U

Bayrik Shan

45°

M o n g o l i

N

Zhangji

Hami

Gongpoquan

Saihan Toroi

G O B I   D E S E R T

I n n e r

Hohot

Jining

BEIJ

10

Huang He (Yellow River)

Baotou

Datong

ZHOUKOUDIA

Hunyuan

Baodin

Anxi

C

Minghoshan

Yumen

G

Jiayuguan

a

Zhangye

n

Shizuishan

Wuhai

Yinchuan

Yulin

Shijiazhuang

40°

H

Qilian Shan

5803

Wuwei

TAIYUAN

Pingyao

Suide

Xingtai

Handan

I

ije

5030

Tianjun

Qinghai Hu

Xining

Ningxia Huizu Zizhiqu

Yan'an

S h a n x i

Any.

11

Mangnai

Qaidam Pendi

Huangyuan

LANZHOU

Yan'an

Huang He (Yellow River)

Linfen

ZHENGZ

Golmud

Huang He

Baoji

Shaanxi

Luoyang

Xuchan

Qinghai

Gyaring Hu

Ngoring Hu

Magèn Gangri

6282

M i n   S h a n

TERRACOTTA ARMY

XI'AN

H e n a n

Nanyang

35°

B a y a n   H a r   S h a n

Golog Shan

5369

Hanzhong

Shiquan

Shiyan

Xian

Qin Ling

Daba Shan

Hub

12

Tanggula Shan

Jinsha Jiang

5527

Lot)gmen Shan

Bärkam

Guangyuan

Daxian

Mianyang

Wan Xian

Fengjie

Chang Jiang (Yangtze)

Three Gorges Da

Sh

| Pc | 95° | Pd | 100° | Qa | 105° | Qb | 110° |

25° 130° 135° 140° 145°

+ 5000 4000 3000 2000 1000 500 250 100 0 Depression 0 200 2000 4000 6000 **+ 8000**

Amur

Šimanovsk
Zejsko-
Bureinskaja
ravnina

Birobidžan
Habarovsk

Blagoveščensk

Jewish
Autonomous
Region

Jagdaqi

Bikin

Yichun

Sakhalin

o. Kunašir

10542

La Perouse Strait

Wakkanai
Abashiri

HOKKAIDO

Asahikawa
2290
△ Asahi dake

Obihiro

Hegang

Hiran Hinggan Range

Lesser Hinggan Range

Bei'an

Heilongjiang

Jiamusi

Dal'nerečensk

Dal'negorsk

Kushiro

SAPPORO

Tomakomai

Hakodate

Zhalantun

Mingshui

Suihua

Tonghe

Jixi

Rudnaja
Pristan'

Tsugaru Strait

Hachinohe

Anda

HARBIN

Shangzhi

Lake
Khanka

Spassk-
Dal'nij

Aomori

Morioka

Kesenuma

Ulanhot

Mudanjiang

Ussurijsk

Nahodka

Akita

Ishinomaki

Baicheng

Jilin

Yanji

Vladivostok

3600

Sakata

Sendai

Kailu

Tongliao

CHANGCHUN

Liaoyuan

Dunhua

Cheongjin

Japan Basin

Yamagata

Fukushima

Naiman Qi

SHENYANG

FUSHUN

Ganggye

NORTH
KOREA

Niigata

Iwaki

Hitachi

feng

Fuxin

Liaoning

Anshan

Hamheung

Sea of
Japan

Shirane-san
2578 △

Nikko

TOKYO

Chaoyang

Jinzhou

Yingkou

Dandong Gaecheon

Wonsan

Fukui
2702

Fuji-san
3776

Mae-
bashi

KAWASAKI

Chengde

PYONGYANG

Nampo

Gangneung

SOUTH
KOREA

Tottori

KYOTO

NAGOYA

YOKOHAMA

Linxi

Qinhuangdao

DALIAN

Sariwon

Haeju

Wonju

Andong

Yonago

Okayama

KOBE

OSAKA

Matsuzaka

TANGSHAN

Lüshun

SEOUL

Cheonan

DAEGU

Gyeongju

HIROSHIMA

Nachi-Katsuura

TIANJIN

Bo Hai

Yantai

Weihai

Daejeon

BUSAN

Matsuyama

Tokushima

JAPAN

Cangzhou

Binzhou

Rushan

Weifang

Yellow Sea

Jeonju

Gwangju

Mokpo

Suncheon

Matsuyama

Kochi

SHIKOKU

ezhou

ZIBO

QINGDAO

KITAKYUSHU

Sukomo

JINAN

Xuejiadao

FUKUOKA

Beppu Oita

Shandong

Tai'an

Jeju

Nagasaki

Yatsushiro

Jining

Lianyungang

Jeju Do

Kagoshima

KYUSHU

China Plain

Xuzhou

East China

Tanega-jima
Yaku-jima

Suzhou

Huai'an

Jiangsu

Yangzhou

Nantong

Sea

Ryukyu Islands

HUAINAN

Bengbu

NANJING

SHANGHAI

O-jima

umadian

Anhui

Wuxi

Suzhou

Shanghai
Deepwater Port

Tokuno-jima

inyang

Lu'an

Hefei

Tongling

Ningbo

able Shan

Anqing

HANGZHOU

Zhejiang

Jiaojiang

Okinawa-
jima

WUHAN

Huangshan

Zhejiang

Jinhua

Naha

Huangshi

Jingdezhen

Quzhou

Jiujiang

Wenzhou

Southern East Asia
Asia

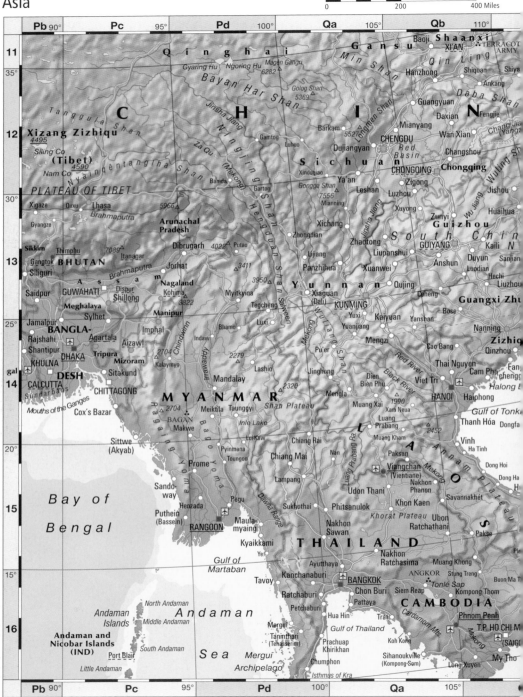

Scale 1:16,000,000

| 0 | 200 | 400 | 600 Kilometers |

| 0 | 200 | 400 Miles |

+ 5000 4000 3000 2000 1000 500 250 100 0 Depression 0 200 2000 4000 6000 + 8000

Henan HUAINAN Bengbu NANJING SHANGHAI
Nanyang Zhumadian Anhui Wuxi Suzhou Shanghai
Xinyang Hefei Shanghai Deepwater Port
Xiangfan Dable Shan Lu'an Anqing Tongling Ningbo East China
Hubei WUHAN HANGZHOU HANGZHOU
ges Dam Huangshi HUANGSHAN Zhejiang Jiaojiang Sea
Shashi Jiujiang Jingdezhen Quzhou Wenzhou
Yueyang LUSHAN NANCHANG Rui'an
Tungting Lake WUYISHAN
ngde CHANGSHA Jiangxi FUZHOU O-jima
nan Pingxiang Nanping Keelung Tokuno-jima
aoyang Zhuzhou Ji'an Sanming Hsinchu TAIPEI Okinawa Islands Okinawa-jima
Hengyang Ruijin Fujian Taichung Hualien Naha
gzhou Leiyang Ganzhou 1870 Quanzhou TAIWAN Ryukyu Trench
Chenzhou Longyan Zhangzhou Xiamen Changhua Tropic of Cancer
Mountains 1510 Shaoguan Meizhou (Amoy) Chiayi
Lian Xian Zhangzhou Chaozhou Tainan Taitung Philippine Basin
Guangdong Huizou Shantou KAOHSIUNG
Wuzhou CANTON Shenzhen
u Foshan Kowloon (Jiulong) Luzon Strait Philippine
lin Zhongshan HONG KONG
MACAO Sea
hai Yangjiang
Maoming Sea
Zhanjiang Aparri
Hai'an Strait Banqui Tuguegarao
ainan Haikou Laoag 2234 Ilagan LUZON
Qionghai Mt. Sicapoo Banaue
Hainan Dao Vigan PHILIPPINES
nan San Fernando Baguio
anya San Carlos San Jose
South China Tarlac Cabanatuan Bagamanoc
Paracel Angeles Catanduanes
Islands 14 Polillo Is.
South China Mt. Pinatubo MANILA Naga Mayon
1600 Olongapo Legazpi Allen Catbalogan
4635 Basin San Pablo Lucena 2462 Matnog Calbayog
Nang Batangas Marin- Masbate Samar
An Sea duque Masbate Tacloban
VIETNAM Mamburao Odiongan Sibuyan Masbate Visayas Ormoc Leyte
Quang Ngai Mindoro Tablas Roxas Cadiz Sogod Dinagat
San Jose Pandan Cebu Surigao
Qui Nhon Coron Panay Cebu Bohol 10830
Calamian Iloilo Bacolod Santander Butuan
Tuy Hoa Group Negros Bislig
Nha Trang El Nido Taytay Basay Siaton Iligan Cagayan de Oro
Lat Roxas Dipolog Pagadian Tagum
Phan Thiet Palawan Puerto Princesa 2956 Mt. Apo Davab
Spratly Aborlan MINDANAO
Islands Quezon Zamboanga Cotabato
Brooke's Tubbataha Reef Peninsula Isulan
Point Zamboanga General Santos
Balabac Sulu Sea Basilan 6220 Karakelong
Balabac Banggi Jolo Jolo

110° Qc 115° Qd 120° Ra 125° Rb

Scale 1:16,000,000

| 0 | 200 | 400 | 600 Kilometers |

| 0 | 200 | 400 Miles |

Pj 95° **Pk** 100° **Qa** 105° **Qb** 110° **Qc**

Henzada
Puthein
(Bassein)
Pegu
Maula-myaing
Kyaikkami
RANGOON
Ye
Dawna Range
Sukhothai
Phitsanulok
Nakhon Sawan
Udon Thani
Nakhon Phanon
Khon Kaen
Savannakhét
L A O S
Annam Plateau
Dong Ha
Hue
Da Nang
Hoi An
Quang Ngai
VIETNAM

MYANMAR
THAILAND
Khorat Plateau
Ubon Ratchathani
Pakse
Pleiku
Qui Nhon
S o u t h

Gulf of Martaban
Ayutthaya
Kanchanaburi
BANGKOK
Nakhon Ratchasima
Muang Khong
Siem Reap
ANGKOR
Stung Treng
Buon Ma Thuot
Tuy Hoa
Nha Trang

Tavoy
Ratchaburi
Chon Buri
Pattaya
Siem Reap
Tonlé Sap
CAMBODIA
Kompong Thom
Da Lat

Petchaburi
Merqui
Taninthari
(Tenasserim)
Hua Hin
Trat
Prachuap Khirikhan
Cardamom Mts.
Phnom Penh
Mekong
Phan Thiet

A n d a m a n
Mergui Archipelago
Chumphon
Koh Kong
Sihanoukville
(Kompong-Som)
T.P. HO CHI MINH
(SAIGON)

Khuraburi
Isthmus of Kra
Lang Suan
Long Xuyen
My Tho

S e a
4510
Takua Pa
Phang Nga
Surat Thani
Nakhon Si Thammarat
Koh Samui
Mui Ca Mau
55

Phuket
Krabi
Trang
Songkhla
Pattani

Little Nicobar
Great Nicobar
Hat Yai
Narathiwat
M
A
L
A
Y
S
I

Great Channel
245
Langkawi
Betong
Kota Bharu
Kuala Terengganu
Natuna Besar
Subi Besar
Sibu

Sigli
Lhokseumawe
Penang
Georgetown
Taiping
Kuala Dungan
Malay
Kep. Natuna

Banda Aceh
Meulaboh
G. Leuser
3404
MEDAN
Peureulak
Langsa
Ipoh
Gua Musang
Kuala Lipis
Kampar
Temerloh
Kuantan
Tioman
Peninsula
Kep. Anambas

Kuching
Bandar Sri Ama

Labuhanhaji
Tebingtinggi
Pematang Siantar
KUALA LUMPUR
Padang Endau
Sambas
Serian
Sengau
Simta

Simeulue
Sinabang
Lake Toba
S
Rantauprapat
Melaka
Kluang
Johor Bahru
Singkawang
Mempawah

Tuangku
Sibolga
Dumai
SINGAPORE
Bintan
Pontianak
Nanga Tayap

Gunungsitoli
Nias
Padangsidempuan
Pekanbaru
Kep. Lingga
Natuna Sea
Kep. Karimata
Maya
Ketapang
Pangkalanbun

Pini
Natal
Rengat
Lingga
Sinkep
50
Karimata Strait
Tg. Pu

Tanahmasa
Bukittinggi
Padangpanjang
Sungaidareh
Muarabungo
Simpang
Bangka
Muntok
Pangkalpinang
Tanjungpandan
Belitung
Tg.
Sambar

Tanahbala
Siberut
Muarasiberut
G. Kerinci
3800
Bangko
Jambi
I N D O

Sipura
Pagai Ulatan
Sungai-penuh
Muaraenim
Palembang
Toboali
Java Sea

Pagai Selatan
Padang
Curup
Martapura
Kayuagung
Kep. Karimunjawa

Mentawai Archipelago
Bengkulu
3159
Manna
Menggala
Bandarjaya
Jepara

Enggano
Bandar Lampung
Kep.Seribu
JAKARTA
Cirebon
SEMA-RANG
Mad

I N D I A N   O C E A N
Merak
Serang
Bogor
Purwakarta
3022
BANDUNG
Ciamis
Pekalongan
3078
BOROBUDUR
Yogyakarta
Sol

Krakatau
Cilacap
Java Trench
J
A
V

Pj 95° **Pk** 100° **Qa** 105° **Qb** 110°

Color/elevation scale (top):
+5000 4000 3000 2000 1000 500 250 100 0 Depression 0 200 2000 4000 6000 +8000

South China
Basin
PHILIPPINES
China Sea
Mamburao
Mindoro
San Jose
Coron
Calamian
Group
El Nido
Taytay
Roxas
Palawan
Puerto Princesa
Aborlan
Quezon
Brooke's
Point
Balabac
Balabac
Banggi
Kudat
G. Kinabalu 4095
2569
Ranau
Kota Kinabalu
Beaufort
dar Seri Begawan
Tenom
Sapulut
BRUNEI
uala Belait
Miri
Longbawan
Niah
Mulu
ulu
Belaga
Longnawang
2130
Sangkulirang
K A L I M A N T A N
Range
2240
G. Liangpran
A.G. Liangpran
Putussibau
Sengata
Samarinda
(B O R N E O)
Muarateweh
Balikpapan
Kuaro
N D S
Amuntai
Kandangan
Palangkaraya
Pagatan
Banjarmasin
Laut
alapembuang
Tg. South
Kep.
Laut Kecil
N E S I A
Bawan
RABAYA
Madura
obolinggo
G.Merapi
△2329 3332
lang
G.Bromo
Banyuwangi
A
4865

Marin-
duque
Odiongan
Sibuyan
Masbate
Matnog
Allen
Calbayog
Samar
Tablas
Masbate
Romblon
Tacloban
Ormoc
V i s a y a s
Roxas
Pandan
Cadiz
Cebu
Sogod
Leyte
Dinagat
Panay
Iloilo
Bacolod
Cebu
Surigao
10830
Butuan
Negros
Basay
Santander
Bohol
Cagayan
de Oro
Bislig
Dipolog
Siaton
Iligan
Pagadian
Zamboanga
Peninsula
Cotabato
Isulan
2956 △
Mt. Apo
Davao
Zamboanga
General Santos
Basilan
Jolo
Jolo
6220
Tawi-Tawi
Sandakan
Lahad Datu
Tawau
Sulu Archipelago
C e l e b e s S e a
Tarakan
Tanjungredeb
Tolitoli
Minahasa
2207
Kotamobagu
Gorontalo
Tomini
2490
Soal
3000
Tg. Mang-
kalihat
Gulf of
Tomini
Toboli
Ampana
Donggala
Poso
Palu
Baturube
2275
S U L A W E S I
(CELEBES)
Kakali
Wotu
Mamuju
Masamba
Makale
3074 △
G. Mekongga
Makassar Strait
Majene
G. Rantekombola
2790
Parepare
3440
Gulf of
Bone
Kolaka
Watampone
Muna
UJUNG PANDANG
(MAKASSAR)
Bulukumba
Selayar
F l o r e s
S e a
Kep.
L E S S E R   S U N D A   I S L A N D S
Flores
Kep. Kangean
Lombok
Sumbawa
Jangkar
Sumbawa
Besar
Mataram
Raba
Denpasar
Bali
Bondokodi
Komodo
Lubaanbajo
Maumere
Ende
Sumba
△1225
Waingapu
Sawu
Roti

6595
PALAU
3660
Sonsorol I.
Pulo Anna
Helen Reef
Tobi
Karakelong
Kep. Talaud
Sangihe
Kep. Sangihe
Morotai
Galela
1335 △
Kao
Halmahera
Waigeo
Manado
Bitung
Ternate
Nosliku
Gebe
Sorong
Halmahera
Sea
Batanta
Salawati
Gani
Kwandong
Obi
Misool
Adua
Ceram Sea
Molucca
Sea
Mangole
Kasiruta
Bacan
Wahai
Waru
Taliabu
Dofa
Sanana
Kep. Sula
Amahai
G. Binaia
3019
Luwuk
Kep.
Banggai
Buru
Ambon
Seram
(CERAM)
Ambon
Kep.Banda
M O L U C C A   I S L A N D S
5215
B a n d a   S e a
Bayu
Kendari
Butung
Baubau
Kep. Daya Barat
Wetar
Damar
Moa
Babar
Sermata
Kep.Babar
Alor
EAST TIMOR
3310
Lomblen
Dili
Aliambata
Antar
Timor
Tutuala
Bathurst I.
Nikiniki
Kupang
Kabaena
Savu Sea
Beagle
Gulf
T i m o r   S e a
Hibernia Reef
Cartier I.
Ashmore
Islands
AUSTRALIA
Joseph
Bonaparte
Gulf

Sulu Sea
Zamboanga
Peninsula
Tubbataha Reef

Makassar Strait
Meratus
Mtns.
Laut
Pagatan

17
5°
18
0°
19
5°
20
10°
21
15°

Australia/Oceania
Physical map

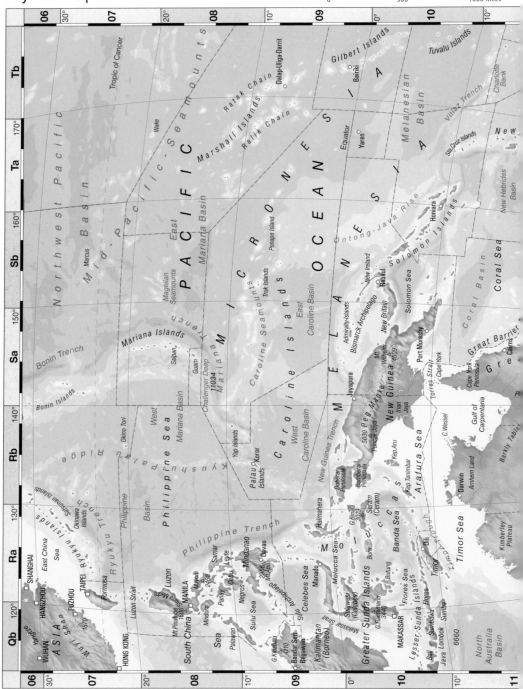

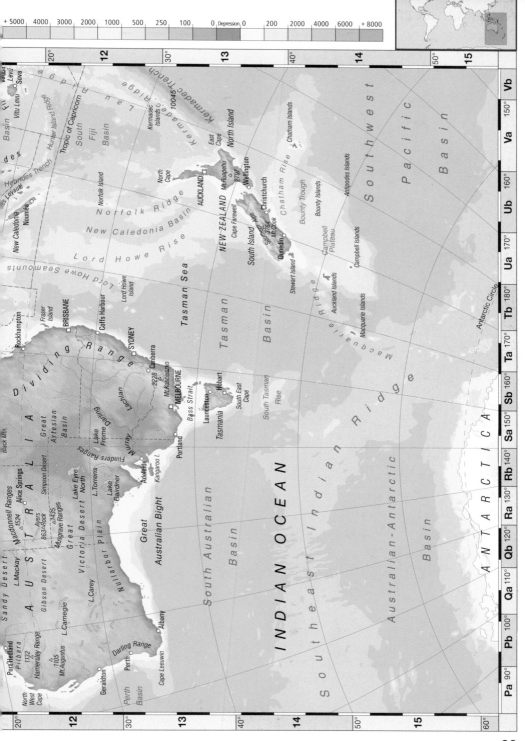

+ 5000 4000 3000 2000 1000 500 250 100 0 Depression 0 200 2000 4000 6000 **+ 8000**

20° **12** 30° **13** 40° **14** 50° **15**

Tonga
Levu
Vitu Levu
Suva

Basin Fiji

Hunter Island Ridge

Lau Ridge

Hebrides Trench
e Loyaute

New Caledonia

Nouméa

Tropic of Capricorn

South Fiji Basin

Kermadec Islands

Kermadec Trench

10045

Norfolk Island

North Cape

Norfolk Ridge

AUCKLAND

North Island

Mt. Ruapehu 2797

Wellington

East Cape

NEW ZEALAND

Cape Farewell

Chatham Islands

Chatham Rise

Christchurch

Southern Alps 3764 Mt. Cook

Dunedin

South Island

Stewart Island

New Caledonia Basin

Lord Howe Rise

Lord Howe Island

Lord Howe Seamounts

Tasman Sea

Tasman Basin

Bounty Trough

Bounty Islands

Antipodes Islands

Campbell Plateau

Campbell Islands

Auckland Islands

Macquarie Ridge

Macquarie Islands

Southwest Pacific Basin

Antarctic Circle

Rockhampton

Fraser Island

BRISBANE

Coffs Harbour

SYDNEY

Canberra

Mt. Kosciuszko 2228

MELBOURNE

Portland

Adelaide

Kangaroo I.

Bass Strait

Launceston

Tasmania

Hobart

South East Cape

South Tasman Rise

Great Dividing Range

Black Mtn.

AUSTRALIA

Great Artesian Basin

Darling

Lachlan

Murray

Lake Frome

Flinders Ranges

L. Torrens

L. Gairdner

Lake Eyre North

Macdonnell Ranges
1524

Alice Springs

Simpson Desert

Ayers Rock 863

Musgrave Ranges 1435

Great Victoria Desert

Nullarbor Plain

Great Australian Bight

South Australian Basin

INDIAN OCEAN

Southeast Indian Ridge

Australian-Antarctic Basin

ANTARCTICA

Sandy Desert

L. Mackay

Gibson Desert

L. Carnegie

L. Carey

Pilbara 1132

Hamersley Range

Mt. Augustus 1105

Port Hedland

North West Cape

Geraldton

Perth

Darling Range

Cape Leeuwin

Albany

Perth Basin

90° **Pa** 100° **Pb** 110° **Qa** 120° **Qb** 130° **Ra** 140° **Rb** 150° **Sa** 160° **Sb** 170° **Ta** 180° **Tb** 170° **Ua** 160° **Ub** 150° **Va** **Vb**

20° **12** 30° **13** 40° **14** 50° **15** 60°

Australia/Oceania
Political map

Scale 1:40,000,000

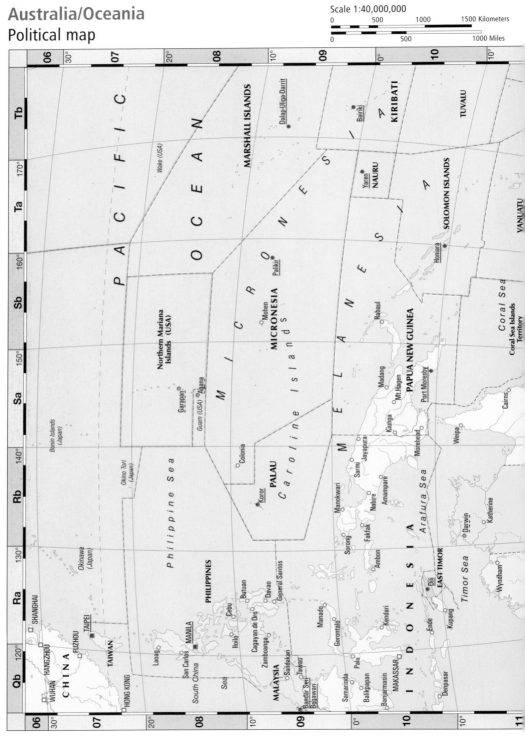

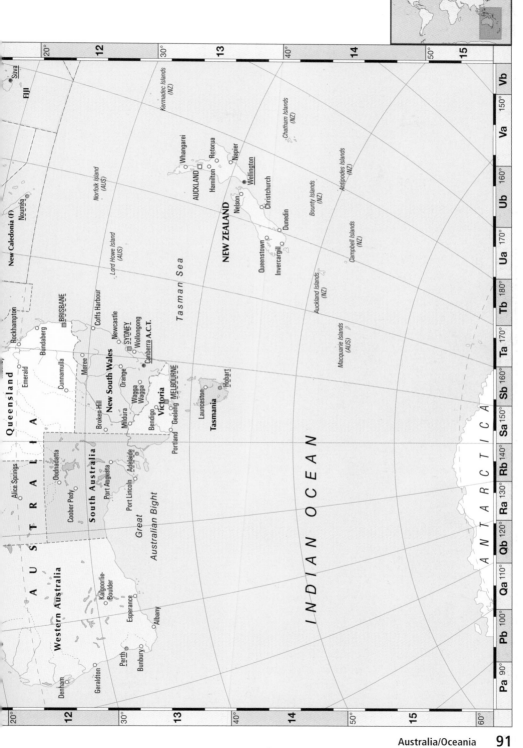

Micronesia, New Guinea
Oceania

Scale 1:16,000,000

0   200   400   600 Kilometers

0   200   400 Miles

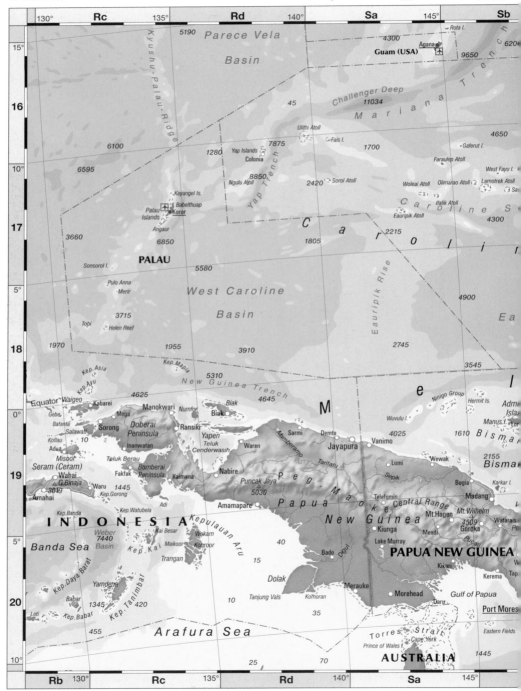

	Rc		Rd		Sa		Sb
130°		135°		140°		145°	

5190 Parece Vela

Basin

Rota I.

4300

Guam (USA) Agana 620

9650

Kyushu-Palau-Ridge

Challenger Deep
11034

M a r i a n a   Trench

45

6100

1280 Yap Islands 7875 Ulithi Atoll Fais I. 4650

Colonia 1700 Gaferut I.

6595 Faraulep Atoll West Fayu I.

8850 Sorol Atoll 2420

Ngulu Atoll Woleai Atoll Olimarao Atoll Lamotrek Atoll

Kayangel Is. Ifalik Atoll

Palau Babelthuap C a r o l i n e S

Islands Koror Eauripik Atoll 4300

3660 Angaur 1805 2215

6850 C a r o l i

PALAU 5580

Sonsorol I. *Eauripik Rise*

Pulo Anna 4900

Merir West Caroline

3715 Basin E a

Tobi Helen Reef 2745

1970 1955 3910 3545

Kep. Mapia

5310

New Guinea Trench

Kep. Asia 4625 4645 M e l

Kep. Ayu Biak Ninigo Group Hermit Is. Adm

Equator Waigeo Kabarei Numfor Biak Wuvulu I. Isla

Gebe Mega Mangkwari Sarmi Demta Manus I. Lor

Batanta Salawati Sorong Doberai Ransiki 4025 1610 Bisma

Kofiau 10 Peninsula Waren Vanimo Jayapura

Adua Inanwatan Yapen Mamberamo

Misool Teluk Berau Teluk Taritatu Lumi Wewak 2155

Seram (Ceram) Cenderwasih Sepik Bisma

Wahai Bomberai Nabire Bogia Karkar I.

G.Binaia Peninsula Kaimana Puncak Jaya Telefomin Madang

3019 Waru 1445 Adi Amamapare 5030 P e g . M a o k e Central Range Mt.Hagen Mt.Wilhelm

Amahai Kep.Gorong Papua Kiunga Mendi Goroka 3509 Watarais

Kep.Banda Kep.Watubela New Guinea Lake Murray Pucak

I N D O N E S I A Kepulauan Aru 40 Bado Ogul PAPUA NEW GUINEA

Weber Kai Besar Wokam 15 Kikori

Banda Sea 7440 Maikoor Kohroor Kerema Tap

Basin Kep.Kai Trangan Dolak Daru

Kep.Daya Barat Yamdena Tanjung Vals Kofhoran Morehead Gulf of Papua

Babar 1345 420 Merauke Port Mores

Leti Kep.Babar Kep.Tanimbar 10 35

455 Arafura Sea Torres Strait Eastern Fields

Prince of Wales I. Cape York

25 70 AUSTRALIA 1445

| | Rb | 130° | Rc | 135° | Rd | 140° | Sa | 145° |

5000 4000 3000 2000 1000 500 250 100 0 Depression 0 200 2000 4000 6000 + 8000

6045

6035

970

935

MARSHALL ISLANDS

16

1390   440   Eniwetok Atoll

Bikini Atoll   Rongelap
Atoll

MICRONESIA   Ailinginae Atoll Rongerik Atoll

1025   Ujelang Atoll   Wotho Atoll

10°

uito Atoll   Fayu I.   Murilo Atoll   Ujae Atoll   Kwajalein Atoll

Nomwin Atoll Hall Islands   1135   Lae Atoll

Ulul Atoll   Minto Reef   17

Kuop Atoll   Oroluk Atoll

640   Mohen   Pakin Atoll   5020

Losap Atoll   Palikir   Ponape I.   Mokil Atoll

Pulusuk I.   Pingelap Atoll

60   Senyavin Islands

Namoluk I.   Ngatik Atoll   Lelu   5°

4665   Kosrae (Kusaie)

Satawan Atoll

245

PACIFIC OCEAN   4310   18

5750   1385

aroline Basin   2705

6920   6680

6310   3945   2790   Nauru   0°
Saint Matthias Group   1685   Yaren

Mussau I.   3710

Lyra Reef   **NAURU**

New Hanover I.   Lihir Group   1670   4320   19

Namatanai
New Ireland   Tabar Is.   3145

Rabaul   Tanga Is.   Nuguria Is.   2250

Witu Islands   Feni Is.

Green Is.   Kilinailau Is.   Tauu Is.   5°

Kimbe   C.St.George
Bay   Hoskins   Buka I.

Sag Sag   Nakanai Mts. Pomio   Tinputz   Bougainville I.   Ontong Java Atoll

Kandrian   8320   2715   Arawa
New Britain   9140 Mt.Balbi   2470   3600

chhafen   Buin   Vuranggo

Gulf   Solomon Sea   Choiseul   20
be   Vella Lavella New Georgia Group Santa Isabel   4515

Trobriand   4900   Gizo   Buala   5705
Popondetta   Is.   New Georgia Vangunu

Tufi   Kiriwina I.   Russell Is.   Auki   Stewart Is.

Goodenough I.   Woodlark I.   Malaita
3676   d'Entrecasteaux   Mara-
Ra.   Fergusson I.   Honiara   masike   2560 **SOLOMON ISLANDS**
Kupiano   Alotau   Islands   3745   Guadalcanal   San Cristobal

Salamo Normanby I.   Pocklington Reef?   Reef Islands   10°
The Calvados   Nendo
Chain   Misima I.   Bellona I.   Haurahu
Louisiade Archipelago   Rennell Rise   8310   21
Tagula I.   Yela I.

Western Australia
Australia

Scale 1:16,000,000

| 0 | 200 | 400 | 600 Kilometers |

| 0 | 200 | 400 Miles |

Rd
Rc
Rb
Ra
Qd
Qc

21 22 23 24
20

Arafura Sea
Gulf of Carpentaria
Timor Sea
Savu Sea
Indian Ocean

INDONESIA
Lesser Sunda Islands

Arnhem Land
KAKADU N.P.
Darwin
Melville I.
Bathurst I.
Van Diemen Gulf
Beagle Gulf
Adelaide River
Pine Creek
Katherine
Maningrida
Jabiru
Roper
Roper Bar
Larrimah
Mataranka
Daly Waters
Timber Creek
Top Springs
Kununurra
L.Argyle
Wyndham
Kalumburu
Kalkaringi
Halls Creek
Sturt

Barkly Tableland
Calvert
Borroloola
Barkly Homestead Roadhouse
Camooweal

Northern Territory
Tanami Desert
Tennant Creek
Elliott
Wauchope
Lander
Sandover
Hale

Alice Springs
Mt.Liebig
Mt.Zell 1524
1511
Macdonnell Ranges
Amadeus
Yulara
Mt.Olga Ayers Rock
1066 863
ULURU N.P.
Mt.Woodroffe 1435
Musgrave Ranges
Tomkinson Ranges
Mt.Sir Thomas 772

Erldunda
Kulgera
Finke
Maria

Simpson Desert
Lake Eyre
Peera Peera
Poolanna L.
Macumba R.
Dodonadatta
Lake Eyre Basin

A U S T R A L I A

Great Sandy Desert
L.White
L.Mackay
L.MacDonald
L.Hopkins

Gibson Desert
L.Disappointment
L.Carnegie
L.Dora
L.Way
L.Wells

Great Victoria Desert

Western Australia

Kimberley
KIMBERLEY PLATEAU
Mt.Hann 779
Mt.Ord 936
King Leopold Ranges
Fitzroy Crossing
Fitzroy
Derby
Dampier Land
C.Leveque
Broome
La Grange

PURNULULU N.P.
Bungle Bungle Ranges

Joseph Bonaparte Gulf
Cape Londonderry
Bonaparte Archipelago
Ashmore Is.
Cartier Is.
Sunday Strait

Timor Trough
North Australia Basin

Java Trench

Scott Reef
Rowley Shoals

De Grey
Marble Bar
Nullagine
Telfer
Sandfire Flat Roadhouse
Larrey Pt.
Port Hedland
Dampier Archipelago
Dampier
Roebourne
Wittenoom
Pannawonica
Newman
Pilbara
Hamersley Range
Mt.Bruce 1132
Tom Price
Paraburdoo
Mt.Essendon 906

Barrow I.
North West C.
Exmouth
Onslow
Montebello Is.
Mary Anne Pass.
Exmouth Plateau

Carnarvon
Wooramel Roadhouse
Denham
Dirk Hartog I.
Shark Bay
Geographe Chan.
Gascoyne
Meekatharra
Mt.Hale 732
Wiluna
Mt.Augustus 1105
Nanutarra Roadhouse

West
Mt.McLeod
North West Basin

Tropic of Capricorn

94   Australia

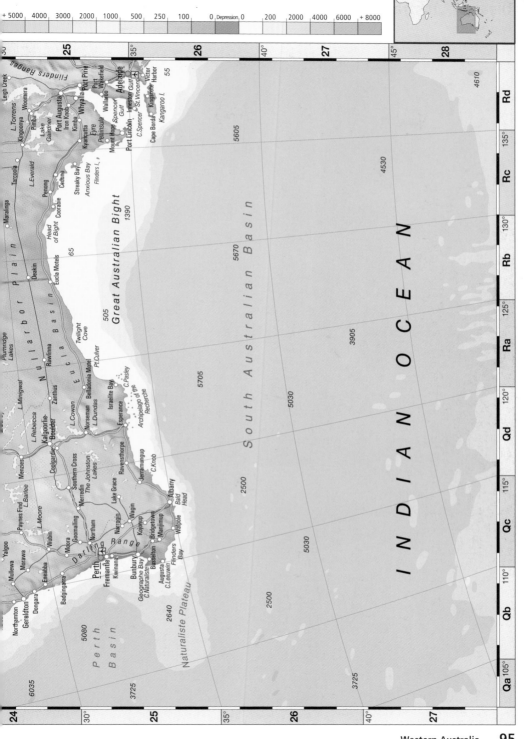

+ 5000 | 4000 | 3000 | 2000 | 1000 | 500 | 250 | 100 | 0 Depression 0 | 200 | 2000 | 4000 | 6000 | + 8000

Flinders Ranges
Leigh Creek
L. Torrens
Kingoonya
Woomera
Pimba
Lake Gairdner
L. Everard
Tarcoola
Maralinga

Port Pirie
Port Augusta
Iron Knob
Whyalla
Kimba
Kyancutta
Cowell
Mount Hope
Port Lincoln
Cape Borda
Cape Jervis

Pt. Pirie
Wakefield
Wallaroo
Adelaide
C. Spencer
Kangaroo I.
Kingscote
Victor Harbor
55

Investigator Strait
Spencer Gulf
St. Vincent Gulf
Eyre Peninsula
Flinders I.

Penong
Cooradie
Head of Bight
Eucla Motels
Deakin

Streaky Bay
Anxious Bay
Ceduna

Great Australian Bight
1390
65
505

N u l l a r b o r   P l a i n

Plumridge Lakes
L. Mingwal
L. Rebecca
L. Cowan
Rawlinna
Zanthus
Kalgoorlie
Boulder
Menzies
Coolgardie
Norseman
L. Dundas
L. Barlee
Southern Cross
The Johnston Lakes
Merredin
Goomalling
Northam
Kellerberrin Motel
Balladonia Motel
Pt. Culver
Twilight Cove
Israelite Bay
C. Pasley
Esperance
Archipelago of the Recherche

E u c l a   B a s i n

5705
5670
5605
4530
5030
3905

S o u t h   A u s t r a l i a n   B a s i n

2500

Yalgoo
Mullewa
Morawa
Paynes Find
Eneabba
Dongara
Geraldton
Northampton
Badgingarra
L. Moore
Wubin
Dalwallinu
Moora

Kwinana
Perth
Fremantle
Geographe Bay
C. Naturaliste
Bunbury
Busselton
Augusta
C. Leeuwin
Flinders Bay
Naturaliste Plateau
2640

D a r l i n g   R a n g e
Wagin
Narrogin
Kojonup
Bridgetown
Manjimup
Walpole
Jerramungup
C. Knob
Ravensthorpe
Lake Grace
Albany
Bald Head

P e r t h   B a s i n
5080
6035
3725
3725
5030
2500
3725

4610

I N D I A N   O C E A N

Rd
Rc
Rb
Ra
Qd
Qc
Qb
Qa

105° 110° 115° 120° 125° 130° 135°

24 25 26 27 28

24 25 26 27

30° 35° 40°
30° 35° 40° 45°

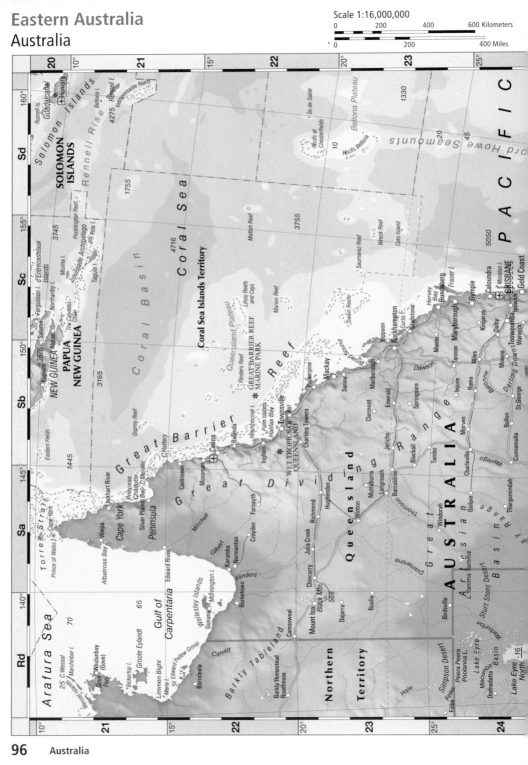

Eastern Australia
Australia

Scale 1:16,000,000

0   200   400   600 Kilometers
0   200   400 Miles

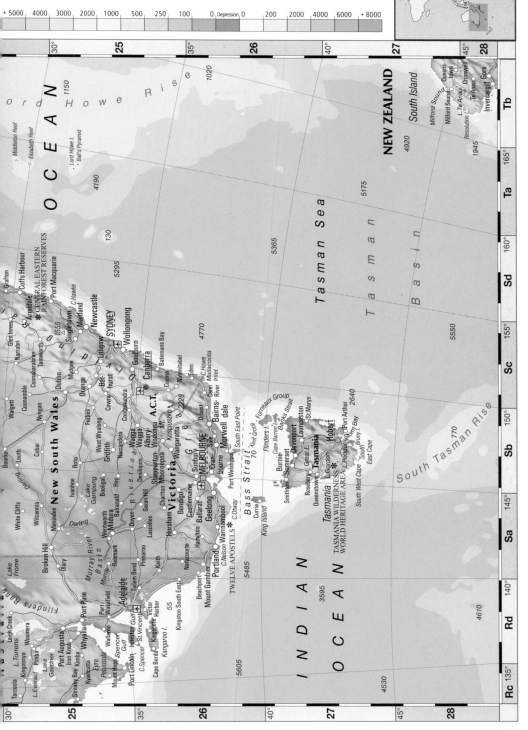

+ 5000 4000 3000 2000 1000 500 250 100 **0** Depression **0** 200 2000 4000 6000 **+ 8000**

30° 25 35° 26 40° 27 45° 28

Lord Howe Rise

1150

Middleton Reef

Elizabeth Reef

Lord Howe I.

Ball's Pyramid

4190

130

5295

1020

O C E A N

NEW ZEALAND

South Island

Milford Sound
Milford Sound
Resolution I.
L. Te Anau
Te Anau
Queens-town
Cromwell
Gore
Invercargill

Tb

4920

1945

Ta

5175

Tasman Sea

Tasman Basin

165° Ta 160° Sd 155° Sc 150° Sb 145° Sa 140° Rd 135° Rc

Grafton
Coffs Harbour
Port Macquarie
C. Hawke
Singleton
Maitland
Newcastle

Glen Innes
Armidale
★ CENTRAL EASTERN RAINFOREST RESERVES
Narrabri
Tamworth
1555
SYDNEY
Wollongong

Coonabarabran
Mudgee
Lithgow
Goulburn
Batemans Bay

Walgett
Dubbo
Orange
Bathurst
Canberra
A.C.T.
Cooma
Nimmitabel

Coonamble
Nyngan
Forbes
Cowra
Mt. Kosciuszko ▲ 2228
Eden

Bourke
Cobar
West Wyalong
Young
Tumut
Cann River
C. Howe
Mallacoota Inlet

4770

Louth
Condobolin
Wagga Wagga
Wodonga
Orbost
Bairns-dale
South East Point

New South Wales

Ivanhoe
Hay
Deniliquin
Albury
Wangaratta
Morwell

Wilcannia
Lake Garnpung
Booligal
Shepparton
Moorabna
Bendigo
Sale

White Cliffs
Menindee
Balranald
Swan Hill
Charlton
Castlemaine
Sunbury
MELBOURNE
Geelong
Port Welshpool

Broken Hill
Wentworth
Mildura
Lascelles
Horsham
Ballarat
Cranbourne

Olary
Murray River
Ouyen
Ballarat
Hamilton
Warrnambool
C. Nelson
C. Otway
TWELVE APOSTLES ★

Riverina

Victoria

Great Dividing Range

Bass Strait

Kent Group
70
Flinders I.
Furneaux Group
Cape Barren I.
Banks Strait

King Island
Currie

Smithton
Burnie
Somerset
Wynyard
Devonport
Launceston
St. Marys

Stanley
Rosebery
Great Lake
Port Arthur
2640

Queenstown
Tasmania
TASMANIA WILDERNESS WORLD HERITAGE AREA
Gordon
Pedder
Bruny I.
Hobart
Storm Bay

South West Cape
South East Cape

Lake Frome
Leigh Creek

Tarcoola
Kingoonya
Woomera
L. Torrens
Pimba
Lake Eyre
L. Everard
Kingoonya

Kyancutta
Streaky Bay
Kimba
Iron Knob
Port Augusta
Whyalla
Port Pirie
Wallaroo
Crystal Brook
Wakefield

Mount Hope
Port Lincoln
Cowell
Spencer Gulf
C. Spencer
Cape Borda
Kangaroo I.
Eyre Peninsula
Yorke Peninsula

St. Vincent Gulf
Port Wakefield
Adelaide
Victor Harbor
Kingscote

Investigator Gulf
Murray Bridge
Tailem Bend
Keith
Pinnaroo
Naracoorte
Penola

Meningie
Kingston South East
Beachport
Portland
Mount Gambier
3595

INDIAN

OCEAN

5485

5605

4530

4610

770

South Tasman Rise

Flinders Ranges

55

5550

5365

3595

30° 25 35° 26 40° 27 45° 28

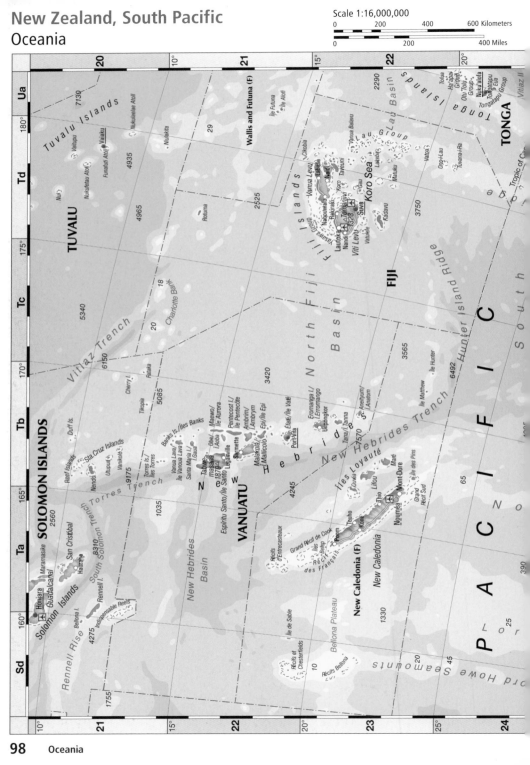

New Zealand, South Pacific
Oceania

Scale 1:16,000,000

0 200 400 600 Kilometers
0 200 400 Miles

TONGA

Lau Islands

2290

Totoa
Ha'apai Group
Otu Tolu Group
Tongatapu Group
Nuku'alofa

Vitiaz II

Ua

180°

Lau Basin

Vanua Balavu

Cikobia

Td

Lau Group

7130

Tuvalu Islands

Vaitupu
Vaiaku
Funafuti Atoll
Nukufetau Atoll
Niulakita

Nanumea Atoll

4935

Île Futuna
Île Alofi

Wallis and Futuna (F)

29

Koro Sea

Vanua Levu
Labasa
Rabi
Koro
Taveuni
Gau

Vatoa

Ongo-i-Lau

Tuvana-i-Ra

Tropic of Ca

Nul

Rotuma

2525

Vanua Levu
Nabouwalu
Tavua
Nadi 528
Lautoka
Suva
Viti Levu
Vatulele
Kadavu

Matuku

3750

TUVALU

4965

Nukufetau Atoll

Vaitupu

5340

Charlotte Bank

18

FIJI

Hunter Island Ridge

Tc

North Fiji Basin

Fiji Islands

20

Vitiaz Trench

6150

Fataka

Cherry I.

3420

New Hebrides Trench

Île Matthew

Île Hunter

6492

3565

South

Tb

Tikopia

5085

Torres Is.
Îles Torres

Banks Is./Îles Banks

Maewo/
Île Aurora
Oba/
I.Aoba
Pentecost I./
Île Pentecôte
Ambrim/
Ambrym
Epi/Île Epi
Éfaté/Île Vaté
Port-Vila

Eromanga I./
I.Erromango

Utupingkor

Tana/I.Tanna

Anei
Anatom

9175

1570

SOLOMON ISLANDS

Duff Is.

Reef Islands

Sta Cruz Islands

Vanikolo

Utupua

Nendö

Vanua Lava/
Île Vanua Lava
Santa Maria I./
I.Gaua

Tabwemasana
1879
Espíritu Santo/Île Santo

Malakula/
I.Mallicolo

4245

Îles Loyauté

Ouvéa
Lifou
Maré
Île des Pins

65

PACIFIC

Ta

San Cristobal

Maramasike

2560

Torres Is.
Îles Torres

Luganville

VANUATU

1035

Touho
Koné
Thio
Nouméa
Mont-Doré

Grand
Récif Sud

390

Homiara
Guadalcanal
Hauro

Solomon Islands

Bellona I.

Rennell I.

South Solomon Trench

8310

New Hebrides Basin

Grand Récif de Cook
Îles
Récif Bélep
Ouen

Récifs
d'Entrecasteaux

New Caledonia (F)

New Caledonia

1330

Lor

25

Sd

Rennell Rise

4275

Indispensable Reefs

1755?

Bellona Plateau

Île de Sable

Récifs et
Chesterfields

10

Récifs Bellona

ord Howe Seamounts

20

45

No

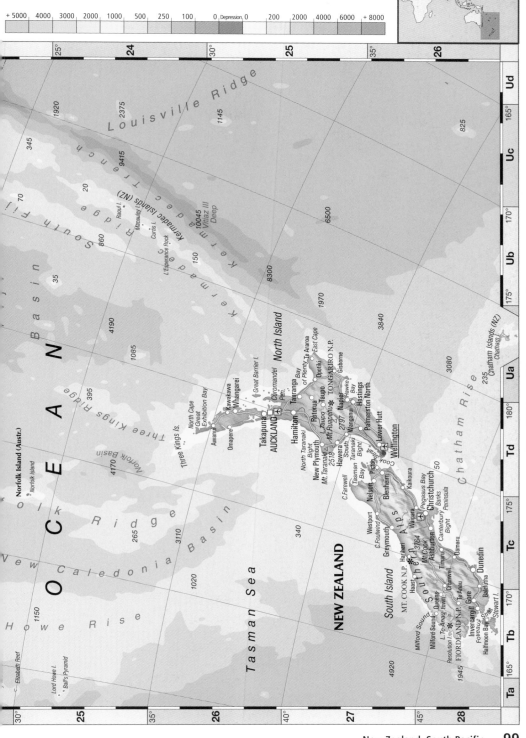

Africa
Physical map

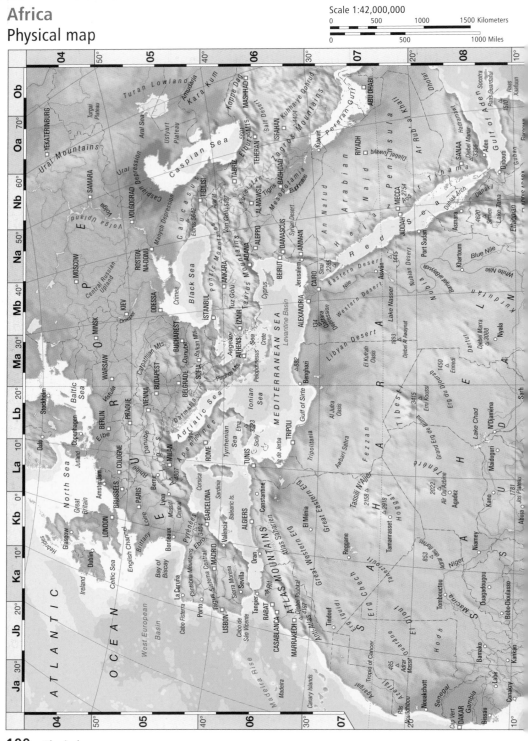

Scale 1:42,000,000

0 500 1000 1500 Kilometers

0 500 1000 Miles

Africa
Political map

Scale 1:42,000,000

| 0 | 500 | 1000 | 1500 Kilometers |
| 0 | | 500 | 1000 Miles |

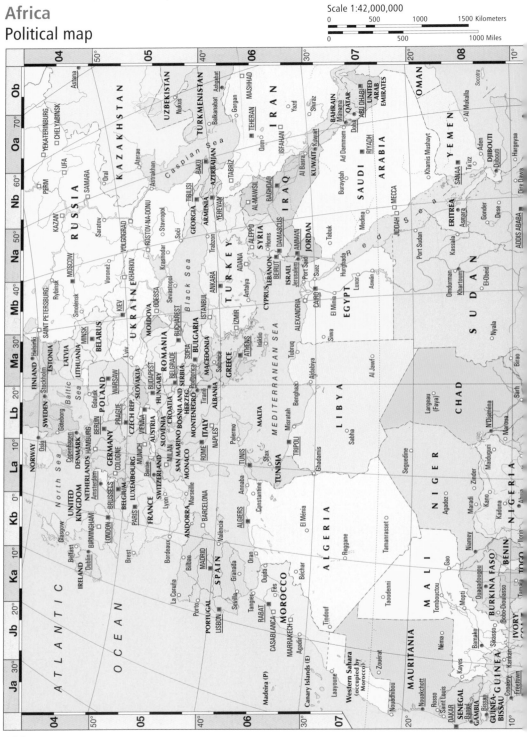

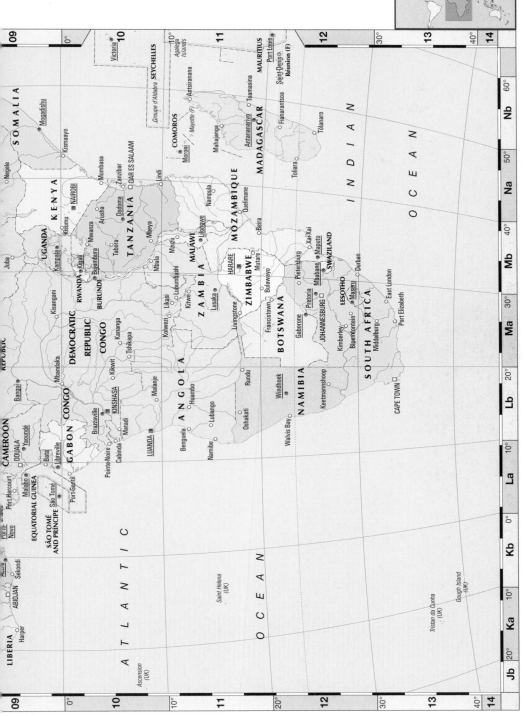

Scale 1:16,000,000

0   200   400   600 Kilometers

0   200   400 Miles

MEDITERRANEAN SEA

PORTUGAL
SPAIN
Murcia
Cartagena
Cabo de Gata
Almería
Granada
Sierra Nevada
Sevilla
Huelva
Faro
Cádiz
Jerez d.l.Fr.
Algeciras
Gibraltar (UK)
Strait of Gibraltar
Tangier
Ceuta (E)
Tétouan
Melilla (E)
Al-Hoceima
2407

ALGIERS
Blida
2814
Chlef
Ténès
Mostaganem
Oran
Sidi Bel Abbès
Tlemcen
Oujda
Mechería
Aïn Sefra
Figuig

Béjaïa
Sétif
2305
Batna
Cap Bougaroun
Biskra
Chott el Hodna
Chott Melrhir
El Oued
Touggourt
Ouargla
Ghardaïa
Djelfa
Tiaret
Aflou
Ech Cheguig
El Bayadh
El Goléa
El Ménia

Bou Saada
Laghouat

Bordj Omar Driss
Bordj Mokhtar

TELL ATLAS
SAHARA ATLAS
Great Eastern Erg
Great Western Erg
Plateau du Tademaït

In Salah
Timimoun
Reggane
Timiadi
O.Saoura
Adrar
Timimoun

ALGERIA
HOGGAR
Tahat 2978
Tamanrasset
Assamakka

MOROCCO
RABAT
CASABLANCA
El Jadida
Safi
Cap Beddouza
MARRAKECH
4165
Khouribga
Meknes
Fès
Taza
Azrou
AÏT BEN HADDOU
Ouarzazate
VOLUBILIS
Kénitra
El-Araich
Djebel Toubkal 4165
Taroudannt
Agadir
Tizila
Cap Rhir
4433

MIDDLE ATLAS
HIGH ATLAS
ANTI ATLAS

Goulimine
Tan Tan
Tarfaya
Oued Drâa
Djebel Ouarkziz
Hamada du Guir
Béchar
Tindouf

Western
Sahara
(occupied by Morocco)
Al-'Ayun
Boukra
Bir Moghrein
Smara
Snara
Cap Boujdour
Ad-Dakhla
Oued el Khatt
Zouérat
Fdérik
Guelb er Richât 485
Choûm
Massif de l'Adrar
Atâr
Akjoujt
Cape Verde Plateau
Nouâdhibou
Râs Nouâdhibou
Nouâmghâr

MAURITANIA
El Djouf
Erg Iguidi
Erg Chech
El Hank
Aoukâr Tanezrouft
Chegga
Taoudenni
Araouane

ATLANTIC OCEAN
Canary Islands (E)
Lanzarote
Fuerteventura
Las Palmas
Gran Canaria
Tenerife
Santa Cruz de Tenerife
La Palma
La Gomera
Hierro
Madeira Islands
Funchal
Madeira (P)
Porto Santo
Desertas
Ilhas Selvagens (Port.)

Monaco Deep
Madeira Rise
Canary Basin
Dacia Seamount
Ampère Seamount
Azores-Cape St. Vicente Ridge
Cabo de São Vicente
Cap St. Vincent

5187
2450
172
85
263
1145
20
35
55

Tropic of Cancer

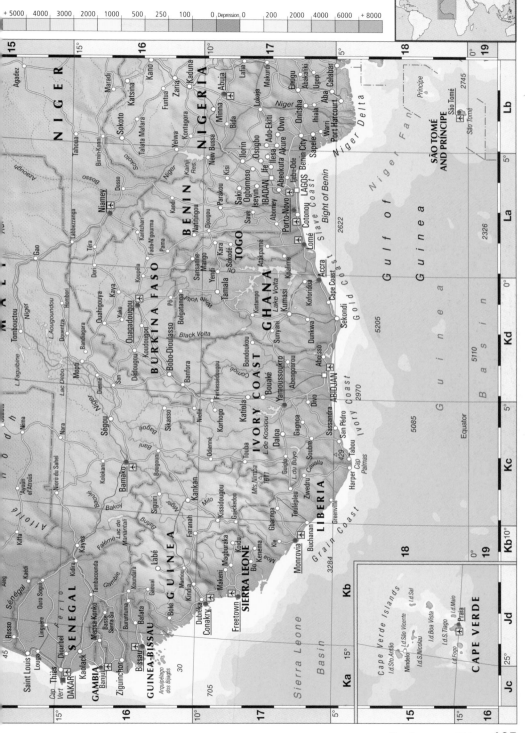

+ 5000   4000   3000   2000   1000   500   250   100   0   Depression   0   200   2000   4000   6000   + 8000

N I G E R

Agadez

Tahoua

Maradi

Katsina

Kano

Sokoto

Birnin-Konni

Talata Mafara

Zaria

Kaduna

Funtua

Lafia

Abuja

Minna

Abakaliki

Enugu

Ugep

Calabar

Yelwa

Kontagora

Kisi

Ilorin

Saki

Abeokuta Akure

Owo

Benin City

Sapele

Warri

Port-Harcourt

Aba

Onitsha

Ihiala

Lokoja

Bida

Ado-Ekiti

Ife Ilesha

Oshogbo

Ogbomoso

Iseyin

Ibadan

Abomey

Porto-Novo

Cotonou LAGOS

Lomé

N I G E R I A

B E N I N

T O G O

Niger

Niger Delta

Niger Fan

Gulf of Guinea

São Tomé

Príncipe

SÃO TOMÉ AND PRÍNCIPE

2745

São Tomé

Lb

La

2622

2326

G u l f   o f   G u i n e a

G u i n e a   B a s i n

Bight of Benin

Slave Coast

G H A N A

Accra

Cape Coast

Sekondi

Kumasi

Koforidua

Dunkwa

Sunyani

Kintampo

Tamala

Yendi

Sansanné-Mango

Kara

Sokodé

Atakpamé

Kpalimé

Bolgatanga

Lake Volta

White Volta

Black Volta

Gold Coast

5205

5110

Kd

Equator

Abidjan

Yamoussoukro

Bouaké

Abengourou

Divo

Gagnoa

Daloa

Sassandra

San Pédro

Tabou

Harper

Cap Palmas

429

I V O R Y   C O A S T

Korhogo

Katiola

Odienné

Touba

Man

Bondoukou

Ferkessédougou

Comoé

Nielé

Sikasso

Ivory Coast

5085

2970

Kc

M A L I

Tombouctou

Gao

Mopti

Ségou

Bamako

Niafunké

Niger

L. Faguibine

Lac Débo

Niger

Bani

Djenné

San

Koutiala

Bobo-Dioulasso

Banfora

Sikasso

Kankan

Siguiri

Kouroussa

Kissidougou

Guéckédou

Faranah

Kindia

Mamou

Labé

Bafing

Bakoy

Milo

B U R K I N A   F A S O

Ouagadougou

Koudougou

Ouahigouya

Kaya

Dori

Déddougou

L'Aougoundou

G U I N E A

Conakry

Dubréka

Kankan

Mts. Nimba
1611

L I B E R I A

Monrovia

Buchanan

Greenville

Zwedru

Ganta

Gbarnga

Kenema

Bo

Makeni

Magburaka

Koidu

SIERRA LEONE

Freetown

Grain Coast

3284

Kb

Sierra Leone Basin

Cape Verde Islands

I.d.Sto.Antão

Mindelo

I.d.São Vicente

I.d.S.Nicolau

I.d.Sal

I.d.Boa Vista

I.d.Maio

Praia

I.d Fogo

I.d.S.Tiago

CAPE VERDE

Jd

Jc

Ka

Kb

Kb 10°

18

19

15

16

SENEGAL

Saint Louis

Rosso

Louga

Linguère

Thiès

Diourbel

DAKAR

Kaolack

GAMBIA

Banjul

Ziguinchor

GUINEA-BISSAU

Bissau

Arquipélago dos Bijagós

Kédougou

Tambacounda

Kolda

Kayes

Kaédi

Kiffa

Néma

Ayoûn el-Atroûs

Nioro du Sahel

Nara

Sénégal

Gambie

Ferlo

S E N E G A L

45

705

30

Baoulé

Koulikoro

Kati

Kolokani

A f r o l l é

O o d h

Azougui

15°

10°

5°

0°

Northwestern Africa   105

Scale 1:16,000,000

0 200 400 600 Kilometers
0   200   400 Miles

La 5° **Lb** 10° **Lc** 15° **Ld** 20° Pátra **Ma** 25°

Cap Bougaroun La Galite Sicily *Linos* 3324 **ITALY** Korinthos Piraeus **ATHENS**
Bejaia Skikda Annaba Bizerte Catánia Pírgos Peloponnesus
2305 Constántine KARTHAGO Agrigento Siracusa Kalamáta Spárti *Aegéa Sea*
Sétif Souk El Kef *di Pantelleria* Gela Areópoli 5054 *Cyclaa* *Sea*
Bou Saada Batna Ahras Sousse Valletta Kíthira Crete 1838
Chott Tebessa Kasserine **MALTA** Khaniá Iráklic 2450
et Hodna Biskra Kairouan *Iles de Kerkenah* 4152 *Akra Krios*
35° *Chott Melrhir* **TUNISIA** Sfax 2719
Touggourt Gafsa *Golfe de Gabès* **M E D I T E R R A N E A**
El Oued Gabès 178 Al Bayda **CYRENE**
Ouargla Hassi Messaoud *Chott El Jerid* *Île de Jerba* Darnah
Medenine Zuwarah **TRIPOLI** Al Khums Benghazi Al Marj 882 3 Tubruq
12 Dehiba Gharyan Misratah Al Qaryat Abu Cyrenaica Umm Sa'ad
Bordj Messouda Nalut **LEPTIS MAGNA** Qurays *Gulf* Marsqa Bi'r Ben Ghimah
Great Eastern Erg Ghadamis Bani Surt *of Sirte* al Burayqah Ajdabiya
Walid *Tarhunah* *Wadi Zamzam* *Sahra Surt* Al Jagbub

30° Hamada de Tinrherr Al Qaryah *Tripolitania*
Oued Irharhar ash Sharqiyah
Bordj Omar Driss In Amenas Hun Al Jufra Awjilah *Libyan Desert*
13 Oasis
A L G E R I A Awbari **L I B Y A**
Awbari Sahra Sabha *Wadi ar Ru'ays* *Grea*
TASSILI N'AJJER Umm al Aranib Zighan
2158 Waw al Kabir *Si*
Adrar Ghat Ramlat Rabyanah El Kufrah *Oa*
25° Djanet *Fezzan* Oasis
Tahat GRAVURES Al Jawf
2918 RUPESTRES Sarir Tibesti Djebel Arknu
Tamanrasset O.Tafassasset **S** **A** **H** **A** **R** 1435
O.Tadrart Al Awaynat
14 **HOGGAR** Plateau du Tarso Emissi Ma'tan as Sarah Djebel Al Awa
Tassili du Hoggar Djado 3376 Chirfa Pic Touside △
Ténéré du 3315 △
Tafassasset Seguedine Zouar *Erdi*

20° Assamakka 3415 Emi Koussi Ounianga Kébir
Iferouâne Fachi Grand Erg de Bilma Largeau (Faya)
Aïr ou **T I B E S T I** Fada 1450
Mts. Bagaane △ Ennedi
2022 Bodélé
15 Azbine Erg du Djourab Zagaoua
Agadez **N I G E R** Oum-Chalouba
S **A** **R** **H** **E** **L** Massif du Kapka
Tanout 1220 Darfur
15° **C H A D** Abéché Al Fash
Maradi Zinder Mao Am Djemena Ati Al Junaynah
Katsina Nguru Lake Chad *Batha* Adré Djebel Marr
Talata Mafara Kano Ngala **N'Djaména** Mongo Zalingei 3088 △ Nyala

Lb 10° **Lc** 15° **Ld** 20° **Ma** 25°

Central Africa
Africa

| La | 5° | Lb | 10° | Lc | 15° | Ld | 20° | Ma |

16 Katsina — Talata Mafara — Nguru — Lake Chad — Am Djemena — CHAD — Zaling
Kano — Birnin Kudu — Potiskum — Maiduguri — Ngala — Mongo — N'Djaména — Baguirmi — Am Timan — Bahr Salamat — Birao
Funtua — S — U — Waza — D — Umm Ti
10° Yelwa — Kontagora — Zaria — Kaduna — Jos — Bauchi — Biu — Mubi — Maroua — Bongor — Chari — Sarh — Bahr Aouk — Massif des Bongo — Ouadda
New Bussa — Minna — Abuja — Jos Plateau — 1699 — Gombe — Pala — Logone — Doba — Ndélé
Bida — N I G E R I A — Numan — Yola — Garoua — Kelo — Moundou — Goré — Batangafo — CENTRAL AFRICA
Ilorin — Lafia — Benue — 2049 — Ngaoundéré — 1113 — Bossangoa — Kaga Bandoro — Bria — Kotto
17 Osogbo — Ado-Ekiti — Lokoja — Makurdi — Wukari — 2460 — Massif de l'Adamaoua — Tibati — Bouar — Sibut — Bossembélé — REPUBLIC — Bambari
Ilesa — Akure — Owo — Enugu — Katsina-Ala — 3010 — Bamenda — Derem — Berbérati — Carnot — Bangassou
Benin City — Onitsha — Abakaliki — Ugep — Bafoussam — Nkongsamba — Bertoua — Lobaye — Bangui — Gbadolite — Monga
Sapele — Ihiala — Aba — Calabar — Bafia — Sanaga — Businga — Ebola
5° Warri — Port Harcourt — Kumba — DOUALA — Yaoundé — Gemena — Lisala — Bumba
Niger Delta — Cameroon Mountain 4095 — Limbe — Edéa — CAMEROON — Quesso — Ngoko — 470 — Basankusu — DEMOC
Malabo — Isla de Bioco — Kribi — Ebolowa — Oubangui — Lulonga — Congo
18 Niger Fan — Bight of Bonny — Ambam — Ngoko — Lopori — Bas
SÃO TOMÉ AND PRÍNCIPE — Príncipe — Bata — Ncue — Oyem — Makokou — Mékambo — Mbandaka — Maringa — Ikela — REPU
São Tomé — Cabo San Juan — Baie de Corisco — EQUATORIAL GUINEA — Libreville — Ivindo — CONGO — Lac Ntomba — Boende — Tshuapa
0° São Tomé — 2745 — Cap Lopez — Lambaréné — Booué — Kéllé — Owando — Lac Mai-Ndombe — Luilaka — Co
Pagalu — Port-Gentil — GABON — Njolé — Alima — Gamboma — Selenge — Lodj
Goumbi 820 — Koulamoutou — Moanda — Lukenie — Kasai
19 Tchibanga — Ndende — Franceville — Djambala — Bandundu — Lulua — CON
1805 — Nyanga — Mayoumba — Kibangou — Kasai — Ilebo — Sankuru — Kananga
Loubomo — Brazzaville — Congo — Idiofa — Logende — Lulua — Mbuji-Ma
Pointe-Noire — Kinkala — KINSHASA — Kenge — Kikwit — Kwilu — Tshikapa — Kasai — Mwene-Dit
5° Cabinda (ANG) — Cabinda — Mbanza-Ngungu — Plateau — Kasa
1250 — Boma — Matadi — Damba — Kwango — Wamba — Chiumbe
20 ATLANTIC — 4720 — 3995 — Mebridege — Camabatela — Cuango — Luangue — Lulua
OCEAN — Malanje — Saurimo — Ka
10° Dondo — Cuanza — Cacolo — Muconda — Dilolo
21 4915 — Quibala — ANGOLA — Cassai — Zambezi
Sumbe — Luena — Bailundo

| La | 5° | Lb | 10° | Lc | 15° | Ld | 20° | Ma |

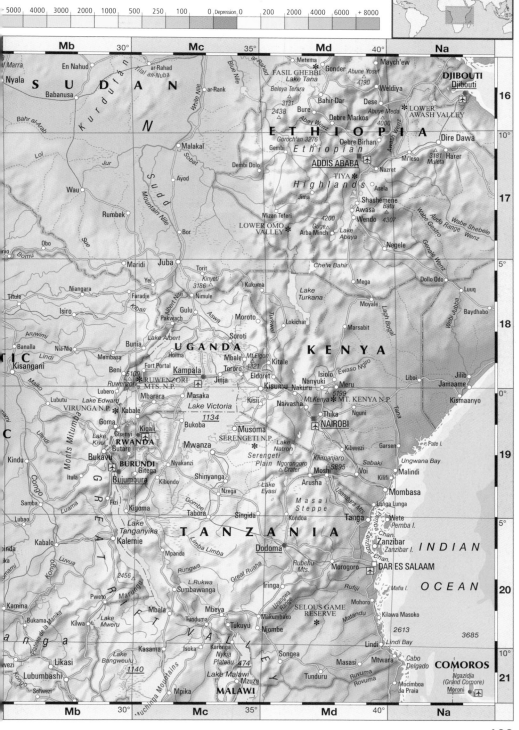

Central Africa **109**

Southern Africa, Madagascar
Africa

+5000 4000 3000 2000 1000 500 250 100 0 Depression 0 200 2000 4000 6000 +8000

Karonga
asama Isoka Nykia
Plateau
Mpika Mzuzu
Lake Malawi
Lake Nyassa
Kasungu Nkhotakota
Chipata Lichinga
tete Dedza Mandimba
ARE Zomba
Cabora Bassa Massano
Tete Blantyre
Changara
Mutare Chimoio
Mt.Binga
2436
Beira
Save
Mapinhane
RUGER N.P.
Xai-Xai Inhambane
AZILAND
Maputo
Baia do Maputo

Songea
Tunduru
Masasi
Lindi Bay
Lindi
3685

Mtwara
Cabo Delgado
Ruvuma
Mocimboa
da Praia
5
Pemba
Metoro
Nacaroa
Lúrio
Monte Namuli
Mt.Mulanje 2420
3001 Alto Molócuè
Nampula
Mocuba
Quelimane

COMOROS
Ngazidja
(Grand Comore)
Moroni
2361
Mwali
(Mohéli)
Mayotte
Mayotte (F)

Grande Terre
Assomption
Cosmoledo Atoll
Astove I.
Groupe d'Aldabra
4030

Îles Glorieuses (F)

T.Babaomby
Ambohitra
1475
Antsiranana
Ambilobe
Ambanja
2876
Maromokotro
Sambava
Marbantsetra
T.Masoala
Helodrano Atongila
Nosy Ste-Marie

MOZAMBIQUE 380
T.Vilanandro
10
Besalampy

Antsalova

Mahajanga
Ambondromamy
F.Alaotra
Ambatondrazaka
Toamasina
Antananarivo
Moramanga
Antsirabe
MADAGASCAR

I.Juan de
Nova (F)
2623
51
993
3412
Ilhas do Bazaruto
Ponta São Sebastião
Réunion (F)
Bassas da India
I.Europa

Tsiroano-
mandidy
Miandrivazo
Morondava
Fianarantsoa Mananjary
Manja Manakara
Morombe
Mangoky Boby
2658
Ihosy Farafangana

2126
3390 Toliara Vangaindrano
3670

Antsohihy

Nosy Mitsio
Nosy Be

3375
3200

2643

Mozambique Channel

4721

Ambovombe
Tanjona
Vohimena
70 Tôlanaro

5393

3260

Mozambique
Basin

Madagascar Ridge

Madagascar
Basin

I N D I A N
O C E A N

Mascarene Plain

1217
20

2592 Inyangani Gorongosa
1863
rgwiza
Caia

Mandimba
Cuamba

474

Lilongwe
MALAWI
Chilwa

Mozambique Plateau

Mozambique Ridge

Lake Malawi

Lilongwe

North and Central America
Physical map

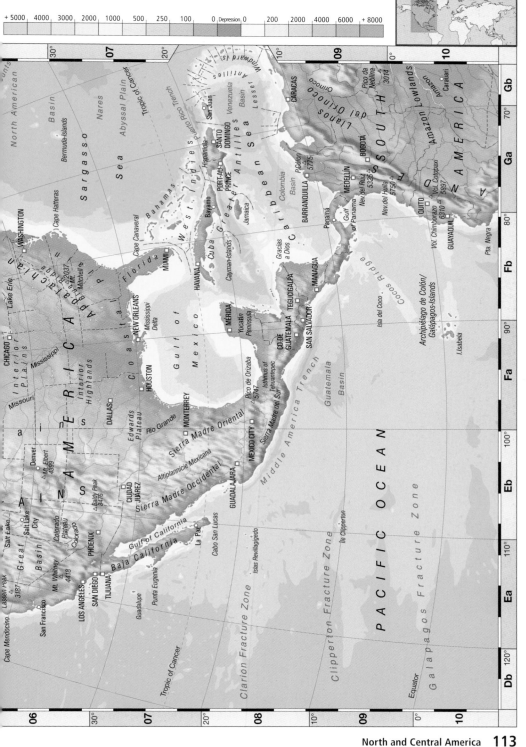

North American

Basin

Sargasso Sea

Bermuda-Islands

Nares

Abyssal Plain

Tropic of Cancer

Windward Is.

Antilles

Lesser

San Juan

CARACAS

Pico da Neblina
3014

Llanos del Orinoco

SOUTH

Amazon Lowlands

Carúari

Amazon

Venezuela

Basin

Hispaniola

SANTO DOMINGO

Greater Antilles

BOGOTÁ

Nev.del Ruiz 5325

MEDELLIN

Pico Cristóbal Colón 5775

AMERICA

PORT-AU-PRINCE

Colombia

BARRANQUILLA

Nev.del Huila 5750

West Indies

Puerto Rico Trench

Cape Hatteras

WASHINGTON

Bahamas

Cuba

Bayamo

Jamaica

Cayman-Islands

Caribbean Sea

Colombia Basin

Panamá

Gulf of Panama

QUITO

Vol.Cotopaxi 5897

Vol.Chimborazo 6310

GUAYAQUIL

Pta. Negra

Lake Erie

Appalachia

Mt. Mitchell 2037

Florida

Cape Canaveral

MIAMI

HAVANA

Gracias a Dios

MANAGUA

Cocos Ridge

Archipiélago de Colón/
Galápagos-Islands

I.Isabela

Coastal

NEW ORLEANS

Mississippi Delta

Gulf of Mexico

MÉRIDA

Yucatán Peninsula

CD.DE GUATEMALA

SAN SALVADOR

TEGUCIGALPA

Isla del Coco

CHICAGO

Interior Plains

Missouri

Interior Highlands

Mississippi

HOUSTON

DALLAS

Edwards Plateau

Rio Grande

MONTERREY

M e x i c o

Pico de Orizaba 5747

Isthmus of Tehuantepec

Sierra Madre del Sur

Guatemala

Middle America Trench

Guatemala Basin

P A C I F I C   O C E A N

Denver

Mt. Elbert 4399

A   M   E   R   I   C   A

N   S

Great Basin

Salt Lake

Salt Lake City

Lassen Peak 3187

Colorado

Colorado Plateau

Baldy Peak 3476

PHOENIX

CIUDAD JUÁREZ

Sierra Madre Occidental

Altiplannicie Mexicana

Sierra Madre Oriental

MEXICO CITY

GUADALAJARA

Mt. Whitney 4418

SAN DIEGO

TIJUANA

LOS ANGELES

San Francisco

Cape Mendocino

Guadalupe

Punta Eugenia

Baja California

Gulf of California

Cabo San Lucas

La Paz

Islas Revillagigedo

Isla Clipperton

Clipperton Fracture Zone

Clarion Fracture Zone

Galápagos Fracture Zone

Tropic of Cancer

Equator

North and Central America
Political map

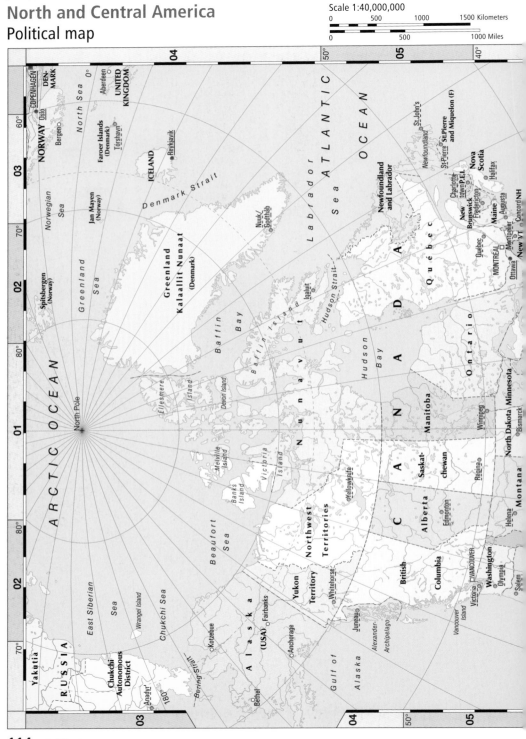

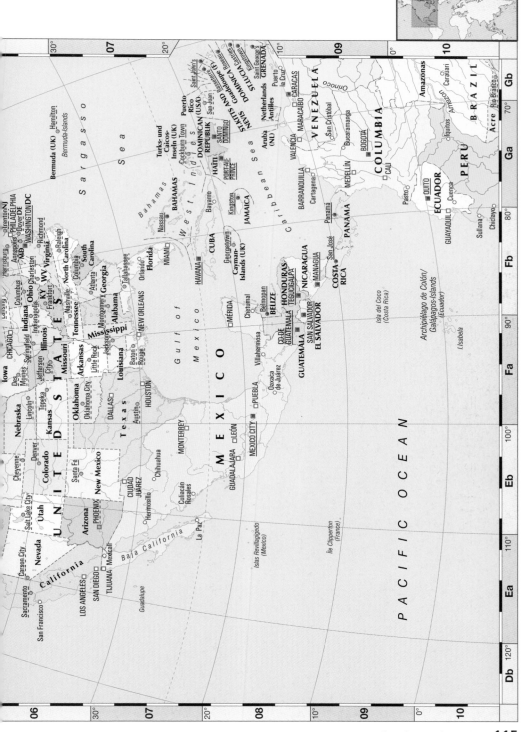

Scale 1:16,000,000

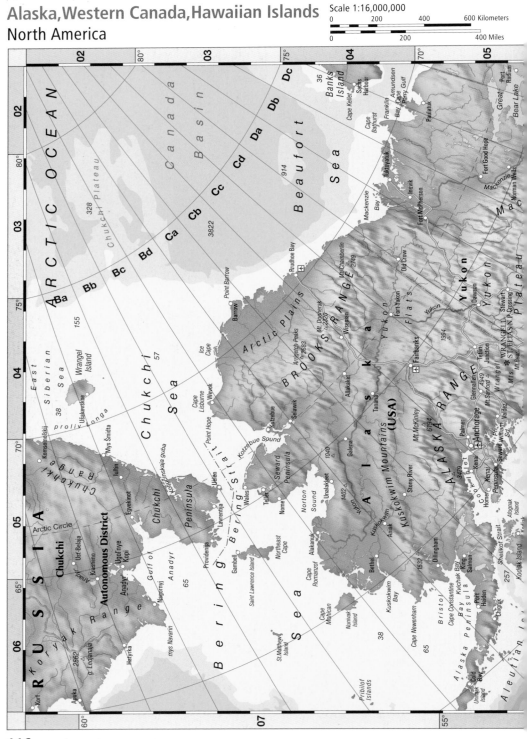

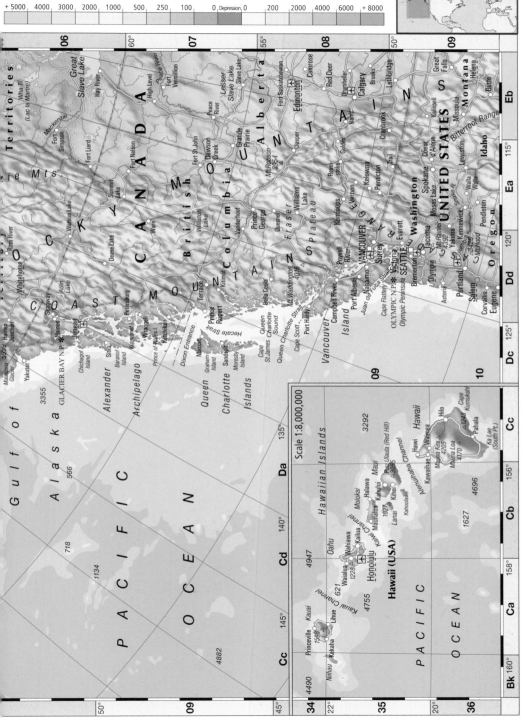

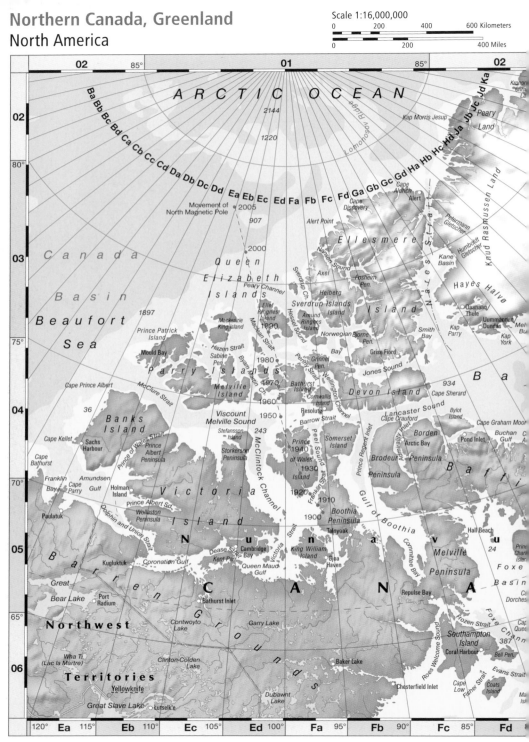

Northern Canada, Greenland
North America

Scale 1:16,000,000

0   200   400   600 Kilometers
0   200   400 Miles

A R C T I C   O C E A N

2144
1220

Lomonosov Ridge

Kap Morris Jesup

Peary Land

Ba Bb Bc Bd Ca Cb Cc Cd Da Db Dc Dd Ea Eb Ec Ed Fa Fb Fc Fd Ga Gb Gc Gd Ha Hb Hc Hd Ja Jb Jc Jd Ka

Kronprins Christian Land

Cape Aldrich
Cape Discovery
Cape Alert
Alert

C a n a d a

Movement of North Magnetic Pole
2005
907
2000

Alert Point

Knud Rasmussen Land

B a s i n

Queen Elizabeth Islands

Nansen Sound
Axel

Ellesmere Island

Petermann Gletscher

B e a u f o r t

1897

Peary Channel

Sverdrup Ch.

Heiberg

Fosheim Pen.

Humboldt Gletscher
Kane Basin

S e a

Prince Patrick Island

Mackenzie King Island
1990

Ellef Ringnes Island

Sverdrup Islands
Hessen Sound

Amund Ringnes Island

Bjorne Pen.

Hayes Halvø

Qaanaaq/ Thule
Uummannaq/ Dundas

Kap Parry

Mel Bu

Mould Bay

Hazen Strait
Sabine Pen.

Byam Martin Ch.

Norwegian Bay

Smith Bay

Kap York

P a r r y   I s l a n d s

1980
1970
1960

Perry Strait
Grinnell Pen.

Grise Fiord

Jones Sound

B a

Cape Prince Albert

McClure Strait

Melville Island

Bathurst Island
Cornwallis Island

Devon Island

934
Cape Sherard

36

Viscount Melville Sound

1950
243

Resolute
Barrow Strait

Lancaster Sound
Cape Crauford

Bylot Island

Cape Graham Moor

B a n k s   I s l a n d

Stefansson Island
Storkerson Peninsula

Prince 1940 of Wales 1930 Island 1920

Somerset Island

Prince Regent Inlet

Admiralty Inlet
Arctic Bay

Borden Peninsula

Pond Inlet

Buchan C
Gulf

Cape Kellet
Cape Bathurst

Sachs Harbour

Prince Albert Peninsula

Brodeur Peninsula

B a f f i

Franklin Bay
Cape Parry

Amundsen Gulf

Holman Island

1910
1900

Boothia Peninsula

Gulf of Boothia

Paulatuk

Prince Albert Sd.
Wollaston Peninsula

V i c t o r i a   I s l a n d

Taloyoak

Hall Beach

24

Melville Peninsula

Prince Charl Islar.

Dolphin and Union Strait

N

King William Island

u

n

Committee Bay

a

v

u

F o x e

B a s i n

B a r r e n

Kugluktuk

Coronation Gulf

Dease St.
Kent Pen.

Cambridge Bay

Victoria Strait

Gjoa Haven

Queen Maud Gulf

Repulse Bay

C

A

N

A

Ca Dorches

Great Bear Lake

Port Radium

G r o u n d s

Bathurst Inlet

Frozen Strait

Southampton Island

387

Cap Low

Bell Pen.

N o r t h w e s t

Contwoyto Lake

Garry Lake

Baker Lake

Roes Welcome Sound

Coral Harbour

Coats Island

Evans Strait

Foxe Chann

Mal

Wha Ti (Lac la Martre)

Clinton-Colden Lake

Chesterfield Inlet

Cape Low
Fisher Strait

T e r r i t o r i e s

Yellowknife

Dubawnt Lake

Great Slave Lake
Lutselk'e

02 85°   01   85° 02
120° Ea 115°   Eb 110°   Ec 105°   Ed 100°   Fa 95°   Fb 90°   Fc 85°   Fd

80°
75°
70°
65°

02
03
04
05
06

03 75° **04** 70° **05** 65°
80°

Jan Mayen (N)

G r e e n l a n d
1344
Arctic Circle
465

Kap Bismarck
Dove Bugt
Kong Frederik VIII Land

Icelandic
Sea
Plateau
Iceland
Faroe Rise

Droning
Louise
Land
Kong Wilhelm
Land

Fontur
Raufarhöfn
Rifstangi
Seydisfjördur

06

Ittoqqortoormiit/
Scoresbysund
627
Scoresby
Land
Kong Christian X Land
Scoresby Sound
Kap Brewster

Saudarkrókur
Akureyri
Grimsvötn
1719
Höfn

Hornbjarg
ICELAND
Vik

G r e e n l a n d

K a l a a l l i t N u n a a t

(DK)

Kong Christian IX Land

Ísafjördur
Akranes
Reykjavik

Ólafsvik
Hafnarfjördur
Keflavik

Denmark Strait

Kangerlussuaq
Breidafjördur

Steenstrup
Gletscher

Kap Gustav Holm
2544

Reykjanes Ridge
1323

Upernavik

Ammassalik
Ikerssuaq

Irminger Basin

60°

i n
B a y

Umanak Fjord
Sullorsuaq Vaigat
Disko Ø
Iulissat/
Jakobshavn
Iulissat Icefjord

Qeqertarsuaq/
Godhavn
Disko
Bugt

Pikiutdleq/Køge Bugt
Guldenløves Fjord
Kap Møsting Tvillingøen
3125

a f f i n
Cape Christian
2907
Cape Raper

Kong Frederik IX

D a v i s S t r a i t

Kangerlussuaq
Land
Kangerlussuaq/
Søndrestrømfjord

Tingmiarmiut Fjord

Kong Frederik VI Kyst

07

Home
Bay

Sisimut/
Holsteinsborg

Droning Ingrid
Land

I s l a n d A

Cape Dyer

Manitsoq/
Sukkertoppen
64

Nuuk/
Godthåb

Narsarsuaq

Cumberland
Peninsula
Pangnirtung

967

Cape Mercy
Paamiut/
Frederikshåb

Quaqortoq/
Julianehåb

Uummannarsuaq/
Kap Farvel

Great Plain
of the
Koukdjuak
Nettiling
Lake
Amadjuak
Lake
Hall
Peninsula

Iqaluit

L a b r a d o r **ATLANTIC**

D

Foxe
ninsula
Cape Dorset

Meta Incognita
Peninsula
Kimmirut
Frobisher Bay
3115

L a b r a d o r

55°

H u d s o n S t r a i t

Cape Labrador
133

S e a

OCEAN

08

Ivujivik

Péninsule
d'Ungava

Quaqtaq
Saglek Bay
Hebron
84

Ungava
Bay

B a s i n
4374

Ga 75° **Gb** 70° **Gc** 65° **Gd** 60° **Ha** 55° **Hb** 50° **Hc**

Southeastern Canada
North America

Scale 1:16,000,000

0   200   400   600 Kilometers
0   200   400 Miles

06

Yellowknife

Great
Slave Lake

Łutselk'e
Nonacho
Lake

Hay River   Fort Resolution

Dubawnt
Lake

Chesterfield Inlet

Coats
Island

Mansel
Island

Cape Smith

H u d s o n

60°

Fort Smith

Uranium City

Nueltin
Lake

Arviat

224

Ottawa
Islands

Inukjuak
(Port Harris

07

Peace River
Fort Chipewyan

Athabasca

Lake
Athabasca

Č

Stony
Rapids

Wollaston
Lake

Caribou

Churchill

Button
Bay

A

257

N

Churchill

Port
Nelson

B a y

Fort Severn

A

Belcher
Islands

Fort McMurray

La Loche

Cree Lake

Reindeer
Lake

Wollaston Lake

Southend   Lynn Lake

Southern
Indian Lake

Nelson

Northern
Indian Lake

Gillam

Peawanuck

107

55°

Saskatchewan

La Ronge

Lac la
Ronge

Flin Flon

M a n i t o b a

Gods
Lake

Gods Lake Narrows

Kasabonika

Attawapiskat

Akim

Grand Centre

N. Saskatchewan
Fort
Saskatchewan

Meadow Lake

Norway
House

Island
Lake

Sandy   Sandy
Lake   Lake

Kashechewan

08

Camrose
Lloyd-
minster

North
Battleford

Prince
Albert

Saskatchewan

The Pas
Cedar Lake

Lake

Winnipeg

Fort Hope

Cla

Drumheller   Kindersley

Saskatoon

Hudson Bay

Lake
Winnipegosis

Swan River

Berens
River

O n t a r i

Brooks

Swift
Current

South Saskatchewan

Lake
Diefenbaker

Yorkton

Dauphin

Lake
Manitoba

Red Lake

Sioux
Lookout

Nakina

Hearst

50°

Moose Jaw

Regina

Portage
la Prairie

Winnipeg

Lac Seul

Lake
Nipigon

Longlac

Havre

Weyburn

Estevan

Brandon

Steinbach

Red R.

Kenora

Dryden

Fort
Frances

Nipigon

Wawa

Malta

Williston

Minot

Devils
Lake

International Falls

Thunder Bay

Lake Superior

Chaple

09

Great Falls

Missouri

Fort Peck
Lake

Glendive

North Dakota

Dickinson

Bismarck

Jamestown

Fargo

Grand
Forks

Minnesota

Bemidji

Virginia

Duluth

Houghton

Upper Peninsula

Sault
Ste.Marie

La

Montana

Roundup

Yellowstone

Miles City

Bowman

Buffalo

Mobridge

Aberdeen

Fergus Falls

Moorhead

Brainerd

Minnesota

St.Cloud

Superior

Rhinelander

Ashland

Escanaba

Cheboygan

Lower

Alpe

Bozeman

Billings

Sheridan

Spearfish

South
Dakota

Watertown

Minneapolis

St.Paul

Wausau

Eau Claire

Green
Bay

Oshkosh

Lake Michigan

Traverse C

Michiga

45°

Cody

Buffalo

Gillette

Rapid City
Hot Springs

Pierre

Huron

Mitchell   Sioux Falls

Wisconsin

Rochester

Winona

La Crosse

Mankato

Milwaukee

Sagina

Peninsu

Grand Rapids

Wyoming

Riverton

Casper

Lusk

Valentine

Niobrara

Mason City

Waterloo

Madison

Dubuque

Rockford

Kenosha

CHICAGO

Lansin

Ann Art

South
Bend

10

Rock
Springs

Rawlins

U N I T E D   S T A T E S

Scottsbluff

North Platte

Norfolk

Sioux City

Ames

Cedar Rapids

Iowa

Davenport

Gary

Fort Way

Laramie

Fort Collins

Cheyenne

North Platte

Nebraska

Grand Island

Council
Bluffs

Des Moines

Burlington

Peoria

Illinois

Bloomington

Muncie

Indian

40°

Greeley

Sterling

Kearney

Hastings

Lincoln

Omaha

Quincy

Champaign

India
poli

09

Steamboat
Springs

Boulder

Denver

Grand
Junction

Mt.Elbert
4399

Salida

Colorado Springs

Pueblo

Colorado

Oakley

Norton

Hays

Manhattan

Salina

Topeka

Lawrence

Emporia

K a n s a s

Kansas
City

St.Joseph

Jefferson
City

Interior

Plains

St.Louis

Alton

CAHOKIA
MOUNDS

Springfield

TerreHaute

New
Albany

Lou
vill

Monticello

Colorado

Lamar

Missouri

Mount
Vernon

Evansville

Owens-
boro

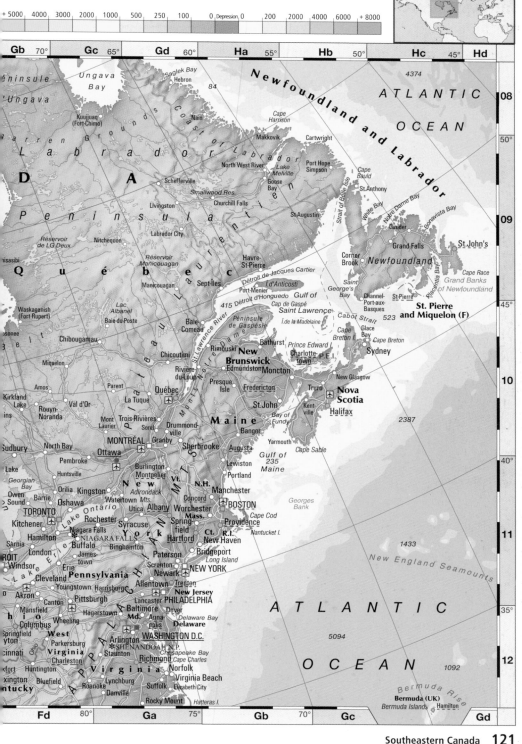

+ 5000   4000   3000   2000   1000   500   250   100   0 Depression 0   200   2000   4000   6000   + 8000

ATLANTIC

Péninsule
d'Ungava

Ungava
Bay

Saglek Bay
Hebron

Nain

Cape
Harrison

Makkovik

Cartwright

4374

OCEAN

Barren Grounds

Kuujjuaq
(Fort-Chimo)

84

50°

Labrador

Coast of Labrador

North West River

Port Hope
Simpson

Newfoundland and Labrador

Schefferville

Scheffervil

Lake
Melville

Goose
Bay

Cape
Bauld

St.Anthony

White Bay

Notre Dame Bay

09

D   **A**

Livingston

Churchill Falls

St-Augustin

Strait of Belle Isle

Gander

Grand Falls

Bonavista Bay

St.John's

Réservoir
de LG Deux

Nitchequon

Labrador City

Smallwood Res.

Corner
Brook

Grand Falls

Newfoundland

Péninsule

Q   **u**   **é**   **b**   **e**   **c**

Réservoir
Manicouagan

Havre-
St-Pierre

Détroit de Jacques Cartier

I.d'Anticosti

Saint
George's
Bay

Cape Race

Grand Banks
of Newfoundland

Waskaganish
(Fort Rupert)

Manicouagan

Sept-Îles

Port-Menier

415 Détroit d'Honguedo

Gulf of

Channel-
Port-aux-
Basques

St-Pierre

523

**St. Pierre
and Miquelon (F)**

Lac
Albanel

Baie-du-Poste

Baie-
Comeau

Cap de Gaspé

Saint Lawrence

Î.de la Madelaine

Cabot Strait

45°

Chibougamau

Péninsule
de Gaspésie

Cape
Breton I.

Cape Breton

Plateau Laurentien

Chicoutimi

Rimouski

Bathurst

Prince Edward I.

Glace
Bay

Miquelon

Rivière-
du-Loup

**New
Brunswick**

Charlotte-
town

P.E.I.

Sydney

Kirkland
Lake

Amos

Parent

Québec

Edmundston

Moncton

New Glasgow

Rouyn-
Noranda

Val-d'Or

La Tuque

Presque
Isle

Fredericton

Truro

**Nova
Scotia**

10

Mont
Laurier

Trois-Rivières

Sorel

St.John

Maine

Kent-
ville

Halifax

2387

North Bay

Drummond-
ville

Bangor

Bay
of Fundy

Sudbury

Pembroke

MONTRÉAL

Granby

Sherbrooke

Augusta

Cape Sable

Pembroke

Ottawa

Burlington

Vt.

Lewiston

Gulf of
235
Maine

40°

Huntsville

Montpelier

N.H.

Portland

Georgian
Bay

Orilia

Kingston

New

Adirondack

Concord

Manchester

Owen
Sound

Barrie

Oshawa

Watertown Mts.

Albany

BOSTON

Georges
Bank

TORONTO

Utica

Worcester

Kitchener

Rochester

Syracuse

York

Spring-
field

Mass.

Cape Cod

11

Hamilton

Niagara Falls

Binghamton

Hartford

Ct.

R.I.

Nantucket I.

Sarnia

London

NIAGARA FALLS

Buffalo

Jamestown

Scranton

Paterson

New Haven

1433

New England Seamounts

DETROIT

Windsor

Erie

Cleveland

Youngstown

Harrisburg

Allentown

Newark

NEW YORK

Long Island

Bridgeport

Akron

Canton

Pennsylvania

Pittsburgh

Lancaster

Trenton

New Jersey

Mansfield

Columbus

Wheeling

Hagerstown

Baltimore

Md.

PHILADELPHIA

Dover

Ohio

Springfield

West

Parkersburg

Anna-
polis

Delaware

Delaware Bay

35°

Dayton

WASHINGTON D.C.

Arlington

Cincinnati

Charleston

Virginia

Staunton

Richmond

Chesapeake Bay

Cape Charles

ATLANTIC

5094

Frankfort

Huntington

Virginia

Norfolk

Lexington

Bluefield

Roanoke

Lynchburg

Virginia Beach

Suffolk

Elizabeth City

1092

Kentucky

Danville

Rocky Mount

Hatteras I.

OCEAN

12

Bermuda Rise

Bermuda (UK)
Bermuda Islands   Hamilton

08

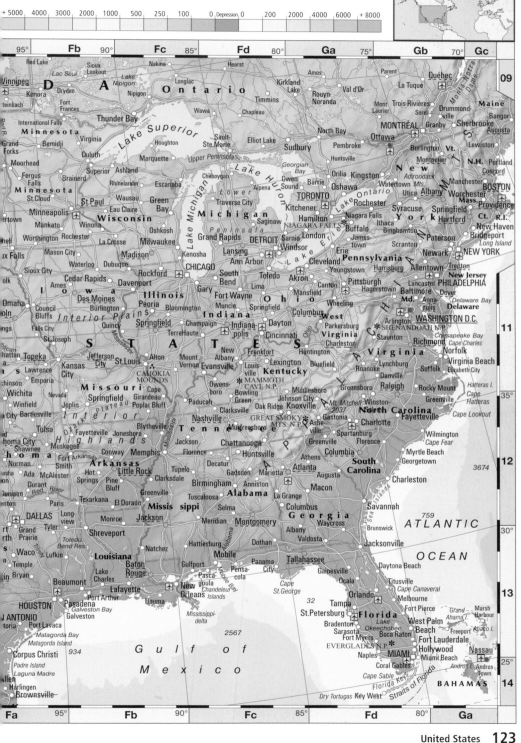

Mexico
Central America

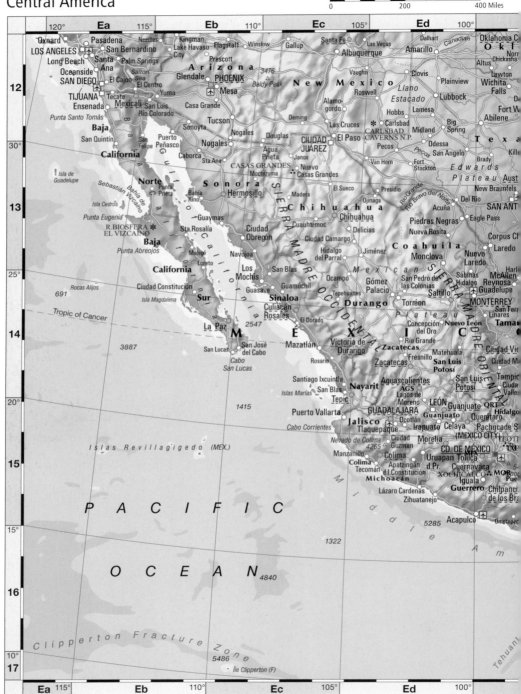

Scale 1:16,000,000

| 0 | 200 | 400 | 600 Kilometers |
| 0 | | 200 | 400 Miles |

Oxnard, Pasadena, Needles, Kingman, Flagstaff, Winslow, Gallup, Santa Fe, Las Vegas, Dalhart, Canadian, Oklahoma C
LOS ANGELES, San Bernardino, Lake Havasu City, Albuquerque, Amarillo, O K I
Long Beach, Santa Ana, Palm Springs, Prescott, A r i z o n a, Altus, Chickasha, Norr
Oceanside, Salton Sea, 3476, Vaughn, Clovis, Lawton, Wichita
SAN DIEGO, El Cajon, El Centro, Glendale, PHOENIX, Baldy Peak, N e w M e x i c o, Roswell, Plainview, Lubbock, Falls
TIJUANA, Tecate, Yuma, Mesa, Llano, Hobbs, Lamesa, Big, Fort W
Ensenada, Mexicali, Casa Grande, Alamo-gordo, Estacado, Spring, Abilene
Punta Santo Tomás, Rio Colorado, Sonoyta, Tucson, Deming, Las Cruces, Carlsbad, Midland, Odessa, T e x a
Baja, Nogales, Douglas, CIUDAD, CARLSBAD, Pecos, San Angelo, Killeen
San Quintín, Puerto Peñasco, Nogales, Agua Prieta, JUAREZ, El Paso, CAVERNS N.P., Van Horn, Fort Stockton, Brady, Aust
California, Caborca, Sta.Ana, Janos, Nuevo, Casas Grandes, Pecos, E d w a r d s, New Braunfels
Isla de Guadelupe, Punta Prieta, CASAS GRANDES, Moctezuma, Casas Grandes, Presidio, Rio Grande, Acuña, Del Rio, P l a t e a u, SAN ANT
Norte, Bahía, Madera, El Sueco, Ojinaga, Rio Bravo del Norte, Piedras Negras, Eagle Pass
Sebastián Vizcaino, Bahía de, Kino, H e r m o s i l l o, S O N O R A, C h i h u a h u a, Chihuahua, Nueva Rosita, Corpus Ch
Isla Cedros, S i e r r a, Cuauhtémoc, Delicias, C o a h u i l a, Monclova, Nuevo, Laredo
Punta Eugenia, Guaymas, Ciudad Obregón, Ciudad Camargo, Hidalgo del Parral, Jiménez, M e x i c a n, San Pedro de las Colonias, Saltillo, Sabinas, Hidalgo, McAllen, Reynosa
R.BIOSFERA, EL VIZCAINO, Sta.Rosalía, Navojoa, Ocampo, Gómez Palacio, Torreón, Concepción, Nuevo León, San Fer
Baja, Mulegé, Los Mochis, San Blas, Guamúchil, Tepehuanes, Durango, P l a t e a u, Linares, Tama
Punta Abreojos, Loreto, Guasave, Sinaloa, Culiacán, El Dorado, Rio Grande, Victoria de, Matehuala, Ciudad Vic
California, Ciudad Constitución, Rosales, Zacatecas, Durango, Fresnillo, San Luis Potosí, Ciuda
Rocas Alijos, 691, Isla Magdalena, Sur, 2547, La Paz, M É X I C, Mazatlán, Durango, Zacatecas, San Luis Potosí, Tampic
Tropic of Cancer, 3887, San Lucas, San José del Cabo, Rosario, Aguascalientes, AGS, Lagos de Moreno, Guanajuato, QRT, Hidalgo
Cabo San Lucas, Santiago Ixcuintla, San Blas, Tepic, Nayarit, GUADALAJARA, LEÓN, Guanajuato, Querétaro, Pachuca
Islas Revillagigedo (MEX.), 1415, Puerto Vallarta, Tlaquepaque, Ocotlán, Celaya, (MEXICO CITY), TEOTI
Cabo Corrientes, Jalisco, Ciudad Guzman, Morelia, CD. DE MÉXICO
Nevado de Colima, 4265, Colima, Uruapan, Toluca, Cuernavaca, MOR
Manzanillo, Colima, Apatzingán, XOCHICALCO, Iguala, Pue
Tecomán, d.Pr., I.Constitución, Michoacan, Guerrero, Chilpanci
P A C I F I C, Lázaro Cardenas, Zihuatanejo, de los Bra
5285, Acapulco, Ometepec
O C E A N, 4840
1322
C l i p p e r t o n   F r a c t u r e   Z o n e, M i d d l e   A m, Tehuan
5486, Île Clipperton (F)

Caribbean Islands
Central America

Scale 1:16,000,000

0   200   400   600 Kilometers

0   200   400 Miles

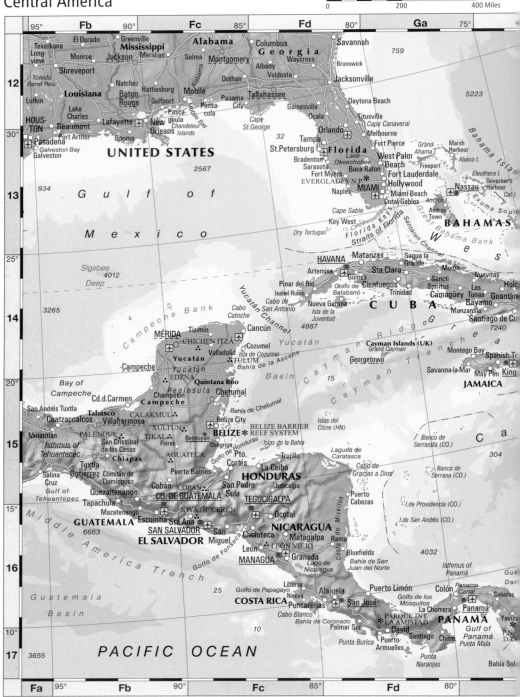

	Fb		Fc		Fd		Ga	
	95°	90°		85°		80°		75°

El Dorado Greenville **Alabama** Columbus Savannah 759
Texarkana Mississippi Georgia
Long- Monroe Jackson Meridian Selma Montgomery Waycross Brunswick
view Shreveport Dothan Albany Valdosta 5223

Natchez Hattiesburg Mobile Panama Tallahassee Jacksonville
Lufkin Louisiana Baton Gulfport Pensa- City
Lake Rouge Pasca- cola Gainesville Daytona Beach
HOUS- Charles goula Chandeleur Cape Ocala Titusville Cape Canaveral
TON Beaumont New Islands St.George 32 Tampa Orlando Melbourne
Pasadena Fort Arthur Orleans St.Petersburg **Florida** Fort Pierce Grand Marsh
Galveston Bay Houma Lake West Palm Ahama I. Harbour
Galveston 2567 Bradenton Okeechobee Beach Freeport Abaco I.
Sarasota Boca Raton Fort Lauderdale Eleuthera I.
934 Fort Myers Hollywood Governor's
G u l f   o f Naples MIAMI Miami Beach Nassau Harbour
Coral Gables Andros Cat I.
Town **BAHAMAS**
M e x i c o Cape Sable Andros I.
Key West Great Bahama Bank W
Dry Tortugas Florida Keys e s
Straits of Florida Santaren Channel

HAVANA Matanzas Sagua la Morón
Sigsbee Artemisa Sta.Clara Grande Nuevitas
4012 Guines Cienfuegos Sancti Las
Deep Pinar del Río Golfo de Trinidad Spíritus Camagüey Tunas Holg
Isabel Rubio Batabanó **C U B A** Bayamo Guantán
3265 Cabo de Nueva Gerona Manzanillo Santiago de Cu
San Antonio Isla de la 7240
Juventud 4887 G r e a
Tizimín Cancún Yucatán Cayman Islands (UK) Ridge
MÉRIDA CHICHEN ITZÁ Grand Cayman Montego Bay
Cozumel Valladolid Isla de Cozumel Georgetown Savanna-la-Mar Spanish T
Yucatán TULUM Cayman Basin 15 May Pen King
Campeche Bahía de la Ascens. **JAMAICA**
Yucatán Cayman Trench
Bay of EDZNA Peninsula Chetumal
Campeche Cd.d.Carmen Quintana Roo Islas del Banco de C a
San Andrés Tuxtla Champotón **Campeche** Bahía de Chetumal Cisne (HN) Serranilla (CO.) 304
Tabasco CALAKMUL Belize City **BELIZE BARRIER**
Coatzacoalcos Villahermosa XULTÚN **REEF SYSTEM** Banco de
Minatitlán PALENQUE TIKAL Belmopán Islas de la Bahía Serrana (CO.)
Chiapas San Cristóbal Flores **BELIZE** Dangriga Laguna de
Isthmus of de las Casas AGUATECA Golfo de Honduras Trujillo Caratasca
Tehuantepec Tuxtla Comitán de Puerto Barrios La Ceiba Cabo de I.de Providencia (CO.)
Salina Gutiérrez Domínguez COPÁN San Pedro Pto. Gracias a Dios
Cruz Quezaltenango Sula Cortés **HONDURAS** Puerto I.de San Andrés (CO.)
Gulf of Tapachula Cobán CD. DE GUATEMALA Juticalpa Cabezas 4032
Tehuantepec JOYA DE CERÉN **TEGUCIGALPA** Costa de Miskitos
Mazatenango Escuintla Sta.Ana Ocotal Isthmus of
GUATEMALA 6663 SAN SALVADOR San **NICARAGUA** Rama Panamá Gul
Choluteca Matagalpa Dar
EL SALVADOR Miguel LEÓN VIEJO Bluefields
San José León Granada Bahía de San Colón Panamá Canazas
Liberia **MANAGUA** Juan del Norte Canal
COSTA RICA Lago de Golfo de los La Chorrera **PANAMÁ** Yaviz
Puntarenas San José Nicaragua Mosquitos P.N
Cabo Blanco Nicoya Puerto Limón David DA
Bahía de Coronado Alajuela Santiago Chitré Gulf of
PACIFIC OCEAN Palmar Sur PARQUE INT. Panamá Punta Mala
Punta Burica Puerto LA AMISTAD Punta Bahía Sol
3655 Armuelles Naranjas
Middle America Trench Guatemala Basin Golfo de Fonseca Golfo de Papagayo Golfo de

	Fa		Fb		Fc		Fd	
	95°		90°		85°		80°	

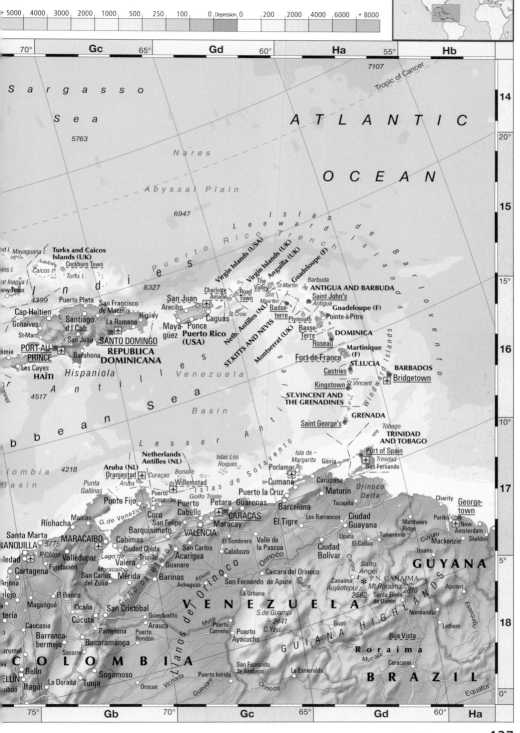

5000 4000 3000 2000 1000 500 250 100 0 Depression 0 200 2000 4000 6000 +8000

70°

14
20°

S a r g a s s o

S e a

5763

Nares

Abyssal Plain

A T L A N T I C

O C E A N

Tropic of Cancer

7107

15

6947

Islas

Leeward

Trench

Islands

de

Barlovento

nd I. Mayaguana

Turks and Caicos
Islands (UK)

Cockburn Town

Caicos I.

Turks I.

at Inagua I.
ew Town

ins I.

West

Puerto Rico

Lesser

15°

I n d i e s

4399

8327

San Juan

Arecibo

Charlotte
Amalie

Road
Town

The
Valley

St-Martin

Anguilla (UK)

Virgin Islands (USA)

Virgin Islands (UK)

Guadeloupe (F)

Barbuda

ANTIGUA AND BARBUDA

Saint John's

Antigua

Puerto Plata

San Francisco
de Macoris

Cap-Haïtien

Gonaïves

St-Marc

Santiago
d.l.Cab.

San Juan

Higüey

La Romana

Caguas

St.Croix

Sint
Maarten

Neth. Antilles (NL)

Basse-
terre

Plymouth

Guadeloupe (F)

Pointe-à-Pitre

Maya-
güez

Ponce

Puerto Rico
(USA)

ST.KITTS AND NEVIS

Basse-
Terre

Roseau

DOMINICA

SANTO DOMINGO

REPUBLICA
DOMINICANA

Montserrat (UK)

Martinique
(F)

Fort-de-France

ST.LUCIA

PORT-AU-
PRINCE

Barahona

Hispaniola

Venezuela

Castries

BARBADOS

Bridgetown

emie

Les Cayes

HAÏTI

4517

A n t i

l l e s

C a r i b b e a n   S e a

Basin

Kingstown

St.Vincent

ST.VINCENT AND
THE GRENADINES

GRENADA

Saint George's

Tobago

TRINIDAD
AND TOBAGO

16

10°

b

b e a n

Lesser

A n t i l l e s

Windward Islands

Netherlands
Antilles (NL)

Aruba (NL)

Oranjestad

Curaçao

Bonaire

Willemstad

*Islas Los
Roques*

Isla de
Margarita

Porlamar

Güiria

Carúpano

*Orinoco
Delta*

Port of Spain

Trinidad

San Fernando

Charity

George-
town

Parika

17

lombia
Basin

4218

Punta
Gallinas

G. de Venezuela

Punto Fijo

Puerto
Cumarebo

Golfo Triste

Puerto
Cabello

Cumaná

Puerto la Cruz

Petare

Guarenas

Barcelona

Maturín

Tucupita

Matthews
Ridge

New
Amsterdam

Mackenzie

Skeldon

Ríohacha

Maicao

Coro

San Felipe

CARACAS

Maracay

El Tigre

Los Barrancos

Ciudad
Guayana

Upata

Tumeremo

Cuyuni

Issano

Santa Marta

ANQUILLA

5775

MARACAIBO

Cabimas

Barquisimeto

VALENCIA

Valle de
la Pascua

Ciudad
Bolívar

El Callao

GUYANA

5°

ledad

Cartagena

P.Cólon

Valledupar

Fundación

Ciudad Ojeda

Lago de
Maracaibo

Trujillo

San Carlos

El Sombrero

Calabozo

Caicara del Orinoco

Orinoco

Caroní

Salto
Ángel

P.N. CANAIMA

Matthews

Apoteri

rjona

elejo

El Banco

Magangué

Ocaña

Mérida

Cord de Mérida

San Carlos
del Zulia

Barinas

Apure

Guanare

Acarigua

Achaguas

San Fernando de Apure

Apure

La Urbana

Auyántepui

2562

Mt.Roraima
2810

Santa Elena
de Uairén

Normandia

Lethem

Essequibo

tería

Caucasia

Barranca-
bermeja

San Cristóbal

Guasdualito

Pamplona

Arauca

Puerto
Carreño

Meta

Guati

GUIANA   HIGHLANDS

Boa Vista

arumal

Cúcuta

Puerto
Rondón

S. de Guampi

△ 2441

C. Yavi

Puerto
Ayacucho

Mucajaí

Caracaraí

18

COLOMBIA

Bucaramanga

Socorro

V E N E Z U E L A

Llanos del Orinoco

San Fernando
de Atabapo

La Esmeralda

R o r a i m a

B R A Z I L

ELLIN

Bello

Itagüí

ibido

La Dorada

Sogamoso

Tunja

Orocue

Vichada

Puerto Inírida

Guaviare

Orinoco

Equator

0°

75° Gb 70° Gc 65° Gd 60° Ha

South America
Physical map

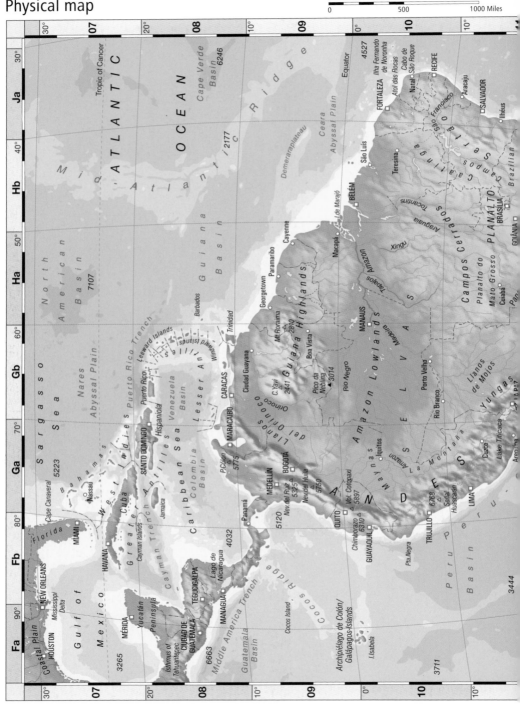

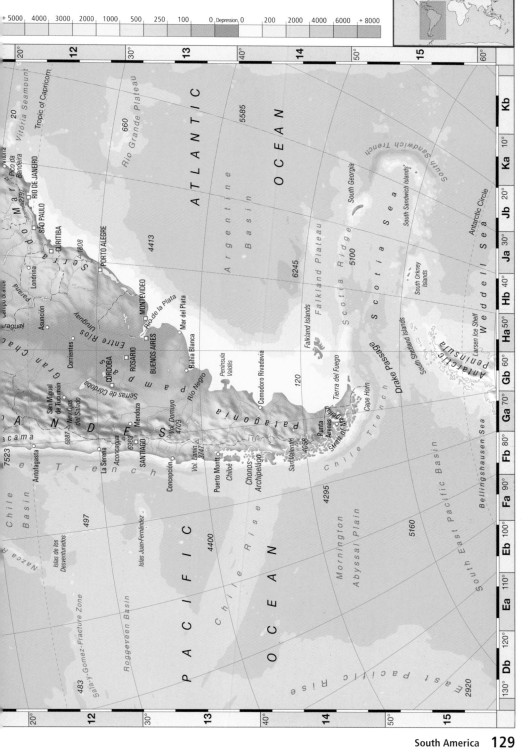

South America
Political map

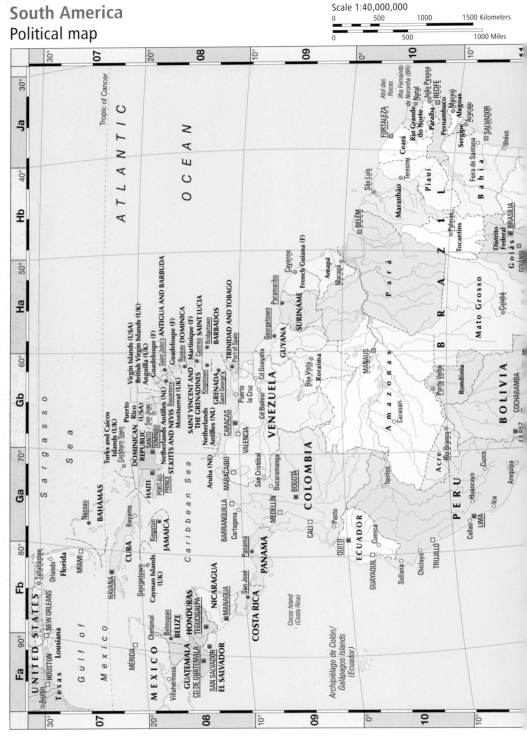

Scale 1:40,000,000

0   500   1000   1500 Kilometers
0   500   1000 Miles

Tropic of Cancer

ATLANTIC

OCEAN

Atol das Rocas
Ilha Fernando de Noronha (BR)
FORTALEZA
Rio Grande do Norte
Natal
João Pessoa
Paraíba
RECIFE
Pernambuco
Maceió
Alagoas
Aracaju
Sergipe
SALVADOR
Ceará
Ilhéus

São Luís
Teresina
Maranhão
Piauí
Feira de Santana
B a h i a

BELÉM
Palmas
Tocantins
Distrito Federal
BRASÍLIA
Goiás
GOIÂNIA

Cayenne
French Guiana (F)
Amapá
Macapá

P a r á

Paramaribo
SURINAME
Cuiabá
Mato Grosso

Georgetown
GUYANA
B   R   A   Z   I   L

Cd Guayana
Cd Bolívar
Boa Vista
Roraima

MANAUS
A m a z o n a s

Port of Spain
TRINIDAD AND TOBAGO
BARBADOS
Bridgetown
Castries SAINT LUCIA
SAINT VINCENT AND THE GRENADINES
GRENADA
Saint George's
Kingstown

Virgin Islands (USA)
British Virgin Islands (UK)
Anguilla (UK)
Saint John's ANTIGUA AND BARBUDA
Guadeloupe (F)
DOMINICA
Roseau
Martinique (F)
Basseterre
ST KITTS AND NEVIS
Montserrat (UK)
Netherlands Antilles (NL)

Puerto
Rico
San Juan

Turks and Caicos
Islands (UK)
Cockburn Town

DOMINICAN
REPUBLIC
SANTO
DOMINGO

HAITI
PORT-AU-PRINCE

CARACAS
VALENCIA
Puerto la Cruz
Aruba (NL)
MARACAIBO
San Cristóbal
V E N E Z U E L A
Carauari
Porto Velho
Rondônia

B O L I V I A
LA PAZ
COCHABAMBA

NASSAU
BAHAMAS
Bayamo

CUBA
HAVANA
Georgetown
Cayman Islands (UK)

JAMAICA
Kingston

C a r i b b e a n   S e a

Cartagena
BARRANQUILLA
Bucaramanga
MEDELLÍN
BOGOTÁ
CALI
Pasto
C O L O M B I A

Iquitos
Rio Branco
Acre
Cuzco
P E R U

QUITO
ECUADOR
Cuenca

GUAYAQUIL
Sullana
Chiclayo
TRUJILLO
Huancayo
LIMA
Callao
Ica
Arequipa

S a r g a s s o   S e a

MIAMI
Florida
Orlando
Tallahassee
New Orleans
Lousiana
Texas
HOUSTON
Austin
U N I T E D   S T A T E S

G u l f   o f
M e x i c o

MÉRIDA
Villahermosa
Chetumal
BELIZE
Belmopan
GUATEMALA
CD DE GUATEMALA
SAN SALVADOR
EL SALVADOR
HONDURAS
TEGUCIGALPA
NICARAGUA
MANAGUA
COSTA RICA
San José
PANAMA
Panamá

Cocos Island
(Costa Rica)

Archipiélago de Colón/
Galápagos Islands
(Ecuador)

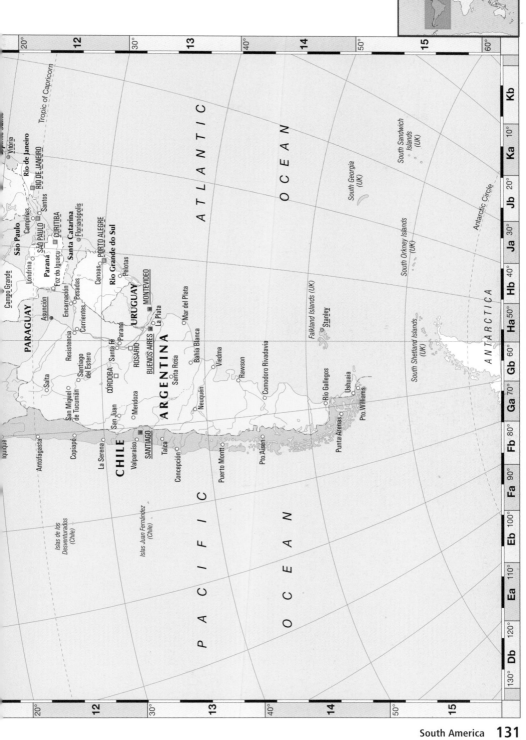

South America **131**

Venezuela, Colombia, Ecuador, Peru
South America

Scale 1:16,000,000

0	200	400	600 Kilometers

0	200	400 Miles

Caribbean Sea

BARBADOS Bridgetown
St. Vincent Kingstown
ST. VINCENT AND THE GRENADINES
GRENADA Saint George's
Tobago
TRINIDAD AND TOBAGO
Port of Spain
Trinidad

Netherlands Antilles (NL)
Aruba (NL) Oranjestad
Willemstad
Curaçao Bonaire
Islas Los Roques

Isla de Margarita
Porlamar
Cumaná
Barcelona
Puerto la Cruz
Cd. Guayana
Ciudad Bolívar
El Tigre
Los Barrancos

Georgetown
New Amsterdam
Mackenzie
Parika
Charity

GUYANA
Mt Roraima 2810
La Gran Sabana
Auyantepui 2562
Salto Ángel
PN. CANAIMA

GUIANA HIGHLANDS

Roraima
Boa Vista
Sta Elena de Uairén

Riohacha Maicao
Santa Marta
BARRANQUILLA
Soledad
Cartagena
Sincelejo
Montería
MARACAIBO
Cabimas
Lago de Maracaibo
Valledupar
Ocaña
Cúcuta
Pamplona
Bucaramanga
MÉRIDA
San Cristóbal
Barinas
Barquisimeto
VALENCIA
Maracay
CARACAS
Puerto Cabello
Coro
Punto Fijo
Guarenas
Maiquetía

VENEZUELA
Llanos del Orinoco
San Fernando de Apure
Calabozo
El Sombrero
Valle de la Pascua
San Carlos
Acarigua
Guanare
San Juan de los Morros

Puerto Ayacucho
San Fernando de Atabapo
Puerto Páez
La Unión
Puerto Carreño
Puerto Inírida

Orinoco
Río Negro
Pico da Neblina 3014

MANAUS
Rio Negro
Amazonas

AMAZON LOWLANDS

COLOMBIA
BOGOTÁ
MEDELLÍN
CALI
Bello
Itagüí
Manizales
Pereira
Armenia
Tuluá
Palmira
Buenaventura
Popayán
Pasto
Tumaco
Florencia
Neiva
Ibagué
Girardot
La Dorada
Honda
Barrancabermeja
Yarumal
Turbo
Quibdó
Villavicencio
San José del Guaviare
Buenos Aires
Leticia

Nevado del Huila 5750
Vol. Puracé 4600
Nev. del Ruiz 5326
Nevado del Tolima 5215

PANAMA
PANAMÁ
Colón
Canal de Panamá
David
La Chorrera
Chitré
Santiago
Gulf of Panama
Yaviza
PN. DEL DARIÉN

ECUADOR
QUITO
GUAYAQUIL
Cuenca
Machala
Milagro
Ambato
Riobamba
Manta
Portoviejo
Jipijapa
Loja
Esmeraldas
Sto. Domingo d.l. Colorados
Vol. Cayambe 5790
Vol. Cotopaxi 5897
Chimborazo 6310
Vol. Sangay 5230
PN. SANGAY
Equator

PERU
Iquitos
Nauta
Pebas

Río Marañón
Río Napo
Río Putumayo
Río Caquetá
Río Amazonas

Golfo de Guayaquil
Isla Puná
Tumbes
Talara

Punta Gallinas
Golfo de Venezuela
G. of Venezuela

Isla de Malpelo (CO)
I. de San Andrés (CO)
I. de Providencia (CO)
Golfo de los Mosquitos
Gulf of Darién

Lesser Antilles
Islas de Sotavento

Serra Acara ou Acari
Caroni

132   South America

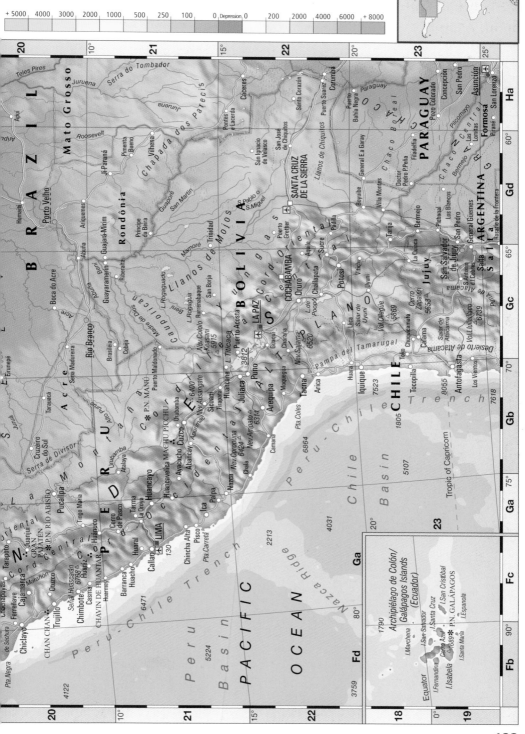

Suriname, Brazil
South America

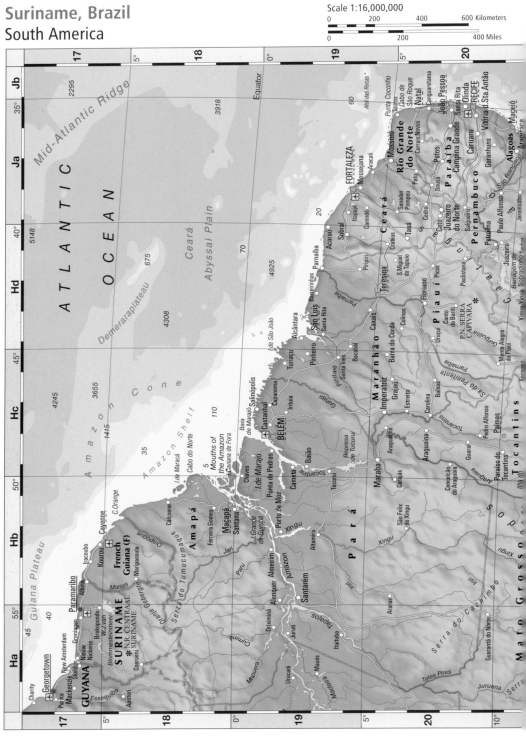

Scale 1:16,000,000

0   200   400   600 Kilometers
0   200   400 Miles

ATLANTIC OCEAN

Mid-Atlantic Ridge

2295

3918

Equator

5148

Ceará Abyssal Plain

675

Demerara plateau

4308

4925

Amazon Cone

4245

3655

1415

Amazon Shelf

35

110

5

Mouths of the Amazon

FORTALEZA
Messejana
Aracati
Mossoró
Rio Grande do Norte
Natal
Cabo de São Roque
Santa Antão
Olinda
RECIFE
Vitória d.Sta.Antão
Maceió
Alagoas
Paraíba
João Pessoa
Campina Grande
Santa Rita
Caruaru
Garanhuns
Pernambuco
Paulo Afonso
Ceará
Pacajus
Caninde
Sobral
Acaraú
Parnaíba
Piripiri
Teresina
Piauí
P.N. SERRA CAPIVARA
Canto do Buriti
Floriano
S. Miguel do Tapuio
Tauá
Cedro
Crato
Juazeiro do Norte
Patos
Sousa
Picos
Oeiras
Caxias
Codó
Colinas
Barra do Corda
Grajaú
Balsas
Maranhão
Imperatriz
Carolina
Estreito
Pedro Afonso
Araguaína
Palmas
Paraíso do Tocantins
Tocantins
São Luís
Santa Rita
Alcântara
I.de São João
Pinheiro
Santa Inês
Turiaçu
Cururupu
Salinópolis
Castanhal
Capanema
Irituia
BELÉM
I.de Marajó
Baía de Marajó
Caviana de Fora
Cabo do Norte
I.de Maracá
Chaves
Ponta de Pedras
Cametá
Baião
Tucuruí
Represa de Tucuruí
Marabá
Carajás
São Félix do Xingu
Conceição do Araguaia
Ilha do Bananal
Pará
Altamira
Porto de Moz
Gurupá
Almeirim
Alenquer
Santarém
Óbidos
Oriximiná
Monte Alegre
Juruti
Itaituba
Maués
Madeira
Tapajós
Teles Pires
Juruena
Serra do Cachimbo
Mato Grosso
Xingu
Araras
Guaraná do Norte
Cuminá
Mapuera
Uruçuí

Georgetown
Charity
Parika
Mackenzie
New Amsterdam
Skeldon
Corentyne
Nieuw Nickerie
GUYANA
Guiana Plateau
Essequibo
Apoteri
Coeroeni
SURINAME
N.R. CENTRAAL SURINAME
Paramaribo
Groningen
Albina
Brokopondo
W.J.van Blommestein meer
Moengo
Maripasoula
French Guiana (F)
Kourou
Cayenne
Iracoubo
Calçoene
Amapá
Ferreira Gomes
Macapá
Santana
I.Grande de Gurupá
Serra do Tumucumaque
Oyapock
Maroni
Jari
Paru
Amazon
Trombetas

134   South America

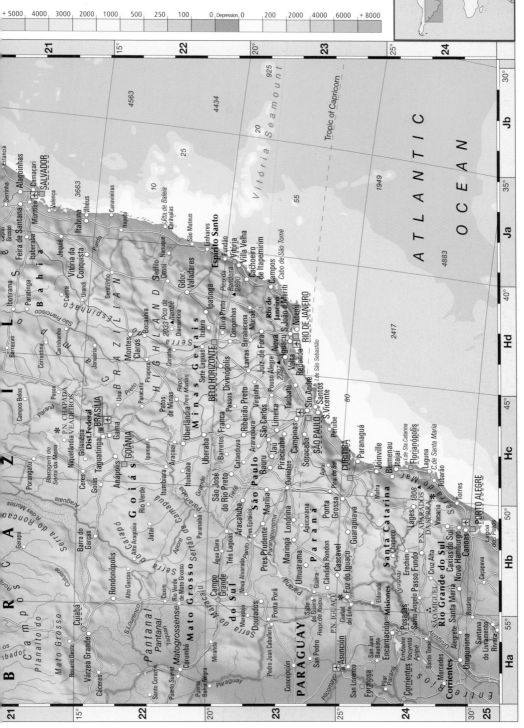

Scale bar (top): + 5000 4000 3000 2000 1000 500 250 100 0 Depression 0 200 2000 4000 6000 + 8000

Map labels:

ATLANTIC OCEAN

Tropic of Capricorn

Vitória Seamount 925

SALVADOR
Camaçari
Alagoinhas
Feira de Santana
Serrinha
Santo Amaro
Murituba
Itaberaba
Ibotirama
Paratinga
Bahia
Jequié
Itabuna
Vitória da Conquista
Ilhéus
Canavieiras
Itapetinga
Pta. de Baleia
Caravelas
São Mateus
Linhares
Espírito Santo
Vitória
Villa Velha
Cachoeiro de Itapemirim
Cabo de São Tomé
Campos
Sedhio
Otoni
Nanuque
Gdor. Valadares
Ipatinga
Fundão
Pico da Bandeira 2890
Itambé
Pico da
Pedra Azul
Teófilo Otoni
Diamantina
Itabira
Ouro Preto
Barbacena
Muriaé
Rio de Janeiro
São João d'Meriti
Nova Iguaçu
Niterói
RIO DE JANEIRO
Volta Redonda
Juiz de Fora
Pouso Alegre
Taubaté
I. de São Sebastião
Sto. André
S. Vicente
Santos
São Paulo
SÃO PAULO
Campinas
Sorocaba
Peruibe
CURITIBA
Paranaguá
Joinville
Blumenau
Itajaí
Florianópolis
I. de Sta Catarina
Laguna
C. de Santa Maria
Tubarão
Santa Catarina
Lages 1808
Chapecó
Erechim
Vacaria
PORTO ALEGRE
Canoas
Novo Hamburgo
Caxias do Sul
Cruz Alta
Passo Fundo
Rio Grande do Sul
SÃO MIGUEL
Santo Ângelo
Santa Maria
Misiones
Posadas
Encarnación
Santa Rosa
Uruguaiana
Alegrete
Santana do Livramento
Rivera
Corrientes
Mercedes
Capão
Rosario
Entre Ríos
PARAGUAY
ASUNCIÓN
Concepción
San Pedro
San Juan Bautista
Pilar
Formosa
San Lorenzo
Pedro Juan Caballero
Ciudad del Este
P.N. IGUAÇU
Foz do Iguaçu
Cascavel
Cândido Rondon
Guaíra
Pres. Epitácio
Dourados
Ponta Porã
Maracaju
Campo Grande
Três Lagoas
Presidente Prudente
Marília
Bauru
Araçatuba
Londrina
Maringá
Umuarama
Paraná
Ponta Grossa
Apucarana
Guarapuava
Jaú
Piracicaba
Limeira
Araraquara
Ribeirão Preto
São Carlos
Franca
Catanduva
São José do Rio Preto
Barretos
Uberaba
Ituiutaba
Araguari
Uberlândia
São Paulo
Minas Gerais
BELO HORIZONTE
Divinópolis
Lavras
Sete Lagoas
Patos de Minas
Pirapora
Três Marias
Montes Claros
Januária
Corrente
Carinhanha
Barreiras
Correntina
BRASÍLIA
Dist. Federal
N. QUELÂNDIA VEADEIROS
P.N. CHAPADA
Niquelândia
Goianésia
GOIÂNIA
Anápolis
Ceres
Goiás
Rio Verde
Jataí
Alto Araguaia
Barra do Garças
Rondonópolis
Alto Garças
Coxim
Corumbá
Miranda
Várzea Grande
Cuiabá
Cáceres
Puerto Suárez
Santo Corazón
Bahía Negra
Rosario Oeste
Pantanal
Matogrossense
Mato Grosso do Sul
Serra do Roncador
Serra do Mar
Planalto do Mato Grosso
Campos
Serra do Amambaí
B R A Z I L
B R A Z I L I A N H I G H L A N D
Serra do Espinhaço
São Francisco
Goiás
Paraná
Paraguay
Paraná

Elevations / numbers:
4563
4434
925
1949
4883
2417
3663
2033
2307
2890
80
55
20
25
10

Grid references (right margin): Jb Ja Hd Hc Hb Ha

Grid references (top): 21 22 23 24
Grid references (bottom): 21 22 23 24 25

Latitude labels: 15° 20° 25° 30°
Longitude labels (top): 15° 20° 25°
Longitude labels (bottom): 15° 20° 25° 30° 35° 40° 45° 50° 55°

Chile, Argentina, Paraguay, Uruguay
South America

Scale 1:16,000,000

0   200   400   600 Kilometers
0   200   400 Miles

22 20° 23 25° 24 30° 25 35°

BRAZIL

GOIÂNIA · Ipameri · Araçatuba · Uberaba · Barretos · Franca · Ribeirão Preto · Uberlândia · Itumbiara · São Carlos · Araraquara · São José do Rio Preto · Limeira · Jaú · Piracicaba · Campinas · SÃO PAULO · Sorocaba · Bauru · Marília · Presidente Prudente · Apucarana · Londrina · Maringá · CURITIBA · Paranaguá · Joinville · Blumenau · Itajaí · Florianópolis · I. de Sta. Catarina

Mato Grosso do Sul · Campo Grande · Dourados · Ponta Porã · Ponta Grossa · Guarapuava · Cascavel · Foz do Iguaçu · P.N. IGUAZU · P.N. DO IGUAÇU

Santa Catarina · Lages · Vacaria · Erechim · Passo Fundo · Chapecó

Rio Grande do Sul · Caxias do Sul · Novo Hamburgo · Canoas · PORTO ALEGRE · Lagoa dos Patos · Rio Grande · Pelotas · Bagé · Santa Maria

Pantanal · Corumbá · Miranda

PARAGUAY · ASUNCIÓN · Concepción · Pedro Juan Caballero · San Pedro · Villarrica · Encarnación · Pilar · Formosa · TRINIDAD · POSADAS

Chaco Boreal

BOLIVIA · SANTA CRUZ DE LA SIERRA · SUCRE · POTOSÍ · ORURO · COCHABAMBA · Tarija · Uyuni · Altiplano

URUGUAY · MONTEVIDEO · Rivera · Salto · Paysandú · Melo · Minas · Florida · Durazno · Mercedes

ARGENTINA · BUENOS AIRES · Quilmes · La Plata · ROSARIO · San Nicolás · Córdoba · CÓRDOBA · Santa Fe · Paraná · Entre Ríos · Corrientes · Resistencia · Formosa · Santiago del Estero · Tucumán · San Miguel de Tucumán · Salta · Jujuy · San Salvador de Jujuy · Catamarca · La Rioja · San Juan · Mendoza · San Luis · San Rafael

CHILE · SANTIAGO · Valparaíso · Viña del Mar · San Bernardo · Rancagua · La Serena · Coquimbo · Antofagasta · Calama · Iquique · Arica · Tocopilla · Desierto de Atacama · Peru-Chile Trench · PARANAL OBSERVATORY

Cerro Aconcagua 6963 · 5653 · 5869 · 6739 · 6100 · 6887 · 6198 · 6231 · 6380 · 6864 · 5189 · 7523 · 8055 · 7618 · 4312 · 1805 · 3593 · 4413

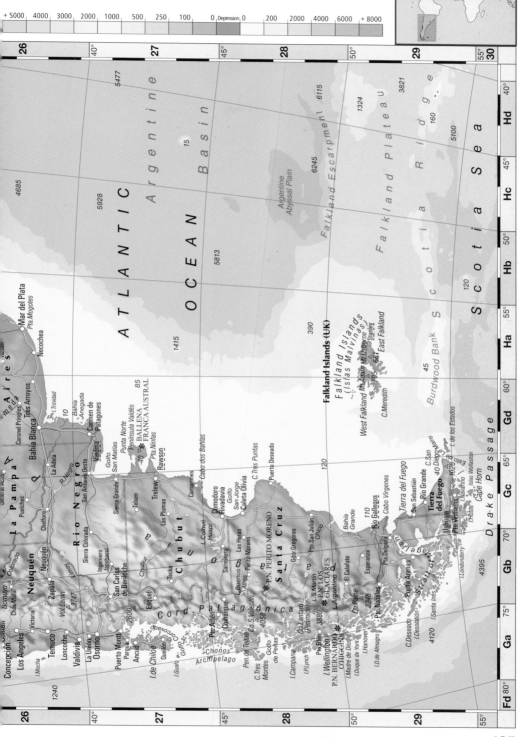

Arctic Region
Polar zones

Scale 1:24,000,000

0 200 400 600 Kilometers

0 200 400 Miles

Map labels (reading across the map):

Top border zones: Dc 130° Db 135° Da 140° Cd 145° Cc 150° Cb 155° Ca 160° Bd 165° Bc 170° Bb 175°, 125°

Left border zones: Dd, Ea 120°, Eb 115°, Ec 110°, Ed 105°, Fa 100°, Fb 95°, Fc 90°, Fd 85°, Ga 80°, Gb 75°, Gc 70°, Gd 65°, Ha 60°

Bottom border zones: Ha 55° Hb 50° Hc 45° Hd 40° Ja 35° Jb 30° Jc 25° Jd 20° Ka 15° Kb 10° Kc 5° K

British Columbia · R O C K Y · Watson Lake · Stewart Crossing · Yukon Territory · Alaska (USA) · BROOKS RANGE · Arctic Plains · Chukchi Sea · Fort Yukon · Barrow Point Barrow · Prudhoe Bay

Dawson Creek · Fort Nelson · M O U N T A I N S · Mackenzie Mts · Fort McPherson · Mackenzie Bay · 4683 · Chukchi Plateau · 328

Alberta · Fort Liard · Mackenzie · Norman Wells · Fort Simpson · Inuvik · B e a u f o r t · 914

Peace River · Hay River · N o r t h w e s t · T e r r i t o r i e s · Great Bear Lake · Cape Bathurst · S e a · Cape Parry · Cape Kellet

Fort Chipewyan · Lake Athabasca · Great Slave Lake · Yellowknife · Amundsen Gulf · Banks Island · Cape Prince Albert · C a n a d a

Stony Rapids · Bathurst Inlet · Coppermine Gulf · Victoria Island · McClure Strait · Prince Patrick Island · B a s i n

C A N A D A · Dubawnt Lake · Storkerson Peninsula · Melville Island · Queen · A R C T I C

Garry Lake · King William Island · McClintock Channel · Prince of Wales Island · Mackenzie King I. · Elizabeth Islands · Alpha Cordillera · Make

Baker Lake · Barren Grounds · 1930 1940 1950 · 1970 1980 1990 · Bathurst I. · Eff Ringnes I. · 2000 · 2005 · Movement of North Magnetic Pole

Nunavut · 1900 · 1920 · Boothia Peninsula · Somerset Island · Sverdrup Islands · Axel Heiberg Island · Nansen Sound · 02 85° · 01

Chesterfield Inlet · 06 65° · 05 70° · 04 · Gulf of Boothia · 03 · Devon Island · Alert Point

Hudson · Roes Welcome Sound · Repulse Bay · Brodeur Peninsula · Arctic Bay · Jones Sound · Ellesmere Island · Cape Discovery · Lincoln Sea

Bay · Southampton Island · Melville Peninsula · Borden Peninsula · Cape Sherard · Nares Strait

Coats Island · 352 · Foxe Basin · Bylot Island · Qaanaaq/Thule · Humboldt Gletscher · Petermann Gletscher · Kap Morris Jesup

Mansel Island · Foxe Peninsula · Prince Charles I. · Baffin Bay · Hayes Halvø · Knud Rasmussen Land · Peary Land

Péninsule d'Ungava · Baffin Basin · Melville Bugt · Kronprins Christian Land

Baffin Island · Cape Christian · Cape Raper · Home Bay · 2907 · Upernavik · Greenland · Kalaallit Nunaat · Kong Frederik VIII Land

Ungava Bay · Iqaluit · Hall Peninsula · Hudson Strait · Cumberland Peninsula · Cape Mercy · Disko Ø · Disko Bugt · (DK) · Droning Louise Land · Dove Bugt · Greenland

Cape Labrador · Frobisher Bay · Cumberland Sound · Godhavn · 64 · Ilulissat/Jakobshavn · Kong Christian X Land

Hebron · Newfoundland and Labrador · 2595 · Davis Strait · Sisimut/Holsteinsborg · Maniitsoq/Sukkertoppen · Kangerlussuaq/Søndrestrømfjord · Kong Frederik IX Land · Scoresby Land · 3069 · No

Labrador · Droning Ingrid Land · Arctic Circle · Iittoqqortoormiit/Scoresbysund · Greenla

Sea · Nuuk/Godthåb · Kong Christian IX Land · Scoresby Sound

3115 · Paamiut/Frederikshåb

Antarctica
Polar zones

Scale 1:24,000,000

0 200 400 600 Kilometers

0 200 400 Miles

Ha
Gd
Gc
Gb
Ga
Fd
Fc
Fb
Fa
Ed
Ec
Eb
Ea
Dd

ATLANTIC OCEAN

Scotia Sea
South Scotia Ridge
5100
5840
Drake Passage
Elephant Island
King George I.
South Shetland Islands
1-14
I.Joinville
Livingston I.
Hero Fracture Zone
G.Gonzalez Videla (RCH)
Palmer Station(USA)
Faraday (UK)
Biscoe Islands
Rothera (UK)
San Martin (RA)
Adelaide I.
Marguerite
Teniente Luis Carvajal (RCH) Bay
Fossil Bluff (UK)
Alexander I.
Carcot I.
Latady I.
Matienzo (RA)
Larsen Ice Shelf
Graham Land
Antarctic Peninsula
Palmer Land
Mt.Jackson
△4190
Soyuz (RUS)
Wilkins Ice Shelf
Ronne Bay
Behrendt Mts.
Mt.Edward
△1637
Sky Blu (UK)

Weddell Sea

3846

Druzhnaya II (RUS)

Ronne Ice Shelf

1 Aguirre Cerda (RCH)
2 Arctowski (PL)
3 Artigas (ROU)
4 Bellingshausen (RUS)
5 C.A.Prat (RCH)
6 Com.Ferraz (BR)
7 Escudero (RCH)
8 Esperanza (RA)
9 Gral.B.O'Higgins (RCH)
10 Great Wall (CHN)
11 Jubany (RA)
12 King Sejong (ROK)
13 Marambio (RA)
14 Presidente Eduardo Frei (RCH)

SANAE IV (SA
Georg von Neumayer (D)
Druzhnaya III (RUS)
Kapp Norvegia
Sarie Mar Base (SA
Rit
Ice
Borgma
Drescher (D)
Aboa (FIN)
Wasa (S)
Svea (S)
Halfrontfjella
Maudheimvidda
Halley (UK)
Brunt Ice Shelf
Belgrano II (RA)
Filchner (D)
Berkner Island
Filchner Ice Shelf
Shackleton Range
Recovery Glacier
Argentina Range
Support Force Glacier
Pensacola Mountains

Ronne Ice Shelf

Korff Ice Rise
Fowler Ice Rise
Evans Ice Stream
Haag Nunataks
Carlson Inlet
Skytrain Ice Rise
Institute Ice Stream

Bellingshausen Abyssal Plain
5245

Bellingshausen
Sea
31 65°
De Gerlache Seamounts
Bryan Coast
Venable Ice Shelf
32 70°
Abbot Ice Shelf
33 75°
Jones Mountains
Walker Mts.
Cape Palmer △1036
Pine Island Bay
Cape Flying Fish
Ellsworth
Land
△1115
Ellsworth Mountains
4897
34 80°
Hudson Mts.
Hollick-Kenyon Plateau
Mt.Seelig
3022
Pine Island Glacier
Marie
35 85°
Thiel Mts.
2812
Horlick Mts.
Wisconsin Range
A
Byrd
Land
West Antarctica
△1920
Byrd (USA)
Rockefeller Plateau
Ice Stream A
Ice Stream B
Ice Stream C
Ice Stream D
Ice Stream E
Siple Coast
Queen Maud
Mt.H
3022
Mt.
Na
4069
Axel Hel
Glac
36 South
Pol

South East Pacific Basin
4830
5226

PACIFIC
OCEAN

Amundsen Ridge
Amundsen
Sea
Crosson Ice Shelf
Mt.Takahe
3398
Mt.Frakes
3677
Cape Felt
Mt.Sidley
4181
Mt.Petras
2875
Getz Ice Shelf
Mt.Siple
3100
Cape Dart
Wrigley Gulf
2000
Russkaya (RUS)
Ford Ranges
Rupert Coast
Mt.Berlin
3498
Sulzberger Ice Shelf
Nickerson Ice Shelf
Sulzberger Bay
Shirase Coast
Ross I
Roosevelt Island
550
Bay of Whales
Cape Colbeck

4460

Heezen Fracture Zone
Amundsen Abyssal Plain
4260
3810
4059
Antarctic Circle
3365
Ross Sea

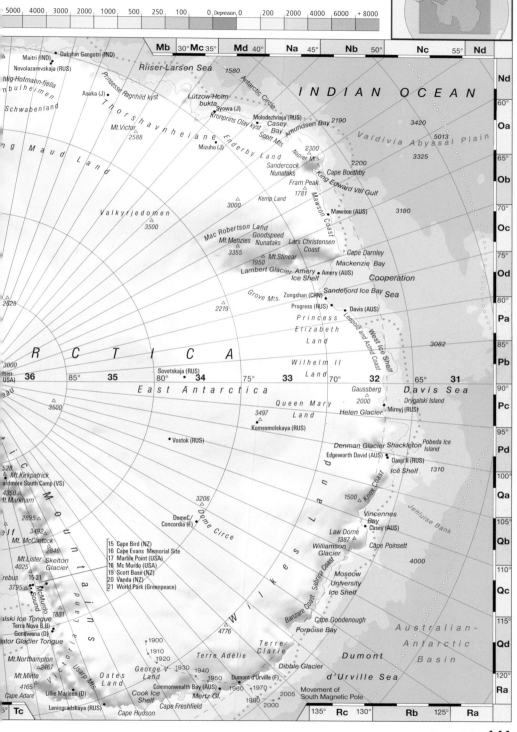

The scale bar at top:

| 5000 | 4000 | 3000 | 2000 | 1000 | 500 | 250 | 100 | 0 | Depression | 0 | 200 | 2000 | 4000 | 6000 | + 8000 |

| Mb | 30° Mc 35° | Md 40° | Na 45° | Nb 50° | Nc 55° | Nd |

INDIAN OCEAN

Maitri (IND)
Dakshin Gangotri (IND)
Novolazarevskaja (RUS)
hlig-Hofmann-fjella
nbulheimen
Schwabenland

Riiser-Larsen Sea
1580
Antarctic Circle

Prinsesse Ragnhild kyst
Asuka (J)
Lützow-Holm bukta
Kronprins Olav kyst
Syowa (J)
Molodezhnaja (RUS)
Casey Bay
Scott Mts.
Amundsen Bay 2190
3420

Thorshavnheiane
Mt.Victor 2588
Mizuho (J)
2300
Napier Mts.
Sanderock Nunataks
Fram Peak 1781
King Edward VIII Gulf
Cape Boothby
2200

ng Maud Land
Enderby Land
Valdivia Abyssal Plain
5013
3325

Valkyrjedomen
3500
Kemp Land
Mawson Coast
Mawson (AUS)
3000
3180

Mac Robertson Land
Goodspeed
Mt.Menzies Nunataks
3355
Lars Christensen Coast
Cape Darnley
Mackenzie Bay

R C T I C A
2628
1950 Mt.Stinear
Lambert Glacier Amery
Ice Shelf
Amery (AUS)
Cooperation

Grove Mts.
Zongshan (CHN)
Sandefjord Ice Bay
Sea
Progress (RUS)
Davis (AUS)
2219

Princess
Elizabeth
Land
West Ice Shelf
Leopold and Astrid Coast
3082

3000
Isen-
USA)
36 85° 35
Sovetskaja (RUS)
80° 34
75° 33
70° 32
65° 31
Wilhelm II
Land

East Antarctica
Davis Sea
Gaussberg
2000
Drygalski Island
Helen Glacier
Mirnyj (RUS)
3500
Queen Mary
Land
3497
Komsomolskaya (RUS)
Denman Glacier Shackleton
Pobeda Ice
Island
Vostok (RUS)
Edgeworth David (AUS)
Oasis II (RUS)
Ice Shelf
1310
528
Mt.Kirkpatrick
ardmore South Camp (VS)
4350
t.Markham
1500 Knox Coast
Jenuise Bank

2895
Vincennes
Bay
Casey (AUS)
3206
DomeC/
Concordia (F)
Dome Circe
Law Dome
1387
Williamson
Glacier
Cape Poinsett

elf
3492
Mt.McClintock
2846
Mt.Lister Skelton
4025 Glacier
rebus 15-21
3795
4000
Moscow
University
Ice Shelf

15 Cape Bird (NZ)
16 Cape Evans Memorial Site
17 Marble Point (USA)
18 Mc Murdo (USA)
19 Scott Base (NZ)
20 Vanda (NZ)
21 World Park (Greenpeace)

McMurdo
Sound
1831
lski Ice Tongue
Terra Nova B.(I)
Gondwana (D)
ator Glacier Tongue
Mt.Northampton
2467
Mt.Minto
4165
Cape Adare
Lillie Marleen (D)
Leningradskaya (RUS)

Cape Goodenough
Porpoise Bay
Australian-
Antarctic
Basin
Dumont
d'Urville Sea

Banzare Coast Sabrina Coast

4776
Terre
Clarie
1900
1910
1920
George V
Land
Terre Adélie
1930
1940
Oates
Land
1950
Dibble Glacier
Commonwealth Bay (AUS)
Cook Ice
Shelf
Mertz Gl.
1980 1970
2005
1980 2000
Movement of
South Magnetic Pole
Cape Freshfield
Cape Hudson

| Tc | 135° Rc 130° | Rb 125° | Ra |

Right margin codes (top to bottom):
Nd, Oa, Ob, Oc, Od, Pa, Pb, Pc, Pd, Qa, Qb, Qc, Qd, Ra

Our planet has experienced countless changes and transformations during its 4.5 billion year history. Natural climate shifts and the powerful forces of plate tectonics have repeatedly altered and continue to shape the topography, vegetation zones, and geology of the Earth.

The first human societies emerged arund 10,000 years ago. Humanity has significantly altered the face of our planet in a relatively short period of time through agriculture and industria-lization. Recent advances in technology have brought the many cultures of our planet closer together than ever before. Our world is now a global community with an incredible diversity of nations, cultures, religions, and ethnicities.

142

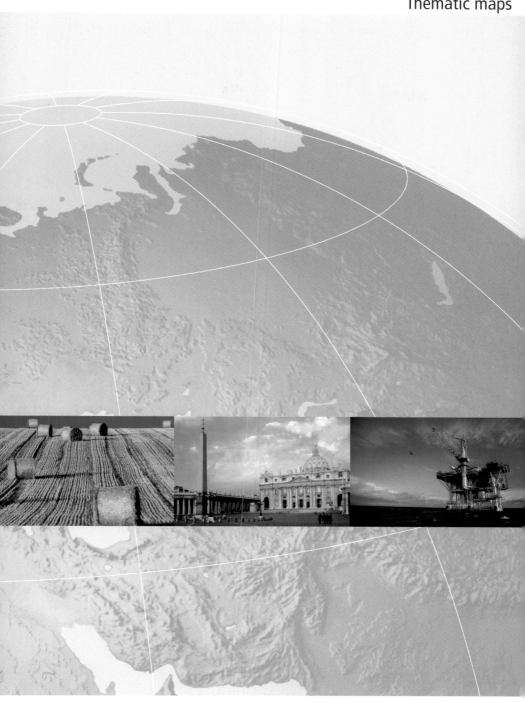

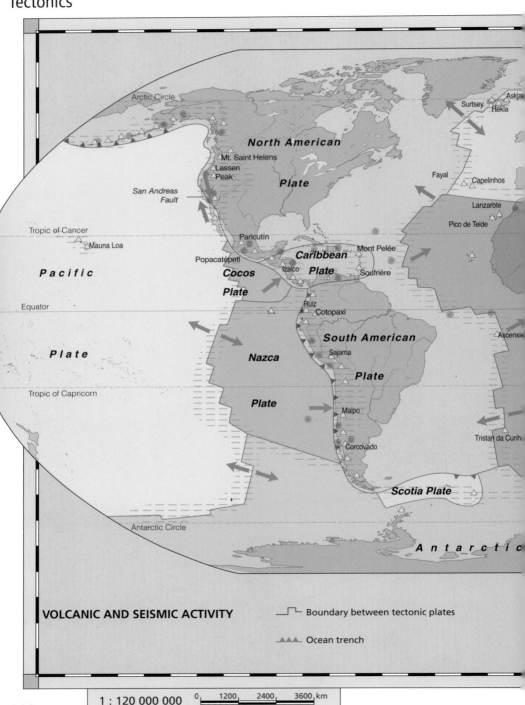

Arctic Circle

Surtsey
Askja
Hekla

North American

Mt. Saint Helens
Lassen
Peak

Plate

Fayal
Capelinhos

San Andreas
Fault

Lanzarote

Pico de Teide

Tropic of Cancer

Mauna Loa

Pacific

Paricutín

Popacatépetl

Caribbean

Mont Pelée

Cocos

Izalco

Plate

Soufrière

Plate

Equator

Ruiz
Cotopaxi

South American

Ascensi

Plate

Nazca

Sajama

Plate

Tropic of Capricorn

Plate

Maipo

Tristan da Cunh

Corcovado

Scotia Plate

Antarctic Circle

A n t a r c t i c

VOLCANIC AND SEISMIC ACTIVITY

Boundary between tectonic plates

Ocean trench

1 : 120 000 000   0   1200   2400   3600 km

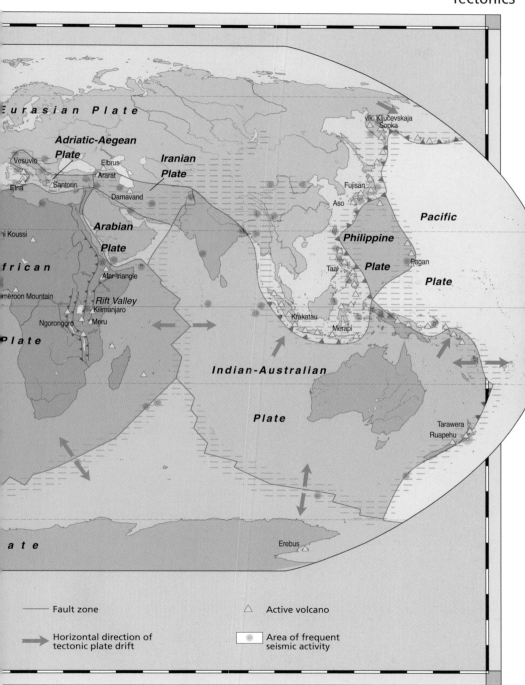

Eurasian Plate

Adriatic-Aegean Plate

Iranian Plate

Vesuvio
Etna
Elbrus
Ararat
Santorin
Damavand

Arabian Plate

ni Koussi

frican

Afar-triangle

meroon Mountain

Rift Valley
Kilimanjaro
Ngorongoro
Meru

Plate

vlk. Ključevskaja
Sopka

Fujisan
Aso

Pacific

Philippine

Taal
Plate

Krakatau
Merapi

Plate

Pagan

Plate

Indian-Australian

Plate

Tarawera
Ruapehu

Erebus

ate

	Fault zone	△	Active volcano
→	Horizontal direction of tectonic plate drift	⊙	Area of frequent seismic activity

145

Thematic Maps
Climate

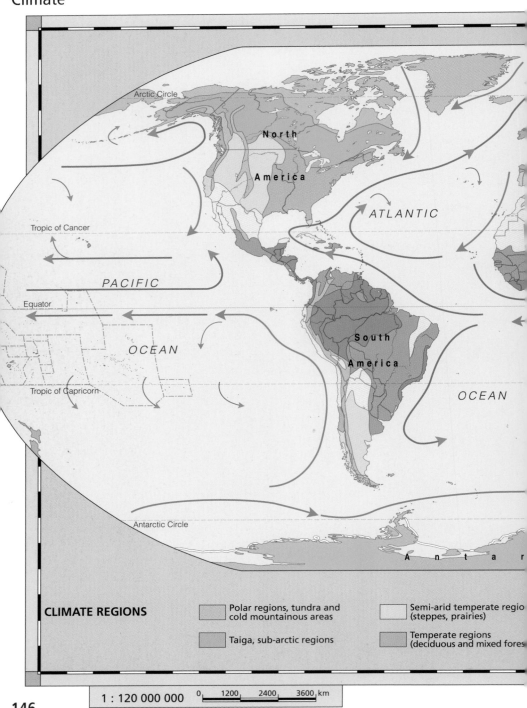

Arctic Circle

North
America

ATLANTIC

Tropic of Cancer

PACIFIC

Equator

OCEAN

South
America

Tropic of Capricorn

OCEAN

Antarctic Circle

A n t a r

CLIMATE REGIONS

Polar regions, tundra and
cold mountainous areas

Taiga, sub-arctic regions

Semi-arid temperate regio
(steppes, prairies)

Temperate regions
(deciduous and mixed fores

1 : 120 000 000   0   1200   2400   3600 km

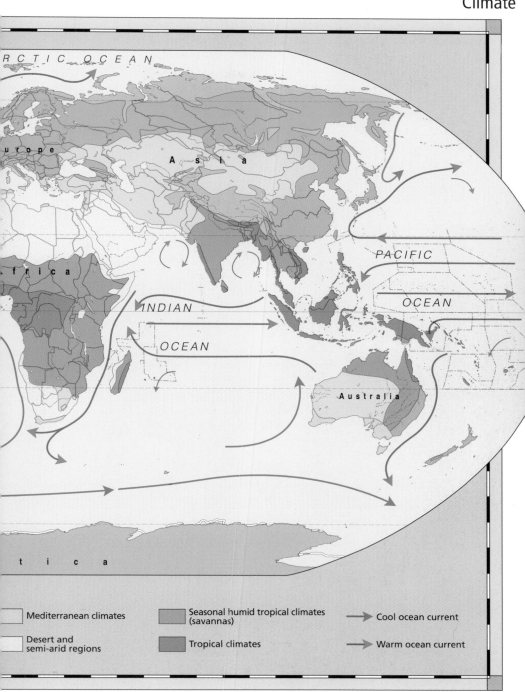

Mediterranean climates

Desert and
semi-arid regions

Seasonal humid tropical climates
(savannas)

Tropical climates

→ Cool ocean current

→ Warm ocean current

Thematic Maps
Vegetation

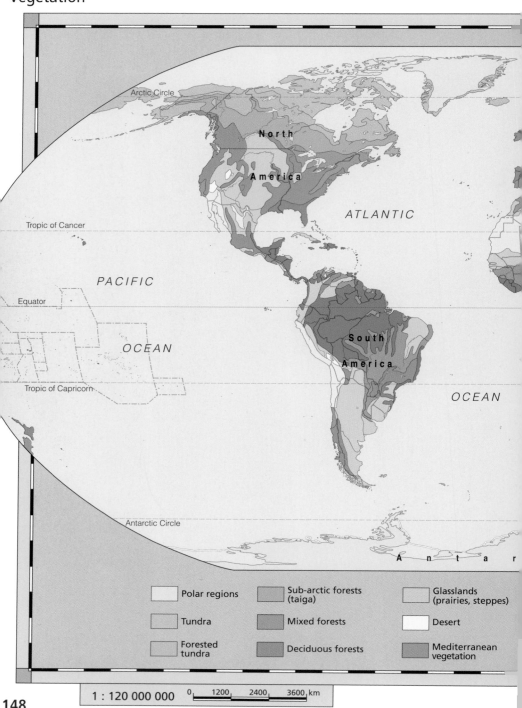

North America

ATLANTIC

Arctic Circle

Tropic of Cancer

PACIFIC

Equator

OCEAN

South America

Tropic of Capricorn

OCEAN

Antarctic Circle

A n t a r

	Polar regions		Sub-arctic forests (taiga)		Glasslands (prairies, steppes)
	Tundra		Mixed forests		Desert
	Forested tundra		Deciduous forests		Mediterranean vegetation

1 : 120 000 000   0   1200   2400   3600 km

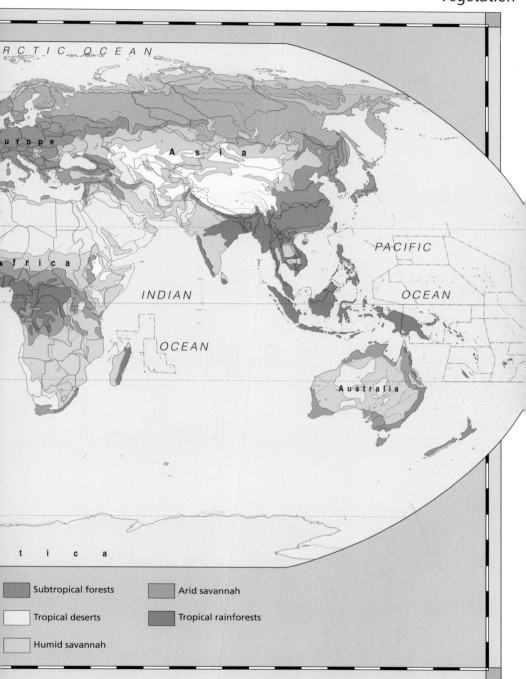

ARCTIC OCEAN

Europe

Asia

Africa

INDIAN

OCEAN

PACIFIC

OCEAN

Australia

Antarctica

	Subtropical forests		Arid savannah
	Tropical deserts		Tropical rainforests
	Humid savannah		

Thematic Maps
Population Density

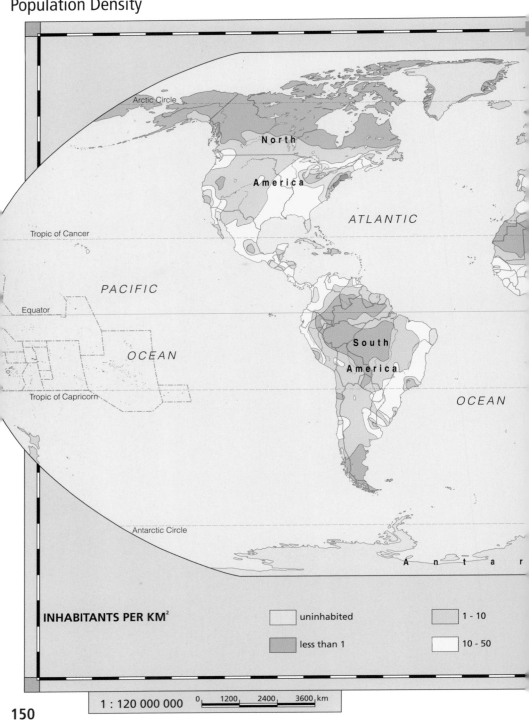

Arctic Circle

North

America

ATLANTIC

Tropic of Cancer

PACIFIC

Equator

OCEAN

South

America

Tropic of Capricorn

OCEAN

Antarctic Circle

A n t a r

INHABITANTS PER KM²

| | uninhabited | | 1 - 10 |
| | less than 1 | | 10 - 50 |

1 : 120 000 000   0 ⎵ 1200 ⎵ 2400 ⎵ 3600 ⎵ km

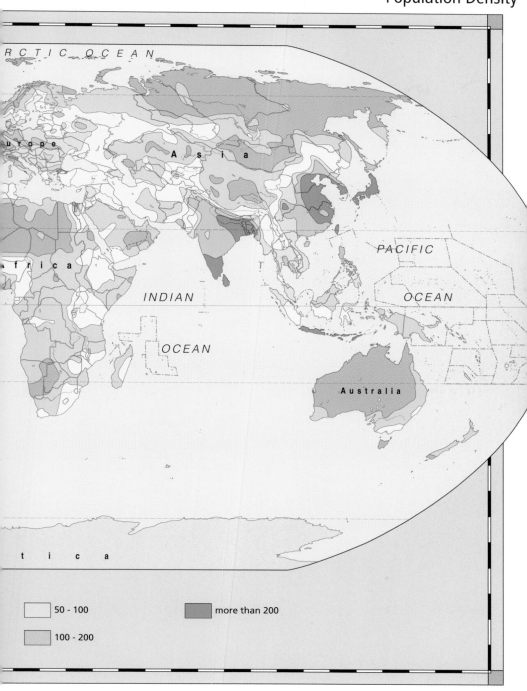

ARCTIC OCEAN

Europe

Asia

Africa

INDIAN

OCEAN

PACIFIC

OCEAN

Australia

Antarctica

50 - 100

100 - 200

more than 200

Thematic Maps
Energy

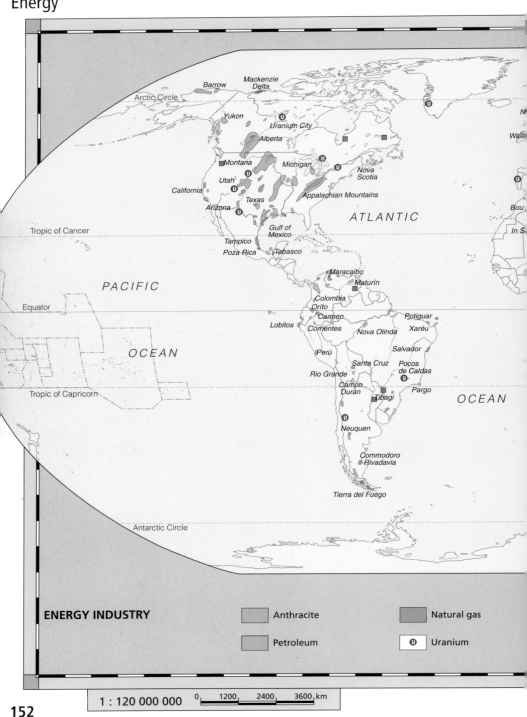

Barrow

Mackenzie Delta

Arctic Circle

Yukon

Uranium City

Alberta

Montana

Michigan

Nova Scotia

Utah

California

Appalachian Mountains

Arizona

Texas

ATLANTIC

Tropic of Cancer

Gulf of Mexico

Tampico

Poza Rica

Tabasco

Maracaibo

Maturín

PACIFIC

Colombia

Orito

Equator

Carmen

Lobitos

Corrientes

Nova Olinda

Potiguar

Xaréu

Perú

Salvador

OCEAN

Santa Cruz

Pocos de Caldas

Rio Grande

Campo Durán

Tibagi

Pargo

Tropic of Capricorn

OCEAN

Neuquen

Commodoro Rivadavia

Tierra del Fuego

Antarctic Circle

N

Wale

Bou

In S.

ENERGY INDUSTRY

Anthracite

Natural gas

Petroleum

Ⓤ Uranium

1 : 120 000 000

0   1200   2400   3600 km

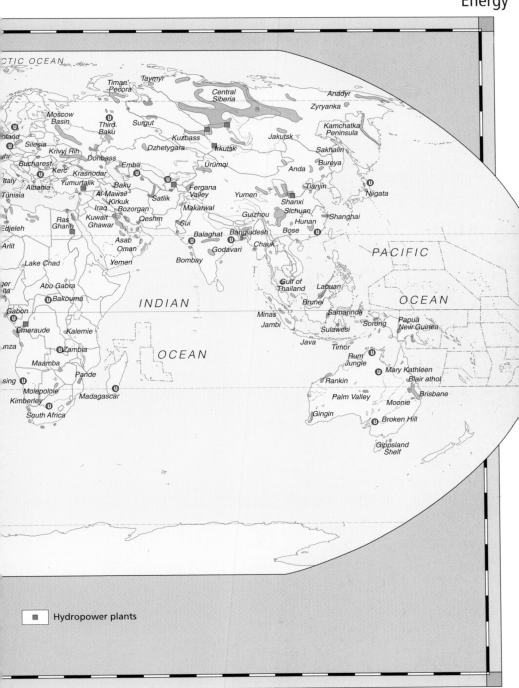

ARCTIC OCEAN

Timan'-Pecora
Taymyr
Central Siberia
Anadyr
Zyryanka

Moscow Basin
Third Baku
Surgut
Kamchatka Peninsula
Poland
Silesia
Krivyj Rih
Kuzbass
Jakutsk
Ihr
Donbass
Dzhetygara
Irkutsk
Sakhalin
Bucharest
Kerc
Krasnodar
Emba
Ürümqi
Bureya
Italy
Yumurtalik
Baku
Anda
Tianjin
Albania
Al-Mawsil
Fergana Valley
Yumen
Niigata
Tunisia
Kirkuk
Satlik
Yumen
Shanxi
Iraq
Bozorgan
Makarwal
Guizhou
Sichuan
Shanghai
Ras Gharib
Kuwait
Qeshm
Sui
Hunan
Edjeleh
Ghawar
Balaghat
Bangladesh
Bose
Arlit
Asab
Oman
Godavari
Chauk
PACIFIC

Lake Chad
Yemen
Bombay

Abu Gabra
Gulf of Thailand
Labuan
OCEAN
Bakouma
INDIAN
Brunei
Gabon
Minas
Samarinda
Papua New Guinea
Emeraude
Kalemie
Jambi
Sulawesi
Sorong
unza
Java
Timor
OCEAN
Zambia
Rum Jungle
Maamba
Pande
Mary Kathleen
Blair athol
sing
Rankin
Molepolole
Madagascar
Palm Valley
Brisbane
Kimberley
Moonie
South Africa
Gingin
Broken Hill

Gippsland Shelf

■ Hydropower plants

Thematic Maps
Religions

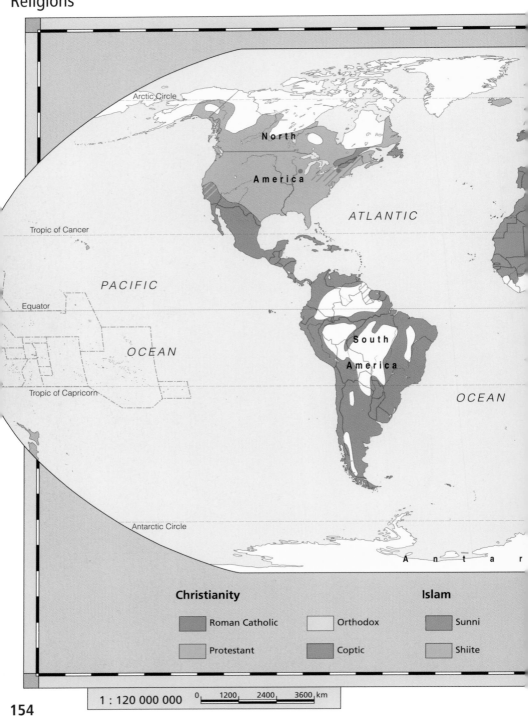

Christianity
- Roman Catholic
- Protestant
- Orthodox
- Coptic

Islam
- Sunni
- Shiite

Arctic Circle

North
America

ATLANTIC

Tropic of Cancer

PACIFIC

Equator

OCEAN

South
America

OCEAN

Tropic of Capricorn

Antarctic Circle

Antar

1 : 120 000 000

0   1200   2400   3600 km

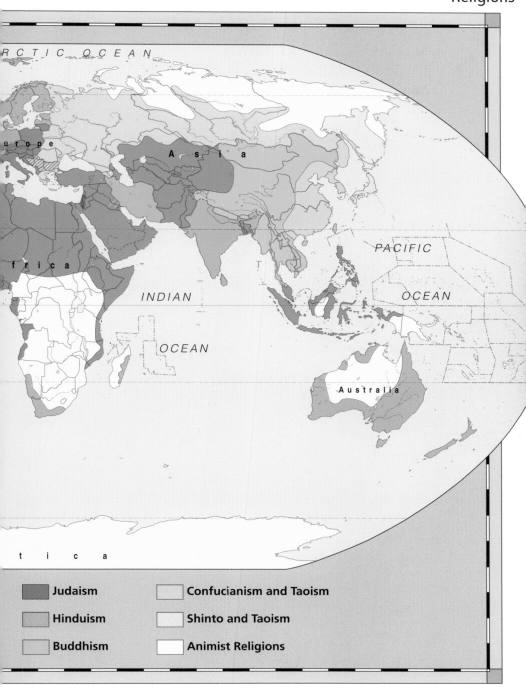

ARCTIC OCEAN

Europe

Asia

Africa

PACIFIC

INDIAN

OCEAN

OCEAN

Australia

tica

▦	**Judaism**	▦	**Confucianism and Taoism**
▦	**Hinduism**	▦	**Shinto and Taoism**
▦	**Buddhism**	▦	**Animist Religions**

Thematic Maps
Languages

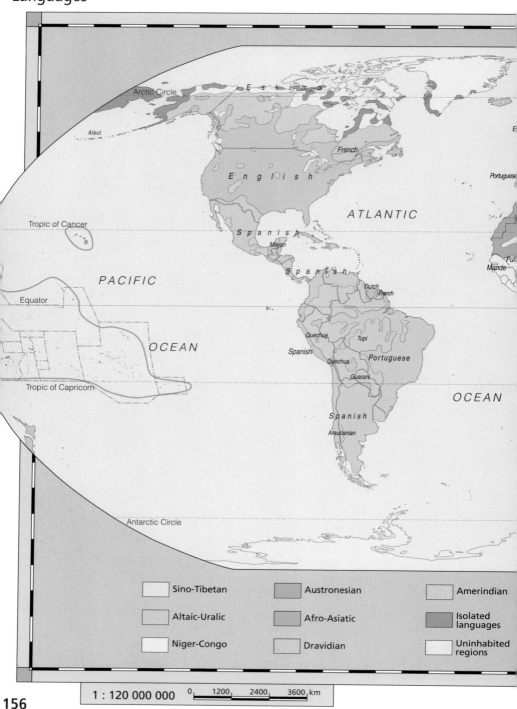

Eskimo

Arctic Circle

Aleut

French

English

ATLANTIC

Portuguese

Tropic of Cancer

Spanish

Mayan

E

Spanish

Ful
Mande

PACIFIC

Spanish

Dutch
French

Equator

OCEAN

Quechua

Tupi

Spanish

Quechua

Portuguese

Guarani

Tropic of Capricorn

OCEAN

Spanish

Araucanian

Antarctic Circle

Sino-Tibetan	Austronesian	Amerindian
Altaic-Uralic	Afro-Asiatic	Isolated languages
Niger-Congo	Dravidian	Uninhabited regions

1 : 120 000 000   0   1200   2400   3600 km

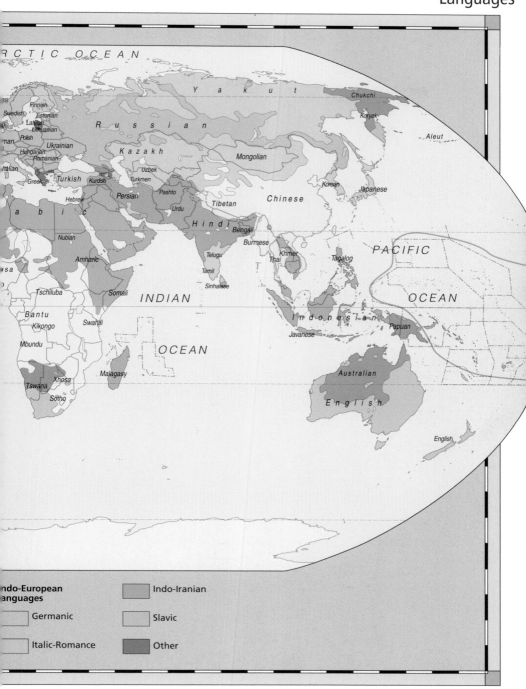

Thematic Maps
Agriculture

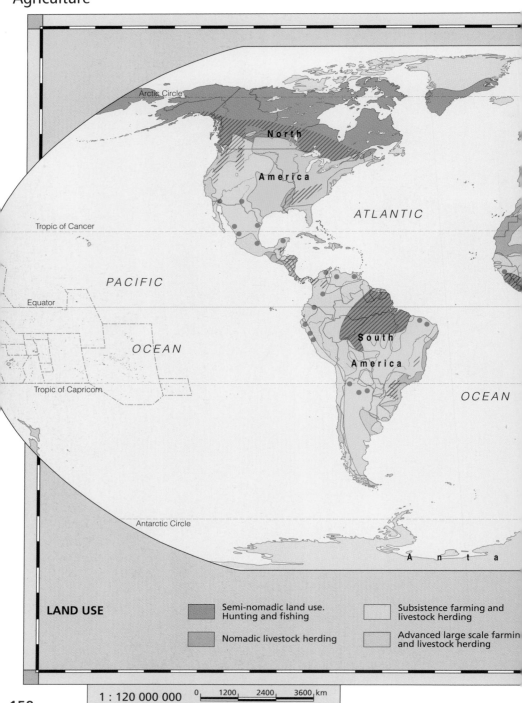

Arctic Circle

North

America

ATLANTIC

Tropic of Cancer

PACIFIC

Equator

OCEAN

South

America

Tropic of Capricorn

OCEAN

Antarctic Circle

A n t a

LAND USE

Semi-nomadic land use.
Hunting and fishing

Nomadic livestock herding

Subsistence farming and
livestock herding

Advanced large scale farming
and livestock herding

1 : 120 000 000   0   1200   2400   3600   km

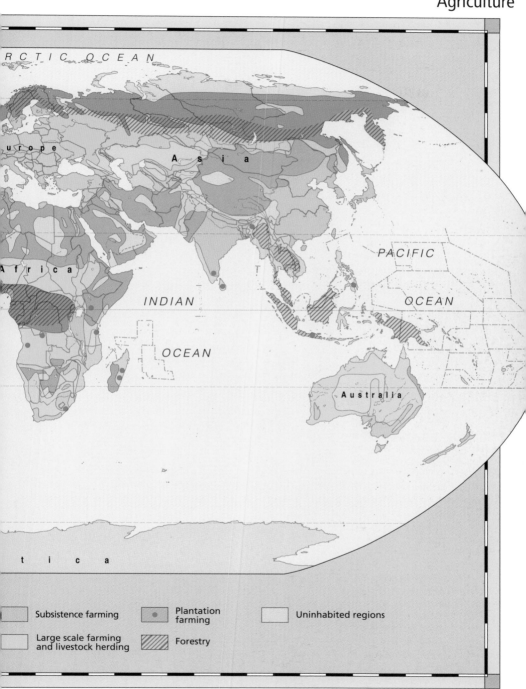

Subsistence farming

Plantation farming

Uninhabited regions

Large scale farming and livestock herding

Forestry

There were 196 sovereign nations on six continents at the start of the 21st century. During the 20th century, the political makeup of our planet changed frequently and the borders of many nations were redrawn. Two world wars, the end of European colonialism, and the decline of communism lead to the creation and collapse of numerous nations and political entities.

Although most of Africa was under the control of European powers at the start of the 20th century, it is now the continent with the most states: 54. Europe is only slightly behind Africa with 47 states and is followed by Asia (46), North America (23), Australia/Oceania (14), and South America (12). Inhospitable Antarctica is the only "stateless" continent.

160

Nations of the world
Index of local country names

The local or indigenous name of a country often varies from its English name or designation. The following index lists the English-language names of all the world's nations, followed by their official local names in the second column.

English	Local	Continent	Page
Afghanistan	Afghānistān	Asia	212
Albania	Shqipëria	Europe	201
Algeria	Al-Ğazā´ir/Algérie	Africa	270
Andorra	Andorra	Europe	168
Angola	Angola	Africa	272
Antigua and Barbuda	Antigua and Barbuda	Central America	308
Argentina	Argentina	South America	308
Armenia	Armenija (Hayastan)	Asia	215
Australia	Australia	Australia	257
Austria	Österreich	Europe	194
Azerbaijan	Azerbajdzan	Asia	216
Bahamas	Bahamas	Central America	308
Bahrain	Al-Bahrain	Asia	212
Bangladesh	Bangladesh	Asia	216
Barbados	Barbados	Central America	310
Belarus	Belarus	Europe	168
Belgium	België/Belgique	Europe	168
Belize	Belize	Central America	310
Benin	Benin	Africa	274
Bhutan	Bhutan	Asia	217
Bolivia	Bolivia	South America	311
Bosnia - Herzegovina	Bosna i Hercegovina	Europe	170
Botswana	Botswana	Africa	275
Brazil	Brasil	South America	313
Brunei	Brunei	Asia	218
Bulgaria	Bŭlgarija	Europe	170
Burkina Faso	Burkina Faso	Africa	276
Burundi	Burundi	Africa	276
Cambodia	Kâmpŭchéa	Asia	225
Cameroon	Cameroun/Cameroon	Africa	277
Canada	Canada	North America	315
Cape Verde	Cabo Verde	Africa	277
Central African Republic	République Centrafricaine	Africa	294
Chad	Tchad	Africa	300
Chile	Chile	South America	317
China	Zhongguo	Asia	248
Colombia	Colombia	South America	318
Comoros	Comores	Africa	278
Congo	Congo	Africa	278
Congo, Dem. Rep.	Congo, Rép. démocr.	Africa	279
Costa Rica	Costa Rica	Central America	318
Côte d´Ivoire	Côte d´Ivoire	Africa	280
Croatia	Hrvatska	Europe	184
Cuba	Cuba	Central America	319
Cyprus	Kypros/Kibris	Europe	186

Czech Republic	Česká Republika	Europe	171
Denmark	Danmark	Europe	174
Djibouti	Djibouti	Africa	280
Dominica	Dominica	Central America	321
Dominican Republic	República Dominicana	Central America	332
East Timor	Timor-Leste	Asia	244
Ecuador	Ecuador	South America	322
Ecuatorial Guinea	Guinea Ecuatorial	Africa	284
Egypt	Al-Miṣr/Egypt	Africa	270
El Salvador	El Salvador	Central America	322
Eritrea	Eritrea	Africa	280
Estonia	Eesti	Europe	177
Ethiopia	Îtyopya	Africa	285
Fiji	Fiji	Australia/Oceania	259
Finland	Suomi/Finland	Europe	204
France	France	Europe	180
Gabon	Gabon	Africa	281
Gambia	Gambia	Africa	282
Georgia	Gruzija (Sakartvelo)	Asia	220
Germany	Deutschland	Europe	174
Ghana	Ghana	Africa	282
Greece	Elláda (Hellás)	Europe	178
Grenada	Grenada	Central America	323
Guatemala	Guatemala	Central America	324
Guinea	Guinée	Africa	284
Guinea-Bissau	Guinea-Bissau	Africa	283
Guyana	Guyana	South America	324
Haiti	Haïti	Central America	325
Honduras	Honduras	Central America	326
Hungary	Magyarország	Europe	188
Iceland	Ísland	Europe	184
India	India (Bhărat)	Asia	220
Indonesia	Indonesia	Asia	223
Iraq	ʿĪrāq	Asia	224
Iran	Îrân	Asia	224
Ireland	Éire/Ireland	Europe	178
Israel	Yisraʾel	Asia	248
Italy	Italia	Europe	184
Jamaica	Jamaica	Central America	326
Japan	Nippon/Nihon	Asia	234
Jordan	Urdunn	Asia	245
Kazakhstan	Kazahstan	Asia	226
Kenya	Kenya	Africa	286
Kiribati	Kiribati	Australia/Oceania	260
Korea, North	Choson	Asia	218
Korea, South	Taehan-Minʾguk	Asia	241
Kosovo	Kosovo	Europe	186
Kuwait	Al-Kuwait	Asia	212
Kyrgyzstan	Kyrgyzstan	Asia	226
Laos	Lao	Asia	227
Latvia	Latvija	Europe	186

Nations of the world
Index of local country names

Lebanon	Al-Lubnān	Asia	213
Lesotho	Lesotho	Africa	286
Liberia	Liberia	Africa	286
Libya	Lîbîyâ	Africa	287
Liechtenstein	Liechtenstein	Europe	187
Lithuania	Lietuva	Europe	188
Luxembourg	Luxembourg	Europe	188
Macedonia	Makedonija	Europe	190
Madagascar	Madagasíkara	Africa	288
Malawi	Malawi	Africa	288
Malaysia	Malaysia	Asia	229
Maldives	Maldives (Divehi Rajje)	Asia	229
Mali	Mali	Africa	289
Malta	Malta	Europe	190
Marshall Islands	Marshall Islands	Australia/Oceania	260
Mauritania	Mawrītāniyah	Africa	290
Mauritius	Mauritius	Africa	290
Mexico	México	Central America	326
Micronesia	Micronesia	Australia/Oceania	261
Moldova	Moldova	Europe	191
Monaco	Monaco	Europe	192
Mongolia	Mongol Ard Uls	Asia	230
Montenegro	Crna Gora	Europe	174
Morocco	Al-Maģrib/Maroc	Africa	270
Mozambique	Moçambique	Africa	291
Myanmar (Burma)	Myanmar	Asia	232
Namibia	Namibia	Africa	292
Nauru	Nauru (Naoero)	Australia/Oceania	262
Nepal	Nepal	Asia	232
Netherlands	Nederland	Europe	192
New Zealand	New Zealand	Australia/Oceania	262
Nicaragua	Nicaragua	Central America	329
Niger	Niger	Africa	292
Nigeria	Nigeria	Africa	294
Norway	Norge	Europe	194
Oman	Saltanat 'Umān	Asia	237
Pakistan	Pākistān	Asia	236
Palau	Palau	Australia/Oceania	263
Panama	Panamá	Central America	330
Papua New Guinea	Papua New Guinea	Australia/Oceania	264
Paraguay	Paraguay	South America	330
Peru	Perú	South America	331
Philippines	Pilipinas	Asia	236
Poland	Polska	Europe	197
Portugal	Portugal	Europe	198
Qatar	Qaṭar	Asia	236
Rumania	Rômânia	Europe	198
Russia	Rossija	Europe	199
Rwanda	Rwanda	Africa	294
Saint Kitts and Nevis	Saint Kitts and Nevis	Central America	332
Saint Lucia	Saint Lucia	Central America	333

St. Vincent and the Grenadines	St. Vincent and the Grenadines	Central America	334
Samoa	Samoa	Australia/Oceania	264
San Marino	San Marino	Europe	201
Sao Tome and Principe	São Tomé e Príncipe	Africa	295
Saudi-Arabia	Al-Mamlaka al-'Arabiya as-Sa'ūdiya	Asia	214
Senegal	Sénégal	Africa	296
Serbia	Srbija	Europa	203
Seychelles	Seychelles	Africa	296
Sierra Leone	Sierra Leone	Africa	297
Singapore	Singapore	Asia	238
Slovakia	Slovenská Republika	Europe	202
Slovenia	Slovenija	Europe	202
Solomon Islands	Solomon Islands	Australia/Oceania	265
Somalia	Soomaaliya	Africa	298
South Africa	South Africa/Suid-Afrika	Africa	298
Spain	España	Europe	180
Sri Lanka	Śrī Laṅkā	Asia	238
Sudan	As-Sūdān	Africa	274
Suriname	Suriname	South America	334
Swaziland	Swaziland (kaNgwane)	Africa	300
Sweden	Sverige	Europe	205
Switzerland	Suisse/Schweiz/Svizzera	Europe	204
Syria	Suriya	Asia	240
Taiwan	Taiwan	Asia	243
Tajikistan	Tadžikistan	Asia	240
Tanzania	Tanzania	Africa	300
Thailand	Muang Thai	Asia	230
Togo	Togo	Africa	301
Tonga	Tonga	Australia/Oceania	266
Trinidad and Tobago	Trinidad and Tobago	Central America	335
Tunisia	Tūnisiyah/Tunisie	Africa	302
Turkey	Türkiye	Europe	206
Turkmenistan	Turkmenistan	Asia	244
Tuvalu	Tuvalu	Australia/Oceania	266
Uganda	Uganda	Africa	302
Ukraine	Ukrajina	Europe	206
Uruguay	Uruguay	South America	342
Uzbekistan	Uzbekistan	Asia	246
Vanuatu	Vanuatu	Australia/Oceania	267
Vatican City	Città del Vaticano	Europe	173
Venezuela	Venezuela	South America	343
Vietnam	Viêt-Nam	Asia	246
United Arab Emirates	Daulat al-Imārāt al-'Arabiya Al-Muttahida	Asia	218
United Kingdom	United Kingdom	Europe	208
United States of America	United States of America	North America	336
Western Sahara	Al-Saharaw	Africa	272
Yemen	Al-Yaman	Asia	214
Zambia	Zambia	Africa	304
Zimbabwe	Zimbabwe	Africa	305

Europe is the second smallest continent and most densely populated landmass on our planet. The continent has a total land area of 10,5 million sq km and is home to at least 700 million people, making it the third most populous continent.

While the eastern and northern sections of the continent are dominated by vast plains, a series of mountain systems including the Massif Central, the Alps, and the Carpathian Mountains stretches through the continent's interior. Southern Europe boasts stunning coastlines along the Mediterranean and its adjacent seas.

Islands and peninsulas make up more than a third of the continent's total area. The Volga and Danube are the longest rivers on the continent, while Russia's Lake Ladoga is the largest body of water on the continent.

At least 120 languages are spoken in the 44 sovereign nations of Europe. The small continent features an incredible array of cultural, scenic and historic attractions.

Albania see Shqipëria

Andorra
Andorra

Area: 467.7 sq km
Population: 67,600
GDP per capita: 28,000 US$
Capital: Andorra la Vella
Government: Parliamentary principality
Language: Catalan (official), Spanish, French
Currency: 1 euro = 100 cents

Geography: The small principality of Andorra consists of three valleys surrounded by high mountains in the eastern Pyrenees (Coma Pendrosa, 2,946 m). More than half of the country's territory is situated above the tree line.

Politics: Several states vied for control of Andorra before the 13th century. An agreement in 1278 left the area under the joint control of the French monarchy and the bishops of d'Urgell in Catalonia. A new constitution in 1993 established Andorra as an independent parliamentary democracy.

Economy: Andorra's mountainous topography limited the growth of industrial activity and large-scale agriculture in the country. Sheep herding and tourism are the country's largest industries. The capital city and the city of Les Escaldes are the country's most popular tourist destinations.

Austria see Österreich

Belarus
Belarus

Area: 207,600 sq km
Population: 10.3 million
GDP per capita: 4,600 US$
Capital: Minsk

Government: Republic
Language: Belarusian (official), Russian, minority languages
Currency: 1 Belarusian rouble = 100 kopecks

Geography: Belarus is situated on the vast East European Plain and consists largely of flat lowlands. The country features numerous rivers, canals and lakes in all of its regions. The Palesse marsh in southern Belarus is the largest marshland in Europe. The capital city of Minsk and the country's lakes are Belarus' principal tourist attractions.

Politics: The Slavic ancestors of the modern Belarussians were able to preserve their language and culture despite centuries of foreign domination by the Polish and Lithuanian Commonwealth. The country came under the control of the Russian Empire at the end of the 18th century. In 1922, Belarus became a Soviet republic in the USSR. Belarus was declared an independent republic in 1991, following the collapse of the Soviet Union. The repressive policies of Belarus' government have been repeatedly criticized by the European Union and numerous human rights organizations.

Economy: Belarus faced a severe economic crisis, including high inflation rates and rising foreign debts, during most of the 1990s. The country has experienced stable growth in recent years but the economy remains heavily regulated and is largely closed to foreign investment. The agricultural sector accounts for approximately one third of the country's GDP. Manufacturing produces just over half (56%) of the national GDP. The government has failed to implement the reforms necessary for stable economic development.

België / Belgique
Belgium

Area: 30,528 sq km
Population: 10.3 million
GDP per capita: 42,500 US$
Capital: Brussels
Government: Parliamentary monarchy
Languages: French, Flemish, German
Currency: 1 euro = 100 cents

The old town of Minsk, Belarus' capital city, on the Svislach River

Geography: Belgium's smooth North Sea coast is lined by sand dunes and sandy beaches. The west and north are dominated by fertile marshy plains, polders, and moorlands. Further south lies the central plateau, a region of fertile

Brussels, the capital of Belgium, was an important European economic and political center long before NATO and the European Union decided to place their headquarters in the city. **1** The Grand Place, Brussels' main square, is ringed by historic buildings and was designated a UNESCO world heritage site in 1998. **2** The beautiful Maison du Rui, a historic building on the Grand Place. **3** The neo-classical Palace of Justice was completed in the late 19th century. **4** The Atomium, the most famous modern landmark of the city, was built for the 1958 World's Fair.

valley crossed by numerous rivers and canals. The third major region of Belgium, the Ardennes, is a heavily forested area of low mountains. Belgium's major tourist attractions include the historic towns of Flanders, the Ardennes countryside, and the capital city Brussels.

Politics: The cities of Flanders were among Europe's leading commercial and cultural centers during the late Middle Ages. Between the Middle Ages and the 19th century, Belgium was under the control of several foreign nations – Spain between the 16th and 17th centuries, followed by Austria, France and finally the Netherlands. Belgium became an independent kingdom in 1833. Modern Belgium is a federal state divided into three distinct regions – Flanders, Brussels, and Wallonia. The capital city of Brussels houses the European Union and NATO headquarters.

Economy: Belgium's highly productive agricultural sector produces less than 2% of the country's GDP. The industrial areas along the Sambre and Meuse (Maas) Rivers are important centers of the chemical, glass, and machinery industries. The expanding service sectors currently account for around 68% of the country's annual GDP. Belgium has one of the world's most modern transportation networks.

Bosna i Hercegovina
Bosnia-Herzegovina

Area: 51,129 sq km
Population: 3.9 million
GDP per capita: 3,700 US$ (estimated)
Capital: Sarajevo
Government: Republic
Languages: Bosnian, Croatian, Serbian (all official)
Currency: 1 convertible mark

Geography: Bosnia-Herzegovina is a largely mountainous country with large stretches of dense forests and a continental climate. Because of poor soils and the mountainous terrain, only a few sections of the country, such as the Sava Valley, are suitable for large-scale agriculture.

Politics: Bosnia was dominated by foreign powers during most of its history. A large percentage of Bosnia's population converted to Islam during more than 400 years under the control of the Turkish Ottoman Empire. The region came under the control of the Austro-Hungarian Empire in the 19th century. Bosnia was a republic of Yugoslavia dur-ing most of the 20th century. Following the collapse of Yugoslavia, Bosnia experienced a period of ethnic conflict that escalated into a bloody war and widespread "ethnic cleansing". The country has been divided into an ethnic Serb republic and a Croat-Muslim federation since 1995. A lasting peace in the region won't be for tomorrow, not to mention the country's accession to the EU.

Economy: Most of the country's infrastructure and industrial facilities were damaged in the civil war of the 1990s. Foreign aid remains important for the country.

Bŭlgarija
Bulgaria

Area: 110,910 sq km
Population: 7.5 million
GDP per capita: 5,200 US$
Capital: Sofia
Government: Republic
Language: Bulgarian
Currency: 1 lev = 100 stotinki

Geography: The marshy Danube basin forms the northern border of Bulgaria. South of this region lie vast fertile plains. Southern Bulgaria is largely mountainous: the Balkans, Rhodope Mountains, and other highlands cover over a third of the country. Bulgaria has a

Bulgaria: The brightly-coloured frescoes of Rila Monastery

continental climate with warm summers and cold winters. The country's major tourist attractions include the beaches along the Black Sea, cities Varna and Sofia and the Pirin National Park.

Politics: The first Bulgarian state was formed in the 7th century by Slavs and Bulgars from the Volga basin. Bulgaria was dominated by the Turkish Ottoman Empire for over five centuries before it achieved independence in 1878. After decades as a kingdom, Bulgaria was declared a people's republic in 1947. The country was closely aligned to the Soviet Union before 1991. Bulgaria is now a multi-party parliamentary republic and a candidate for EU membership.

Economy: Bulgaria has faced several economic crises since its transition to democracy in the early 1990s. The fall of the socialist government in 1996 was followed by fiscal discipline and economic reforms. Despite recent impressive growth and successful reforms, most Bulgarians still live in poverty. Manufacturing and services account for over three-quarters of GDP. Major agricultural products include wine, fruits, and tobacco.

Česká Republika
Czech
Republic

Area: 78,866 sq km
Population: 10.2 million
GDP per capita: 17,000 US$
Capital: Prague
Government: Republic
Language: Czech (official), Slovakian
Currency: 1 Czech koruna = 100 haleru

Geography: The central plateau and the populous Bohemian basin are surrounded by the Sudetes, Bohemian forest, and the Ore Mountains. Moravia, in the east, is a fertile and largely hilly region. The Elbe and Vltava (Moldau) rivers are the most important waterways. The Czech Republic's leading tourist attractions include the historic towns of Bohemia, the natural landscapes of the country's

mountainous regions, and the capital city Prague.

Politics: Great Moravia, a powerful Slavic state, emerged in the 9th century and was closely aligned to the German-dominated Holy Roman Empire for most of its history. Following the domination of the Hussites in the 15th century, the Czech lands were ruled by the Austrian Hapsburg Empire. They

1 Romania, Bulgaria, and the Balkan countries are home to large Roma minorities. Also known as gypsies, the Roma today live in all of Europe's regions and nations. Most European Roma are Roman Catholics and less than 10% are migratory.

2 The large monastery complex of Rila is an important Bulgarian national monument. Most of the monastery was reconstructed in the 19th century. The Hrelyo Tower was built in the middle ages and is one of the oldest structures in the complex.

3 Alexander Nevski Cathedral in Sofia was completed in 1912. The cathedral is the largest Christian-Orthodox church in the Balkans.

171

Widely considered one of the most beautiful cities in Europe, Prague has also become one of the continent's most visited destinations since the fall of European communism. The capital city of the Czech Republic features stunning architecture and countless historic sites. **1** The Church of Our Lady before Tyn in Prague's old town was built in the 14th century. **2** Prague has many masterpieces of baroque and gothic architecture, including the famous **3** Charles Bridge with its **5** beautiful statues. Prague's old town features many medieval buildings such as the palaces and merchant homes around **4** Town Hall Square. **6** The astronomical clock of Prague's old town hall, a popular tourist attraction, was built in 1410.

united with Slovakia to form the first Czechoslovak republic in 1918 following the collapse of the Austro-Hungarian Empire. Czechoslovakia was occupied by Germany during the Second World War and assigned to the Soviet bloc in 1945. In 1948, Czechoslovakia was declared a socialist republic under the Communist party. An attempt at political liberalization during the Prague Spring of 1968 was brutally repressed by Soviet troops. Czechoslovakia was dissolved in 1993 and the Czech Republic joined the EU in 2004.

Economy: The Czech Republic is one of the most successful transition countries in Europe, with steady growth and an increase in living standards since the 1990s. Manufacturing accounts for a third of GDP, and services for over 60%. Leading industries include the production of textiles, glass and metal.

Città del Vaticano
Vatican City

Area: 0.44 sq km
Population: 920
GDP per capita: not available
Capital: Vatican City
Government: Sovereign diocese since 1929
Language: Latin, Italian
Currency: 1 euro = 100 cents, and own currency

Geography: The world's smallest sovereign state is situated in the center of the Italian capital city Rome. Vatican City's major tourist attractions include St. Peter's Basilica, St. Peter's Square, and the Sistine Chapel.

Politics: The history of the Vatican begins with the founding of the Roman Catholic Church. For cen-

turies, popes ruled the Papal States on the Italian peninsula. The territory of the Vatican and the popes was mostly lost in the creation of the modern Italian state. An agreement with Italy in 1928 guaranteed Vatican sovereignty. Vatican City, the center of the Roman Catholic church, is ruled by the Pope.

Economy: Vatican City's existence as a sovereign state is funded

1 Golden statues atop a column in Olomouc, the former capital city of the region Moravia in the Czech Republic.

2 The Czech town of Ceske Budejovice (German: Budweis) is not only famous for its beer and breweries but also for its medieval layout and charming baroque architecture. Samson's Fountain in Ceske Budejovice's centre is one of town's many attractions.

3 St. Peter's Square, the famous area in Vatican City. Located in the middle of Rome, Vatican City is an important pilgrimage site for millions of Roman Catholics each year.

Nations of the World
Europe

mostly by church investments and holdings as well as other contributions from around the world. Tourism and the sale of postage stamps are also important sources of income which make Vatican City a blossoming enclave.

Crna Gora
Montenegro

Area: 13,812 sq km
Population: 620,000
GDP per capita: 3,800 US$
Capital: Podgorica
Government: Republic
Languages: Serbian, Albanian
Currency: 1 euro = 100 cents

Geography: The central mountainous terrain, with high peaks of up to 2,500 m, descends steeply towards the Adriatic Sea. The large Lake Scutari borders Albania.

Politics: Until 2006, Montenegro's history was quite similar to Serbia's, from which it gained independence in 2006 after a referendum.

Economy: In 2005, GDP was 2 billion US dollars. To date, only a few statistics are available for the emerging state with a bright economic outlook.

Croatia see Hrvatska
Cyprus see Kypros
Czech Rep. see Ceska Republica

Danmark
Denmark

Area: 43,094 sq km;
Greenland 2.176 million sq km;
Faroe Islands 1,398 sq km
Population: 5.4 million;
Greenland 55,400; Faroes 43,700
GDP per capita: 57,000 US$
Capital: Copenhagen
Government: Parliamentary monarchy

Language: Danish
Currency: 1 Danish krone = 100 øre

Geography: The Kingdom of Denmark consists of the Jutland peninsula and at least 400 islands located between the North and Baltic seas. Only a fourth of Denmark's islands are inhabited and 40% of the country's population live on the most populous island, Seeland. Denmark is a flat country and consists mostly of meadows, moorlands, sandy coastlines and forests. The capital city, Copenhagen, and the beaches of Jutland are the country's major tourist attractions.

Politics: The history of the Danish kingdom begins around 800 AD. In the 14th century, the Danish monarchy was able to expand its territory through a series of conquests and unions. The country was occupied by Germany during the Second World War. Both Greenland and the Faroe Islands are currently administered by Denmark.

Economy: The generous welfare state of modern Denmark guarantees all Danish citizens access to excellent social services. Only around 5% of the country's population works in the agricultural sec-

tor. Textile, machine and metal production are the country's leading industries. The service sector currently generates more than 70% of the country's annual GDP.

Deutschland
Germany

Area: 357,021 sq km
Population: 82.4 million
GDP per capita: 40,500 US$
Capital: Berlin
Government: Parliamentary federal republic
Language: German
Currency: 1 euro = 100 cents

Geography: The northern most region of Germany includes coastal areas along the North and Baltic seas and numerous islands. Germany's south is dominated by the Alps and Alpine foothills. Most of northern Germany consists of flat and fertile plains, bordering a series of mountains that stretch through much of central and eastern Ger-

A typical romantic German castle: Burg Eltz, in a tributary valley of the Mosel.

many. Southern Germany begins in its northern sections with low rolling hills giving way to the higher Alpine foothills and the Alps. The country's major waterways include the Rhine, Elbe, and Weser rivers. Germany's tourist attractions include the capital city, Berlin, and the capital of Bavaria, Munich,

Copenhagen, Denmark's capital and largest city, is located on the island of Seeland, one of more than 400 Danish islands. **1** The Nyhavn and Frederiksstaden districts contain the city's old harbour and **2** Amalienborg Palace, the residence of Denmark's royal family. **3** The statue of Hans Christian Andersen's Little Mermaid, a popular tourist attraction, is located near the **4** bars, cafes and restaurants of Nyhavn. **5** Tivoli park in the city centre is one of Denmark's most visited tourist attractions.

175

From a divided city to the symbol of German reunification: Berlin, Germany's old and new capital, can look back on a turbulent history. Its population is drawn from over 180 countries, giving the city its unique cosmopolitan flair and vitality. **1** The Brandenburg Gate is the most poignant symbol of Germany's new unified status. Berlin's new center is once more **2** Potsdamer Platz, a major city square, was redesigned by top international architects in the 1990s. The picture shows the interior courtyard of the Sony Center. After the Second World War, the **3** ruined Kaiser-Wilhelm Memorial Church became the emblem of West Berlin. **4** Schloss Charlottenburg was presented by the Prussian King Frederick I to his wife as a gift.

s well as important cultural centers such as Dresden, Weimar, and Cologne. The Bavarian Alps, the Black Forest, and the coastal areas along the North and Baltic seas are also popular attractions.

Politics: Germany was originally settled by a variety of Germanic, Celtic, and later Slavic peoples. Large areas were controlled by the Romans for centuries, who founded many of Germany's oldest cities. Charlemagne was able to unite much of Germany into one empire during the 9th century. Between the 10th and 12th century, German nobles and the popes vied for control. During most of the middle ages, Germany was a collection of kingdoms known as the Holy Roman Empire, ruled by an elected Kaiser. The Thirty Years War, which devastated Germany and left a third of its population dead, weakened the Holy Roman Empire and left Germany divided for many centuries. The formation of the German Empire in 1871 was followed by a period of rapid economic and social progress as part of the industrial revolution. Following Germany's defeat in the First World War, the Kaiser was forced to abdicate and the country became a republic. One of the darkest chapters in German history began in 1933 when the National Socialist party and Adolf Hitler came to power, leading the country to a devastating defeat in the Second World War and to the Holocaust. Following the Second World War, the country was divided into two states – East and West Germany. While West Germany, an ally of the USA, prospered under capitalism and democracy, the East was transformed into a repressive communist state. The two German states were reunited in 1990 and the country currently consists of sixteen federal states.

Economy: Germany is one of the world's wealthiest industrialized nations and has the largest economy in Europe. Services and manufacturing account for most of Germany's GDP. Tourism is also an important source of income in several German regions, while agriculture plays a marginal role.

Eesti
Estonia

Area: 45,226 sq km
Population: 1.3 million
GDP per capita: 16,000 US$
Capital: Tallinn

1 The modern skyline of Frankfurt, Germany's leading financial center.

2 The beautiful and historic riverside of Dresden.

3 Cologne's famous cathedral is a popular attraction.

4 Tallin, Estonia's medieval capital city on the Baltic Sea.

Nations of the World
Europe

Government: Parliamentary republic
Language: Estonian (official), Russian
Currency: 1 Estonian krone = 100 senti

Geography: Estonia mainly consists of low-lying plains, moorlands and marshes. More than 1,500 islands are situated off the country's coast. The fresh climate gives way to a continental climate in the country's interior. The country's main tourist attractions are the capital city, Tallinn, and the cities of Narva and Tartu.

Politics: This small country on the Baltic Sea was conquered by the Danes in the 13th century. During the 15th century the country was ruled by Sweden and after 1721 by Russia. Estonia declared its independence from Russia in 1918 but was occupied by the Soviet Union in 1940. Estonia was declared an independent republic in 1991. The country is now a multiparty democracy.

Economy: Estonia has been largely successful with its transition from a planned economy to free market capitalism. The country experienced strong growth and foreign investment rates in the 1990s. The service sector now accounts for most of Estonia's GDP.

Éire / Ireland
Ireland

Area: 70,280 sq km
Population: 4 million
GDP per capita: 60,000 US$
Capital: Dublin
Government: Parliamentary republic
Language: Irish Gaelic, English (both official)
Currency: 1 euro = 100 cents

Geography: Ireland is a medium-sized island situated in the North Atlantic with a temperate maritime climate. The country's terrain consists mostly of rolling hills, meadows, and moorlands. The northern half of the island features numerous lakes. Ireland's historic monuments and attractive countryside are the island's leading tourist attractions.

Politics: Archeological finds show the island was settled by Celts no later than the 3rd century BC. The island's people were converted to Christianity during the 5th century. The English conquest of Ireland in 1171 was followed by a series of revolts and centuries of British domination. Devastating famines in the mid-19th century largely decimated the population and caused thousands of people to emigrate, mostly to the United States and Canada. In December 1922, the Republic of Ireland was finally declared an independent state, while several northern Irish countries in the province of Ulster remained within the territory of the United Kingdom.

High crosses in the cemetery of Clonmacnoise in western Ireland

Economy: Ireland experienced a remarkable economic transition in the 1990s. The country is today one of Europe's richest due to foreign investment, competitive tax rates, and EU regional aid. While agriculture once dominated the Irish economy, services and manufacturing (primarily the computer, chemical and pharmaceuticals industries) now account for over 90% of Ireland's GDP, making it a role model of economic success.

Elláda (Hellás)
Greece

Area: 131,940 sq km
Population: 10.6 million
GDP per capita: 28,000 US$
Capital: Athens
Government: Parliamentary republic
Language: Modern Greek
Currency: 1 euro = 100 cents

Geography: Greece consists of a large peninsula on the southern edge of the Balkans, the Peloponnese peninsula, and numerous islands. Heavily forested mountains and hills cover over three-quarters of the land. The Pindus Mountains occupy much of central and western mainland Greece. Most of the country has a warm Mediterranean climate, while the northernmost regions have a con-

The cradle of western civilization, Athens, is more than 4,000 years old – the first settlements around the Acropolis were founded as early as 3000 BC. The city, host of the 2004 Olympic Games, is home to more than four million residents and boasts a fascinating mixture of tradition, modernity, and cosmopolitanism. The **1** Parthenon on the Acropolis was founded during the 5th century BC in honour of the goddess Athena. **2** The Caryatid statues of the Erechtheum are reproductions; the originals are housed in an Athens museum. The **3** Olympieion and the **4** Odeon of Herodus Atticus are both located at the base of the Acropolis. The Odeon, an open air theatre, was founded around 160 AD. Vegetable dealers **5** are a common sight in many of the city's older neighborhoods.

tinental climate. Ancient monuments and the Greek islands are the country's main attractions.

Politics: The powerful Greek city-states of the classical era profoundly influenced European culture. Alexander the Great (356-323 BC) conquered vast territories and spread Greek (Hellenic) culture through the Near East and Mediterranean. Greece was a Roman province from 148 BC-396 BC, then a province of the Byzantine Empire. Conquered by the Ottoman Turks in 1356, Greece remained an Ottoman province for almost five centuries. A sovereign Greek kingdom was created in 1832. After a military coup in 1964, the monarchy was abolished. Greece became a democratic republic in 1974 after several years of repressive dictatorship.

Bilbao's distinctive Gugenheim Museum was designed by Frank O. Gehry

Economy: Despite a move towards greater privatization a large segment of Greece's economy is under government control. Traditional crops including olives, wine, citrus fruits and tobacco account for more than a quarter of Greece's exports. Greece's manufacturing sector is dominated by small businesses. The rapidly growing service sector accounts for more than

60% of the country's GDP. Greece currently has the world's largest fleet of commercial sailing vessels. Tourism remains an important sector of the national economy.

España
Spain

Area: 504,782 sq km
Population: 40.3 million
GDP per capita: 32,000 US$
Capital: Madrid
Government: Parliamentary monarchy
Language: Spanish (Castilian), Catalan, Basque (Euskara), Galician
Currency: 1 euro = 100 cents

Geography: The Pyrenees mountains form a natural boundary between the mountainous Iberian Peninsula and the rest of Europe. Northern Spain is dominated by the plateaus of Castille, while the Sierra Nevada mountains stretch over much of the country's south. The south consists largely of semi-arid areas with steppe vegetation. The northernmost coastal areas have a distinct temperate climate with heavy rainfall. Spain is one of the world's most popular tourist destinations, with its leading attractions including islands such as

Majorca and large cities such as Barcelona.

Politics: Spain was settled by a variety of European groups including Basque, Celts and Iberians before the 3rd century BC. Most of Iberia became a Roman province in the 1st century BC. Large sections of the country fell under the control of Muslim Arabs during the 8th century. The Reconquista, a long military campaign led by Christian nobles, eventually succeeded in expelling the Arabs by 1492. Spain was Europe's most powerful nation by the 16th century and the ruler of vast territories in the Americas. By the 18th century, however, Spain was in a period of decline that culminated with the loss of its empire in the 19th century. A civil war between nationalists and Spanish republicans ended with a victory for the reactionary nationalists. The country returned to democracy following the dictator Franco's death in 1978.

Economy: After a period of high unemployment and rising foreign debts, the Spanish economy has become increasingly strong in recent years. Agriculture and fishing account for around one-tenth of the country's GDP, although this is falling. Manufacturing produces around a third of the country's GDP, and the service sector more than half. Tourism remains a major industry and provides employment for a large number of Spaniards.

Estonia see Eesti
Finland see Suomi

France
France

Area: 547,030 sq km
Population: 60.4 million
GDP per capita: 41,500 US$

Madrid's grand architecture and wide boulevards reflect it role as the proud capital and commercial center of Spain. Chosen to be the capital of Spain in the 16th century, Madrid is now the country's largest city. Madrid was once the political center of Spain's vast global empire and is a city of commerce, government, education and the home of the Spanish monarchy. **1** The city's main post office, the Palacio de Communicaciones, is one of Madrid's most famous buildings. **2** The Cybele fountain at the center of Plaza de Cibeles is named after a mythical goddess of fertility and is one's of Madrid's most famous landmarks. **3** Plaza Major, the largest square in Madrid, served as the model for many similar central squares throughout the Spanish-speaking world. Until the 20th century, the square was the site of spectacular and sometimes bloody events: the square was often used for public executions and traditional Spanish bullfights. **4** A prominent statue in the center of Madrid pays tribute to the two most famous characters of Spanish literature, Cervantes' Don Quixote and Sancho Panza.

Many important international organizations such as UNESCO have their headquarters in Paris, the economic and political center of France. The city is also a major cultural center and is home to countless musicians, artists, writers, and designers from around the world. **1** IM Pei's glass pyramid in the courtyard of the Louvre was quite controversial when it was completed in 1989. **2** The Arc de Triomphe was built to celebrate Napoleon's successful military campaigns throughout Europe. **3** The bridges on the Seine offer spectacular views of the Eiffel Tower **4** The gothic cathedral Notre Dame was built between the 12th and 14th centuries in the center of medieval Paris. **5** Paris' neo-baroque opera house, one of the world's largest, was completed in 1875.

Capital: Paris
Government: Parliamentary republic
Language: French
Currency: 1 euro = 100 cents

Geography: France is a mostly hilly country situated between the Atlantic Ocean, English Channel, and the Mediterranean Sea. Two high mountain ranges form natural borders along the country's edges – the Pyrenees in the south and the Alps in the east. Large basins cover a large segment of France's territory, including the densely populated Paris Basin. The Rhone, Seine and Loire are the country's principal rivers. France is an extremely popular tourist destination and its main attractions include the city and surrounding of Paris, the Loire river valley, the French Riviera and the country's Atlantic coast.

Politics: The history of modern France can be directly connected to the division of the Frankish Empire in the year 843 AD. France emerged victorious from the Hundred Years' War (1338-1453) with England. In the centuries that followed, France greatly expanded its territory and was ruled by absolutist monarchs. The French Revolution of 1798 brought an end to the monarchy and established the first French republic. The French general Napoleon was declared emperor in 1804 and launched a series of military campaigns that changed the political structure of Europe. The country switched between monarchy and republicanism several times during the 19th century. The country was occupied by Germany during the Second World War. France is currently governed by the so-called fifth republic, a presidential democracy established in 1958.

Economy: France rapidly made the transition from a largely agricultural economy to an industrialized nation following the Second World War. Modern France is now one of the world's most affluent nations with a diverse economy. Despite the country's wealth, unemployment remains high and the French people are heavily taxed. Tourism continues to play an important role

1 The Pont du Gard (45 meters high and 275 meters long) is the most impressive Roman aqueduct in France and a stunning monument to Roman engineering skills.

2 Mont Saint Michel monastery is situated on a small island off the coast of Normandy.

3 Chambord Chateau, one of the world's most beautiful and famous castles, was built by King Francois I.

4 Cannes on the French Riviera is most famous for its annual film festival. Every year film makers and actors from around the world gather here to introduce their latest works.

in the national economy. The French government retains significant influence over the economy with many under government control. The service sector now accounts for most of France's GDP.

Germany see Deutschland
Greece see Elláda (Hellás)
Hungary see Magyaroszag

Hrvatska
Croatia

Area: 56,542 sq km
Population: 4.5 million
GDP per capita: 11,500 US$
Capital: Zagreb
Government: Republic
Language: Croatian
Currency: 1 kuna = 100 lipa

Geography: Croatia borders the Adriatic Sea to the west. The country's narrow coastal strip stretches south from Dalmatia to the Bay of Kotor. Croatia's territory also includes at least 600 islands in the Adriatic. Northeastern Croatia is a largely mountainous region that borders the fertile plains between the Sava and Danube rivers. The Croatian coast is an increasingly popular tourist destination.

Politics: Croatia was first settled by Slavic groups in the 7th century. The first Croatian kingdom was established in the 9th century. The country came under the control of the Hapsburg Empire in 1527. Between 1918 and 1991, Croatia was a republic in the kingdom and later socialist republic of Yugoslavia. The country's declaration of independence was followed by a brutal civil war that lasted until 1995.

Economy: Croatia's economy was severely affected by the war of the early 1990s but has since made a gradual recovery. Agriculture remains an important economic sector, although the service sector is the fastest growing segment of the economy. After the war tourism has been boosting.

Ísland
Iceland

Area: 103,000 sq km
Population: 294,000
GDP per capita: 64,000 US$
Capital: Reykjavik
Government: Republic
Language: Icelandic
Currency: 1 Icelandic krone = 100 aurar

Iceland: Ofaernfoss waterfall

Geography: Iceland is a volcanic island situated in the Atlantic Ocean. The northernmost sections of the country are located above the Arctic Circle. Most of the population is concentrated on the coast, while the rugged interior is largely uninhabited. Approximately 27 of the country's 140 volcanoes are active. Geysers, hot springs, lava and ash fields are common throughout the country. Around one-half of the island is covered by glaciers.

Politics: Norwegians, the first permanent settlers of Iceland, arrived on the island during the 9th and 10th centuries. The Althing, an assembly of chiefs, was founded in 930 BC and exists to this day. The population of Iceland was converted to Christianity around 1000 BC. The island was ruled by Denmark between the 13th century and 1944, when independence was declared.

Economy: Fishing and the manufacture of fish products is the largest industry in Iceland. Around one-quarter of the local workforce work directly or indirectly for the fishing industry. Livestock herding (sheep and horses) is also an important industry. The economy has become increasingly diverse.

Ireland see Éire

Italia
Italy

Area: 301,230 sq km
Population: 58 million
GDP per capita: 36,000 US$
Capital: Rome
Government: Republic
Language: Italian
Currency: 1 euro = 100 cents

Geography: The Alps stretch along the northern border of Italy. Further south, the alpine foothills extend south to the fertile Po River Valley. The Apennine Mountains stretch from north to south through the center of the Italian peninsula. In addition to mainland Italy, the country also consists of several large islands such as Sicily and many smaller islands in the Mediterranean and Adriatic seas. Major tourist attractions include the historic sites, cities and coastal areas.

Politics: Italy was dominated by the Catholic Church for centuries following the collapse of the Roman Empire. Several Italian city-states – including Venice and Florence – emerged as important centers of cultural and commercial progress during the late middle

The city of Rome is located in the central section of the Italian peninsula near the Tyrrhenian Sea. Once the center of Europe's greatest empire, the city is still the center of a major religion and modern capital city with more than two million residents. **1** A panoramic view of the city on the banks of the Tiber with the memorial to Victor Emanuel II in the center of the photo. **2** The Spanish Steps are a popular public meeting place in the city center, while the Piazza Navona with the **3** Fountain of Neptune is possibly the city's most beautiful square. **4** The Pantheon was first completed in the year 27 BC and later remodeled during the reign of Emperor Hadrian **5** Castel Sant' Angelo was originally built as a burial site for Roman emperors and later became a fortress used to defend the Vatican. The Greec Ponte Sant' Angelo leads to the charming district of Trastevere.

185

Nations of the World
Europe

ages. The popes and several foreign powers vied for control of Italy between the 16th and 19th centuries. A united Italian kingdom was created in 1861 and Rome was declared the national capital in 1870. A series of domestic crises led to the rise of Mussolini's fascist government in the 1920s. The country was occupied by German troops before the end of the Second World War. In 1946, Italy was declared a republic. Despite frequent changes in government during recent decades, Italy remains an open multi-party democracy.

Economy: The dramatic wealth gap between the industrialized north and the poorer, agricultural south of the country remains a major problem for modern Italy. Italy's highly productive agriculture sector now contributes less than 3% of the country's GDP, while the diverse service sector accounts for at least 70% of national GDP. Major exports include automobiles, electric goods, chemical products, textiles, and machinery. Tourism is blossoming.

Kosovo
Kosovo

Area: 10,887 sq km
Population: approx. 3 million
GDP per capita: 1,300 US$
Capital: Pristina
Government: Republic
Languages: Albanian, Serbian
Currency: 1 euro = 100 cents

Geography: In the centre of the Balkan Peninsula, Kosovo is a terrain characterized by high valleys with surrounding mountains and no outlets to the sea. The climate is continental and the temperatures vary considerably, depending on the season and altitude. Its capital Pristina is located in the heart of Kosovo.

Politics: Kosovo became an Ottoman province after the Battle of Amselfeld in 1389 and was occupied by Albanians. After the First World War, it formed part of Yugoslavia and became an autonomous province in 1974. Due to the nationalistic policies of Slobodan Milošević, the conflicts between the Albanians and Serbians intensified. After the Kosovo War in

Italy: Vernazza on the Ligurian coast

1999, when NATO intervened on the side of the UCK independence movement, Kosovo became a UN protectorate before its declaration of independence in 2008. Independence is disputed under international law and is not recognized by the Serbian minority.

Economy: The country is agricultural and mainly survives from money transfers by international organizations and Kosovars resident abroad. Natural resources, including rich reserves of brown coal, offer new prospects.

Kypros / Kibris
Cyprus

Area: 9,250 sq km
Population: 776,000
GDP per capita: 27,000 US$
Capital: Nicosia

Government: Presidential republic
Language: Greek, Turkish (both official), English
Currency: 1 euro = 100 cents

Geography: The island of Cyprus is located in the Mediterranean Sea to the south of Turkey. Mesaoria, a large plain, stretches through central Cyprus and borders the Kyrenia mountains to the north. The Troodos mountains stretch through most of southern and western Cyprus. The mediterranean climate makes the island a popular tourist destination.

Politics: Cyprus is a melting pot of cultures including Persians, Romans, Arabs and Christians. The island was a British colony between 1925 and 1960. In 1974, Turkey occupied the northern sections of the island. Since then, the island has been divided between a Greek-speaking republic in the south and an ethnic Turkish state.

Economy: Greek Cyprus has experienced rapid growth in recent decades, while the Turkish north has generally stagnated due to its political isolation and corruption. The service sector dominates the economy of both areas and tourism is an important industry.

Latvija
Latvia

Area: 64,589 sq km
Population: 2.3 million
GDP per capita: 12,000 US$
Capital: Riga
Government: Republic
Language: Latvian (official), Russian
Currency: 1 lats = 100 santims

Geography: Latvia is bordered to the west by the Baltic Sea. The country's coast is mostly smooth and lined by wide sandy beaches. Latvia's interior is dominated by large fertile plains. Around 40% of the country's land area is covered by forests of birch, fir, and pine trees. Riga, the historic capital city, and Latvia's national parks are the country's leading tourist attractions.

Politics: The German speaking Teutonic Knights and the Hanseatic League dominated Latvia during the middle ages. Latvia was annexed by Russia in the 18th century and became independent in 1920. The country was reoccupied by Russia in 1940 and declared a republic of the USSR. Latvia declared its independence from the Soviet Union in 1991.

Economy: Agriculture and fishing remain important sectors of the Latvian economy and together account for around 10% of national GDP. The services sector now accounts for 66% of the country's GDP and is expanding. Major exports include agricultural products, electronics and machinery. Most of former state enterprises have been privatized since 1991.

Liechtenstein
Liechtenstein

Area: 160 sq km
Population: 33,400
GDP per capita: 100,000 US$ (estimated)
Capital: Vaduz
Government: Parliamentary monarchy
Language: German
Currency: 1 Swiss franc = 100 rappen

Geography: Liechtenstein is a small principality in the highlands of the Alps, located between Austria and Switzerland. The Rhine River forms the country's northwe-

stern border. Liechtenstein attracts mountain tourists all year round.

Politics: Liechtenstein's existence as a sovereign principality began in 1719. The country remained neutral during both world wars and joined a customs and monetary union with Switzerland in 1923. Liechtenstein's ruling monarch has broad sweeping powers in contrast to

1 Restoration work in recent years has preventing the famous Leaning Tower of Pisa from collapsing.

2 Cyprus: The small town of Girne with its medieval castle and charming harbor is one of the most picturesque destinations on the northern coast of Cyprus.

3 Riga, the capital city of Latvia, is located near the country's Baltic Sea coast and boasts an attractive medieval city center.

4 An imposing castle towers above the Vaduz, the small capital city of Liechtenstein. The medieval castle is home to the country's ruling prince.

187

Nations of the World
Europe

most other European constitutional monarchies.

Economy: Liechtenstein has a highly developed economy, attracting 30% of its workforce from Switzerland, Germany and Austria.

Lietuva
Lithuania

Area: 65,200 sq km
Population: 3.6 million
GDP per capita: 11,500 US$
Capital: Vilnius (Tbilisi)
Government: Parliamentary republic
Language: Lithuanian (official), Russian
Currency: 1 litas = 100 centas

Geography: Lithuania has a 100-kilometer coastline along the Baltic Sea and the Curonian Lagoon. The

stretching from the Baltic to the Black Sea during the 17th and 18th centuries. Lithuania came under the control of the Russian Empire in 1772. The country declared its independence from Russia in 1918 and was annexed by the Soviet Union in 1940. Lithuania became the first Soviet republic to declare its independence (1991).

Economy: On its long way to free market capitalism in the 1990s the country has achieved a strong economic growth. Agriculture accounts for 10% of GDP, while the services contribute ca. 66% of GDP.

Luxembourg
Luxembourg

Area: 2,586 sq km
Population: 462,700
GDP per capita: 105,000 US$

The bell tower and front entrance of Vilnius cathedral in Lithuania

country is largely flat. Most of the country's terrain is covered by forests, moorlands, and meadows. The coastal areas have a mild maritime climate, while the interior has a drier continental climate.

Politics: The Polish-Lithuanian Commonwealth ruled a vast territory

Capital: Luxembourg
Government: Constitutional monarchy
Language: Letzebuergesch, French, Germany (all official)
Currency: 1 euro = 100 cents

Geography: Luxembourg, one of the smallest states in Europe,

shares borders with France, Germany, and Belgium. Northern Luxembourg is a heavily forested area with rolling hills while the south is dominated by river valleys. The country's main attractions include its river valleys and capital city.

Politics: Once a region of the German-dominated Holy Roman Empire, Luxembourg came under the control of France in the 18th century. The country achieved its formal independence in 1867. It was occupied by the German army in both world wars and abandoned its neutrality when it joined the NATO defence alliance in 1949. The Grand Duke of Luxembourg is the country's official head of state.

Economy: Foreign workers – most from other EU countries – form more than 25% of Luxembourg's population. The country's economy is heavily dependent on foreign trade. The steel industry was once the largest in the country but the economy is now its focus on services, including the large banking and financial services sector.

Magyarország
Hungary

Area: 93,030 sq km
Population: 10 million
GDP per capita: 14,000 US$
Capital: Budapest
Government: Parliamentary republic
Language: Hungarian
Currency: 1 forint = 100 filler

Geography: The vast Pannonian plain/Carpathian Basin stretches over most of Hungary's national territory. Low mountains rising up to 1,000 meters above sea level stretch along the Slovakian border

The capital city of Hungary has a population of 1.8 million and is divided
by the Danube River into two distinct
sections, Buda in the west and Pest in
the east. The city is the country's leading economic and cultural center **1**
The Danube flows a dis-tance of 28
kilometers through the city. **2** The
Chain Bridge became the first bridge
to span the Danube in the city when it
was completed in 1849. **3** Built between 1880 and 1902, the Hungarian
parliament building is one of the
world's largest government buildings.

and in northern Hungary. The Danube and the Theiss river are the country's principal waterways. Budapest, Lake Balaton, and the pristine landscapes of Hortobagy National Park are the country's leading tourist attractions.

Politics: The Magyar ancestors of the Hungarians arrived in the Carpathian Basin during the 9th century. Hungary was one of Europe's most powerful states by the 13th century. The country was divided and controlled by the Hapsburg Empire and Ottoman Turks during the 16th century. After a failed Hungarian revolution in 1867, the Hapsburg Empire was reorganized into the Austro-Hungarian Empire. Hungary became an independent kingdom in 1918 at the end of the First World War and was governed by a re-

Economy: Hungary is one of the wealthier transition countries in Europe. The country has privatized most former state industries and receives impressive levels of foreign investment. The service sector accounts for more than 62% of Hungary's GDP, while the manufacturing sector accounts for 34%. The country remains a major supplier of the European food industry.

Makedonija
Macedonia

Area: 25,333 sq km
Population: 2 million
GDP per capita: 3,700 US$
Capital: Skopje
Government: Republic
Language: Macedonian (official), Albanian, Turkish, Serbian
Currency: 1 Macedonian denar = 100 deni

Valletta, the capital city of Malta, boasts fascinating architecture

actionary nationalist government in the 1930s. Hungary was allied to the axis powers in the Second World War and was placed in the Soviet sphere of influence after the war. Hungary was the first communist state in Eastern Europe to begin the transition to democracy and capitalism, and joined the European Union in 2004 along with nine other countries in Central and South-East Europe plus Malta.

Geography: The former Yugoslav republic of Macedonia is a largely mountainous republic with several peaks rising 2,000 meters or more above sea level. The southern sections of the country and the Vadar Valley have Mediterranean climates, while the rest of the country has a cooler continental climate. More than a third of the country's terrain is covered by forests. The monasteries around Lake Ohrid,

the country's national parks, and the capital city, Skopje, are Macedonia's leading attractions.

Politics: Macedonia was a region in the Ottoman Empire between the 14th and 19th centuries. The country was widely known as Vadarska before 1929 when it was renamed Macedonia. The country has been in dispute with Greece over the name Macedonia since its independence in 1991.

Economy: Macedonia was one of the poorer republics in Yugoslavia. The country's economy stagnated throughout the 1990s because of its poor infrastructure, conflicts in the Balkans, and a Greek embargo. Ethnic conflict and instability continue to undermine sustained economic development. Textiles, steel and agricultural produce are the country's leading export commodities.

Malta
Malta

Area: 316 sq km
Population: 397,000
GDP per capita: 18,000 US$
Capital: Valletta
Government: Republic
Language: Maltese, English
Currency: 1 euro = 100 cents

Geography: The island republic of Malta is situated in the southern Mediterranean Sea and consists of three islands – Malta, Gozo, and Comino. The ancient islands are the remnants of a large land bridge that once stretched between North Africa and Europe. Malta has few freshwater sources and most of the islands consist of arid plains with poor soils. Most of Malta's indigenous vegetation was cleared during the middle ages. All of the Maltese islands have a distinctly

Mediterranean climate with hot, dry summers and mild winters.

Politics: The ancient megaliths of Malta are remnants of an ancient stone age culture that once inhabited the islands. Malta was ruled by numerous foreign powers throughout its history including the Romans, Egyptians, Phoenicians, Arabs, Spaniards, and the British. The country was an important center of the Christian wars against the Ottoman Turks during the middle ages. The country joined the EU in 2004.

Economy: Malta's agricultural sector consists mostly of small farms and produces less than 5% of the country's GDP. The services sector accounts for more than 74% of the national GDP. Due to the island's rich culture and coastal areas, tourism remains the single most important industry in the country and provides jobs for more than a quarter of the population. The country's leading export commodities include citrus fruits and machinery.

Moldova
Republic of
Moldova

Area: 33,700 sq km
Population: 4.4 million
GDP per capita: 1,300 US$
Capital: Chisinau
Government: Republic
Language: Moldavian (official), Russian
Currency: 1 Moldau leu = 100 bani

Geography: This small country in Eastern Europe consists primarily of plains and marshes. Moldova is crossed by several rivers including the Danube, the Dniester, and the Prut River. Most of the country is covered by grasslands, marshes, and deciduous forests.

Politics: The area of modern Moldova was part of Principality of Moldovia during the middle ages. Moldova was conquered by the Ottomans in the 16th century. The eastern part of the country was annexed by Russia in 1812 and became a Soviet republic in 1918. The country declared its independence from the Soviet Union in 1991.

1 Lake Ohrid in Macedonia is surrounded by scenic beaches and marshlands. Macedonia's tourist industry remains underdeveloped but the lake is a popular destination for Macedonian tourists.

2 The Macedonian town of Ohrid has a long history and is a designated world heritage site with interesting architecture.

3 Eger in northern Hungary is one of the most attractive and historic cities in the country. The city's cathedral is the second largest in the country and houses the country's second largest organ.

191

Economy: Moldova is one of the poorest states in Europe despite strong growth in recent years. The country has few mineral resources and agriculture contributes more than a quarter of national GDP. The country's agricultural sector stagnated during the 1990s due to a loss of its traditional markets in the former Soviet republics. Moldova's service sector remains undeveloped and the manufacturing is relatively unproductive. Major exports include fruits, grain, wine, tobacco, and machinery.

Monaco
Monaco

Area: 1.95 sq km
Population: 32,300
GDP per capita: 60,000 US$
Capital: Monaco City
Government: Constitutional hereditary monarchy
Language: French (official), Monegasque, Italian
Currency: 1 euro = 100 cents

Geography: Monaco is a small principality situated on the Mediterranean coast of Southern France. Most of the country's land area was created by reclaiming land from the sea. The densely populated country consists mostly of urban landscapes, although wines and olives are grown in a few areas. Monaco is a popular tourist destination.

Politics: The ruling Grimaldi dynasty gained control of Monaco in 1454. Monaco achieved complete independence in 1861 after periods of Spanish and French domination. Monaco lost most of its territory to France during the 19th century. The constitutions of 1911 and 1962 limited the power of Monaco's princes and transformed the country into a modern constitutional monarchy.

Economy: Only around 17% of Monaco's residents are citizens of the country. Monaco has a high standard of living and low taxes that attract many residents and investors. Tourism is an important industry for the country and the principality's famous casino in the Monte Carlo area is the country's largest single business. Royals and riches from all over the world contribute their part to its glamour.

Nederland
Netherlands

Area: 41,526 sq km
Population: 16.3 million
GDP per capita: 46,000 US$
Capital: Amsterdam
Government: Parliamentary monarchy
Language: Dutch
Currency: 1 euro = 100 cents

Geography: The Netherlands is situated on a vast plain that extends through large sections of western and central Europe. Reclaimed land situated below sea level comprises more than a quarter of the country's territory. The highest point in the country, the Vaalserberg hill, rises just 320 meters above sea level. Several major rivers flow through the country including the Rhine and the Meuse. The Netherlands has a temperate-maritime climate with frequent precipitation throughout the year. The capital city, Amsterdam, is by far the most visited destination in the country.

Politics: The Netherlands gained its independence from the rulers of the German-dominated Holy Roman Empire in 1648. During much of the 16th and 17th centuries, the Dutch controlled Europe's most powerful trading and naval fleet. The country lost control of Belgium in 1831 but retained control of its largest overseas territories until the 1950s. The country was occupied by Germany during the Second World War. The Netherlands was one of the founding members of NATO and the EU.

Economy: The Netherlands has one of the most diverse and highly developed economies in the world. The people of the Netherlands enjoy one of the highest standards of

Monaco: The famous Casino of Monte Carlo attracts tourists and gamblers

living in Europe. Most of the country's population is concentrated in the heavily-populated Randstad, an urban conglomerate in the western section of the country. The

Only a small segment of Amsterdam's 735,000 inhabitants live in the city's world famous center with its picturesque canals and charming historic architecture. The official capital city of the Netherlands is the home of the Dutch royal family and boasts many fascinating attractions including museums and distinctive local architecture. **1** Amsterdam's many canals are the most famous landmarks of the city. Large amounts of money and energy are invested into maintaining the water level. **2** This wooden drawbridge, known as the "Skinny Bridge", was built in the 17th century. **3** Only a lucky minority of the city's people are able to live in the houseboats along Amsterdam's canals. **4** Many of the city's bridges are illuminated during the night.

country's service sector contributes more than 70% of national GDP. The Rhine Delta is one of the world's busiest centers of shipping and Rotterdam is the site of Europe's busiest harbour. Agriculture contributes less than 4% of national GDP but remains an important industry. Major agricultural exports include flowers and vegetables. Fishing also remains an important industry. Machinery, electronics, and chemical products are important industrial exports.

Norge
Norway

Area: 324,220 sq km
Population: 4.6 million
GDP per capita: 84,000 US$
Capital: Oslo
Government: Parliamentary monarchy
Language: Norwegian
Currency: 1 Norwegian krone = 100 øre

The northernmost sections of the country are situated above the arctic circle. Most of Norway's landscapes were formed by glaciers during the last ice ages. Large fjords cut deep into the country and it is surrounded by numerous islands. Most of Norway's interior is dominated by mountains and hills. Northern Norway has a severe sub-arctic climate and the far north consists of treeless tundras. Most of the country, however, has a mild maritime-temperate climate. The country's main tourist attractions include its impressive landscapes as well the cities of Bergen and Oslo.

Politics: Norway came under the control of the Danish monarchy in the late 14th century. The country was joined with Sweden in a political union between 1814 and 1915. Norway was neutral during the First World War but was occupied by Germany in the Second World

Economy: Less than 3% of Norway's terrain consists of arable land. The agricultural sector is protected from foreign competition by tariffs and subsidies. Oil from Norway's North Sea reserves is the country's most important export commodity and the country is the third largest oil exporter in the world. The service sector accounts for most of the country's GDP.

Österreich
Austria

Area: 83,870 sq km
Population: 8.2 million
GDP per capita: 45,000 US$
Capital: Vienna
Government: Federal republic
Language: German
Currency: 1 euro = 100 cents

Geography: Austria is a small mountainous republic located in Central Europe. The Alps and alpine foothills cover more than half of the country's terrain. A small section of the flat Carpathian Basin stretches through eastern Austria. The Danube and Inn rivers are the most important waterways in the country. Austria's major tourist attractions include the capital city Vienna and the country's many excellent winter sports facilities.

Politics: Austria emerged as the center of the Habsburg Empire in the 13th century. The Habsburgs were able to rapidly expand their empire through numerous alliances and marriages. The vast multi-cultural empire was reorganized into the Austro-Hungarian Empire during the 19th century. The German-speaking provinces of the empire became the Republic of Austra in 1918. A second Austrian republic gained its sovereignty in 1955. Austria joined the European Union in 1995.

Dusk at the North Cape, considered to be the northernmost point of Europe.

Geography: Norway occupies the western section of the Scandinavian peninsula and has more than 2,650 kilometers of coastline.

War. The country was a founding member of NATO in the 1950s. Norway is a constitutional monarchy and a multi-party democracy.

Vienna is one of Europe's most beautiful and charming cities and the capital of Austria. For centuries, the city was the political center of the Austro-Hungarian Empire. Several important international organizations including OPEC have headquarters in the city. **1** The Karlskirche is the most famous baroque building in the city **2** St. Stephan's cathedral, one of the city's most important landmarks, was founded in the 12th century and completed in the 16th century. **3** The Austrian parliament building and the **4** Hofburg imperial palace are two of the most important 19th-century buildings in the city. **5** Schoenbrunn Palace was modeled after the palace at Versailles. **6** The annual Vienna Opera Ball takes place in the city's famous opera house.

Special
Warsaw

Warsaw replaced Krakow as Poland's royal capital in the 16th century. Today Warsaw is the largest city in the country with a population of 1.6 million. **1** Zygmunt's Column rises above Royal Castle Square in the old town of Warsaw. **2** The beautiful and historic Market Square is a popular attraction. Warsaw was virtually de-stroyed during the Second World War but the city's old town was meticu-lously restored in the 1950s. **3** Many of the historic buildings standing around the Market Square were built in the 16th and 17th centuries. **4** The banks of the Vistula in the old town. The river flows through the heart of the city.

Economy: Austria has a highly developed and diverse economy. The country has attracted significant levels of foreign investment in recent years because of its proximity to the transition countries of Central Europe. The service sector contributes more than 65% of the national GDP. Tourism alone contributes 8% of Austria's GDP.

Polska
Poland

Area: 312,685 sq km
Population: 38.6 million
GDP per capita: 11,000 US$
Capital: Warsaw
Government: Republic
Language: Polish
Currency: 1 zloty = 100 groszy

Geography: Poland consists mostly of vast plains and is bordered to the north by the Baltic Sea. A series of medium-height mountains stretches along the country's southern border. Several major rivers, including the Oder and the Vistula, flow through Poland. Poland's leading tourist atractions include the country's Baltic coast, the mountainous regions in the south, and historic cities such as Gdansk, Warsaw, and Krakow.

Politics: Poland emerged as a distinct nation around the 10th century. The country, together with Lithuania, ruled a vast empire that stretched from the Baltic to the Black Sea. Poland was divided between Prussia, Austria, and Russia during in 1795 and did not exist as an independent state during most of the 19th century. The country regained its independence in 1918. Poland was occupied by Germany in the Second World War and five million Poles died during the war. Communist rule was ended in 1989. Poland joined the EU in 2004.

Economy: Around 40% of the country's terrain is used for agricultural purposes. More than a fourth of the Polish labor force works in the agricultural sector, although agriculture contributes less than 5% of GDP. Major industries in the country include the chemical, steel, and shipbuilding industries. The rapidly growing service sector now contributes more than half of the country's GDP. Reforms in the 1990s have

1 Mountains cover around one half of Austria's territory: the pristine glaciers of the Stubaier Alps are situated between southern Austria and Italy.

2 The historic market square in the center of Krakow (Poland) is the largest market square in Central Europe and features impressive architecture

3 The historic port city of Gdansk was founded around 1,000 years ago. Photo: the historic harbour was reconstructed after the Second World War.

from several different eras. The Cloth Hall, built in renaissance style, is one of the largest and grandest buildings on the square.

opened the economy to increased foreign investment. As a strong economic partner of neighboring Germany, Poland is expected to become one of the major players in Europe's economy.

Portugal
Portugal

Area: 92,391 sq km
Population: 10.5 million
GDP per capita: 21,000 US$
Capital: Lisbon
Government: Republic
Language: Portuguese
Currency: 1 euro = 100 cents

Geography: Portugal occupies the westernmost section of the Iberian

The many hills of Lisbon offer beautiful views of the charming city

Porto (Oporto) is situated on the banks of the Douro River

Peninsula. The Sierra de Estrela mountain range stretches through the center of the country. The Tejo, Portugal's principal river, flows from Spain to its delta at the Atlantic Ocean near Lisbon. The country has a mediterranean climate with hot, dry summers. In addition to the mainland, Portugal

also consists of two island groups in the Atlantic Ocean: the Azores and Madeira Islands. Lisbon, the Algarve region, and the coastal areas are the country's most important tourist destinations.

Politics: Portugal was dominated by Arabs between the 8th and 13th centuries. The country gained its independence from the Spanish kingdom of Castille in the 14th century. Portugal was one of Europe's most powerful nations during the 15th and 16th centuries. Portugal was declared a republic in 1910 but a military coup in 1926 left the country under military rule for decades. Portugal is now a multiparty democracy.

Economy: The areas between the Tejo and Duoro rivers are an important agricultural area where wine, olives, and citrus fruits are produced. The country's economy, which was once dominated by agriculture, has become increasingly diverse since the 1980s. Today, the service sector accounts for more

than 65% of national GDP. Major exports include textiles, cork, machinery and agricultural products.

România
Romania

Area: 237,500 sq km
Population: 22.4 million
GDP per capita: 7,700 US$
Capital: Bucharest
Government: Republic
Language: Romanian (official), Hungarian, Germany
Currency: 1 leu = 100 bani

Geography: Romania is situated in south-eastern Europe and borders the Black Sea in the east. The Transylvanian basin is surrounded by the Carpathian Mountains and other highland areas. Several large plains dominate the rest of the country including the Moldovian plain in the north and Wallachian plain in the south. The Danube flows along most of the country's southern border. Most of the country has a continental climate.

Politics: The principalities of Moldovia, Wallachia, and Transylvania were conquered by the Ottoman Empire in the 14th century. In 1878, Wallachia and Moldovia united to form the Kingdom of Romania. The country was dominated by the Soviet Union after the Second World War and was declared a socialist republic in 1947. Romania was ruled by the dictator Nicolae Ceausescu for more than 24 years before he was overthrown in 1989. The country is now a candidate for membership in the EU.

Economy: Romania's economy is now gradually developing, after years of difficult transition to free market capitalism. The service sector now contributes more than half of Romania's GDP. Major exports include natural resources, machinery, and agricultural products.

Rossija
Russia

Area: 17,075,200 sq km
Population: 143.7 million
GDP per capita: 9,000 US$
Capital: Moscow
Government: Federative presidential republic
Language: Russian (official), other national languages
Currency: 1 rouble = 100 kopecks

Geography: Russia, the largest nation on Earth, stretches from the Baltic Sea in the west to the Pacific Ocean in the east and from the Black Sea in the south to the Arctic Ocean in the north. The country's territory includes vast areas on two continents and a variety of climate and vegetation zones. The Caucasus Mountains stretch along the country's south-eastern border while the Urals separate the European and Asian sections of Russia. Most of northern Russia consists of forested Taiga areas and arctic tundras. Russia's two largest cities, Moscow and St. Petersburg, are the country's most popular tourist destinations.

Politics: The Kiev Rus, an alliance of Slavic groups, emerged in the 9th century and gained power and influence through its trade with the Byzantine Empire. Christianity arrived in Russia during the 10th century and encouraged the formation of a formal state. The duchy of Moscow gained increased political power in the 14th century. Russia developed into a vast empire in the following centuries. The imperial era, however, came to an end in 1918 during the Bolshevik Revolution. The Russian-dominated Soviet

Union was one of the world's two superpowers before it collapsed in 1991. Russia is now a multi-party democracy consisting of 21 republics.

Economy: Russia has an incredible wealth of natural resources and a large manufacturing sector. The country faced a series of economic crises throughout the 1990s. The ef-

1 The distinctive Castelo da Pena was built by Prince Ferdinand in the middle of the 19th century. It is now a popular tourist attraction.

2 Putna Monastery, located near Romania's border to Ukraine, is one of the country's many beautiful monasteries.

3 The monastery of Sergiev Posad was founded in the 14th century. The tomb of Russian Czar BorisGodunov is located at the center of the monastery.

4 Braganca in northeastern Portugal was founded in the 12th century as the headquarters of a powerful aristocratic family.

Special
Moscow

Moscow is by far the largest city in Russia, with an official city population of 8.7 million. Moscow was the capital of Russia for centuries before it was replaced by St. Petersburg in the 18th century. In 1918 the city was once again designated as the capital. **1** The Kremlin, originally a fortress, is the headquarters of Russia's government. The Kremlin imperial palace was built between 1838 and 1849. **2** Red Square is the site of the Kremlin and the 16th-century Saint Basil's Cathedral. **3** Seven monumental skyscrapers were built in the city's center between 1938 and 1949 under the orders of Stalin. **4** Ice sculptures in front of Saint Basil's Cathedral.

fects of a severe financial crisis in 1997 have been mostly overcome. High global oil prices and foreign investment have led to stable growth in recent years but the country's economy is still in need of major reforms.

San Marino
San Marino

Area: 61.2 sq km
Population: 28,500
GDP per capita: 22,000 US$
Capital: San Marino Città
Government: Republic
Language: Italian (official), Romagnol
Currency: 1 euro = 100 cents

Geography: The smallest republic in Europe is dominated by Mount Titano (756 meters). The country comprises ten separate towns, including the small capital city San Marino Città. The principal rivers are the Marano and the Ausa. The country's small and historic capital city is a popular destination.

Politics: San Marino, first settled around 600 AD, achieved its independence in 1400 and become a republic in 1600. Its independence was affirmed at the Congress of Vienna in 1815. The neutral country was occupied by the German army and later the allies during the Second World War. San Marino's status as an Italian protectorate was ended in 1968.

Economy: Tourism and the sale of postage stamps are the two largest industries in San Marino, with tourism accounting for more than half of the country's GDP. Agriculture is only on a small scale and contributes little to the economy. San Marino has a relatively high standard of living which is based on a strong GDP per capita.

Serbia see Srbija

Shqipëria
Albania

Area: 28,748 sq km
Population: 3.5 million
GDP per capita: 3,400 US$
Capital: Tirana
Government: Republic
Language: Albanian
Currency: 1 lek = 100 quindarka

1 The Alexander Column, the world's tallest victory column, rises in the middle of Winter Palace Square in St. Petersburg, Russia.

2 The Winter Palace on the Neva River in St. Petersburg was built for Czar Peter the Great by the Italian architect Rastelli.

3 San Marino: The small capital city is located 750 meters above sea level atop Mount Titato. The city has preserved most of its medieval character including fascinating narrow alleys and numerous historic buildings. La Guaita castle was built in the 11th century and is the oldest large structure in the city.

Nations of the World
Europe

Geography: Albania is situated in south-eastern Europe along the Ionian and Adriatic Seas. The country is largely mountainous and features more than 40 mountains rising more than 2,000 meters above sea level. Numerous rivers flow through the country, most of which are not navigable. The coun-

during the second world war and was declared a communist republic in 1946. The country returned to democracy in 1991 after decades of dictatorship and repression.

Economy: Albania remains one of the poorest countries in Europe and has one of the continent's

Ljubljana has a wealth of beautiful Baroque and Art Nouveau buildings.

The historic city of Gjirokaster is located in southernmost Albania.

try's coast is bordered by expansive marshlands and swampy plains. Albania boasts several large lakes including Lake Ohrid.

Politics: The area of modern Albania was once a region of the Roman and later Byzantine Empire. Albania was dominated by the Ottoman Empire for several centuries after 1502. The country declared its independence from the empire in 1913. Albania was occupied by German and Italian forces

least developed infrastructures. Agriculture is an important industry and contributes more than a third of national GDP. A majority of the labour force works in agriculture.

Slovenija
Slovenia

Area: 20,273 sq km
Population: 2 million
BSP pro Kopf: 23,000 US$
Capital: Ljubljana
Government: Republic

Language: Slovenian
Currency: 1 tolar = 100 stotin

Geography: The Julian Alps dominate much of northern Slovenia. More than half of the country is covered by forests, one of the highest ratios of woodland coverage in Europe. The flat Pannonian Plain covers sections of eastern Slovenia. Slovenia's narrow Adriatic coast has a Mediterranean climate, while the rest of the country has a cooler continental climate. The Slovenian Alps, Ljubljana, and the coast are all major tourist destinations.

Politics: The territory of modern Slovenia was under Austrian domination between the 13th century and 1918. Slovenia was joined in a united kingdom with Serbia, Croatia, and Macedonia after the First World War. The Yugoslav regions were reunited after the Second World War as a communist federation. Slovenia was the first Yugoslav republic to declare its independence. The country is now a member of NATO and the EU.

Economy: Slovenia has a highly developed and diversified economy and a high standard of living. The country also boasts the highest GDP per capita of any former communist state in Europe. Agriculture and forestry contribute around 5% of national GDP, while the services sector accounts for 65%. Slovenia's major exports include machinery, electronic goods, and chemical products. Tourism is an important industry in several regions.

Slovenská Republika
Slovakian
Republic

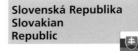

Area: 48,845 sq km
Population: 5.4 million

GDP per capita: 14,000 US$
Capital: Bratislava
Government: Republic
Language: Slovakian (official), Hungarian, Ruthenian
Currency: 1 Slovakian krone = 100 heller

Geography: Slovakia is a largely mountainous country; the country's terrain is dominated by the western Carpathian Mountains. Large basins separated by mountains also cover large sections of the country. The Vah is the country's longest river, while the Danube flows along the country's south-western border. Slovakia has a continental climate with cold winters and warm summers. The country's mountains and the towns of eastern Slovakia are the main tourist destinations.

Politics: Slovakia was settled by Slavs in the 6th century AD and came under the control of Hungary in the year 908. The country, together with Hungary, became a region of the Habsburg Empire in 1526. The country was merged with the Czech lands in 1918 to form Czechoslovakia. After the second world war, Czechoslovakia became a communist state. Democracy was restored to Czechoslovakia in 1989 and Slovakia became an independent state in 1993.

Economy: Like many other former communist states in Europe, Slovakia experienced a difficult transition to capitalism in the 1990s. Major reforms in recent years have opened the economy to foreign investment and led to stable growth. Most of the country's former state enterprises have been privatized and the service sector now contributes 60% of the country's GDP. High levels of unemployment are a major challenge for the country.

Spain see España

Srbija
Serbia

Area: 88,361 sq km
Population: 10.2 million
GDP per capita: 4,400 US$
Capital: Belgrade
Government: Republic
Languages: Serbian (official), Albanian, Hungarian
Currency: 1 new dinar = 100 paras

1 Kotor is one of the most beautiful areas in Montenegro. The city is situated on the southern shore of the Kotor Bay and boasts well preserved medieval architecture.

2 The medieval castle of Slovakia's capital, Bratislava, sits atop a hill in the city centre. St. Maria's cathedral (right) was built between 1302-1452 along the banks of the Danube .

3 The Baroque church on an island in the middle of Slovenia's Lake Bled is one of the area's most famous and beautiful attractions. Lake Bled is a popular tourist destination with beautiful scenery.

Nations of the World
Europe

Geography: Apart from the Vojvodina and the area around the intersection of the rivers Sava and Danube, Serbia is a landlocked, mountainous terrain. The climate is predominantly continental.

Politics: A kingdom of Serbia already existed in the 12th century and came under Ottoman rule. At the end of the 19th century, the principality gained independence and in 1918 was unified with Croatia and Slovenia. Conflicts between the different nationalities were ongoing until unification in the state of Yugoslavia (1946). In 1991, after a new outbreak of the conflicts and dissolution into the republics of Croatia, Slovenia, Macedonia and Bosnia-Herzegovina, a bloody war broke out in which the remainder of Serbian-dominated Yugoslavia aimed to regain control. The 1995 peace accord set out a solution for territorial disputes with Croatia and Bosnia-Herzegovina. In 1998, the conflicts intensified in the province of Kosovo. In 1999, ethnic cleansing of Kosovar Albanians led to the war in which NATO defeated Serbia. Subsequently, KFOR troops secured UN-administered Kosovo. From 2003, Serbia and Montenegro formed a state union. In 2006 Montenegro declared independence, followed by the Kosovo in 2008.

Economy: In 2005, GDP was 26 billion US dollars. Despite a rich supply of natural resources, Serbia continues to struggle with the consequences of a severe economic crisis.

Suisse/Schweiz/Svizzera
Switzerland

Area: 41,290 sq km
Population: 7.3 million
GDP per capita: 58,000 US$
Capital: Berne
Government: Parliamentary federation
Languages: German, French, Italian, Rhaetoromanian (all of them official languages)
Currency: 1 Swiss franc = 100 rappen/centimes

View of the northern face of Mount Eiger (3,790 metres) in the Berner Oberland.

Geography: Switzerland is a mostly mountainous country and contains some of the highest mountains in Europe. The country consists of three distinct geographic regions: the Jura mountains, the central plateau, and the Alps. Several of Switzerlands's higher mountains rise 4,000 meters or more above sea level including the famous Matterhorn (4,478 meters). The densely-populated central plateau between the Jura mountains and the Alps is home to several large lakes including Lake Geneva and Lake Constance. Switzerland is a popular tourist destination.

Politics: In 1291, three German-speaking areas – Uri, Schwyz, Unterwalden – formed a confederation that would later evolve into Switzerland. The country later acquired French and Italian speaking regions in the 18th century. Switzerland became a federal republic in 1848 and maintained its neutrality through both world wars. The individual cantons maintain a large degree of sovereignty.

Economy: Switzerland is one of the world's wealthiest nations and its people enjoy a high standard of living. The small but productive agricultural sector accounts for less than 3% of the country's GDP. Despite its land-locked location, Switzerland is a major trading nation and an important centre of the global banking and financial services industries. Major exports include timepieces, machinery, chemical products, and electronic goods. Tourism is an important industry in many Swiss regions with an excellent infratstructure.

Suomi/Finland
Finland

Area: 337,031 sq km
Population: 5.2 million
GDP per capita: 46,500 US$
Capital: Helsinki
Government: Republic
Language: Finnish, Swedish (both official)
Currency: 1 euro = 100 cents

Geography: Finland is located in northern Europe and borders the Gulf of Bothnia in the east as well as the Gulf of Finland and Baltic Sea in the south. The country's terrain is dominated by forests and thousands of lakes and swamps. The northernmost section of the country consist of treeless tundra with an arctic climate. While most of the country is flat, central and some sections of eastern Finland feature rolling hills. Finland's pristine landscapes attract numerous tourists to the country. Helsinki and the country's rural areas are its most popular tourist attractions.

Politics: Finland was under the control of the Swedish monarchy between the 12th and 18th centuries. Sweden relinquished control of the country to Russia after a series of wars. Finland achieved independence from Russia in 1918. Finland, a capitalist country, was closely aligned to its powerful neighbour, the USSR, after the Second World War. The country joined the EU in 1995.

Economy: Finland has a diverse and advanced free market economy. The country suffered a major economic crisis in the early 1990s but quickly rebounded and has experienced steady growth since then. Trade is vital for the Finish economy with exports accounting for around 15% of the national GDP. Major exports include paper, electronics, and machinery.

Geography: Sweden is located in northern Europe between the Gulf of Bothnia and Norway. More than two-thirds of the country's land area is covered by forests. In addition to the mainland, Sweden also consists of numerous islands including Gotland and Oland. The country's interior has a continental climate with often severe winters, while the southern coasts have a milder maritime climate. The capital city of Stockholm as well as the country's many lakes and pristine

Sverige
Sweden

Area: 449,964 sq km
Population: 9 million
GDP per capita: 49,500 US$
Capital: Stockholm
Government: Constitutional monarchy
Language: Swedish
Currency: 1 Swedish krone = 100 øre

1 Bern, the capital city of Switzerland, has a wealth of historic and beautiful architecture.

2 Oberhofen Castle is situated on the picturesque shore of Lake Thun.

3 The architect Carl Ludwig Engel was hired in the 19th century by Czar Nicholas I to plan the city center of Helsinki. The area now boasts many impressive neo-classical buildings such as the university and national library.

4 Hundreds of small islands are located near Sweden's capital city, Stockholm.

Nations of the World
Europe

forests are the most popular tourist destinations in Sweden.

Politics: Sweden was united with Norway and Denmark in the Kalmar Union between 1389 and 1520 AD. The country emerged as a major European power during the 17th century. Sweden eventually lost its role as the leading power of northern Europe to Russia. The country remained neutral through both world wars despite the occupation of its neighbors Finland and Denmark during the Second World War. Sweden joined the EU in 1995.

Economy: Sweden faced a major economic crisis in the 1990s but remains one of world's most prosperous nations. Swedish citizens have access to a generous social network and an excellent public education system. Sweden has a modern infrastructure and a wealth of hydroelectric power sources and natural resources. The country's diverse service sector accounts for more than 70% of the Swedish national GDP.

Türkiye
Turkey

Area: 780,580 sq km
Population: 68.9 million
GDP per capita: 9,600 US$
Capital: Ankara
Government: Republic
Language: Turkish
Currency: 1 Turkish lira = 100 kurus

Geography: Turkey occupies the Anatolian peninsula, a small section of Europe, and numerous islands in the Mediterranean Sea. A large central plateau covers most of mainland Turkey and is surrounded by the Taurus and Pontus Mountains. The country has a Mediterranean climate with mild winters, although some areas on the Black Sea coast have a distinct humid subtropical climate. Turkey is a popular tourist destination and its major attractions include countless ancient historic sites as well as popular beach resorts.

Politics: The first Turkish state emerged around the year 552 AD. The Ottoman Empire became one of the world's most powerful states in the centuries that followed. After centuries of conquest, however, the Ottoman Empire faced a series of military defeats and territorial losses in the 19th century. Mustafa Atatürk, a young soldier, founded the Turkish republic in 1923 after the country's defeat in the first world war. The republic has ex-

perience several military coups in its history; the last took place in 1980.

Economy: Turkey is in the midst of a rapid transition from an agrarian economy to one centered on industry and services. Around 40% of the Turkish labour force currently works in the agricultural sector, which accounts for a fifth of the country's GDP. The rapidly growing service sector now accounts for just over half of the country's GDP. The country's leading exports include both agricultural products and mineral resources. Tourism is a rapidly growing industry in many parts of the country.

Ukrajina
Ukraine

Area: 603,700 sq km
Population: 47.7 million
GDP per capita: 3,000 US$
Capital: Kiev
Government: Republic
Language: Ukrainian (official), Russian
Currency: 1 hryvnia = 100 kopijken

Geography: Ukraine is situated in Eastern Europe and has a long coastline along the Black Sea. Most of the country consists of plains and scattered plateaus. The country is crossed by many significant rivers including the Dniepr, Donets, and Dnister rivers. Odessa in southern Ukraine has one of the largest harbors on the Black Sea. The Crimean Peninsula is a popular destination for tourists from Ukraine and neighboring countries.

Politics: Much of Ukraine was once controlled by the Kievan Rus, a Slavic alliance that existed between the 9th and 13th centuries. Later the country came under the control of the Mongols, the Polish-Lithuanian Commonwealth,

Swallow's Nest Castle is located near the town of Yalta on the Crimean peninsula.

Turkey's largest city is home to 8.2 million people and is geographically both European and Asian. The city was once the center of the Eastern Roman/Byzantine Empire. **1** Numerous ferries traverse the Golden Horn between the Galata and Beyoglu districts of the city. **2** The Galata Tower offers magnificent views of the city's historic old town. **3** The Hagia Sophia was built in 532 during the reign of the Emperor Justinian. **4** The Sultan Ahment Mosque, also known as the Blue Mosque, is one of the world's finest examples of Ottoman architecture. **5** The walls of the mosque, which was built between 1609 and 1616, are decorated with 21,000 tiles. **6** Istanbul's marketplace, the Great Bazaar, is the largest roofed marketplace in the world – 500,000 shoppers visit the bazaar every day

and eventually the Russian Empire. Ukraine was declared a Soviet Republic in 1922 and remained one of the most influential republics in the USSR up until the union's collapse in the 1990s. Ukraine declared independence in 1991.

Economy: Ukraine's economy has mostly stagnated since the country achieved independence in 1991. The economy remains largely closed to foreign investment and previous governments have been ineffective at implementing desperately needed reforms. Ukraine is rich in mineral resources and arable land. Agriculture accounts for a large percentage of Ukraine's national GDP per capita. Russia is the country's leading trading partner and supplies most of its energy imports including natural gas. Natural resources and agricultural products are the country's leading exports.

United Kingdom
United Kingdom

Area: 241,752 sq km
Population: 60.2 million
GDP per capita: 45,500 US$
Capital: London
Government: Constitutional monarchy within Commonwealth
Language: English (official), Welsh, Scots Gaelic
Currency: 1 pound sterling = 100 pence

Geography: Great Britain is separated from mainland Europe by the English Channel and the North Sea. The United Kingdom consists of four main divisions: England, Wales, Scotland, and Northern Ireland. England, which comprises around two-thirds of Great Britain's land area, consists mostly of rolling hills. Scotland and Wales both feature medium-height mountain systems and numerous valleys. The capital city of London and scenic rural areas such as the Scottish Highlands are the country's leading tourist destinations.

Politics: England was successfully invaded by a Norman army in the year 1066 AD. The end of the English Civil War left England without a monarchy before its restoration less than two decades later. England emerged as an important world power by the early 1700s and the 1800 Act of Union united Britain and Ireland. Great Britain was the world's premier power throughout the 19th century and ruled a vast empire with large territories on several continents. The country emerged exhausted but victorious from both world wars. Britain's vast colonial empire was gradually relinquished in the decades after the

The exact history of Stonehenge remains a mystery.

The picturesque ruins of Eilean Donan Castle in the Scottish Highlands.

Second World War and Queen Elizabeth II was crowned in 1952. The country is now a member of NATO and the EU.

Economy: Britain was the world's first industrialized nation and the leading trading nation throughout much of the 19th century. The country experienced a painful transition during the 1970s and 80s as it shifted from a manufacturing to a services-based economy. The United Kingdom enjoyed stable growth throughout most of the 1990s and London is one of the world's most important financial services and banking centers. The country has a small but productive agricultural sector. The diverse service sector produces more than 70% of the country's GDP and provides employment for most of the population. Recent reforms target the health and education sector.

London is Western Europe's largest city and one of the world's great cultural centers. The hectic and cosmopolitan city is home to 7.6 million people, including a large immigrant population. **1** Trafalgar Square and Nelson's Square are reminders of Britain's past as a great imperial power. **2** The Tower Bridge is the city's most famous bridge. **3** Westminster Bridge, Big Ben and the Houses of Parliament. **4** Central London is a leading center of international finance and business.

With an area of 44.7 million sq km – about one third of the earth's overall landmass – and more than 3 billion inhabitants, Asia is the biggest, most populous continent.

Mighty mountain ranges such as those of the Pamir, Karakorum, the Hindu Kush and the Himalayas with the highest mountains in the world (Mt. Everest, 8,846 m) divide the continent into the continental – sub-polar North Asia, and the tropical – sub-tropical South Asia. Asia's flora and fauna are as varied as its climate. Vegetation ranges from the mosses and lichens of the tundra to the world's oldest rain forest in Malaysia. Polar foxes, elks, reindeer, camels, elephants, rhinoceroses, orangutans and tigers are representative of the fauna in the various biotopes.

The scope of the continent's peoples, cultures, languages and religions is impressive: Judaism and Christianity, Islam, Buddhism, Hinduism, and the philosophies of Confucius and Lao-Tse originated in Asia.

Nations of the World
Asia

Afghānistān
Afghanistan

Area: 652,225 sq km
Population: 28.5 million
GDP per capita: 400 US$
Capital: Kabul
Government: Republic
Languages: Pushtu, Dari
Currency: 1 afghani = 100 puls

Geography: The mountainous interior, with a large part of the Hindu Kush and pass summits of up to 4,000 m, features steppes and gravel deserts with only sparse vegetation. Great climatic differences exist in a relatively limited space, ranging from arid to subtropical and alpine climates depending on altitude. Tourist destinations include the Islamic buildings in Ghazni, the Caliph Mausoleums in Kabul and the pilgrimage sites of Kandahar and Mazar-e Sharif.

Politics: Settled by Iranian tribes since the 2nd millennium BC, Afghanistan has been under a succession of foreign dominations. The Afghan Emirate, established in 1747, later came under English influence. In 1919 it became a kingdom independent of Great Britain, and in 1973 a republic. The civil war from 1979 to 1992 and the struggle against the Russian army on its own soil to 1989 have brought lasting changes; the radical Islamist Taliban gained increasing influence from 1994. Their terror regime was overthrown at the end of 2001 in an offensive by the US and the Afghan Northern Alliance.

Economy: Afghanistan is one of the poorest countries in the world. Agriculture and fruit cultivation is practiced in the irrigated valleys, and livestock breeding in the mountain areas. Natural resources include coal, lapis lazuli, petroleum and natural gas. The continuous fighting has wreaked enormous damage on the economy – more than three quarters of the industrial plants lie in ruins today.

Al-Bahrain
Bahrain

Area: 665 sq km
Population: 699,000
GDP per capita: 26,000 US$
Capital: Al-Manama
Government: Emirate
Language: Arabic
Currency: 1 Bahrain dinar = 1,000 fils

Geography: The Emirate in the Persian Gulf is composed of 33 islands, 13 of which are inhabited. Bahrain, the main island, has a desert-like landscape with expansive salt marshes and sand dunes, whilst the archipelago enjoys a mild desert climate. Artesian wells permit oasis agriculture in the northern coastal area. Tourism is concentrated in the capital Al-Manama.

Politics: The city of Dilmun was a trading hub as early as the 3rd century BC. Occupied by the Portuguese in the 16th century and later by the Persians, the emirate was a British protectorate from 1816 to 1971 and joined the Arab League after declaring independence in 1971. The Emir in power since 1999 has ushered in political reforms including a constitution (in force since 2002), making the country a constitutional monarchy.

Economy: The rich petroleum reserves discovered in 1932 have provided a solid base for the country's economy, with the oil and gas sector generating 80% of exports but only 2% of employment. Because of the climatic conditions, the agricultural sector accounts for only 1% of GDP, whilst industry contributes 14%. The services sector (banking) plays an important role as part of diversification, anticipating the end of the oil reserves.

Al-Kuwait
Kuwait

Area: 17,820 sq km
Population: 2.4 million
GDP per capita: 34,000 US$

The Blue Mosque in Mazar-e Sharif, Afghanistan.

Capital: Kuwait City
Government: Emirate
Language: Arabic
Currency: 1 Kuwait dinar = 100 dirhams = 1,000 fils

Geography: This emirate on the Persian Gulf consists of dry steppes and sandy deserts. Summers inland are extremely hot and dry, while the more humid coastal areas have some of the lowest precipitation on the planet. Destinations include the old town of Kuwait City as well as the Island of Faylakah (holiday facilities with beaches). The 1991 Gulf War left ecological devastation in its wake.

Politics: A British protectorate from 1899, Kuwait gained independence in 1961. Executive power lies with the Emir, a member of the Al Sabbah dynasty that has reigned since 1756, and has been elected by it; a house of representatives, elected in 1996, enjoys limited powers. Invaded and occupied by Iraq in 1990, Kuwait was freed by allied forces in the (first) Gulf War in early 1991.

Economy: 62% of the people living and working in Kuwait come from neighboring countries. Because of the terrain, agricultural use is limited to only 0.2% of the overall area where there is coastal irrigation. Most food is imported. Oil, drilled in Kuwait since 1946, accounts for the country's wealth. Kuwait has many large-scale oil harbors. Shrimps also form an important export. Kuwait does not levy taxes or social security contributions.

Al-Lubnān
Lebanon

Area: 10,452 sq km
Population: 3.8 million
GDP per capita: 6,500 US $
Capital: Beirut
Government: Republic
Languages: Arabic (official), French
Currency: 1 Lebanese pound = 100 piasters

Geography: Dominated by mountain ranges on the eastern edge of the Mediterranean, the country has only a narrow, fertile coastal strip, with a Mediterranean climate in this region and a continental climate in the hinterland, with high snowfalls in the winter. Tourist destinations include Baalbek (excavations of Roman sites), the old harbor city of Beirut and Tripoli.

1 The Orient's bazaars arose in the era of the caravans. Many are multi-storey commercial buildings with large courtyards, the market quarter of an Oriental city.

2 The emirate of Kuwait has become one of the richest Persian Gulf states by exporting petroleum and natural gas.

3 Boomtown Beirut: The Comanche, the famous promenade along the Mediterranean coast, is now marked by skyscrapers with shops, offices and restaurants. In the civil war of 1975-1976 the city was almost completely razed; though the situation is still tense, economic development is positive.

Nations of the World
Asia

Politics: After the end of the Ottoman Empire, Lebanon came under a French mandate in 1920 until it gained independence in 1944. Since 1958 it has been continuously shaken by external political crises and internal conflicts, attributable to the overall Middle East conflict. After a peace treaty with neighboring Syria, Lebanon is also negotiating a comprehensive peace settlement with Israel.

Economy: The country's economic fabric and infrastructure was almost completely destroyed by the civil war. Agriculture covers only part of the country's needs. Fruit and vegetables are grown on the irrigated land on the coast. Industry is limited to products for domestic consumption. Services are the largest contributor to GDP. Tourism will need some time to recover after the July War (2006) where it was used again as a scapegoat for the uncanny incompetence of the Arab world.

Al-Mamlaka al-'Arabiya as-Sa'ūdiya
Saudi Arabia

Area: 1,960,582 sq km
Population: 27 million
GDP per capita: 15,000 US$
Capital: Riyadh
Government: Islamic absolute monarchy, largely influenced by the Al Saud Family with 6,000 members
Language: Arabic
Currency: 1 Saudi riyal = 20 qirshes = 100 hallalas

Geography: The country's territory, covering a large part of the Arabian Peninsula, features stony and sandy deserts traversed by wadis, in a hot and dry climate. The only natural vegetation is found in the oases. Tourist destinations are restricted almost entirely to pilgrimages to holy sites.

Politics: The history of Saudi Arabia begins with the Prophet Mohammed, who in the 7th century not only founded the new religion of Islam, but also united various Arab tribes. The Ottomans conquered the north and west of the peninsula, as well as the holy sites, in the 16th century. The ruling Saud dynasty, still in power today, founded the Islamic State of the Wahhabites in the 18th century. The Kingdom of Saudi Arabia was proclaimed in 1932.

Economy: More than three quarters of the almost exclusively Muslim population live in the cities. A small proportion engage in nomadic livestock breeding, 13% generate nearly one-tenth of GDP through agriculture. The petroleum and natural gas reserves in the Persian Gulf make Saudi Arabia the world's largest oil exporter.

Al-Yaman
Yemen

Area: 527,970 sq km
Population: 21.5 million
GDP per capita: 1,000 US$
Capital: Sanaa
Government: Republic
Languages: Arabic (official), English
Currency: 1 Yemeni rial = 100 fils

Geography: Yemen lies at the south-western edge of the Arab peninsula. North Yemen occupies a sandy, flat coastal strip on the Red Sea, behind which rise craggy highlands meeting the Rub al-Khali desert. Ample monsoon rain falls on the highlands. South Yemen extends behind a narrow, coastal area with high rainfall to meet a mountain plateau, giving way to the sandy desert in the north. The country enjoys a tropical desert climate. The preferred tourist destinations are the numerous Islamic sites and a great many of ancient sights of the Kingdom of Sheba.

Saudi Arabia: The Ka'bah in Mecca, the religious center of the Islam world.

Politics: In pre-Christian times, Yemen belonged to the Kingdom of the Minoans and Shebans. In the 7th century it was conquered by the Abbasids, and in the 16th century became part of the Ottoman Empire. Under British control, the Kingdom of Yemen was created in 1918 in Northern Yemen, and became a republic in 1962 after a coup d'état. A socialist republic was created in South Yemen in 1967. The tortuous process of unification to the Republic of Yemen lasted from 1990 to 1994. In 1999 for the first time the head of the state was appointed by free elections.

Economy: Yemen is one of the most underdeveloped countries in the world. Agriculture is still the most important economic sector. Nomadic livestock breeders roam the hinterland. Industrialization is still in its infancy, with the export of oil from

farmlands and a favorable climate. Owing to the continental climate, steppe and semi-desert vegetation dominate. Armenia frequently suffers earthquakes and drought.

Politics: In the 7th century Turks and Persians contested the country; in the 19th century, Russia's attempt at conquest was repulsed. In 1922 Armenia was divided, with a part becoming a Soviet Republic, and the other part remaining with Turkey. Armenia declared its inde-

reserves developed in 1984 and 1993 playing the most important role.

Armenija (Hayastan)
Armenia

Area: 29,800 sq km
Population: 3 million
GDP per capita: 2,300 US$
Capital: Yerevan
Government: Republic
Languages: Armenian (official), Russian, Kurdish
Currency: 1 dram = 100 luma

Geography: The Ararat highlands extend to the west, with the peaks of the Lesser Caucasus in the north. The central depression in the south-east is dominated by Lake Sevan. The south has fertile

1 Traditional dress is becoming rare in modern Yemen, but the veil is still an important part of women's clothing.

2 Yemen's capital Sana, its largest city (population 950,000), enclosed by high walls, has magnificent architecture including the Great Mosque of al-

Kebir. Richly decorated house fronts are the rule. The city is a flourishing commercial and market center.

3 Much of the Geghard Monastery in Armenia is medieval, hewn out of the rocks; the monastery played a key role in the Christianization of Armenia as early as the 4th century.

pendence in 1991, but retained the socialist-tinted constitution. The enclave of Nagorno Karabakh has in recent times been the object of conflict with Armenia's Islamic neighbor Azerbaijan.

Economy: The economy is characterized by the difficult transition from the Soviet planned economy to a market economy. Half of GDP is generated by industry, only a fifth by services. Important exports are light industry products. The country imports oil, gas and foodstuffs. The country will need some time to achieve economic success.

Azerbajdzan
Azerbaijan

Area: 86,600 sq km
Population: 7.9 million
GDP per capita: 3,700 US$
Capital: Baku
Government: Republic
Languages: Azeri (official), Turkish, Russian
Currency: 1 manat = 100 gepik

Geography: Over half the country's area is covered by the Greater Caucasus (4,466 m) in the north, the Lesser Caucasus with Karabakh in the west, and the southern mountains extending to Iran. The plains of the Kura and Arax rivers in the east are bordered by the Caspian Sea in the south. The climate ranges from subtropical and humid to arid-dry. Large-scale irrigation is necessary for agriculture.

Politics: A settlement in early times, the area was briefly a Roman province. Islamization commenced in the 7th century. After 300 years of Mongol rule, Azerbaijan was besieged first by the Ottomans and then by the Russians, who in 1813 divided the country with the Persians. The

Soviet Republic of Azerbaijan was founded in 1920. Ethnic conflicts over the Nagorno Karabakh enclave and its annexation by Armenia in 1988 led to the declaration of independence and a more pronounced turn towards Islam.

Economy: The economy concentrates on wine-making, cotton, tobacco, vegetables, olives and tea. Canned fish products from the Caspian Sea (caviar) are exported. The country's real wealth, however, lies in its mineral resources such as oil, iron ore, copper and manganese. These resources form the basis of the remaining industry (chemical, mechanical engineering). The main oil fields lie in the Apseron peninsula and near Baku.

Bahrain see Al-Bahrain

Bangladeshis call their country "Golden Bengal".

Bangladesh
Bangladesh

Area: 144,000 sq km
Population: 147 million
GDP per capita: 500 US$
Capital: Dhaka

Government: Republic
Languages: Bengali (official), Urdu and Hindi
Currency: 1 taka = 100 poisha

Geography: The entire country consists of fertile lowlands in a monsoon region with high rainfall; the unprotected coast with few harbors is threatened by flooding, often with catastrophic consequences. The south-west at the Indian border comprises part of the flood plains of the Ganges and Brahmaputra. Tourist destinations include Dhaka with its interesting old town, and the coastal city of Chittagong for swimming. Part of the Sundarban National Park, with unique fauna, is on Bangladeshi territory.

Politics: The former Bengal belonged to the British colony of India (1757-1947). In the division that followed Indian independence, West Bengal remained part of India, whereas East Bengal went to Pakistan. After bloody riots following the great flood of 1970, East Bengal separated from Pakistan, and the Republic of Bangladesh was declared in 1971. After 15 years of authoritarian presidential rule, characterized by frequent coups d'état, the first democratically elected government took office in 1991. Relations with neighboring India have visibly improved in recent years.

Economy: The education system has been seriously neglected, and only one fourth of the population is literate. One of the poorest national economies in the world, Bangladesh relies essentially on agriculture, which employs 66% of the working population in small companies and generates one third of GDP. The most important exports are rice, jute and seafood. 12% of the workforce are employed in industry, comprising small handicraft concerns (jute products, cotton yarn and fabrics, textiles, sugar and tea), and generating about one third of GDP. Heavy industry processes the available raw materials (natural gas, oil, coal and ores) but is of minor importance.

Bhutan
Bhutan

Area: 47,000 sq km
Population: 2.2 million
GDP per capita: 2,000 US$
Capital: Thimphu
Government: Constitutional monarchy
Languages: Dzongkha (official), Tibetan dialects
Currency: 1 ngultrum = 100 chetrum

Geography: The small kingdom on the southern incline of the Himalayas is accessible only with extreme difficulty. The mighty mountain chains (Jomo Lhari, 7,314 m) flank the high plateau, which slopes down only gradually to the southern foothills on the Indian border. Interesting destinations include the monasteries and temples in the vicinity of the capital.

Politics: In a country initially ruled by Indian princes, Tibetan conquerors founded a lamaist state in the 9th century. In the wake of 19th century civil wars, a hereditary monarchy emerged under British influence, which today governs the land together with the National Assembly (parliament of estates). There is close cooperation with India over foreign affairs and defense.

Economy: Nearly half of GDP is generated by agriculture, which also accounts for 90% of all jobs and covers domestic needs. A few products (maize, wheat, cardamom) are also exported. Wood from the extensive forest areas is exported to India. The poorly developed industrial sector consists of small handicraft concerns (weaving, metalwork, mask carving). Bhutan has been open to tourism to a limited extent since 1974, and the 5,000 annual tourists are the most important source of foreign currency. Technical and mechanical work traditionally occupies a lowly status.

1 Narrow lanes lead through the historical terraced district of Azerbaijan's capital Baku.

2 In the Kingdom of Bhutan, temples are not only places of worship but also administrative centers for the small country. The picture shows the 17th-century Paro Dzong.

3 Bhutan: The state religion in Bhutan, the kingdom on the southern slopes of the eastern Himalayas, is lamaism – Tibetan-style Buddhism. The picture shows a monk from the Taktshag Monastery, Gomchen. The wooden beads help the memory in prayers and recitations from the Scriptures.

Nations of the World
Asia

Brunei
Brunei

Area: 5,765 sq km
Population: 379,000
GDP per capita: 32,000 US$
Capital: Bandar Seri Begawan
Government: Sultanate
Languages: Malay (official), English
Currency: 1 Brunei dollar = 100 cents

Geography: The Sultanate of Brunei comprises two non-adjoining territories on the northern coast of Borneo, surrounded by the Malaysian Sarawak mountains. The hill country, covered by tropical rain forests, is the habitat of a rich fauna. The densely settled coast consists of alluvial land with mangrove forests, broken by coral sand beaches. The country has an equatorial rainy climate. The capital (old town, Sultan's palace and mosque) is worth visiting.

Politics: Muslim Malays founded the Sultanate of Brunei in the 15th century, which became a British protectorate in 1888. After Japanese occupation in 1941-1945, it became a British colony until the constitution of 1959, which initially guaranteed autonomy. Brunei finally gained independence in 1984. Enthroned in 1967, the Sultan took over the affairs of state in 1973, and has reigned as an absolute monarch since 1984, supported by a Council. He is one of the world's richest men. The country has no political parties and no suffrage.

Economy: Islam plays an important role in the life of the predominantly Malay population, which, owing to the country's enormous riches, enjoys full social protection. Agriculture is of subordinate importance. A large part of the foodstuffs are imported. Brunei has extensive petroleum and natural gas reserves.

Cambodia see Kampuchea
China see Zhongguo

Choson
Korea, Democratic
People's Republic

Area: 120,538 sq km
Population: 22.2 million
GDP per capita: 1,000 US$
Capital: Pyongyang
Government: People's democracy
Language: Korean
Currency: 1 won = 100 chon

Geography: The country covers the north of the Korean peninsula and a part of the Asian mainland. It is largely mountainous with peaks of up to 2,541 m (Gwammo), but be-

Kim Il Sung Stadium, Pyongyang, holds 100,000 people.

comes considerably flatter to the south-west. It has a cool, moderate monsoon climate. The country's flora and fauna have been seriously affected by industrialization. Primary destinations for the scarcely developed tourist trade are Pyongyang and the old capital of Kaesong.

Politics: Owing to the country's geographic location, the history of Korea has always been influenced by the tensions between China and Japan. After the Japanese occupation (1910-1945), the north of the country was occupied by Soviet troops, and the Democratic People's Republic was established in 1948. The conflict with South Korea reached a climax during the Korean War (1950-1953). Initially close to China and the Soviet Union, the country has become increasingly isolated.

Economy: The country has a Socialist planned economy. 65% of the population live in cities. Agriculture, which employs 34% of the workforce population and generates 20% of GDP, produces staples (rice, corn, potatoes) for domestic consumption. 7% of the industrial production is state run. The industrial sector generates two thirds of GDP; main branches include heavy industry, food, textiles, and increasingly the electrical goods industry. Reasons for the food shortages include poor planning and enormous arms spending, which led to a serious famine in 1997.

Daulat al-Imārāt
al-'Arabiya Al-Muttahida
United Arab
Emirates

Area: 82,880 sq km
Population: 2.6 million
GDP per capita: 43,000 US$
Capital: Abu Dhabi
Government: Federation of independent sheikdoms
Language: Arabic (official)
Currency: 1 dirham = 100 fils

Geography: The flat, coastal strip on the Persian Gulf is followed by salty clay plains inland, which meet the extensive dunes of Rub' al-

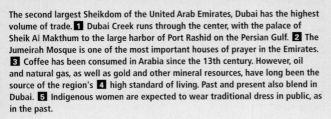

The second largest Sheikdom of the United Arab Emirates, Dubai has the highest volume of trade. **1** Dubai Creek runs through the center, with the palace of Sheik Al Makthum to the large harbor of Port Rashid on the Persian Gulf. **2** The Jumeirah Mosque is one of the most important houses of prayer in the Emirates. **3** Coffee has been consumed in Arabia since the 13th century. However, oil and natural gas, as well as gold and other mineral resources, have long been the source of the region's **4** high standard of living. Past and present also blend in Dubai. **5** Indigenous women are expected to wear traditional dress in public, as in the past.

Nations of the World
Asia

Khali. On the eastern border, the Al-Hajar mountains rise to 1,100 m. Vegetation in this hot, dry climate is possible only in the irrigated coastal area. The chief tourist destination is the Emirate of Sharjah.

Politics: The seven sheikdoms of Abu Dhabi, Dubai, Sharjah, Ajman, Umm-el-Qaiwain, Fudjaira und Ras' al-Khaimah became a British protectorate in the 19th century. When the British withdrew, the emirates formed a federation in 1971. The seven emirates have constituted the Upper Council since the adoption of the constitution (1975), electing one of their number as president.

Economy: Three quarters of the inhabitants are migrant workers from the Indian subcontinent. Agriculture plays only a subordinate role, and contributes 2.5% to GDP. Oil has been drilled in the Persian Gulf since 1962. This industry employs 2% of the working population, and generates 40% of GDP. The modest processing industries produce textiles, leather goods and clothing.

East Timor see Timor-Leste

Gruzija (Sakartvelo)
Georgia

Area: 69,700 sq km
Population: 4.7 million
GDP per capita: 2,400 US$
Capital: Tbilisi (Tiflis)
Government: Republic
Languages: Georgian (official), Russian, Ar
Currency: Lari

Geography: The western border is formed by the Black Sea coast, which runs into the Kura lowlands. The climate here is sub-tropical and humid. The north is dominated by the southern slope of the

Greater Caucasus (Kasbe 5,033 m). The country extends into part of the Lesser Caucasus in the south. To the east of Tbilisi, the country is characterized by dry forests in an increasingly continental climate, becoming grassy steppe. In addition to 15 nature reserves, winter sports and hiking regions, towns such as Suchumi and Batumi on the Black Sea coast are very popular. Important historic sites are at Kutaisi and Mzcheta.

Politics: After the Roman era (from 65 BC), the country became part of the Byzantine Empire in the 4th century. In the 14th century it came under Mongol rule. Following the division of the country between the Ottomans, Persians and Russians (1555), an Eastern Georgian Kingdom was founded in the 18th century and annexed by the Russian Empire (1801-1810). Georgia declared its independence in 1918, and the Soviet Socialist Republic of Georgia was founded in 1921. Since independence (1991), efforts

The 13th-century Metechi Church in Georgia's capital Tblisi.

towards autonomy by the Islam-oriented Republics of Abkhazia and South Ossetia have led to warring confrontations. Ethnic conflicts hamper the peace process.

Economy: Most of the agricultural land consists of grain, beet and potato fields. In addition, tropical fruits, tea, tobacco, grapes and wine are cultivated, with eucalyptus, bamboo and bay trees on the coast. Mining yields coal, copper, manganese, barite, diatomite and semi-precious stones. The processing industry produces foodstuffs and textiles. Chief exports are raw materials and foodstuffs. A third of the population lives from the traditionally important sector of tourism.

India (Bhărat)
India

Area: 3,287,263 sq km
Population: 1.095 billion
GDP per capita: 1,000 US$
Capital: New Delhi
Government: Republic
Languages: Hindi, English
Currency: 1 Indian rupee = 100 paisa

Geography: The Indian subcontinent is divided into three regions; the mountain area of the Himalayas follows the plain of the Indus and the Ganges, which in the south rises to a plateau crossed by rivers, whose coasts are hemmed by

1 New Delhi, Delhi's southern district, has been the capital of India since 1947. The city was planned in the 1930s. More than 7 million people live here, many of them below the poverty line. Old Delhi was the centre of the Sultanate of Delhi from the 13th to the 16th century, and boasts beautiful palaces and mosques that are masterpieces of Islamic architecture. Shah Jahan, the uncle of the great Moghul Akbar and builder of the Taj Mahal, built the **2** Friday Mosque in the 17th century, and also shaped Delhi's cityscape with other buildings. **3** The India Gate in the government district was built during the British colonial period. **4** The 72-meter-high Qutar Minar minaret at the Quwwat al-Islam Mosque, built by a Ghurid ruler around 1200 AD.

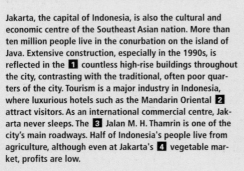

Jakarta, the capital of Indonesia, is also the cultural and economic centre of the Southeast Asian nation. More than ten million people live in the conurbation on the island of Java. Extensive construction, especially in the 1990s, is reflected in the **1** countless high-rise buildings throughout the city, contrasting with the traditional, often poor quarters of the city. Tourism is a major industry in Indonesia, where luxurious hotels such as the Mandarin Oriental **2** attract visitors. As an international commercial centre, Jakarta never sleeps. The **3** Jalan M. H. Thamrin is one of the city's main roadways. Half of Indonesia's people live from agriculture, although even at Jakarta's **4** vegetable market, profits are low.

wide plains. The climate is subtropical to tropical. In addition to nature reserves with a rich variety of fauna, India has countless cultural and historical monuments.

Politics: Aryan nomads displaced the Indus civilization from the 15th century BC. The Islamization of India began in the 12th century AD. The advance of the Europeans in the beginning of the 16th century led to the weakening of the Mogul rulers. In 1858 India was brought directly under the British crown. The struggle for independence started at the end of the 19th century, and inspired Mahatma Gandhi's movement after World War I. After Islamic Pakistan broke away, India finally gained independence in 1950. Although the country has enjoyed relative political stability since then, the conflict with Pakistan over Kashmir continues to the present day.

Economy: The caste system dominates the life of the population. Three fourths of the inhabitants live from agriculture, generating some 32% of GDP. India is the world's number one tea exporter, and second largest exporter of dairy produce. The rich natural resources, which are little exploited, constitute the basis for the largely state-owned heavy industry. India has highly developed weapons, nu-clear and space exploration industries. Tourism is an important branch of the services sector (40% of GDP) and is likely to increase in the coming years.

Government: Presidential republic
Languages: Indonesian (official), Javanese, other
Currency: 1 rupiah = 100 sen

Geography: More than 13,600 islands, about half of which are inhabited, span the Equator in a 5,000 km arc. Over half the overall area is covered by forests, and the lowland plains of Sumatra and Borneo

Indonesia
Indonesia

Area: 1,919,440 sq km
Population: 245.4 million
GDP per capita: 2,000 US$
Capital: Jakarta

1 Rice is the principle staple throughout South-East Asia, although its cultivation, unchanged for centuries, is labor-intensive and toilsome; the seedlings must be planted and the crops harvested by hand. Weeds flourish in the wet, fertile rice paddies and ducks are used to keep them down.

2 Dasashwamedh Ghat in Varanasi is one of the seven holy places of the Hindu religion. Here the faithful gather to perform cleansing rituals in the River Ganges.

3 Char Minar Gate in Hyderabad, historic capital of the Indian state of Andhra Pradesh.

also feature extensive marsh and freshwater swamp forests. The climate is tropical and always humid. Indonesia is a popular tourist destination, especially Bali, the main island of Java, with Borobudur Temple and the Lesser Sunda islands.

Politics: In early times, the country was under Hindu and Buddhist influence, becoming Islamic in the 13th century, with the exception of Hindu Bali. The Dutch conquered the entire archipelago in the 16th – 19th century to control the spice trade. In World War II, Japan occupied the Dutch East Indies, which became independent in 1949 as the Republic of Indonesia. The country's history since then has been characterized by unrest and military coups. The military hold extensive power, and occupy several seats in the unicameral government.

Economy: The multiethnic state is predominantly inhabited by Malays,

plantations for export. Other important exports include wood, rattan and copal from the rain forest regions. Rich ore, mineral, oil and natural gas reserves form the basis of the highly developed heavy industry, solely directed to export.

Îrân
Iran

Area: 1,648,000 sq km
Population: 68 million
GDP per capita: 4,200 US$
Capital: Teheran
Government: Islamic republic
Languages: Farsi (official), Luri, Balochi, Kurdish
Currency: 1 rial = 100 dinar

Geography: Iran, between the Caspian Sea and the Persian Gulf, is bordered to the north by the Elburz Mountains (up to 5,064 meters high), and the Zagros Mountains to the south. The arid highlands in the interior meet the Lût Desert in the east. In addition to the

Iranians in the 2nd millennium BC, who established the first Persian empire in the 6th century. Islamization began with the Arab conquest in the 7th century AD. In 1907 Russia and Great Britain divided the country into areas of influence. Extensive western-style reforms were introduced by Shah Pahlewi from 1925. The Islamic Revolution (1978) led to the flight of the Shah and the establishment of the Islamic Republic.

Economy: Only 10% of the area is used for agriculture through artificial irrigation. In addition to wheat, barley, vegetables and sugar beet, tobacco, tea, pistachios and dates are grown for export; the Caspian Sea yields caviar, whitefish and ray. The country's heavy industry is based on the rich petroleum and natural gas reserves, together with coal, copper, nickel and chromium mining, and accounts for 85% of exports.

'Irāq
Iraq

Area: 438,072 sq km
Population: 26.7 million
GDP per capita: 1,800 US$
Capital: Baghdad
Government: Presidential republic
Language: Arabic
Currency: 1 Iraqi dinar = 1,000 fils

Geography: The heartland of the country in the north-east of the Arabian Peninsula is formed by the floodplain of the Tigris and Euphrates rivers, which turns into desert to the west. There is a narrow access route to the Persian Gulf in the south-east. The sites of ancient Mesopotamia are of immense cultural importance.

Curving rice terraces, a familiar sight on Bali.

with Polynesian-Melanesian peoples in the eastern islands. More than half of the population work in agriculture, producing rice, corn, cassava and sweet potatoes for domestic consumption, and coffee, cocoa, tea and rubber from the

pilgrim cities of Qom and Masshad, popular destinations include the ancient ruins of Persepolis and the royal mosque in Isfahan.

Politics: The country's chequered history began with its settlement by

Politics: Mesopotamia was founded in the 3rd millennium BC by the

Sumerians; in the 2nd-1st millennium BC, the area was ruled by the Babylonians and Assyrians, and then conquered by the Persians in the 6th century BC. In the 7th century AD, the country fell under the Arabo-Islamic sphere of influence; the Ottomans ruled from the 16th to the 19th century. The monarchy established by the British in 1921 was overthrown by a bloody coup in 1958. Under the dictatorial president Saddam Hussein (in power from 1979), Iraq waged war with Iran over the oil regions from 1980-1988. In 1990 Iraq annexed Kuwait. The result was the Second Gulf War (1991), which ended with the defeat of Iraq by the USA. The conflict with the USA escalated in 2002, with the USA accusing Iraq of holding concealed stocks of weapons of mass destruction. In 2003 the USA in conjunction with Great Britain and other states began a war which, within a short time, led to the end of the regime. In 2005 the first free elections for over 40 years were held, but the political situation remains unstable as before. Dozens fall victim to terrorist attacks daily.

Economy: Iraq has the third largest oil reserves in the world. Its recovery in the aftermath of the war remains slow and after decades of war economy new building is not making progress due to the difficult security situation.

Israel see Yi'sra'el
Japan see Nippon/Nihon
Jordan see Urdunn

Kâmpŭchéa
Cambodia

Area: 181,035 sq km
Population: 13.8 million
GDP per capita: 600 US$
Capital: Phnom Penh

Government: Constitutional monarchy
Languages: Khmer (official), Vietnamese
Currency: 1 riel = 10 kak = 100 sen

Geography: The lowlands of the Tônlé-Sap basin and the Mekong Delta are bounded to the north by the Dangrek mountain range, and to the south-west by the Cardamom mountains, sloping down to the

1 Women, heavily veiled in the Iranian tradition, prepare for Friday prayers in the courtyard of the Royal Mosque, Isfahan.

2 The magnificent mausoleum of Ayatollah Khomeini, founder of the "Islamic Republic", in south Teheran – a shrine and place of pilgrimage.

3 Despite the friendly smile of this Baghdad trader, the economic situation and supplies for the Iraqi people are devastated after two Gulf Wars, a trade embargo and the 2003 war. Reconstructing industry and infrastructure will take years; investment is likely to hold back until the continuing outbreaks of violence abate.

Nations of the World
Asia

Gulf of Thailand. In the tropical, humid climate, vegetation ranges from mangrove forest swamps on the coast to monsoon forests in the central region and rain forests in the mountains. The most important destination is Angkor, the former capital of the old Khmer Empire.

Politics: The Khmer Empire was established in the 7th century and was overrun in the 17th century after repeated attacks by neighboring countries. In 1867 it was occupied by the French and incorporated into the Union of Indochina. The country gained independence in 1964. The civil war triggered in 1970 by the Indochina conflict was won by the communist forces of the Khmer Rouge. In 1975,

the workforce, who, in addition to growing rice, cultivate soybeans, corn and pepper for export. Tobacco, seafood and valuable tropical hardwoods are also exported goods. The industrial sector comprises small companies and factories supplying the domestic market.

Kazahstan
Kazakhstan

Area: 2,717,300 sq km
Population: 15.2 million
GDP per capita: 6,900 US$
Capital: Astana
Government: Republic
Languages: Kazakh, Russian
Currency: 1 tenge = 100 tiin
Geography: Much of the country,

autonomous Socialist Republic was proclaimed in 1920 and joined the USSR in 1936, from which it again gained independence in 1991.

Economy: Grain, sugar beet, tobacco and fruit are cultivated by means of irrigation, with vineyards in the northern mountain areas. Large copper and iron deposits, oil and natural gas form the basis of the country's heavy industry.

Korea, Dem. Rep. see Choson
Republic of Korea see
Taehan-Min'guk
Kuwait see Al-Kuwait

Kyrgyzstan
Kyrghyzstan

Area: 198,500 sq km
Population: 5.2 million
GDP per capita: 700 US$
Capital: Biskek
Government: Presidential republic
Languages: Kyrghyz (official), Russian, minorities
Currency: 1 Kyrghyzstan som = 100 tyin

Geography: This Central Asian republic lies mostly in the Tianshan mountains. 50% of the landmass is at an altitude of over 3,000 m, with only the western and northern promontories falling under 1,200 m. At 3,000 m, the landscape turns from desert and semi-desert into mountain steppes, meadows and forests. The mountainous tundra lying beyond gives way to a glaciated region.

Luang Prabang, residence of the Buddhist leader of Laos.

they set up a terror regime, which was ended only when Vietnamese troops marched in. Despite free elections in 1993, the democratization process launched with the Vietnamese withdrawal and the introduction of a new constitution in 1989 has not stabilized to the present day.

Economy: Agriculture accounts for 50% of GDP and employs 85% of

which comprises extensive steppes and deserts and includes part of the Tianshan mountains in the south-east, has a continental, dry climate. The south-west border is formed by the Caspian Sea.

Politics: In the mid 18th century, the country, settled since the 6th century, came under Russian sovereignty, and was incorporated into the Czarist empire in 1873. The

Politics: The country, settled early by nomadic peasants and hunters, achieved modern statehood only after the October Revolution of 1917. The Soviet Socialist Republic (from 1936) proclaimed its independence from the USSR in 1991. The amendment of the 1993 constitution granted far-reaching powers to the head of state.

Economy: Agriculture, which is possible on only 7% of the area, is the most important sector of the economy. In addition to grain and fodder for the extensive livestock breeding, fruit, vegetables, cotton, hemp, poppies, oil-giving plants and tobacco are grown for export and for domestic consumption. Light industry is of great importance in this country with few natural resources.

Lao
Laos

Area: 236,800 sq km
Population: 6.3 million
GDP per capita: 700 US$
Capital: Vientiane
Government: People's republic
Languages: Lao (official), minorities
Currency: 1 kip

Geography: The country is bordered in the north by the Tramin Plateau which rises up to 2,820 m, and in the south by the Boloven Plateau, about 2,000 m high with a tropical monsoon climate. 40% of the area is covered by forests; dense deciduous forest gives way to rain forests at higher altitudes. The most important travel destination is Luang Prabang, but the diversity of landscapes in Central Laos or the Khmer temple Vat Phou in the south also attract travellers for discovery tours and trekkings.

Politics: Buddhism was introduced in the 14th century with the establishment of the first Laotian Kingdom. After occupation by the Thais, Laos became a French protectorate in the 19th century and gained independence in 1954. During the Vietnam War, Com-munist revolutionary troops overran large parts of the country. The last king abdicated in 1975.

Economy: Around 78% of the population work in agriculture, which accounts for 57% of GDP. A large part of the arable land comprises rice fields. Wood such as rattan and bamboo is felled for export.

 Many Kazakhs are hunters or nomad herders and still hunt with eagles today.

 Angkor has the largest complex of buildings in South-East Asia, the Angkor Vat temple from the 12th century. From the 9th – 15th centuries, the city was the religious and political center of Hindus and Buddhists in the Khmer Empire, today known as Cambodia.

 A Kyrgyz family gathers for dinner. Family life is important for the Kyrgyz since many retain the clan-focused nomadic lifestyle. Three-quarters of the population are Muslims, and one-quarter Russian Orthodox.

Special
Kuala Lumpur

The Malaysian capital Kuala Lumpur stands witness to an eventful colonial past – the Portuguese, Dutch and British vied for a foothold on the trade route to the Far East. In 1957, the Malaysian national flag was hoisted on **1** the former cricket grounds of Dataran Merdeka as a sign of independence. The British colonial administration built the **2** Suntan Abdul Samad Palace in a fascinatingly eclectic style in 1897. Exactly 100 years later, the **3** Petronas Twin Towers were completed – the tallest building in the world, standing 452 meters high.

Lebanon see Al-Lubnān

Malaysia
Malaysia

Area: 329,758 sq km
Population: 24.3 million
GDP per capita: 7,000 US$
Capital: Kuala Lumpur
Government: Constitutional elected monarchy in the Commonwealth
Languages: Malay (official), Chinese, Tamil, Iban, English
Currency: 1 Malay ringgit = 100 sen

Geography: Malaysia extends over the southern part of the Malacca Peninsula and the north-west part of the island of Borneo 600 km away, separated by the China Sea. The predominantly mountainous country is largely covered by evergreen tropical rain forests, which flourish in lush abundance in the hot and humid climate with average temperatures of 27° C. Flora and fauna are highly varied. With many beaches, nature reserves and cities such as Kuala Lumpur or Malacca, Malaysia has a host of tourist destinations.

Politics: Malaysia was created in 1963 from the union of newly independent principalities on the Malacca peninsula, the British territories of Sabah and Sarawak, Borneo and Singapore, which however left the union two years later. The country is governed by a king elected for a five-year term, who then appoints the head of government nominated by the lower house and also appoints some members of the upper house. The more influential lower house is elected directly for a five-year term.

Economy: Exported forestry and agricultural products such as tropi-

cal hardwoods, rubber, palm oil and coconut products have helped Malaysia gain an economic upswing. The country is also the world's leading producer of tin. The services sector, which has hitherto generated 20% of GDP, will gain in importance as the infra-structure of this emerging country expands.

Maldives (Divehi Rajje)
Maldives

Area: 298 sq km
Population: 359,000
GDP per capita: 3,000 US$
Capital: Malé

1 2 While Borneo's indigenous peoples, including the Penan and Dyak, retain traditional techniques such as blowpipe hunting, "Western" work and interests are part of life for the inhabitants of Kuala Lumpur (population approx. 1.2 million). The two sides have little in common besides being part of Malaysia.

3 Hardy plants like the coconut palm chiefly thrive in the sandy soil of the Maldives' 2,000-plus islands.

4 5 The Batu Caves in Malaysia are the scene of the most important Hindu festival, Thaipusam, attended by thousands of faithful in the tenth month of the Hindu calendar.

Government: Presidential republic in the Commonwealth
Languages: Divehi (official), English
Currency: 1 rufiyaa = 100 laari

Geography: The country's territory is divided into 19 atoll groups with about 2,000 islands, only about one tenth of which are inhabited. The tropical climate ensures an average annual temperature of 30° C. In contrast to the limited land fauna, there are many species of sea fauna in the coral reefs. The Maldives have a very well developed tourism industry, and boast a site of cultural and historical interest in the 17th century mosque in the capital Malé, as well as idyllic beaches.

Politics: The expansion of Islam, which has been the state religion since 1153, dates back to traveling Arab merchants of the 12th century. The British protectorate, on the other hand, which ruled from

Economy: One fourth of the population lives in the capital. Owing to soil conditions, agriculture can only cover domestic needs (coconuts and betel nuts, cassava, onions and chili peppers). Part of the fishing catches are processed for export, the second highest foreign currency earner after tourism. The Maldives have no railway, and cars only on Malé and Gan. The most important economic sector on the Maldives is tourism, with 20% of GDP.

Mongol Ard Uls
Mongolia

Area: 1,565,000 sq km
Population: 2.8 million
GDP per capita: 1,500 US$
Capital: Ulan Bator
Government: Republic
Languages: Mongolian (official), Kazakh, Russian, minorities
Currency:
1 tugrik = 100 mongo

taiga vegetation grows in the north-east. The mountain desert and steppe vegetation that dominates the remaining area gives way to the Gobi Desert in the south.

Politics: Settled early by nomadic horsemen, Mongolia was united in 1206 by Genghis Khan and formed the core of a large empire with Beijing as the center. After the fall of the Mongolian imperial dynasty in 1368, the country became insignificant and fell under Chinese rule. In 1911, Outer Mongolia separated from China. The People's Republic of Mongolia was created in 1924. In the wake of the collapse of the USSR, a multi-party system was introduced and the Republic of Mongolia founded in 1992. The country has a unicameral parliament.

Economy: The population consists predominantly of Mongols, followed by Kazakhs, Chinese and Russians. The transition from a socialist planned economy to a market economy has proved difficult. Traditional animal husbandry (goats, sheep, camels and horses) predominates, as only 1% of the area can be used for agriculture (grains, vegetables, feedstuffs). The rich coal, copper, molybdenum, gold and tin deposits are mined and form the basis of the industry. Tourism is almost non-existent; services account for 34% of GDP.

In agricultural Mongolia, the people primarily live from livestock breeding.

1887 until independence in 1965, had little influence on the state system. The 1975 constitution vests the directly elected president with extensive powers. There are no political parties or parliamentary supervisory authorities.

Geography: The country also known as Outer Mongolia is dominated in the west by the Altai mountains, up to 4,300 m in height and the Changai mountains (over 3,500 m). Highlands with peaks of 1,000-1,500 m cover the east, and

Muang Thai
Thailand

Area: 513,115 sq km
Population: 64.8 million
GDP per capita: 3,700 US$
Capital: Bangkok
Government: Constitutional monarchy
Languages: Thai (official), English, Chinese dialects
Currency: 1 baht = 100 stangs

The royal and political capital of
Bangkok on the Gulf of Thailand is a
treasure trove of Asian architecture.
1 The demonic-looking figures at
the Great Palace protect the "Emerald
Buddha" inside. **2** The buildings of
the royal palace are situated in the
center of Bangkok. **3** Skyscrapers
are reflected in the waters of the
Chao-Phraya River at night. **4** King
Rama I, the founder of the Chakri
Dynasty, built this palace at the end
of the 18th century.

Geography: The west of the country consists of foothills of the Southeast Asian central mountain range, which reaches as far as the Malacca peninsula. The fertile lowland plain running from north to south and watered by the Menam is the most densely populated area of the country. The Korat plateau lies to the east, sloping gently into the Mekong. Rain and monsoon forests flourish in the tropical climate, with high temperatures all year round. In addition to tourist sites like Pattaya and Phuket, Thailand boasts numerous cultural sights such as Ayutthaya and Sukhotai. Rare animals can be seen in the Khao-Yai National Park.

Politics: The Kingdom of Siam was founded in the 13th century. Bangkok became its capital in 1782. In the 19th century, Siam ceded areas to France and Great Britain, without being colonized itself. In 1932, a coup d'état led to a constitutional monarchy. The emergence of a modern state since the Second World War has been delayed time and again by unrest. A new constitution has been in force since 1998, vesting power in a bicameral parliament. The monarch is the head of state. 95% of Thais are Buddhists.

Economy: 80% of the population live outside the cities. Some 60% of the workforce are employed in agriculture, cultivating rice, corn, manioc, sugar cane and rubber. The country's main exports are rubber and tin. Illegal poppy growing is a not insignificant economic factor. In addition to foodstuffs, the industry produces paper, computer parts, building materials, and motor vehicles, and accounts for 40% of GDP. Tourism is the main branch of the services sector, contributing 50% of GDP.

Myanmar
Myanmar (Burma)

Area: 678,500 sq km
Population: 47.3 million
GDP per capita: 300 US$
Capital: Yangon
Government: Republic
Languages: Burmese (official), local languages
Currency: 1 kyat = 100 pyas

Geography: The land is surrounded by high mountains at the borders and opens up on the coast. The Arakan mountains in the southwest (Hkakabo Razi, 5,881 m), covered with virgin forest, are foothills of the Himalayas. The Irawadi river valley flows through a densely populated lowland plain to the east, irrigating the world's largest rice-growing region. Myanmar belongs to the tropical monsoon zone. Popular tourist destinations include the Buddhist monuments in Yangon and Pagan and the beautiful landscapes on the Shan Plateau.

Politics: Settled by Burmese invaders from China in the 8th century, the country was conquered by the Mongols in the 13th century. Power struggles between the Arakan and Ava empires ended in 1752 with the union of the entire country under a Burmese dynasty. Burma was under British rule from 1866 to 1948. In the civil war that followed after independence, the military emerged victorious and has hampered all attempts at democratization since 1962 under a succession of leaders.

Economy: The population is predominantly Buddhist. The leading economic sector is agriculture, the main products of which (rice, pulses, beans) are processed by the small-scale industrial sector for export. Forests yield hardwoods such as teak for export. Diamonds and natural gas reserves generate the highest export earnings. Illegal opium is grown in the area known as the Golden Triangle.

The magnificent Shwedagon Pagoda at Yangon, Myanmar.

Nepal
Nepal

Area: 140,800 sq km
Population: 28.2 million
GDP per capita: 400 US$
Capital: Kathmandu
Government: Constitutional monarchy
Languages: Nepali (official), Maithili, Bhojpuri
Currency: 1 Nepalese rupee = 100 paisa

Nepal's capital is also the center of a conurbation of some 800,000 inhabitants. **1** The stupa in Buddhanath is a Tibetan Buddhist temple. **2** The Nyatapola Temple in Bhaktapur was built in the 16th century. **3** The Krishna Temple in Patan. **4** The streets of Kathmandu unfurl the religion-dominated life of Nepal – the only land to have Hinduism as its official religion.

Nations of the World
Asia

Geography: Nepal consists of a narrow strip of land 853 km long and 160 km wide, on the southern slopes of the Central Himalayas. The flood plain of the Terai to the far south follows the Siwalik chain and the broad, medium-altitude Fore-Himalayas. The national territory ends in the north at the crest of the Himalayas with some of the world's highest peaks (Mt. Everest, 8,846 m). The core economic and social region is the Kathmandu Valley, extending through the Fore-Himalayas for 30 km in length and 25 km breadth. Increasing numbers of Himalayan trekking tours are beginning to take their toll on the environment.

Politics: The principalities and tribal societies in the Valley of Kathmandu were united for the first time in 1756 under the rule of the Gurkhas. From the beginning of the 19th century, Great Britain exercised its influence on the Nepalese government. A constitutional monarchy followed a change

have been permitted since 1990, with representatives running for election to the National Assembly every five years.

Economy: The Nepalese economy is based on the poorly developed agricultural production (livestock breeding). Gold, copper and iron ore deposits are mined and slate and limestone quarried for export. The modest industrial sector consists of textile companies, carpet weaving concerns, and brickworks, plus jute, tobacco and grain processing. Tourism is emerging as the leading economic sector.

Nippon/Nihon
Japan

Area: 377,801 sq km
Population: 127.3 million
GDP per capita: 34,000 US$
Capital: Tokyo
Government: Constitutional monarchy
Language: Japanese
Currency: 1 yen = 100 sen

less hot springs, there are also some 40 active volcanoes in this earthquake-prone country. Industrialization has almost completely destroyed the original natural landscapes. The extensive geographical area includes a variety of climates; the south is subtropical and hot, the north temperate and cool. Monsoon winds bring rain in summer, which falls as snow in winter. The numerous tourist destinations range from hot springs in the Beppu spa, to the ancient imperial cities of Nara and Kyoto and the metropolis Tokyo.

Politics: An early target for settlement, the country came under Chinese influence in the 6th-7th century, and was ruled by powerful warring clans from the 12th century. In the 16th – 19th century, under the rule of the Tokugawa Shogunate, Japan moved into international isolation. After the restoration of imperial power (1868), the country underwent industrialization. At the end of World War II, two American atomic bombs were dropped on Japan (Hiroshima, Nagasaki). A new constitution was introduced in 1947, and the emperor now is only a figurehead.

Economy: Japan is one of the richest industrialized nations in the world. Agriculture (grains, rice, tea, fruit and vegetables) is practiced primarily for domestic consumption. The northern island of Hokkaido is the centre of an extensive cattle breeding industry. Part of the fleet of this major fishing nation is stationed abroad. The highly developed industry of a country with little raw materials produces the most important export products: ships, cars, steel, computers, and artificial fibers and materials.

Breathtaking Fuji is Japan's highest mountain, at 3,776 m.

of dynasty in 1951. The democratic constitution of 1959 was replaced in 1962 by a markedly monarchist constitution. Civil war has raged for years between the government and Maoist rebels. Political parties

Geography: Japan's territory comprises some 4,100 mainly mountainous islands, the peaks of an underwater mountain range. The highest mountain is the volcano of Fuji (3,776 m); in addition to count-

Oman see Saltanat 'Uman

Tokyo and Yokohama lie on Tokyo Bay in the east of Japan's main island. **1** Home to eight million people, Tokyo is to the north of the Keihin industrial area, which includes Yokohama (3.3 million inhabitants) and Kawasaki (1.1 million). **2** Yokohama has one of Japan's most important export harbors. A symbol of the Japanese enthusiasm for technology: **3** the Shibuya District in Tokyo. **4** High-speed trains connect these business centers.

Nations of the World
Asia

Pākistān
Pakistan

Area: 803,940 sq km
Population: 165.8 million
GDP per capita: 900 US$
Capital: Islamabad
Government: Islamic republic
Languages: Urdu (official), English, Punjubi, Sindhi, other minority languages
Currency: 1 Pakistani rupee = 100 paisa

Geography: Pakistan is bounded to the north by part of the Himalayas, the Hindu Kush and Karakorum, and to the West by the mountains bordering Iran and Afghanistan. The eastern part of the country is taken up by the Indus basin. The country has a high-altitude climate in the mountains, and a dry hot to arid climate in the Indus basin. Only 4% of the area is wooded. In addition to Lahore, possible tourist destinations include the ancient sites of Mohenjodaro and the northern mountains.

Politics: Pakistan was created in 1947 by the partition of former British India. After a civil war, the eastern part split off in 1971 as Bangladesh. Not even free elections since 1988 have succeeded in bringing peace to the country, which has been torn by politically motivated acts of violence since its independence. Atomic bomb tests and the Kashmir conflict affect relations with neighboring India.

Economy: Agriculture, which employs some 50% of the population, generates 25% of GDP. A fifth of the land is used for agriculture. The Indus basin has one of the largest artificial irrigation systems in the world. In addition to wheat, cotton and sugar cane, the main product is rice. The industrial sector, which is gaining in importance, processes agricultural products for export.

Pilipinas
Philippines

Area: 300,000 sq km
Population: 89.4 million
GDP per capita: 1,600 US$
Capital: Manila
Government: Presidential republic
Languages: Filipino (official), Spanish, English
Currency: 1 Philippine peso = 100 centavos

Geography: The Philippines extend along the northern part of the Malaysian Archipelago. The predominantly mountainous islands are often hit by earthquakes and volcanic eruptions. The humid climate favors tropical forests, which have largely been replaced by grass savanna as a result of land clearing. Primary tourist destinations are the scenic areas and the capital Manila.

Politics: The Philippines were under Spanish rule from the 16th to the 19th century. The colony was transferred to the United States in the late 19th century and granted independence in 1946. A 30-year dictatorship that ruined the country's economy was overturned in 1986.

Economy: 45% of the population live from agriculture, cultivating grains, vegetables and coconut trees – the country is the world's biggest producer of coconut products. The rich natural resources (copper, nickel and petroleum) form the basis of a major industrial sector; high-tech electronic products generate the highest export revenues.

Qaṭar
Qatar

Area: 11,437 sq km
Population: 886,00
GDP per capita: 73,000 US$
Capital: Doha
Government: Emirate (Absolute monarchy)
Language: Arabic
Currency: 1 Qatar riyal = 100 dirham

Pakistan: The Wazir Khan Mosque in Lahore, built in 1634.

Geography: The small penins. country extends into the Persian Gulf from Arabia's east coast. Rolling hills about 100 m high are found only in the east of this otherwise flat country, which has a hot, dry desert climate.

Politics: The peninsula has been ruled by the al-Thani family since the 18th century. After interruptions by Ottoman (1872-1916) and British occupations (until 1971), members of the family have returned to reign over the stable country as a hereditary monarchy.

Economy: More than 50% of the population are migrant workers from neighboring Arab states. Social security, health and educa-

Geography: Oman's natural borders are the Gulf of Oman in the east, the Arabian Sea in the south, and the Rub' al-Khali Desert in the west. 15 km of fertile coast extend to the 3,000 meter-high Oman Mountains. The territory includes the Mussandam exclave, enabling Oman to control the Straits of Hormuz, the exit from the Persian Golf. Oman has an extreme desert climate, with temperatures of up to 50° C in summer, and a subtropical climate in the highlands. Monsoon rains fall in the south and west.

tion systems are good. Agriculture is insignificant; the majority of foodstuffs are imported. The economy as a whole is based on oil drilling; Qatar's natural gas reserves are thought to be the largest in the world.

Salţanat 'Umān
Oman

Area: 212,457 sq km
Population: 3.1 million
GDP per capita: 15,000 US$
Capital: Maskat
Government: Sultanate (absolutist monarchy)
Languages: Arabic (official), Farsi, Urdu
Currency: 1 Omani rial = 1,000 baizas

1 Just recognizable under the decoration: a bus in Pakistan.

2 A sampan, typical boat in the Philippines, in El Nido Bay.

3 Skilfully carved rice terraces in the Philippines' Banaue Valley are a harmonious connection between primeval nature, human aesthetics and agricultural function.

4 A mixture of the Baroque and Oriental: St. Augustine's Church in Paoay, on the Philippine island of Luzon.

Nations of the World
Asia

Politics: Settled around 2500 BC, the region fell under Islamic influence in the 7th century and became independent in 751. Ahmed bin Said founded the current reigning dynasty after the end of Portuguese rule, from the 16th century. Oman was a British protectorate from 1891 to 1951. Progress has been registered in all areas since Sultan Qabus became the ruling monarch in 1970.

Economy: Oman's economy is a liberal free market economy with some state influence. Only 5% of the national territory is inhabited. The oil sector has dominated the economy since oil was discovered in the 1950s, and registers a 38% share of GDP. As the oil reserves will be exhausted in 30 years at most, efforts are already under way to diversify the economy.

Saudi Arabia see Al-Mamlaka al-'Arabiya as-Sa'udiya

Singapore
Singapore

Area: 692.7 sq km
Population: 4.5 million
GDP per capita: 35,000 US$
Capital: Singapore
Government: Republic in the Commonwealth
Languages: Malay, English, Chinese, Tamil (all official)
Currency: 1 Singapore dollar = 100 cents

Geography: The main island of Singapore, with 54 smaller islands, only two dozen of which are inhabited, lies at the southern outlet of the Malacca Straits. The country is low-lying. A railway and road dam connects the main island with the Malaysian peninsula. The tropical flora and fauna have been seriously affected by settlement.

Politics: The first British trading settlement was founded in 1819, and in 1824 the East India Company took over Singapore. In 1955 the British crown colony was given a constitution with election rights for the entire population, as well as extensive self-government. After gaining autonomy in 1959 and independence in 1963, Singapore became a republic in 1965. Its president has been elected in general

Sri Lanka: Buddhist temple site of Raja Maha Vihara in Kelaniya.

elections since 1991. The parliament is elected every five years.

Economy: Inhabited largely by Chinese, this city-state is a leading industrial and service center, as well as an important air traffic hub in Asia. The agricultural sector today accounts for less than 1% of GDP, owing to rapid industrialization in the 1960s and 1970s. Export revenues are predominantly generated by electronic products in addition to tools, machinery and shipbuilding. The services sector (banks) accounts for 62% of GDP.

Srī Lankā
Sri Lanka

Area: 65,610 sq km
Population: 20.2 million
GDP per capita: 1500 US$

Capital: Colombo
Government: Socialist presidential republic in the Commonwealth
Languages: Singhalese, Tamil
Currency: 1 Sri Lankan rupee = 100 cents

Geography: Sri Lanka is separated from the Indian subcontinent by the Palk Straits and the Gulf of Mannar. Its territory includes 22 smaller islands off its coasts. Extensive lowlands broken by isolated peaks join the coastal areas to the north and the east. The central mountain region rises over several terraces to the Pidurutalagala peak (2,524 m). The country has a monsoon-influenced tropical climate. The Buddhist sites of Kandy, Polonnaruva and Dambulla are fascinating.

Politics: Settled by Tamils since the 2nd century, the island was discovered by the Portuguese in 1505. At the end of the 18th century, it became a British crown colony. The country gained its independence in 1948. Discrimination of Tamils by the Singhalese is destabilizing, resulting in terrorist acts and military conflict. Before the introduction of the republican constitution in 1972, Sri Lanka was named Ceylon.

Some three million inhabitants, mostly of Chinese origin, live in the extremely strictly governed and extremely prosperous city-state of Singapore. In the city's architecture **1** the present has largely ousted the past shaped by Portuguese and British colonial rulers. Space on the peninsula is at a premium, which encourages appropriately vertical architecture, and older, traditional buildings are now rare in the city. There are, however, numerous modern buildings **2** in the city that have been clearly influenced by the city-state's East and Southeast Asian heritage.

Nations of the World
Asia

Economy: Compared with the percentage of GDP generated by agriculture (tea and rubber plantations; 24%), industry (15%) is still insignificant, although steadily growing. The most important industrial exports are textiles. The services sector accounts for nearly half of GDP.

and its tributaries flow for 675 km through the north-east. Syria lies at the transition zone between the Mediterranean climate, with its moist winters, and the continental dry climate. Chief travel destinations include important historical and cultural cities such as Damascus, Aleppo and Palmyra.

only slowly. Agriculture, which is still the mainstay of the economy at 28% of GDP, is dependent on highly fluctuating rainfall, and artificial irrigation is employed to produce cotton and fruit for export in addition to grain. Oil extraction and processing account for the highest export revenues. Half of GDP is generated by the services sector, which is greatly boosted by the tourism industry.

Shopping street in Sri Lanka's metropolis, Colombo.

Sūriya
Syria

Area: 185,180 sq km
Population: 18 million
GDP per capita: 2,000 US$
Capital: Damascus
Government: Presidential republic
Languages: Arabic (official), Kurdish, Armenian
Currency: 1 Syrian pound = 100 piasters

Geography: 90% of Syria's area is uncultivated; while steppes dominate in the north and north-west, the Syrian Desert extends through the south-east. The remaining territory to the west is essentially mountainous (Mt. Hermon, 2,814 m). Rising in Turkey, the Euphrates

Politics: A Persian satrapy since the 6th century BC, the country became the centre of the Seleucid empire in 323, and later came under Roman, Byzantine, Arab and Ottoman rule. Declared part of the French mandate in 1922, Syria gained independence in 1946. The politically unstable years up to 1970 were marked by coups, a temporary union with Egypt and the 6 Days' War in June 1967. The possibility of reconciliation with Israel did not emerge until the 1990s.

Economy: The socialist-planned economy provides for an amalgam of state, collective and private ownership. Economic reforms and attempts at industrialization and diversification are progressing

Tadžikistan
Tajikistan

Area: 143,100 sq km
Population: 7.3 million
GDP per capita: 600 US$
Capital: Dushanbe
Government: Presidential republic
Language: Tajik
Currency: 1 Tajik rouble = 100 kopeks

Geography: An extremely mountainous land to the south of the CIS, 90% of which has an altitude of over 1,000 m; almost the entire population lives in the narrow mountain valleys. In the south-east, the Pamir mountains cover an area of 64,000 sq km. The western mountain ranges boast the highest peaks of the CIS: Communism Peak (7,495 m), and Lenin Peak (7,134 m). The continental climate is characterized by hot, dry summers and cold winters. Tourism is largely limited to trekking expeditions.

Politics: Settled as early as the 1st millennium BC, the region was ruled by the Persians, Greeks, Macedonians and Arabs until the 9th century. After centuries of Mongol and Uzbek rule, the north of Tajikistan came under Russian control in 1870, and in 1918 became part of the Soviet Republic of Turkestan. In 1929, the Tajik Soviet Socialist Republic became part of the USSR, from which it broke away in 1991 to become an independent state and a member of CIS. It underwent changes of government and a civil war, before achieving relative stability.

Economy: Owing to poor infrastructure and the cotton monoculture of the USSR era, Tajikistan is today the poorest republic of the

Taehan-Min'guk Republic of Korea (South)

Area: 98,480 sq km
Population: 48.8 million
GDP per capita: 20,000 US$
Capital: Seoul
Government: Presidential republic
Language: Korean
Currency: 1 won = 100 chon

CIS. Agriculture still accounts for some 40% of GDP. The important industries are wool processing, foodstuffs and textiles. Raw materials include uranium and gold, and to a small extent petroleum, natural gas, lead, zinc, tungsten and tin.

1 The bazaars are the market quarters of Oriental cities. Shops are crowded along open or roofed alleys, some in multi-storey buildings with large courtyards.

2 Rugaija Mosque in Damascus is a gift by the Iranian government to the Shiite minority.

3 Portraits of President Hafis a-Assad, who died in 2000, are everywhere in Syria.

4 Bedouins, the nomads of the Arab world, travel through the deserts of many Middle Eastern countries with their camels. They are traditionally herders of sheep, camels or goats.

Special
Seoul

Tradition and modernity meet in the South Korean capital city, Seoul. Founded at the end of the 4th century by the newly powerful Yi Dynasty, the city boasts several impressive historic palaces and temples. The more than ten million inhabitants account for a large part of the country's enormous economic power, and highly qualified young students are educated in the capital's 300 or so tertiary education institutions. **1** Seoul suffered extensive damage in the Korean War, and was later rebuilt in a modern and international style. The Changdeok-gung Palace was an imperial residence for some time. The **2** Ingjoyngyon throne room is located in the centre of the complex.

Geography: The landscape in the southern part of the Korean peninsula is predominantly mountainous. Unlike the uniform east coast, the south and west coasts are highly fragmented. A hilly, fertile basin in the south is traversed by the Naktong, with a 50-100 km costal plain to the west. Extensive deciduous and coniferous forests dominate the landscape. The major rivers flow into the Yellow Sea and are only partly navigable. With the exception of the subtropical south, the climate is continental and cool to moderate. Cultural cities other than Seoul of interest to tourists include Taegu or Kyongju.

Politics: Tradition dates the founding of the Korean empire at 2333 BC, although the date 57 BC is historically documented. Under the influence of China and Japan, Korea has nonetheless developed its own independent culture. In 1910 Korea was annexed by Japan. In 1945, occupation by the USSR and the USA led to the division of the country, then in 1948 to the establishment of the Republic of Korea in the US-controlled south. After the Korean War (1950-1953), the military held sway in South Korea. Democratization, launched in the mid 1980s, led to a new constitution in 1988.

Economy: Rice cultivation in smallholdings cannot meet domestic needs. Industrialization has taken off in the last 30 years; initially in cheap, labor-intensive products, now export production is shifting from manufactured products in the food, textile and clothing industry to individualized technologies and brand articles for the automobile and electronics industry. In addition, the share of the financial, service and real-estate sector in GDP is rising (48%).

Taiwan
Taiwan

Area: 35,980 sq km
Population: 23 million
GDP per capita: 17,000 US$
Capital: Taipei
Government: Republic
Language: Chinese
Currency: 1 New Taiwanese dollar = 100 cents

1 South Korea's most important and most visited temple, the Pulguk Temple, is a fine example of Buddhist civilization in the Silla dynasty (668-918), together with the neighboring Sokkuram Grotto. Pulguk Temple is guarded by four Heavenly Kings, including the Kings of the East and South. It is now a world heritage site.

2 Near the Pulguk Temple is the artificial Sokkuram Grotto. The 8th century Buddha is 3.40 m high, housed in a temple of mighty granite blocks.

3 Some of Taipeh's citizens practice qigong on the square before the Chiang-Kai-Shek Monument commemorating Taiwan's first president.

Geography: Taiwan lies off the south-east coast of China. The center has thickly wooded mountain ranges with more than 60 peaks over 3,000 m in height (Jade Mountain or Yushan, 3,997 m). The climate is subtropical with high rainfall in the north, but tropical with winter monsoons in the south. Apart from the capital, chief tourist destinations are the magnificent inland and coastal landscapes.

Politics: Settled by the Chinese in the 9th century and the focus of colonization attempts by Portugal, Spain and Holland, Taiwan became part of the Chinese empire in 1661. China ceded the island to Japan in 1895, but it became Chinese territory again in 1945. Defeated in the civil war, the Kumointang moved its seat of government to Taiwan in 1949. Relations between the People's Republic and Taiwan remain tense. Despite the constitution of 1946, the president retains significant political power.

Economy: Privatization is gradually replacing state economic control. On this densely populated island with few natural resources, agriculture mainly produces rice to cover domestic needs. While industry accounts for 37% of GDP, services generate 60%, and 50% of employment.

Thailand see Muang Thai

Timor-Leste
East-Timor

Area: 15,007 sq km
Population: 1 million
GDP per capita: Estimated at 500 US$
Capital: Dili
Government: Republic
Languages: Indonesian, Portuguese
Currency: 1 US dollar = 100 cents

Geography: The island republic occupies the eastern part of the Lesser Sunda Island of Timor. The central mountains attain an altitude of 2,960 m in Ramelan.

Politics: East Timor was a Portuguese colony from 1695; the west of the island was occupied by the Dutch. After World War II, this part was given to Indonesia. When the Portuguese withdrew in 1975, civil war broke out, with the Fretilin Party fighting for independence. Indonesia annexed East Timor in 1975/76, resulting in a bloody conflict with many lives lost. In 1999 the majority of the population voted for independence, and East Timor became a sovereign state in 2002.

Economy: There are great hopes for the petroleum and natural gas reserves in the Timor Sea. Hitherto the economy has relied on the cultivation of coffee, rice, manioc and coconut trees.

View of Jordan's crowded capital Amman.

Turkmenistan
Turkmenistan

Area: 488,100 sq km
Population: 5 million
GDP per capita: 5,200 US$
Capital: Ashgabat
Government: Presidential republic

Language: Turkmen
Currency: 1 manat = 100 tenge

Geography: Turkmenistan is located between the Caspian Sea in the west and the Amu-Darja River on the Uzbek border in the east. 80% of the country is lowlands covered by the Kara-Kum sand desert. The coastal area on the Caspian Sea is flat and sandy. The country has a continental desert climate with extreme temperature fluctuations.

Politics: Settled by Turkic peoples since the 5th century and Islamic since the 7th century, Turkmenistan became part of Czarist Russia during that country's expansion in 1877-1881. In 1918 it became a part of the Autonomous Soviet Republic of Turkestan and in 1991, after the dissolution of the USSR, an independent member of the CIS. However, the old Communist regime is still in power, even after the new constitution of 1992.

Economy: Agriculture is concentrated around cotton production in irrigated areas. Formerly supplying raw materials to the USSR, industry is still underdeveloped. Key economic factors are the natural gas, petroleum, sulphur and mineral reserves. The petrochemicals and textile sectors are also major industries in the country.

United Arab Emirates see Daulat al-Imārāt al-'Arabiya Al-Muttahida

Urdunn
Jordan

Area: 92,300 sq km
Population: 5.9 million

navigable River Jordan flows through the valley into the Dead Sea. Jordan has an outlet to the Red Sea through a small coastal strip on the Gulf of Aqaba. Most areas of the country have a desert climate, although the Mediterranean climate in the west enables agriculture to be practiced. Tourist destinations, other than the capital Amman and Aqaba, include the ruins of Petra in the south.

GDP per capita: 2,800 US$
Capital: Amman
Government: Constitutional monarchy
Language: Arabic
Currency: 1 Jordanian dinar = 1,000 fils

Geography: The Jordan rift valley separates the country at the northwest of the Arabian peninsula into a hilly landscape with 600-800 m peaks in the west, and a mountain range rising to 1,745 m in the east, gradually sloping down to the Arabian desert. The twisting, non-

Politics: Jordan's constitutional hereditary monarchy has existed since the country gained independence from Great Britain in 1946. According to the constitution in force since 1952, only the king exercises executive power, and in theory shares legislative power with the national assembly. In 1994 King Hussein concluded a peace treaty with Israel.

Economy: Jordan consists mostly of non-arable deserts and mountainous landscapes, and because it has no oil reserves, it is one of the

poorest states in the Arab world. Because opportunities in industry and agriculture are lacking, economic activities tend to concentrate in the services sector, which accounts for 65% of GDP and employs 72% of the workforce. Tourism is one of the most important sources of foreign revenue.

1 The island of Taiwan is home to the Tsou, Paiwan and Atayi, and the small Ami people.

2 Impressive rock graves in Petra, Jordan, bear witness to the Nabatean culture in the 2nd century BC.

Nations of the World
Asia

Uzbekistan
Uzbekistan

Area: 447,400 sq km
Population: 27 million
GDP per capita: 800 US$
Capital: Tashkent
Government: Presidential republic
Language: Uzbek
Currency: 1 Uzbek sum = 100 tijin

Economy: Uzbekistan is an agricultural country with little industry. The cultivation of cotton plays a major role in the economy – Uzbekistan is the world's third largest exporter of cotton. Agriculture accounts for 32% of GDP and employs at least 44% of the workforce. Aside from the manufacture of cotton harvesting machinery, the industrial sector also produces

Viêt-Nam
Vietnam

Area: 329,560 sq km
Population: 84.4 million
GDP per capita: 800 US$
Capital: Hanoi
Government: Socialist republic
Language: Vietnamese
Currency: 1 dong = 10 hào = 100 xu

Three madrasas from the 15th – 17th century frame Registan Square in the Uzbek city of Samarkand.

Geography: This Central Asian republic comprises the center of the Turan basin with the south western part of the Kysyl-Kum Desert. The Amu-Darja River flows through the desert on the south-west border with Turkmenistan and into the Aral Sea. In the east, the country is bounded by the foothills of the Tianshan and Altai mountains. The climate is continental, with hot summers.

Politics: When Uzbekistan was made a republic of the USSR (1924), the term "Uzbeks" was introduced for the Turkic speaking populations round Bukhara and Kokand. When the Soviet Union collapsed in 1991, Uzbekistan declared its independence.

Uzbekistan: modern architecture in the ancient oasis of Tashkent

fertilizers. Gold and oil production are becoming increasingly important sectors of the economy.

Geography: The Red and Black River delta lies on the Gulf of Tongking. To the south extends the central region of Annam, formed by a deeply indented costal strip that is 40 km wide at its narrowest point. In the south lies the Mekong Delta, 70,000 sq km in area. In the long rainy season, tropical rain forests and mangrove forests flourish in the coastal areas. Vietnam has a host of cultural monuments in Ho Chi Minh City (Saigon) and Hue, plus areas of natural beauty.

Economy: The transition from the socialist-planned economy has meant a surplus in rice production in recent years. Vietnam is today the world's third largest rice exporter. Wood and rubber reserves are industrially processed. Private companies are increasing, but the economy remains underdeveloped.

Yemen see Al-Yaman

Politics: In the 10th century, Vietnamese rebels drove out their Chinese overlords. Rivalries between two families caused a split in the country in the 15th century, which was reunited only in 1802 with French help. After World War II, the country was partitioned into Communist-ruled North Vietnam, and dictator-led South Vietnam. The Vietnam War (1957/58-1975), in which the USA and the SEATO states played an important role, ended with the Vietcong taking power in South Vietnam and the unification of the country under Communist leadership. The invasion of Cambodia in 1979 led to acts of war with China.

1 The imperial graves in Hue, capital of the feudal sovereignty of Vietnam from 1744, date from the 19th and first half of the 20th century and are modeled on those of China's Ming dynasty. In a spacious park, stone sculptures depicting guards, attendants, ministers and horses line the avenues to the grave-mound.

2 Chua Thien Mu Pagoda, the pagoda of the ancient Goddess of the Sky, in the Vietnamese imperial city of Hue. It is part of a 17th century Buddhist monastery.

3 Women in a "street café" on a business street in Vietnam's bustling capital, Hanoi.

247

Nations of the World
Asia

Yiśra'el
Israel

Area: 21,946 sq km
Population: 6.3 million
GDP per capita: 22,500 US$
Capital: Jerusalem
Government: Republic
Languages: Hebrew,
Arabic (official), English
Currency: 1 new shekel =
100 agorot

Geography: The highlands of Galilee extend to the Mediterranean in the north, with a narrow, fertile coastal strip to the south that meets the Negev Desert, occupying the country's largest area. Israel is bounded to the east by the Red Sea and the Jordan plains. The coast has a Mediterranean climate, while a desert climate reigns to the south. Important tourist destinations, other than the Dead Sea scenery, are sites from Jewish, Roman and Byzantine eras and the Crusades.

Politics: The Republic of Israel was proclaimed by the Jewish National Council in 1948 at the end of the British Mandate in Palestine. A large part of the Arabs living in the national territory who had fought for the creation of their own state thereupon left the country. Irreconcilable differences with their neighbors have led to a total of four Israeli-Arab wars. The peace process, initiated in 1993 by Arafat and Rabin with a mutual agreement to recognize Israel and the PLO, slowed down in 1996 when a conservative coalition came to power. Clashes escalated in 2001, and Palestinian suicide bombers aggravated the situation. A peaceful solution seems to have receded. In the meantime, the establishment of a Palestinian State has become the focus of international efforts, with a crucial aspect being how to draw the borders of a country when large areas are still under Israeli control. The role and influence of PLO leader Yasser Arafat can scarcely be overestimated in this conflict.

Economy: Once solely agricultural, Israel is developing into a modern industrialized country; cooperative agriculture accounts for just 3% of GNP; industry for over 30%. Important areas of industry include the food, metal, and aircraft industries. Tourism is the most reliable source of foreign exchange, at 2 billion US$.

An Orthodox Jew in Jerusalem

A Palestinian in the Israeli-occupied Gaza Strip

This young woman in Bethlehem proudly displays her traditional dress.

Zhongguo
China

Area: 9,596,960 sq km
Population: 1.3 billion.
GDP per capita: 2,500 US$
Capital: Beijing
Government: Socialist people's republic
Language: Mandarin Chinese (official), Cantonese and other dialects
Currency: 1 yuan renminbi = 10 jiao = 100 fen

Jerusalem is the most important city for three great religions of the world. But the city has more to offer than cornerstones of faith; Jerusalem is a modern metropolis with some 630,000 inhabitants. **1** The Dome on the Rock in the Temple Mount is crowned by a 31 meter golden cupola. **2** The "Wailing Wall", the western wall of the Old Temple in Jerusalem, is a central shrine, and not only for Orthodox Jews. Access to it was restored in 1967. It stands as a reminder of the spot where King Solomon built the first temple for the Ark of the Covenant. **3** The 12th century Church of the Holy Sepulchre, the most important shrine for Christians, was built over the spot where the tomb of Jesus is believed to have been.

Since the mid-20th century Beijing, the capital of the People's Republic, has grown from a classical imperial city into a modern megalopolis of 9.3 million inhabitants. Not all fascinating monuments were sacrificed to the increasing needs of space for industry. **1** The square in front of the Gate of Supreme Harmony in the Forbidden City was used for the Emperor's largely public representation. **2** Tiananmen Square is of central significance for China, the world's most populous country; here Chairman Mao Tse Tung proclaimed the People's Republic on October 1, 1949, and more recently, demonstrations for greater freedom were brutally crushed on the same spot. **3** Up to 1911, Tiantan, the "Temple of Heaven", could be entered only by the emperor, the "Son of Heaven." Today, the buildings and park form a popular excursion for the capital's inhabitants. **4** Gatekeepers: the two lions in the palace compound represent Yin and Yang.

eography: From the fertile lownds in the east, the landscape ses to meet the Himalayas in the est. High plateaus and mountains f over 1,000 m occupy one third of ie area. The coast at the Yellow ea is flat at the mouths of China's vo major rivers, the Huanghe and ie Yangze. The southern coast is ountainous, with many offshore lands. The testimonials of 5,000 ears of civilization and a richly aried landscape offer a vast numer of fascinating travel destinaons. Rapid industrialization, eroon and pollution have decimated ie rich flora and fauna.

olitics: As early as 2000 BC, small tates existed in what is now hina. Since the formation of a unied empire in 221 BC, accompaied by standardized systems for veights, measures and writing, hina has twice fallen to foreign ule; the Mongols governed from 280 to 1368, and the Manchurians rom 1644-1911. The fall of the emire was followed by a republic in 911. After the end of World War I, he country was the scene of epeated civil wars. In 1937 war roke out with Japan, and in 1941 China declared war on Germany. he Chinese civil war between Kuomintang and the Communists nded in 1949 with the withdrawal of the Kuomintang to Taiwan, later he National Republic of China. In October 1949, the People's Republic of China was established under Mao Tse Tung. In the 1960s internal struggles resulted in the Cultural Revolution. Since 1978, the Communist leadership has been pursuing economic liberalization, although without relinquishing any of their political power. In 1997, China took over the former British crown colony Hong Kong, undertaking to retain the existing economic system for another 50 years.

Economy: Most of the population lives and works in rural regions. Rice and grain cultivation covers basic needs, and surpluses are exported. The country is opening up rapidly to world markets after having a strict planned economy. In a low-wage country such as China, the lion's share of exports is accounted for by processed goods, chiefly machinery and electronic appliances, but also textile products. Thanks to foreign trade and tourism, the services sector is gaining in importance.

1 The one-child rule for families, intended to slow China's population growth.

2 The restored terracotta army of Xian. The weapons carried by the 8,000 soldier figures, some larger than life-size, were stolen by grave robbers before excavation of the 2000-year-old figures began in 1974. In the 3rd century BC China's first emperor, Qin Shi Huang Di, ordered the soldiers to be made as grave goods.

3 A Zhuang woman surveys the terraced rice paddies in the province of Guangxi. The spectacular region is fringed with limestone mountains.

Special
Shanghai

Shanghai has a fascinating past. The birthplace of the Communist Party, it is China's new boomtown, with 13 million inhabitants: An all-new **1** residential and business district has been constructed in just a few years on the east bank of the Huangpu River, with skyscrapers rivaling Hong Kong's. The 400-meter **2** television tower soars above the Pudong business district. **3** Shanghai, China's second largest and most Westernized mainland city, boasts an enormous harbor and booming foreign trade.

The former British crown colony of Hong Kong was returned to China in a solemn ceremony on July 1, 1997. Under the motto "one country – two systems," the region was promised economic and political freedom for the next 50 years. Thanks to its international connections, Hong Kong, with 6.7 million inhabitants, 98% of whom are Chinese, boasts a fascinating blend of Far Eastern and Western lifestyles with a definite focus on business. **1** The skyline never stops growing. The business and service metropolis has continued to expand even after its transfer to China. Land reclamation projects are in operation. **2** 554-meter high Victoria Peak affords breathtaking views of the Kowloon peninsula. **3** The city's most thrilling attractions include the groundbreaking skyscraper architecture, such as the Bank of China Building (1991), contrasting with French and British buildings from colonial times.

Australia is the smallest of the world's continents, with a total area of just over 7.6 million sq km. The continent's indigenous people, the Aborigines, arrived on the continent more than 40,000 years ago. European explorers arrived in Australia in the 17th century and ushered in an era of colonization and set-tlement that would have devas-tating effects for the aborigines.

The Australian interior is dominated by the deserts and semi-arid regions. Central Australia features numerous fascinating rock formations, including Ayers Rock (Uluru). The world's largest coral reef, the Great Barrier Reef, is situated just off the continent's eastern coast. Australia's unique indigenous flora and fauna includes kangaroos, koalas, and Tasmanian devils.

The more than 100,000 islands of Oceania have a combined area of less than 800,000 sq km.

Micronesia, Polynesia, Melanesia, New Zealand, and Hawaii are, however, located in a vast stretch of ocean covering more than 70 million sq km. Oceania's beaches, tropical landscapes, and colorful cultures draw tourists from around the world to the region.

1

2

Almost one-fifth of Australia's population – around four million people – live in the metropolitan area of Sydney, the continent's largest city and host city of the 2000 Olympic Games. Sydney is located on Australia's southeastern coast approximately 300 kilometers north of the capital city of Canberra. **1** The city's modern skyline is an indication of its role as Australia's leading economic center. **2** Sydney Opera House has become a landmark of the city and the nation since its construction in the 1970s. The Harbour Bridge, another landmark of Sydney, was completed in 1932. **3** A copy of the legendary ship Bounty can now be seen in Sydney's harbor.

3

ustralia
ustralia

ea: 7,686,850 sq km
pulation: 20.2 million
)P per capita: 43,000 US$
pital: Canberra
vernment: Parliamentary
mocracy
nguages: English, Asian and
original languages
rrency: 1 Australian dollar =
0 cents

eography: Deserts and semi-arid
nd cover around 70 percent of
e world's smallest continent,
cluding most of western and
entral Australia. The 3,000-kilo-
eter-long Great Dividing Range
retches along the continent's
ast coast, while the Great Barrier
eef extends 2,000 kilometers from
orth to south directly off the
oast. Northern Australia features
xtensive grassy and forested sa-
annas as well as humid rain
rests along the coast. The
lurray and Darling rivers in the
outh are Australia's most impor-
ant rivers. The island state of Tas-
ania is located south of mainland
ustralia's south-eastern coast. In
ddition to numerous national parks
nd wilderness areas, Australia
lso features countless beaches
nd diving sites open to tourists.

olitics: The Aborigines, Australia's
ndigenous inhabitants, arrived on
he continent during the last ice
ge. In 1770, British captain James
Cook claimed the colony of New
South Wales for Great Britain. The
colony served as a British penal
colony until 1865. The first free set-
lers arrived – in the Sydney area –
n 1793. The six Australian colonies
united in 1901 to form the Commonwealth of Australia. In the following
decades, Australia achieved increased political independence

but the British monarch remains
the country's official head of state.
The Aborigines have been granted
increased political rights in recent
decades, including citizenship and
voting rights after generations of
political and social neglect.

Economy: Immigrants from more
than 120 nations have settled in
Australia during the past two centuries. The country's standard of

1 Koala bears are among the most
famous of Australia's many unique
indigenous animal species.

2 Large transporter trucks are common on the isolated highways that
stretch across vast distances through
the Australian interior. The Stuart
Highway is perhaps the most famous

route in the country's 913,000 kilo-
meter-long network of roads.

3 Australian Aborigines now form
less than 1.6% of the continent's
population. A minority of the Aborigines live in small traditional communities where their ancient languages
and customs are rapidly disappearing.

257

1 Melbourne in southeastern Australia is the country's second largest city with a population of 3.8 million. **2** The Victorian architecture of Flanders Street Station contrasts starkly with the modern architecture of Melbourne's skyscrapers. **3** The Australian parliament building in the capital city of Canberra is a beautiful example of 20th-century architecture.

iving is one of the world's highest. The country's leading export products include agricultural goods, and mineral resources such as iron, uranium, nickel, and opals. Australia, the world's leading wool exporter, is also an important producer of grain, meat and dairy products. Around 25% of the country's labor force works in the manufacturing sector, while at least 70% of Australians now work in the service sector.

Fiji
Fiji

Area: 18,270 sq km
Population: 900,000
GDP per capita: 3,900 US$
Capital: Suva
Government: Republic
Languages: English, Fijian, Hindi
Currency: 1 Fijian dollar = 100 cents

Geography: Fiji consists of more than 320 islands, including volcanic and coral islands. Around 110 of the islands are inhabited. The mountains on the largest islands, Viti Levu and Vanua Levu, rise to over 1,300 meters. Fiji is a major tourist attraction with a tropical climate and countless sandy beaches.

Politics: In 1643, Abel Tasman was the first European to visit the islands. More than a century later, James Cook claimed the islands for Great Britain. From 1874 to 1970 the islands were a British colony. Following independence, the country experienced periods of political instability including several military coups. A new constitution was created in 1997 in an attempt to ease tensions between the country's indigenous Melanesian population and the large Indo-Fijian community. Political power is now divided between the Senate, House of Re-

presentatives, and President. Fiji's President, the official head of state, is chosen by the national council of chiefs, a non-elected body of mostly hereditary members. This council also appoints one-third of the country's senators. The role of the council is controversial because it excludes the country's Indo-Fijian majority. Elections to the House of Representatives are based on a mixture of universal direct elec-

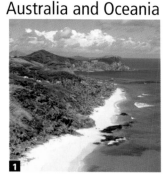

1 Many of Fiji's islands are covered by lush tropical rain forests

2 Mossman Gorge in the rain forests of Queensland

3 Uluru-Kata Tjuta National Park in Central Australia features the famous monolith Ayers Rock (Uluru) and other

interesting natural attractions.

4 The Pinnacles: Thousands of spectacular limestone formations rising above the golden sand of Nambung National Park

5 The Great Barrier Reef near the northeastern coast of Australia

tions and electoral rolls divided between the country's ethnic groups.

Economy: Around half of the Fijian labor force works in the country's large agricultural sector. Sugar and fish are among the country's main exports. The country's industrial sector consists primarily of sugar refining, rice milling, and textile production. Mining – primarily gold and copper – also plays a limited but important role in Fiji's economy. The service sector generates at least 62% of the Fiji gross domestic product. Tourism remains an important industry and a major source of employment for many Fijians.

Kiribati
Kiribati

Area: 810.5 sq km
Population: 105,000
GDP per capita: 700 US$
Capital: Tarawa
Government: Presidential republic
Languages: I-Kiribati, English
Currency: 1 Australian dollar = 100 cents

Geography: Kiribati consists of 33 atolls scattered over an area of 5 million sq km in the Pacific Ocean. Kiribati is generally divided into the Gilbert, Phoenix, and Line island groups. Most of the islands are unsuited for large scale agriculture because of their poor soils. The capital is located on the island of Tarawa.

Politics: The islands of Kiribati were first settled during the prehistoric era. During the 19th century, the first European traders arrived on the islands. The islands were declared a British protectorate in 1892, together with the Ellis Islands. After several decades as a British colony, the islands were granted independence in 1975.

Economy: The majority of Kiribati's population works in agriculture. Coconuts and fish are the leading exports. Manufacturing currently generates less than 10% of the country's gross domestic product. The country's geographic isolation is an obstacle to trade and increased foreign investment. Aid from the industrialized countries is an important source of currency.

Marshall Islands
Marshall Islands

Area: 181 sq km
Population: 60,000
GDP per capita: 2,300 US$
Capital: Majuro
Government: Republic
Languages: Marshallese dialects, English
Currency: 1 US dollar = 100 cents

Politics: The islands were first sited by Europeans in 1529 and became a German protectorate 1884. After the First World W the islands were transferred Japanese control. Between 19 and 1980 the islands were admir stered by the United States. In 19 the Marshall Islands were d clared an independent state b the United States provides th country's defense and much dev opment aid.

Economy: More than half of th Marshall Islands' population concentrated on the islands Ebeye and Majuro. Much of th country's population works in agr culture. Bananas, papayas, an coconuts are the most widely pr duced crops. The islands have fe mineral resources, but phosphat

The inhabitants of the Fiji Islands have retained their traditional way of life.

Geography: The Marshall Islands consist of two atolls that stretch over a distance of 1,200 kilometers. The Ratak island group comprises 16 atolls, while the large Ralik group consists of 18 atolls and more than 100 coral reefs. The Marshall Islands all have humid tropical climates with heavy rainfall.

is mined on the Ailinglaplap atoll. Coconuts and fish are the leading exports. Tourism is a small but important industry for the islands and the industrial sector consists mostly of fish processing. Development aid from the United States is the country's main source of government funding.

Micronesia
Mikronesia

Area: 702 sq km
Population: 110,000
GDP per capita: 2,300 US$
Capital: Palikir
Government: Constitutional government
Languages: English, local Polynesian and Micronesian languages
Currency: 1 US dollar = 100 cents

centuries before they were sold to Germany in the 19th century. The islands were administered by Japan after the end of the First World War, and were transferred to the United States after the Second World War. Micronesia became an independent federal republic in 1990, although the United States continues to maintain responsibility for the country's defense.

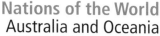

Geography: The territory of the Federated States of Micronesia are scattered over an area of 2.6 million sq km in the Pacific Ocean. The country comprises four states – Chuuk (294 islands), Yap (145 islands), Kosrae (5 islands), and Pohnpei (163 islands). The country consists of both volcanic and coral island groups. All of the islands have humid tropical climates with heavy rainfall, and tropical storms are common in the regions. Ancient ruins and the diverse marine life in Micronesia's coral reefs are the country's main tourist attractions.

Politics: The islands of Micronesia were under Spanish control for

Economy: Small-scale farming of coconuts, cassava and other crops provides most of Micronesia's food demands and employs a significant segment of the local population. The selling of fishing licenses to foreign companies, chiefly Japan, is an important source of income for the country. Tourism and the export of crops are both major industries in Micronesia.

1 Melanesian man wearing a traditional headdress during a ceremony. The majority of Melanesia's people are Christians but indigenous spiritual beliefs are still maintained.

2 The Caroline Islands are the largest island group in Micronesia, with more than 963 islands including

islands of volcanic origin and coral atolls. Archeological discoveries have indicated a long history of human settlement on the islands.

3 Coconut palms are the most common vegetation on the islands of Kiribati. Their leaves, nuts, and wood are harvested by the islanders.

Nations of the World
Australia and Oceania

Nauru (Naoero)
Nauru

Area: 21.3 sq km
Population: 13,000
GDP per capita: 5,000 US$
Capital: Yaren
Government: Parliamentary democracy
Languages: Nauruan, English
Currency: 1 Australian dollar = 100 cents

Geography: This small coral island is surrounded by a large reef. Nauru's coast consists of sandy beaches that border a broad strip of fertile land stretching between 150-300 meters inland. Most of the island is covered by a plateau that rises 70 meters above sea level. Large sections of Nauru's interior are uninhabitable, covered with barren patches of land created as a result of phosphate mining. The island has neither rivers nor natural harbours.

Politics: In 1798, after centuries of isolation, European whale hunters arrived on the island. Nauru was incorporated into the German protectorate of the Marshall Islands in 1888. The island's first phosphate mining operation began in 1905. Nauru achieved independence in 1968 after decades of Japanese and later Australian administration. The country's parliament is directly elected every three years. The traditional Polynesian clan system is still in operation on the island.

Economy: The economy of Nauru is dominated almost entirely by phosphate mining. The local mining industry is controlled by the Nauru Phosphate Corporation, the country's largest company and employer, and a major investor in fishing and tourism. With most of its phosphate deposits depleted, Nauru is now facing serious economic challenges that could threaten its survival as a viable independent nation.

New Zealand
New Zealand

Area: 268,680 sq km
Population: 4 million
GDP per capita: 30,000 US$
Capital: Wellington
Government: Parliamentary democracy
Languages: English, Maori
Currency: 1 New Zealand dollar = 100 cents

Geography: New Zealand consists of two large islands (North and South Islands) separated by the Cook Strait, and several smaller islands. The terrain on both of the large islands is dominated by a series of mountain ranges. The North Island features several active volcanoes as well as numerous hot springs and geysers. The South Island features the 300-kilometer chain of the Southern Alps, New Zealand's largest mountain system. The country's largest mountain, Mount Cook, rises 3,764 meters above sea level. Most of New Zealand's virgin forests were cleared by settlers to create farmland. New Zealand is home to an array of unique flora and fauna, with a host of fascinating bird species including the Kiwi. The North Island has a mild subtropical climate, while the South Island features a cooler, more temperate climate.

Politics: The Polynesian ancestors of today's Maori people first arrived in New Zealand during the 9th century. During the late 18th century, Captain James Cook explored the islands, and the first European settlers, mostly British, arrived on the islands shortly thereafter. The Treaty of Waitangi (1840) granted

The volcanic island of Kayangel to the north of Palau is a 6km-long atoll.

Great Britain control over most of New Zealand. A series of violent conflicts between the Maori and British forces was brought to an end in 1874. New Zealand achieved independence in 1931 but the British monarch remains the country's official head of state. New Zealand has one of the few unicameral parliaments in the world and elections are held every three years.

:onomy: New Zealanders of Euro-ean descent comprise around % of the country's population. he country's advanced agricul- ral sector is one of the world's ost productive. New Zealand is w the only developed nation hich does not subsidize its dome- ic agricultural industry. sportant crops include grains, uits, and dairy products. The ma- ufacturing and service sectors ave both grown substantially in cent decades. Important indu- rial exports include chemical and ectronic products. New Zealand so exports wood products from e country's forests. The country's xtensive hydroelectric resources re being increasingly exploited nd could eventually have a major npact on New Zealand's economy.

islands were under American ad- ministration between 1947 and 1982, when they became an inde- pendent republic with close ties to the United States.

Economy: Fishing and agriculture (fruit, manioc, coconuts) generate around half of Palau's gross domes- tic product. Most of the country's national budget, however, is gener- ated from annual payments from the United States government.

Palau
Palau

Area: 458 sq km
Population: 20,000
GDP per capita: 8,500 US$
Capital: Koror
Government: Democratic state associated with the United States
Languages: Palauan, English, Japanese
Currency: 1 US dollar = 100 cents

Geography: Palau consists of 343 islands stretching over a distance of 200 kilometers. Most of the is- lands are volcanic in origin. Many of the country's coral islands feat- ure extensive sand beaches and interesting diving sites including numerous coral reefs.

Politics: The islands were settled as early as 1000 BC and were first visi- ted by European explorers in the 18th century. Palau was adminis- tered by Germany at the beginning of the 20th century and came under Japanese control after 1914. The

1 The ancestors of the Maori origi- nated in eastern or central Oceania and first arrived in New Zealand around 900 AD. Traditional tattooing is rare among modern Maori but Maori culture and language have experienced a strong revival in recent decades.

2 The two main islands of New Zea- land feature an astonishing diversity of beautiful landscapes.

3 A lawn bowling match in Rotorua. The sport remains popular in New Zea- land and is evidence of its strong cul- tural connections to Great Britain.

4 Fjordland is the southernmost region in Te Wahipounamu National Park. The area's impressive landscapes were created during the last ice ages and were featured in the motion pic- ture The Lord of the Rings.

Nations of the World
Australia and Oceania

Papua New Guinea
Papua New Guinea

Area: 462,840 sq km
Population: 5.6 million
GDP per capita: 1,000 US$
Capital: Port Moresby
Government: Democracy
Languages: Pidgin, English, Motu
Currency: 1 kina = 100 toea

Geography: Papua New Guinea comprises the eastern half of New Guinea, the Bismarck Archipelago, and numerous small Melanesian islands. The mainland is dominated by volcanic mountain ranges and large swampy plains. The majority of the population is concentrated in the central highlands. Vast tropical rainforests and savannas cover most of the islands.

Politics: The island of New Guinea has been continuously inhabited for at least 40,000 years. In 1884 the eastern section of the island was divided and occupied by Germany and Great Britain. In 1975, Papua New Guinea became an independent nation after decades of Australian administration.

Economy: A significant percentage of Papua New Guinea's population continues to live in isolated rural communities with little or no access to modern technology or education. At least 66% of the population works in the agricultural sector, which generates 33% of the country's GDP. Major export crops include coconuts, coffee, and tea. Around 80% of the country's income from exports is generated by mineral resources including gold, copper, and oil. Other major exports include timber and palm oil. Economic growth has slowed in recent years, but the government is now working to reform the economy.

Samoa
Samoa

Area: 2,944 sq km
Population: 180,000
GDP per capita: 2,100 US$
Capital: Apia
Government: Constitutional monarchy
Languages: Somoan, English
Currency: 1 tala = 100 sene

Geography: Samoa consists of two large islands – Upoli and Savai'i – and seven small islands in the southern Pacific Ocean. All of Samoa's islands are of volcanic origin, and the country's tallest mountain, Silisili, rises 1,857 meters above sea level. The island group has a tropical climate with high humidity and warm temperatures throughout the year.

Politics: Samoa was frequently visited by European traders and explorers throughout the 18th century. During the 19th century, the island was disputed between Germany, the United States, and Great Britain. Samoa became an independent nation in 1961, after decades under the administration of New Zealand. Samoa is now a constitutional monarchy where local traditions play an important role in the nation's government.

Economy: More than 70% of Samoa's people live on the island of Upolu. Fishing and agriculture are the primary sources of income.

In Papua New Guinea, evil spirits are driven away by warlike rituals.

for most of the population. Coffee and bananas have traditionally been the leading export crops of Samoa but cocoa production is becoming increasingly important for the economy. Tourism is now a major source of income for the country, but Samoa still maintains a large trade deficit.

Solomon Islands
Solomon Islands

Area: 28,450 sq km
Population: 550,000
GDP per capita: 700 US$

Politics: Originally settled more than 30,000 years ago, the Solomons are home to a blend of Polynesian and Melanesian cultures. The isolated island group was largely avoided by Europeans until the 19th century. Towards the end of that century, the islands were declared a British protectorate. Since independence in 1978, the Solomon Islands have experienced sporadic periods of political instability, including a coup in 2000.

Economy: The economy of the Solomon Islands is dominated by

Capital: Honiara
Government: Parliamentary democracy
Languages: Pidgin, English
Currency: 1 Solomon Islands dollar = 100 cents

Geography: The Solomon Islands comprise two long island chains stretching over a distance of 1,450 kilometers in the western Pacific. The largest islands – including Guadalcanal, San Cristobal, Santa Isabel, Malaita, New Georgia and Choiseul – are all of volcanic origin. The country also comprises numerous small coral islands and islets. Because of their tropical climate, heavy rainfall and high humidity are common throughout the year on the islands.

1 The indigenous people of Polynesia settled in the region between 500 BC and 300 AD.

2 A Papuan couple with traditional beads and headwear. The man's colorful face paint is a symbol of mourning for the death of a relative; the woman's ocher paint expresses condolences.

3 Elaborate wigs and colorful face paint are among the traditions of the Huli people in Papua New Guinea.

4 The islands of Western Samoa are among the most undeveloped in the southern Pacific. The country also boasts a well-maintained and vibrant local culture.

agriculture, which generates 70% of the country's GDP. The country's most important crops include cocoa, coconuts, rice, and spices. Fishing accounts for at least 25% of the country's gross domestic product and is a major source of foreign income. Forestry is a rapidly growing industry on the island, while the government strictly regulates the exploitation and export of mineral resources.

Tonga
Tonga

Area: 748 sq km
Population: 115,000
GDP per capita: 2,200 US$
Capital: Nuku'alofa
Government: Constitutional monarchy
Languages: English, Tonga dialect
Currency: 1 pa'anga = 100 seniti

Geography: Tonga consist of two long island chains encompassing 172 islands in the southern Pacific. While the western islands are mostly of volcanic origin, the smaller eastern islands are mostly flat coral islands. Tonga's capital city Nuku'alofa is located on Tongatapu, the country's largest and most populous island. Tonga has a tropical climate and the country's beaches and coral reefs attract a growing number of tourists.

Politics: The Tongans once ruled vast sections of the southern Pacific under the reign of powerful monarchs. In 1793, the British Captain James Cook visited and explored the islands. During the 19th century European missionaries exerted major control on the islands and converted the majority of the population to Christianity. The islands became a British protectorate in 1900 and an independent kingdom in 1970.

Economy: Polynesian Tongans constitute 98% of the ethnically homogenous population. Agriculture dominates the local economy and at least half of all Tongans work in this sector. Key export crops are bananas and coconuts. Tonga has a major trade deficit, mostly because much of the country's food needs must be imported. Foreign aid and wages from Tongans working abroad are the country's two most important sources of income. Development of the country's industry is limited by Tonga's isolation and lack of natural resources – most manufactured goods used on the islands are imported. Tourism remains small and undeveloped.

Geography: This island group in the south-western Pacific consists of nine atolls and numerous coral islets. Most of the islands are surrounded by coral reefs and are situated just a few meters above sea level. Tuvalu has a hot and humid tropical climate.

Politics: The population of Tuvalu was devastated by slave traders and diseases following the arrival of European traders and explorers in the 16th century. Great Britain declared the islands a protectorate in 1892 and officially annexed Tuvalu in 1916. Tuvalu was formally granted its independence from Great Britain in 1978.

Sweet potatoes, taro, manioc and spices are sold in Tonga.

Tuvalu
Tuvalu

Area: 26 sq km
Population: 11,000
GDP per capita: 1,600 US$
Capital: Vaiaku (Funafuti)
Government: Constitutional monarchy
Languages: Tuvaluan, English
Currency: 1 Australian dollar = 100 cents

Economy: The population of Tuvalu consists primarily of Polynesians and a Melanesian minority. Most of the country's people work as small-scale farmers. Fishing and the sale of postage stamps are major sources of income for Tuvalu but the country remains highly dependent on foreign aid. Tourism and the export of mineral resources could help develop the country's economy. The country's isolated

location prevents the development of large-scale tourism and industry. A significant number of Tuvalan citizens now work in other countries and contribute to the country's economy through remittances. The licensing of the internet domain tv. has become another important source of income.

export crops produced on the islands. The local service industry is rapidly expanding because of increased tourism. Vanuatu has become a minor financial services center because of its lax financial disclosure and tax laws, but the country has faced pressure to regulate the industry.

Vanuatu
Vanuatu

Area: 12,190 sq km
Population: 210,000
GDP per capita: 2,000 US$
Capital: Port Villa
Government: Republic
Languages: English, French, Bislama
Currency: 1 vatu = 100 centimes

Geography: Vanuatu comprises twelve main islands and at least 70 smaller ones located 2,000 kilometers east of Australia. The country includes both coral islands and islands of volcanic origin. Except for the more arid islands of Eromanga and Aneityum in the south, most of Vanuatu has a humid tropical climate. The country's major tourist attractions include volcanic landscapes and beaches.

Politics: The islands were visited by Portuguese explorers in 1606 and Captain James Cook in 1774, who named the islands the New Hebrides. In 1906, France and Great Britain agreed to jointly administer the islands. An independent state since 1980, Vanuatu is governed by an elected parliament and a council of local chiefs.

Economy: Agriculture and fishing are the most important segments of Vanuatu's economy and the sources of employment for most of the country's people. Cocoa and coconuts are the most important

1 Vanuatu: The islands – formerly known as the New Hebrides – have been settled by more than 100 Melanesian peoples since the first people arrived more than 3,000 years ago. More than half of the country's population works in agriculture and timber is the country's leading export.

2 The people of the Solomon Islands carefully maintain many of their Melanesian traditions. Melanesians form more than 90% of the country's population. The Solomons, in the South-West Pacific, are also home to small Polynesian, European, and Micronesian communities.

The third largest continent, Africa has an area of 30.4 million sq km – around a fifth of the earth's surface – and more than 700 million inhabitants.

Its chief geographical features are the Sahara, the world's larg-est desert, and the Chad, Congo and Kalahari Basins. Kilimanjaro is the continent's highest mountain at 5,895 m, and Lake Victoria its largest freshwater lake. The Nile is the world's longest river, at 6,671 km. The humid rain forests in Central Africa's equatorial zones give way to rolling savanna to the north and south, and to deserts in the tropical regions. Africa's rich animal life is today confined to its extensive national parks.

Africa's cultural heritage includes the sites of Egypt, among the world's most ancient cultures, and the discovery of arch-eological evidence of the earliest humans in sub-Saharan Africa.

Nations of the World
Africa

Al-Ǧazā'ir/Algérie
Algeria

Area: 2,381,741 sq km
Population: 32.9 million
GDP per capita: 3,800 US$
Capital: Algiers
Government: Presidential republic
Language: Arabic
Currency: 1 Algerian dinar =
100 centimes

Geography: Settlements are concentrated in the Mediterranean climate of the fertile coastal areas to the north, extending along 1,300 km of bays and inlets. 85% of the south is occupied by the Sahara. In addition to the Sahara's unique landscape and beautiful oases, other places of interest are the many cultural sites from the Roman and Phoenician eras.

Politics: First settled by the Phoenicians and later by Carthaginians and Romans, the coastal areas fell under Arab rule from the 7th to 15th centuries, were conquered by the French in 1830 and became French territory from 1881 to 1962. Although uprisings and resistance activities reached their peak in 1945 and 1958, political unrest continued after 1962 and terrorism by Islamic fundamentalists has increased since 1990.

Economy: Although constraints of climate and soil quality restrict agriculture to a narrow coastal area, it is the country's second largest industry. Algeria is among the world's largest cork exporters; the sparse forests are state-run. Natural gas and petroleum exports from the Sahara's extensive reserves form Algeria's main source of foreign currency. The country is now the world's second largest exporter of natural gas. Recent reforms may eventually help to diversify the economy but Algeria's unemployment and poverty rates remain critically high.

Al-Maġrib/Maroc
Morocco

Area: 446,550 sq km
Population: 33.2 million
GDP per capita: 2,400 US$
Capital: Rabat
Government: Constitutional monarchy
Languages: Arabic, French (both official), Berber dialects
Currency: 1 dirham = 100 centimes

Geography: Fertile countryside with a Mediterranean climate extends to the Rif Mountains in the north. To the south of the coastal strip, three chains of the Atlas Mountains mark the transition to the steppes and deserts in the extreme south-west. The most popular tourist destinations are Agadir, Fez, Marrakesh, Meknes and Rabat.

Politics: Conquered by the Arabs in the 7th century, Morocco fell under the rule of Islamic dynasties until the end of the 19th century, became a French protectorate from 1912 and gained independence in 1956. The country's monarch is its political and spiritual leader. In 1996, the current monarch ushered in a phase of liberalization.

Economy: Agriculture accounts for less than 20% of GDP, with the chief exports being citrus fruit, wine, fruit and vegetables. Industry, though underdeveloped, contributes 32% of GDP. Morocco has the largest phosphate reserves in the world. Services, principally tourism, form the chief economic sector. Trade with Europe is an important economic factor for the country.

Al-Miṣr/Egypt
Egypt

Area: 1,001,450 sq km
Population: 78.8 million
GDP per capita: 1,800 US$
Capital: Cairo
Government: Presidential republic
Language: Arabic
Currency: 1 Egyptian pound =
100 piasters

Market in Adrar, one of the important Touat oases in the Algerian Sahara

Geography: The fertile Nile valley between three and 20 km wide and extending over 1,000 km from the river delta in the north deep into the south, has been settled since earliest times. The Arabian Desert lies to the north-west, while th-

Morocco's royal cities of Fez, Marrakesh, Rabat and Meknès contain some of the finest works of Islamic architecture in existence, mosques and palaces built by the rulers of the great dynasties. The historic centers of Marrakesh, Fez and Meknès are designated world cultural heritage sites. **1** Marrakesh was founded in 1063 as the residential city of the Almoravides dynasty, and was capital of the Almohades until the end of the 13th century. Jemaa-el-Fna Square is the heart of one of Morocco's most beautiful souks. **2** The tanners of Fez still use traditional methods to dye leather, hides and wool. **3** The impressive Bab el-Mansur city gate in Meknès, completed in 1732.

Libyan Desert in the west occupies one-quarter of the country's area. Egypt is in a subtropical zone of high pressure, with only the Mediterranean coastal areas receiving rain in winter. The Aswan Dam enables the country's agricultural areas to be irrigated. Places of interest include sites associated with the Pharaohs, but also Cairo and Alexandria.

Politics: The cradle of one of the earliest major cultures from the 3rd millennium BC, Egypt fell under Libyan, Persian and Assyrian rule from the 1st millennium BC. At the turn of the millennium, the fertile Nile region was the granary of Ancient Rome. Islam took effect after the conquest of Egypt by the Arabs in the 7th century. In 1517 the country came under Ottoman rule. British influence increased after the opening of the Suez Canal in 1869. Egypt became an independent kingdom in 1922. After conflicts with neighboring Israel over the latter's occupation of the Sinai peninsula in 1967, a peace treaty was concluded in 1979.

Economy: The high level of education in the cities contrasts with the lifestyle of the nomads, who principally raise livestock. Only the fertile Nile valley yields grain, sugarcane and cotton – the latter being Egypt's principal export after oil. Agriculture accounts for 18% of GDP. The Suez Canal is a major source of revenue. Tourism, although contributing the majority of service sector revenues, is suffering from Islamic acts of terrorism. Remittances from overseas Egyptians have also decreased due to the political and economic instability in the near east. Successful economic reforms in the 1990s led to an increase in foreign investment levels and growth rates.

Al-Saharaw
Western Sahara

Area: 266,000 sq km
Population: 280,000
GDP per capita: not available
Capital: El Aaiún
Government: Republic/annexed by Morocco in 1979
Languages: Arabic, Spanish, Hassani
Currency: Saharaui peseta; unofficial currency:
1 Moroccan dirham = 100 centimes

Geography: This almost uninhabited country largely consists of semi-desert. Rocky outcrops feature in the north, sand deserts in the south.

Politics: The territory belonged to the Islamic empires that ruled over what is now Morocco from the 11th century. It was declared Spanish in 1885 and became the overseas province of Spanish Sahara in 1958. The Polisario Liberation Front was founded in 1973. Spain withdrew in 1975 and designated Morocco and Mauretania as administrative powers. In 1979 Mauretania waived its share in favour of Polisario, only to have its share annexed by Morocco. After a UNO peace plan Polisario and Morocco agreed a cease-fire in 1991, to be followed by a referendum on independence.

Economy: The country has rich phosphate reserves and fishing grounds in coastal waters. Oasis cultivation and nomadic animal husbandry are practised as subsistence farming.

Angola
Angola

Area: 1,246,700 sq km
Population: 12.1 million
GDP per capita: 3,800 US$

Egypt: The Sphinx near the Pyramid of Cheops in Gizeh, 2500 BC

Capital: Luanda
Government: Republic
Languages: Portuguese (official), Bantu languages
Currency: 1 kwanza = 100 lwei

Geography: The high plateau is traversed by rivers and slopes steeply down to the rain forests along the narrow coastal region. The tropical climate of Angola's interior is moderated by the altitude

Egypt's capital is the largest city in Africa, with 6.8 million inhabitants. Almost as many tourists visit Cairo every year, principally as a starting-point for tours of the Ancient Egyptian sites along the Nile. **1** The Sultan Hassan Mosque is considered the most beautiful of Cairo's 500-plus mosques. **2** The Old City has been designated a world cultural heritage site by UNESCO. Mulid is one of the greatest Islam festivals at which the faithful celebrate the birth of the prophet Mohammed, **3** crowding into the Hussein Mosque and all other places of worship throughout the Islamic world.

Nations of the World
Africa

Savanna to the far south-west gives way to desert. Nine national parks and animal reserves provide protection for indigenous wildlife.

Politics: Discovered in 1483 by Diego Cao, Angola remained a Portuguese province. Its independence in 1975 triggered a civil war lasting over 15 years. The country is currently ruled by UN mandate, but the peace process is making only slow progress.

Economy: The long civil war has ravaged the economy, and the population depends on foreign aid. Agricultural products are sisal, sugar and tobacco. Key exports are coffee, diamonds, petroleum and iron ores. The small industrial sector primarily processes agricultural goods. Development of the country's poor infrastructure is desperately needed for greater economic progress.

As-Sūdān
Sudan

Area: 2,505,813 sq km
Population: 41 million
GDP per capita: 1,200 US$
Capital: Khartoum
Government: Republic
Languages: Arabic (official), English, Hamitic and Nilotic languages
Currency: 1 Sudanese pound = 100 piastres

Geography: The Sudan is the largest African countriy in terms of area. It is divided into north and south by the great swamps of the Sudd, a flood plain of the White Nile. Almost one-third of the country consists of barren sand desert, although rain forests grow in the mountainous southern regions. The climate is largely continental tropical. The game reserves in the south are the chief tourist destinations. Desertification is a major environmental issue throughout the country, which can only be solved with the help of aid organizations to help people help themselves by careful water management.

Politics: Sudan's early history was shaped by Egypt; an independent kingdom was not formed until 1000 BC. Christian empires ruled from the 6th century onwards until the country was Islamicized by Arab settlers at the end of the 13th century. Sudan was ruled by the British in the 19th and 20th centuries. Since Sudan acheived independence in 1956, religious and ethnic differences have led to frequent political unrest and armed conflicts; human rights violations are commonplace in the country.

Economy: Subsistence agriculture and nomadic animal husbandry are

Sudan: Koran study at the El-Sheik-Deffa-Allah Mosque in Omdurman

practised. Agricultural products are the chief exports, comprising cotton, peanuts, sesame and oilseed as well as 80% of the world's gum resin production. The small industrial sector, which did not begin its slow development until after independence, is still rudimentar and employs 5% of the workforce The perspectives can only become better with sustainable peace.

Benin
Benin

Area: 112,622 sq km
Population: 7.8 million
GDP per capita: 700 US$
Capital: Porto Novo
Government: Presidential republic
Languages: French (official), Fon, Yoruba and other tribal languages
Currency: 1 CFA franc = 100 centimes

Geography: Benin's coast alon the Gulf of Guinea consists of hu mid, swampy lowlands fringed b lagoons. To the north the countr rises to fertile clay highlands tha form a plateau in the north. In th west the land slopes gently dow to the Niger basin. Tourist destina tions are the nature parks in th North, and the cities of Ouidah an Porto Novo in the south.

Politics: In the 17th century th kingdom of the Fon, based in th city of Aborney, increased i power. The Fon delivered slaves t European trading centers. In 189 the region became part of the colo ny of French West Africa, and wa decolonized and awarded inde pendence in 1960. The Republic o Benin was established in 1975 afte a coup d'État. Torn by tribal wars the country held its first free parlia mentary elections in 1991.

Economy: Benin is inhabited b more than 60 ethnic populations Attempts to nationalize the econ omy in the 1970s failed. The coun try primarily lives from the agricul tural sector, which produces fo the domestic market, as well as coffee, oils, and cotton for export. The industrial and service sectors are both relatively undeveloped. Tourism is strongly promoted.

Botswana
Botswana

Area: 600,370 sq km
Population: 1.6 million
GDP per capita: 7,900 US$

cause of its key strategic location to the north of the Boer state. The country was administered by the British Ambassador to South Africa from 1964, and gained independence in 1966 as the Republic of Botswana. The government comprises the National Assembly and the House of Chiefs.

Economy: 95% of the population are Bantu, with over 80% living out-

Capital: Gaborone
Government: Republic
Languages: Setswana, English (both official)
Currency: 1 pula = 100 thebe

Geography: The Kalahari semi-desert covers almost 80% of Botswana, which extends over the chiefly flat continental plateau (800-1,300 m). Agriculture is restricted to small areas in the southeast. Around one-fifth of the country is a registered national park. The Okavango forms a freshwater delta on the northern rim of the Kalahari. The climate is subtropical and extremely dry, with maximum termperatures of 40°C in summer and 6°C in winter.

Politics: English missionary territory since 1820, Botswana became a British protectorate in 1885 be-

1 Voodoo, a spiritual sect that originated in Benin, has followers throughout the world, including many in the Americas. The sect, with an estimated 50 million believers today, is based on unwritten rites and respect for ancestral spirits and is now registering increased interest in many regions including West Africa.

2 The Okavango rises in the Angolan uplands. Its swampland delta in Botswana is home to an exceptionally rich fauna.

3 The royalty of Aborney is still a living tradition in Benin; the influence of its royal families remains almost unbroken.

side the urban centers. Agriculture largely consists of extensive cattle farming. However, the backbone of the economy are the rich diamond mines of the Kalahari, which have made Botswana the second largest exporter in the world. Iron ore and anthracite are also important export commodities. Botswana is a member of the Southern African Customs Union.

Burkina Faso
Burkina Faso

Area: 274.200 sq km
Population: 13.6 million
GDP per capita: 500 US$
Capital: Ouagadougou
Government: Republic
Languages: French (official), Fulbe, More and further tribal languages
Currency: 1 CFA franc = 100 centimes

Geography: Wet savannas in the south-west give way to dry savannas in the country's center and main settlements. The Black Volta is the only river that carries water all year. Part of the Sahel desert region lies in the north-east, where a semi-desert climate reigns. Tourist centers are the cities of Ouagadougou and Bobo-Dioulasso and the national parks with their rich animal life.

Politics: The heart of today's Burkina Faso was the state of Ouagadougou, founded in the 11th century by the Mossi and conquered by the French in the 19th century. The former colony of Upper Volta (1919-1960) was renamed Burkina Faso in 1984. After independence, Burkina Faso was weakened by frequent attempted coups succeeded by years of military dictatorship; the political situation seems to have stabilized.

Economy: Among the most densely populated countries in West Africa, Burkina Faso is inhabited by around 160 tribes, around half of whom practice natural religions. Despite regular periods of drought, the country's economy is based on agriculture, with 90% of the population practising subsistence farming. Small amounts of cotton are exported. Apart from gold, the rich natural resources are largely untapped. The country's poor infrastructure and widespread corruption have impaired development.

Burundi
Burundi

Area: 27,834 sq km
Population: 6.8 million
GDP per capita: 150 US$
Capital: Bujumbura
Government: Presidential republic
Languages: Kirundi, French (official), Kiswaheli
Currency: 1 Burundi franc = 100 centimes

Cap Verde: The economy is weak, the selection of goods limited.

Geography: Lying to the north-east of Lake Tanganyika, the country comprises uplands with wet and dry savannas in the interior and humid tropical rain forests to the

north-east. The humid, tropical climate is moderated by the country's relatively high average elevation above sea level.

Politics: Tutsi tribes invaded the territory of Burundi in the 15th century and established feudal rule over the indigenous Hutus. In 1890, the country became part of the German colony of East Africa, and subsequently fell under Belgian administration. Since Burundi's independence in 1962, the political situation has been determined by repeated conflicts between the Hutu (85 % of the population) and Tutsi (15%). Despite a new constitution (1992) and international efforts, the civil war finds no end cannot be regarded as over.

Economy: Agriculture is the chief economic sector. The mild climate favors tropical fruit farming and extensive animal husbandry. The industrial center around the city of Bujumbura produces textiles and small amounts of agricultural products for export, with coffee the most important of these. The government of Burundi is heavily dependent on foreign aid and invest

...nts to help the population fulfil ...eir basic needs.

abo Verde
ape Verde

...ea: 4,033 sq km
...pulation: 400,000
...DP per capita: 2,900 US$
...pital: Praia
...overnment: Republic
...nguages: Portuguese (official), ...eole
...urrency: 1 Cape Verde escudo = ...0 centavos

...eography: Cape Verde, an archi-...elago off the west coast of Africa, ...omprises nine large islands and ...ve uninhabited islets, all of volca-...ic origin. The landscape is domi-...ated by bush, steppe, and semi-...esert vegetation. Cape Verde has ...ne of the lowest rainfalls in the ...orld, and drought periods often ...ast for years. The sandy beaches ...n Sal, Boa Vista and Maio and the ...sland of Fogo attract tourists.

...olitics: After the islands' discov-...ry by the Portuguese in 1460, it ...emained under Portuguese rule ...or over 500 years. The slave trade ...vith America brought long pros-...erity. Cape Verde did not become ...ndependent until 1975. The parlia-...ment, elected for a five year term, ...elects the executive body and the ...President of State.

...Economy: Over 70% of the popula-...tion are descended from Portu-...guese immigrants and African sla-...ves. Over 60% of Cape Verdians ...live and work abroad owing to the ...sparse natural resources. The rich ...fishing grounds account for 50% of ...export revenues, but almost all ...foodstuffs must be imported. Most ...of the country's GDP is generated ...by the service sector. Local tourism ...is gradually expanding.

Cameroun/Cameroon
Cameroon

Area: 475,442 sq km
Population: 17.3 million
GDP per capita: 1,100 US$
Capital: Yaoundé
Government: Presidential republic
Languages: French, English (both official), Bantu languages
Currency: 1 CFA franc = 100 centimes

1 In Burkina Faso agriculture has been heavily subsidized since the 1980s. The land's chief resource is its livestock, although poultry farming is also important.

2 The north of Cameroon is inhabited by semi-nomadic herdspeople. Their round stone or clay huts, called sarés, serve as dwellings or grain stores. Such traditional dwellings are chiefly found in the country's rural regions.

3 The mosques of Burkina Faso are built of clay in typical West African style. Around 25% of the population are Muslims.

Nations of the World
Africa

Geography: The narrow coastal plain is covered by tropical rain forests that give way to wet savanna in the largely mountainous interior. To the north are dry grassland savannas that meet Lake Chad in the north-east and the Sahel to the far north. The highest point is the volcano Mount Cameroon (4,070 m). Cameroon's natural beauty and diversity of cultures offer a wide range of tourist attractions.

Politics: In the 15th century the coast of Cameroon was a center of the slave and ivory trade for European colonial powers. It became a German protectorate in 1884. From 1918 Britain and France shared the former colony under the mandate of the League of Nations, awarding the country independence in 1960. After a period as a federal republic, Cameroon has been a presidential republic since 1972.

Economy: The population is composed of roughly 200 tribes. Agriculture plays a significant role, with the principal exports coffee and cocoa. The country's petroleum resources brought only temporary economic growth. The industrial and services sectors are underdeveloped. Cameroon has experienced steady and strong growth in recent years and the country has made progress in reducing its foreign debt burden.

Central African Republic see République Centrafricaine
Chad see Tchad

Comores
Comoro Islands

Area: 2,170 sq km
Population: 690,000
GDP per capita: 700 US$
Capital: Moroni
Government: Islamic

Presidential republic
Languages: Comorian, French (both official), minority languages
Currency: 1 Comorian franc = 100 centimes

Geography: The territory comprises the three large islands of Ngazidja, Ndzuani and Mwali and other islets off the East African coast. They are largely of volcanic origin, with the highest volcano the still-active Karthala (2,361 m). Rain forests cover the craggy mountain massifs. The narrow coastlines are fringed by coral reefs.

Politics: The islands fell under Persian and Arab rule from the 16th century. The colony founded by France in 1843 on the neighboring island of Mayotte was extended in 1912 to encompass the Comoro Islands. Most of the Islands declared their independence in 1975, while Mayotte remained French.

Economy: The educational, health and social security system are inadequate (50% of the population are illiterate). 78% of the population work in agriculture, many as subsistence farmers. Large areas of the agricultural land are under state control. Major agricultural export commodities include vanilla, coconuts, and spices. The country's underdeveloped infrastructure is a major hindrance to investment and development.

Congo
Congo

Area: 342,000 sq km
Population: 3.7 million
GDP per capita: 2,200 US$
Capital: Brazzaville
Government: Republic
Languages: French (official), Bantu languages
Currency: 1 CFA franc = 100 centimes

Geography: A narrow coastal plain where mangroves and tropical rain forests flourish gives way in the country's interior to rolling hills of an average height of 800 m with savanna vegetation. The swampy lowlands of the Congo Basin are covered mostly by vast tropical rain forests.

Friday Mosque in Mutsamudu on the small Comorian island of Anjouan

...litics: After the Congo was di-...overed in the 15th century, ...ropeans established trading ...sts there. The region did not be-...me a French colony until 1880. ...ter independence in 1960, the re-...blic first modeled itself on ...ance, but declared itself a ...cialist People's Republic in 1970. ...91 saw the introduction of demo-...acy and a multiple-party system.

Economy: The agricultural sector ...counts for 12% of GDP, with ...ops being yams, plantains and ...ain. Petroleum forms the basis of ...e economy, with drilling, proces-...ng and export bringing in around ...0% of foreign currency. Hard-...oods are also exported. The ...ountry's industrial sector pro-...uces chemicals and foodstuffs. ...ervices account for 51% of GDP. ...olitical instability hampers econo-...ic development in Congo.

Congo, République démocratique
Congo, Democratic Republic

Area: 2,345,410 sq km
Population: 62 million
GDP per capita: 200 US$
Capital: Kinshasa
Government: Presidential republic
Language: French
Currency: 1 Congo franc

Geography: The third largest coun-try in Africa is shaped by its lo-cation in the Zaire Basin, a plain at an altitude of 200-400 m which ex-tends to the Central African rift val-ley in the east and is bounded to the west by the Congo and Kwango rivers. The highest peaks are the Virunga volcano (4,507 m) and the Ruwenzori (5,109 m). Tourism is restricted to the capital and the national parks. Tropical rain forests cover much of the country.

Politics: In 1885 the Congo was owned by the King of Belgium, but received independence in 1960 as Congo-Kinshasa. A military coup in 1965 was followed in 1971 by the foundation of the Republic of Zaire. The dictator Mobutu was over-thrown in 1997 by rebels, whose leader Kabila proclaimed the Demo-cratic Republic of Congo; after his murder in 2001, responsibility for solving the Congo conflict now lies with his son Joseph Kabila.

Economy: In agriculture, subsist-ence farming produces the bare minimum necessary, with coffee and rubber produced for export. The country is rich in natural resources (copper, zinc, precious metals, diamondsand petroleum.

1 In the Ituri Forests, Democratic Republic of Congo, many ancient rituals still survive. Epulu women, for instance, paint their faces white during menstruation ceremonies.

2 A wide array of products are sold in traditional markets. The sales-woman in the photo is selling oil in bottles of all shapes and sizes.

279

Côte d'Ivoire
Côte d'Ivoire

Area: 322,462 sq km
Population: 17.6 million
GDP per capita: 1,000 US$
Capital: Yamoussoukro
Government: Presidential republic
Languages: French (official),
Dioula and further languages
Currency: 1 CFA franc =
100 centimes

Geography: From its 550 km of coastline, fringed by lagoons to the east, the country rises to an altitude of 300-400 m. Around half the country's area consists of table-land covered by wet savannas. Intensive farming is practiced along the coast. Tourist destinations include the animal reserves (Comoé, Nimba) and beaches.

Politics: Before its colonization by the French from 1893, the north belonged to the old kingdom of Mali and the south was ruled by the Ashanti. European influences were introduced by missionaries who traveled through the country from the 17th century. The Republic of the Ivory Coast gained independence from France in 1960 and became a role model of political stability and economic prosperity. However in 1999 and 2001, this sta-

bility has been destroyed by two coups and a civil war since 2002.

Economy: 33% of national GDP is produced by agriculture and fishery sectors, in which more than half of the workforce is employed. Ivory Coast is the world's fourth largest producer of coffee and has the highest level of industrialization in West Africa; agricultural products and petroleum processing account for 29% of GDP. One-third of the population is employed in the service sector.

Djibouti
Djibouti

Area: 23,200 sq km
Population: 500,000
GDP per capita: 1,100 US$
Capital: Djibouti
Government: Republic
Languages: French, Arabic
(both official), Cushitic languages
Currency: 1 Djibouti franc =
100 centimes

Geography: The Tadjoura Basin, among the world's hottest areas, is covered by sand and stony deserts in the interior. 95% of the country is covered by steppe. Hot springs and active volcanos can be found throughout the country.

Politics: In 1896, French protectorates on the Gulf of Aden were merged to form the state of Djibouti. Although the country became independent in 1977, the French army maintains military bases there and is still responsible for national defense.

Economy: Over half the population are nomads. Djibouti has to cope with waves of Ethiopian refugees who make up almost one-fifth of the population. Frequent drought means that agriculture accounts for only around 2% of GDP, while industry contributes around 18%. The country aims to concentrate on services, which already account for 80% of GDP thanks to the French military presence.

Egypt see Al-Misr
Equatorial Guinea see Guinea
Ecuatorial

Eritrea
Eritrea

Area: 121,320 sq km
Population: 4.7 million
GDP per capita: 300 US$
Capital: Asmara
Government: Republic
Languages: Arabic, Tigrinja
(official)
Currency: 1 birr = 100 cents

Geography: The Red Sea forms the country's north-eastern border. The narrow coastal plain extends in the north to the Abyssinian Highlands, with mountains over 2,600 m in height. The main settlements are located here because of the relatively high rainfall. Desert lowlands are found to the south in the foothills of the Denakil Mountains. The Dahlak Islands in the Red Sea also belong to Eritrea. Tourist destinations are Asmara, the nearby ancient city of Cohaito,

A camel caravan transports salt from Lake Assal in Djibouti.

e historic colonial architecture in
assawa and the coral reefs of
e Dahlak archipelago.

litics: What is today Eritrea was
rt of the Italian colony from 1890
1941, and subsequently under
itish administration until 1952.
ter ten years as an autonomous
gion within Ethiopia, it was an-
xed as the 14th province, finally
ining independence as a repub-
c in 1993 after a long battle for
eedom. The Provisional National
uncil, in power since 1991, is
orking on a democratic constitu-
n and on the establishment of a
multiple-party system to form a
sis for a more sustainable eco-
omic development and higher po-
tical stability.

conomy: Illiteracy is around 80 %.
he war caused particularly exten-
ve damage to agriculture; while
0% of the population are tradition-
lly small farmers, millet, wheat
nd pulse production is currently
ufficient for only about 20% of the
opulation. A current development
rogram subsidizes coffee and to-
acco farming for export. Industrial
rocessing and consumer goods
roduction account for 18% of GDP.
uarrying (marble industry) is plan-
ed for expansion. There are reali-
tic perspectives and hopes of
ttracting foreign investors and ot-
er forms of development aid to
upport the quick reconstruction of
he infrastructure, which was com-
letely destroyed in the war.

Ethiopia see Ityopya

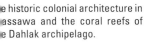

Gabon
Gabon

Area: 267,667 sq km
Population: 1.4 million
GDP per capita: 7,900 US$
Capital: Libreville

Government: Presidential republic
Languages: French (official),
Bantu languages
Currency: 1 CFA franc =
100 centimes

Geography: The mangrove swamps
and lagoons of the coastal lowlands give way to coastal savanna.
The interior tableland with an altitude of up to 1,000 m is largely covered with tropical rain forests

1 The Rashaida, an isolated and
largely nomadic ethnic group of Arab
origin, make up less than 0.3% of
Eritrea's total population.

2 Next to cocoa and wood, cotton
is an important export for the Ivory

Coast, although methods of transport-
ing are often limited in capacity.

3 One-quarter of Eritrea's 3.5 million inhabitants are nomads and semi-
nomads, chiefly living in the south-
east in the semi-desert Afar region.

Nations of the World
Africa

(Birougou Mountains 1,190 m). There are dry savannas to the south-east. The climate is tropical. Tourist destinations are the capital city, the Albert Schweitzer Hospital in Lambaréné and the three national parks.

Politics: After the coast was discovered by the Portuguese in 1470, several European powers established trading points for raw material and slave trading. The country became a French colony in 1885, and gained independence in 1960. Under the new constitution (1991), the National Assembly is elected for five years and the President is appointed by direct election.

Economy: Around half of the predominantly Bantu population lives in the cities. Agriculture accounts for only 8% of GDP; 20% of the

one of Africa's richest countries. The mining industry produces uranium, manganese, iron ore and gold.

Gambia
The Gambia

Area: 11,295 sq km
Population: 1.6 million
GDP per capita: 400 US$
Capital: Banjul
Government: Presidential republic
Languages: English (official), Mandingo, Wolof, other local languages
Currency: 1 dalasi = 100 butut

Geography: Africa's smallest country, located along the banks of the Gambia River, is completely enclosed by Senegal, and no more than 50 km wide at its widest point. Mangrove swamps extend far in-

scovered by the Portuguese in the 15th century and became a British colony in 1765, received independence in 1965 as a Commonwealth state and became a republic in 1970. The British-style constitution (1970) was repealed in 1994 after the military coup. Parliamentary elections were resumed in 1997.

Economy: The majority of the population are small farmers growing subsistence crops of millet, sorghum, rice and maize; peanuts are the main export product, and like fishery products are processed by the underdeveloped industry. Tourism accounts for 15% of GDP and the industry has largely recovered from a major decline that followed a military coup in the 1990s.

Ghana
Ghana

Area: 239,460 sq km
Population: 22.4 million
GDP per capita: 700 US$
Capital: Accra
Government: Presidential republic
Languages: English (official), over 70 further languages and dialects
Currency: 1 cedi = 100 pesewas

Geography: The 535 km-long coastline along the Gulf of Guinea, rendered near impassable by lagoons, forms a natural border to the south. From here, grassland gives way to the tropical rain forests that cover the Ashanti Highlands rising to the west. Lake Volta lies in the wet savanna to the east. The climate is tropical. Tourism concentrates on the partly preserved forts at the colonial trading outposts of Cape Coast, Elmina and Accra.

The ancient architecture of the Mossi people still survives in northern Ghana.

country's area is taken up by subsistence crops of manioc, yams, plantains and maize, and coffee, cocoa, sugar-cane and palms for export. Rain forest timber is a major source of export revenue. The backbone of the economy, however, is the export of petroleum and refinery products, which accounts for 80% of GDP and makes Gabun

land from the Gambia delta. The Atlantic beaches, said to be the most beautiful in Africa, attract tourists.

Politics: In the 8th century a number of kingdoms arose in what is today The Gambia, and were annexed to the kingdom of Mali in the 12th century. The Gambia was di-

Politics: The Ashanti people founded a powerful kingdom in what is now Ghana, engulfing neighboring tribes to extend their territory to the coast, from where they conducted slave trading with Europe from the 15th century. In 1850 the British conquered the country and founded the colony of Gold Coast. After early independence in 1957, the republic initially profited from its rich natural resources until economic decline set in from 1966. The new constitution (1993) is intended to promote the process of democratization by introducing a multiple-

party system. Ghana has enjoyed a period of political stability since 1993 and is now one of the most open democracies in Africa.

Economy: Half of the population are small farmers, cultivating basic subsistence crops of rice, millet, yams and plantains. 50% of the agricultural land is taken up by cocoa. Animal husbandry is primarily conducted in the north. Tropical rain forest timber is exported. The mining industry supplies mineral raw materials (bauxite, manganese) and rich yields of gold. The small industrial processing sector produces foodstuffs, textiles and shoes for the country's own needs. Services cover almost half of GDP with six main branches (transport, trade, finance, real estate etc.)

1 The Ashanti, Ghana's largest ethnic group, still maintain many of their ancient traditions.

2 In 1482 Portuguese gold-hunters and traders built this fort in Elmina, on the Gold Coast in what is now Ghana. The fort, a UNESCO world cultural heritage site, commemorates the cruelty of the transatlantic slave trade, for which the fort was once a major center.

3 Traditional ceremonies still take place in this Ashanti village near Kumasi in South Ghana.

Nations of the World
Africa

Geography: The broad coastal plain traversed by rivers is bounded to the east by wet savanna and to the south-east by hills. Freshwater swamps in the interior give way to mangrove swamps at the coast. Tourist attractions are the old colonial city of Bissau and the islands of the Bijagos Archipelago off the coast.

Politics: Portuguese outposts for the slave trade were founded in the 16th century. Guinea-Bissau was a Portuguese colony from 1879-1974 and later became a parliamentary democracy after gaining independence, which ended abruptly in a military coup. After the approval of new parties in 1991, the first free elections of a National Assembly were held in 1994.

Economy: 80% of the population cultivate subsistence crops of rice, maize and other grain. Animal husbandry accounts for nearly a third of GDP, and peanuts and cashews are significant exports. There are plans to attract foreign investors to tap the bauxite, phosphate and petroleum reserves. The country's economy was thrown into a major crisis by a civil war in the late 1990s.

Guinea Ecuatorial
Equatorial Guinea

Area: 28,051 sq km
Population: 540,000
GDP per capita: 8,700 US$
Capital: Malabo
Government: Presidential republic
Languages: Spanish (official), pidgin English, Bantu languages
Currency: 1 CFA franc = 100 centimes

Geography: The country's territory comprises the mountainous region of Mbini and the volcanic islands of

Bioko and Pagalu. The higher elevated areas of Mbini are covered with savanna and the rest with tropical rain forests, giving way to mangrove swamps on the coast.

Politics: Discovered in 1470, Bioko and Pagalu became Spanish in 1778, and the mainland in 1885. After independence (1968) the country was ruled by a dictatorship until a military coup in 1979. The 1991 constitution's plans for a democratic multi-party system were limited prior to the country's first free elections in 1993.

Economy: The majority of the population are Bantu-language speak-

Guinée
Guinea

Area: 245,857 sq km
Population: 9.6 million
GDP per capita: 500 US$
Capital: Conakry
Government: Republic
Languages: French (official), tribal languages
Currency: 1 Guinea franc = 100 cauris

Geography: The coastal plain to the west gives way to the plateau of Fouta Djalon, up to 1,500 m high and the source of the Senegal, Niger and Gambia rivers, which slopes away to the east. The coast

Vibrant colors at the market of Mamou, a small town in Guinea

ers and 85% are Catholics. The economy is founded on cocoa and coffee plantations and valuable timber reserves. Livestock farming on the mainland is gaining in significance. 5% of the population is employed in industry, primarily processing agricultural products. Modest gold reserves are mined. The service sector accounts for 42% of employment but the export of oil now accounts for most economic growth.

is swampy; the country's north-east is covered by savanna and the south-east by tropical rain forests.

Politics: For centuries, the Fulbe people defended their territory against the mighty kingdoms of Ghana and Mali. In the 19th century Guinea became a French colony. After independence in 1958 a single-party system was established which was overturned by a military coup in 1984. The republican constitution of 1991 led to the first democratic elections in 1995. Conflicts in neighbouring states could threaten Guinea's current stability.

Economy: Three-quarters of the population live from agriculture, which barely covers domestic needs. The country has rich natural

(Omo, Awash, Bale), the ruins at Axum and the Christian sites at Lalibela.

Politics: The legendary Kingdom of Sheba was succeeded in the 1st century by the mighty Axum, which lasted for over 1,000 years, was Christianized as early as the 4th century and subsequently defied

resources and is the second largest bauxite producer in the world. Other mining products are iron ore, uranium, cobalt, gold. Foodstuffs and textiles play a minor role.

Îtyopya
Ethiopia

Area: 1,127,127 sq km
Population: 74.7 million
GDP per capita: 250 US$
Capital: Addis Ababa
Government: Federal republic
Languages: Amharic (official), 70 further languages and dialects
Currency: 1 birr = 100 cents

Geography: The territory of Ethiopia extends over a mountain range divided by the East African Rift Valley. The north is dominated by desert and savanna, the south by rain forests. The chief tourist destinations are the landscapes and fauna of the national parks

1 The Bidjogo people on the Bissago Islands off the coast of Guinea-Bissau are said to be expert fishers, boat-builders and craftspeople.

2 Ethiopia: Some of the riches in the treasury of the church of Saint Mary of Zion in Axum. The historic building is one of many important Christian structures in the country.

3 The church of Debre Berhan Selassie was built in Gondar by Emperor Yasu the Great at the end of the 17th century and richly ornamented. It is still a religious center today.

4 The rock churches at Lalibela, Ethiopia, were built in the 12th-13th centuries. St. George, "Beta Ghirgis", is cruciform in shape.

Nations of the World
Africa

Islamization. Not until the 19th century did a mighty state again rise to resist colonialization. A Socialist people's republic was founded after the 1974 abdication of the last emperor; its leader was overthrown in 1991. Zenawi's government was elected in 2000 in Ethiopia's first ever multiparty elections, however the results were heavily criticized as fraudulent.

Economy: Agriculture in this multinational state accounts for over half of GDP and employs 80% of the labor force, yet barely produces the basic foodstuffs. Coffee is the main export. The country's underdeveloped service industry primarily produces goods for the domestic market.

Kenya
Kenya

Area: 582,646 sq km
Population: 34.7 million
GDP per capita: 800 US$
Capital: Nairobi
Government: Presidential republic
Languages: Kiswaheli (official), English, tribal languages
Currency: 1 Kenya shilling = 100 Cents

Geography: Kenya, situated on Africa's eastern coast, is divided into four distinct geographic zones: dry plains in the north-east, mountainous foothills around Lake Turkana to the north-west, south-eastern savannas with forests and thorny scrub vegetation, and high plateaus in the west that rise to altitudes of over 3,000 m and then slope down to Lake Victoria.

Politics: The former British colony gained full independence in 1963, and proclaimed itself a republic. From 1982 the single-party system was gradually broadened in favor of democracy, at the urging of international aid contributors. The 2002 elections were a major transition in Kenyan politics and ended the decades of government by the KANU political party.

Economy: Kenya's agriculture produces tea, coffee, sisal and sugarcane for export. Cattle farming is practised at a high level. Processing industries (petroleum, agricultural products) account for 11% of GDP. The service sector, including tourism, is the largest segment of the national economy. Tourism has lost momentum owing to political unrest and loss of stability.

Lesotho
Lesotho

Area: 30,355 sq km
Population: 2 million
GDP per capita: 700 US$
Capital: Maseru
Government: Constitutional monarchy within the Commonwealth; the king serves a largely ceremonial function.

Languages: Sesotho, English
Currency: 1 loti = 100 lisente

Geography: Lesotho is a completely enclosed by South Africa and is in the extreme south of the continent. The predominant forms of vegetation are grass savanna and mountain pastures.

Politics: The kingdom of the Basotho was formed in the 19th century and gained independence from British rule in 1966. It has been a constitutional monarchy since 1993.

Economy: Owing to the limited land area and repeated droughts, agriculture (maize, wheat, millet and livestock) is poorly developed; supplies are imported. The majority of the country's GDP is derived from the wages of Lesotho citizens working in South Africa.

Liberia
Liberia

Area: 111,369 sq km
Population: 3.4 million
GDP per capita: 200 US$
Capital: Monrovia
Government: Presidential republic
Languages: English (official), tribal languages

Nairobi is Kenya's economic and administrative center.

Currency: 1 Liberian dollar = 100 cents

Geography: The coastal areas are characterized by savanna, while much of the interior is covered by tropical rain forest. The climate is humid and tropical. The nature reserves in the Nimba Mountains were once tourist attractions but the tourist industry is now virtually non-existent due to political instability.

Politics: Africa's oldest republic, Liberia was established in 1822 by freed American slaves. The country gained independence in 1847 but retained close ties to the USA for many years. After nine years of civil war following the 1990 fall of President Doe, the dictator who had ruled since 1986, a peace-keeping force was provided by ECOWAS. After special elections in 1997, the National Patriotic Party came back to power. Rebels groups made President Taylor resign and flee the country

Economy: Agriculture (rice, manioc) barely covers two-thirds of the country's needs. Large-scale plantations principally supply rubber for export. Other exports are coffee, cocoa and palm kernels. Timber and iron ore are also exported. The services sector profits from the world's largest trading fleet in terms of tonnage.

Lîbîyâ
Libya

Area: 1,759,540 sq km
Population: 5.9 million
GDP per capita: 9,400 US$
Capital: Tripoli
Government: Islamic people's republic
Languages: Arabic (official), Berber dialects
Currency: 1 Libyan dinar = 1,000 dirham

Geography: The Mediterranean climate favors relatively lush vegetation along the narrow coastal region, which gives way in the south to steppes and ultimately to the de-

sert that cover 90% of the country's area. In the extreme south, foothills of the Tibesti Massif on the northern fringes of the Sahara reach altitudes of up to 2,285 m. The ancient historical sites along the coast (Leptis Magna, Cyrene) and capital of Tripoli are the main tourist destinations.

Politics: Settlements were established in the coastal regions by the 9th century BC, and fell to Roman

1 A medicine man from the Kikuyu tribe in Kenya.

2 The Libyan oasis Ghadames, on the borders of Algeria and Tunisia, was formerly an important watering hole for camel caravans owing to its prolific springs.

3 After the start of the Liberian civil war in 1989, around 80% of the population fled, chiefly to neighboring Guinea and Ivory Coast. Some have now been able to return to their homes. A peace treaty was concluded in 1995 under pressure from the UN, but the region remains unstable.

rule in the 1st century AD. Libya was conquered by the Ottomans (1517) and ruled by an Islamic order in the 19th century. The country was an Italian protectorate for 40 years before receiving independence as a monarchy. The king was overthrown in 1969 by a military coup led by Colonel al-Gaddafi.

Economy: 90% of the population lives in the coastal area. Only 2% of the land is cultivatable. Privatization of most state-owned operations is planned to secure subsistence quantities of fruit, vegetables, grain and fruit. The Libyan economy is centered on the country's enormous petroleum reserves (25% of the GDP).

Madagasikara
Madagascar

Area: 587,041 sq km
Population: 18.5 million
GDP per capita: 500 US$
Capital: Antananarivo
Government: Republic
Languages: Malagasy, French (both official official), Howa
Currency: 1 Madagascar franc = 100 centimes

Geography: The world's fourth largest island is largely composed of sloping mountains, with coastal plains to the west. The climate is tropical; the island's east has high rainfall and is covered with lush rain forest. The unique, partly endemic flora and fauna of the island is threatened by slash and burn agricultural techniques, cyclones, flooding and earthquakes.

Politics: Originally settled by South Asian peoples, the island was discovered in 1500 by Portuguese who established settlements with the French on the coast. The indigenous population successfully re-

sisted colonization until 1896; then a colony of France, the country gained independence in 1960. Its 1992 constitution specifies a bicameral parliament, with elections held every five years.

Economy: Social and healthcare services are as inadequate as the provision of basic foodstuffs. The agriculture forms the basis of existence for 75% of the largely Malayan / Indonesian population, who cultivate rice, cassava, maize, sweet potatoes, mangos, bananas and sugar cane in smallholdings. Key exports are coffee, vanilla, cotton, and tobacco. Prawns, tuna and lobster are processed by the poorly developed industrial sector.

Madagascar is divided from north to south by mountain chains.

Political instability and corruption have slowed economic growth. Reforms of liberalization are due.

Malawi
Malawi

Area: 118,484 sq km
Population: 13 million
GDP per capita: 300 US$
Capital: Lilongwe

Government: Presidential republic within Commonwealth
Languages: Chichewa, English (both official), Chitumbuka, other Bantu languages
Currency: 1 Malawi kwacha = 100 tambala

Geography: The majority of the country's area is occupied by Lake Nyasa. The regions to the west and south of the lake are mountainous, with peaks of up to 2,670 m (Nylka Plateau). Grasslands and dry forests are the principal forms of vegetation; dense forests can be found in the mountains. The rich animal life is protected in four national parks; tourist centers are Lake Nyasa and Blantyre, with its beau-

Butchers and baskets; street vendors in Madagascar

tiful surroundings. Its geographic situation makes it a wonderful add-destination for nature lovers and fishing enthusiasts.

Politics: In 1891 the region surrounding Lake Nyasa became a British protectorate, and was incorporated into Rhodesia as Nyasaland in 1907. Malawi was declared independent in 1964

e president's extensive powers ⸱arded by the Constitution in ₅6 were repealed in 1993, partly the urging of creditor countries. ₑ first free elections were held in ₉4.

onomy: 70% of Malawi's popula-n lives from smallholder farming, oducing 35% of GDP. Subsist-ⁱce is threatened by periods of ⸱ought. 90% of export revenues

Geography: Between Ségou and Timbuktu, the Niger forms a large freshwater delta with fertile alluvi-al deposits. Mali's north is domi-nated by dry Saharan zones, while the south has tree savannas and gallery forests. Tourist attractions are the areas of natural beauty and the ancient royal cities of Timbuktu, Mopti and Bamako. Desertification is a major environmental issue in the country.

⸱e derived from coffee; other ex-⸱rts are tea, sugar and tobacco. ₗbsistence fishing is practiced on ₑ country's three lakes. The indu-⸱rial sector processes domestic ₉ricultural products (tea, beer, to-⸱cco). Tourism is well-developed, ⸱ntributing 25% to GDP. The servi-ₑ sector is underdeveloped but ₒw contributes half of GDP. Ma-ₗwi is heavily indebted.

⸱ali
⸱ali

⸱rea: 1,240,192 sq km
⸱opulation: 12 million
⸱DP per capita: 500 US$
⸱apital: Bamako
⸱overnment: Presidential republic
⸱anguages: French (official),
⸱amakan, further Mandé languages
⸱urrency: 1 CFA franc =
⸱0 centimes

1 Among the Dogon in Mali, impor-tant decisions are made by the Coun-cil of Elders and the Hogon.

2 The vibrant marketplace of Bama-ko, Mali's capital city, offers a wide variety of goods, mostly domestic. Many visitors still try the traditional art of bargaining.

3 The Dogon in Mali build their vil-lages on the cliffs of the Bandiagara Plateau in a loop of the Niger. The straw-roofed buildings are granaries.

4 Lake Malawi is Africa's third larg-est lake, a plentiful fishing ground. A large segment of the local popula-tion survives from fishing.

Nations of the World
Africa

Politics: The legendary kingdom of Mali arose in the 11th century. Its trading center – Timbuktu – became famous far beyond the borders of Africa in the 14th century. At the end of the 19th century the French conquered the country and incorporated it into the colony of French West Africa. The Republic of Mali gained independence in 1960 and was ruled by a dictator-ship until 1991. After the first free elections in 1992, conflicts with the Tuareg were reconciled by the assurance of partial autonomy.

Economy: The north is inhabited only by the Tuareg, while 90% of the largely Islamic population live in the south. Because of Mali's poverty migration into neighboring countries is very high. Over 80% of the population subsists from agriculture. Desertification is reducing the amount of cultivatable land, and grain cultivation in the savannas is frequently affected by drought. Nomadic animal husbandry in the Sahel and fishing in the Niger delta and lakes are major contributions to subsistence. The industrial sector processes domestic agricultural products. Mali is heavily dependent on foreign aid, remittances from overseas workers, and global prices for agricultural goods. Government reforms have led to steady growth in national rates in recent years.

Mauritius
Mauritius

Area: 2,040 sq km
Population: 1.2 million
GDP per capita: 5,500 US$
Capital: Port Louis
Government: Republic
Languages: English (official), Creole, Hindi, Urdu
Currency: 1 Mauritius rupee = 100 cents

Geography: This tropical island, a volcanic formation in the Indian Ocean, has a humid tropical climate. Its highest mountain is the Cocotte (771 m) in the south. The white beaches of the coastline's many bays are fringed by lagoons. Parts of the original rain forest have survived only in the nature reserves. The island's capital is the center of its thriving tourism industry, and the nature reserves at Rivière Noire and Ile Aigrettes are easily accessible.

Politics: The island was captured in the 16th century by the Dutch, who introduced plantation cultivation. The French took over the colony in the 18th century, while Mauritius came under British rule from 1810 until its independence in 1968. The Republic of Mauritius was founded in 1992, although the country remained a member of the Commonwealth.

Economy: Sugar-cane cultivation has primary importance, employing 14% of the labor force. Three-quarters of foodstuffs are imported; cultivation of potatoes, vegetables, bananas and pineapple is subsi-

dized. The country's industrial sector focuses on textile production and sugarcane processing. 10% of the workforce are already employed in the well-developed tourism sector.

Mawrītāniyah
Mauretania

Area: 1,030,700 sq km
Population: 3.1 million
GDP per capita: 1,000 US$
Capital: Nouakchott
Government: Islamic presidential republic
Languages: Arabic (official), Niger-Congo languages
Currency: 1 ouguiya = 5 khoums

Malawi's capital Bamako has around 1.8 million inhabitants.

Geography: The eastern Atlantic coast gives way to flat coastal plains and extensive tableland with steppe vegetation. The majority of the country is occupied by the Sahara with sand and scree deserts. Its highest elevations are the plateaus of Adrar and Tagant, at around 500 m. Owing to the extremely dry climate, palms and baobab flourish only in the far south in the savannas on the Senegal. Of interest for tourists are the cities of Chinguetti, Oualâta, Tîchît and

Oudâne. The bird sanctuary of Djoudj and Banc d'Arguin national park are on the coast. Desertification is a major environmental problem in Mauretania.

Politics: The country was Islamicized by Arab settlers in the 11th century. In 1902 the French acquired the territory and incorporated it into the colony of French West Africa in 1920. Mauretania gained independence in 1960. The new constitution of 1991 smoothed the path from dictatorship to democracy; the first elections were held in 1992.

Economy: Persistent droughts have reduced the proportion of traditional nomadic populations; urbanization is increasing. Only 0.2% of the country's area is cultivatable. The fertile land in the catchment area of the Senegal and the oases of the south is cultivated for subsistence agriculture supplying basic needs. Animal husbandry is practised in the southern steppe belt. Fishery accounts for the majority of export revenues, and forms the basis of a small processing industry. Iron ore exports are the major source of foreign currency.

Moçambique
Mozambique

Area: 801,590 sq km
Population: 19.6 Million
GDP per capita: 400 US$
Capital: Maputo
Government: Republic
Languages: Portuguese (official), Bantu languages
Currency: 1 metical = 100 centavos

Geography: The many bays of the coast along the Indian Ocean give way to savanna and dry forests inland. To the north are mountains of

up to 2,000 m. Mangrove forests grow in the swampy regions of the river deltas. In the summer, monsoons dominate the tropical climate. The once-rich animal life (antelopes, gazelles, elephants, leopards) has been decimated by big game hunting. Tourism concentrates on nature reserves such as Gorongosa and the broad beaches, but also the old colonial cities of

1 Many Mauretanian women have joined women's cooperatives, leaving traditional structures in favor of labor efficiency.

2 Mauretania: The Tuareg are called "the shrouded ones" or, after their indigo robes, the "Blue Knights of the Desert".

3 Mozambique: The Zambesi is dammed in the gorge of Cabora Basse. The reservoir has an area of 2,700 sq km and a volume of 160 billion cubic meters. Its enormous capacity is designed to solve annual flooding problems and irrigate 15,000 sq km of land. The dam also supplies valuable electricity to the country.

Moçambique and Maputo. The country's climate ranges from sub-tropical to tropical with significant differences between the coastal and interior regions. Severe flooding and periods of drought are common in many regions.

Politics: Occupied in the 16th century by the Portuguese, the country did not gain independence until 1975 after a long guerilla war. In the same year the liberation movement proclaimed a people's republic, which was replaced in 1990 by a parliamentary democracy with a new constitution. After a long civil war, a peace treaty was signed with the right-wing rebels in 1992.

Economy: Although the largest sector of the economy, agriculture is barely at subsistence level. Over half the export revenues are derived from prawns and shrimps. The rich natural resources (precious and semi-precious stones, iron ores, minerals, metals) are largely untouched. After improvement to the infra-structure, the services sector will profit from the ports and tourism.

Morocco see Al-Magrib/Maroc

Namibia
Namibia

Area: 824,292 sq km
Population: 2 million
GDP per capita: 3,600 US$
Capital: Windhoek
Government: Republic within Commonwealth
Languages: English (official), Afrikaans, German
Currency: 1 Namibian dollar = 100 cents

Geography: The sandy, rocky expanse of the Namib Desert extends parallel to the coast. A steep escarpment (Brandberg, 2,574 m) rises in the interior to rolling highlands that slope down in the east to the Kalahari basin at 1,000 m. To the north is the Etoscha Pan, one of Africa's largest salt pans. The climate is subtropical. Around 7% of the country's area comprises animal reserves principally inhabited by antelopes, lions and elephants. The country's major tourist attractions include the seaside towns of Swakopmund and Walvis Bay as well the extensive desert wildernesses in the interior, providing nature circuits and ecologdes.

Traditional and modern: Himba women in a Namibian supermarket

Politics: European traders and missionaries first entered the country in the mid-19th century; Namibia became a German colony in 1884. It was occupied by South Africa during the First World War and was subsequently annexed as the Boer state's 5th province. The guerilla war which raged from the 1960s ended in a cease-fire in 1989; Namibia gained independence in 1990, and a democratic constitution followed. SWAPO, which led the resistance movement from the outset (1959), is today the most influential political force.

Economy: The economy is still suffering the separation from South Africa. Agriculture is the most important area, accounting for 73% of employment, and beef is the main agrarian export. Natural resources (diamonds, metal ores) are mined. The profitable fishing industry is expanding further after the inclusion of the port of Walvis Bay in the country's territory (1994). The country's economy is closely linked to that of South Africa. Government reforms are now liberalising the economy and privatizing many state industries.

Niger
Niger

Area: 1,267,000 sq km
Population: 12.5 million
GDP per capita: 300 US$
Capital: Niamey
Government: Presidential republic

Languages: French (official), Haussa and further tribal languages
Currency: 1 CFA franc = 100 centimes

Geography: The country extends from the middle reaches of the Niger through the Sahel and deep into the Sahara. Oases are fed by rivers rising in the Aïr Mountains (1,944 m) to dry up in the desert. The north is dominated by sand and

Economy: The country's economy is dominated by traditional nomadic animal husbandry and small-scale farming, principally in the Niger Valley and largely for subsistence. Fisheries and the fishing licence business are profitable. The mining industry supplies the country's main exports in the form of diamonds, copper and uranium. Niger is heavily dependent on foreign loans and aid.

stony deserts, the south by dry savanna. The chief settlement areas are the Niger and Komadougo basins. Popular tourist sights are the ancient city of Agadez, former hub of caravan routes, prehistoric rock drawings in the Aïr Massif and the W nature reserve.

Politics: In the 16th century, the political structure which had stood in the Niger area since the 12th century came under Islamic influence before the country was conquered by the Fulbe in the 19th century. The French colony of Niger was founded in 1922. The constitution brought in after independence in 1960 was suspended until 1991. The National Assembly was dissolved in 1996 following a coup. A new constitution restored civilian rule to the country in 1999.

1 The Bororo people of Niger are traditionally nomadic cattle farmers, less Islamicized than the sedentary Fulbe people. They often form economic communities with farmers. The Bororo men are noted for their complex face painting.

2 The Namib Desert extends along the Atlantic coast of Namibia. The interior has less than 20 mm of rainfall per year. Low temperatures and dense fog are common in this coastal desert region.

3 Camel caravans still cross the Sahara in the Republic of Niger below the Air Massif as they have done for hundreds of years – also a popular tourist trip.

Nations of the World
Africa

Nigeria
Nigeria

Area: 923,768 sq km
Population: 132 million
GDP per capita: 1200 US$
Capital: Abuja
Government: Presidential federal republic
Languages: English (official), Arabic, tribal languages
Currency: 1 naira = 100 kobo

Geography: This country on the Gulf of Guinea has a humid tropical climate. The coast is fringed by a strip of mangroves 15-90 km wide, which gives way to primeval forest further inland. The plateau in the country's interior is marked by savannas, steppes and desert-like regions. Lake Chad lies to the northeast. The Niger flows through the country for 1,168 km and ends in 24,000 sq km of delta. Tourist destinations are the northern Haussa cities of Kano and Katsina.

Politics: The kingdoms of Nigeria, in existence since the early Middle Ages, were gradually conquered by the Fulbe. In 1885 the country was declared a British protectorate. Since its independence in 1960 Nigeria has been ravaged by military coups, unrest and religious conflict. The elections of 1992 were annulled by the country's leaders but the military dictatorship ended in 1999 with new elections.

Economy: Nigeria is inhabited by three major peoples: the Christian Yoruba and Igbo in the south, and the Muslim Haussa in the north. Agriculture consists of subsistence smallholdings and plantations that supply export goods such as cocoa and rubber. The main basis of the economy, at 90% of export revenue, is the petroleum and natural gas reserves which

have been exploited since the 70s. Corruption and the poor infrastructure are major obstacles to the country's economic development.

République Centrafricaine
Central African Republic

Area: 622,984 sq km
Population: 4.3 million
GDP per capita: 400 US$
Capital: Bangui
Government: Presidential republic
Languages: French, Sangho (both official), Bantu and Sudan languages
Currency: 1 CFA franc = 100 centimes

Central African Republic exports include coffee, cotton and livestock.

Geography: The interior consists of low, rolling hills 500-1100 m in height, broken by isolated outcrops. Great rain forests flourish in the humid tropical climate of the south. The remaining country is covered by wet savannas, giving way to dry savanna in the northeast. Manovo-Gounda St. Floris National Park and the capital are the chief areas of interest for tourism, a sector that remains largely undeveloped. Floods are common throughout the country.

Politics: The French conquered the country and incorporated the region into what is now Chad; liberation movements gained the country's independence in 1960. The single-party system, in place since 1962, was replaced after a military coup in 1965 by a dictatorship under General Bokassa, who was overthrown in 1979. The country's first mulit-party democratic elections were held in 1993.

Economy: Agriculture is primarily subsistence, with coffee and cotton cultivated for export. Small quantities of uranium, iron, copper and nickel are mined, as are diamonds. The poorly developed industrial sector produces basic and semi-luxury foodstuffs, leather and wood products. The service sector also remains largely undeveloped.

Rwanda
Rwanda

Area: 26,338 sq km
Population: 8.6 million
GDP per capita: 400 US$
Capital: Kigali
Government: Presidential republic
Languages: Kinyarwanda, French (both official), Kiswaheli, English
Currency: 1 Rwanda franc = 100 centimes

Geography: The highest peaks in this mountainous country are the Virunga volcanoes (4,507 m) in the west. Much of central and eastern Rwanda consists of low, hilly tableland. Rain forests and wet savannas flourish in the humid tropical climate up to a height of 2,500 m, giving way to bamboo forests at higher altitudes. Virunga National Park is the home of the mountain gorilla, a rare species that is now threatened with extinction due to widespread poaching.

Politics: In the 15th century the Tutsi people established feudal rule in the territory settled by the Hutu, which survived colonization by the Germans and Belgians. When the Tutsi (9% of the population) lost their position of power in the 1950s, sustained and bloody conflicts erupted which have continued to the present day and which reached a terrible climax in the 1994 massacres.

Economy: A civil war which began in the spring of 1994 completely destroyed the economy in Africa's most densely populated country; rebuilding of the economy with foreign aid began in 1996. Coffee is the main export, followed by tea, pyrethrum, beans, maize and bananas. The developing industrial sector mostly processes agricultural products in small and medium-sized enterprises.

São Tomé e Príncipe
São Tomé and Príncipe

★ ★

Area: 1,001 sq km
Population: 200,000
GDP per capita: 900 US$
Capital: São Tomé
Government: Republic
Languages: Portuguese (official), Creole
Currency: 1 dobra = 100 centimos

Geography: The archipelago off the coast of Gabun near the Equator consists of the two main islands of São Tomé and Príncipe and some smaller islands, all volcanic in origin and part of the Cameroon line. The landscape is dominated by rain forests, favored by the climate and the numerous rivers. A leisure and sports fishing center was built in the north of Príncipe in 1992. Soil erosion due to farming is a major environmental issue in the country.

Politics: The islands were settled by the Portuguese from 1485, and in the 16th-18th centuries were the world's largest sugar suppliers and a center of the slave trade with Brazil. A Portuguese overseas province from 1951, the islands became independent in 1975. Recent years have seen major political reforms. In 1990 a multiple-party system was established and Príncipe received a statute of autonomy in 1995.

1 African pygmies were among the first humans to settle in the Congo basin. Under 4 ft 11 in height, they are the smallest ethnic groups in the world.

2 Lagos is a major industrial center and Nigeria's foremost port. The metropolis is sited on four islands interconnected by bridges. Like many Africa cities, Lagos has grown dramatically in recent decades.

3 With a total area of over 25,000 sq km, the Niger delta is the largest river delta in Africa. Its plentiful fishing grounds sustain many of the area's inhabitants.

Economy: Cocoa is almost the only significant economic factor, accounting for 78% of export revenues. Agricultural land passed into state control in 1975 and was partly awarded to small farmers; foreign investors receive administration licences. Since 1987 the slump in world cocoa prices has generated structural reorganization initiatives supported by the World Bank. However, 80% of foodstuffs are imported. Tourism and offshore oil reserves could both become important economic factors.

Sénégal
Senegal

Area: 196,722 sq km
Population: 12 million
GDP per capita: 900 US$
Capital: Dakar
Government: Presidential republic
Languages: French, Wolof
Currency: 1 CFA franc =
100 centimes

Domestic produce is sold at Senegal's many markets.

Geography: Senegal, bounded by the Senegal river and its tributary, the Falémé, is at the western extremity of the continent of Africa. Largely flat, it rises in the northeast to the Guinean Fouta Djalon.

Senegal is in the Sahel zone; rainfall increases to the south, while Casamance has a humid tropical climate. Tourism is chiefly concentrated in Casamance, Dakar and Petite Côte.

Politics: The home to European settlements, Senegal came under French colonial rule in the 17th-19th centuries. In 1958 Senegal was awarded autonomy within the French Communauté and became independent in 1960. Senegal became a single-party state in real terms in 1966; opposition parties were not permitted until 1975. The country joined with Gambia from 1982-1989 to form the confederation of Senegambia.

Economy: Agriculture and fishery account for the majority of export revenues, with raw materials (gold, iron ore) increasing in significance. The service sector (tourism) is the country's primary economic focus, at 61% of GDP. Key economic tasks for the future are the reduction of subsidies and industrial privatization. Government reforms have led to strong growth rates in recent years and the country's government has successfully held inflation in check since the 1990s.

Seychelles
Seychelles

Area: 454 sq km
Population: 80,000
GDP per capita: 8,600 US$
Capital: Victoria
Government: Republic within the Commonwealth
Languages: English, French, Creole
Currency: 1 Seychelles rupee =
100 cents

Geography: The archipelago in the Indian Ocean consists of over 90 islands, fewer than half of which are inhabited. Only the larger islands are mountainous and covered with sparse vegetation. The climate is tropical marine. The territory covered by the archipelago includes more than 1 million sq km in the Indian Ocean. The sandy beaches of Mahé, the nature reserve on Praslin and the island of Silhouette are the primary tourist destinations.

Politics: Discovered by Vasco da Gama in 1501, the islands were colonized by the French from 1756 and by the British from 1794-1811, and became a British Crown colony in 1903. Independence in 1976 was followed by years of political unrest in which the constitution was overturned by a coup. Although other parties have been allowed since 1991, the Unity Party SPPF has held power since 1977.

Economy: The main exports continue to be fish, cinnamon and copra. The greatest economic potential lies in tourism services. The economy has stagnated since 1991, leading to an extensive program of privatization. Tourism remains the most important industry but the government is now attempting to diversify the economy to achieve a better balance.

Sierra Leone
Sierra Leone

Area: 71,740 sq km
Population: 6 million
GDP per capita: 300 US$
Capital: Freetown
Government: Republic within the Commonwealth

one-party state after 1973, Sierra Leone received a democratic constitution in 1991, shortly followed by a military coup and another in 1997. A system of parliamentary democracy was reintroduced in 1998. Elections held in August 2007 were initially judged by official observers as "free, fair and credible".

Economy: Sierra Leone is one of the poorest countries in the world, with an economy originating from

Languages: English (official), Creole
Currency: 1 leone = 100 cents

Geography: Sierra Leone is on Africa's west coast, and includes small islands off the flat, wooded coastal region with strips of alluvial deposits. The higher savannas in the country's interior are traversed by rivers that rise in the Talla and Falaba plateaus in the north and east. The tropical climate on the coast provides relatively constant temperatures.

Politics: European contacts with Sierra Leone were among the first in West Africa. England acquired land in the region from 1787-1788 and established settlements of freed slaves. British crown colony from 1808, independence in 1961. A

1 Senegal: 78% of the workforce is employed in agriculture, cultivating rice, millet, peanuts, sugar-cane and cotton.

2 Mahé is the only island of the Seychelles with steep granite crags as well as palm-fringed beaches. The largest island, it is an ideal resort for divers.

3 The Temne, a ethnic group consisting mostly of farmers, make up one-third of Sierra Leone's total population. Temme communities are governed by chiefs whose territory often includes one larger and several smaller villages. Male and female social and community groups are formed according to traditions; here to organize religious ceremonies.

colonial times, based on raw materials and oriented to global markets. Mining products are titanium ore, diamonds, bauxite and gold. Initial signs of economic stabilization were destroyed by the Liberian war. The industrial sector remains undeveloped, despite the country's mineral wealth. Sierra Leone's service sector contributes one-fifth of national GDP and its development is blocked by political instability and corruption. The economy is now dependent on foreign aid.

Soomaaliya
Somalia

Area: 637,657 sq km
Population: 8.8 million
GDP per capita: 200 US$
Capital: Mogadishu
Government: Republik
Languages: Somali (official), Arabic, English, Italian

An impressive range of spices from the traders in Hargeisa, Somalia.

Currency: 1 Somalia shilling = 100 centesimi

Geography: The largely steep, craggy coast of Somalia runs along the Gulf of Aden and Indian Ocean

for over 3,000 km. The country's highest peak is Surud Add (2,408 m). The two largest rivers, Yuba and Shebeli, form great swamps along the flat southern coast. The climate is desert-like in the north west, with monsoon conditions in other regions. Before the civil war, the beaches, natural landscapes and cultural heritage sites were important tourist destinations.

Politics: Following Portuguese and Turkish influences in the 16th century, the country came under the rule of the Sultan of Oman in the 17th-19th centuries. At the end of the 19th century the colonial territories of French and British Somaliland were founded on the Gulf of Aden, and Italian Somaliland on the Indian Ocean. The Republic of Somalia was founded in 1960. The military dictatorship in power from 1969 was overthrown in 1991. The civil war which has raged since then has resisted even UN intervention.

Economy: One of the world's poorest countries, Somalia has seen its animal husbandry and agriculture

destroyed by drought and the long civil war. UN aid provided only temporary relief in the famines of 1992-1993. Political instability impedes substantial development.

South Africa/Suid-Afrika
South Africa

Area: 1,219,912 sq km
Population: 44 million
GDP per capita: 5,900 US$
Capital: Pretoria
Government: Republic
Languages: English, Afrikaans, Zulu, Bantu languages (all official)
Currency: 1 rand = 100 cents

Geography: South Africa is divided into three main regions: the plateau of the interior, the Rand ridge and the coastal area. The extensive interior plateau of the Karoo (veld), 1,000-1,800 m in height, is broken by isolated peaks and bordered by the Drakensberg mountains to the east. The coastal region, generally narrow and straight, joins this region further east. The country has a warm, temperate subtropical climate. Krueger National Park, the Garden Route and Cape Town are only two of South Africa's many tourist attractions.

Politics: The Dutch colony was founded in the 17th century. Conquered by the British in 1795, the region was divided into the crown colony of Natal and the Boer republics of Transvaal and Oranje, which were defeated in the Second Boer War. The racist apartheid policy introduced in 1911 was fiercely opposed by the ANC. The policy of reconciliation launched in 1989 led in 1993 to a new constitution and the end of government-enforced racial discrimination.

Economy: Agriculture (citrus fruits, wine, fruit, wool and cotton) ac-

Cape Town lies to the far south of the African continent, in one of the world's most beautiful locations. 2.3 million people live in the city, the majority still in townships into which the black and mixed-race population were forced at the end of the 1940s. **1** The beautiful Camps Bay below the "Twelve Apostles" are located in a Cape Town suburb. **2** The best view of the city is from the plateau. **3** Socializing beneath Table Mountain – the legacy of apartheid doesn't dominate the lives of all young South Africans.

counts for only 4.6% of GDP, covering both subsistence needs and exports. South Africa is the world's primary supplier of gold and platinum. The industrial sector contributes 44% of GDP, while services are catching up.

Sudan see As-Sudan

Swaziland (kaNgwane)
Swaziland

Area: 17,363 sq km
Population: 1.1 million
GDP per capita: 2,500 US$
Capital: Mbabane
Government: Constitutional monarchy within Commonwealth
Languages: English, Siswati (both official)
Currency: 1 lilangeni = 100 cents

Geography: Swaziland, enclosed by South Africa and Mozambique, is on the eastern side of the Drakensberg Mountains and has a warm, moderately subtropical climate. The country is divided into four zones of varying altitudes; the western highlands have large forestry plantations, while. the main settlement area is the savanna of the adjacent Middle Veld, giving way to the Low Veld to the east on the border with Mozambique. The dry savanna of the Lebombo Plateaus is used for grazing. The mountains and game reserves (Mlilwane and Ehlane) are popular tourist destinations.

Politics: The area was settled by the Bantu people of Swazi from the mid-18th century before the first Boers entered the country in 1868, followed by the British in 1877. Swaziland was named a British protectorate in 1907 and gained independence in 1968. Since 1978, monarchy is given absolute power, while political opposition is banned.

Economy: Swaziland's economy is dependent on global markets and its neighbor South Africa. It is traditionally dominated by the cultivation of agricultural and forestry products, which are processed by the industrial sector, contributing 38% to GDP. Services (tourism) account for 47% of GDP. More than 75% of the population works in agriculture and animal husbandry.

The nomadic Masai people live in southern Kenya and Tanzania.

Tanzania
Tanzania

Area: 945,087 sq km
Population: 37.5 million
GDP per capita: 400 US$
Capital: Dodoma
Government: Federal Presidential republic
Language: Kiswaheli
Currency: 1 Tanzanian shilling = 100 cents

Geography: Situated on the Indian Ocean, the country rises from the coast towards the west and is divided by highland plateaus and mountains. Its highest peak is Kilimanjaro (5,895 m). It is bordered by the three great lakes of Lake Victoria, Lake Nyasa and Lake Tanganika. The territory also includes the islands of Zanzibar, Pemba and Mafia. The climate is tropical, and temperate in the uplands. Tanzania is a popular safari destination.

Politics: In 1884 Tanganika became the main constituent of the colony of German East Africa. The country was taken over by Britain in 1920 under a League of Nations mandate and became a UN trustee territory in 1946, and acheived independence in 1962. The presidential republic of Tanzania was formed in 1964 by merging Tanganika and the British protectorate of Zanzibar, independent since 1963. The one-party system of the 1977 constitution was replaced by a multiple-party system in 1992.

Economy: Agriculture, forestry and fishery account for around 53% of GDP and 60-70% of export revenue. Tanzania's food production is self-sufficient. Industry, at 4.3% of GDP, is insignificant, while services account for 23%. The government has endeavoured since 1986 to accelerate development in line with IMF requirements by restructuring the economy as a market economy. Major export commodities include gold and coffee. Government reforms have led to higher growth rates in recent years.

Tchad
Chad

Area: 1,284,000 sq km
Population: 10 million
GDP per capita: 750 US$
Capital: N'Djamena
Government: Presidential republic
Languages: French, Arabic (both official)
Currency: 1 CFA franc = 100 centimes

Geography: The Republic of Chad lies in the Sahara, Sahel and Sudan regions along the east of the Chad Basin. The basin, an average of 200-500 m above sea level, is broken by a few isolated peaks. Lake Chad to the west is an important water reservoir. Tourist centers include the national parks of Zakouma and Manda, the game reserves of Abou-Teflan, Siniaka-Minia and Bahr-Salamat and the northern desert regions.

Politics: Chad was settled by Arabs, Berber and Bantu from the 15th century and became a French protectorate in 1900. After gaining independence in 1960 the country was torn by military struggles for political power, in which Libya, France and the USA intervened. After international pressure a transitional charter was passed in 1993 that paved the way for the introduction of a multiple-party system.

Economy: The country today is one of the poorest and least-developed in the world. Agriculture is still largely at subsistence level, and is dominated by arable farming and animal husbandry, with marginal links to world markets through products such as cotton and peanuts. The economy is dependent on foreign aid, although the establishment of oil drilling and export offers a perspective for the future. Currently more than 80% of Chad's labor force works in the agricultural sector, most as subsistence farmers. The service industry is the main source of growth.

Government: Presidential republic
Languages: French (official), Kabyé, Ewe
Currency: 1 CFA franc = 100 centimes

Geography: Togo lies in West Africa on the Atlantic Ocean between Ghana and Benin. Its narrow, 53 km-long coastal region gives way to a 50 km-wide strip of hills and a sandstone plateau traversed by the Togo-Atakora moun-

Togo
Togo

Area: 56,785 sq km
Population: 5.5 million
GDP per capita: 400 US$
Capital: Lomé

1 Proud and confident, most Masai women enjoy a great range of freedom from their early teens. Married women are free to take several lovers. If a woman is physically abused by her husband, she can demand a divorce (kitala) and return to the home and communities of her parents.

2 The Ngorongoro Crater is one of the greatest natural attractions in the East African country of Tanzania. The ancient crater has a total diameter of 22 km.

3 The Arabic Tubu people live in the north and east of Chad, in the Tibesti mountains and Ennedi uplands.

301

tains (Mont Agou, 986 m). The tropical climate has created a wet savanna in the south, merging into dry savanna in the north. Forests are found only in the mountains and along the rivers. The major tourist destinations are the sandy beaches and former colonial cities such as Lomé.

Politics: Discovered by the Portuguese in 1481 and first settled by Europeans from the 16th century, Togo became a German protectorate in 1884. In 1922 the region was divided between the French and British under a League of Nations mandate, and became a UN territory of the French Union in 1946. Since its independence (1960) oppositional forces have battled for democracy. The 1992 constitution was planned as a transition from the single-party dictatorship to a democratic republic.

Economy: The 40 or so tribes and peoples that make up Togo's population live in one of the poorest countries in the world. The less developed north is chiefly given to subsistence farming. Agriculture accounts for 70% of employment, yet generates only 36% of GDP. Togo is highly dependent on the export of a few raw materials, with the main exports phosphate, cotton, coffee and cocoa. Trade and services account for 42.7% of GDP. The government has encountered major difficulties in enacting a series of planned reforms to open the economy in recent years.

Tūnisiyah / Tunisie
Tunisia

Area: 163,610 sq km
Population: 10 million
GDP per capita: 3,400 US$
Capital: Tunis
Government: Presidential republic

Languages: Arabic (official), French
Currency: 1 Tunesian dinar = 1,000 millimes

Geography: The Tell-Atlas mountains, up to 1,200 m in height, join the north coast and give way to the Medjerda plain in the south, an agricultural area. Further south is a central ridge of mountains up to 1,500 m in height, which also marks the boundary of the humid Mediterranean climate. Beyond this border the south is characterized by dry steppes and deserts. Tourist centers are Tunis, Sousse, Kairouan and Djerba.

Politics: A country with a great Carthaginian and Roman past, Tunisia experienced Arab and Turkish rule from the 7th century before becoming a French protectorate in 1881. Independent since 1956, Tunisia finally began to abandon the single-party system in 1981. The constitutional reform of 1987 was aimed at increasing democracy. Tunisia's largest political party, the Constitutional Democratic Assembly, has dominated politics since independence.

Economy: Agriculture accounts for around 15 % of GDP and is export-oriented, cultivating grain, fruit, wine and olives. Products from the textiles, food and electrical engineering industries deliver around half of export revenues and have increased in importance over petroleum and natural gas exports. The service sector, including the tourism industry, has the largest share of GDP, at 50%.

Uganda
Uganda

Area: 236,040 sq km
Population: 28.1 million
GDP per capita: 400 US$
Capital: Kampala
Government: Presidential republic within the Commonwealth
Languages: Kiswaheli, English (both official), Luganda
Currency: 1 Uganda shilling = 100 cents

The prayer hall of the Great Mosque of Kairouan, built in the 7th century

Geography: Most of the country is made up of a high plateau from 1,000-3,000 m in height, broken by isolated peaks. The highest elevations in this savanna landscape are Mt. Elgon (4,321 m) to the east and the Ruwenzori Massif in the west,

Tunis was shaped chiefly by the Hafsides dynasty and by waves of Spanish Muslim immigrants from the 13th – 17th centuries. Today it is a modern metropolis with 670,000 inhabitants as well as the political center of Tunisia. **1** The "Olive Tree Mosque" was completed in 864. **2** Avenue Habib Burgiba. **3** The Great Mosque Djamâ ez-Zituna is a major religious center.

up to 5,119 m high. Half of Lake Victoria lies within the south-east of Uganda's territory. The climate is temperate owing to the altitude. The rich animal life of Ruwenzori National Park is a magnet for tourists fond of nature.

Politics: A number of centralized African kingdoms had already existed for centuries in Uganda when the British conquered the country and declared it a protectorate in 1894. After independence (1962) the situation in the 70s and 80s under the terror regimes of Amin and Obote was characterized by civil war before the political situation stabilized in the 1990s. The last presidential elections were held in February 2006. According to national and international observers, the elections were predominanty free and fair.

Economy: Agricultural production continues to dominate the economy, although half of agriculture's 50% share of GDP is accounted for by subsistence farming, with 5% directed to exports (90% of it coverd by coffee), but also cotton, tea and tobacco. The industrial sector con-tributes 11-12% to GDP. Since 1987 the government has applied a policy of economic liberalization in coordination with the IMF, and an economic community with Kenya and Tanzania has been in existence since 2001.

Western Sahara see Al-Saharaw

Zambia
Zambia

Area: 752,614 sq km
Population: 11.5 million
GDP per capita: 900 US$
Capital: Lusaka
Government: Presidential republic within Commonwealth

Languages: English (official), Bantu languages
Currency: 1 kwacha = 100 ngwee

Geography: The high plateau (1,000-1,500 m) rising from south to north is broken up by isolated-mountains of up to 2,300 m. The basins of the Zambezi and Kafue rivers have shallow lakes and swamps. The north-east of the country is part of the East African Rift Valley. The altitude causes an almost tropical climate; the highland savannas experience prolonged dry periods. Tourist attractions include Victoria Falls, Lake Tanganika and the national parks.

Politics: Today Zambia is a Commonwealth republic. The country

Around half of Zambia's population are rural.

was formed from the original territories of Barotseland, North-West Rhodesia and North-East Rhodesia to the north of the Zambesi River, which were declared a British protectorate in 1911. In 1923 the region came under direct British colonial rule. From 1953 to 1963 North Rhodesia was part of the Central African Federation before gaining independence in 1964. Its president, K. D. Kaunda, established a single-party system in 1972/73. National and international pressure for democracy led in 1990 to the approval of previously prohibited opposition parties. A new constitution guarantees the multi-party system and specifies the simultaneous holding of presidential and parliamentary election.

Economy: The majority of the African population, composed of 73 different ethnic groups, practices subsistence farming. Only the minority of European farmers use modern methods of cultivation. Zambia's economy is based on copper mining and export, which accounts for 65% of the total export volume. The government has privatized the country's largest mining company and some progress has been made in liberalizing the economy. Service industries, including tourism, are the country's fastest growing industries.

Zimbabwe
Zimbabwe

Area: 390,757 sq km
Population: 12.2 million
GDP per capita: 400 US$
Capital: Harare
Government: Presidential republic within the Commonwealth
Languages: English (official), Bantu languages
Currency: 1 Zimbabwe dollar = 100 cents

Geography: Zimbabwe, bounded to the north by the Zambesi and to the south by the Limpopo lowlands, mainly consists of a high plateau belonging to the rim of the Kalahari Basin. The highlands of the interior consist of rolling tableland with rocky outcrops and savanna vegetation. The climate is tropical but moderate thanks to the altitude. The preferred tourist destinations include the nature reserves, Victoria Falls and the ruins of Great Zimbabwe.

Politics: A British protectorate from 1891, the country became the colony of Rhodesia in 1923, named after the British South African colonial politician Cecil Rhodes. In 1930 Rhodesia was divided into European and African territories, favoring the Europeans. After long negotiations and a struggle for freedom the country achieved independence in 1980 and was renamed Zimbabwe. Its president, Robert Mugabe, rules the country autocratically. From 2000 onwards the regime has tolerated the illegal seizure of white Zimbabweans' farmland as well as clashes with the opposition parties and Zimbabwe has been plunged into deep internal crisis.

Economy: With an export-oriented economy that exploited mineral resources (gold, copper, nickel, coal) and with its industry diversifying, Zimbabwe was once a prosperous African country. However, due to its erratic political situation it is today in serious crisis – since 1998 the economy has shrunk by a third; inflation and unemployment are both extremely high.

1 Over 120,000 children and young people under 18 are used as soldiers in countless conflicts throughout Africa. Stable peace between Uganda and Congo is still a long way off.

2 "Scenes so lovely must have been gazed upon by angels in their flight" wrote Livingstone on discovering Victoria Falls, where the Zambesi falls 110 m. The world's largest falls are a popular tourist attraction.

3 The Ndebele, one of southern Africa's Ngni ethnic groups, live in Zimbabwe and South Africa. The women wear traditional bright clothing and lavish jewellery.

The double continent of the Americas covers an area of 42 million sq km (including Greenland) and is inhabited by 680 million people.

North America's main geographical features are its mountainous plateaus, including the Grand Canyon, the Rocky Mountains and the Great Plains. The southern continent's principal features are the Andes Mountains (Aconcagua, 6,960 m), the Amazon basin with the world's largest rain forests, and savannas and steppes. The volcanic Cordillero Mountains are up to 5,000 m high, and the idyllic islands of the West Indies in the Caribbean Ocean are also volcanic in origin.

Many magnificent nature reserves have been founded to preserve the breathtaking scen-ery and its unique animal and plant life, such as the Galapagos Islands off the west coast of South America.

The country's first inhabitants, the native American Indians, today live mainly in reservations. The richly diverse population incorporates immigrants from Europe and Asia and the descendants of African slaves.

Nations of the World
America

Antigua and Barbuda
Antigua and Barbuda

Area: 442 sq km
Population: 69,000
GDP per capita: 13,000 US$
Capital: St. John's
Government: Constitutional monarchy within the Commonwealth
Languages: English (official), Creole
Currency: 1 Eastern Caribbean dollar = 100 cents

Geography: This tiny country in the Caribbean Ocean includes the islands of Antigua (280 sq km), Barbuda (161 sq km) and Redonda (1 sq km) in the Lesser Antilles. Uninhabited Redonda is part of the region's volcanic arc. The island's south has craggy mountains with lush vegetation. The climate is tropical, moderated by the sea winds but with frequent hurricanes. Beaches and ocean are ideal for bathing and diving, and the coastline is fringed by coral banks.

Politics: Discovered by Columbus in 1493, the islands were only settled 150 years later by the English, who established plantations there. Antigua and Barbuda was a British colony from 1667, and did not gain independence until 1981. The country is governed by a bicameral parliament, elected every five years; the British monarch is the head of state.

Economy: Because of the country's history, the majority of the population is of African descent. Vegetables, tropical fruit, cotton and sugar-cane are cultivated. However, the largest contribution to the economy comes from tourism, which contributes 50% to GDP and employs 80% of the inhabitants. Exports include petroleum products.

Argentina
Argentina

Area: 2,766,889 sq km
Population: 40 million
GDP per capita: 6,600 US$
Capital: Buenos Aires
Government: Federal republic
Language: Spanish
Currency: 1 Argentinean peso = 100 centavos

Geography: The country is around 3,700 km long from north to south; the Andean mountains form its western border with Chile. To the south-east, the main settlement area is the treeless plains of the pampas with their fertile steppes, giving way in the south to Patagonia's tableland. In the north, the pampas meet the densely wooded, rainy area between the Paraná and Uruguay rivers and the swamp forests along their banks, terminating in the Brazilian mountains. Favorite tourist destinations are the beaches along the Atlantic Ocean, the ski resorts and nature reserves in the Andes and the game reserves on Tierra del Fuego.

Politics: The arrival of the Spanish in 1516 heralded two centuries of foreign rule that ended in 1816 with the Proclamation of Independence by the United Provinces. After conquering Patagonia in 1880, Argentina became a major destination for immigrants. Until 1982 the country was ruled by a succession of military juntas and conservative large-scale landowners. Argentina's defeat by Britain in the Falklands War led to the end of military rule and to free presidential elections in 1983. Since 1999 Argentina has faced a deep economic recession, resulting in the country's inability to pay back foreign debts and an exploding crime rate.

Economy: 90% of Argentina's population are descended from European immigrants. The country has extensive agricultural and industrial capacities. Agriculture (principally livestock) accounts for 8% of GDP, and services 63%. The country's industry concentrates on processing agricultural products and on mechanical engineering. Exports are primarily from the agricultural sector.

Argentina: Perito Moreno Glacier in Los Glaciares National Park

Bahamas
Bahamas

Area: 13,939 sq km
Population: 305,000
GDP per capita: 20,000 US$

Magnificent boulevards and impressive colonial architecture hark back to the long-gone heyday of Argentina's capital. Immigrants, chiefly from Italy and Spain, made Buenos Aires into one of the world's great economic centers. More recently, life is becoming catastrophic for the 12 million and more inhabitants of Greater Buenos Aires on the La Plata delta. **1** The 67m high obelisk on Plaza de la Republica commemorates the city's foundation in 1536. Demonstrators from all over the country frequently gather at Plaza del Mayo in front of the **2** Congress Building. **3** The district of San Telmo lies directly adjacent to the harbour quarter La Boca, where the tango originated 150 years ago. **4** The city's spacious, generously proportioned design is modeled on that of a European metropolis.

Nations of the World
America

Capital: Nassau
Government: Parliamentary monarchy within the Commonwealth
Language: English
Currency: 1 Bahamian dollar = 100 cents

Geography: The island state comprises 30 large and 700 small to tiny islands and thousands of reefs extending over 1,200 km from Florida's east coast down to Haiti. Tourist centers with bathing or sailing facilities can be found on the Exumas and around Nassau. Angling is popular around the Bimini Islands, and the Inagua Islands has a rich variety of tropical fauna.

Politics: It was here that Columbus first stepped onto American soil in 1492. The islands were depopulated by Spanish slave traders; the British established a crown colony in the 17th century. The Bahamas have been independent since 1973. The parliament is bicameral, modeled on its British counterpart, with elections held every five years.

Economy: Agriculture is restricted by the barrenness of the steppes. In addition to tourism, which accounts for around half of GDP, the economy is principally driven by the resale of imported petroleum and petroleum products, chiefly to the USA.

Barbados
Barbados

Area: 430 sq km
Population: 275,000
GDP per capita: 13,500 US$
Capital: Bridgetown
Government: Parliamentary monarchy within the Commonwealth
Languages: English (official), Bajan
Currency: 1 Barbados dollar = 100 cents

Geography: The easternmost island of the Lesser Antilles, 36 km long and 24 km wide, is volcanic in origin and largely (80%) composed of fossilized coral and fringed by coral reefs. The impermeable bedrock prevents the formation of watercourses. Only the north of the island has rolling hills, some up to 340 m high. The island's climate and natural features make it a holiday paradise.

Politics: Discovered in the 16th century by Spain, Barbados became a British crown colony in 1652. In the 17th century the first settlers established sugar-cane plantations worked by imported African slaves; the slave economy ended in 1838. Barbados gained independence in 1966.

Economy: The traditional sugar-cane cultivation employs only 6% of the workforce and is dwindling

from deposits in the interior and the north and east coasts. Services, principally tourism, contribute two-thirds of GDP.

Belize
Belize

Area: 22,965 sq km
Population: 290,000
GDP per capita: 4,100 US$
Capital: Belmopan
Government: Constitutional monarchy
Languages: English (official), Creole, Spanish, minorities
Currency: 1 Belize dollar = 100 cents

Geography: Belize, to the southeast of the Yucatán peninsula, is composed of swampy coastland with large rivers and countless lagoons enclosing hilly landscapes (altitudes around 1,000 m) in the interior. Rainforests and dense man-

The sea is the main source of protein for the Caribbean people.

in significance. The island is heavily dependent on imports, including foodstuffs, machinery and crude oil. Its exports include sugar, cotton and peanuts, but also electronic components and petroleum

grove forests flourish in the humid, tropical climate. A major natural phenomenon is an island chain of coral reefs extending 300 km down the coastline. Hurricanes are frequent.

litics: Before its discovery by e Spanish conqueror Cortèz ›24/25) the region was the heart-1d of the Mayan civilization. :ttled from the 17th century by itish colonists, it became a own colony in 1862 as British ›nduras. Renamed Belize in 1973, gained independence in 1981.

:onomy: While 38% of the area is itable for cultivation, only around .% is actually utilized. Citrus

Geography: The west of the country is taken up by the Bolivian Andes, divided by the Altiplano plateau with average altitudes 3,000-4,000 m. The lowlands to the east of the Andes give way to the plain of La Plata in the south and the Amazon basin in the north. The climate ranges from cold to tropical. Tourist attractions are Lake Titicaca, Inca sites in Tiahuanaco and the ancient silver-mining center of Potosí.

ruits, seafood, bananas, sugar-:ane, cocoa and tropical hard-voods are key exports. The under-developed industrial sector employs 10% of the workforce and is primarily oriented towards products for export, comprising sawmills, sugar factories, rum distilleries and textiles. Services, including tourism, account for 57% of GDP.

Bolivia
Bolivia

Area: 1,098,581 sq km
Population: 9 million
GDP per capita: 1,300 US$
Capital: Sucre
Government: Presidential republic
Languages: Spanish, Quechua and Aymará (all official)
Currency: 1 boliviano = 100 centavos

1 The traditional ponchos and blankets of the Bolivian Indios are produced from naturally dyed llama or sheep's wool.

2 Belize's 250-kilometer-long Barrier Reef and famous Blue Hole, one of the world's largest and most spectacular coral reefs.

3 The impressive ruins of the Maya city Xunantunich, one of Belize's main attractions, perch on a mountain in the jungle.

4 One of the world's highest metropolitan cities, La Paz in Bolivia, lies in a valley 4,000 m above sea level near Lake Titicaca.

Special
Rio de Janeiro

Rio de Janeiro was the capital of Brazil until Brasilia was awarded that status in 1960. Now a major port with over 5.5 million inhabitants, the city was founded in the 16th century by Portuguese settlers. It attracts tourists from all over the world, particularly at carnival time. When winter is at its worst in the northern hemisphere, **1** Copacabana beach on the Atlantic Ocean is crowded with swimmers. The beach has a good view of the city's emblem – the statue of Christ the Redeemer on the 710 m high **2** Corcovado. The **3** Sugarloaf's peak towers 395 m over Guanabara Bay. At **4** carnival time in Brazil, samba sets the pace. Processions may last for days and are crammed with gorgeous costumes which are lovingly fashioned throughout the year.

itics: Bolivia's history has ways been closely linked to that neighboring Peru. The end of the h century saw the first Indian risings against Spanish colonial e, brought to an end in 1825 with foundation of the republic. The sent-day political situation is rked by ideological conflicts, erilla warfare and military coups.

onomy: Almost 40% of the work-ce supply 17% of GDP in agricul-e on the plateau and in the val-s. The most important crop is obably coca cultivation aimed to gal drug traffic. Mining includes c, tin, lead and precious metals. troleum and natural gas exports e an important economic factor in day's globalized world. The pro-ssing industry primarily compri-s small and medium-sized enter-ises (foodstuffs, textiles).

rasil
razil

ea: 8,511,996 sq km
pulation: 188 million
DP per capita: 6,900 US$
apital: Brasília
overnment: Federative republic
nguages: Portuguese (official), gional Indian languages
urrency: 1 real = 100 centavos

eography: The Atlantic forms the astern border of the world's fifth rgest country; the narrow coastal rip is densely populated. To the orth, in the mountains of Guyana, opical rain forests dominate the ndscape. Further south is the mazon basin, home to a unique cosystem with countless species. ourism centers are Rio de aneiro, the coastal regions, the mazon, and the Iguazú Falls.

olitics: Brazil was settled as early s the 8th century BC. The Spanish

reached the coast in 1500, the first Europeans to do so; however, the region became a Portuguese colo-ny in the 17th century. In 1825 Brazil declared independence, and econ-omic prosperity began as coffee exports grew. The military seized power in 1961; the first general elections were held in 1982, and the country had a civil president in 1985. The new constitution of 1988 confirmed the presidential system,

1 The Caiapo Indians in Brazil paint their faces elaborately and wear impressive, brightly colored head-dresses and ceremonial jewelry to intimidate their enemies in war.

2 The well-preserved colonial archi-tecture in Salvador da Bahia, the for-mer capital of Brazil from 1549 to

1763, has been a world heritage site since 1985.

3 One of Brazil's oldest cities, the coastal resort of Olinda is also among its finest bathing locations. The palm-fringed Benedictine monastery of São Bento is a masterpiece of late Baroque architecture.

Special
Brasilia

Brazil's new capital of Brasilia was designed on the drawing board from 1956-1960 and sited at the dead center of Brazil, in an area which up to then had been scarcely settled. The most impressive building, designed by Oscar Niemeyer, is the **1** Congresso Nacional with its "twin-shell" roof; the shell facing upwards seems to collect the voices of the people, while the dome under the second shell is a conference center. Niemeyer's aim was to design the congress building as a **2** work of art. The architecture of the **3** + **4** cathedral is also strongly symbolic.

although the military still retains extensive influence. Voting is compulsory between the ages of 18 and 69.

Economy: The country is inhabited by many ethnic groups, the smallest of which are the indigenous Indians. Agriculture is highly profitable; coffee, cocoa, soybeans, sugar, tobacco, maize and cotton are cultivated in addition to livestock farming. Rich natural resources (iron, manganese) are as yet not fully exploited. Economic reforms introduced from the mid-1990s are showing initial success. The industrial sector of this highly industrialized country (textiles, leather goods) is dominated by the automotive industry and its suppliers. Other key exports are metals and metal products.

Canada
Canada

Area: 9,984,670 sq km
Population: 33 million
GDP per capita: 43,500 US$
Capital: Ottawa
Government: Parliamentary monarchy in the Commonwealth
Languages: English, French (both official)
Currency: 1 Canadian dollar = 100 cents

Geography: Canada is the second largest country in the world, fringed to east and west by two great mountain chains and dotted with the world's biggest number of lakes, mainly in the province of Québec. The foothills of the Appalachian Mountains extend to the Atlantic coast in the east, giving way in the west to the broad plains and lakes of the Great Plains and bounded by Hudson Bay to the north. The plains rise further to the west, meeting the Rocky Mountains (highest peak: Mt. Logan (6,050 m)

at an altitude of 1,500 m. To the far north, the Arctic islands border the North Polar Sea. 80% of the country consists of forests and tundra; the remainder is arable land and the polar islands. The continental climate fluctuates considerably, with average temperatures often falling below zero. Canada offers many tourist attractions; count-

 The Inuit people of the eastern Canadian Arctic were highly skilled at surviving in the hostile environment. Isolated from other Eskimo peoples, they developed a unique culture and language. Today, the Inuit chiefly live in mixed settlements, and their traditional clothing, language and customs are gradually forgotten. They represent only a minority of the population.

 Mount Assiniboine in Alberta, Canada (3,618 m), on the western flank of the Rocky Mountains in the Kootenay National Park.

 Banff National Park in the Canadian Rockies. Founded in 1885, it is Canada's oldest nature reserve, with the glacial Lake Louise and Lake Moraine.

Special
Montreal, Quebec, Toronto

The major cities of the world's second largest country lie in the south near the US border. **1** Toronto, prosperous capital of the province of Ontario, is Canada's New York, where almost 70 nationalities coexist peacefully. The city has a population of almost 5 million. **2** In Québec, capital of Québec province, the French roots of its founders can still be seen. The luxury hotel Château Frontenac was built in 1893 by a railway company. In **3** Montreal, site of the 1976 Olympic Games, 60% of the inhabitants speak French. The city successfully fuses **4** traditional and modern elements in its architecture, lifestyle, art and culture.

ess national parks of unspoiled cenery, Niagara Falls and cosmoolitan cities such as Québec, Montreal and Vancouver.

Politics: Up to the arrival of the first ettlers in the 17th century, the country was inhabited by Indians nd Inuit. Conflicts over British and rench territorial claims were decided in 1763 by the British. Canada id not gain full political independence until 1931. The country is overned by a bicameral parliament, the lower house of which is elected every five years, with the British monarch as the formal Head of State. Given increasing alls for autonomy in the province of Québec, a key goal of domestic politics is to achieve equilibrium etween the French Canadian and English-speaking populations.

Economy: Canada is one of the world's most prosperous nations, with rich natural resources, forests and vast tracts of arable land. Agriculture employs 3% of the workforce; in addition to extensive livestock farming, grain (wheat, maize) and potatoes are cultivated. Ontario, Québec and British Columbia are the main industrial areas, where 2% of the workforce produces around 30% of GDP. Petroleum and natural gas drilling are important. The commercial and services sector accounts for 60% of GDP per capita.

Geography: Chile extends 4,230 km along the west coast of South America, with an average width of only 176 km. The country encompasses five highly diverse climatic zones. The northern desert zone is among the most arid places on earth; the semi-desert can only be cultivated with the help of artificial irrigation. The main cities are in Central Chile between Illapel and

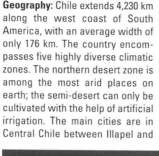

Chile
Chile

Area: 756,950 sq km
Population: 16.1 million
GDP per capita: 9,900 US$
Capital: Santiago de Chile
Government: Presidential republic
Language: Spanish
Currency: 1 Chilean peso = 100 centavos

1 A child of the Algonquin tribe, painted for a ritual. This tribe already lived on the banks of the River Ottawa before our chronology began; today they live in poverty on the fringes of Ontario's capital.

2 The llamas and alpacas of Chile's uplands were bred by the area's native Indians as hardy beasts of burden, but chiefly for their meat and wool.

3 Chile's capital Santiago de Chile at night. Over one-third of Chile's population, 5 million people, live in the Andean metropolis, founded in 1541. The city is frequently visited by earthquakes.

Concepción; to their south is a panorama of lakes. The great forests of the south have high rainfall and a cold climate. The south also has many active volcanoes. The Easter Islands are a travel destination worth adding to Chile's many areas of natural beauty.

Politics: Conquered in 1544 by the Spanish, Chile gained independence in 1818 after a long struggle. The following decades were dominated by conflicts between the great landowners and farm workers. The Socialist President Allende was overthrown in 1973 and power was seized by a military regime; the country has faced the painful duty of addressing its political heritage since the process of democratization began in 1990. Chile has been a presidential republic since 1925, with a bicameral parliament. Voting is compulsory from age 18.

Economy: Only 23% of the area is cultivatable; in Central and South Chile fruit is grown for export and grain (wheat, maize) for subsistence. Yields from the rich fishing grounds are chiefly for export. The industry primarily processes foodstuffs (fishmeal, fish canning). Chile is the world's largest copper exporter (40% of foreign trade). Commerce and services account for over half of GDP.

Colombia
Colombia

Area: 1,138,910 sq km
Population: 43.5 million
GDP per capita: 3,600 US$
Capital: Bogotá
Government: Republic
Language: Spanish
Currency: 1 Colombian peso = 100 centavos

Geography: The northern foothills of the Andes divide the country into a western coastal plain and eastern lowlands, extending in the far south-east into the Amazon basin through the pastures of Llanos del Orinoco. Tropical rain forests flourish here and on the Pacific coast. The main settlements are in the Andes basins. The tropical climate has few temperature fluctuations. Tourist centers are the Caribbean coast to the north (Santa Marta), the pre-Colombian sites (San Augustín), and colonial cities (Cartagena, Bogotá).

Politics: Colombia was the site of early Indian civilizations. Discovered by the Europeans in 1499, it became a Spanish colony in the mid-16th century. After successfully fighting for independence under Simon Bolivar in 1819, the country gained its first republican constitution in 1886. Reforms in the 1930s were succeeded by years

Economy: Agriculture accounts for 20% of GDP and employs 30% of the workforce. Colombia is the world's second largest coffee exporter, with bananas and flowers also cultivated for export. 30% of agricultural production is devoted to livestock farming (cattle breeding, goats, sheep). The industrial sector (automotive, foodstuffs, petroleum processing) accounts for 20% of GDP. Imports include machinery and chemicals. The rich natural resources (gold, iron ore, oil) are almost untouched. The service sector accounts for 40% of GDP. Despite of the country's rich heritage, tourism has diminished in the last decades due to persistent reports on violence and crimes.

Costa Rica
Costa Rica

Area: 51,100 sq km
Population: 4 million
GDP per capita: 5,900 US$

Villa de Leyva (Colombia), colonial settlement from the 18th cent.

of bloody civil war. The military junta which took over power resigned in 1957; however, the uprisings and civil war which characterized the 1960s still recur today.

Capital: San José
Government: Presidential republic
Language: Spanish
Currency: 1 Costa Rica colón = 100 centavos

Geography: Humid savannas up to 700 m in altitude and dry forest lie on the Pacific side of Costa Rica, while the main settlements are found in the Valle Central, with fertile land and a mild climate. Rain forests dominate the Caribbean coast.

Politics: Costa Rica was discovered by Columbus in 1502 and became a Spanish colony in the mid-16th century. It became a republic ten years

Capital: La Habana
Government: Socialist republic
Language: Spanish
Currency: 1 Cuban peso = 100 centavos

Geography: The largest island of the Western Antilles, Cuba has an interior of craggy mountain chains (over 1,900 m) met by a swampy, fertile plain that gives way to the rain forests of the mountainous

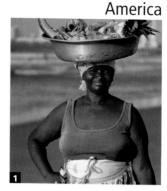

after gaining independence (1838). The constitution of 1949 stipulates political neutrality. The country is governed by the parliament and a directly elected president.

Economy: The predominantly white population is relatively well-educated. Agriculture accounts for 16% of GDP and 64% of export revenues. The industrial sector contributes 26% of GDP from processing agricultural products, and textile and chemical production. Tourism is undergoing a dramatic increase.

Cuba
Cuba

Area: 110,860 sq km
Population: 11.3 million
GDP per capita: 3,500 US$

 1 Fruit seller on Cartagena Beach, Colombia.

2 Cartagena: The well-preserved colonial architecture of the Old City, with its walls and bastions. The church of San Pedro Claver is a memorial against slavery. Cartagena was a key trading center of the colonial empire

when Colombia was still a Spanish colony. The port is still a major economic factor today.

3 Costa Rica: The Central American Cordilleras are largely covered by tropical evergreen mountain and rain forests, with a wide variety of flora and fauna.

Cuba's capital Havana – La Habana – is full of picturesque reminders of its colonial past, but also signs of the country's current economic problems. Great hopes are placed in the tourism industry. The dome of the **1** Capitol affords a view of the **2** Old City's colonial architecture, designated a world cultural heritage site in 1982. The **3** Plaza de la Catedral is also here. The former **4** Presidential Palace is today a Museum of the Revolution. The **5** »Bodeguita del Medio« bar preserves Ernest Hemingway's memory as the spot where the American Nobel Prizewinner discovered his fondness for the mojito, the Cuban cocktail he made world-famous.

ast. High, rolling hills dominate he west. Arable land and savanas have replaced much of the rain orests. The climate is tropical nd humid. Tourist centers are La labana (Havana), Trinidad and antiago de Cuba.

Politics: Discovered in 1492 by Columbus, the island was settled y the Spanish from 1511. In 1902 he republic of Cuba fell under the nfluence of the United States, but ecame a Socialist republic after Castro's revolution (1959). The disntegration of the USSR has caused Cuba many problems since the trale US trade embargo, although the ountry has emerged from isolation since the end of the Cold War.

Economy: The healthcare and edu- cational system are exemplary. 0% of agricultural operations are owned by the state. The main crop s sugarcane (73% of export reve- nues). The processing industry (tex- iles, leather, tobacco goods) ac- counts for 46% of GDP. Tobacco nd nickel are important exports. Tourism is now the second largest source of foreign currency.

Dominica
Dominica

Area: 750 sq km
Population: 70,000
GDP per capita: 4,300 US$
Capital: Roseau
Government: Republic within he Commonwealth
Languages: English (official), Patois, Cocoy
Currency: 1 East Caribbean dollar = 100 cents

Geography: The volcanic island is part of the Lesser Antilles. It is pre- dominantly mountainous (Morne Diablotins, 1,447 m), almost un- touched at the center and covered

with evergreen rain forests. The main settlements are on the coast. The climate is tropical and humid; cyclones may occur in the rainy season from June to November. The country's principal attraction is the Morne-Trois-Pitons National Park in the interior, with over 100 species of birds and a huge biodi- versity. The volcanic island located half way between Martinique and Guadeloupe has many hot springs and a picturesque crater lake.

1 Equanimity is essential in Cuban life. With public transport almost always crammed, an old car is a prec- ious asset; getting spare parts is an art in itself.

2 Cuba: The most famous landmark of the city of Trinidad, the campanile of San Francisco monastery church.

Many of the city's buildings bear wit- ness to area's former prosperity from the sugar trade in the 18th and 19th centuries.

3 The Lesser Antillean island of Dominica, just 750 sq km in area; every inch of space is used. Soufrière church is directly on the beach.

Nations of the World
America

Politics: Discovered by Columbus on a Sunday in 1493, Dominica successfully resisted all attempts at colonization into the 18th century. It became a British colony in 1805 and gained independence in 1978.

Economy: The economy is founded on agriculture, with 50% of export revenues produced by small farmers from banana cultivation. Other crops such as ginger, coconuts, copra, fruit juices, cocoa, and citrus fruits are industrially processed, partly for export. Plans to expand the weak industrial sector through incentives for foreign investors are under way. Trade and tourism generate 63% of GDP.

Ecuador
Ecuador

Area: 283,560 sq km
Population: 13.5 million
GDP per capita: 3,200 US$
Capital: Quito
Government: Presidential republic
Languages: Spanish, dialects
Currency: 1 sucre = 100 centavos

Geography: The country is divided into three main geographical zones: the densely settled coastal region on the Pacific, the mountainous Andean region (Chimborazo 6,310 m, an extinct volcano) and the Oriente lowlands in which tropical rain forests flourish up to the Peruvian border. The climate has no significant temperature fluctuations. Ecuador's territory includes the Galapagos Islands, around 1,000 km away in the Pacific, with their unique animal life (tortoises, giant lizards, birds). The country's chief tourist attractions are these islands, rain forest areas of natural beauty and the old colonial cities (Cuenca, Quito; today a world heritage site).

Politics: Ecuador was conquered in the 15th century, first by the Incas and 100 years later by the Spanish, who founded today's capital of Quito. The country received independence in 1822 but found only brief interludes of peace; not until the second half of the 20th century did Ecuador have long periods of political stability. The 1979 constitution appoints the parliament as the legislative power, elected every four years; the President of State is the head of government.

Economy: Agriculture accounts for 18% of GDP and employs one-third of the workforce. In addition to grain, potatoes, vegetables and fruit as subsistence crops, coffee, cocoa, sugar cane and bananas are cultivated for export. Prawns are also exported at important volumes. A major source of foreign currency are the natural resources in the Amazon basin, where gold, silver, zinc and copper are mined. Around 60% of the population live below the poverty line, which makes Ecuador dependent on aid.

El Salvador
El Salvador

Area: 21,041 sq km
Population: 6.8 million
GDP per capita: 2,900 US$
Capital: San Salvador
Government: Presidential republic
Languages: Spanish (official), Indian languages
Currency: 1 El-Salvador colón = 100 centavos

Geography: El Salvador largely consists of fertile hills and grassland, apart from a narrow coastal strip of mangrove forest with a hot, humid climate. In the interior, a high plateau with grassland enclosed by mountains forms the main settlement area. Much of the natural vegetation has given way to arable land. The country has one of the most frequent incidences of earthquakes in the world. The humid, hot climate extending to an altitude of 1800 m is ideal for agriculture. Tourist destinations are the volcanoes and the Indian cult sites.

Quito, with fascinating traces of Ecuador's colonial past.

Politics: From the country's conquest in 1524 to its independence in 1821, El Salvador was part of the Spanish colony of Guatemala. Its history is marked by recurring periods of unrest, in which the economic and social situation deteriorated considerably. A military dictatorship ruled from 1931 to 1967. The military coup in 1979 resulted in 14 years of civil war, with a high toll of victims. The 1983 constitution states that the president is directly elected by the people for a term of five years.

Economy: 95% of the population of Central America's most densely populated country are mestizos. Agriculture employs 50% of the workforce and generates 14% of GDP. Rice, maize, beans and millet are grown for domestic markets, and coffee, sugar, cotton and more recently flowers and ornamental plants for export. The industrial sector chiefly comprises small and medium-sized companies which account for 3% of GDP. Well over half the population works in the services sector. The tourism industry is still in its infancy.

Grenada
Grenada

Area: 344 sq km
Population: 90,000
GDP per capita: 5,600 US$
Capital: St. George's
Government: Constitutional monarchy
Languages: English (official), Patois
Currency: 1 East Caribbean dollar = 100 cents

Geography: The volcanic island is part of the Lesser Antilles. The highest peak in its mountainous interior (Mt. St. Catherine) is 840 m high. Mountain and rain forests

grow in the mountainous interior. The climate is tropical, with an extended rainy season. The island's many beaches are visited primarily by cruise tourists.

Politics: Discovered in 1498 by Columbus, Grenada was first settled by the French. The island was occupied by the British in 1762 and remained a British crown colony until its independence in 1974. It was invaded by US American troops in 1983 following a Social-

1 Carriacou island, off the Caribbean island of Grenada; ideal for diving and swimming.

2 Quechua-speaking Indians in Peru and Ecuador live from potato farming and alpaca breeding. Woolen garments woven from alpaca yarn and dyed in bright colors protect them from the harsh weather conditions in the High Andes, and are also their chief trade at city markets.

3 St. George's, Grenada's capital, one of the Caribbean's loveliest cities on the wooded bay, overshadowed by tall palm trees. Despite its scenic beauty, hurricanes are a danger.

ist revolution. According to the reinstated constitution of 1974, the parliament is composed of the Senate and the House of Representatives. The British monarch is the head of state.

Economy: The majority of Grenada's inhabitants are descended from Black African slaves. The country's flag depicts its main export: nutmeg, cultivated by small farmers in addition to bananas and cocoa. The underdeveloped industrial sector chiefly manufactures semi-luxury goods, but also electronic components and pharma products.

Guatemala
Guatemala

Area: 108,889 sq km
Population: 13 million
GDP per capita: 2,500 US$
Capital: Guatemala City
Government: Presidential republic
Languages: Spanish (official), Maya languages
Currency: 1 quetzal = 100 centavos

Geography: The plains to the north are covered with tropical rain forests. The Central American Andes traverse the country's south from east to west. To the far south, the high plains of the Sierra Madre extend to the Pacific coastal plains. Tourist attractions are the intact Indian cultures (Chichicastenango), sites of the Mayan civilizations (Tikal) and the colonial architecture in the cities of Antigua and Quezaltenango.

Politics: The center of the ancient Mayan culture was conquered by the Spanish in 1524 and remained a Spanish colony until its independence in 1821. Since then Guatemala has been ruled by a succession of military dictatorships. The government has been democratically elected since 1986, but the war led by the guerrilla movement URNG did not end until a peace treaty was signed in 1997.

Economy: Over half of the inhabitants work in agriculture; peas, broccoli, tobacco and flowers are cultivated in addition to traditional export crops of coffee, sugar, bananas and cardamom. Natural resources are largely untapped. The industrial sector processes foodstuffs, rubber and textiles for export. Tourism is the main source of foreign revenue.

Guyana
Guyana

Area: 214,969 sq km
Population: 770,000
GDP per capita: 1,400 US$
Capital: Georgetown
Government: Presidential republic within the Commonwealth
Languages: English (official), Hindi, Urdu, dialects
Currency: 1 Guyana dollar = 100 cents

Geography: The fertile coastal region gives way to mountain chains in the west and far south. Savannas dominate the south-west. 80% of the country is covered by largely untouched rain forest. Land reclaiming for arable use has been practiced since the 17th century.

Politics: Guyana's history of colonization began in the early 17th century, when British colonizers were followed by French and Dutch. As part of the former colony of Dutch Guyana, the country returned to Great Britain, gaining independence in 1966 and adopting South America's only socialist constitution in 1980.

Economy: Over half the population is descended from Indian immigrants, who came in the 19th century to work in the plantations. 25% of the workforce are employed in agriculture (cane sugar and rice for export). Hardwoods from the extensive forests, gold, sugar, bauxite and manganese are the prima-

Antigua, Guatemala's former capital, lies between three volcanoes.

sources of export revenue. Trade nd services are underdeveloped.

Haïti
Haiti

rea: 27,750 sq km
opulation: 8.3 million
OP per capita: 600 US$
apital: Port-au-Prince
overnment: Presidential republic

pendence in 1804 as the Empire of Haiti. After an era of revolutions, dictatorships and civil war the country now appears to be gaining political stability. Democratic parliamentary elections were introduced in 1996.

Economy: Agriculture, although employing over half the population, is barely at subsistence level. Sugar

anguages: French (official), Creole
Currency: 1 gourde = 100 centimes

Geography: Haiti occupies the western third of the island of Hispaniola and includes the two neighboring islands of Gonâve and Tortue. The country is divided from east to west by four mountain chains, accounting for around 80% of the country's area. Vegetation is dominated by savannas, with the remaining tropical rain forests limited to a few mountain areas. Cruise ship tourism concentrates in the capital of Port-au-Prince.

Politics: After its discovery by Columbus, Hispaniola was a Spanish colony; the western part became a French colony in 1697, rose to prosperity and declared its inde-

1 Almost 25% of Guatemala's people are the descendants of the Maya, who once ruled a powerful kingdom in Central America.

2 Antigua has been repeatedly devastated by earthquakes. The monastery church La Merced was badly damaged but rebuilt in the 18th cent.

3 "Temple of Jaguars" in the Mayan city of Tikal, Guatemala, a relic of the mighty and powerful civilization of the Mayas.

4 Lively, bustling and colorful: Chichicastenango, North Guatemala, the indigenous peoples' main market.

cane, coffee, coca and sisal are exported. Industry principally comprises local small trade companies. Raw materials and semifinished products (textiles, electrical goods) are processed for reexport.

Honduras
Honduras

Area: 112,088 sq km
Population: 7.3 million
GDP per capita: 1,600 US$
Capital: Tegucigalpa
Government: Presidential republic
Languages: Spanish (official), English, Indian languages
Currency: 1 lempira = 100 centavos

A Mayan ruler ornaments this column in ruined Copàn, Hunduras.

Geography: Honduras is bounded to the north by the Caribbean and to the south-west by the Pacific. Its territory includes the Bahía Islands and Swan Islands. The country is primarily mountainous, with only a narrow coastal strip along the Pacific, and rivers, lagoons and swamps on the Caribbean side. The main settlement area is concentrated in the valleys of the Central American Andes.

Politics: In 1524 the country was conquered by Spain; in 1821 Honduras proclaimed its independence and became an independent republic in 1838 after leaving the Central American Federation. Over 100 governments and military dictatorships have seized power as a result of coups to the present day. The 1982 constitution specifies a term of four years for elected members of the National Assembly.

Economy: Agriculture primarily produces bananas and coffee for export, with seafood the second most important export product. The extensive livestock farming also exports its overstocks. The rich natural resources (lead, zinc, silver) are almost untapped. Industry is insignificant, directed chiefly at the national market.

Jamaica
Jamaica

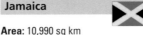

Area: 10,990 sq km
Population: 2.7 million
GDP per capita: 4,200 US$
Capital: Kingston
Government: Parliamentary monarchy within the Commonwealth
Languages: English (official), Patois
Currency: 1 Jamaica dollar = 100 cents

Geography: The 235 km-long island extends from east to west. The east is dominated by the volcanic Blue Mountains (up to 2,257 m); impenetrable gorges cleave the densely wooded western foothills. Rolling karst highlands in the west slope down to craggy sea cliffs. The Caribbean holiday paradise, with its tropical climate and idyllic sandy beaches, primarily attracts swimming enthusiasts.

Politics: Jamaica was discovered by the Spanish in 1494, who eradicated the indigenous population and introduced slaves. The island was conquered by the British in 1655 and became a crown colony in 1866. Jamaica has been independent since 1962 and has a bicameral parliament, with elections for the House of Representatives held every five years.

Economy: The educational and social systems are well-developed. Export crops are bananas, citrus fruits, coffee, cocoa, coconuts and allspice (pimento), as well as large-scale sugar-cane plantations. Jamaica is the world's third largest bauxite supplier. The industrial sector comprises foodstuffs, but increasingly electronics and data processing products. Tourism is significant, accounting for just under 50% of GDP.

México
Mexico

Area: 1,972,550 sq km
Population: 108 million
GDP per capita: 8,500 US$
Capital: Mexico CIty
Government: Presidential federal republic
Languages: Spanish (official), minority languages
Currency: 1 Mexican new peso = 100 centavos

eography: Mexico lies between e Gulf of Mexico and the Pacific. ridge of high mountains, with the erra Madre to the west, south nd east, surround the tableland at comprises most of the coun-y's interior, with the highest peak Popocatépetl (5,452 m) – at its enter. The peninsula of Yucatán, ordering the Caribbean in the outh-east, is composed of a chalk yer. The southern foothills of the

volution, which ended in 1920 after the proclamation of a presidential federal republic. The country's states have their own constitutions, with a relatively high degree of autonomy. The president is elected by a bicameral parliament for a term of six years.

Economy: Agriculture forms the livelihood of half the population, with maize, wheat, pulses, vege-

oastal American Cordilleras form he peninsula of Baja California, ivided from the remaining territory y the Gulf of California. Northern Mexico has desert vegetation; ropical rain forests grow along he coast of the Gulf of Mexico. ourist attractions are princi-ally the capital, the many sites of ncient civilizations (Uxmal, Teoti-uacán, Palenque) and the lively eaches (Acapulco, Tampico).

Politics: At the start of the 16th century the Spanish conquered the seat of the Maya and Aztec civilizations and plundered its rich silver reserves, overthrowing the native ruler to establish an extensive colony under Hernán Cortez. Mexico declared independence in 1821. The civil war in the following era culminated in 1911 in a bloody re-

1 The majority of Jamaica's population are descended from slaves imported up to the mid-18th century to work in the country's many plantations.

2 Popocatépetl was once the backdrop of a Toltecan pyramid, over which the Spanish built the church of

Nuestra Senora de los Remidios, Cholua. Pre-Colombian wall paintings survive in the older building's subterranean passages.

3 In Mexico, December 12 is the feast day of Our Lady of Guadalupe. The celebrations are typical of Mexico's religious culture.

Mexico's capital is the fourth largest city in the world, with 20.7 million inhabitants. Originally an Aztec city, then the residence of the Spanish Viceroy, Mexico City is today a modern, if crisis-torn metropolis. The city in the form we see it today was founded in 1521. **1** To the north of Zócalo central square is the Baroque cathedral; the eastern **3** Palacio Nacional dates from the 17th century. **2** In its courtyard, Diego Rivera's 1930s frescoes depict the history of the Mexican people.

tables and fruit grown for subsistence in smallholdings and private plantations cultivating coffee, tobacco and cotton for export. Extensive and largely untapped reserves of minerals and ores have already made Mexico a major supplier of silver, feldspar and graphite. The rich petroleum and natural gas reserves make a significant contribution to the economy, accounting for around 30% of export revenues and forming the basis of the chemical industry. Tourism is well-developed and accounts for a large share of the services sector.

Nicaragua
Nicaragua

Area: 129,494 sq km
Population: 5.6 million
GDP per capita: 1,000 US$
Capital: Managua
Government: Presidential republic
Languages: Spanish (official), Chibcha
Currency: 1 córdoba = 100 centavos

Geography: Central America's largest country is bounded to the west by the Pacific, to the east by the Caribbean Ocean. Two-thirds of the population live on the plains of the Pacific coast. A 240 km-long arc of volcanic mountains, eleven of which are active, lie to the east. Earthquakes are relatively frequent. The Caribbean coast is rich in lagoons and swamps, with savannas on the Pacific coast. 40% of the country is covered by rain forests. Tourist destinations are the Pacific and Caribbean beaches, the capital Managua and the nearby Lake Nicaragua.

Politics: Nicaragua was discovered by Columbus in 1502 and conquered 20 years later by the Spanish. In the early 19th century the country joined the Central American Federation. Nicaragua was torn by civil war from the early 20th century; the overthrow of the dictator Somoza in 1979 after 40 years' rule triggered military conflict between the left-wing Sandinistas and the Contra rebel forces, which did not end until 1990. The first free democratic elections, won by the opposition party UNO, were held the same year.

1 Christian and pre-Colombian traditions mingle on the feast day of Our Lady of Guadalupe, the Patroness of the Americas, held on December 12.

2 The "snail shell" El Caracol was used by the priests of Chichén-Itzá as an observatory.

3 The Spanish named the mighty, forbidding pyramid of Chichén-Itzá "El Castil" – fortress. Now a world heritage site.

4 Uxmal's richly decorated "Governor's Palace" and soothsayer's pyramid in the background.

Nations of the World
America

Economy: Agriculture supplies 28% of GDP and comprises basic food crops, but also coffee, sugarcane, cotton and bananas for export. The industrial sector is poorly developed and chiefly processes foodstuffs. Tourism, although as yet in its infancy, is undergoing gradual expansion. 80% of the population live in poverty.

Panamá
Panama

Area: 78,200 sq km
Population: 3.1 million
GDP per capita: 5,900 US$
Capital: Panama City
Government: Presidential republic

Languages: Spanish (official), English
Currency: 1 balboa = 100 centésimos

Geography: The west of Panama is taken up by the foothills of the Central Cordilleras, with peaks of up to 3,475 m, falling to the tropical lowlands of the Darien Jungle. In the northern rain forests, rainfall is high owing to the climatic divide formed by the Cordilleras. Only 46 km wide, the Panama isthmus is the narrowest point between the Atlantic and Pacific Oceans.

Politics: 1501 saw the first Spanish colonies on the Panama coast. The country joined Greater Colombia in 1821. After the Panama Canal was completed, Panama became nominally independent in 1903 on intervention from the USA, and has been a sovereign state since 1982. The US military maintained a strong presence in the canal region (part of US territory until 1977) until 2000.

Economy: The commercial and services sector is the economy's largest at 70% of GDP, thanks to the Canal, opened in 1914, and the free trade area around Colón. Bananas, cane sugar, coffee, cocoa, prawns and tuna are the main exports. Industries process foodstuffs and petroleum.

Paraguay
Paraguay

Area: 406,752 sq km
Population: 6.5 million
GDP per capita: 1,800 US$
Capital: Asunción
Government: Presidential republic
Languages: Spanish, Guaraní (all official)
Currency: 1 guaraní = 100 céntimos

Geography: The Río Paraguay, surrounded by swamp, divides Paraguay into an eastern region, with mountains and plateaus, and the western plains of Gran Chaco. The north-west has tropical rain forests giving way to savanna and grassland in the south. Tourist destinations are the areas of natural beauty and many sites dating from the colonial era.

Politics: Conquered by the Spanish in 1536, Paraguay housed a Jesuit state in the early 17th century, which was dissolved in 1759. Paraguay became independent in 1811. 1989 saw the end of over 30 years of dictatorship. The country has a bicameral parliament.

Ciudad del Este, a new city on the borders of Paraguay and Brazil.

Panama's economy is heavily dependent on the Canal.

Economy: Agriculture is the principal economic sector, dominated by monocultures (extensive livestock farming, coffee, rice, soybean and cotton cultivation). The profitable export of tropical hardwoods has led to widespread clearing of rain forest areas. Industrial development has advanced little owing to lack of exploitation of the rich natural resources. River shipping is a popular transport method in trading with neighboring countries.

Languages: Spanish, Quechua (official), Aymará
Currency: 1 nuevo sol = 100 céntimos

Geography: The Andes Mountains (Nevado Huascarán, 6,768 m) in Peru's interior follow the coastline and slope down to the broad expanse of the Amazon basin in the north-west. Grasslands are found at higher altitudes. Tourist destinations are cultural monuments such

Perú
Peru

Area: 1,285,216 sq km
Population: 28.5 million
GDP per capita: 3,900 US$
Capital: Lima
Government: Presidential republic

1 Palm-fringed beaches and idyllic islands; Panama is discovering its tourist attractions and is becoming a popular cruise destination. Merengue musicians supply Caribbean atmosphere.

2 Machu Picchu, Peru's "Forgotten City"; walls, stairs, alleys and temples at an altitude of 2,900 m. US explorers discovered the mysterious Inca city in 1911. Its temple precincts were surrounded by dwellings. The countless artifacts give an insight into the ancient civilization.

3 Lake Titicaca in the Andean uplands, 190 km long. The world's largest upland lake belongs to Bolivia and Peru.

as Machu Picchu and Chan-Chan, and colonial cities such as Lima and Trujillo.

Politics: The Inca's kingdom was destroyed by Spanish conquerors in 1572. In 1821 Peru declared its independence from Spanish colonial rule, and since then the country has been ruled by a succession of military and civil governments. Moves towards neo-liberalism have been met by social unrest.

Former sugar mill in Montpelier, on the Caribbean island of Nevis.

Economy: The main agricultural crops are sugar-cane, maize, cotton and coffee. Illegal coca cultivation is increasing dramatically. Fisheries account for 24% of export revenues; other key exports are copper, zinc, silver and petroleum. The industrial sector processes textiles, foodstuffs, chemicals and metals.

República Dominicana
Dominican Republic

Area: 48,730 sq km
Population: 9.1 million
GDP per capita: 4,200 US$
Capital: Santo Domingo

Government: Presidential republic
Language: Spanish
Currency: 1 Dominican peso = 100 centavos

Geography: The Dominican Republic covers two-thirds of the island of Hispaniola, and is bounded by Haiti to the west. The highest peaks of the four parallel mountains that transverse the island are on Dominican territory. The dense forests have largely been replaced by sugar-cane plantations. Although frequently hit by earthquakes, the Dominican Republic is a popular tourist destination thanks to its beautiful beaches.

Politics: The island's history from the 17th century was dominated by colonial conflicts, revolutions and US military intervention, the latter continuing after independence (1844). The murder of the dictator Trujillo in 1961 led to a period of deceptive stability, but social tensions continually disrupt the peace.

Economy: 32% of the workforce is employed in the agricultural sector, with the main exports being sugar, honey, coffee and cocoa. Despite rich natural resources (gold and silver ores, ferronickel) mining is poorly developed. The services sector (tourism) is the only growth industry and a major source of revenue; it accounts for 24% of jobs.

Saint Kitts and Nevis
Saint Kitts and Nevis

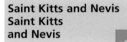

Area: 261.6 sq km
Population: 40,000
GDP per capita: 10,100 US$
Capital: Basseterre
Government: Federation/ constitutional monarchy within the Commonwealth
Language: English
Currency: 1 East Caribbean dollar = 100 cents

Geography: These mountainous islands, 5 km apart in the Eastern Caribbean, are volcanic in origin (Mt. Liamuiga, 1,156 m; an extinct volcano with crater lake) and have many sulphurous springs. Rain forests grow at higher altitudes; the coastal plains are used for agriculture. The white, sandy beaches represent the popular tourist attractions.

Politics: Discovered by Columbus in 1493, the islands were ruled for centuries by the Spanish, who enslaved the indigenous population. The islands became Britain's first West Indian colony in 1623. Long years of striving for independence were finally successful in 1983. A Governor-General still represents the British monarch. Nevis also has its own parliament and prime minister.

Economy: Illiteracy has been reduced to 10 %, a key condition for advanced economic development.

The islands' economy is principally based on agriculture (sugar-cane) and tourism. Cruise passengers are the main source of foreign currency, so that the services sector employs 43.1% of the workforce. Exports are sugar-cane and textiles.

Saint Lucia
Saint Lucia

Area: 616.3 sq km
Population: 165,000
GDP per capita: 5,700 US$

lonial rulers in the 17th century; the island was subsequently British and French in succession before finally becoming a British colony in 1814. A member of the West Indian Federation in 1958, St Lucia gained independence in 1979.

Economy: The economy chiefly consists of banana exports and tourism. While tourism has delivered around half of St. Lucia's foreign currency revenues since the early 1990s, banana cultivation

Capital: Castries
Government: Constitutional monarchy within the Commonwealth
Languages: English (official), Patois
Currency: 1 East Caribbean dollar = 100 cents

Geography: Located in the East Caribbean island arc, St. Lucia is volcanic in origin. Agriculture is practiced in the coastal regions and in the broad mountain valleys in the north and south. Rain forests are confined to higher altitudes. The climate, influenced by the North-West Passage, has average temperatures of 25-30° C. The main tourist destination is the cruise terminal of Pointe Seraphine in Castries.

Politics: The indigenous Caribbean inhabitants were wiped out by co-

1 The Dominican Republic is ideal for divers. Near the border, Parque Nacional del Este national park offers untouched coral reefs with crayfish, giant crabs, rays, and manatees.

2 Islands in the wind; the islands of St. Lucia, St. Kitts and Nevis and St. Vincent and the Grenadines lie in the arc of the Lesser Antilles. Tourism is

increasingly important for all three scenic Caribbean locations, with their white beaches and deep blue waters. The largest resort hotel in the Eastern Caribbean was opened on St. Kitts in 2003.

3 Saint Lucia; an enchanting view of the deep blue waters and gleaming beaches of Soufrière Bay.

and export is primarily practiced on small holdings and is highly vulnerable to crises.

Saint Vincent and the Grenadines
Saint Vincent and the Grenadines

Area: 389 sq km
Population: 120,000
GDP per capita: 5,200 US$
Capital: Kingstown
Government: Constitutional monarchy in the Commonwealth
Language: English
Currency: 1 East Caribbean dollar = 100 cents

Politics: St. Vincent was discovered by Columbus in 1498. Fought over by the French and English in the 17th century, in 1748 the island was initially awarded to the Carib Indians as neutral territory before becoming a British colony in 1783. From 1958–1962 the islands joined the West Indian Federation, and became an Associated State of the British Commonwealth in 1969 before gaining independence in 1979.

Economy: The islands' principal sources of revenue are agriculture and tourism. 28% of the area is given over to agriculture. The ba-

GDP per capita: 4,600 US$
Capital: Paramaribo
Government: Presidential republic
Languages: Dutch (official), Hindustani, Javanese, English
Currency: 1 Surinam guilder = 100 cents

Geography: Surinam, on the Caribbean Ocean, is named after the Suriname river that forms a great lake at Brokopondo before flowing into the Atlantic at Paramaribo. Behind the coastal plain, where around 80% of the population live, the interior rises to meet the Tumuc-Humac Mountains, covered with dense rain forest and largely unexplored. The climate is tropical and humid, moderated only by the north-eastern trade winds.

Politics: After a turbulent colonial history from the 16th century, Surinam fell to the Dutch in 1814. In 1974 around 50,000 Surinamese utilized their Dutch citizenship to emigrate to Europe, after which, in 1975, Surinam became independent. Bitter ethnically motivated power struggles developed, as a result of which one-third of the population continued to emigrate in the following years in search of a better life. The 1992 overthrow of Desi Bouterse, who had gained power in 1980 in a military coup, failed to restore stability. Parliamentary elections are held every five years.

Economy: The agricultural sector produces key exports of rice, sugar, bananas and coffee. Bauxite reserves, exploited almost exclusively by US companies, generate the majority of export revenues. Waterways are an important method of transport. Tourism is almost non-existent. The consumer goods industry is directed solely a

Impenetrable rain forests in Central Surinam nature reserve.

Geography: Part of the arc of the Lesser Antilles, the islands consist of the main island of St. Vincent, 345 sq km in area, and the smaller Grenadine Islands, seven of which are inhabited. The active volcano Soufrière (1,234 m) lies in the north of St. Vincent. The mountains there are covered by tropical rain forests with a moist tropical climate, while the Grenadines are considerably drier.

nana crop is frequently endangered by hurricanes. Other important exports are flour, cotton and arrow-root. Tourism is increasing in importance as a source of foreign currency.

Suriname
Surinam

Area: 163,265 sq km
Population: 440,000

he home market. Since 85% of the country is wooded, forestry could be a potential factor given appropriate development.

Trinidad and Tobago
Trinidad and Tobago

Area: 5,128 sq km
Population: 1.1 million
GDP per capita: 16,000 US$

coming a notorious center of piracy in the 17th century and a British crown colony in 1803. From 1958-1962 Trinidad and Tobago were members of the West Indian Federation, gaining independence in 1962 as a British Commonwealth state. The country received a republican constitution in 1976. Tobago has held autonomy since 1987. The islands have a bicameral parliament elected for a five-year term.

Capital: Port of Spain
Government: Presidential republic within the Commonwealth
Language: English
Currency: 1 Trinidad-and-Tobago dollar = 100 cents

Geography: The islands of Trinidad and Tobago, off the coast of Venezuela, form the southern end of the east Caribbean island arc. Trinidad's mountainous north has rain forests, while the flat east coast at the Gulf of Paria is mainly occupied by industrial plants and harbors. Tobago too has hilly rain forest country. The climate is tropical, with minor seasonal temperature fluctuations. Tourism focuses on Tobago as a diving paradise.

Politics: Discovered by Columbus in 1498, the islands were initially ruled by the Spanish before be-

1 Trinidad's annual carnival is the island's major cultural event, with fascinating parades rivaling Rio de Janeiro in their riotously colorful, elaborate costumes.

2 Tourism on Tobago benefits from its unique diving and swimming locations.

3 "Son", Cuba's most popular music in the 1920s, is played today in Trinidad. The origin of salsa, it features a mixture of solo and harmony vocals. The fame of this seductively melancholy music spread throughout Europe after the runaway success of Wim Wenders' film "Buena Vista Social Club".

Nations of the World
America

Economy: The population is hetero-geneous, with 41% black and 41% Indian. Although export-oriented, agriculture (cocoa, sugar, citrus fruits) and fisheries contribute a mere 2.7% to GDP. Trinidad's econ-omy remains dependent on petro-leum and natural gas exports from the relatively small deposits in the country's ocean shelf, generating at least 23% of GDP. The country also has the world's largest natural asphalt deposits at Pitch Lake, a 95-acre tar lake. The economy has grown at around 5% p.a. in recent years.

United States of America
United States
of America

Area: 9,631,418 sq km
Population: 300 million
GDP per capita: 46,000 US$
Capital: Washington
Government: Presidential federal republic
Languages: English (official), Spanish, tribal languages
Currency: 1 US dollar = 100 cents

Geography: The United States ex-tend from the Canadian border in the north to the Caribbean Ocean in the south, a distance of 2,500 km; the country is 4,500 km wide from the eastern Atlantic to the western Pacific coast. The USA can be di-vided into six major landforms: the coastal plains on the Atlantic and Gulf of Mexico, the craggy, low Appalachian mountains, the inland plains, the high Rocky Mountains, the basins and plateaus of the west, and the Coastal Cordilleras. The country's territory includes the mountainous Arctic and sub-Arctic region of Alaska, and Hawaii, a group of tropical volcanic islands. Almost every climatic type, with the exception of tropical, is repre-sented. The USA offers an enor-mous variety of tourist destina-tions, from major cities such as New York, Chicago or Los Angeles to Florida's bathing beaches and the breath-taking scenery of the Colorado plateau.

Politics: Since the first European settlers arrived in the early 17th century, the country's history has been dominated by the rivaling interests of European colonists. The Declaration of Independence in 1776 heralded the USA's new status as an independent power. In the 19th century the country ex-tended its territory significantly by waging war, acquiring lands and displacing the Native Indian popu-lation, and expanded towards the west coast. The civil war of 1861-1865 (War of Secession) led to the abolition of slavery. The USA be-came a military and economic superpower by entering the global political stage in both World Wars. The Constitution of 1788 and Bill of Rights of 1791 still determine the political system today. The country has a bicameral parliament, with direct elections to the House of Representatives held every two years. At the start of the new mil-

Breathtaking views in Yosemite National Park, Northern California.

Indian summer; golden aspens in the Colorado Rockies.

Pacific breakers at Big Sur on the Californian coast.

The center of the global superpower USA is its capital, Washington D. C. on the Potomac River. Spacious parks and a museum avenue were built as a counterpart to the dominant government buildings; the historical Georgetown quarter also forms a fascinating contrast. **1** The Lincoln Memorial: 36 columns surrounding the monumental statue of Abraham Lincoln symbolize the 36 states united by the President after the Civil War. **2** Congress, the legislative body of the USA, meets in the Capitol. **3** »Washington Crossing the Delaware« by E. G. Leutze depicts America's first president taking the decisive step to gain independence from the English in 1776. **4** The White House is the traditional residence of the world's most powerful politician.

With 21.5 million inhabitants, the urban center of New York is the world's second largest city; for most people, however, New York is Manhattan – though even here an area of just under 60 sq km houses 1.5 million people, hence the record height of the district's **1** residential and office buildings. The world's first skyscraper, the 1913 Woolworth Building at 232 m, has long been overshadowed. **2** The Wall Street Stock Exchange is the epicenter of the USA's economic power. **3** Manhattan is located on an island between the Hudson and East Rivers. **4** Times Square and **5** the skyline seen from Brooklyn – a city that truly never sleeps, as bright as day even at night, and bustling with life.

Chicago, the Midwest metropolis with the largest inland
harbour of the USA, is a business and geographical center,
as well as a richly diverse cultural metropolis. The city
attracted German, Polish and Italian immigrants. Famous for
its blues and jazz, Chicago is also home to the famous
Chicago Symphony Orchestra. After a devastating fire in
1871 the **1** city on Lake Michigan began to build upwards.
In 1974 the **2** Sears Tower was completed, at 442 m high
the world's highest building until 1997. In the prohibition
era, Chicago was ruled by Mafia clans; today, its rulers are
the **3** brokers at the world's second largest commodity
exchange. Chicago has expanded into a leading trade center since the 1980s. It is also the location of the world's
largest airport.

Despite its international significance as a Pacific seaport, parts of San Francisco have retained an almost small-town flair. Its inhabitants' famed liberalism is rooted in movements such as the 1960s peace movement; San Francisco was the capital of hippiedom. Like Los Angeles, San Francisco is in an earthquake zone, so that the striking **1** Transamerican Pyramid is on flexible foundations. The claim to 'Frisco's most famous emblem is shared by the **2** Golden Gate Bridge (crossed by over 1 million cars since its opening in 1937), the **3** brightly painted Victorian-style houses and the **4** historic cable cars.

Los Angeles seems to be a city without end or beginning – a vast mega-metropolis. The **1** sea of houses along the Pacific coastal strip extends over 1,200 sq km. Over 12 million people live here, spending twice as much time in their cars as the inhabitants of an average large American city. **2** The golden skyline at sunset gave Hollywood's Sunset Boulevard its name. Less than 450 km east of L. A. is **3** gamblers' paradise Las Vegas, and only 30 km to the south, the **4** dream world of Disneyland, which now attracts 60,000 visitors per day, and was built in the 1950s by the famous cartoon artist.

lennium, the USA regards itself as the world's economic and military leader and strives to implement western ideals of democracy and human rights throughout the world. The country was confronted by a new situation on September 11, 2001 when terrorists attacked the World Trade Center in New York and the Pentagon in Washington.

Economy: The country has the richest economy in the world despite of the growing competition. The geographical structure of the USA enables a variety of agriculture to be practiced in all areas, with large-scale livestock farming and highly mechanized grain cultivation (wheat, rice) playing key roles. Vast natural resources (petroleum, coal, ores) have hastened the development of high-performance industries, particularly in the north (chemicals, mechanical engineering, automotive, electronics). In the USA's post-industrial economic structure, services account for almost 80% of GDP, employing an equivalent percentage of the workforce.

Uruguay
Uruguay

Area: 176,215 sq km
Population: 3.4 million
GDP per capita: 7,200 US$
Capital: Montevideo
Government: Presidential republic
Language: Spanish
Currency: 1 Peso Uruguayo = 100 centésimos

Geography: Uruguay lies to the north of Río de la Plata. The foothills of the Brazilian highlands extend into the country from the north, creating rolling hills. Wet grasslands or pampas dominate the landscape at the coast and along the Uruguay River. Uruguay

is the least forested country in South America. The climate is temperate, influenced by the ocean. March, April, October and November are particularly good months to visit coastal resorts or the capital of Montevideo.

Politics: Discovered in 1515 by the Spanish, Uruguay was part of the viceroy of Rio de la Plata after 1777, passed to Brazil in 1817, and gained independence in 1830. In 1967, Uruguay regained the status of a presidential republic with a bicameral parliament, under its fifth

constitution since its independence. A civil head of state was not elected until eleven years after the 1973 coup. In the intervening period, two presidents were appointed by a "Council of Ministers".

Economy: Around 80% of the area is used for agriculture, mainly grazing. Despite this, only 8.5% of the population work in agriculture. Chief exports are agricultural products (beef, rice) and industrial goods (leather goods, wool and textiles), while the service sector accounts for most of GDP, at 69%.

USA: Water-mill in the thick Appalachian forests, West Virginia.

Breathtaking natural sculptures: Sandstone arches in Arches National Park, USA

Uruguay: Punta del Este, a popular resort on South America's Atlantic coast.

Venezuela
Venezuela

Area: 912,050 sq km
Population: 26 million
GDP per capita: 8,600 US$
Capital: Caracas
Government: Presidential federal republic
Language: Spanish
Currency: 1 bolívar = 100 céntimos

by attempted coups, high crime and inflation and social unrest. General strikes in 2003 triggered an economic crisis.

Economy: Long neglected, agriculture is now receiving new attention. Petroleum and its derivates account for 71% of GDP. The government's efforts to promote industry have met with little success.

Geography: To the north-west is the oil-rich Maracaibo Basin with shallow Maracaibo Lake, 13,600 sq km in area. These lowlands are bordered by the Cordillera de Mérida (Pico Bolívar, 5,002 m). To the south-east are the Orinoco lowlands and the Llanos, giving way in the south to the Guayana mountains, which occupy almost half the country's area. Canaima National Park is the main tourist attraction.

Politics: Discovered in 1498 by Columbus, Venezuela has been independent since 1830 following a succession of colonial and territorial claims. The 1961 constitution places legislative power with the National Congress, comprising the Senate and House of Representatives. The country is still dogged

1 The Yanomami live in the Amazon forests of Venezuela and Brazil. Land-grabbing and slash-and-burn clearance is threatening their homeland and lifestyle. Gold deposits have attracted countless treasure-hunters. Many Yanomami die of illnesses carried by outsiders, with which their immune systems cannot cope.

2 Venezuela's east is largely uninhabited. The region around Auyan Tepui (2,953 m) is only accessible by air or water.

3 The metropolis of Caracas, Venezuela's political and economic center and among South America's most modern cities.

Antarctica, the coldest continent, combines over 90% of the Earth's ice at the South Pole. Its underlying land mass, the same size as Europe, is covered by a sheet of ice around 2 km thick, increasing up to 4.5 km thick towards the continent's center, and depresses its rocky base well below sea level with its enormous weight.

The continent's size fluctuates with the seasons; in the winter months it accumulates ice masses and roughly doubles in size. Only the mountain ranges on the Pacific Ocean are not wholly embedded in ice.

The Antarctic ice desert is divided into five regions, primarily differing in the consistency of their ice layers, and two mighty shelves consisting solely of ice with no continental land mass as a base.

Nations of the World
Antarctica

Area: 12,500,000 sq km,
14 million sq km including ice
shelves

Geography: Antarctica was part of
the paleocontinent of Gondwana,
which split around 180 million years
ago to form Antarctica, Africa,
South America, Australia and Near
India. Antarctica, the world's highest continent, is bounded by the
Antarctic Circle. 90% of the world's
store of freshwater ice is here,
equal to 80% of the earth's fresh
water. To the east is a plateau of
104 million sq km covered in inland
ice; to the west is the Antarctic
peninsula, 2.69 sq km in area, disin-
tegrating into countless islands
and peninsulas towards the north.
West Antarctica has a glaciated
chain of fold mountains over 4,000
m high at some points. The still-
active volcano Mount Erebus,
4,023 m high, stands on Ross Island
in the Ross Sea. Around the pole,
the inland ice sheet forms a tableland of around 3,000 m in height,
glaciated around the perimeter
and finally breaking up into icebergs and floes. With 30-70 mm
precipitation per year and average
temperatures of between -50 and
-60° C, Central Antarctica is an extremely cold, extremely arid desert.
While coastal temperatures are
around 10 to -20° C, the region's
storms, scarce sunshine and persistent fog are hardly favorable
conditions. Apart from scientific

Melting ice in the Antarctic causes world sea levels to rise.

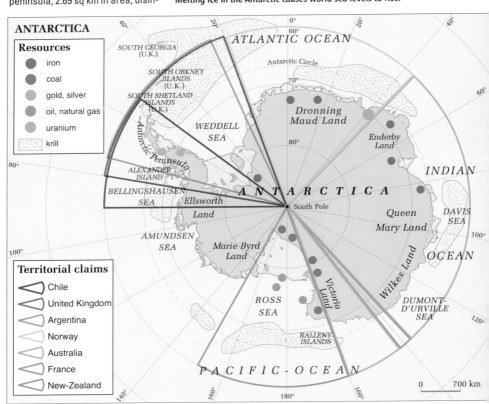

ANTARCTICA

Resources
- iron
- coal
- gold, silver
- oil, natural gas
- uranium
- krill

Territorial claims
- Chile
- United Kingdom
- Argentina
- Norway
- Australia
- France
- New-Zealand

personnel – around 1,000 in summer and 4,000 in winter – at the 42 research stations, the Antarctic is uninhabited.

Politics: Although in ancient times land was believed to exist at the southern polar regions, it was not until 1772-1775 that James Cook reached the Antarctic Circle. In 1820 the continent was sighted sources (iron, nickel, platinum, gold, coal, copper, titanium, chromium, natural gas, uranium). Fishing is extremely restricted and strict ecological regulations apply to the limited tourist activities. There are currently no plans for permanent settlement of Antarctica and most nations support leaving the continent as an unspoilt natural area closed to development.

almost simultaneously by the British explorer Bransfield, the American Palmer and the Russian Bellinghausen. Research on the area did not begin until the 20th century. On December 14th, 1911, the Norwegian Amundsen was the first to reach the South Pole, only a few weeks before Scott's expedition for Britain. Seven countries lay claim to around 80% of Antarctic territory, although these claims are not recognized under international law. The Antarctic is a demilitarized zone, and nuclear testing is banned.

Economy: On December 1, 1959, twelve countries signed a treaty to regulate the commercial exploitation of the Antarctic and other issues. Supplementary treaties protect and conserve flora and fauna and prohibit commercial exploitation of the rich natural re-

1 No land mammals live in the Antarctic ice desert; only penguins are occasional visitors to the mighty ice masses at the South Pole.

2 Icebergs several square miles in area constantly break away from the Ross Shelf on the Pacific side of Antarctica and are held by pack ice. The pack ice freezes into a continuous ring in winter. Large icebergs can be sighted off of most of Antarctica's coastal areas.

3 When icebergs "calve" into thousands of smaller pieces, climatic changes are probably the cause. Global warming has extended summers and increased the quantities of meltwater.

In April 1919, shortly after the end of the devastating First World War, the victorious Allied powers signed a declaration for the establishment of the League of Nations, the first global organization for international cooperation, at the Paris Peace Conference. The organization was succeeded in 1945 by the United Nations Organization, with headquarters in New York. The principal goals of the United Nations are the establishment and maintenance of peace and international security as well as the fostering of peaceful international relations in accordance with the principles of equality of states and the right to self-determination of peoples and nations.

UNO
United Nations Organization
Founded: 1945
Members: 191 countries
Headquarters: New York

In 1942, the effects of the Second World War moved 26 countries to form a joint organization. On October 24, 1945, 45 countries signed the United Nations Charter transforming the former war alliance into a global forum to replace the 1919 League of Nations. The goals of the Organization are the establishment of world peace and international security, the promotion of human rights and basic freedoms "without distinction of race, sex, language or religion". In 1948 it formulated the Universal Declaration of Human Rights, under the heading of "all human rights for all". Peaceful resolution of conflicts is a key goal. The UN may not intervene in the right to self-determination of peoples.

The UN General Assembly (UNGA), in which each member is represented by one vote, meets annually. China, France, Great Britain, Russia and the USA are permanent members of the Security Council, with ten further members elected for a two-year term. The Security Council acts on behalf of all members and awards and extends mandates of the UN forces. In 1988 the UN peace-keep-ing forces were awarded the Nobel Peace Prize.

ECOSOC
Economic and Social Council
Founded: 1945
Members: 54 countries
Headquarters: New York

A central organization of the UNO, presiding over a number of Special Committees. Responsible for co-ordinating member states on economic, social, cultural and humanitarian issues.

FAO
Food and Agricultural Organization
Founded: 1945
Members: 187 countries
Headquarters: Rome

Improvement of the nutritional situation, achievement of food security and promotion of agriculture in developing countries. It both stores and mobilizes expertise to aid rural development.

IAEA
International Atomic Energy Agency
Founded: 1957
Members: 137 countries
Headquarters: Vienna

Monitoring of nuclear power plants and their waste disposal policies, plus compliance with the non-proliferation treaty of 1970.

ICAO
International Civil Aviation Organization
Founded: 1947
Members: 188 countries
Headquarters: Montreal

Coordination and development of international civil aviation with regard to specific issues of health policy and security technology.

IFAD
International Fund for Agricultural Development
Founded: 1977
Members: 163 countries
Headquarters: Rome

Promotion of agriculture and nutritional situation in developing countries. A leader in effective, sustainable poverty-alleviation strategies for rural areas, aimed at ultimately eradicating rural poverty.

ILO
International Labour Organization
Founded: 1919, re-founded 1946
Members: 177 countries
Headquarters: Geneva

Promoting and implementing standards, fundamental principles and rights for workers. Improvement of working conditions and opening

Many UN organizations are headquartered in the Palace of Nations in Geneva.

new fields of employment in Third World countries and the transformation countries of Central and Eastern Europe, under the heading of "decent work for all". Further areas of focus: Programs to combat child labor (IPEC) and forced labor (SAP-FL), and protection of maternity leave for working women throughout the world.

O
ergovernmental
ritime Organization
nded: 1948
mbers: 163 countries
adquarters: London
janization for shipping issues
luding maritime security and en-
onmental issues. Draws up
ernational regulations aimed at
vancing shipping safety.

IMF
International Monetary Fund
Founded: 1944
Members: 184 countries
Headquarters: Washington
Organization responsible for monitoring the international currency
system and promotion of development aid. The IMF also produces
bi-annual reports on the international economic situation.

CB
ternational Narcotics
ntrol Board
unded: 1961
embers: 13 countries
eadquarters: Vienna
pervises compliance with nar-
tics control measures.

J
ternational Court of Justice
unded: 1945
eadquarters: The Hague
he UNO's principal judicial organ
omprises 15 judges from different
ountries, who may take action
ly if both parties agree on the
eatment of the issue at hand. The
ourt of Justice also offers legal
pinions to queries from other UN
odies including the General
ssembly. It can pronounce judge-
ents on contentious issues bet-
een countries.

1 The UNO flag was designed in 1946. Its olive branch symbolizes peace, and the globe from the perspective of the North Pole shows all the countries of the Earth.

2 The General Assembly meets at least once a year in the United Nations Assembly Hall. All of the United Nations' 191 member states are represented in the assembly.

3 Since the early 1970s the General Assembly of the UN members has held its plenary session at its headquarters at UN Plaza, New York.

4 The United Nations Security Council, where the five permanent and ten rotating members discuss peace missions to the world's crisis points. Its goal is to maintain international peace and security.

UNCTAD
United Nations Conference on Trade and Development
Founded: 1964
Members: 192 countries
Headquarters: Geneva
Promotion of international trade, particularly with developing countries, and interrelated issues of finance, technology, investment and sustainable development.

UNDP
United Nations Development Programme
Founded: 1965
Headquarters: New York
Executive Council for the coordination and financing of technological and other forms of aid for developing countries. Its global network seeks to ensure the most effective use of UN and international aid resources.

UNEP
United Nations Environment Programme
Founded: 1972
Headquarters: Nairobi
Administrative council for international environmental issues, including those outside the UN system.

UNESCO
United Nations Educational, Scientific and Cultural Organization
Founded: 1946
Members: 190 countries
Headquarters: Paris
Special UNO organization fostering cooperation with member states on cultural affairs and managing the continuously expanding "World Heritage List" of cultural and natural sites. Also contributes special support to educational and learning programs in developing countries and works on forging universal agreements on ethical issues.

UNFPA
United Nations Fund for Population Activities
Founded: 1967
Headquarters: New York
The Fund promotes education on family planning and mother/child healthcare and monitors world population and economic development. UNFPA advocates mobilizing resources to solve population issues, with the ultimate goal of reproductive health for all.

In 1988 the UN troops under Javier Perez de Cuéllar won the Nobel Peace Prize.

UNHCR
United Nations High Commissioner for Refugees
Founded: 1949
Headquarters: Geneva
Assists those persecuted for reasons of race, religion or political views. Regular monitoring of refugee movements throughout the world and organization of aid campaigns. Leads and coordinates international action to protect refugees and resolve refugee problems worldwide.

UNICEF
United Nations International Children's Fund
Founded: 1946
Headquarters: New York
Secures food and medical supplies for children and mothers in need in around 160 countries and is largely financed by private donations. Demands ban on recruitment of "child soldiers". Educational, child development and training programs, promotion of children's rights, emergency assistance in crises.

UNIDO
United Nations Industrial Development Organization
Founded: 1966
Members: 171 countries
Headquarters: Vienna
Promotes projects supporting industrial development and competitiveness, and fighting poverty and marginalization.

World Bank Group
Headquarters: Washington
Comprises five institutions:
- **IBRD**
International Bank for Reconstruction and Development
Founded: 1944
Members: 184 countries
- **IDA**
International Development Association
Founded: 1959
Members: 163 countries
- **IFC**
International Finance Corporation
Founded: 1956
Members: 176 countries
- **MIGA**
Multilateral Investment Guarantee Agency
Founded: 1985
Members: 163 countries
- **ICSID**
International Centre for Settlement of Investment Disputes
Founded: 1966
Members: 154 countries
The World Bank Group support

economic development in less developed member countries by granting loans and supplying consulting and technical assistance, with the goals of combating poverty and improving the standard of living. The World Bank Group institutions are governed by a single president.

WFP
World Food Programme
Founded: 1961
Headquarters: Rome
World's largest organization for securing food production and supplying emergency famine relief and rehabilitation for disaster-hit areas. Promotes food aid as a deterrent to long-term poverty.

WHO
World Health Organization
Founded: 1948
Members: 192 countries
Headquarters: Geneva
WHO's objective, as set out in its constitution, is the attainment by all peoples of the highest possible level of health. Its constitution defines health as a state of complete physical, mental and social well-being, and not merely the absence of disease or infirmity. The WHO maintains a global atlas of infectious diseases and is active in expanding medical research and care, for example in the struggle against AIDS (UNAIDS Program). It also supplies emergency aid in disease outbreaks and crises.

WIPO
World Intellectual Property Organization
Founded: 1967
Members: 179 countries
Headquarters: Geneva
Organization dedicated to promoting the protection of intellectual property. WIPO is financed by the provision of services.

WMO
World Meteorological Organization
Founded: 1985
Members: 185 countries
Headquarters: Geneva
Organization dedicated to maintaining a network of meteorological stations and the exchange of meteorological and environmental data.

1 Kofi Annan (r.), UN Secretary-General from 1997 to 2006, was succeeded by Ban Kimoon (l.) in 2007.

2 UNICEF's responsibilities include providing water supplies for 250 million people in Africa. The organization's goals are protection of rights and creation of adequate living standards for children around the world.

3 Workers of the United Nation's "World Food Programme" prepare a load of emergency food aid for transport to an African region devastated by floods.

International Organizations
European Union

EU
European Union
Founded: 1993
Members: Germany, France, Great Britain, Finland, Italy, Spain, Netherlands, Belgium, Austria, Sweden, Denmark, Portugal, Greece, Ireland, Luxembourg, Latvia, Estonia, Lithuania, Hungary, Poland, Czech Republic, Slovakia, Slovenia, Malta and Cyprus
Headquarters: Strasbourg, Brussels, Luxembourg

The EU is a development of the original European Coal and Steel Community, which joined with the European Economic Community (EEC) in 1957. In 1967, these bodies merged with the European Atomic Energy Commission (EURATOM) to form the European Community – renamed the EU in 1993. The organization strives towards a common foreign and security policy and fosters cooperation in issues of national policy and law.

EU Commission
Founded: 1993
(previously EC Commission)
Members: 30 Commissioners; one for each of the 25 EU members plus an additional one for Germany, France, Italy, Spain and the UK.
Headquarters: Brussels
The Commission is responsible for meeting budgets, directing EU policy, submiting bills, and monitors the member states' compliance with EU legal directives.

Flags of the member states at EU headquarters in Brussels

The European Parliament has met in Strasbourg since 1978.

The euro circulates in bills of 5, 10, 20, 50, 100, 200 and 500.

The European Parliament Plenary. The Parliament's influence extends to many areas of European politics such as legislation, budget and supervision of the executive.

Council of Ministers
Founded: 1993
(Previously EC Council of Ministers)
Headquarters: Brussels
The Council comprises the ministers of EU member countries with responsibility for specific areas (e.g. ECOFIN, Council of Economics and Finance Ministers). Presidency held by each country for six months in rotation. The Council passes laws on supranational

European Court of Justice
Headquarters: Luxembourg
The highest legal institution in the EU deals with disputes involving EU law, ensuring that it is uniformly interpreted and applied throughout the Union. The Court hears actions against member countries, the EP, the Council or Commission. Its verdicts cannot be overturned by national courts. All member states are represented by one judge, presided over by a president.

issues. The EU Council is subordinate to the Council of Europe, of which the EU Commission President is a member.

P

European Parliament
Founded: 1952
Members: total of 732 elected members from all EU countries
Headquarters: Strasbourg, Luxembourg, Brussels
The EP has far-reaching legislative powers and supervises the executive. Together with the European Council, it forms the EU budgetary authority and supervises budget spending. The EP also presides over EU issues of foreign and security policy and plays a key role in the enlargement discussion.

1 The twelve stars symbolize not the number of EU members, but unity.

2 Euro banknotes are in seven denominations: 5, 10, 20, 50, 100, 200 and 500 euro. Their design is identical in all countries and depicts the architectural styles of seven periods throughout Europe's cultural history.

3 José Manuel Barroso, president of the EU commission

Other International Organizations

AfDB/AsDB
African/Asian Development Bank
Founded: 1963/1966
Members: 53 African and
24 non-African countries/44 Asian
and 17 non-Asian countries
Headquarters:
Abijan/Mandaluyong City
Granting and coordination of development aid in Africa and Asia.

ai
amnesty international
Founded: 1961
Members: around 1.8 million in 140
countries throughout the world
Main headquarters: London
The largest human rights organization, staffed by volunteers, fights for freedom for prisoners of conscience and for the abolition of torture and the death penalty. Independent of any government, it is concerned with the universal protection of human rights.

Amnesty international (ai) protest against human rights violations

AOSIS
Alliance of Small Island States
Founded: 1990
Members: 43 small island and
coastal states
Headquarters: New York
The organization is a coalition of small island and low-lying coastal countries, and seeks solutions for problems created by natural disasters and global warming.

APEC
Asia-Pacific Economic Cooperation
Founded: 1989
Members: 21 Pacific Rim states
Headquarters: Singapore
The Cooporation's goal is to create a free trade area in the Asia Pacific region by 2020, reduce tariffs and other trade barriers in the region, and create efficient domestic economies. Commitment is voluntary and decisions are consensus-based.

Arab League
Founded: 1945
Members: 22 Arab countries in
Africa and Asia
Headquarters: Cairo
Voluntary association of independent Arab countries fostering cooperation on cultural, economic, political and scientific issues and representing common interests.

ASEAN
Association of South East Asian Nations
Founded: 1967
Members: Brunei, Cambodia, Indonesia, Malaysia, Philippines, Myanmar, Singapore, Thailand, Vietnam, Laos
Headquarters: Jakarta
Promotion of economic growth, social progress and political stability

by means of political and security dialogue and cooperation. A free trade area is planned by 2010.

CEFTA
Central European Free Trade Association
Founded: 1993
Members: Poland, Slovakian Republic, Slovenia, Czech Republic, Hungary, Bulgaria, Romania
Headquarters: none
The Free Trade Agreement entered into force in 1993. The long-term goal of all members is EU and NATO membership, whereupon CEFTA would be dissolved.

CFA
Communauté Financière Africaine
Members: 13 West and
Central African countries
Headquarters: none
Currency union of former French colonial states in Africa. Valid currency is the CFA franc of the West and Central African central banks.

CIS
Commonwealth of Independent States
Founded: 1991
Members: Armenia, Ukraine, Azerbaijan, Georgia, Russia, Kazakhstan, Kyrgyzstan, Moldavia, Tajikistan, Turkmenistan, Uzbekistan, Belarus
Headquarters: none
Association of twelve former Soviet republics under the presidency of Russia. Cooperation on political cultural, military and economic issues. The 1993 founding charter strives towards common foreign and economic policies.

Commonwealth of Nations
Founded: 1931
Members: 53 countries
Headquarters: London

Other International Organizations

Fostering of political, economic and cultural cooperation as well as the securing of democracy in the former territories of the British Empire. The foundation of the Commonwealth in 1931 coincided with the beginning of decolonization. Most colonies had gained independence by 1984 but retained their close ties to Great Britain and the Commonwealth.

COE
Council of Europe
Founded: 1949
Members: 41 countries
Headquarters: Strasbourg
Organization with almost all European countries as members. Based on the law of nations and founded in London as a private initiative. Its goal is to foster cooperation, preserve items of common cultural heritage, defend human and minority rights as well as support the spread of democracy throughout Europe.

ECO
Economic Cooperation Organization
Founded: 1985
Members: Afghanistan, Azerbaijan, Iran, Kazakhstan, Kyrgyz Republic, Pakistan, Tajikistan, Turkey, Turkmenistan, Uzbekistan
Headquarters: Teheran
Cooperation of Islam nations on economic, agricultural, industrial, transport, technological, scientific and educational issues.

EFTA
European Free Trade Association
Founded: 1960
Members: Iceland, Liechtenstein, Norway, Switzerland
Headquarters: Geneva
Promotion of an extensive network of free trade agreements between member states and associated EU and non-EU countries.

FTAA
Free Trade Area of the Americas
Members: USA, Canada, all Latin and South American countries
Headquarters: none
The agreement signed in Miami in 1994 is aimed at interconnecting the planned North and South American free trade areas (NAFTA and Mercosur), with the goal of incorporating most countries in the

Americas to create the world's largest international free trade zone by 2005.

ICRC
International Committee of the Red Cross
Founded: 1863 as "Committee of Five"
Members: 25 members

1 Queen Elizabeth II is the head of the Commonwealth, a largely representative function in many countries.

2 The Palace of Europe in Strasbourg has housed the Council of Europe since 1977.

3 Volunteers with the International Red Cross. Hard assignments in crisis areas have led to a shortage of new recruits.

Other International Organizations

Headquarters: Geneva

The organization, which developed in 1880 from the "Committee of Five" founded to support wounded soldiers in Europe, is a neutral and independent association formed to promote humanitarian rights and prevent suffering. It is the umbrella organization for the International Red Cross and Red Crescent movements.

IOC
International Olympic Committee
Founded: 1894
Members: 201 National Olympic Committees (NOCs)
Headquarters: Lausanne

International, non-governmental, non-profit organization and umbrella organization of the Olympic Movement. Decides the locations, rules and programs of the Summer and Winter Olympic Games and supervises their organization.

striving to win more influence within the UN. NAM fosters economic and political ties between its members, and advocates solutions to global economic, political and social problems.

NATO
North Atlantic Treaty Organization
Founded: 1955
Members: 19
Headquarters: Brussels

The military pact was initiated by the USA and several Western European states in response to the formation of the Warsaw Pact during the Cold War. NATO has cooperated with the former Eastern Bloc countries since the early 1990s within the NATO Partnership for Peace. The organization has also extended membership to several former Warsaw Pact members. NATO's fundamental role is the safeguarding of its members' freedom and security by

Members: 30 countries
Headquarters: Paris

Successor to the Organization for European Economic Cooperation (OEEC) founded in 1948. Its goal is the economic development and improvement of living standards in member countries, fostering good governance and multilateral agreement. It produces individual country reviews and surveys, monitors trends and analyzes economic developments. It spearheads efforts to help countries respond to new economic challenges.

OPEC
Organization of Petroleum Exporting Countries
Founded: 1960
Members: 11 countries
Headquarters: Vienna

Oil cartel organization serving the interests of its member states with economies heavily reliant on oil. Aims to bring stability and harmony to the oil market by adjusting oil output to help ensure a balance between supply and demand.

OSCE
Organization for Security and Cooperation in Europe
Founded: 1975 (CSCE), since 1995 OSCE
Members: 55 countries
Headquarters: Vienna

The world's largest regional security organization, the Conference for Security and Cooperation in Europe, began its work with the signing of the Helsinki Final Act. It deals with many security and stability-related issues. The OCSE has played an important role in assisting the former communist states of Europe in their transition to democracy.

NATO members join military operations in collective defense issues.

NAM
Non-Aligned Movement
Founded: 1961
Members: 114 countries
Headquarters: in rotation

The majority of UN members, most Third World countries, are not members of military pacts and are

political and military means as well as upholding democracy, political stability and the rule of law.

OECD
Organization for Economic Cooperation and Development
Founded: 1961

UNPO
Unrepresented Nations' and Peoples' Organization

Other International Organizations

Founded: 1991
Members: 52 nations and peoples
Headquarters: The Hague
UNPO represents peoples, countries and minorities that are unrepresented by the United Nations and other international forums.

WEU
Western European Union

ments concerning exchange of goods and services and agreements on patents and other property rights. The WTO also provides arbitration services in trade conflicts. Its promotion of global trade prompts many countries to apply for membership.

Founded: 1954
Members: 10 countries holding both NATO and EU membership
Headquarters: Brussels
Once planned as NATO's "European pillar", the defense pact will be superseded by the establishment of the European Security and Defence Identity (ESDI).

WTO
World Trade Organization
Founded: 1995
Members: 146 countries and the EU Commission
Headquarters: Geneva
Replaced the GATT world trade agreement of 1947 and since then has supervised multilateral agree-

1 The NATO flag has flown at its Brussels headquarters since 1953. It symbolizes the global defense alliance – now with 19 members.

2 The interests of OPEC's eleven members in mutually beneficial pricing and trade policies has become a

key element in world politics. Its members supply over 40% of the world's oil output from over 75% of its proven crude oil reserves.

3 The Commonwealth of Independent States of the former Soviet Union was founded in Minsk in 1991.

359

During the 3rd century BC, the Byzantine Philon compiled a list of the seven wonders of the world including the Great Pyramids of Giza, the Hanging Gardens of Babylon, the Statue of Zeus at Olympia, the Temple of Atemis, the Halicarnassus Mausoleum, the Colossus of Rhodes, and the lighthouse of Alexandria. Philon chose his wonders, not for their aesthetic beauty, but instead because they were the boldest achievements of engineering and construction that he knew of.

The world has always been fascinated by the largest and grandest achievements of nature and mankind. Tourists travel the globe to stare and be amazed by these superlative structures and the human urge to build ever larger and bolder wonders remains.

The World in Records
Man-made and natural highlights

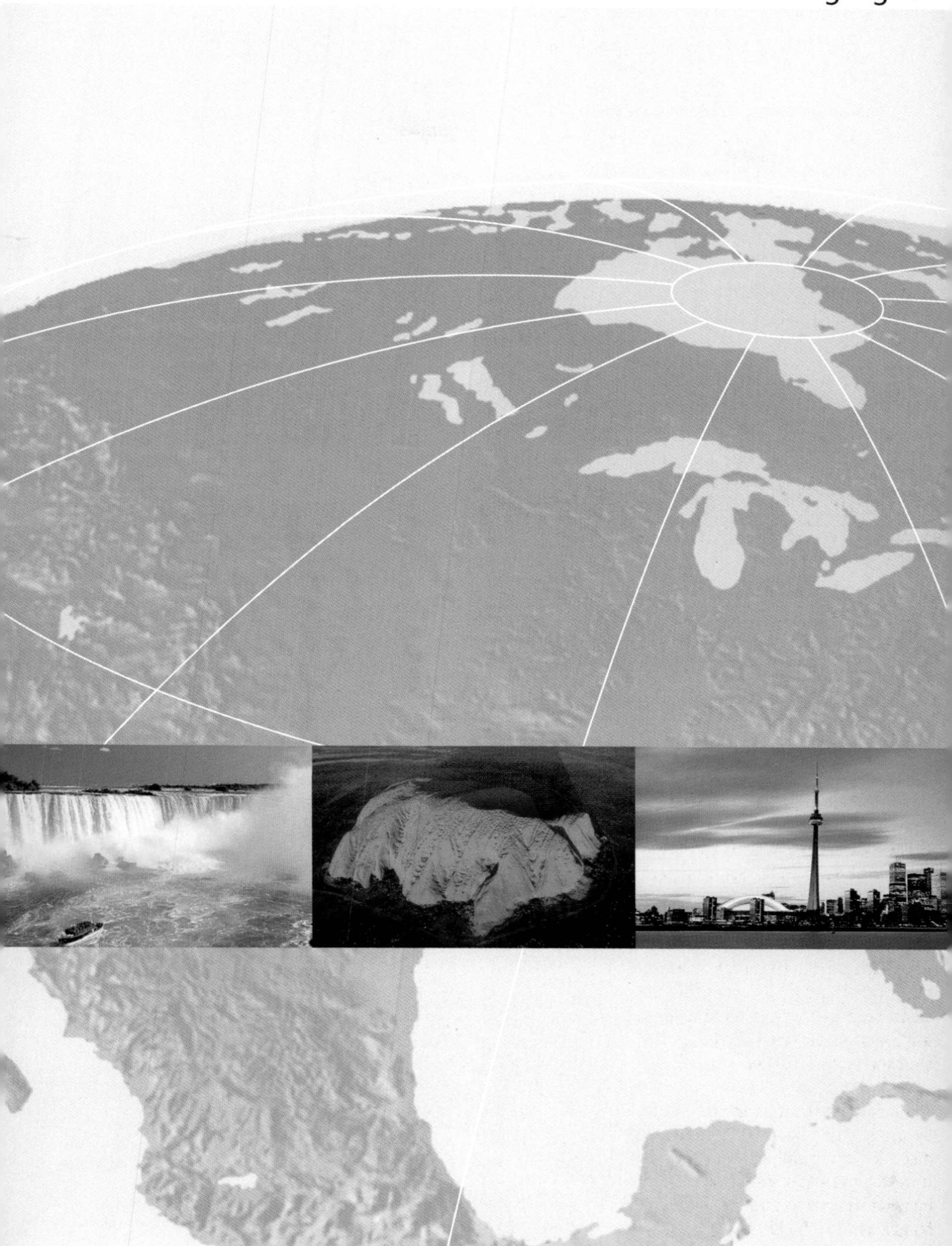

The Universe
Infinite Space

Like many other cultures, the Babylonians were intrigued by the movements of the heavenly bodies in the night sky. The ancient Babylonians produced incredibly accurate maps of the night sky and relied on the movements of the stars to keep pace of time.

More than 13 billion years have passed since the big bang occurred, the moment at which our universe was born. The incredible vastness of our universe is almost as incomprehensible as the notion that the universe has not always existed. In recent years, humanity has been able to view even the most distant galaxies with the use of modern astronomical equipment. The galaxy RD1 is situated around 12.2 billion light years away from our planet. The largest known galaxy, located in the Abell Cluster, has a diameter of 5.6 million light years. In comparison, our galaxy the Milky Way has a diameter of "only" 100,000 light years.

But what is the structure of our gigantic universe and the space surrounding our Earth? The Sun, around which our planet and eight others revolve, is just one of many billions of stars in the universe. There are 40 more stars in the area within 16 light years of the Solar System. Alpha Centauri is located 4.3 light years from the sun and Proxima Centauri is even closer but the dim star is invisible to the naked eye.

Our sun and the surrounding stars are part of a large group of more than 100 million stars – the Milky Way galaxy. Our galaxy is so large that light takes 100,000 years to travel from one end to the next. The Milky Way galaxy has a shape similar to that of an elongated disc and is only a few thousand light years wide at some points. The sun is situated 25,000 light years from the galaxy's centre.

The Milky Way is just one of many galaxies. Together with 30 other galaxies, the Milky Way is part of a galaxy cluster called the Local Group. Even galaxy clusters are often part of larger groups of galaxies – the Local Group is part of the Virgo or Local Supercluster. Even these superclusters, however, are not evenly distributed throughout the galaxy and are surrounded by inconceivably vast voids of relatively empty space that contains few galaxies.

Superlatives in Space

The largest galaxies in the Local Group

Andromeda Galaxy (M 31)
130,000 light years diameter
Milky Way Galaxy (our galaxy)
100,000 light years diameter
Maffei 1
100,000 light years diameter
Triangulum Galaxy
52,000 light years diameter
Large Magellanic Cloud
30,000 light years diameter
Small Magellanic Cloud
16,000 light years diameter
M32
12,000 light years diameter
NGC 205
8,000 light years diameter
NGC 1613
8,000 light years diameter
Fornax
7,000 light years diameter

The largest known star Betelgeuse in the constellation Orion has a diameter of 700 million kilometers.

The heaviest star Eta Carinae in the Eta Carinae Nebula has 150 to 200 times more mass than the sun.

The nearest star Proxima Centauri 4.22 light years (40 billion kilometers)

The Brightest Stars

Sirius -1.46 magnitude
Canopus -0.72 magnitude
Alpha Centauri -0.27 magnitude
Arcutus -0.04 magnitude
Vega 0.03 magnitude
Capella 0.08 magnitude
Rigel 0.12 magnitude
Procyon 0.38 magnitude
Achernar 0.46 magnitude
Hadar 0.61 magnitude
Altair 0.77 magnitude
Aldebaran 0.85 magnitude
The visible brightness of stars as seen from the Earth is measured in magnitude – the lower the value, the brighter the star

Astronomical Measurements

Astronomical Unit (AU) A measurement equal to the mean distance between the Sun and the Earth. One Astronomical Unit is equal to around 150 million kilometers or 93 million miles.

Light year (ly) A measurement equal to the distance that light travels in one year. Light speed equals 300,000 km per second and 1 ly equals 9,460,528,000,000 kilometers.

The Solar System
Planets Orbiting the Sun

The Earth and eight other planets travel in different orbits and at different speeds around our Sun.

Closest to the Sun is the planet Mercury. It needs only 88 days to complete one orbit around the Sun. Following Mercury are the planets Venus and Earth, respectively. Beyond the Earth's orbit are Mars, Jupiter, Saturn, Uranus, and Neptune.

The planet farthest from the Sun is Pluto. This small planet needs 247 years to complete one orbit around the Sun. The immense dimensions of our Solar System can be illustrated by the time that sunlight needs to travel through it and to the different planets. Sunlight reaches the Earth in 8.2 minutes, Pluto after almost 6 hours, and Alpha Centauri A in 4.3 years. Incredible distances when you realize that light can circle the Earth 7.5 times in a second.

In the 16th century Copernicus discovered that the planets orbit around the sun. Johannes Kepler realized in the 17th that the orbits of the planets were not circular but elliptical. In the same century Newton confirmed that the planets were held in their orbits around the sun by the forces of gravitational pull.

Today we know that the planets are a by-product from the development of stars. Our solar system was formed around 4.5 billion years ago from a large cloud of gas and dust. Most of the material in this cloud formed the sun but much of the rest became rotating masses that eventually solidified and formed planets.

The Sun
Maximum Diameter: 1,392,700 sq km
Mass: 332,270 times Earth's Mass – 743 times the combined mass of all other known bodies in the solar system
Core Density: 1.41 g/cm³
Temperature: In the core minimum 15 mil-

lion K, on the visible surface (photosphere) 5,785 K, in the chromosphere 8,000 K, the outermost layer (corona) has temperature between 1 and 3 million K.

The Planets from Largest to Smallest

Jupiter (5th Planet)
Diameter: 142,700 km
Median distance from the sun: 778.3 million km
Revolution around the sun: 4,333 days
Rotation: 9.8 hours
Surface Temperature: -130° C
Satellites: Jupiter has at least 60 satellites, including the largest satellite in the solar system Ganymede (larger than the planet Mercury), Europa, Io, and Callisto; all of which are larger than our moon. Jupiter is generally considered the planet with the largest number of satellites in our Solar System.

Saturn (6th Planet)
Diameter: 120,800 km
Median distance from the sun: 1,428 million km
Revolution around the sun: 10,756 days
Rotation: 10.2 hours
Surface Temperature: -185° C
Seven ring systems with a total diameter of 270,000 km.
Satellites: Saturn has at least 30 moons. Saturn's moon Titan, also the second largest satellite in the Solar System, is the only known moon with a significant atmosphere.

Uranus (7th Planet)
Diameter: 51,600 km
Median distance from the sun: 2,872 million km
Revolution around the sun: 30,685 days
Rotation: 17.24 hours
Surface Temperature: -215° C
Rings: Ten ring systems
Satellites: Uranus has at least 15 satellites, ten of which were first discovered by the NASA space probe Voyager 2.

Neptune (8th Planet)
Diameter: 48,600 km
Median distance from the sun: 4,498 million km
Revolution around the sun: 60,189 days
Rotation: 19.1 hours
Surface Temperature: -110° to -220° C
Rings: One ring system
Satellites: Neptune has eight satellites, five

of which have diameters less than 100 kilometers. Six of the planet's moons were first discovered in 1989.

Earth (3rd Planet)
Diameter: 12,756 sq km
Median distance from the sun: 149.6 million km
Revolution from the sun: 365.26 days
Rotation: 23.93 hours
Surface Temperature: 15° C
Satellites: One moon

Venus (2nd Planet)
Diameter: 12,100 km
Median distance from the sun: 108.2 million km
Revolution around the sun: 224.7 days
Rotation: 243.2 days
Surface Temperature: circa 460° C, the hottest planet
Rings: Venus like all of the other inner planets has no ring systems.
Satellites: Venus has no moons.

Mars (4th Planet)
Diameter: 6,800 km
Median distance from the sun: 227.9 million km (Mars has a highly elliptical orbit and the planet travels at distances between 206.6 and 249.2 million km away from the sun)
Revolution around the sun: 686 days
Rotation: 24.6 days
Surface Temperature: -50° C
Satellites: Mars has two moons, Phobos with a diameter of 27 km and Deimos with a diameter of 15 km. Scientists predict that Phobos will eventually crash into the planet's atmosphere, while the other moon Deimos appears to be slowly drifting away from its orbit around Mars.

Mercury (1st Planet)
Diameter: 4,900 km
Median distance from the sun: 56.9 million km
Revolution around the sun: 87.9 days
Rotation: 58.6 days
Surface Temperature: 430° during the day and -170° C at night
Satellites: Mercury has no satellites

Pluto (9th Planet)
Diameter: 2,300 km
Median distance from the sun: 5,910 million km
Revolution around the sun: 90,465 days; since the planet's discovery no complete orbit around the sun has been observed.

Rotation: 6.37 days
Surface Temperature: -230° C
Satellites: Charon has a diameter of 1,186 km and is only slightly smaller than Pluto — many astronomers consider the two twin planets or bodies because of their similar sizes and synchronized orbits

The Largest Moons in our Solar System

Ganymede (Jupiter) 5,262 km diameter
Titan (Saturn) 5,150 km diameter
Callisto (Jupiter) 4,800 km diameter
Io (Jupiter) 3,630 km diameter
Moon/Luna (Earth) 3,476 km diameter
Europa (Jupiter) 3,138 km diameter
Triton (Neptune) 2,720 km diameter
Titania (Uranus) 1,610 km diameter
Oberon (Uranus) 1,550 km diameter
Rhea (Saturn) 1,530 km diameter
Iapetus (Saturn) 1,435 km diameter
Charon (Pluto) 1,200 km diameter
Umbriel (Uranus) 1,190 km diameter
Ariel (Uranus) 1,160 km diameter
Dione (Saturn) 1,120 km diameter
Tethys (Saturn) 1,048 km diameter

Earth
The Blue Planet

The Earth was formed around 4 billion years ago from the leftover materials in our solar system. Around the same time the moon was formed and since then has followed the Earth from a distance of 350,000 km.

After the early development of the planet Earth, an atmosphere of carbon dioxide and nitrogen was formed containing little oxygen. 3.6 billion years ago the first primitive forms of life appeared on the Earth. This early life relied on photosynthesis and inorganic substances such as water and carbon dioxide for survival. Our planet is the only planet that we know of to contain liquid water, a key ingredient for the development of organic life, because it was only after algae and other aquatic plants produced sufficient oxygen that more advanced animal life forms could evolve. The moon is the closest heavenly body to the Earth and the gravitational pull between the two bodies is significant. On the Earth the moon's

The World in Records
Earth, The Continents, The Oceans

gravitational pull produces tides and floods, and the Earth's gravity creates earthquakes on the moon. The moon today is a geologically inactive body with no active volcanoes. The many craters on the surface of the moon are the result of countless meteor impacts. Unlike Earth, the moon has no significant atmosphere or bodies of liquid water. From the Earth, we can only see one side of the moon and it is only through space exploration that we have been able to discover the dark side of the moon in recent decades.

Facts about the Earth

Age: around 4.3 billion years old
Diameter: 12,756 km at the equator
Distance from the sun: Maximum distance 152 million km; minimum distance 152 million km, estimated mean distance 149.6 million km
Rotation: 23.93 hours
Revolution around the sun: 365.26 days
Surface: 510,083 million sq km
Water Coverage: 361,445 million sq km (71 % of surface)
Land Area: 148.628 million sq km (29%)
Mass: 5,973 · 10^{27}g
Core Density: 5,520 kg/m^3
Speed: 11,200 m per second
Layers:
Inner Core 5,100 km
Outer Core 2,900-5,100 km
Lower Mantle 950-5,100 km
Upper Core 40-2,900 km
Crust 0-40 km
Hottest Point: 4,530° C (Inner Core)
Atmosphere: Contents: nitrogen 78.09%, oxygen 20.95%, argon 0.93%, carbon dioxide 0.03%. The troposphere extends up to 11 km, the stratosphere up to 50 km, the mesosphere up to 80 km, the thermosphere up to 400 km, and the exosphere, the outermost layer, extends between 100 and 400 km above the Earth's surface.

The Moon

Diameter: 3,476 km
Median distance from the Earth: 384,403 km
Revolution around the Earth: 29.5 days
Surface: 37.69 million sq km
Mass: 7.35 ·10^{23}g
Surface Temperature: 117° C to -163° C
Deepest Crater: Newton 7,000-8,500 m
Largest Crater: Mare Orientale, 965 km diameter

The Moon Landings

Apollo 11: July 20, 1969
Armstrong, Collins, Aldrin
Apollo 12: November 11, 1969
Conrad, Gordon, Bean
Apollo 14: February 2, 1971
Shepard, Roose, Mitchell
Apollo 15: July 30, 1971
Scott, Worden, Irwin
Apollo 16: April 4, 1972
Young, Mattingly, Duke
Apollo 17: December 11, 1972
Cernan, Evans, Schmitt

The Continents
The Blue Planet

The modern continents were formed around 245 million years ago as the mega-continent Pangaea broke apart and the continents drifted into their present positions.

As the continents drifted away from one another most of their low-lying edges were submerged but some remained above water to form continental islands such as the British Isles or Newfoundland off the coast of mainland Canada. Most islands are younger and were created through underwater volcanic activities. The planet's tectonic plates continuously collide with one another. For this reason regions near the borders of plates such as the western coast of North America are sites of frequent geological activity. This leads to earthquakes, volcanic eruptions, and the gradual formation of mountain chains.

Continents from Largest to Smallest

Asia
Area: 44,614,000 sq km (without Papua New Guinea)
The largest and most populated continent covers almost a third of Earth's land surface. It is also the continent with the highest mountain chain (Himalayas).

Africa
Area: 30,273,000 sq km
Africa, the birthplace of humanity, is the hottest continent with average temperatures between 25 and 28° C.

North America
(Including Greenland)
Area: 24, 219, 000 sq km

South America
Area: 17, 839,000 sq km

Antarctica
Area: 13, 200,000 sq km
Antarctica is the windiest and coldest continent on our planet with an average temperature of -40° C. Antarctica holds almost 90% of the Earth's ice and is with an average elevation of 2,280 m the highest elevated continent.

Europe
Area: 9,839,000 sq km

Australia/Oceania
Area: 8, 937,000 sq km
Australia is the world's flattest and smallest continent.

The Oceans
The Source of all Life

Water covers almost two-thirds of the Earth's surface, approximately 361,445,000 sq km. The seven continents divide this mass of water into four oceans, each with its own independent currents and tides.

The Pacific Ocean, the largest of the four oceans, dominates almost half of the Earth's surface. The water of the oceans differs from the fresh water of most lakes and rivers because of its high salt content. In some regions the salt content of ocean water can exceed 35g per 1,000g of water. The oceans are also the source of all life on our planet because it was there, billions of years ago, that the first primitive life began to evolve.

Oceans from Largest to Smallest

Pacific Ocean
Area: 181,349,000 sq km
Average Depth: 4,000 m

Atlantic Ocean
Area: 106,575,000 sq km
Average Depth: 3,292 m

Indian Ocean
Area: 74,120,000 sq km
Average Depth: 3,800 m

Arctic Ocean
Area: 13,950,000 sq km
Average Depth: 1,328 m

Ocean Depths

Pacific Ocean
Mariana Trench
Challenger Deep 11,033 m
Tonga Trench
9,100 m

Atlantic Ocean
Puerto Rico Trench
Milwaukee Depth 9,219 m
South Sandwich Trench
Meteor Deep 8,264 m
Cayman Trench
7,680 m

Indian Ocean
Sunda Trench
Planet Deep 7,455 m
Southeast Asian Basin
6,857 m
North Australian Basin
6,840 m

Arctic Ocean
Eurasian Basin
5,449 m
Greenland Basin
Sweden Deep 4,846 m

Largest Ocean Animals

Mammal
Blue Whale – this species, the world's largest mammals, can grow to weigh between 100-150 tons and reach lengths between 25-35 meters.

Fish
Great White Shark, 18 meters long

Turtle
Leatherback Turtle, up to 560 kg heavy

Cephalopod
Giant Squid, up to 35 meters long

Jellyfish
Lion's Mane Jellyfish, up to 4 meters long and more than 1,000 tentacles

Crab
Japanese Giant Crab, its legs can grow to almost 2 meters

Mussel
Tridacna Clams, up to 300 kg heavy and 1.5 meters wide

Islands
Oases in the Sea

Scientists distinguish between two types of islands, continental and oceanic. The first group includes islands such as Ireland, Great Britain, and the two main islands of New Zealand. Oceanic islands are created as a result of volcanic activity.

The relatively short history of most oceanic islands is fascinating. These islands go through a rapid cycle of formation and expansion. The birth of an oceanic island begins with the eruption of a large underwater volcano. Hot magma from the Earth's crust released by an eruption forms layer upon layer of stone until this underwater mountain breaches the ocean's surface as a new island. The world's highest volcanoes and highest mountains, when measured from the ocean floor, are the volcanoes of the Hawaiian Islands in the Pacific Ocean. Mauna Kea for example is 10,205 meters tall from its base on the ocean floor to its peak, which is situated 4,205 meters above sea level.

The Largest Islands

Greenland 2,175,600 sq km
New Guinea 771,900 sq km
Borneo 746,950 sq km

Europe
Britain 219,801 sq km
Iceland 103,000 sq km
Ireland 84,426 sq km
Spitsbergen 39,368 sq km
Sicily 25,400 sq km

Asia
Borneo 746,950 sq km
Sumatra 425,979 sq km
Honshu 230,636 sq km
Celebes 174,000 sq km
Java 129,000 sq km

Africa
Madagascar 587,041 sq km
Reunion 2510 sq km
Bioko 2043 sq km

Australia/Oceania
New Guinea 771,900 sq km
New Zealand – South Island
153,947 sq km
New Zealand – North Island
114,729 sq km

The Americas
Greenland 2,175,600 sq km
Baffin Island 517,890 sq km
Victoria Island 217,290 sq km

Coral Reefs and Atolls
Living Islands

Coral reefs cover around 600,000 sq km of the Earth's surface. They are common in many tropical bodies of water.

Coral reefs are living Islands that formed by large amounts of organic coral. Coral grows mostly in mineral and oxygen-rich water with a minimum temperature of 20° C. Atolls are ring-shaped coral reefs that encircle lagoons.

The Largest Coral Reefs

The Great Barrier Reef is located off the north-eastern coast of Australia and with an area of 250,000 sq km and a length of 2024 km is the world's largest reef.

Barrier Reef located near the island Grand Terre in New Caledonia is the world's second longest coral reef with a length of 802 km.

The Belize Barrier Reef (Grande Recife Maya) stretches along the coast of Belize and the Yucatan. The 300 km-long reef is the longest in the western hemisphere.

The Largest Atolls

Kwajalein Atoll in the Marshall Islands has a land area of 16 sq km and encircles the world's largest lagoon.

Kiritimati in Polynesia has the largest land area of any atoll covering 388 sq km.

Coastal Areas
Shaped by the Seas

The world's coasts are the areas where land and bodies of water meet and merge. Coastal areas have always been shaped by the effects of wind and water erosion. Erosion and storms often cause coastlines to rapidly and dramatically change their form.

The Longest Bays

Bay of Bengal 1,850 km
Hudson Bay 1,560 km
Gulf of Mexico 1,330 km

The Largest Tides

Bay of Fundy, Canada: on average between 16 and 18 meters, 21 meter tides have been observed
Shelikof Strait: high tide averages 12.9 meters in the area
Gulf of Alaska: 12 meters
Bay of Bengal: 10.7 meters
Bay of Mezen: 10 meters

Vegetation Zones
Living Landscapes of the Earth

The Earth's land areas can be divided into several distinct vegetation zones. These zones are identified by their different climates, flora, and fauna. It is also significant that similar vegetation zones are usually found along or near the same latitudes.

The polar regions of Antarctica and the Arctic are covered by glaciers and icecaps. In the northern hemisphere this region is bordered by tundra, a zone with extremely cold temperatures in winter and where the frost-covered ground only briefly thaws in summer.

The mild climate of the temperate zones is home to mixed forests and extensive shrubbery growth. Large-scale agriculture is common in these regions. The temperate regions are located primarily in the northern hemisphere; in Europe and North America but also in New Zealand, southern South America, and parts of Australia. Around and beyond the twentieth latitudes lie the world's subtropical regions. The subtropics are characterized by a diverse variety of ecosystems and landscapes. The Everglades in Florida and the eucalyptus forests of Australia are located in this zone.

The tropical belt of the Earth stretches along and above the equator through the Amazon rain forest, Central Africa, and South Asia. Most tropical regions are bordered by extensive grasslands such as savannah landscapes or semi-arid regions. The Llanos of South America, the Serengeti in East Africa, and large sections of Australia are typical savannahs. The various regions between the 15th and 35th latitudes with less than 250 mm annual precipitation are classified as deserts.

Polar Regions

Around 15 million sq km of the Earth's surface is covered by ice and glaciers, of this amount the vast majority or around 12.7 million sq km is located in Antarctica. The rest of this amount is scattered around the globe including 1.8 sq km of ice coverage in Greenland, 300,000 sq km in the areas surrounding the Arctic Ocean and Antarctica, 120,000 sq km in Asia, 100,000 sq km in North and South America, and 10,000 sq km in Europe. Because of its inhospitable climate and terrain, Antarctica remains the world's only continent without permanent human inhabitants.

The Largest Glaciers
Vatnajokull, 8,540 sq km
Iceland
Malaspina Glacier, 3,900 sq km
Alaska
Siachen Glacier, 1,150 sq km
India
Fedchenko Glacier, 907 sq km
Tajikistan
Nabesna Glacier, 819 sq km
Alaska
Baltoro Glacier, 754 sq km
Pakistan
Biafo Glacier, 620 sq km,
Pakistan
Muldrow Glacier, 516 sq km
Alaska
Jostedalsbreen, 415 sq km
Norway

Polar Wildlife
Largest Land Mammal: Polar Bear
Largest Aquatic Bird: Emperor Penguin
Largest Seals: Southern Elephant Seals

Tundra

Tundra is the name of the regions bordering the Polar Regions and above the tree lines of many mountainous areas. The tundra of Canada and Siberia alone cover nearly 10 percent of the Earth's land area. The climate of the tundra is characterized by cold temperatures and low levels of precipitation. The ground in the tundra is not always covered by ice and hardy plants such as mosses, lichens, and shrubs can thrive in this hostile environment. Reindeer, moose, caribous, and wolves are among the animals that populate tundra regions. On the coast around tundra you might find seals, walruses, and a variety of aquatic birds.

Taiga

Taiga or boreal forests are forest landscapes consisting of coniferous trees that lie south of the polar regions in North America and Eurasia. 70% of the world's taiga regions are located in Russia. These expansive landscapes contain one third of the world's forests. Pines, fir trees, and spruces are all abundant in this type of vegetation zone. The ground of the taiga is usually covered by weeds, moss, and shrubbery.

Northern Wildlife
Largest Bear: Kodiak Brown Bear, Alaska
Largest Feline: Siberian Tiger, Russia

Temperate Forests

The world's temperate broadleaf deciduous forests, or simply temperate forests, are located mostly in the Northern Hemisphere. These regions contain approximately 18% of the world's forests.

In the past, far larger regions of North America and Europe were covered by temperate forests but as the population density of Europe rose and North America opened up to European settlement most of these forests were leveled. Today the most intact temperate forests can be found in eastern North America. The forests there are famous for the color changes their leaves display particularly in autumn.

Forest Wildlife

Largest Predator: Brown Bear
Largest Canine Predator: Wolves
Largest Songbirds: Common Raven
Fastest Birds: Peregrines
Largest Land Mammal (Europe): Bison
Largest Deer Species (Europe): Red Deer
Largest Canine Species (Europe): Lynx
Largest Trees: Giant Sequoia (Redwood)
Oldest Tree Species: Ginkgo

Between Temperate and Tropics

Between the temperate forest and the tropics lie a variety of vegetation zones. There are the humid and warm subtropical regions including areas like Florida and South China. There are also numerous deserts and semiarid grasslands in the area between the tropics and temperate zone.

Subtropical Wildlife

Largest Felines: Bengal Tiger
Largest Reptile (North America): American Alligator
Highest Tree Species: Eucalyptus, up to 130 meters
Largest Fern Species: Giant Tree Ferns

Tropical Forests

Tropical forests comprise almost half of the world's forests. The rain forest belt that stretches along the equator covers 6% of the Earth's land area. The largest area of continuous tropical rain forest is located in the vast Amazon River basin of South America and covers an area of approximately 3.6 million sq km.
Other large tropical rain forests are located in Guyana, West and Central Africa, South and Southeast Asia, and Oceania. The most fascinating aspect of the rain forests is their remarkable diversity of plant and animal life. More than half of the world's known plant and animal species inhabit the tropical rain forests.

Tropical Wildlife

Largest Land Mammal: African Elephant
Largest Mammal (South America): Baird's Tapir
Largest Predator (South America): Jaguar
Largest Primate: Western Gorilla
Longest Reptile: Anaconda
Largest Insect: Pharnacia serratipes, up to 35 cm in length

Savannas

Between many of the world's tropical forest and deserts you can find extensive grasslands called Savannas. Among the world's major savannas are the Serengeti in Africa, Brazil's Campos, and the arid grasslands on Australia. A distinctive characteristic of the savannas are the distinct dry and wet seasons. Various grasses thrive in the savannas, and oases of trees dot these landscapes. Once the rainy season begins the savannas are transformed into seas of green grass.

Wildlife of the Savanna

Largest Land Mammal: African Elephant
Largest Feline: Lion
Fastest Land Animal: Cheetah
Tallest Land Animal: Giraffe
Largest Bird: African Ostrich

Deserts

Deserts cover 30% of the Earth's surface. Most of the deserts are located between the 15th and 35th latitudes. Deserts are the warmest and driest regions on our planet. Day and night-time temperatures in deserts can differ by as much as 50° C. Seasons are less distinctive in the deserts than in other regions.

The Largest Deserts

Sahara: 9.7 million sq km; this figure includes the Libyan and Nubian deserts. The Sahara is the world's largest desert and grows 10,000 sq km larger every year. The desert has a maximum length of 5,150 km from east to west and 2,250 km from north to south. Daytime temperatures in the Sahara often exceed 40° C.
Gobi: 1.3 million sq km; this Asian desert lies at an average height of 1,000 m above sea level.
Kalahari: 1 million sq km; the large arid basin in southern Africa lacks outflowing waterways.

Africa

Sahara 9.7 million sq km
Kalahari 1 million sq km
Arabian Desert (Egypt and Sudan) 182,000 sq km
Namib 135,000 sq km; this desert along the coast of south-western Africa stretches more than 1,300 km from north to south and has an average width of around 100 kilometers. The Namib is one of the world's driest deserts.

Asia

Gobi (China and Mongolia) 1.3 million sq km
Rub al Khali (Saudi Arabia) 800,000 sq km
Taklamakan (China) 400,000 sq km
Karakum (Turkmenistan) 350,000 sq km
Kyzylkum (Kazakhstan and Uzbekistan) 300,000 sq km
Kevir (Iran) 260,000 sq km
Syrian Desert 260,000 sq km
Thar (India and Pakistan) 250,000 sq km
Negev (Israel) 12,300 sq km

Australia

Great Sand Desert 520,000 sq km
Gibson 330,000 sq km
Great Victoria Desert 274,000 sq km
Simpson 250,000 sq km

Americas

Atacama (northern Chile) 400,000 sq km
Sonora, including the Colorado and Yuma Deserts (USA) 310,000 sq km
Mojave (USA) 38,900 sq km

Europe

The only true deserts in Europe are located in the Russian republic of Kalmykia. These deserts are manmade, the result of overuse of the region's once fertile soils. Today deserts cover at least 80% of Kalmykia's territory.

Climate
Hot and Cold

The word weather describes the atmospheric condition of an area for a specific relatively short period of time. Climate on the other hand is a general description of the dominant atmospheric conditions in a region year-round. Mountains and large bodies of water are important.

Climatic Extremes

Lowest Temperature Recorded

In 1983 at Vostok in Antarctica and at a height of 3,420 meters temperatures -89.2° C/-128° Fahrenheit were recorded. This is the lowest temperature ever measured on the Earth's surface.

The World in Records
Climate, Natural Disasters, Volcanoes

Highest Temperature Recorded
In Al' Azziyah, Libya the temperature reached 58° C/ 136° Fahrenheit on September 13, 1922.

Hottest Region
During an average year Dallol in Ethiopia is the warmest place on the Earth's surface. The average temperature between 1960 and 1966 at any time of the year was 34° C/94° Fahrenheit.

Coldest Region
The coldest area in Anarctica is located at the coordinates 78° south, 96° east, where the average temperature is -58° C/-72.4° Fahrenheit.

Rainiest Region
On the Hawaiian Island of Kauai it rains an average 350 days in the year.

Sunniest Region
In Yuma, Arizona, the sun is visible during 91% of the daytime hours.

Most Rainfall
The area around Mawsynram in the Indian state of Megalaya receives an average of 11,873 milimeters of rainfall in a year.

Driest Region
The driest place on Earth is located on Chile's pacific coast between Arica and Antofagasta. During an average year less than one millimeter of precipitation falls in this arid region.

Windiest Region
Commonwealth Bay in Australia is the windiest place on Earth. Storms in this bay can produce winds reaching speeds up to 320 km/h.

Natural Disasters:
Wind and Weather

On average one meter of precipitation falls to the Earth's surface during a year. In reality, however, this rain and snowfall is unevenly distributed across the globe.

The greatest levels of precipitation occur in the tropics. Countries such as Bangladesh are often devastated by floods and typhoons.

Every year powerful storms form off the coast of West Africa; many of these storms become immense tropical cyclones capable of crossing the Atlantic Ocean. These storms often reach land in the Caribbean Sea and continental North America. With winds that can reach 300 km/h, tropical cyclones – more commonly known as hurricanes and typhoons – are one of the most destructive forces of nature. Hurricanes and typhoons can devastate entire regions in a matter of hours. The heavy rainfall and severe floods that usually accompany hurricanes add to their destructive power.

Deadly Storms and Floods
Resulting deaths

Yellow River, China: 1887 flood 900,000
Bangladesh: 1970 typhoon 300,000
Bangladesh: 1991 typhoon 150,000
Japan: 1896 tsunami 22,000
Galveston, Texas: 1900 hurricane 6,000
Yangtze River, China: 1998 4,000
Papua New Guinea: 1998 tsunami 3,000
England, The Netherlands: 1953 flood 2,000
Midwestern United States: 1925 Tri-State tornado 689
United States, Canada, Caribbean: 1993 "Storm of the Century" 220

Natural Disasters:
An active planet

Our planet is an active and energetic world. In the subterranean layers of the Earth huge masses of stones and magma are constantly on the move. The massive tectonic plates beneath the Earth's surface move along and collide into one another, often creating earthquakes. These quakes originate from sources between 5 and 30 kilometers under the surface.

Around 500,000 instances of seismic activities occur every year. Of this number only about 100,000 can be felt on the Earth's surface. Unfortunately, there is still no effective method to predict the occurrence of earthquakes.
Volcano eruptions are also difficult to pre-

dict but not impossible. In 1991 the population living near Mt. Pinatubo was evacuated before a violent eruption devastated the area. The ash released from this one eruption affected the world's climate long afterwards. At present there are 1,343 active volcanoes around the world.

The Strongest Earthquakes: 20th Century
Magnitude on the Richter Scale

Chile: May 22, 1960 (9.5)
Alaska: March 28, 1964 (9.2)
Alaska: March 3, 1957 (9.1)
Russia: April 11, 1952 (9.1)
Ecuador: Jan. 01, 1906 (8.8)
Japan: Nov. 06, 1958 (8.7)
Alaska: Feb. 02, 1965 (8.7)
India: August 08, 1950 (8.6)
Argentina: Nov. 11, 1922 (8.5)
Indonesia: Jan. 02, 1938 (8.5)

Volcanic Eruptions
Resulting deaths

Tambora, Indonesia: 1815 90,000
Miyi, Indonesia: 1793 53,000
Pelè, Martinique: 1902 40,000
Krakatau, Indonesia: 1883 36,300
Nevado del Ruiz, Columbia: 1985 22,000
Mt. Etna, Italy: 1669 20,000
Laki, Iceland: 1783 20,000
Unzen, Japan: 1792 15,000
Vesuvius, Italy: 75 A.D 10,000
El Chicón, Mexico: 1982 3500

Volcanoes
Smoke and Fire

The world's numerous active volcanoes are the most dramatic reminders of the violent natural processes that occur beneath the surface of our planet. These mountains of fire are often unpredictable. Some active volcanoes like Hawaii's Kilauea constantly release lava, while others are prone to powerful and sudden eruptions.

The regions near the border of tectonic plates are also the regions with the most volcanic activity. One such area is the so-called Ring of Fire along the coasts of the Pacific. Many countries in this region including Japan, Indonesia, and the Phillipines are home to active volcanoes.

The Tallest Active Volcanoes
(worldwide)

Volcan Guallatiri, Chile: 6,060 m
Volcan Láscar, Chile: 5,990 m
Tupungatito, Chile: 5,900 m
Cotopaxi, Ecuador: 5,897 m
Popcatepetl, Mexico: 5,452 m

(Europe)
Mt. Etna 3,350 m
Beerenberg 2,277m
Mt. Hekla 1,491 m

Asia
Kluchevskaya Sopke 4,750 m
Kerinci 3,800 m
Tolbachik 3,682 m

Oceania
Mauna Loa 4,170 m
Mt. Ruapeha 2,797 m

Africa
Mt. Cameroon 4,070 m
Mt. Nyirangongo 3,475 m
Emi Koussi 3,415 m

North America
Popocatépetl 5,452 m
Mt. Rainier 4,392 m
Volcan Colima 3,984 m

South America
Volcan Guallatiri 6,060 m
Volcan Lascar 5,990 m
Cotopaxi 5,897 m

Antartica
Mt. Erebus 3,795 m

Geysers
Erupting Wonders

Geysers are geological wonders that can be found in many regions around the world. These spectacular gushing fountains of water often erupt in regular cycles.

Geysers are formed when extremely hot magma approaches the Earth's surface and warms underground water sources. These eventually reach boiling point and gradually force their way to the surface as an explosive plume. Minerals in the water fall to the ground, gradually forming the stone structure of a geyser. A large number of the world's geysers are concentrated in America's Yellowstone National Park. Yellowstone's largest geyser, Old Faithful, is also the world's most famous geyser. Iceland and New Zealand are also home to a large number of geysers. The largest known geyser was once located in the New Zealand city of Waimangu. Before it became inactive in 1917, the Waimangu Geyser regularly produced a 450-meter-high plume of water.

The Tallest Geysers
(Water Plumes)

United States, Yellowstone National Park
Service Steamboat 60-115 meters
Old Faithful 50 meters

Iceland
Geysir 60 meters
Strokkur 25-30 meters

New Zealand
Pohutu 31 meters
Lady Knox 10-15 meters

Russia
Velican 40 meters

Mountains
Stone Giants

Humanity has always been in awe of the majestic beauty of mountains. Even today many people around the world view mountains as the home of gods and other spirits.

Far into the last century many peaks of the world's most famous mountains, including the Himalayas, remained unconquered. In 1953 Edmund Hillary and Norgay Tenzing became the first men to reach the summit of Mount Everest. The Himalayas like most mountain chains were formed by the convergence of tectonic plates. When tectonic

plates push into one another an enormous amount of pressure is put on the surrounding earth. With no way to go but up, this process eventually leads to the formation of mountain systems. Mountains formed in this way are referred to as folded mountains. Because this process continues today, most of the world's highest mountains continue to expand upwards by an average of one centimeter every year.

Major Mountain Systems
(including highest mountains)

Asia
Himalayas (main range)
Mt. Everest 8,861 m
Karakoram Range
K2 8,610 m
Kunlun Mountains
Kongur Tagh 7,719 m

North America
Alaska Range
Mt. McKinley 6,194 m
St. Ellas Mountains
Mt. Logan 5,951 m
Sierra Madre Oriental
Citlaltepetl 5,700 m

South America
Andes
Aconcagua 6,960 m
Sierra Nevada de Santa Maria
Pico Cristobal 5,800 m

Africa
Mt. Kilimanjaro
Kibo 5,963 m
Mt. Kenya
Batian 5,201 m
Ruwenzori Range
Mount Stanley 5,109 m

Europe
Caucasus Mountains
Mount Elbrus 5,633 m
Alps
Mont Blanc 4,807 m
Sierra Nevada
Cunbre de Mulhacen 3,478 m
Pyrenees
Pico de Aneto 3,404 m

Oceania
Surdiman Range
Puncak Jaya 5,030 m
Southern Alps
Mount Cook 3,764 m

Antarctica
Elisworth Range
Vinson Massif 5,140 m
Queen Alexandra Range
Mount Markham 4,350 m
Executive Committee Range
Mount Sidley 4,181 m

The Highest Mountains

Mount Everest (Nepal) 8,863 m
first successful ascent in 1953
K2 (Pakistan) 8,610 m
first successful ascent in 1954
Kangchenjunga (Nepal) 8,586 m
first successful ascent in 1955
Lhotse (Nepal) 8,511 m
first successful ascent in 1956
Makalu (Nepal) 8,463 m
first successful ascent in 1955
Dhaulagiri (Nepal) 8,167 m
first successful ascent in 1960
Manaslu (Nepal) 8,125 m
first successful ascent in 1956
Cho Oyu (Nepal) 8,153 m
first successful ascent in 1954
Nanga Parbat (Nepal) 8,125 m
first successful ascent in 1953
Annapurna I (Nepal) 8,091 m
first successful ascent in 1950
Gasherbrum I (Pakistan) 8,068 m
first successful ascent in 1958
Broad Peak (Pakistan) 8,047 m
first successful ascent in 1957
Gasherbrum II 8,035 m
first successful ascent in 1956
Sishapangma (China) 8,027 m
first successful ascent in 1964

Basins and Depressions
Areas Below Sea Level

Depression and basin are the terms used to describe an area of land that is situated at a significant depth below sea level. The world's depressions were formed through tectonic activity or wind erosion.

The Deepest Basins/Depressions
(distance below sea level)

Dead Sea, -400 m below sea level
Israel, Jordan

Assal Depression, -155 m
Djibouti
Turfan Depression, -154 m
China
Qattara Depression, -133 m
Egypt
Mangyshlak Basin, -132 m
Kazakhstan
Lake Asal, -116 m
Ethiopia
Death Valley, -86 m
California, United States
Salton Sink, -85 m
California
Ustyurt Basin, -70 m
Kazakhstan
Caspian Depression, -67 m
Kazakhstan
Al Fayyum Oasis, -50 m
Egypt
Salinas Grande, -40 m
Argentina

The Largest Basins/Depressions

Caspian Depression 394,000 sq km
Kazakhstan
Qattara Depression 20,000 sq km
Egypt

Canyons and Gorges
Wonders of Erosion

Rivers have played a major role in the shaping the world's surface. Canyons are valleys surrounded by stone walls and cliffs. The world's gorges and canyons were created over many centuries by rivers. The powerful eroding effects of rivers cut through the hardest of surfaces over time forming large gashes in the land.

The shape of a canyon or gorge is determined by the flow of the river that forms it and the nature of stone it is carved from. The hardness of the stone determines the direction of the eroding effects that produce a canyon. The upper course of a river is usually the section with the fastest speed and the section with the greatest eroding power. Most of the world's deep canyons were formed on the upper course of a large river.

Because there are so many factors that can influence the formation of a canyon, these natural wonders come in a variety of shapes and sizes. The Colorado River began eroding the ground near what is now the Grand Canyon around 26 million years ago. After numerous centuries the canyon began to emerge out of the hard stone in the region. The 24-kilometer-wide Grand Canyon is now one of world's most visited and famous natural attractions.

The Deepest Canyons
(maximum depth in meters)

North America
Grand Canyon 1,800 m – the world's largest canyon
USA
Hell's Canyon 1,700 m
USA
Barranca del Cobre 1,400 m
Mexico
Black Canyon 700 m
USA
Bryce Canyon 600 m
USA

Africa
Fish River Canyon 600 m
Namibia
Dades Gorge 400 m
Morocco
Wadi Kantara 400 m
Algeria

Asia
Wu Gorge 900 m
China
Black River Canyon 800 m
Vietnam
Sanmen Gorge 600 m
China

Europe
Vicos Gorge 900 m
Greece
Via Mala 700 m
Switzerland
Neretva Canyons 800 m
Bosnia and Herzegovina
Grand Canyon du Verdon 700 m
France

Oceania
Milford Sound 600 m
New Zealand
Vaihiria 550 m
Tahiti, French Polynesia

South America
Colca Canyon 3,400 m – the world's deepest canyon
Peru

Rivers
The Arteries of our Planet

Rivers bring life to large areas of land; they nurtured ancient civilizations, and have functioned throughout history as the important means of transportation for people around the world. Many of the world's great rivers begin as small creeks before merging with other rivers and flowing into the seas and oceans.

97.5% of the world's water is saltwater. On top of this at least 70% of the world's freshwater is frozen in the polar ice caps and most of the remaining 30% lies in underground sources that are practically inaccessible. Only around 0.007% of the world's water is currently available for human use. The world's rivers contain 42,700 km^3 of water. That is more water than the amount contained in Lake Tanganyika, Baikal, and Victoria together.

The world's longest river is the Nile in Africa. Its source was sought by explorers for many centuries before its discovery in the 19th century. The Nile River Valley is a fertile oasis surrounded by barren deserts.

The world's largest river is the Amazon in South America. The Amazon is 200 km shorter than the Nile but contains far more water – the river contains at least one-fifth of the world's river water. In addition to its size the Amazon is noteworthy because it is the foundation of an amazing and important ecosystem, the vast Amazon rain forest.

The Longest Rivers
(Worldwide)

Nile 6,672 km
Amazon 6,437 km
Yangtze 6,300 km
Mississippi/Missouri 6,020 km

North America
Mississippi/Missouri 6,020 km
Mackenzie-Peace River 4,241 km

Yukon 3,185 km
St. Lawrence 3,058 km
Rio Grande 3,034 km
Colorado 2,334 km

Africa
Nile 6,672 km
Zaire (Congo) 4,374 km
Niger 4,184 km
Zambezi 2,736 km
Ubangi-Uele 2,300 km

Asia
Yangtze 6,300 km
Irtysch 5,410 km
Huang He 4,875 km
Mekong 4,500 km
Amur 4,416 km

Europe
Volga 3,351 km
Danube 2,858 km
Ural 2,428 km
Dnieper 2,200 km

Australia
Darling 2,740 km
Murray 2,570 km
Murrumbidgee 2,160 km

South America
Amazon 6,437 km
Parana-La Plata 4,264 km
Madeira 3,240 km
Rio Purus 3,211 km

Waterfalls
Rivers in Freefall

Waterfalls are formed when a stream of water flows over an area with a sudden drop in elevation. There are several types of waterfalls and many of the most famous and beautiful are popular natural attractions. Every year, millions of tourists around the world enjoy the awe-inspiring beauty of these natural spectacles

The Largest Waterfalls (width)

Khone Pha Pheng 10,800 m
Laos

Iguacu Falls 4,000 m
Brazil, Argentina
Victoria Falls 1,700 m
Zambia, Zimbabwe
Niagara Falls 1,150 m
United States, Canada

The Highest Waterfalls
(by continent)

North/South America
Angel Falls 948 m – the world's highest waterfalls
Venezuela
Yosemite Falls 739 m
United States
Cuquean Falls 610 m
Guyana, Venezuela
Roraima Falls 457 m
Guyana
Kaieteur Falls 226 m
Guyana

Africa
Tugela 411 m
South Africa
Maletsunyane 192 m
Lesotho
Augrabies 146 m
South Africa
Ruacana 120 m
Namibia, Angola
Victoria Falls 110 m
Zambia, Zimbabwe

Asia
Falls of Gersoppa 253 m
India
Cauvery Falls 101 m
India
Kegon Falls 101 m
Japan
Juizhaigou 78 m
China
Gokaks 52 m
India

Australia/New Zealand
Sutherland Falls 580 m
New Zealand
Wollomombi Falls 335 m
Australia
Wallaman Falls 285 m
Australia
Tully 270 m
Australia
Wentworth Falls 187 m
Australia

The World in Records
Waterfalls, Lakes, Reservoirs

Europe
Mardalsfossen 517 m
Norway
Gavarnie Falls 422 m
France
Krimmler Falls 380 m
Austria
Giessbach Falls 300 m
Switzerland
Skykkjedalsfoss 300 m
Iceland

Lakes
Inland Seas

Most of the world's large lakes are gla-cial lakes, formed as huge glaciers melted after the last ice age. But the world's oldest lakes including Lake Baikal and Victoria were formed as a re-sult of tectonic activity. Lake Tangayika, the world's longest lake with a length of 655 km, owes its unusual narrow shape and existence to tectonic activity. Endorheic lakes are lakes with no out-flowing waterways. Such lakes, located mostly in deserts, often exhibit rapid changes in shape and depth.

The Largest Lakes
(With area and maximum depth)

Caspian Sea 371,800 sq km – the world's largest lake, salt water lake, maximum depth 1,025 m
Kazakhstan, Russia, Azerbaijan, Turkmeni-stan, Iran
Lake Superior 82,103 sq km, 406 m
USA, Canada
Lake Victoria 69,484 sq km, 406 m
Kenya, Tanzania, Uganda
Lake Huron 59,570 sq km, 229 m
USA, Canada
Lake Michigan 58,140 sq km, 282 m
USA
Lake Tanganyika 34,000 sq km, 1,435 m
Tanzania, Burundi, Zaire, Zambia

North America
Lake Superior 82,103 sq km, 406 m
USA, Canada

Lake Huron 59,570 sq km, 229 m
USA, Canada
Lake Michigan 58,140 sq km, 282 m
USA

Africa
Lake Victoria 69,484 sq km, 406 m
Kenya, Uganda, Tanzania
Lake Tanganyika 34,000 sq km, 1,435 m, the world's longest lake with a maximum length of 655 km
Tanzania, Burundi, Zaire, Zambia
Lake Malawi 30,800 sq km, 706 m
Malawi, Tanzania

Asia
Caspian Sea 371,800 sq km, 1,025 m
Russia, Turkmenistan, Iran, Azerbaijan, Kazakhstan
Aral Sea 33,640 sq km, 52 m – the lake is rapidly declining is size and has become increasingly saline due to man-made en-vironmental damage
Kazakhstan, Uzbekistan
Lake Baikal 31,500 sq km, 1,620 m
Russia

Australia
Lake Eyre 9,323 sq km, 12 m
Lake MacKay 3,494 sq km, N.A
Lake Amadeus 1,032 sq km, N.A
All three of Australia's largest lakes are dry salt lakes which only periodically contain water and reach maximum depths less than one meter.

Europe
Lake Ladoga 18,180 sq km, 230 m
Russia
Lake Onega 9,950 sq km, 127 m
Russia
Lake Vaenern 5,564 km, 92 m
Sweden

South America
Lake Maracaibo 13,512 sq km, 50 m
Venezuela
Lake Titicaca 8,559 sq km, 281 m – the world's highest elevated lake
Peru, Bolivia
Lake Popoo 2,530 sq km, 3 m
Bolivia

Reservoirs
Man-Made Lakes

Reservoirs are large man-made lakes and are usually created by constructing dams to obstruct rivers. Most reservoirs are used to store drinking water or for flood prevention.

In addition to these benefits, reservoirs also provide recreational opportunities. But the construction of reservoirs often brings dis-advantages for some regions and people. The resettlement of entire communities and the destruction of ecosystems are issues that arise with the creation of reservoirs. The Three Gorges Dam in China has resulted in the resettlement of over one million people.

The Largest Reservoirs

Owens Falls 204,800 million m³
Uganda
Lake Kariba 180,600 million m³
Zambia, Zimbabwe
Bratsk 169,270 million m³
Russia
Lake Nasser 168,900 million m³
Egypt
Lake Volta 148,000 million m³
Uganda
D. Johnson 141,852 million m³
Canada
Tarbela 141,000 million m³
Pakistan
Guri 138,000 million m³
Venezuela
Krasnoyarsk 73,000 million m³
Russia

The Largest Dams
(with names of obstructed rivers)

Rogun Dam 335 meters
Tajikistan, Vakhsh River
Nurek Dam 300 meters
Tajikistan, Vakhsh River
Grand Dixence 284 meters
Switzerland, Dixence River
Inguri Dam 272 meters
Georgia, Inguri River
Chicoasen 264 meters
Mexico, Rio Grijalva
Tehri 261 meters
India, Bhagirathi River
Vaiont 259 meters
Italy, Piave River
Mica Dam 250 meters
Canada, Columbia River
Sayano-Shushkenskaya Dam 245 meters
Russia, Yenisei River
Guavio Dam 240 meters
Columbia, Rio Guavio

Nations
The World's Political Patchwork

At the end of the last century there were 193 independent nations on our planet. Throughout the course of the 20th century the world map changed form on many occasions. Two world wars, decolonization in Africa and Asia, as well as the fall of European communism were the most important factors that contributed to the rise and fall of so many nations.

The nations of the world are separated by large division in wealth and political influence. The richest nations on the planet including the United States, Canada, Japan, the EU member nations, and several other states, are collectively referred to as the developed nations. The developing nations – also known as Third World nations – in Africa, Asia, and Latin America are characterized by widespread poverty, economic weakness and the dominant role of agriculture in their economies. The developing countries are home to the majority of the world's population but their political power remains relatively limited due to their lack of economic influence and financial resources. Measurements of GDP (gross domestic product) per capita are often used to rank and compare the wealth of different nations. Unfortunately these measurements do not take into account the often extreme gaps between rich and poor in individual nations. GDP measurements also ignore other important factors that affect the quality of life in a society, including political stability, social mobility, tolerance, and climate. Around 150 of the world's nations are developing nations. Hunger, high mortality rates, and often explosive population rates are among the many widespread problems these nations must solve.

The Largest Countries

Russia/Russian Federation
17,075,200 sq km
Canada 9,984,670 sq km
United States 9,631,418 sq km
China 9,596,960 sq km
Brazil 8,511,996 sq km

North America
Canada 9,984,670 sq km
United States 9,631,418 sq km
Mexico 1,972,550 sq km

Africa
Sudan 2,505,813 sq km
Algeria 2,381,741 sq km
Democratic Republic of Congo 2,345,410 sq km

Asia, excluding Russia
China 9,596,960 sq km
India 3,287,263 sq km
Kazakhstan 2,717,300 sq km

Europe
Russia 17,075,200 sq km
Ukraine 603,700 sq km
France 547,030sq km

Oceania
Australia 7,686,850 sq km
Papua New Guinea 462,840 sq km
New Zealand 268,680 sq km

South America
Brasil 8,511,996 sq km
Argentina 2,766,889 sq km
Peru 1,285,216 sq km

Where are the different nations?

Africa 54 countries
Asia 47
Europe 46 (with Kosovo: 47)
North America/Caribbean 23
Oceania 14
South America 12

The Wealthiest Nations
(GDP per capita)

Luxembourg 105,000 US$
Liechtenstein 100,000 US$
Norway 84,000 US$
Qatar 73,000 US$
Iceland 64,000 US$
Ireland 60,000 US$
Monaco 60 000 US$
Switzerland 58,000 US$

The Poorest Nations
(GDP per capita)

Malawi 250 US$
Ethiopia 250 US$
Myanmar 250 US$
Somalia 200 US$
Guinea-Bissau 200 US$
Liberia 200 US$
Democratic Republic of Congo 200 US$
Burundi 150 US$

The Largest Economies
(By purchasing power parity in US dollars)

USA 13.8 trillion US$
China 7 trillion US$
Japan 4.3 trillion US$
India 3 trillion US$
Germany 2.8 trillion US$
United Kingdom 2.1 trillion US$
Russia 2.1 trillion US$
France 2 trillion US$

Population
Explosive Growth

More than 6.6 billion people live on our planet (2007). United Nations estimates predict a global population between 7.9 and 11 billion in the year 2050. The vast majority of this growth will take place in the developing nations of Africa and Asia.

Increased productivity in agriculture, improved living conditions, and medical advancements were the primary factors behind the dramatic growth of the world's population in the 20th century. The world's population is, however, unevenly distributed across our planet. Some continents such as Europe are densely populated, while others such as Australia are home to relatively few people. The populations of the different continents are also distributed unevenly with populations often concentrated in certain regions while others remain sparsely populated – most Australians for example, live in a few large coastal cities.

World Population (by continent)

Asia 4,000 million
Africa 950 million
Europe 730 million
South America 350 million
North and Central America 550 million
Australia/Oceania 35 million

The World in Records
Population, Cities, Skyscrapers

Most Populous Nations

Europe
Russia 143.7 million
Germany 82.4 million
United Kingdom 60.2 million

Asia
China 1.3 billion
India 1.095 billion
Indonesia 245.4 million

North America
United States 300 million
Mexico 108 million
Canada 33 million

South America
Brazil 188 million
Columbia 43.5 million
Argentina 40 million

Africa
Nigeria 132 million
Egypt 78.8 million
Ethiopia 74.7 million

Oceania
Australia 20.2 million
Papua New Guinea 5.6 million
New Zealand 4 million

Population Density

Highest population density
Monaco: 23,600 inhabitants per sq km

Lowest population density
West Sahara: 1 inhabitant per sq km

Cities
Centers of Growth

At the beginning the 19th century, there were only a handful of cities with more than a million inhabitants. In the past 100 years, however, the numbers of large cities on our planet have increased rapidly and the populations of the world's largest cities have also increased substantially.

Dealing with the rapid growth of urban areas in the developing world will be one of the greatest challenges of the 21st century. Few of these cities have been able to expand their infrastructures fast enough to cope with explosive population growth and the already poor environmental conditions in many third world cities continue to deteriorate.

According the UN estimates, most of the world's population will live in cities by 2015. The trend of people in developing nations abandoning rural areas for better economic and social conditions in large cities will continue for many decades. This rapid urbanization of the developing world will only exacerbate existing urban overcrowding problems. The cities of the developing world lack the housing, transportation networks, and jobs to provide most urban migrants with a substantially better standard of living. Most of these cities are surrounded by vast slums and temporary settlements inhabited by the poor. At least 85% of Cairo's area consists of residential areas with mostly substandard housing. Other cities in the developing world are better able to cope with rapid growth due to improving economic conditions. The population of Shanghai, the center of China's impressive economic boom, has expanded by several million in recent years.

The Largest Metropolitan Areas

Tokyo-Yokohama 34.9 million,
Japan
New York City (Tri-State area) 21.65 million,
United States
Seoul 21.1 million,
Republic of (South) Korea
Mexico City 20.7 million,
Mexico
Sao Paolo 20.2 million,
Brazil
Mumbai (Bombay) 18.1 million,
India
Osaka-Kobe 18 million,
Japan
Delhi 17.1 million,
India
Los Angeles 16.8 million,
United States
Jakarta 15.8 million,
Indonesia

Europe
Paris 9.3 (metro area), 2 million (city)
France
Moscow 8.7 million,
Russia
Istanbul 8.2 million,
Turkey
London 7.6 million (Greater London),
United Kingdom
St. Petersburg 5.5 million,
Russia

Asia
Tokyo-Yokohama 34.9 million,
Japan
Seoul 21.1 million,
Republic of (South) Korea
Mumbai (Bombay) 18.1 million,
India
Osaka-Kobe 18 million,
Japan

Australia
Sydney 3.9 million
Melbourne 3.3 million
Brisbane 1.5 million

Africa
Cairo 14.8 million in metro area,
Egypt
Khartoum 7.3 million in metro area,
Sudan
Lagos 7.2 million in metro area,
Nigeria
Kinshasa 6.1 million in metro area,
Democratic Republic of Congo
Alexandria 4.8 million,
Egypt

North and South America
Mexico City 20.7 million,
Mexico
Sao Paolo 20.2 million,
Brazil
New York City (city only) 9.3 million,
United States
Lima 7.5 million,
Peru
Bogotá 7.2 million,
Colombia

Skyscrapers
Modern Giants

The world's first skyscraper, completed in 1902, had a height just over 180 meters. Improved engineering and construction techniques were the main factors behind the rapid vertical growth of our planet's cities in the 20th century.

The invention of the elevator made the construction of skyscrapers practical and was another major factor behind the development of highrise buildings. New York City is still home to the largest concentration of skyscrapers. However, most of the world's tallest buildings under construction at the moment are in the booming cities of East Asia. The Taipei Financial Center in Taiwan has a height of 508 meters and replaced Malaysia's Petronas Towers as the world's tallest building in 2004. There are currently plans to construct the world's tallest skyscraper on the site of the former World Trade Center towers, but the project could lose the title before it is completed because there are several other projects competing for the title of world's tallest building. With city populations growing rapidly and skyscrapers remaining symbols of progress and wealth it is unlikely the age of the skyscraper will end in the near future.

The Tallest Buildings

Burj Dubai (under construction) 630 m (as of March 2008), 141 floors, Dubai
Taipei Financial Center (Taipei 101) 508 m, 101 floors, Taipei, 2004
Shanghai World Financial Center 492 m, 101 floors, Shanghai, 2008
Petronas Towers 452 m, 88 floors, Kuala Lumpur, 1998
Sears Tower 442 m, 110 floors, Chicago, 1974
Jin Mao Tower 421 m, 88 floors, Shanghai, 1998
Two International Finance Centre 415 m, 88 floors, Hongkong 2003
Citic Plaza 391 m, 80 floors, Guangzhou, 1997
Shun Hing Square 384 m, 69 floors, Shenzhen, 1996

Asia

Burj Dubai (under construction) 630 m (as of March 2008), 141 floors, Dubai
Taipei Financial Center (Taipei 101) 508 m, 101 floors, Taipei, 2004
Shanghai World Financial Center 492 m, 101 floors, Shanghai, 2008
Petronas Towers 452 m, 88 floors, Kuala Lumpur, 1998
Jin Mao Tower 421 m, 88 floors, Shanghai, 1998
Two International Finance Centre 415 m, 88 floors, Hong Kong 2003
Citic Plaza 391 m, 80 floors, Guangzhou, 1997

Shun Hing Square 384 m, 69 floors, Shenzhen, 1996
Central Plaza 374 m, 78 floors, Hong Kong, 1992
Bank of China Tower 367 m, 72 floors, Hong Kong, 1990

The Americas

Sears Tower 442 m, 110 floors, Chicago, 1974
Empire State Building 381 m, 102 floors, New York City, 1931
Aon Center (Amoco Building) 346 m, 83 floors, Chicago, 1973
John Hancock Center 344 m, 100 floors, Chicago, 1969
Chrysler Building 319 m, 77 floors, New York City, 1930
New York Times Tower 319 m, 52 floors, New York, 2007
Bank of America Plaza 312 m, 55 floors, Atlanta, 1992
US Bank Tower 310 m, 73 floors, Los Angeles, 1990
AT&T Corporate Center 307 m, 60 floors, Chicago, 1989

Africa

Carlton Centre 202 m, 36 floors, Johannesburg, 1973
Hassan II Mosque (minaret) 198 m, Casablanca, 1993

Australia

Q1 Tower 323 m, 78 floors, Gold Coast City, 2005
Eureka Tower 297 m, 92 floors, Melbourne, 2006
120 Collins Street 264 m, 52 floors, Melbourne, 1991
101 Collins Street 260 m, 50 floors, Melbourne, 1991
Rialto Towers 251 m, 63 floors, Melbourne, 1986
Central Park 249 m, 52 floors, Perth, 1992

Europe

Naberezhnaya Tower C 268 m, 61 floors, Moscow, 2007
Triumph Palace 264 m, 54 floors Moscow 2004
Commerzbank Tower 259 m, 63 floors, Frankfurt, 1997
Messeturm 257 m, 64 floors, Frankfurt, 1991
Lomonosov University 240 m, 32 floors, Moscow 1953
Torre Espacio 236 m, 57 floors, Madrid 2007

Towers and Antennas
Reaching for the Sky

Towers have been used for thousands of years and for many different purposes, including defensive, navigational, and observation use. Most modern towers were built to transmit broadcast waves over great distances.

Huge radio and television antennas can be found all over the planet. These thin steel structures often rise several hundred meters into the air and play an important part in global communications.

The Tallest Towers

CN Tower 553 m, 1976 Toronto, Canada
Ostakino Tower 540 m, 1967, Moscow, Russia
Oriental Pearl Tower 468 m, 1995, Shanghai, China
Borj-e-Milad 435 m, 2005, Teheran, Iran
KL Tower 421 m, 1996, Kuala Lumpur, Malaysia
Tianjin Tower 415 m, 1991, Tianjin, China
Central Radio & TV Tower 405 m, 1992 Beijing, China
Kiev TV Tower 385 m, 1973, Kiev, Ukraine
Tashkent TV Tower 375 m, 1985, Tashkent, Uzbekistan
Almaty TV Tower 371 m, 1983, Almaty, Kasachstan
Liberation Tower 370 m, 1996 Kuwait City, Kuwait
Riga TV Tower 368 m, 1986 Riga, Latvia
Berlin TV Tower Alexanderplatz 365 m, 1969, Berlin, Germany

Antennas/Transmitting Towers

KVLY/KHTI tower 629 m, Fargo, United States
KXJB tower 628 m, Galesburg, United States
KXTV tower 624 m, Walnut Grove, United States
KLDE tower 615 m, Angleton, United States

375

The World in Records
Bridges and Tunnels

Bridges and Tunnels
Vital Connections

Great bridges span powerful bodies of water, withstand the forces of nature, connect islands to the rest of the world, and could one day even connect entire continents.

Tunnels are in many ways subterranean bridges – they run through mountains or beneath bodies of water.

Satellite technology and future advancements in engineering could one day make it possible to construct gigantic bridges over the deep bodies of water that separate the continents including the Bering Strait and Strait of Gibraltar.

Tunnels are vital transportation links in many of the world's mountainous regions. These underground roadways stretch through mountains, reduce distances, and connect many mountainous areas to the world. Underwater tunnels are especially impressive engineering achievements. The 50-kilometer-long Channel Tunnel was completed in 1994 despite the technical difficulty of its construction. Travelers can now travel by train between northern France and southern England in less than 35 minutes.

Visionary Bridges
(futuristic proposals)

Gibraltar Bridge 10 kilometers, Spain/Morocco
Strait of Messina Bridge 3.3 kilometers, Sicily, Italy

Cable-Stayed Bridges with longest Main Span

Sutong Bridge 1088 m, 2008, China
Tatara Bridge 890 m, 1999, Japan
Pont de Normandie 856 m, 1994, France
Second Nanjing Bridge 628 m, 2001, China
Wuhan Baishazhou Bridge 618 m, 2000, China
Quinzhou-Minjiang Bridge 605 m, 1996 China

Yangpu Bridge 602 m, 1993 China
Xupu Bridge 590 m, 1997 China
Meiko Central Bridge 590 m, 1998, Japan
Rio-Andirrio Bridge 560 m, 2004, Greece

Suspension Bridges with longest Main Span

Akashi Kaikyo 1,991 m, 1998, Japan
Xihoumen Bridge 1,650 m, 2008, China
Store Belt Bridge 1,624 m, 1998 Denmark
Runyang Bridge 1,490 m, 2005, China
Humber Bridge 1,410 m, 1981, United Kingdom
Jiangyin Daqiao Bridge 1,385 m, 1998, China
Ts'ing-Ma Bridge 1,377 m, 1997, China
Verrazano Narrows Bridge 1,298 m, 1964, United States
Golden Gate Bridge 1,280 m, 1937, United States
Yangluo Bridge 1,280 m, 2008, China

Bridges with longest Main Span by Continent
S= suspension bridge, CS= cable-stayed bridge, A= arch bridge, C= cantilever bridge

Europe
Store Belt Bridge (S) 1,624 m, 1998, Denmark
Humber Bridge (S) 1,410 m, 1981, United Kingdom
Hoega Kusten Bridge (S) 1,210 m, 1997, Sweden
Fatih Sultan Mehmet Bridge (S) 1,090 m, 1998, Turkey
Kemal Atatürk Bridge (S) 1,074 m, 2004, Turkey

Asia
Akashi-Kaikyo (S) 1,991 m, 1998, Japan
Xihoumen Bridge (S) 1,650 m, 2008, China
Runyang Bridge 1,490 m, 2005, China
Jiangyin Daqiao Bridge (S) 1,385 m, 1998, China

Australia/Oceania
Sydney Harbour Bridge (A) 509 m, 1932, Australia
West Gate Melbourne (CS) 336 m, 1974 Australia
Gladesville Bridge (A) 305 m, 1964 Australia

North America
Verrazano Narrows (S) 1,298 m, 1964; United States
Golden Gate Bridge (S) 1,280 m, 1937, United States
Mackinac Bridge (S) 1,158 m, 1957, United States
George Washington Bridge (S) 1,067 m, 1931, United States

South America
Puente de Angostura (S) 712 m, 1967, Venezuela
Ponte Hercilio Luz (S) 340 m, 1926, Brazil
Arroyo Cangrejillo Pipeline Bridge (S) 337 m, 1998, Argentina

Africa
Matadi Suspension Bridge (S) 520 m, 1983, Democratic Republic of Congo
Birchenough Bridge (A) 329 m, 1935, Zimbabwe
Chirundu Bridge (S) 328 m, 1939, Zambia/Zimbabwe

The Longest Tunnels
Rail and road tunnels

Seikan Tunnel 53.90 kilometers, Japan
Channel Tunnel 49.94 kilometers, United Kingdom/France
Loetschberg Tunnel 34.57 kilometers, Switzerland
Guadarrama Tunnel 28.30 kilometers, Spain
Iwate-Ichinoe 25.81 kilometers, Japan
Laerdal 24.51 kilometers, Norway
Dai-Shimizu 22.17 kilometers, Japan
Simplon II 19.82 kilometers, Italy/Switzerland
Simplon I 19.80 kilometers, Italy/Switzerland
Vereina Tunnel 19.05 kilometers, Switzerland
Shin-Kanmon 18.68 kilometers, Japan
Apennin Tunnel 18.49 kilometers, Italy
Zongnanshan/Qinling Tunnel 18.45 kilometers, China
St Gotthard Tunnel 16.91 kilometers, Switzerland/Italy

The index explained

All of the places named on the maps in the atlas are listed in the atlas index. The place names are listed alpabetically. Special symbols and letters including accents and umlauts are ignored in the order of the index. For example, the letters Á, Ä, Â are all categorized under A, and Ž, Ż, Z are all treated as the standard Latin letter Z. Written characters consisting of two letters joined together (ligatures) are treated as two separate characters in the index: for example, words beginning with the character Æ would be indexed under A E. Generic geographic terms (sea, bay, etc.) and word

articles (the, le, el etc.) were used in the order of the index: for example, the Gulf of Mexico is listed und **G** and Le Havre, France is listed under **L** . Pictograms make it possible for the user to easily locate and categorize objects in the maps. Each pictogram is followed by the international vehicle number plate code of the country where the object is located. Most of the objects in the atlas can be connected to one country. ISO country codes are used for objects located in regions without a number plate code. Two codes divided by a slash are used if an object is located

within two countries. For geographic features that can not be attributed to one nation, such as the Atlantic Ocean, the name is followed by relevant page numbers and map grid references.

The grid references for towns and cities identify the location of the place name on the map. Grid references for countries and territories identify the location of the first letter of the place name.

Symbols used in the index

- ▲ Mountains
- ▲ Mountain
- ▥ Landscape
- ♠ National Park
- ◁ Desert

- ▨ Oasis
- ◪ Volcano
- ◪ Glacier
- ◣ Cape, Coast
- ▧ River

- ⋯ Canal
- ▨ Waterfall, rapids
- ▤ Lake
- ▨ Sea, Bay
- ▦ Coral reef

- ▨ Island
- ▨ Undersea landscape
- ■ Country
- ▢ Province

- ● National Capital
- ◉ Provincial Capital
- ○ Town, village

A

Å ▢ N 24 Lf14
Aabenraa ▢ DK 26 Le18
Aabybro ▢ DK 26 Le17
Aalborg ▢ DK 26 Le17
Aalen ▢ D 45 Lf21
 Äänekoski ▢ FIN 28 Mc14
Aarau ▢ CH 45 Le22
Aars ▢ DK 26 Le17
Aba ▢ WAN 108 Lb17
Abaco Island ▨ BS 126 Ga13
Abadan ▢ IR 77 Nb12
Abakaliki ▢ WAN 108 Lb17
Abakan ▢ RUS 79 Pc08
Abancay ▢ PE 133 Gb21
Abashiri ▢ J 83 Sa10
Abay Wenz ▧ ETH 109 Md16
Abbeville ▢ F 35 La20
Abbot Ice Shelf ▤ 140 Fa33
Abéché ▢ TCH 106 Ma16
Abengourou ▢ CI 105 Kd17
Abeokuta ▢ WAN 108 La17
Aberdeen ▢ GB 34 Kj17
Aberdeen ▢ USA 120 Fa09
Abergavenny ▢ GB 35 Kj20
Aberystwyth ▢ GB 35 Kh19
Abganerovo ▢ RUS 61 Nc21
Abha ▢ KSA 77 Na15
Abide ▢ TR 64 Me26
Abidjan ▢ CI 105 Kd17
Abilene ▢ USA 122 Fa12
Abington ▢ GB 34 Kj18
Abisko ▢ S 22 Lk11
Abisko fjällstation ◪ S 22 Lk11
Abisko n.p. ♠ S 22 Lk11

Åbo = Turku ▢ FIN 22 Mb15
Aboa ▢ 141 Kb33
Aboisso ▢ CI 105 Kd17
Abomey ▢ DY 105 La17
Aborlan ▢ RP 85 Qd17
Abrantes ▢ P 40 Kf26
Abrene = Pytalovo ▢ RUS 30 Md17
Abruzzo ▢ I 49 Lg24
Abruzzo, P.N. d' ♠ I 48 Lg25
Abu Ajram ▢ KSA 76 Md13
Abu Dhabi ● UAE 77 Nc14
Abu Hadiyah ▢ KSA 77 Nb13
Abu Hamad ▢ SUD 107 Mc15
Abuja ▢ WAN 108 Lb17
Abuña ▧ BOL 133 Gc21
Abuña ▢ BR 133 Gc20
Abune Yosef ▲ ETH 107 Md16
Abu Simbel ▢ ET 107 Mc14
Abuye Meda ▲ ETH 109 Md16
Abyad ▢ SUD 107 Mb16
Acapulco ▢ MEX 124 Fa15
Acaraú ▢ BR 134 Hd19
Acarigua ▢ YV 132 Gc17
Accra ● GH 105 Kd17
Achaguas ▢ YV 132 Gc17
Achill Island ▨ IRL 33 Ke19
Acıgöl ▤ TR 64 Me27
Ačinsk ▢ RUS 73 Pc07
Acireale ▢ I 49 Lh27
Acklins Island ▨ BS 127 Gb14
Acquapendente ▢ I 46 Lf24
Acqui Terme ▢ I 46 Le23
Acre ▢ BR 133 Gb20
Acre ▧ BR 133 Gc20
Acri ▢ I 49 Lj26

Acuña ▢ MEX 124 Ed13
Ada ▢ USA 123 Fa12
Adam's Peak ▲ CL 81 Pa17
Adana ▢ TR 76 Md11
Adana ▢ TR 65 Mh27
Adapazarı = Sakarya ▢ TR 64 Mf25
Ad Dahna ▨ KSA 77 Nb13
Ad-Dakhla ▢ MA 104 Ka14
Ad Dammam ▢ KSA 77 Nb13
Ad Darb ▢ KSA 77 Na15
Ad Dawadami ▢ KSA 77 Na14
Addis Ababa ● ETH 109 Md17
Ad Diwaniyah ▢ IRQ 76 Na12
Addoo Atoll ▨ MV 81 Oc19
Adelaide ▢ AUS 97 Rd25
Adelaide Island ▨ 140 Gc32
Adelaide River ▢ AUS 94 Rc21
Ademuz ▢ E 42 Kk25
Aden ▢ YE 77 Nb16
Adi ▢ RI 92 Rc19
Adigrat ▢ ETH 107 Md16
Adilcevaz ▢ TR 66 Nb26
Adirondack Mountains ▲ USA 121 Gb10
Adi Ugri ▢ ER 107 Md16
Adıyaman ▢ TR 65 Mh27
Adjud ▢ RO 55 Md22
Adler ▢ RUS 66 Mk24
Admiralty Inlet ▨ CDN 118 Fc04
Admiralty Islands ▨ PNG 92 Sb19
Admont ▢ A 52 Lh22
Ado-Ekiti ▢ WAN 108 Lb17
Adra ▢ E 41 Kj27
Adrano ▢ I 49 Lh27
Adrar ▲ DZ 106 Lb13

Adrar des Iforhas ▲ RMM 105 La15
Adré ▢ TCH 106 Ma16
Ádria ▢ I 46 Lg23
Adua ▢ RI 87 Rb19
Adygea ▢ RUS 76 Na10
Aegean Sea ▨ GR/TR 57 Mc26
Čuprija ▢ SRB 54 Ma24
Afándou ▢ GR 64 Me27
Affollé ◣ RIM 105 Kb15
Afghanistan ■ AFG 78 Oa12
Aflou ▢ DZ 104 La12
Afognak Island ▨ USA 116 Cb07
Afşin ▢ TR 65 Mj26
Afyon ▢ TR 64 Mf26
Aga Buryat Autonomous District ▢ RUS 82 Qd08
Agadez ▢ RN 106 Lb15
Agadir ▢ MA 104 Kc12
Agana ▢ USA 92 Sa16
Agargar ▨ MA 104 Kb14
Agartala ▢ IND 84 Pc14
Agde ▢ F 38 Lb24
Agen ▢ F 38 La23
Aggteleki N.P. ♠ H 53 Ma21
Agiá ▢ GR 56 Mb26
Agia Galini ▢ GR 57 Mc28
Agia Pelagia ▢ GR 56 Mb27
Aginskoe ◉ RUS 82 Qc08
Ágios Charalampos ▢ GR 57 Mc25
Ágios Efstrátios ▨ GR 57 Mc26
Ágios Kirikos ▢ GR 57 Md27
Ágios Nikólaos ▢ GR 57 Mc28
Ağlı ▢ TR 65 Mg25
Agnew ▢ AUS 94 Ra24
Agra ▢ IND 80 Od13
Ágreda ▢ E 42 Kk25
Ağrı ▢ TR 76 Na11

Ağrı ▢ TR 66 Nb26
Agrigento ▢ I 48 Lg27
Agrinio ▢ GR 56 Ma26
Agrópoli ▢ I 49 Lh25
Água Clara ▢ BR 135 Hb23
Agua Prieta ▢ MEX 122 Ec12
Aguascalientes ■ MEX 124 Ed14
Aguascalientes ▢ MEX 124 Ed14
Águeda ▢ P 40 Kf25
Aguilar ▢ E 41 Kh27
Aguilar de Campóo ▢ E 40 Kh24
Águilas ▢ E 43 Kk27
Aguirre Cerda ▢ 140 Gd31
Ahaus ▢ D 44 Ld19
Åheim ▢ N 24 Lc14
Ahlat ▢ TR 66 Nb26
Ahmedabad ▢ IND 80 Oc14
Ahmednagar ▢ IND 81 Oc15
Ahtopol ▢ BG 55 Md24
Ahtubinsk ▢ RUS 61 Nd21
Åhus ▢ S 27 Lh18
Ahvaz ▢ IR 76 Nb12
Ahvenanmaa = Åland ▨ FIN 25 Lk15
Ahvenanmeri ▨ FIN 25 Lk15
Aigues-Mortes ▢ F 38 Lc24
Aigüestortes i Estany de Sant Maurici, P.N. de ♠ E 42 La24
Ailinginae Atoll ▨ MH 93 Tb16
Şimleu Silvaniei ▢ RO 54 Mb22
Ainaži ▢ LV 30 Mc17
Ainos N.P. ♠ GR 56 Ma26
Ainsa ▢ E 42 La24
Aïn Sefra ▢ DZ 104 Kd12

Cambrian Mountains – Cassino

Götene – Gulf of Tehuantepec

I

Istiéa – Kachovs'ke vodoschovyšče

Llano Estacado USA 122 Ed12
Llanos de Chiquitos BOL 133 Gd22
Llanos del Orinoco CO/YV 132 Gc17
Llanos de Mojos BOL 133 Gc21
Llay-Llay RCH 136 Gb25
Lleida E 42 La25
Llerena E 41 Kg26
Llica BOL 133 Gc22
Llíria E 43 Kk26
L'Ile-Rousse F 46 Le24
Lloret de Mar E 42 Lb25
Lloydminster CDN 120 Eb08
Llucmajor E 43 Lb26
Lnáře CZ 52 Lg21
Lobatse RB 110 Mb24
Löbau D 44 Lh20
Lobay RCA 108 Ld18
Lobcovo RUS 58 Na17
Łobez PL 50 Lh19
Lobito ANG 110 Lc21
Locarno CH 45 Le22
Lochboisdale GB 34 Kg17
Loch Lomond and The Trossachs N.P. GB 34 Kh17
Loch Ness GB 34 Kh17
Lochvycja UA 62 Mg20
Lockhart River AUS 96 Sa21
Locminé F 36 Kj22
Locri I 49 Lj26
Lodejenoe Pole RUS 29 Mg15
Lodève F 38 Lb24
Lodi I 46 Le23
Løding N 22 Lh12
Lødingen N 22 Lj11
Lodja RDC 108 Ma19
Łódź PL 50 Lk20
Lofsdalen S 24 Lg14
Log RUS 61 Nb21
Logan USA 122 Eb10
Logange RDC 108 Ma19
Logone TCH 108 Ld17
Logroño E 42 Kj24
Logrosán E 41 Kh26
Løgstør DK 26 Le17
Lohja FIN 28 Mc15
Loi-Kaw MYA 84 Pd15
Loimaa FIN 22 Mb15
Loire F 38 Kk22
Loja E 41 Kh27
Loja EC 132 Ga19
Lojmola RUS 29 Mf15
Lokan tekojärvi FIN 23 Md12
Lokichar EAK 109 Md18
Loknja RUS 30 Mf17
Lokoja WAN 108 Lb17
Lokot' RUS 59 Mh19
Lol SUD 109 Mb17
Lom BG 54 Mb24
Lom N 24 Le15
Łomża PL 51 Mb19
Lomami RDC 109 Ma19
Lomami RDC 108 Ma20
Lombardy I 46 Le23
Lomblen RI 87 Ra20
Lombok RI 87 Qd20
Lomé TG 105 La17
Lomela RDC 108 Ma19
Lomonosov RUS 30 Me16
Lomonosov Ridge 138 Hb01
Loncoche RCH 137 Gb26
London CDN 123 Fd10
London GB 35 Kk20
Londonderry GB 33 Kg18
Londrina BR 135 Hb23
Longbawan RI 87 Qd18
Long Beach USA 122 Ea12
Longford IRL 33 Kg19
Longhurst, Mount 141 Sd34
Long Island BS 126 Ga14
Long Island PNG 92 Sb20
Long Island USA 121 Gb10
Longlac CDN 120 Fc09
Longmen Shan CHN 84 Qa12
Longnawang RI 87 Qd18
Longreach AUS 96 Sa23
Longuyon F 37 Lc21
Longview USA 123 Fb12
Longwy F 37 Lc21
Long Xuyen VN 84 Qb16
Longyan CHN 85 Qd13
Longyearbyen N 22 Lf06
Löningen D 44 Ld19
Lönsboda S 27 Lh17
Lons-le-Saunier F 39 Lc22
Lopatino RUS 61 Nc19
Lop Nur CHN 79 Pc10
Lopori RDC 108 Ma18
Lorca E 43 Kk27
Lord Howe Island AUS 97 Sd25
Lord Howe Rise 98 Ta24
Lord Howe Seamounts 97 Sd24
Lorengau PNG 92 Sb19
Loreto I 47 Lg24
Loreto MEX 124 Eb13
Lorica CO 132 Ga17
Lorient F 36 Kj22
Lörrach D 45 Ld22
Lorraine F 37 Lc21
Los S 25 Lh15
Los Alamos USA 122 Ec11
Los Angeles RCH 137 Gb26
Los Angeles USA 122 Ea12
Losap Atoll FSM 93 Sc17
Los Barrancos YV 132 Gd17
Los Blancos RA 136 Gd23
Łosice PL 51 Mb19
Losiny ostrov N.P. RUS 58 Mj18
Los Mochis MEX 124 Ec13
Los Navalmorales E 40 Kh26
Lossen S 24 Lg14
Lossiemouth GB 34 Kj17
Los Vientos RCH 136 Gc23
Los Vilos RCH 136 Gb25
Los Yébenes E 41 Kj26
Lot F 38 La23
Lotošino RUS 58 Mh17
Loubomo RCB 108 Lc19
Loudéac F 36 Kj21
Loudun F 38 La22
Louga SN 105 Ka15
Loughborough GB 35 Kk19
Lough Neagh GB 33 Kg18
Loughrea IRL 33 Kf19
Louhans F 39 Lc22
Louisiade Archipelago PNG 96 Sc21
Louisiana USA 123 Fb12
Louisville USA 123 Fd11
Loulé P 41 Kg27
Louny CZ 52 Lg20
Lourdes F 42 Kk24
Louth AUS 97 Sb25
Louth GB 35 La19
Louviers F 36 La21
Lövånger S 25 Ma13
Lovćen, N.P. SRB 54 Lk24
Loveč BG 55 Mc24
Lower Hutt NZ 99 Td27
Lower Peninsula USA 123 Fc10
Lowestoft GB 35 La19
Łowicz PL 50 Lk19
Loznica SRB 54 Lk23
Lozova UA 63 Mj21
Luama RDC 109 Mb19
Lu'an CHN 85 Qd12
Luanco E 40 Kh24
Luanda ANG 108 Lc20
Luanginga ANG 110 Ma21
Luangoe ANG 108 Ld20
Luang Prabang LAO 84 Qa15
Luang Prabang Range LAO 84 Qa15
Luangwa Z 111 Mc21
Luanshya Z 110 Mb21
Luarca E 40 Kg24
Lubaanbajo RI 87 Ra20
Lubango ANG 110 Lc21
Lubao RDC 109 Mb20
Lubartów PL 51 Mb20
Lubawa PL 50 Lk19
Lübben (Spreewald) D 44 Lg20
Lübbenau (Spreewald) D 44 Lg20
Lubbock USA 122 Ed12
Lübeck D 44 Lf19
Lubefu RDC 108 Ma19
Lubero RDC 109 Mb19
Lubin PL 50 Lj20
Lubjaniki RUS 58 Na18
Lublin PL 51 Mb20
Lubliniec PL 50 Lk20
Lubny UA 62 Mg21
Lubumbashi RDC 110 Mb21
Lubutu RDC 109 Mb19
Lucca I 46 Lf24
Luce Bay GB 34 Kh18
Lucena E 41 Kh27
Lucena RP 85 Ra16
Lučenec SK 53 Lk21
Lucera I 49 Lh25
Luc'k UA 51 Mc20
Lucknow IND 80 Pa13
Luçon F 38 Kk22
Ludbreg HR 52 Lj22
Lüderitz NAM 110 Ld24
Ludhiana IND 80 Od12
Luduş RO 54 Mc22
Ludvika S 25 Lh15
Ludwigsburg D 45 Le21
Ludwigsfelde D 44 Lg19
Ludwigshafen D 45 Le21
Ludwigslust D 44 Lf19
Ludza LV 30 Md17
Luena ANG 110 Ld21
Luena Z 110 Ma21
Lufkin USA 123 Fb12
Luga RUS 30 Me16
Luga RUS 30 Me16
Lugano CH 46 Le23
Luganville VU 98 Tb22
Luganville VU 98 Tb22
Lugenda MOC 111 Md21
Lugo E 40 Kg24
Lugo I 46 Lf23
Lugoj RO 54 Ma23
Luh RUS 58 Nb17
Luh RUS 58 Nb17
Luhans'k UA 63 Mk21
Luhovicy RUS 58 Mk18
Luhuo CHN 84 Qa12
Luiana ANG 110 Ma22
Luilaka RDC 108 Ma19
Luilu RDC 108 Ma20
Lukavac BIH 47 Lk23
Lukenie RDC 108 Ld19
Lukojanov RUS 60 Nc18
Lukovit BG 55 Mc24
Lukovnikovo RUS 58 Mh17
Łuków PL 51 Mb20
Luleå S 19 Mb13
Luleälven S 25 Ma13
Lüleburgaz TR 57 Md25
Lulonga RDC 108 Ld18
Lulua RDC 108 Ma20
Lumbala ANG 110 Ma21
Lumbrales E 40 Kg25
Lumi PNG 92 Sa19
Lund S 26 Lg18
Lüneburg D 44 Lf19
Lunéville F 37 Ld21
Lunga Z 110 Mb21
Lunga Lunga EAK 109 Md19
Lungué-Bungo ANG 110 Ma21
Luninec BY 51 Md19
Lunino RUS 60 Nc19
Luodian CHN 84 Qb13
Luoyang CHN 82 Qc12
Lure F 39 Ld22
Lúrio MOC 111 Md21
Lusaka ZW 110 Mb22
Lushnjë AL 56 Lk25
Lüshun CHN 83 Ra11
Lusk USA 122 Ed10
Lutherstadt Eisleben D 44 Lf20
Lutherstadt Wittenberg D 44 Lg20
Lütjenburg D 44 Lf18
Luton GB 35 Kk20
Lutselk'e CDN 120 Eb06
Lutuhyne UA 63 Mk21
Lützow-Holm bukta 141 Md32
Luumäki FIN 28 Md15
Luuq SP 109 Na18
Luvua RDC 109 Mb20
Luwuk RI 87 Ra19
Luxembourg L 37 Ld21
Luxembourg L 37 Ld21
Luxeuil-les-Bains F 39 Ld22
Luxi CHN 84 Pd14
Luxor ET 107 Mc13
Luzern CH 45 Le22
Luzhou CHN 84 Qb13
Luzon RP 85 Ra15
Luzon Strait RP 85 Ra15
Lycksele S 25 Lk13
Lydney GB 35 Kj20
Lyman UA 63 Mj21
Lynchburg USA 123 Ga11
Lyngdal N 26 Ld16
Lyngen N 22 Ma11
Lyngseidet N 22 Ma11
Lynn Lake CDN 120 Ed07
Lyon F 39 Lc23
Lypci UA 63 Mj20
Lypova Dolyna UA 62 Mg20
Lyra Reef PNG 93 Sc19
Lysekil S 26 Lf16
Lyskovo RUS 60 Nc17
Lysøysundet N 24 Le14
Lysyčans'k UA 63 Mk21
Lysye Gory RUS 61 Nc20
Lyubimets BG 57 Md25

M

Ma'an JOR 76 Md12
Maanselkä FIN 23 Me12
Maanselkä FIN 28 Me14
Maardu EST 30 Mc16
Maarianhamina = Mariehamn FIN 25 Lk15
Maastricht NL 37 Lc20
Mablethorpe GB 35 La19
Macao CHN 85 Qc14
Macapá BR 134 Hb18
Macauley Island NZ 99 Ua25
Macdonnell Ranges AUS 94 Rc23
Macedonia GR 56 Ma25
Macedonia MK 56 Ma25
Maceió BR 134 Ja20
Macerata I 46 Lg24
Machala EC 132 Ga19
Măcin RO 55 Me23
Mackay AUS 96 Sb23
Mackenzie CDN 116 Dc05
Mackenzie GUY 134 Ha17
Mackenzie Bay CDN 116 Da05
Mackenzie Bay 141 Oc32
Mackenzie King Island CDN 118 Eb03
Mackenzie Mountains CDN 116 Dc06
Maclean Strait CDN 118 Ed03
Macomér I 48 Le25
Macon USA 123 Fd12
Mâcon F 39 Lc22
Mac Robertson Land 141 Nd33
Macumba AUS 96 Rd24
Madagascar RM 111 Nb23
Madagascar Basin 111 Nc24
Madagascar Ridge 111 Na25
Madagaskar RM 111 Nb23
Madan BG 57 Mc25
Madang PNG 92 Sb20
Madeira BR 132 Ha19
Madeira P 104 Ka12

Madeira Rise – Mary Anne Passage

Samsu – Sarina

Samsu ◻ TR 66 Nb26
Samsun ◻ TR 65 Mj25
San ◻ RMM 105 Kd16
Sanaa ● YE 77 Na15
SANAE IV ◻ 141 Kd33
Sanaga ⬔ CAM 108 Lc18
Sanana ◻ RI 87 Rb19
Sanandaj ◻ IR 76 Nb11
San Andrés Tuxtla ◻ MEX 125 Fa15
San Angelo ◻ USA 122 Ed12
San Antonio ◻ USA 123 Fa13
San Antonio d.l.Cobres ◻ RA 136 Gc23
San Antonio Oeste ◻ RA 137 Gd27
San Benedetto del Tronto ◻ I 47 Lg24
San Bernardino ◻ USA 122 Ea12
San Bernardo ◻ RCH 136 Gb25
San Blas ◻ MEX 124 Ec13
San Blas ◻ MEX 124 Ec14
San Borja ◻ BOL 133 Gc21
Sancak ◻ TR 66 Na26
San Carlos ◻ RP 85 Ra15
San Carlos ◻ YV 132 Gc17
San Carlos de Bariloche ◻ RA 137 Gd27
San Carlos del Zulia ◻ YV 132 Gb17
Sanchahe ◻ CHN 83 Rb10
San Cristóbal ⬔ SOL 98 Ta21
San Cristóbal ◻ YV 132 Gb17
San Cristóbal de las Casas ◻ MEX 125 Fb15
Sancti Spíritus ◻ C 126 Ga14
Sančursk ◻ RUS 60 Nd17
Sand ◻ N 26 Ld16
Sand ◻ N 24 Lf15
Sandakan ◻ MAL 87 Qd17
Sandane ◻ N 24 Ld15
Sandanski ◻ BG 56 Mb25
Sandefjord ◻ N 26 Lf16
Sandefjord Ice Bay ⊟ 141 Oc32
Sandercock Nunataks ◣ 141 Nc32
Sandfire Flat Roadhouse ◻ AUS 94 Ra22
Sandi ◻ SUD 107 Mc15
San Diego ◻ USA 122 Ea12
Sandıklı ◻ TR 64 Mf26
Sandnes ◻ N 26 Lc16
Sandnessjøen ◻ N 22 Lg12
Sandomierz ◻ PL 51 Ma20
Sandön ➤ FIN 25 Ma14
Sandover ⬔ AUS 94 Rc23
Sandovo ◻ RUS 58 Mj16
Sandoway ◻ MYA 84 Pc15
Šandrivka ◻ UA 63 Mh21
Sandspit ◻ CDN 117 Db08
Sandstad ◻ N 24 Le14
Sandstone ◻ AUS 94 Qd24
Sandvika ◻ N 24 Lg13
Sandviken ◻ S 25 Lj15
Sandy Lake ⬔ CDN 120 Fb08
Sandy Lake ◻ CDN 120 Fb08

San Felipe ◻ CO 132 Gc18
San Felipe ◻ MEX 122 Eb12
San Felipe ◻ YV 127 Gc16
San Fernando ◻ E 41 Kg27
San Fernando ◻ MEX 124 Fa14
San Fernando ◻ RP 85 Ra15
San Fernando ◻ TT 127 Gd16
San Fernando d.Valle de Catamarca ◻ RA 136 Gc24
San Fernando de Apure ◻ YV 132 Gc17
San Fernando de Atabapo ◻ YV 132 Gc18
Sånfjällets n.p. ◼ S 24 Lg14
San Francisco ◻ RA 136 Gd25
San Francisco ◻ USA 122 Dd11
San Francisco de Macoris ◻ DOM 127 Gb15
Sangar ◻ RUS 75 Rb06
Sangaste ◻ EST 30 Md17
San Gavino Monreale ◻ I 48 Le26
Sangazi ◻ TR 57 Me25
Sângerei ◻ MD 55 Me22
Sangerhausen ◻ D 44 Lf20
Sangihe ⬔ RI 87 Rb18
San Giovanni in Fiore ◻ I 49 Lj26
San Giovanni Rotondo ◻ I 49 Lh25
Sangkulirang ◻ RI 87 Qd18
Sangli ◻ IND 81 Oc15
Sangüesa ◻ E 42 Kk24
San Ignacio de Velasco ◻ BOL 133 Gd22
San Isidro ◻ RA 136 Ha25
San Javier ◻ E 43 Kk27
Sanjiang ◻ CHN 84 Qb13
San Joaquin Valley ◻ USA 122 Dd11
San Jose ◻ RP 85 Ra15
San Jose ◻ RP 85 Ra16
San Jose ◻ USA 122 Dd11
San José ● CR 126 Fd17
San José ◻ E 41 Kj27
San José ◻ RA 136 Gc25
San José de Chiquitos ◻ BOL 133 Gd22
San José del Cabo ◻ MEX 124 Ec14
San José del Guaviare ◻ CO 132 Gb18
San Juan ◻ DOM 127 Gb15
San Juan ◻ RA 136 Gc25
San Juan ◻ RA 136 Gc25
San Juan ◻ USA 127 Gc15
San Juan Bautista ◻ PY 136 Ha24
Sankt Gallen ◻ CH 45 Le22
Sankt Johann ◻ A 52 Lg22
Sankt Moritz ◻ CH 45 Le22
Sankt-Peterburg ◻ RUS 29 Mf16
Sankt Peter-Ording ◻ D 44 Le18
Sankt Pölten ◻ A 52 Lh21
Sankt Veit an der Glan ◻ A 52 Lh22

Sankuru ➤ RDC 108 Ma19
Şanlıurfa ◻ TR 76 Md11
Şanlıurfa ◻ TR 65 Mk27
San Lorenzo ◻ PY 136 Ha24
San Lorenzo de Calatrava ◻ E 41 Kj26
Sanlúcar de Barrameda ◻ E 41 Kg27
San Lucas ◻ MEX 124 Eb14
San Luis ◻ RA 136 Gc25
San Luis ● RA 136 Gc25
San Luis Obispo ◻ USA 122 Dd11
San Luis Potosí ● MEX 124 Ed14
San Luis Potosí ● MEX 124 Ed14
San Luis Río Colorado ◻ MEX 122 Eb12
San Marino ● RSM 46 Lg24
San Martín ⬔ BOL 133 Gd21
San Martin ◻ 140 Gc32
San Miguel ⬔ BOL 133 Gd21
San Miguel ◻ ES 125 Fd15
San Miguel de Tucumán ● RA 136 Gc24
Sanming ◻ CHN 85 Qd13
San Nicolas d.l.Arroyos ◻ RA 136 Ha25
Sânnicolau Mare ◻ RO 54 Ma22
Sanok ◻ PL 51 Mb21
San Pablo ◻ RP 85 Ra16
San Pablo o ⬔ BOL 133 Gd22
San Pedro ◻ PY 136 Ha23
San Pedro ◻ RA 136 Gd23
San Pédro ◻ CI 105 Kc17
San Pédro ◻ CI 105 Kc18
San Pedro de las Colonias ◻ MEX 124 Ed13
San Pedro Sula ◻ HN 125 Fc15
San Quintin ◻ MEX 122 Ea12
San Rafael ◻ RA 136 Gc25
San Remo ◻ I 46 Ld24
San Roque ◻ E 41 Kh27
San Salvador ● ES 125 Fc16
San Salvador de Jujuy ◻ RA 136 Gc23
Sansanne-Mango ◻ TG 105 La16
San Sebastián ◻ RA 137 Gc29
San Sebastián = Donostia ◻ E 42 Kj24
Sansepolcro ◻ I 46 Lg24
San Severo ◻ I 49 Lh25
Sanski Most ◻ BIH 47 Lj23
San Stéfano di Camastra ◻ I 49 Lh26
Santa Ana ◻ ES 125 Fc16
Santa Ana ◻ MEX 122 Eb12
Santa Ana ◻ USA 122 Ea12
Santa Barbara ◻ USA 122 Ea12
Santa Catarina ◻ BR 135 Hb24
Santa Clara ◻ C 126 Fd14
Santa Comba ◻ E 40 Kf24
Santa Cruz ◻ RA 137 Gb28

Santa Cruz de la Sierra ◻ BOL 133 Gd22
Santa Cruz de Tenerife ◻ E 104 Ka13
Santa Cruz Islands ⬔ SOL 98 Tb21
Santa Elena de Uairén ◻ YV 132 Gd18
Santa Eugenia ◻ E 40 Kf24
Santa Fe ● USA 122 Ec11
Santa Fé ◻ E 41 Kj27
Santa Fé ◻ RA 136 Gd25
Santa Fé ● RA 136 Gd25
Sant'Ágata di Militello ◻ I 49 Lh26
Santa Ines ◻ BR 134 Hc19
Santa Isabel ⬔ SOL 93 Sd20
Santa Maria ◻ BR 135 Hb24
Santa Maria ◻ USA 122 Dd12
Santa Maria del Camí ◻ E 43 Lb26
Santa Maria Island ⬔ VU 98 Tb21
Santa Marta ◻ CO 127 Gb16
Santana ◻ BR 134 Hb19
Santana do Livramento ◻ BR 136 Ha25
Santander ◻ E 42 Kj24
Santander ◻ RP 85 Ra17
Sant'Antioco ◻ I 48 Le26
Sant Antoni de Portmany ◻ E 43 Lа26
Santanyí ◻ E 43 Lb26
Santa Olalla del Cala ◻ E 41 Kg27
Sant'Arcángelo ◻ I 49 Lj25
Santarém ◻ BR 134 Hb19
Santarém ◻ P 40 Kf26
Santaren Channel ➤ C 126 Ga14
Santa Rita ◻ BR 134 Hd19
Santa Rita ◻ BR 134 Ja20
Santa Rosa ● RA 137 Gd26
Santa Rosa ◻ USA 122 Dd11
Santa Rosalia ◻ MEX 124 Eb13
Santa Teresa Gallura ◻ I 48 Le25
Sant Carles de la Ràpita ◻ E 43 La25
Sant Celoni ◻ E 42 Lb25
Santiago ◻ PA 126 Fd17
Santiago ● RCH 136 Gb25
Santiago de Compostela ● E 40 Kf24
Santiago de Cuba ◻ C 126 Ga15
Santiago del Estero ◻ RA 136 Gd24
Santiago del Estero ◻ RA 136 Gd24
Santiago de los Caballeros ◻ DOM 127 Gb15
Santiago Ixcuintla ◻ MEX 124 Ec14
Sant Mateu ◻ E 42 La25
Santo André ◻ BR 135 Hc23
Santo Ângelo ◻ BR 135 Hb24
Santo Corazón ◻ BOL 133 Ha22
Santo Domingo ● DOM 127 Gc15
Santo Domingo d.l.Colorados ◻ EC 132 Ga19

Santorin ⬔ GR 57 Mc27
Santos ◻ BR 135 Hc23
Santo Tirso ◻ P 40 Kf25
Santo Tomé ◻ RA 136 Ha24
San Vicente de la Barquera ◻ E 40 Kh24
Sanya ◻ CHN 85 Qb15
Sanza ◻ I 49 Lh25
São António da Abunari ◻ BR 132 Gd19
São Carlos ◻ BR 135 Hc23
São Felix do Araguaia ◻ BR 134 Hb21
São Felix do Xingu ◻ BR 134 Hb20
São Francisco ⬔ BR 135 Hd21
São Francisco ⬔ BR 134 Ja20
São João d.Meriti ◻ BR 135 Hd23
São José do Rio Preto ◻ BR 135 Hc23
São Lourenco ⬔ BR 135 Ha22
São Luís ◻ BR 134 Hd19
São Mateus ◻ BR 135 Ja22
São Miguel do Tapuio ◻ BR 134 Hd20
São Paulo ◻ BR 135 Hb23
São Paulo ● BR 135 Hc23
Sao Tomé ⬔ STP 108 Lb18
Sao Tomé ⬔ STP 108 Lb18
São Tomé and Príncipe ● STP 108 Lb18
São Vicente ◻ BR 135 Hc23
Sápai ◻ GR 57 Mc25
Sapele ◻ WAN 108 Lb17
Sapernoe ◻ RUS 29 Me15
Sapiénza ⬔ GR 56 Ma27
Sapožok ◻ RUS 59 Na19
Sapporo ◻ J 83 Sa10
Sapri ◻ I 49 Lh25
Sapulut ◻ RI 87 Qd18
Sarabikulovo ◻ RUS 60 Nf18
Sarai ◻ RUS 59 Na19
Säräisniemi ◻ FIN 28 Md13
Sarajevo ● BIH 47 Lk24
Sarandë ◻ AL 56 Ma26
Saransk ◻ RUS 60 Ne18
Sarapul ◻ RUS 72 Nc07
Sarasota ◻ USA 123 Fd13
Šarašova ◻ BY 51 Mc19
Saratov ◻ RUS 61 Nc20
Saratovskoe vodohranilišče ⊟ RUS 60 Ne19
Saray ◻ TR 57 Md25
Sarayköy ◻ TR 64 Me27
Sárbogard ◻ H 53 Lk22
Sardinia ⬔ I 48 Le25
Sareks n.p. ◼ S 22 Lj12
Sarektjåkka ▲ S 22 Lj12
Sargasso Sea ⊟ 113 Ga06
Sarh ◻ TCH 108 Ld17
Šarhorod ◻ UA 62 Me21
Sari ◻ IR 76 Nc11
Saria ⬔ GR 57 Md28
Sarie Marais Base ◻ 141 Kd33
Sarıgöl ◻ TR 64 Me26
Sarıkamış ◻ TR 66 Nb25
Sarıkaya ◻ TR 65 Mh26
Sarina ◻ AUS 96 Sb23

420 Index of names

Shakhrisyabz – Slovenska Bistrica

PHOTO INDEX:

Abbreviations:
C = Corbis, D = digitalvision/Woodhouse, DFA = Das Fotoarchiv,
G = Getty, Hub = Huber, Mau = Mauritius, P = Premium, U = Uluntuncoc

2 P (1,2,4,5) IFA (3), 6, 128/129, 160/161 G, 166/167 P, 168-169 P, 169.3 Monheim,
170 P, 171.1 G/Dickinson, 2 Evans, 3 P, 172.1 FAN, 2 G, 3 laif, 4 P, 5 laif/Zanetti,
6 FAN, 173.1 Imagine/Janvogt, 2 Huber, 3 G/Layda, 174 G, 175.1,2,3 D, 175.3 DFA,
175.5 laif, 176.1,3 Böttcher, 2 DFA, 4 Huber, 177.1,2 Huber, 177.3 P , 4 P, 178.1 P,
179.1,3 G, 2 W. Kunth, 4 P, 5 Wrba, 180 P, 181.1 D, 2,3 P, 4 laif, 182.1–3 P, 4 Huber,
5 Herzig, 183.1,2 P, 3 Monheim, 4 Mau/Pigneter, 184 P, 185.1 D, 2–5 P, 186 G,
187.1 P, 2 laif/Krause, 3 P, 4 Hub, 188, 189.1 Hub, 2 P/Tarlan, 3 Hub, 190–192 Hub,
193.1,2 D, 3,4 P, 194, 195.1 P, 2 Mau, 3 G/Armand, 4 DFA/Sackermann, 5 P, 6 DFA,
196.1 laif/Hilgner, 2 P, 3, 4 G, 197.1 Klammet, 2 P, 3 Hub, 198 P, 199.1 P, 2 Klammet,
3 Hub, 4 P, 200.1–3 P, 4 G/Carasco, 201.1 P, 2 laif/Puschner, 3 G, 202.1 Freyer,
2 mediacolor's, 203.1 IFA/Strobl, 2 P/Hilger, 3 G/Shano, 204–205 P, 206 Hub, 207.1
Mau/Hollweck, 2 laif/Tophoven, 3–5 P, 6 Mau, 208–210 P, 212 G/Stahl, 213.1
DFA/Scarlandis, 2 DFA/Riedmiller, 3 DFA/Sasse, 214 G/Turner, 215.1,2 P, 215.3 G.
M. Schmid, 216 DFA/Stark, 217.1 G. M. Schmid, 2 G/Chesley, 3 P, 218 DFA/Portnoy,
219.1,2,4,5 DFA/ Sasse, 3 Mau/Cotton, 220 G/Weinberg, 221.1 P, 2–4 IFA, 222.1
DFA/Sasse, 2,3 Mau, 4 DFA/Petterson, 223.1 G/Waugh, 2 G, 3 laif/Hub, 224 G,
225.1 IFA/ Tschanz ,2 IFA, 3 DFA, 226 G/Renaut, 227.1 zefa/Anderle, 2 P, 3 zefa/
Minden/Lanting, 228.1 P/Yamashita, 2 G/Sitton, 3 DFA/Sasse, 229.1 G/Chesley,
3 G, 2,4,5 DFA/Sasse, 230 G/Harris, 231 P, 232 G/Kavanagh, 233.1 DFA/Gordon,
2 DFA/Bolesch, 3 K. U. Müller, 4 P/Buss, 234 G, 235.1 P/Mon Tresor, 2 IFA/Aber-
ham, 3 Ehlers, 4 P, 236 DFA/Bolesch, 237.1,3 G, 2 Hub/Giovanni, 4 Transglobe,
238 DFA/Eisermann, 239.1 P, 2 DFA/Sasse, 240 DFA/Eisermann, 241.1 DFA/Sasse,
2 Krause/laif, 3,4 P, 242.1 G, 2 Mau/Gierth, 243.1,2 DFA/Sasse, 3 Mau/Blokhuis,
244 IFA, 245.1 DFA/ Christoph, 2 Hub, 246.1,2 Mau/O'Brien, 247.1 K. U. Müller,
2 DFA/Lausner, 248.1 P, 2 DFA/Lausner, 3 DFA/Künzig, 249.1 Künzig, 2 mediacolors,
3 Hub/ Schmid, 250.1,2 G, 3 P, 4 Hub, 251.1 P, 2 Hub, 3 G, 252.1,3 P, 2 DFA, 253.1,3
P, 2 G, 254 Hub, 256 G, 257.1 P, 2 FAN/Heinrichson, 3 C/Lloyd, 258 P, 258.1 G/Stra-
chan, 2–5 P, 260 G, 261.1 Schapowalow/Pratt, 2 C/Lloyd, 3 G, 262 G, 263.1–3 P,

4 G, 264 Bilderberg/Leser, 265.1 IFA/ Comnet, 2 Schapowalow/Beisert, 3 Mau,
4 G/Drake, 266 P, 267.1 G, 2 TG/Ryman, 268/269 Alamy/Sanger, 269 FAN (2), 269
M.Graben, 270 pix/Transworld, 271.1,3 Hub/Damm, 2 Mau/Vidler, 272 P/Pictor,
273.1 DFA/Riedmiller, 2 P/Roda, 3 Krause/ laif, 274 U/laif, 275.1 DFA/Christoph,
2 P, 3 DFA, 276 Pix/Bagni, 277.1 Laif/Bessard, 2 DFA/Christoph, 3 DFA/ Müller,
278 Hub/laif, 279.1 Bilderberg, Aurora/Azel, 2 Pix/Bitsch, 280 Mau, 281 Pix/Aber-
ham, 2,3 Hoogte/laif,282 IFA, 283 DFA/Christoph, Stark, 284 Hoogte/laif, 285.1 P,
2 DFA/Scheibner, 3 U/laif, 4 P/Hicks, 286 Pix/Aberham, 287 laif, 288.1 P/Minden/
Lanting, 2,3 pix/Fiala, 289.1 DFA/Christoph, 2 P/Hilger, 3 G/ Rothefeld, 4 DFA, 290
U/laif, 291.1 laif, 2 /U, 3 DFA, 292 laif, 293.1 P/Pictor, 2 P/Wolfe, 3 mediacolor's/
Buck, 294 U/laif, 295.1 Mau/ de Foy, 2,3 Pix/Havi, 296 Hub/laif, 297.1 DFA/ Stark,
2 G, 3 P/Pictor, 298 U/laif, 299.1 P/Hummel, 2,3 laif/Emmler, 300 DFA/Stark, 301.1
Schapowalow/Ponzio, 2 Pix/Minden/Lanting, 3 Pix/Aberham, 302 P/Waldkirch,
303.1 Mau/Vidler, 2 P, 3 Gartung/laif, 304 DFA/Christoph, 305.1 U/laif, 2 Hub/Sie-
wert, 3 laif, 306/307 Laif/Panstock, 308 G/Klevansky, 309.1 P, 2 IFA, 3 G, 4 IFA,
310 P/Roda, 311 Gy, 312.1.2 IFA, 3,4 G, 313.1 Mau, 2 laif, 3 P, 314.1 mau/Wendler,
2,4 look/ Naundorf, 3 Mau/Wittgen, 315, 316.1–3 P, 4 look/Raach, 317.1 G/Swartz,
317.2 NN, 3 zefa/Damm, 318 A.M.Gross, 319.1 Mau, 2 DFA/Zippel, 3 G, 320.1
G/Lewis, 2 G/McIntyre, 3 FAN, 4 Hub, 5 P/Pictor, 321.1 G, 2 FAN, 3 Mau/Pearce,
322 Mau/Fischer, 323.1,2 G, 3 P/Pictor, 324 Hub/Schmid, 325.1 Schapowalow/
Hiller, 2 Hub/Schmid, 3 DFA/Hirth, 4 G/Nelson, 326 P/NGS, 327.1 P/Pictor, 2 P,
3 G/Hiser, 328.1 G/Frerck, 2 Gonzalez/laif, 3 Mayer/laif, 329.1 Gonzalez/laif, 2,3
P/Marr, 4 G/Locke, 330.1 Mau/Raga, 2 /AGE, 331.1 FAN, 2 P/Segal, 3 D, 332 Pic-
tor/P, 333.1 G, 2 mediacolor's, 3 Everts, 334 NN, 335.1,2 G, 3 look/Raach, 336 P,
337.1 Mau/Visa image, 2 G/Armand, 3 AKG, 4 Huber/Bertsch, 338.1–3 P, 4 Hub,
5 corbis, 339 P, 340.1 P, 2 G, 4,5 IFA, 341.1 IFA, 2,3 P, 4 DFA/Tack, 342 P, 343.1 G,
2 P, 3 C/Madere, 344/345 P/Minden, 346–347.2 P, 347.3 Beatty, 348/349 Mau,
349.1 G/stone/ Vikova, 349.2 C/P. Robert, 349.3 f1 online/Prisma, 350 Mau/O'Brien,
351.1,2 NN, 3 G/Armand, 352 dpa, 353.1 G/C. Hondros, 353.2,3 dpa, 354 li REA/
laif, 355 P, 355 u DFA, 356 357.1 dpa, 2 IFA, 3 DFA, 358.1 DFA, 359.2 DFA/Scar-
landis, 3 dpa. 360/361 P.

CREDITS/CONTRIBUTORS:

This edition is published on behalf of APA Publications GmbH & Co.
Verlag KG, Singapore Branch, Singapore
by Verlag Wolfgang Kunth GmbH & Co. KG, Germany

This edition is distributed by:

GeoCenter International Ltd
Meridian House, Churchill Way West
Basingstoke, Hampshire RG21 6YR
Great Britain
Tel: (44) 1256 817 987
Fax: (44) 1256 817 988
sales@geocenter.co.uk
www.insightguides.com

ISBN 978-981-282-025-9

Original edition:
© 2008 Verlag Wolfgang Kunth GmbH & Co. KG, Munich
Königinstr. 11
80539 Munich
Tel: (49) 89 4580 20 0
Fax: (49) 89 4580 20 21
www.kunth-verlag.de

English edition:
Copyright © 2009 Verlag Wolfgang Kunth GmbH & Co. KG
© Cartography: GeoGraphic Publishers GmbH & Co. KG
Thematic maps: Legenda, Novara (Italy)

Texts: Heike Barnitzke, Gesa Bock, Dirk Brietzke, Michael Elser, Ursula Klocker
Text translation: Demetri Lowe, Alison Moffat-McLynn, Karin Weidlich/comtranslate
Printed in Slovakia

The information and facts presented in the book have been extensively researched and edited for accuracy. The publishers, authors, and editors,
cannot, however, guarantee that all of the information in the atlas is entirely accurate or up to date at the time of publication. The publishers are
grateful for any suggestions or corrections that would improve the content of the atlas.

See the world in colour...
Where are *you* going next?

The world's largest range of visual travel guides and maps

WIMBLEDON
2007

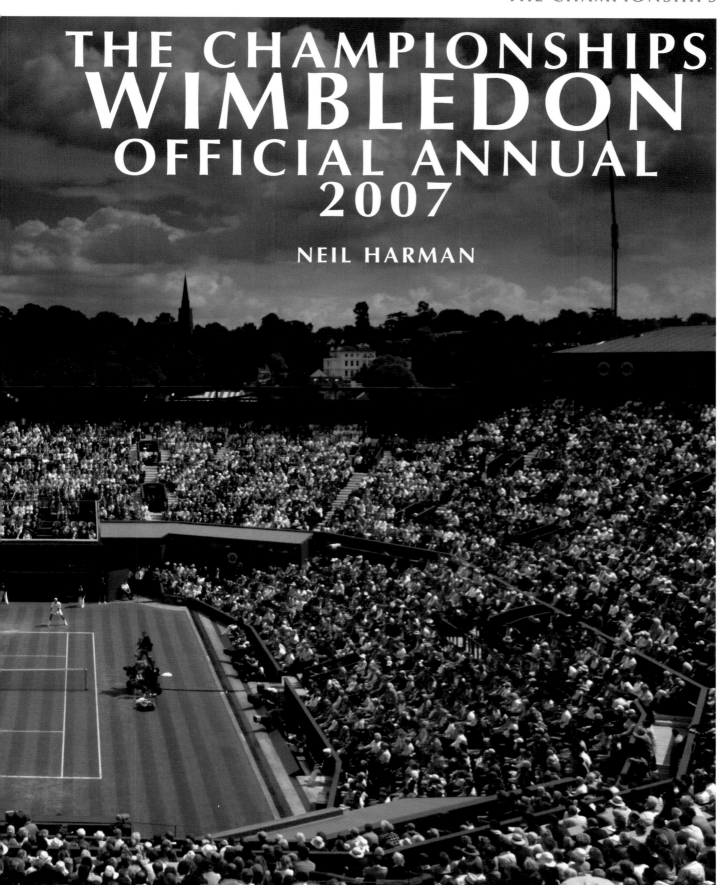

THE CHAMPIONSHIPS
WIMBLEDON
OFFICIAL ANNUAL
2007

NEIL HARMAN

Publisher
PPL Sport & Leisure

Managing Director
Bill Cotton

Art Editor
David Kelly

Design Team
Emma Robinson
Graham Nuttall
Caroline O'Donovan

Photography
PA Photos

Editorial
Neil Harman

Editorial Liaison
Kevin McGoverin

Copyright (c) 2007
The All England Lawn Tennis
and Croquet Club

Photographs Copyright (c)
PA Photos

This edition
published 2007 by
PPL Sport & Leisure
Century Building
Tower Street
Brunswick Business Park
Liverpool L3 4BJ

PPL Sport & Leisure
Bradford House
East Street
Epsom, Surrey KT17 1BL

ISBN 1-903381-17-7

Printed by Butler and Tanner
Caxton Road, Frome,
Somerset BA111NF

CONTENTS

FOREWORD
Tim Phillips

**Chairman of The All England Lawn Tennis and Croquet Club
and Committee of Management of The Championships**

**The 121st Championships enjoyed a magical climax
made all the more intense by the disappointment of the
earlier rain delays.**

The clash of Roger Federer and Rafael Nadal in the
men's singles final produced one of Wimbledon's great
and memorable matches. The world number one player
and current holder of three Grand Slam titles, was
challenged by the number two and recent winner, for
the third time, of the fourth Grand Slam title (the French
Open). In three hours and forty five minutes of sublime
tennis, Roger Federer needed all his great talent to
become only the second men's singles champion, since
the Challenge round format was abolished in 1922, to
win five successive Wimbledon titles – and he did it
with Bjorn Borg (the only other such champion)
watching intently from the front row of the Royal Box.

Venus Williams triumphed in the ladies' singles – for
the fourth time. After a wobbly start (in the first round she
only won 7-5 in the final set), Venus became invincible
as she progressed further into the tournament. In the final
she overpowered the delightful Marion Bartoli, who had
upset world No.1 Justine Henin in the semi-finals.

Arnaud Clement and Michael Llodra, of France, won
the men's doubles in great style, beating the defending

champions and world No.1 pair, Bob and Mike Bryan,
in the final. Earlier in the draw the Frenchmen won
their second round match 14-12 in the fifth set – by
such fine margins can championships be won.
However, Andre Sa and Marcelo Melo of Brazil
(eventual semi-finalists) played the longest men's
doubles ever at Wimbledon when they beat Paul
Hanley and Kevin Ullyett 28-26 in the fifth set in their
102 game second round match.

In the ladies' doubles, Cara Black and Liezel Huber
regained the trophy they won in 2005 with some
wonderful tennis. Cara has now won three ladies'
doubles titles to add to the mixed doubles Wimbledon
title she won with brother, Wayne, in 2004.

And The Championships concluded with a British win
– in the mixed doubles. Jamie Murray became the first
British player since Jeremy Bates and Jo Durie in 1987 to
become a Wimbledon winner. Jamie, partnered by
Jelena Jankovic, won the title by playing excellent tennis
and by enjoying themselves enormously while they did
so. This wonderfully entertaining final brought the
curtain down on another remarkable Wimbledon.

I hope you will enjoy this annual which vividly records
the story of Wimbledon 2007 in words and pictures. ●

INTRODUCTION
Neil Harman

Two months before the flag went down on The 121st Championships, workman's hard hat and yellow vest at the ready, it was time to pick one's way through mud and cement droppings and find a space atop the Centre Court in the company of Tim Phillips, Chairman of the All England Club. The mind drifted back to what the picture would have looked like in 1922, when The Championships first moved to Church Road. To construct the building that would become the Holy Grail of lawn tennis, some 3,000 tons of shingle, 1,700 tons of sand and 600 tons of cement were used and 21 miles of wood slats were required for the three miles of seating. What glories were about to unfold.

What were the conditions like in those days? The pioneers had enormous foresight – the court was placed so that no shadow would appear until 7pm – and a disc of white paper the size of an old farthing (a fourth of a penny in pre-decimal days), placed on the turf, could be seen from each of the initial 9,989 seats. Was it possible to have conceived of a roof, because the weather was to be so bad that year that play was extended to a third Wednesday.

These 85 years on, the grounds had undergone bold and beautiful transformation and yet had done so – as was the club's will – while retaining the unique blend of tennis in an English country garden that was at the heart of Wimbledon. But on hard hat day in May, it still seemed remarkable that everything would be dusted down and pristine in appearance before the first ball was hit. We had everyone's word that it would. Once the last shot of 2007 had been played, the bulldozers would be back and, by 2009, of course, we would have *that* roof.

Phillips, who was to receive a CBE in the Queen's Birthday Honours said: "This is a club with a rich inheritance and what we try to do is build on that

inheritance. We are proud of the standing Wimbledon occupies in the world because there are an awful lot of things that Britain is not best at and, in an extremely cluttered marketplace of major sporting events, we work very hard to make sure Wimbledon retains its status as something the public wants to see and TV wants to buy.

"We do not intend to be left behind. We hang on to the finest of our traditions while leading the way in innovation and enhancement and, with the facilities here, I think we've done quite a good job. You have to ask yourself where Wimbledon would be if we hadn't taken these decisions. Putting a roof on Centre Court might, to the casual observer, be an easy thing to do, but one, we are dealing with an 85-year-old building; two, it had to improve the sunlight getting onto the grass; three, we knew it would mean putting in magnificent new facilities and four, the roof itself had to be right."

Eddie Seaward, the head groundsman, has pronounced that, since the old roof was removed, the grass had never been in better condition at this time of the year. And viewing The Championships this summer would be an unmatched experience, with the former facade

gone, and Centre Court more of an ampitheatre, its new commentary boxes (with awnings in place to shield commentators' eyes from a sun they could only guess was there before) erected and, for those in the top tiers, a warning that they should find room for plenty of suncream in their picnic baskets.

From up there, it was possible to believe that London was the capital of the tennis world and, to Phillips, that was just where it was. "We are the original Grand Slam, the LTA has just moved into its new headquarters in Roehampton, where the ITF has its head office and the ATP has moved its HQ to London as well," he said. "We are hoping to bring the Masters Cup to the capital by 2009 (confirmation of which would come mid-Championships). It is difficult to know how, structurally, British tennis could be in better shape."

Strolling back to his office, the Chairman had a final thought on the equal prize money drama upon which he, and his committee, had finally brought the curtain down to seismic interest with an April announcement. "It was a classic issue, the club wanted to make a positive statement and the timing was right. "Wishful thinking perhaps, but we want to sell the idea that tennis should be a sport for young girls who are athletic because where else could they travel the world and earn the sort of money they can in tennis?

"This is the third time in my chairmanship that the relativities (between pay for men and women) have changed and all we have done is

taken the last step. It wasn't such a drama going from 90% to 95% as it was from 95% to 100. We want our athletes to feel respected, and looked after and if half of them felt they weren't, we are happy that that has been put right."

The infrastructure was ready, the purses were overflowing, the courts were in great shape. What of the players? Local interest had, of course, centred on Andy Murray, the British No.1 and the wrist he had damaged while playing in the Masters event in Hamburg. Murray had become a top ten player, thanks to winning the title in San Jose for a second time, as well as his semi-final run in the elite tournaments in Indian Wells and Miami. Unfortunately, his clay court season would be dogged by physical misfortune – he had played only one full game – before the Hamburg horrors. He damaged a tendon in his right wrist and though, two days before The Championships, he held out a partial hope of participation, the very next day he chose – sensibly – to withdraw.

Roger Federer had a new book out called *Quest for Perfection*, written by Switzerland's premier tennis writer, Rene Stauffer. That quest reached its moment of truth every June in SW19. The defending champion had, once more, endured heartache at the French Open when he was beaten in four sets in the final by Rafael Nadal, his tormentor-in-chief. Amelie Mauresmo, the ladies' champion, had been troubled by illness and lack of form and one wondered if the freshness of the grass would resuscitate her.

The Chairman, as per tradition, invited two special guests, Jack Kramer and Virginia Wade. Kramer had won the title 60 years earlier when, in seven matches, he had lost only 37 games, establishing a record. At 85, he remained utterly sharp and charming, and when one heard him speak, it brought back those happy days first watching The Championships on television, when he was in distinctive harness on the BBC with Dan Maskell.

Was it really 30 summers since Virginia had become the last British women's singles champion, defeating Betty Stove in three sets to crown the Queen's Silver Jubilee? She had played The Championships a record 24 years in singles and, in all, contested 212 matches – the record for a British player. Such excellent company, such unimaginable excitement. We could not wait for the gates to open. ●

THEY ENTER AS PLAYERS AND
LEAVE AS CHAMPIONS.

At Wimbledon, the game begins long before the players walk through the wrought-iron gates. Here, they put on their whites and exorcise their demons on the secluded practice courts. All in preparation for the hallowed grass of Centre Court, where straight-set victories awe millions and players become legends. **THE WIMBLEDON CHAMPIONSHIPS – JUNE 25TH TO JULY 8TH, 2007.**

Roger Federer
Seeded 1st

Age: 25. Born Basel, Switzerland.

The magnificent Swiss was returning for his ninth Wimbledon and it was quite amazing to think that in his first four visits, he was beaten in the first round three times. Now the king of all he surveyed, Federer was seeking a fifth successive title. He had lost in the final of the French Open to Rafael Nadal, thereby losing his chance to become the first man since Rod Laver to hold all four Grand Slam titles at the same time.

Rafael Nadal
Seeded 2nd

Age: 21. Born: Manacor, Majorca.

Had stunned everyone – but not himself – in reaching the final of Wimbledon in 2006, which illustrated what an accomplished player he had become. The left hander from the Balearics, whose fierce top spin, angled strokes and on-court intensity made him a ferocious opponent, had won 81 consecutive clay court matches until Federer defeated him in the final of Hamburg, but recovered to win at Roland Garros, becoming the first player since Bjorn Borg to land that title three times in succession.

Andy Roddick

Seeded 3rd

Age: 24. Born: Omaha, Nebraska, USA.

A fourth title at Queen's Club suggested that Roddick was once more entering Wimbledon with as much right as anyone to consider themelves among the title contenders. A twice losing finalist to Federer, Roddick had turned to Jimmy Connors in the spring of 2006 to help him focus on what he needed to get right, Roddick had the air of a man determined to win the title he cherished above all others. Had become a lot more than just a player with a strong serve and a thumping forehand.

Novak Djokovic

Seeded 4th

Age: 20. Born: Belgrade, Serbia.

What a remarkable year for the Serbian right hander whose promise was brilliantly fulfilled when he reached the final of the Masters tournament in Indian Wells, losing to Nadal and followed that with victory in Miami, beating Guillermo Canas, of Argentina, in the final. Djokovic was a character is every sense of the word, a young man of fierce ambition, a superb mimic, and a wonderfully resilient player who had brought Mark Woodforde, the Australian, into his coaching team to help work on his grass court technique.

Fernando Gonzalez
Seeded 5th

Age: 26. Born: Santiago, Chile.

His Grand Slam breakthrough had come in Melbourne in January, when he reached the final of the Australian Open, in which he played a magnificent first set but crumbled under the awesome power of Federer. Gonzalez, coached by Larry Stefanki, who had spent two years with Tim Henman, possesses one of the meanest forehands in the game but was adding more variety and reliability as well, which makes him a very dangerous customer.

Nikolay Davydenko
Seeded 6th

Age: 26. Born: Severodonezk, Ukraine.

Had no form to speak of on grass and, like Yevgeny Kafelnikov and Marat Safin before him, has some kind of weird mistrust of the surface. Behind his rather surly facade, there is an interesting guy trying to get out. One of the finest athletes on the tour, just watching him chasing everything down wore you out. He had twice reached the semi-finals of the French Open and, in 2006, won a career high five ATP titles and 68 match wins, which illustrated what a competitor he is.

Tomas Berdych
Seeded 7th

Age: 21. Born: Valasske Mezirici, Czech Republic.

It had been a long time since the last Czech winner of the men's singles, Jan Kodes, in 1973, but Berdych bore all the hallmarks of a potential champion. A tall man with boyish features, he had had a staggered year of form, reaching the last 16 of the Australian Open and winning his first title, on grass, in Halle nine days before The Championships. Best known for defeating Nadal in Madrid last year and then lifting a finger to his lips – a gesture that did not go down well with the locals.

James Blake
Seeded 8th

Age: 27. Born: Yonkers, New York, USA.

On the withdrawal of Andy Murray, the American with the English mother was promoted to the eighth seeded spot. Blessed with dashing good looks and a charming man, Blake had all the tools to do well on grass, but somehow had never been able to knit it all together. Won his first tournament of the year, in Sydney, but had subsequently endured what was, for him, a disappointing spell of results.

Justine Henin
Seeded 1st

Age: 25. Born: Liege, Belgium.

The waif-like Justine had won the French Open for a third year in succession and a fourth in total, with some glorious tennis. On grass, she had been twice a finalist at Wimbledon – losing to Venus Williams in 2001 and Amelie Mauresmo last year, but had been working since the start of the year on developing her all court game. The victory at Eastbourne, on the Saturday prior to The Championships, was a fascinating portent.

Maria Sharapova
Seeded 2nd

Age: 20. Born: Nyagan, Russia.

The 2004 champion and reigning US Open champion had come within a whisker of withdrawing from the French Open with a shoulder problem that had plagued her throughout the first half of the year. How would such an injury impact on her chances of a sustained challenge on the lawns? Her fighting spirit is undeniable but so, too, was her brittleness under fire.

Jelena Jankovic

Seeded 3rd

Age: 22. Born: Belgrade, Serbia.

The form girl of the field, entered The Championships having reached 11 semi-finals in her previous 17 tournaments in 2007. A wonderfully exuberant player from Serbia, who had reached the semi-finals in Paris and followed that with a victory on grass in Edgbaston. Her Wimbledon record had been improving each year and with the former Middlesex county player, Richard Brooks in her corner, was highly regarded as one who could mount a serious challenge for her first Grand Slam title.

Amelie Mauresmo

Seeded 4th

Age: 28. Born: St Germain-en-Laye, France.

This was her 38th career singles main draw in Grand Slams but it had been a long and relatively unfulfilled year for the defending champion, not least because she was forced to miss a period out of the game after requiring an appendectomy in March. She had been beaten in the fourth round of the Australian Open by the Czech Repulbic's Lucie Safarova and the same girl was to defeat her in the third round at the French Open. Reached the final of Eastbourne the week before The Championships, falling to Justine Henin.

Svetlana Kuznetsova
Seeded 5th

Age 21. Born: St Petersburg, Russia.

A new braided hairstyle for the fifth seed might perhaps lead to a change of fortune. The two time Wimbledon singles quarter-finalist and runner-up in the 2005 doubles with Amelie Mauresmo, Kuznetsova's year had been highlighted by four runners-up finishes, in Doha, Indian Wells, Berlin (where she defeated Justine Henin, the top seed, in the semi-finals) and Rome. Still best remembered for becoming the first Russian woman to win a Grand Slam, the 2004 US Open.

Ana Ivanovic
Seeded 6th

Age: 19. Born: Belgrade, Serbia.

First played Wimbledon as a 17 year old and the next year she made the fourth round. Was entering her third Championships on the crest of a wave after reaching the final of the French Open – where she was soundly defeated by Henin – the first Serbian woman to achieve such status in a Grand Slam. She had already won the German Open in Berlin, pipping Kuznetsova in a final set tie-break. A tall, elegant right hander with a superb attitude and fighting spirit, she was destined to become a favourite with the photographers.

Serena Williams

Seeded 7th

Age: 25. Born: Saginaw, Michigan, USA.

A staggering triumph in the Australian Open – her eighth Grand Slam title – for which she had barely prepared and yet the American came through to demolish Maria Sharapova in the final, was followed by an equally unrealistic victory in the Sony Ericsson Open in Miami, having lost the first set of the final against Henin 6-0. Lost to the Belgian again in the quarter-finals of the French Open but saw that more as a failing of her game rather than a triumph of Henin's. Appearing at her eighth Wimbledon after missing last year with an injury to her left knee.

Anna Chakvetadze

Seeded 8th

Age: 20. Born: Moscow, Russia.

A quarter-finalist at both the Australian and French Opens this year following her fourth round appearance at the 2006 US Open had marked a significant breakthrough for the Russian right hander. She had won the very first tournament of the year, in Hobart, Tasmania and reached the semi-finals in Miami, where she was pipped by Henin and, on the eve of The Championships, gave Jelena Jankovic a real fright in the finals of S'Hertogenbosch, Holland.

Day **ONE**
25.06.2007

HENMAN
VS
MOYA

FEDERER
VS
GABASHVILI

STEPANEK
VS
MATHIEU

QUERREY
VS
FALLA

HINGIS
VS
CAVADAY

Monday 25 June…

At 9.18pm, Andrew Jarrett, the referee and Mike Morrissey, one of his assistants, strode onto Centre Court and asked the players if they wanted to stay out there. The pictures on television would suggest that it was light enough to keep hitting tennis balls, but to be on location, in the deepening gloom, was to tell a different story. Had they not been dressed in predominantly white, Tim Henman and Carlos Moya would not have been able to distinguish each other.

To say that the pair of thirtysomethings rescued proceedings, was stating the obvious. The worst of the forecasts ushering in the opening day – when tornadoes struck Shropshire of all places – suggested Wimbledon would suffer something similar to the deluges that had left the good folk of Sheffield, Hull and Lincoln up to their waists in floods. It would require a procession of buckets to empty the water from the Royal

Carlos Moya

Box. As it was, as the afternoon progressed, there were showers to the left of SW19 and showers to the right – the partition was the Club itself.

Thank goodness for that, otherwise we would have been unable to witness a brand of tennis from Henman, especially, that re-awakened a long lost sense. The four time semi-finalist came into The Championship on the back of slim pickings. He had registered two victories on the ATP Tour and two more in the Davis Cup against the Netherlands and he had found it so difficult to close matches out, not least in his previous two events, losing in the first round of the French Open to Ernests Gulbis, of Latvia, and, at the same stage, to another 18 year old, Marin Cilic, of Croatia, at the Artois championships at Queen's Club.

When he was asked, on the eve of Wimbledon, if he hoped to be back previewing the event next year, he said that yes, it was a hope. No more than that. So ➤

every bit of Henman we would see in 2007, had to be cherished. He walked out to a standing ovation and proceeded to play from memory. It was altogether really thrilling. The man may drive the crowd to distraction 'Come on Tim, Good Old Tim' but they love him for it.

Wimbledon has invariably given him succour and strength. "It is such a special place and hopefully it will be even better once they've finished it," he had said of the Wimbledon refurbishments. Even as the match against Moya started, both players were casting anxious looks upwards and it was Henman who struck first, breaking to take a 3–1 lead after a protracted fourth game. Having established a first set advantage, Henman was within two points of winning it when the rains began to fall.

Stephen Bierley, the adroit *Guardian* correspondent wrote: "In the Royal Box, shawls and rugs were draped, possibly hiding a strategic hot water bottle or two, while elsewhere there was a plethora of cagoules. As the showers intensified, Henman gave the umpire a long stare and then threw away the balls and made for his chair. It was as routine and instinctive as his volley."

There had been no hesitation from either player in using Hawk-Eye, indeed at one stage there seemed to be a parallel contest between who could hit most winners and who could make the most errors when challenging the line calls. Moya had run out of his quota of challenges before that first break in play came. A 90 minute break obviously hurt the British player rather than the Spaniard, for Moya responded by taking the second set hurriedly.

Now the tennis really picked up. Having missed four of the past five Championships, it was felt that Moya would buckle but it was he who made more forays to the net, who kicked his mule-like serve into brilliantly conceived angles, and when he was 5-4 down in the fourth set, and stood four times within a point of defeat, he put his deliveries where Henman could do nothing about them.

And so into a fifth; Henman hesitant. He was 4-2, 15-40 down, the horrid prospect of defeat stared him squarely between the eyes. It was then that he resorted to type, with great depth on two approaches, skipping forward to pick off Moya's attempted passing shots with forehand volleys. At 5-5, it was clearly too dark to continue. To whom would sleep come easier?

Lest one thinks that Henman against Moya was the only action of the first day we had, of course, been treated to the first sight of the defending champion. Roger Federer had titillated us a couple of days before the event, when revealing that Nike, his clothing manufacturers, had come up with something special. Full length trousers? An overcoat? Silk cravat? Boater? All of the aforementioned? ➤

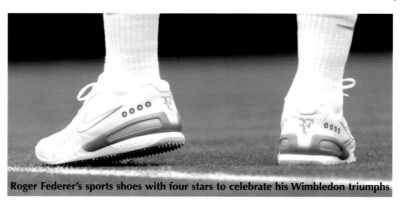

Roger Federer's sports shoes with four stars to celebrate his Wimbledon triumphs

Roger Federer serving to Teimuraz Gabashvili

As it happened, Federer came out in long pants that were unzipped when he chose to play. The jacket was back, adorned with a new logo and his silver bag carried four Federer emblems, designating his four triumphs on the Wimbledon lawns. His opponent, Teimuraz Gabashvili, from Russia, looked far too normal and insignificant to have a chance.

Gabashvili was known on the circuit as Tsunami, because of his tendency to let big matches wash all over him. Simon Barnes, in

The Times wrote: "Federer declined to play the match in his longs – 'it was cold, but not that cold,' he said – all the same his entire style under great grey skies above the oddly naked-looking roofless Centre Court, was one of muted greatness – like a great actor who brings all eyes upon himself by means of the deliberate modesty of his demeanour." Federer won 6-3, 6-2, 6-4.

There were a couple of surprise losses – though Radek Stepanek had endured a

Valentino Rossi, the Italian professional motorcycle racer, who has won seven Grand Prix World Championships, watching Roger Federer

lacklustre few months of form since, incidentally, he had become engaged to Martina Hingis, who had won this title ten years ago. Stepanek was beaten in straight sets by the Frenchman, Paul-Henri Mathieu; and a lot more had been expected of the American, Sam Querrey, all 6'6" of him, but he was also beaten in three, by Alejandro Falla, of Colombia.

For Stepanek there was consolation of a sort in that his fiancee survived her first singles of the tournament, though by the veritable skin of her teeth. Hingis was up against Britain's Naomi Cavaday who, in conversation with myself and Virginia Wade a few days before The Championships, had been engrossed with the tales Wade told of her 16-year career at The Championships that culminated, unforgettably, with victory in 1977.

"I wasn't allowed to play Wimbledon at 16, the rules forbade it," Wade says. "Then, at 18, I won a round and the next morning my father read out an order of play and I fell down the ➤

MARTINA HINGIS, THE CHAMPION IN **1977**, IN REFLECTIVE MOOD:

"I'm happy to be around and still be playing. The older you get, the more fears you have. When I look at the pictures of the past champions, me included, it seems so totally different. I felt like the whole world belonged to me. I was so pleased with myself. I felt I was invincible."

stairs. I was playing Ann Hayden (later Jones) on Centre Court." She asked Cavaday about her first experience at Wimbledon.

"That was last year," she replied. "I was playing in the LTA wild card play-off and I didn't quite appreciate what all the fuss was about. But I beat four players either 7-6 or 6-4 in the final set, on courts at Raynes Park that were so hilly and I made it into the main draw"..."How were your bum muscles?" Virginia asked. "Gosh, mine used to be so tight with all that bending and stretching you had to do on grass." "Yeah, you're right," Cavaday responded.

"And this year you've got a wild card into the event, so you've never played qualifying?" Virginia asked. "That's fortunate because it's rather like having to endure a rather nasty medical procedure. Everybody is so tense there, nobody plays well."

But Cavaday was playing well this day, enough to have Hingis on the rocks at 5-3 down in the second set when it took all of the Swiss player's guile to extricate her from a potential embarrassment. Once she had pulled herself around, Hingis won 6-7 7-5 6-0 but Cavaday – coached by David Felgate, Henman's former mentor – had proved herself one to log under the 'British players with terrific potential' section of one's memory.

The dubious honour of being the first player to have to pack their bags went to Ashley Harkleroad of the United States. The world no.79 picked up only three games in her defeat to Italy's Roberta Vinci (whose surname translates to 'win'). Harkleroad, once touted as the new face of American tennis, said: "Travelling around the tour isn't that glamorous, at least not unless you are in the top 10 or 20 (her career high ranking had been No.39 four years ago). It's actually not a fun life whatsoever. It's a difficult life. It's lonely. You're travelling around with a bunch of girls. What can be the fun in that?"

It depended, one supposed, on what you wanted from life.

Day **TWO**
26.06.2007

SANTORO
VS
KARLOVIC

MAURESMO
VS
JACKSON

V. WILLIAMS
VS
KUDRYAVTSEVA

O'BRIEN
VS
KLOESEL

PREVIOUS SETS

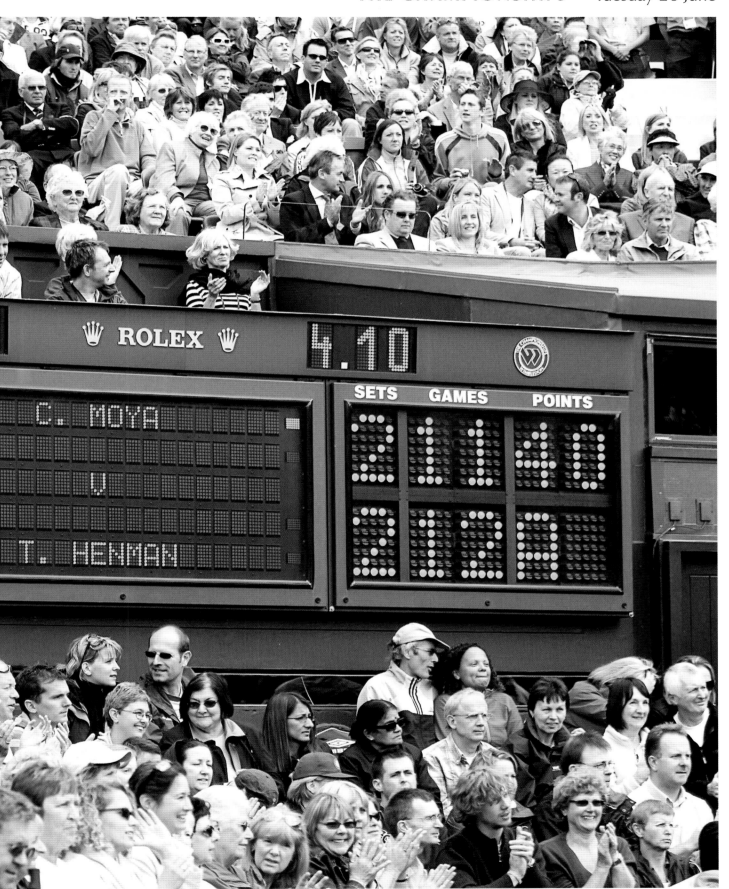

Amelie Mauresmo

Tuesday 26 June…

The image of the day followed the improvised shot of the day performed by a Frenchman, Fabrice Santoro, the greatest improvisor in modern-day tennis. On his second match point at 5-4 in the fifth set against Ivo Karlovic, the tallest man ever to don tennis whites, Santoro nudged a return into play, picked up the Croatian's half volley then flicked the ball over 6'10" of flesh and a couple of inches inside the baseline.

With that, he raced forward, tossing his cap in the air as those teenagers do at American colleges on their graduation day. Santoro remains one of the great entertainers of the modern game, a man who has eschewed convention ever since he came onto the tour with a double-fisted stroke off both flanks, a penchant for doubles (he was the most popular player on the tour to have as a partner, even at the age of 34) and a zest for life.

I recalled that, two years earlier at the Australian Open, he was chatting with a couple of French writers in the media garden when one of them pointed in my direction. Santoro ventured across, shook hands and wondered what could be done to help him in his greatest quest, to play a singles match on Centre Court before he retired. What could one say except that I'd do my best.

Beating Karlovic certainly made him extremely popular with the rest of the players in the draw. One of the worst nightmares at this time of year was the prospect of confronting big Ivo and his impenetrably difficult serve on a greasy grass court, endorsed by the fact that he had won the title at the Nottingham Open the Saturday before The Championships. Getting shot of him this soon was a boon to everyone's chances.

Santoro had won 4-6, 7-6, 7-6, 3-6, 6-4, to set up a second round meeting with Nicolas Kiefer, the German who had just returned to the sport after almost a year's absence with a wrist injury (note to Andy Murray: be careful). And he was not the only French player to be making substantial progress. The country had every reason to be emboldened by its chances in SW19 – for they had the record number of men in the singles, 15, and a further eight in the women's draw. Considering the French Open was played on clay, only 15 per cent of the courts in the country were of that surface, a remarkable statistic.

No wonder, perhaps, the last Frenchman to win at Roland Garros was Yannick Noah, 24 years ago, having spent his formative years playing on clay in Nice, Cote D'Azur. But shift the scene to grass and France has produced a steady stream of high quality players – raised in a vibrant club structure where competition

Fabrice Santoro

and fun are well balanced – who had been able to thrive because they were taught the finest technical fundamentals and so the variables of grass held no fears.

Of the 49 grass court tournaments staged on the two tours since 2001, the French had contested 15 finals – a success ratio of around 30% – winning five titles. At Wimbledon, between 2001 and 2006, 11 French players have reached the quarter-finals, five semi-finals and, of course, Mauresmo topped the bill with her triumph a year ago.

"We are looking at building more clay courts in the south of France because we are aware that we lack a flow of players who feel comfortable on the surface," Patrice Hagelauer, the former LTA director of performance said. "To win on clay you have to develop a great forehand, a lot of top spin and find the angles; we have more players capable of playing well on hard courts, which transfers well to grass."

It is a point taken up by Arnaud Clement, a finalist at the Nottingham Open on Saturday, having reached the semi-finals of the Artois championship eight days earlier. "In France we have players who know how to volley, who are at ease around the net," he said. "It is about having a clean technique because so many balls on grass are played a lot lower than on a clay court where you can win playing one kind of game." Michael Llodra, Clement's compatriot, added: "The whole mentality changes. The Spanish and Argentinians lose one third of their games here because they do not believe in themselves on grass."

Of her 24 titles, Mauresmo had won 12 on hard courts, six on clay, five on hard, and one, the most venerated of them all. Her gladness at returning to the Club as champion and member could not be over-emphasised. "I wrote a great story in 2006 and I come back ➤

33

with a clean white page ready, I hope, to write another great story," Mauresmo, the fourth seed, said. "I was so relaxed last year, I handled it all so well, I was so inspired.

"I feel I am among a group of very privileged people. It is difficult to put into words how I feel about Wimbledon but they show you what a special person you are, something I did not really feel when I won the Australian Open, nor even when I play at the French. The atmosphere here contains so much history and that weighs on you – but not in a bad way – every time you come back. I hope I am ready."

At 1pm precisely, as tradition dictates, we would discover if she was, as Mauresmo made her way onto Centre Court to face Jamea Jackson of the United States. Was it a bit of stage fright when she faced break point in the first game? Mauresmo was not unused to feathery feelings in the tummy. "When I overcame that, I felt I was right into the match," she said. "I was just trying to get into a rhythm." Which she did, safely progressing with a 6-1, 6-3 victory.

Little had been made of Venus Williams' chances this week. The committee had chosen to give her an enhanced seeding of 23, as opposed to the 31st place where she was stationed on the Sony Ericsson WTA Tour. In practice, it was clear that she was striking the ball a lot more cleanly than Serena, her sister. In the first round, she was drawn to face Alla Kudryavtseva, a petite Russian with a big game and very capable of upsetting an apple cart.

And a struggle it was to be for the former champion, as the first set flew past her. "I didn't have any answers," she said later. "My balls were just flying so far and that bothered me because when things go wrong I can figure it out, change my game and adjust. I hadn't played a match for a few weeks, so that could have been a factor." Williams won 2-6, 6-3, 7–5 but, in the second set had trailed 2-0, love-30 and 2-1, 40-15, and twice more the Russian had advantage games on her own serve. It was perilously close.   ➤

QUOTE of the Day

Venus Williams

35

Not as close as the events unfolding on Centre Court where, upon resumption, Tim Henman and Carlos Moya were to indulge in a match that kept the place spellbound. They had left the scene the previous evening locked at 5-5 in the final set in dim light. The sense of reprieve for Henman was evident but still there would be an hour and seven minutes of tennis to play, each moment spent on the edge of one's seat.

This was to be the 33rd five set match of Henman's career and, in the circumstances, one of the most memorable. It encompassed four hours and 11 minutes in total, the twists, turns, peaks, troughs, dazzling lights and shafts of fear that have accompanied Henman through 14 summers in SW19 and that ought to have left an odd line on his face and grey hair on his head.

The stoicism with which Henman has greeted the results of these marathons, good and bad alike, made the rejoicing at his 6-3, 1-6, 5-7, 6-2, 13-11 victory all the more agreeable because imagine had he lost, what a crushing blow to his morale that would have been. "I stuck to my guns and played some great points," he said. "There hasn't been much to get my teeth stuck into this year, but this place is special to me, I always expect good things to happen." ➤

Lucy Henman

There were plenty of spaces vacated in the draw by the rest of the British contingent. It was to become the worst day of participation in The Championships for 17 years, with only Henman's victory and that of Katie O'Brien, as she defeated Sandra Kloesel of Germany in straight sets, preventing a complete cull.

These were difficult days for the LTA and their much-vaunted assembly of many of the top names in the coaching stratosphere. Josh Goodall, Alex Bogdanovic, Jonny Marray, Richard Bloomfield, Jamie Baker and Lee Childs (who successfully qualified) did not win a set between them; Anne Keothavong had the desperate misfortune to have drawn Jelena Jankovic, the No.3 seed from Serbia; Melanie South did not fare much better with the experienced Ai Sugiyama of Japan and Elena Baltacha had the credit of taking a set from Katerina Srebotnik, from Slovakia, the No.19 seed. But it was a pretty inferior report card.

Day **THREE**
27.06.2007

GOLOVIN
vs
HSEIH

S. WILLIAMS
vs
MOLIK

VERDASCO
vs
SEPPI

TIPSAREVIC
vs
SERRA

IVANOVIC
vs
GAJDOSOVA

YAN
vs
GARBIN

Tatiana Golovin

Serena Williams

Wednesday June 27...

Sir, the recent flooding should not be blamed on global warming – it is because of an unfortunate confluence of Glastonbury and Wimbledon, those well known storm-bringers.

A letter to *The Times* summed up the general mood around the first two days of The Championships, as the dark clouds refused to budge, the rain came and went intermittently, where pac-a-macs and umbrellas prevailed and most of the people who had tickets required a humour transplant. And what did Wimbledon have up its sleeve to stir the pulses? Knickers, that's what. And red knickers to boot.

Tatiana Golovin, of France, defeated Su-Wei Hseih, a qualifier from Taipei, 5-7, 6-3, 8-6, a match of considerable fascination on Court No.14, the court from which it is possible to view all the proceedings from the press restaurant. There was plenty of spilled HP sauce that morning, I can tell you.

The first seven questions after the victory of the 17th seed had nothing to do with the fighting qualities of her tennis, that she had been inspired to produce one of the most defiant performances of her Grand Slam career to win a first round match, but about – you've guessed it – her attire. First question: Can I ask you about your knickers? Third question (well not so much a question as a statement): But the dress code is white and the knickers are red. Sixth question: They were lovely, can I have a pair and are you going to keep on wearing them? Eighth question: How about the match then?

Golovin is an attractive girl as well as a pretty fine player. She had not played for six weeks through injury and when she returned – wowee, she made a statement. "I'm happy with my red knickers," she insisted. "They say red is the colour that proves you are strong and confident" Unfortunately, in the next round, she was to lose quite easily to a 16 year old from Austria, so it was *au revoir* a little too soon for the tabloids' liking.

But there were plenty of other amusements

for them to consider, not least Serena Williams' 7-6, 6-3 victory over Australia's Alicia Molik on Court No.1, and whether or not, midway through the first set and trailing 4-1, 15-30, she had pulled one of her earrings off or it had fallen out. "Ordinarily," wrote Martin Johnson in *The Telegraph* "you'd have to think that this wouldn't make a whole lot of difference, but if you combine Serena's size with the pair of earrings that appeared to her Australian opponent to have been hewn from Ayers Rock, merely putting them on must have required a gang of workmen and more scaffolding than they'll need for the Centre Court roof."   ➤

Richard Williams

There was contention, too, on the final point of the match. A call of out on a sideline, that secured Serena's success, was seen by the chair umpire, Sandra De Jenken, but the players didn't realise and the point continued for three strokes before play was halted. As the two players, having shaken hands, approached the chair, the umpire asked Molik if she would like to challenge the call and, in the circumstances, who would refuse such an offer? The technology confirmed the validity of the original call, game, set and match, but Richard Williams, Serena's father, was not best pleased and stormed into the referee's office asking for an explanation.

QUOTE of the Day

ANDY RODDICK COMMENTING ON THE FACT
THAT GORDON BROWN HAD REPLACED TONY
BLAIR AS BRITISH PRIME MINISTER:

*"The funniest thing I saw was they
televised the moving van pulling up,
and they followed it down the street.
That's hilarious. We need to get a
moving van in the States somewhere.
I'd be on the verge of ignorance if I
was to talk about the political views of
Gordon Brown, but I'm a big fan of
televising the moving van."*

It was one of those days to stroll the outside courts, to sniff the breeze and discover what made Wimbledon so different from the other Grand Slams, indeed than any other event anywhere in the world. Alongside Court No.5, on a park bench, sat Manuel Santana, the last Spaniard to win the men's title, in 1966, who had been asked if he would help Fernando Verdasco, the left hander from Madrid, with his grass court strategy.

Here was Verdasco defeating Andreas Seppi, of Italy, no mean opponent, 6-3, 6-2, 6-4 and a delighted Santana revelled in his situation. Spanish players had characteristically given a wide berth to grass, much to the former champion's chagrin. After all, he had been the man who had begun the country's tennis revolution when Spain had come to a standstill acknowledging his success in that summer that we English tend to remember for another sporting triumph in London. Even General Franco, who had regarded tennis a louche sport and the plaything of imperalists, came around to recognise its virtues once Santana prevailed. ➤

45

Janko Tipsarevic and
his Dostoevsky tattoo

Just as fascinating a character was a couple of courts around the corner – Janko Tipsarevic, the leader of the Serbian pack, or at very least the one who had been around the longest of the current crop, though he was still only 23. *The Sun* had already nicknamed him Tipsy, though it had nothing whatsoever to do with alcohol. There are several tattoos on his body and one of those on his arm is a quotation from Dostoevsky, 'Beauty will save the world' in Japanese. He is a voracious reader who also revelled in Nietsche and Goethe. Which made him something of an anomaly in tennis playing terms.

He remembered when tennis in Serbia had been 'born from mud.' The Federation had nothing, they were unable to fund him and it

was only through the love of his parents and the fact that Pavel, his father and a professor, paid for his lessons, clothing and travel, that Tipsarevic was able to tread the professional boards. 'Tipsy' did not stop repeating to anyone who would listen how grateful he was for his parents' support and generosity.

He won his first round match in five sets against Florent Serra, of France, on a day which was to prove another memorable one for his country. Ana Ivanovic, the 19-year-old French Open finalist, Jelena Jankovic, who reached the semi-finals in Paris and had risen to a career high No.3, and Novak Djokovic, who also made the last four at Roland Garros, had been feted, in the meantime, by 15,000 people who crowded around the parliament building in the capital, Belgrade. These athletes were becoming huge in their home country, which usually feted its volleyball or baskeball players with such fanfare.

Ana Ivanovic

Below: Jelena Jankovic serving
to Jarmila Gajdosova

Novak Djokovic

Below: Jelena Jankovic serving
to Jarmila Gajdosova

The Serbians clearly loved every minute of
what they did, which made them rare in
another way. Jankovic, especially, gave a
whole new meaning to that famous line from
Bridge on the River Kwai – 'be happy in your
work.' This girl never stopped smiling. A 6-1,
6-1 victory in the first round against Jarmila
Gajdosova, of Slovakia, was cause enough for
hilarity and it was wonderful to see that, in
the stands, her mother, Snezana, was just as
joyous as her daughter.

Jelena Jankovic

"If you make a big circus about losing, you'll be crazy in a few months," Snezana said as she watched proudly on. "I don't want to make any pressure for her. But she always gives credit to her opponents. Mrs Jankovic also had strong views on how a player ought to deport herself. The fist pump is fine, but never to be directed at the opponent. "I hate that," she said. "So intimidating." And if Jelena chooses to throw her racket? "I say to her 'look, you are breaking rackets. Do you know how many other people have no racket at all'.

"I see a lot of players and they might have won their match, they might be very successful but they are not happy. And I ask: Why? The answer is: the family. You give me bread and happiness and I would have that ahead of champagne and caviar. I like small things. I like to see my daughter smile."

Smiles were evident on the concourse outside the referee's office as Wang Jijun and Ye Xin were introduced to the public. They were two ballkids chosen from the 2,000 from Shanghai, hosts of the Masters Cup, who were flown to Wimbledon in an ambassadorial role to help promote Chinese tennis around the world. A year ago, there were six Chinese women in the top 100 but that number had been halved. The highest ranked Chinese male on the tour, Yu Xinyuan, is No.529. And the day saw the end of China's involvement in this year's championships when Zi Yan, a qualifier, lost 3-6, 6-2, 6-3 to Tathiana Garbin of Italy. Much had been done, much more needed to be done. Where had we heard that one before? ●

Thursday June 28…

It was a tale of borrowed shirts, Booty, O'Brien and a heavy dose of the first Thursday Blues. The day was properly defined by the headline 'Tim Turns Off The Lights' whose tone was self explanatory. The Blues were those felt across the British tennis board as Tim Henman lost in five sets to Feliciano Lopez, of Spain, and Katie O'Brien won only a single game from Holland's Michaella Krajicek.

Borrowed shirts – well that was the story of Werner Eschauer of Austria and Booty, that is Eric Butorac, the American doubles player, of which more later.

Any Henman loss at Wimbledon had become the fulcrum for soul-searching across the land and, now he had reached his 32nd year, they were followed by the inevitable examinations of whether he would – or indeed should – put himself through the tribulations again. Having gone through the mill against Carlos Moya, in the first round, it was hardly unexpected that Henman would find the second test altogether less pleasant. ➤

Tim Henman leaves Wimbledon having been beaten by Feliciano Lopez (below)

James Blake

54

Katie O'Brien

1.01 Court No 3

PREVIOUS SETS			PLAYER	SETS	GAMES
6	6		Miss M.KRAJICEK	2	
0	1		Miss K.O'BRIEN	0	

Curioser and curioser the match became – the final score of 7-6, 7-6, 3-6, 2-6, 6-1 in favour of Rafael Nadal's lodger underscoring how Lopez, who went off for a toilet break before thundering through the decider (amazing what a whiff of Wimbledon's air freshener can do!) had always threatened to hold the decisive upper hand. The only point Henman took off his serve in the final set was a double fault.

Henman, indeed, had waited until he was a break down in the third set before finding his stride. And at 0-2 there was only despair in the air. So he reeled off the next five games and 11 of the next 14. But the final set, oh it was ever so redolent of recent Henmans – the flubbed volley into the net with the court gaping, the killer forehand that takes wing and flies away, the caught-in-two-minds poke and, worst of all, and the most painful shot in the entire repertoire, the suicide 'leave' – the dramatic withdrawal of the racket that permits the ball to clip the line behind or to either side of him.

Simon Barnes in *The Times* observed: "It has been an exciting week then, one way or another, for us and for Henman. And guess

what he was talking about after the match. You've got it, he's staying positive. He's taking a lot of positives from his two matches at Wimbledon this year. Has he ever taken anything else? 'Tim, do you expect to be here next year?' 'Absolutely.'..... Oh God".

Over at the *Daily Mail*, Mike Dickson wrote: "He (Henman) assures you that he will be back next year and, by then, Andy Murray will have recovered and his exploits will provide some cover for what is the true state of British tennis – all fur coat and no knickers."

It prompted the usual pleas to James Blake, the No.8 seed from America, whose mother, Betty, was raised in Banbury, Oxfordshire, to consider strengthening ties with the British but as he had already represented the United States in Davis Cup (as well as attending and distinguishing himself at Harvard University), it was bound to fall on dear ears. "I like the fact that I do have some kinship with this country," Blake said after his 6-4, 6-3, 6-3 defeat of Andrei Pavel, of Romania, settled a third round place which equalled, surprisingly, his best Wimbledon performance. ➢

"It's unbelieveable to see my Mum over here, how much she appreciates it, how her accent comes back, how she remembers times when she was young. I've been to see the house where she grew up, it just makes all the stories she tells and everything about her become so much more real. I really do cherish that." But that was as far as it went.

Meanwhile, the navel-contemplation had set in over at the LTA's new National Tennis Centre at Roehampton. A few of the doubles teams were intact but in singles, where it really mattered, that was it for another year. Henman railed against those players who had generated mediocrity for too long and ought to be working hard towards securing their place in future championships through their ranking, rather than hanging around for a wild card.

Katie O'Brien, from Yorkshire, had been kept waiting four days longer than the other four British recipients of wild cards into the ladies' draw – quite why was not explained. If it was hoped to have the effect of steeling her resolve, then it worked in that O'Brien was the lone woman to emerge into the second round, a window of opportunity that was to be slammed shut by Michaella Krajicek, half sister of Richard, the 1996 men's champion.

O'Brien double faulted in each one of her service games which did not help her cause. She also seemed to be trapped into a baseline routine, even when she had opened up the court and might have moved forward to impose herself on the 32nd seed. It was evident that she would have benefited from more committed coaching help, though she said she had been told she would not receive one-to-help help until she reached No.75 in the world. Was that not the wrong way around?

All the coaching in the world cannot help if you have not got the proper kit to play in. When Werner Eschauer was called to Centre Court to play Nadal late in the afternoon, he was lacking in one or two important essentials. This is a man who had slept under bridges at tournaments when he was younger because he could not afford a hotel room – the LTA now provided very nice accomodation at its NTC for anyone in similar straits in the British game. Drawing on the strength of character instilled during impoverished times, Eschauer had risen 300 spots in two years to his current ranking of No.72 – something he was at a loss to explain.

In 2007, to date, he had made more than a fifth of his career earnings of £250,000. Spread that over 12 years, plus travel and equipment costs and here was a man who played the game for love rather than money.

Fortunately, Pavel was on hand to lend Eschauer a white shirt because he did not have one – it would have got terribly sweaty had he

extended the match to five sets, but he lost 6-2, 6-4, 6-1, so it didn't pose a problem – and Florian Mayer, of Germany, provided him with the properly-pimpled grass court shoes (albeit with traces of clay splattered on them).

Eschauer actually broke serve first but a man with no coach, no physical trainer, and not a Euro in support from the Austrian Federation was hardly likely to keep up that level of dominance. He actually traded games in the second set until Nadal broke at 3-3 and then Eschauer decided not to sit down at changeovers, fearing his legs might lock altogether. He handed back his loaned clothes and headed for the next stop on the tour.

The highest seed in the men's side to fall, Spain's Tommy Robredo, lost to Wayne Arthurs, the veteran Australian, in straight sets but there was consolation to be found across the capital, at Wembley. Robredo had been named Tommy because his father, Angel, was a fervent fan of The Who, whose musical *Tommy* was his favourite. Made sense.

And who was in town that night, but The Who. A frantic car/Underground/sprint journey from Wimbledon made certain that Robredo and son made it to the sell-out concert with a few minutes to spare. Much of the hurt of defeat had been assuaged by the end of the night. ➤

Rafael Nadal

Venus Williams

Maria Sharapova

QUOTE of the Day

MARAT SAFIN, THE RUSSIAN, WHO RAILED AGAINST PRICES IN THE WIMBLEDON PLAYERS' RESTAURANT, FOUND SOME THINGS TO HIS LIKING:

"There are great facilities on the inside. I like the garden upstairs, the restaurant, plenty of space, pretty comfortable. You can go to Aorangi (the practice courts) through a tunnel, great locker rooms, great showers. No, showers are really important – if you see them, you understand what I'm talking about."

Akiko Morigami

It was the end of the road for red knickers as Tatiana Golovin, of France, lost in three sets to Tamara Paszek, an Austrian who was coached by Larri Passos, who helped Brazil's Gustavo Kuerten to three French Open titles and had tried to get him to believe that he could master the grass. Paszek's father had written to Passos pleading with him to come and take a look at his daughter when she was 14; Passos flew to Austria, watched her hit for 15 minutes and was smitten. She was definitely a player to keep an eye on. It was the last sight, too, of Bethanie Mattek, the American who had worn knee-length socks and very short shorts the previous year and set the fashionistas tongues wagging. She was out, in straight sets, to Svetlana Kuznetsova of Russia.

The rest was pretty much straightforward as usual in the second round of a Grand Slam

where the leading lady players were concerned, Maria Sharapova, Venus Williams, Amelie Mauresmo, Nadia Petrova and Ana Ivanovic all winning in straight sets (for the loss of 21 games between them). The most unexpected defeat was that of Dinara Safina, the No.13 seed to Akiko Morigami, of Japan, 6-4, 7-5.

The doubles competitions were starting to hit their stride and much focus was on the partnership of Butorac, the effervescent American and Jamie Murray, elder brother of Andy. The pair had won three titles in 2007, including the recent Nottingham Open and their 6-3, 6-3, 6-3 victory over Spain's Oscar Hernandez and Italian, Potito Starace, though a gentle introduction to the Grand Slam routine, illustrated the sharpening of their undoubted promise. ●

Day **FIVE**
29.06.2007

FEDERER
VS
SAFIN

TIPSAREVIC
VS
GONZALEZ

S. WILLIAMS
VS
SEQUERA

RODDICK
VS
VERDASCO

FERRERO
VS
BLAKE

HINGIS
VS
GRANVILLE

SCHNYDER
VS
BONDARENKO

BARTOLI
VS
PEER

Martina Hingis versus Laura Granville

Roger Federer

Friday 29 June…

Another intermittently cloudy day and the mind was beginning to wander. The Tim Henman two round, three day story apart, nothing much else had grabbed the first week of The Championships by the lapels and given it a shake. A telephone call to Jim Courier, the former world No.1, whose last match on grass was the 1999 fourth round giant against Henman – a five set match of indelible brilliance – made one sit up and think a bit.

The conversation came around to the best male grass court player of all time – if seven Wimbledon titles swung the vote – and whether or not we would ever see Pete Sampras on the courts of SW19 again. The circumstances of his 2002 defeat to Switzerland's George Bastl on Court No.2 continued to eat away at him, even five years on. Courier and Sampras had re-established their friendship playing on the Outback Champions Series, for which Courier was co-founder and having Sampras back in competitive harness was a real coup.

"He's playing with the new string technology which is more forgiving, he is at his playing weight, he's been playing for about a year and he's very competitive," Courier said. "For a start, on grass, who would get his serve back? I'm not talking about a return to the tour proper, because the energy and commitment that entails is what drove Pete away in the first place. But a one-off tournament, on grass? Well, let's not write it off."

Those thoughts reverberated as one watched Roger Federer play Marat Safin on Centre Court. Federer had knocked on Sampras' door in Beverly Hills earlier this year and had a hit with the man whom he had beaten in their only professional meeting, in the fourth round of Wimbledon in 2001, an unforgettable experience for both men. The Swiss pronounced himself awestruck at the American's game and power.

This Championship Federer had won his first two matches with reasonable ease and this, surely, would be the kind of significant test we all wanted to see. But Safin, as ever, maintained a double-edged persona. Andy Fyfe, the Mr Fixit for players like Boris Becker and Goran Ivanisevic in his time, was now looking after Safin and said he had never seen him so relaxed. But, as Stephen Bierley pointed out in *The Guardian*: "Since 2000, when he defeated Sampras in the US Open final, the threads of clarity in his mind have constantly been shredded by storms of doubt and sundry other disturbances. He has all the qualities for a permanent place inside the top ten, but currently maunders outside the top 20."

It was not until 6.35 pm that the two men came onto court – a five set match of utter commitment between Janko Tipsarevic and Fernando Gonzalez, the No.5 seed that the former had won 8-6 in the fifth was followed by a blissfully fast women's singles, with Serena Williams losing but a game to Milagros Sequera, of Venezuela. By now, the best sunshine of the day bathed the stadium in light and Federer's response was to play twinkle-toed tennis and win the first set in 19 minutes.

Safin was in one his moods, twice catapulting his racket into the turf and often looking at it as if he might do it a few more times. He stared at a couple of other times but restrained himself. What he could not do was restrain his opponent who, though Safin broke first in the second set to suggest he might really make a match of it, gathered himself again. Though he required a tie-break in the third set, it was Federer's afternoon 6-1, 6-4, 7-6.

Across on No.1 Court, Andy Roddick was in similarly no-frills mode against Fernando Verdasco, a Spaniard who had taken the American to five distinctive sets in the third round of the previous year's US Open. Like ➤

Serena Williams

Andy Roddick

Jimmy Connors

Federer, Roddick was to win in straight sets but it was something about the manner of his persona on court, and the way he responded to his 6-3, 6-4, 7-6 victory, pounding his chest, exhorting Jimmy Connors, his coach in the players' box, and mouthing a message which went along the lines of 'that was a brave win, young man', meant that you sensed something was really happening for the man from Nebraska.

Perhaps it had something to do with the fact that he had recovered from 5-2 down and saved three set points at 5-3 in the third set that made Roddick's gesturing all the more profound. Perhaps it was because the effort of getting to the staging post of the second week of The Championships – "it makes tomorrow (Saturday) a lot less stressful, it's a bit of a relief," he said. "I'm playing well enough to go in there and fight without worrying how I'm hitting the ball. When you can do that, it's fun."

James Blake

Roddick was the lone American left in the men's draw for James Blake made his annual rather-too-early exit with a four set defeat to Juan Carlos Ferrero, one of the few Spaniards to have considered that playing Wimbledon was important to have on one's C.V. The thought occured watching it that even when Ferrero became the No.1 player in the world, when he had won the French Open, when he reached the final of the US Open, it was unlikely that he had ever served with more consistent depth and bite.

Blake recalled that the only time Ferrero made errors was usually when he was either 40-0, or 0-40 and that it did not much matter because he responded on the very next point. "This guy has won Grand Slams, he's been the best, he raised his game, I tried to weather the storm but he kept pushing," was Blake's analysis and it was not far wrong. "A lot today had to do with how well the other guy played.

But it definitely stings."

As did the 6-4, 6-2 defeat of Martina Hingis, the former champion, to Laura Granville of the United States. Eighteen months on from her vaunted comeback to the competitive tennis world, nothing had really clicked for Hingis the way she would have wanted. Initially, it was something of a breeze, then it occured to the now 26-year-old how hard she had needed to work to restore herself to somewhere near the level she first achieved as a carefree teenager.

It was when Hingis' feet began to hurt her so much that she stopped playing tennis in the first place and now her hips were creaking a bit. It was an injury that had caused her to sidestep (if that's the right word) the French

65

Juan Carlos Ferrero

Anna Wintour, Editor of American Vogue

Open and now she suspected she had been a tad too optimistic in thinking she could last at Wimbledon. There were sure signs that Hingis was slower in stroke preparation and the subsequent lack of weight of shot left her vulnerable to attack, something Granville managed with relish.

The first time they had faced each other, Granville was new to the professional ranks. It

Martina Hingis

was the first round of the US Open and someone recalled there were eight people in the stands. "Yeah and I made eight shots in the court," the 26-year-old from Chicago jested. She recalled, too, having beaten Mary Pierce at The Championships in 2002 when, on her first visit to London, she had reached the fourth round. "It was all so new to me then," she recalled, "so this one means so much more."

Granville railed at suggestions that Hingis may have been a little bit off her game – it does not do to raise the thought in a victor's mind that the player they had just defeated was in any way sub-standard. "But I haven't been able to run that much," Hingis reported, "workouts are just spent on the bike and I used to run a couple of hours a day. When you can't do that, there's cardio-vascular work that needs to be done but I haven't been able to do that yet. During the tournament I didn't want to know how bad I was. I'll get everything checked out when I get home."

For Patty Schnyder, her fellow Swiss, though, this was becoming a Wimbledon to savour.

Jelena
Jankovic

Laura
Granville

MATCH of the Day

Jelena Jankovic (Ser) beat Lucie Safarova (Cz)
5-7, 7-6, 6-2.

A match that see-sawed mightily but never lost any of its intensity, it was the classic left v. right hander but it was the manner of so many of the rallies, the consistency of the ball-striking, the relentless effort that kept the crowd enthralled. The fact that the rains interrupted the play only served to heighten the drama. There had not been a match in the ladies' draw to better it thus far.

"I was feeling heavy in my legs and not moving well," Jankovic said later, but you could have fooled the No.1 Court crowd. "If you are half a step late with your shots, you give her the chance to play the points the way she wants to play them. I just managed to find a way." We had to wait until midway through the third set for the famed Jankovic smile to make its debut. Safarova, girlfriend of the Czech player, Tomas Berdych, had given her all.

Marion Bartoli

Patty Schnyder

The 28-year-old left hander had only been to the third round once in 11 previous visits and with her 6-4, 3-6, 8-6 win over Alona Bondarenko, the No.24 seed from the Ukraine, was into the last 16 – new ground. Schnyder was also in the process of writing a book *The White Mile* which had, on its cover, Schnyder, in tennis gear, standing next to a dilapidated house that backs on to a crop field. She is in colour, the house and field are in black and white. Considering she is married to Rainer Hoffmann, the man who was a private investigator once hired by her parents to snoop into the background of another of her former gurus, it has the makings of a bit of a best-seller.

"We have had tough times," Schnyder said, "but there is also the funny side of the tour. It is going to take us through all the faces of tennis. We have been involved in some things that are not nice, indeed they are pretty scary." As was the thought that her upcoming opponent was Justine Henin, the No.1 player in the world.

There was another woman's result that came onto the radar and made one stop and think. A French girl called Marion Bartoli – who thwacked the ball with two hands on both flanks – defeated Shahar Peer, of Israel, 6-3, 6-2. Peer was well regarded as one of the strongest-willed players on the tour and so to have been beaten that handily struck one as a intriguing outcome. Perhaps there was more to come from Miss Bartoli.

●

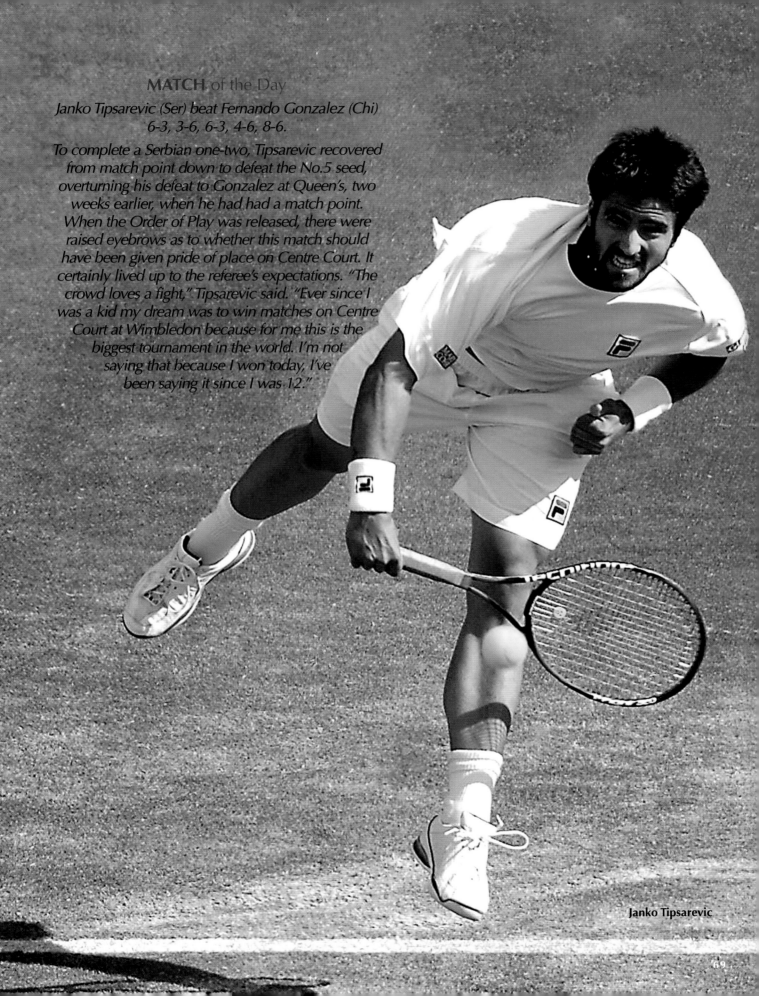

MATCH of the Day

Janko Tipsarevic (Ser) beat Fernando Gonzalez (Chi)
6-3, 3-6, 6-3, 4-6, 8-6.

To complete a Serbian one-two, Tipsarevic recovered
from match point down to defeat the No.5 seed,
overturning his defeat to Gonzalez at Queen's, two
weeks earlier, when he had had a match point.
When the Order of Play was released, there were
raised eyebrows as to whether this match should
have been given pride of place on Centre Court. It
certainly lived up to the referee's expectations. "The
crowd loves a fight," Tipsarevic said. "Ever since I
was a kid my dream was to win matches on Centre
Court at Wimbledon because for me this is the
biggest tournament in the world. I'm not
saying that because I won today, I've
been saying it since I was 12."

Janko Tipsarevic

Day **SIX**
30.06.2007

SHARAPOVA
VS
SUGIYAMA

MAURESMO
VS
SANTANGELO

V. WILLIAMS
VS
MORIGAMI

Maria Sharapova

Saturday 30 June…

There was one word for it. Deplorable. The weather, that is. This was supposed to be the day where Wimbledon set out its stall to the rest of the sporting world and what did it have to show? A £1 million loss, that's what. Only 57 minutes of play was possible on Centre Court and 75 minutes on No.1 Court which meant the Club was liable for a hefty refund under its own rules and regulations.

It was one of those days when you just wanted to head for the hills – and not the one named for Tim Henman. Announcements came and went, people came and went, players came and went, a sunny interval was spotted for a few minutes but that had come and gone before most people noticed it in the first place. It was unutterably miserable.

Ai Sugiyama

The Royal Box was replete with some of the great and good of world sport but there was not even time to announce them to the public, for fear it would just start raining again and ruin the whole shebang. One of the English national papers reproduced a picture of the box at one moment when it was full and it is a long time since so many miserable faces were captured in one place at one time at a sporting venue. Sir Clive Lloyd and Brian Lara, the West Indian cricketers, looked coldest of all.

Two matches were completed – success and high spirits all round for Maria Sharapova and Amelie Mauresmo. They were the fortunate ones. Though there was a tempestuous end to the match between Sharapova and Ai Sugiyama, a Japanese whose face is normally wreathed in smiles but did not have much to find joy in on this occasion.

In the latter stages on No.1 Court, the rain had began to fall steadily again and Lynn Welch, the umpire, decided after an impromptu rubbing of the palm of her hand across the grass that it was safe to continue. Sharapova had just enough of an opportunity to confirm her 6-3, 6-3 victory, though Sugiyama was decidedly unchuffed. "I complained to her at the end because it was very wet," Sugiyama said. "The last two games were slippery." Even Sharapova said she was 'agitated.'

Mauresmo was equally impressive defeating Mara Santangelo, of Italy, for the loss of three games, despatching 11 aces, winning 81 per cent of the points when her first serve was good (exactly the same as Sharapova's average incidentally) and making only nine unforced errors. These were the kind of statistics that indicated a defending champion getting into the groove at just the right time. ➤

Amelie Mauresmo

But that was it. There were seven uncompleted ladies' third round matches – there was one potential upset on the cards as Venus Williams, who had won the first set against Japan's Akiko Morigami trailed 4-1 in the second – only one men's match actually got started and a few doubles encounters had begun. And so one was forced either to look back, or throw The Championship forward. One man who was being pursued across the lawns for a quote or two was Tommy Haas, the German No.13 who had bagged the scalp

on Friday evening of Dmitry Tursunov, the Russian with the dynamite serve and hell-for-leather game.

Haas was next up to play Roger Federer, a fourth round encounter to whet (don't mention that word!) anyone's appetite. "I've had some good battles with Roger in the past and my game is in good shape at the moment," he said. "There's a lot of talk about Roger and Rafael Nadal, which is right, but people who know the sport realise there are more than just two personalities in men's

Mara Santangelo

tennis. I'm still working hard."

But Haas had never been Wimbledon's luckiest competitor and, on the way home on Friday night, he began to feel that something was not quite right with the way his stomach was aching. So much agony was Haas in later that night – as Federer, his family and closest friends, including Yves Allegro, his doubles partner, were treated to a slap up meal in the Member's Enclosure – that he decided to call Dr Erich Rembeck, his personal physician.

Poor Haas, he had had wretched luck ➤

Miss A.MORIGAMI

Miss V.WILLIAMS[23]

Venus Williams

through his career but at this event, where he won on his only previous Centre Court date, against Andre Agassi eight years ago, the 29-year-old had been especially plagued. In June 2002 – a month after reaching a career high No.2 in the world – his parents, Peter and Brigitte, were involved in a motorcycle accident in Sarasota, Florida, which left Peter in a coma for three weeks. Haas had to miss the event. Two years ago, in the warm up to his match against Janko Tipsarevic, of Serbia, he stood on a ball that was being rolled to one of the ball-boys, twisted his ankle and had to forfeit.

Now, he had to step aside again. "I have a pretty severe tear, there has been some serious bleeding," he said. "I didn't know if I was going to be ready to play Wimbledon this year, then they knocked me three spots down the seedings to 13, which I regard as my lucky number, I reached the fourth round for the first time in nine tries and then this happens. Who knows if this opportunity will come again but maybe there will be a happy ending sometime." Federer was granted a walk-over into the quarter-finals.   ➤

Rain doesn't stop an improvised game of cricket

Andrew Jarrett

The withdrawal of Haas prompted yet another re-design of the Order of Play which already comprised 100 matches scheduled for Monday. "We are a long way from desperation," Andrew Jarrett, the referee, said. "The forecast for Monday and Tuesday is not wonderful but we cannot look too far ahead. Of course, there are contingencies for a third week, but they were in place in January."

When Jarrett talked of 'mopping up' the rest of the men's and women's third round matches as a priority, he saw the amusing side of the comment. "We would like to complete those matches and the top half of the ladies' round of 16s tomorrow," he said. "On Tuesday, we'd like to play the bottom half of the ladies' 16s, the entire men's fourth round and the ladies' top half quarter-finals. We would be pretty much back on track then." ●

Day **SEVEN**
2.07.2007

NADAL
VS
SODERLING

S. WILLIAMS
VS
HANTUCHOVA

HENIN
VS
SCHNYDER

BJORKMAN
VS
ARTHURS

NALBANDIAN
VS
BAGHDATIS

Serena Williams

Monday July 2…

If Wimbledon's schedule was in a bit of a chaotic state, it was nothing compared to the centre of London, where a remarkably vigilant ambulance crew had spotted a van that was parked where they thought it should not have been parked, alerted the police and almost certainly averted another catastrophic attack on the city. Security was, therefore, being stepped up, concrete barriers were placed across all the entrances to the All England Club where cars could be used as battering rams. Sections of the concrete were painted Holly Bush green (colour code 6005), the same with which all of the club's masonry and courtside furniture is covered – a nice touch.

Simon Barnes in *The Times* wrote: "The fans came in their umbrella-clutching thousands, defying the rain, defying the terrorists, as if it was the only possible thing to do. It was all rather admirable really, this not giving in. And we did get occasional outbreaks of tennis, coming at us like cliffhanger instalments of *EastEnders*, only classy."

Cliffhangers there were, everywhere. Rafael Nadal, the No.2 seed from Spain, was playing Robin Soderling, of Sweden, on No.1 Court, a match that should have begun on Saturday, the story of which was to be continued, and continued, and continued and of which more, much more, follows later.

But the day's drama was encapsulated in one occasion, when Serena Williams and Daniela Hantuchova collided in a Centre Court clash that contained just about everything you would wish for – and it finished within a day's play which made it a bit of a novelty. Williams won 6-2, 6-7, 6-2, though the scoreline barely scratched the surface of the intrigue that surrounded it.

Justine Henin had sent Patty Schnyder into an extended period of penmanship – the Swiss was writing a book (see Friday, June 29) – with a quick-fire 6-2, 6-2 victory that cleared the path for a seventh meeting between Williams and the 24-year-old from Slovakia who had won just one of the previous six, in the third round of the 2006 Australian Open. The opening set was plagued by delays, rhythm was hard to come by, the continual dashes from warm locker room to cold court was playing havoc with the senses and the muscles.

Hantuchova was doggedly defiant, refusing to bow after the first set and leading the second 4-1, playing tennis of great fortitude. It was then that the power and the noise began to be turned up by Williams, who took on the guise of bully and recovered to 5-5. The next game was to be the most pivotal, when Williams, leaping across the baseline in front of the Royal Box, came to a sudden stop, whacked a bulging left calf with her racket and promptly fell to the turf. The bully had been stopped in her tracks.

And so what was the problem? On came the trainer and it took four minutes to diagnose what many of us courtside knew straightaway, she was having trouble with her left calf. A further three minute medical 'time-out' followed, during which her calf was the subject of much manipulation and concern. Retirement looked a distinct possibility but Williams could move about a bit and decided to hang around and see how the match progressed. At the following changeover, the leg was strapped and Williams managed to hobble to a tie-break, in which she trailed 4-0 and was 4-2 adrift when

another shower arrived.

The pair returned, Hantuchova saw the tie-break through and seemed likely to press home her advantage against a disadvantaged opponent. The drop shot was an excellent tactic but it had the effect of hardening William's resolve. "That set if off for me," Serena said after she had stumbled in vain to ➤

Daniela Hantuchova

Jonas Bjorkman

reach one such Hantuchova effort. "I thought 'I'm going to do this or die trying.' I don't know why it got me so upset but there was no way I was going to go down today."

And so Williams, despite the grimaces, wails, grunts and gnashes of teeth, would not

be beaten and, drawing on some scribbled notes for inspiration – You are the best; You are the No.1; You will win Wimbledon – elbowed her way into the last 16. Hantuchova could only harrumph later that; "in the third set I don't think there was anything wrong with her at all. She was moving very well. There cannot be too much wrong when you serve at 120 miles per hour."

And sister, Venus, was not having it all her own way. Venus, remember, had left her match against Akiko Morigami, of Japan, in the drizzle of Saturday with the first set pocketed but trailing 4-1 in the second. Morigami was another of those who played off both wings with a double handed shot, which often afforded her a disguise with which Williams found it difficult to contend. She soon seized the second set, turning Venus inside out at times and led 5-3 in the third and a real surprise was on the cards.

There were 14 doubles faults and 42

Boris Becker

unforced errors from Venus, which helped Morigami to 23 break point chances. And chances rarely come as often as that against a Grand Slam champion. But that the Japanese converted only four, spoke to the fighting spirit of the American. When her ground-strokes were firing, they *fired*, as she showed at game point to break Morigami to love and pull back to 4-5 in the deciding set. And when she hit her athletic stride, Venus was pure class, as demonstrated in the running passing shot to move 6-5 ahead, the decisive advantage.

"It's definitely invigorating to win a match like that," she said. "This is a good surface for her because she hits the ball so flat and low, she had beaten (Dinara) Safina in the previous round and that's a real good win. When I was 3-5 down, I had to correct myself quickly, there was no time to waste. Personally, I'm not thinking about losing at this point."

Wayne Arthurs, the oldest man in the men's tournament, had contemplated that from the moment he entered the Roehampton qualifying – a competition every bit as competitive as the main event. In the final round the 36-year-old from Adelaide had come from two sets to one ➤

QUOTE of the Day

"A stage was set in the last couple of games. A big cloud sort of ascended over the court and it was all dark. It felt like the end of my career coming over the top of my head. There was a 'Well Done Wayne' on a white board when I came back into the locker room. Neville Fowler, who looks after all the towels here, he's an Aussie, he'd written it. So that was nice."

WAYNE ARTHURS, OF AUSTRALIA, WHO RETIRED AT THE AGE OF 36 HAVING NEVER BEEN BEYOND THE FOURTH ROUND OF ANY GRAND SLAM TOURNAMENT

Wayne Arthurs

Marcos Baghdatis

Arsene Wenger, Arsenal manager

down to defeat Belgium's Christophe Rochus and become one of only five non-seeds among the 16 men advancing.

Against Thiemo de Bakker, the former Wimbledon boys champion from Holland, who had been granted a wild card into the main draw, he was two sets to love down and won by what was a typical Arthurs score, 6-7, 6-7, 7-6, 6-4, 6-4. Then came his victory in straight sets over Tommy Robredo, the 11th seed. And so to a meeting with Jonas Bjorkman, which could properly be described as a match-up of two of the game's real gents, though, strangely, they were not the best of mates. Bjorkman, a year younger and a smidgin fresher, was a semi-finalist in 2006 and had recently equalled a career best fourth round showing at Roland Garros – set in 1996.

The expectation was that these two golden oldies might run each other to a standstill. Instead, Bjorkman eased through 6-2, 6-1, ➤

David Nalbandian

6-4, a victory that brought the curtain down on a career that began for Arthurs in 1989, brought a single singles title, in Scottsdale, Arizona in 2005, 12 doubles titles, a career-high singles ranking of 44, a Davis Cup Final victory for Australia on home soil against Spain in 2003 and bucket-loads of memories.

"I knew it was time," Arthurs said. "My ranking doesn't move pretty much at all because I qualified here and got 60 points which moves me from 200 to 175, something like that. So the time is right. I was too hyperactive today, wanting to play and I came out and could not do anything. It is very hard to be on an even keel for the whole of your career – the general public doesn't see tennis outside the Grand Slams, but there are 30 other tournaments you're losing at. Yes, you need that even keel or you're going to go nuts, you really are."

A lot of players were beginning to lose it over Wimbledon scheduling and the inability to consider playing on the middle Sunday, though The Club had long considered it a rest day – for themselves, the players and the local residents – and were keen to keep that situation sacrosanct and in recent memory, only in 1991, 1997 and 2004 had the day been used because of terrible weather in the first week.

David Nalbandian, the 2002 finalist from Argentina, lost 6-2, 7-5, 6-0 to Marcos Baghdatis, of Cyprus, and led the chorus of complaint. "They don't care about us," he said. "Nobody who takes the responsibility

Kate Middleton and a friend watch the action on No. 1 Court

has to play three days in a row. The bottom half had to play today, tomorrow and after tomorrow – but why? Very tough, very tough." One was tempted to remind Nalbandian that this was a Grand Slam championship, the one that made him as a player, but it would have seemed churlish.

Oh, and over on No.1 Court, Nadal and Soderling were locking horns in what proved to be the first series of a saga of a match. As Federer kicked up his heels, his favoured challenger was indulged in what seemed like an hourly game of 'Beat the Shower.' Having taken the first two sets comfortably enough,

Nadal was stunned by the velocity of the Swede's stroke play in the third. At 5.30 pm, at 7-6 in the third set tie-break, Nadal contrived to open up the court and needed only to make one of his famed spun forehands, but missed it. After one more point, they were called off again.

How he must have stewed on that miss, for, upon the re-start, Soderling nabbed the tie break, won the fourth set with some destructive hitting and the pair were forced off for the night, with Nadal leading the deciding set 2-0, 30-30 on his serve. How much longer this would carry on, we could only guess ●

Sir Clive Woodward watches the Soderling v Nadal match

Rafael Nadal

Day **EIGHT**
3.07.2007

MAURESMO
VS
VAIDISOVA

JANKOVIC
VS
BARTOLI

IVANOVIC
VS
PETROVA

HEWITT
VS
CANAS

V. WILLIAMS
VS
SHARAPOVA

FERRERO
VS
TIPSAREVIC

Tuesday 3 July…

A terrific hailstorm had covered Clapham, about three miles away, in a layer of white. Lightning forked the skies above the All England Club, a double rainbow formed off to the south-west as twilight approached. The sun played peek-a-boo. The Championships were 178 matches behind schedule at the end of the day and Andrew Jarrett, the referee, fished for a description for his situation. "Utterly ghastly," he said. And Rafael Nadal's match against Robin Soderling was still listed under 'unfinished business.' Day Four and counting.

The day had begun with a meeting of the high minds of the sport, Tim Phillips, the Chairman of the All England Club, his Chief Executive Ian Ritchie and the President of the Lawn Tennis Association, Stuart Smith, joined at a top table to welcome the fact that London was to stage the Tennis Masters Cup – re-named, as is tennis' wont – the ATP World Tour Finals, on a four-year deal from 2009.

Etienne de Villiers, ATP President and Chairman, talked of the huge debt he owed to the club 'who put on unquestionably the world's most prestigious and well-known tennis event and to have received their endorsement would have been enough, but their active support in promoting and marketing to ensure the (Tour Finals) event is a success, goes beyond words.' It was about time Britain had another high-profile tournament to help propagate the tennis gospel. The venue would be the O2 arena (the former Millenium Dome) in Greenwich.

As of now, what we wanted was a grass court tournament to write about. Two men's third round matches were completed, two had not concluded, one in the fourth round was over (Juan Carlos Ferrero, of Spain, could relax a bit) and another was still to finish. A total of four matches were played in the

Nicole Vaidisova

ladies' singles and what a reverberation they caused. For, among their foreshortened number, came confirmation that the 2007 title ambitions of Amelie Mauresmo, the reigning champion, and Jelena Jankovic, the Serbian world No.3 had been dashed.

Mauresmo was beaten 7-6, 4-6, 6-1 by Nicole Vaidisova, of the Czech Republic, an 18-year-old who reached the semi-finals of this year's Australian Open and the 2006 Roland Garros to prove she was clearly a star in the final stages of polishing. In the *Daily Mail*, Alan Fraser remarked that 'if ever individual matches were sponsored at Wimbledon, the Centre Court opener would have been perfect for that chocolate bar which crumbles in the mouth of a nubile wench.'

The suggestion was that both Mauresmo and Vaidisova had inclinations towards flaky tennis – that their games would often crumble, with plenty of mess to clear up afterwards. Well, it was clear that the 28-year-old French woman had not been in the sprightliest of form, but the extent of her collapse towards the end was dismal, even for her.

The match itself was full of toe-curling unforced errors and it was the timing of them that got to you. The first set contained six

Marion Bartoli

Ana Ivanovic

Jelena Jankovic

breaks of serve. As the play progressed, it became clear Vaidisova played best on her own serve when she was 0-30 down. Indeed, she became almost unplayable once she had let her opponent build up a sizeable lead. The same was true for Mauresmo – the idea of being ahead induced a sense of panic. Not only that, but, at the start of the second set, after Mauresmo had tossed the first one away, making two horrid forehand errors from 6-6 in the tie-break, the umpire had forgotten whose turn it was to serve first. "It's unbelievable, it's laughable," remarked John McEnroe, from the BBC commentary box, though it was difficult to remember when he had ever laughed at an umpire.

"Everything went wrong today," said Mauresmo, one of whose first serves hit the ground before it reached the net, a boon for those of us who would like to play this game well one day. "I'm struggling to get my confidence back. It always shows when you play a better opponent and when it's a little tighter in terms of the score."

And there had been plenty of hopes held out for Jankovic, on the back of her brilliant run through the French Open, where she reached the semi-finals and the fact she had won the grass court title at Edgbaston the weekend before The Championships. Her

nemesis was to be Marion Bartoli, of France, who coped a good deal better with the six hours the match took to complete – two hours, 24 minutes of court time, the rest spent hanging around in the locker room. Bartoli won 3-6, 7-5, 6-3 (she had won just two games from Jankovic at the same stage of the French Open a month earlier) and brusquely dealt with those who suggested that her victory was 'a big surprise.'

"I'm a top 20 player," she responded, "I'm not 200 in the world. I think I should be in the quarter-finals of a Grand Slam. I am happy, but not over-happy. This is what I have been working 16 years for, to be in this stage, on the big courts with the crowd really happy to see me."

And so, for the second Grand Slam tournament in succession, the Serbian flag was being waved in the ladies' singles by Ana Ivanovic with a 6-1, 2-6, 6-4 victory over Nadia Petrova, the Russian No.11 seed. When she reached the final of Roland Garros a month earlier, Ivanovic had become the first Serbian woman to achieve such status. It was all the more noteworthy in that Ivanovic was stopped in her tracks at 5-4, 15-all serving for match when another dark cloud deposited its contents on the grounds. She returned to complete the job with marked assurance.

Out on Court No.3, late in the evening, murmurings began. Was that Venus Williams and Maria Sharapova making their way towards the court or were we beginning to imagine seeing players when they had actually gone home? No, here they came. "Miss Williams to serve," intoned the umpire. Cue forked lightning and rolling thunder followed, in the words of Giles Smith of *The Times* by 'raindrops the size of canned hams.'

Three points were possible and those on Court No.3 had been blessed, albeit briefly, with stardust. It would be back to doubles from hereonin.

Of the two men's matches completed, arguably the more significant was the victory for Lleyton Hewitt, the 2002 champion, over Guillermo Canas, the Argentinian who had had the rare privilege, earlier in the year, of beating Roger Federer in back-to-back tournaments in Indian Wells and Miami. Some people have retired on less.

Who, from the mangled bottom half of the draw had the temperament and substance to make it all the way to the final? One pace forward Hewitt. The 26-year-old Australian defeated Canas 6-4, 3-6, 6-3, 6-4 on Court No.18 and now had a 6-2 head-to-head record over a man regarded as the toughest piece of Argentinian steak on the tour. If anything was designed to illustrate Hewitt's powers, it is that he had gone through the

card of Argentines with sustained conviction –
playing 26 times against the pick of their crop
in his career and winning 20 of those
matches.

An example of how tough this Wimbledon
had become – for anyone other than Federer –
was that Hewitt and Canas started their match
six times and, according to Hewitt, probably
warmed up on ten to 15 other occasions.
"There's a lot of nervous energy wasted, just
going out there to stay in the tournament," he
said. "A lot has been taken out of me mentally
in the last couple of days. I feel like I've
handled it all really well.

"But you've just got to be prepared to do it,
this is how you win majors. It's about not
getting frustrated with the situation. Whatever
hand you're dealt, you deal with it and keep
positive. In the locker room, it's important to
stay in the match frame. On two of the rain
delays I was up a break but down breakpoint
and ended up going out there and losing my
serve both times. Obviously, I didn't do the
right thing in the locker room." ➤

Lleyton Hewit

Guillermo Canas

Juan Carlos Ferrero

Since his defeat in the third round of this year's Australian Open – before which Roger Rasheed, his coach, had walked out on him saying Hewitt wasn't giving enough of himself to make the partnership work – Hewitt was out of sorts through the American hard court spring but grooved his game to its nitty-gritty essence on the clay and did not worry that he lost early at Queen's Club to Jo-Wilfried Tsonga, the dynamic Frenchman. Hewitt knew his game was in shape, that *he* was in shape, that he was in settled company with Bec, his wife, Mia, his 19-month-old daughter, and with John Fitzgerald and Darren Cahill, the country's Davis Cup captain and coach, speaking in his ear when they knew the time was right to speak.

A round ahead, Ferrero was ending the inspired challenge of Janko Tipsarevic, of Serbia, in three sets and would not play Federer. Writing of the champion, who had not been spotted since the previous Friday, the

Daily Mail's Paul Hayward said: "It may sound frivolous in the present climate, but the age-spanning ease and refinement of the world's best player is the best antidote you're going to find to the suspicion that this year's tournament belongs on a spike of soggy non-events. As long as Roger Federer is in it, it's worth any number of bag searches and drenchings."

Oh, and Nadal and Soderling were still at it on No.1 Court. Their match was to resume on Wednesday, some 92 hours after it was first called, the players now level at 4-4 in the fifth. One match, five days, seven interruptions, no conclusion. They were beginning to call Nadal the Rain Man. ●

QUOTE of the Day

"Ladies and gentlemen, here is an update from the referee's office. We can see from our window that a lot of you are walking around with your umbrellas up and because there is lightning around, we don't think it is such a good idea."
Cue the loudest groan of The Championships from hundreds of saturated patrons.
MIKE MORRISSEY, ASSISTANT REFEREE AND GENERAL WEATHER FACTOTUM

The Rain Man

99

Day **NINE**
4.07.2007

NADAL
VS
SODERLING

DJOKOVIC
VS
KIEFER

RODDICK
VS
MATHIEU

GASQUET
VS
TSONGA

S. WILLIAMS
VS
HENIN

BARTOLI
VS
KRAJICEK

Wednesday 4 July…

At long last we could celebrate a winner. Rafael Nadal defeated Robin Soderling and sank to his knees as if the title itself had been earned. The third round match took 96 hours, 22 minutes from the time it was called until Hawk-Eye raised the chequered flag deeming a Soderling backhand had landed an inch long; the actual time on court was four hours and a minute, there had been six rain interruptions; Soderling said he had been kept waiting 200 times while Nadal went through his rituals; six was the number of millimetres Nadal's hair grew during its course and 30.2 the estimated rainfall in millilitres that fell between first ball and last.

Soderling struck his serves an average 10 mph faster, won more points when his first serve landed in, claimed ten more winners, had 16 more aces, won more points (176-174) and yet he was the loser. What was that about lies, damn lies and statistics?

What made the whole thing even more extraordinary was that, as the match laboured on, it became clear the two players liked each other less. Soderling took the mickey out of Nadal's famed pant-pulling tic by mimicking it, which drew a titter from the crowd but was much to the Spaniard's displeasure. When he won a point in the final set, thanks to a net cord, rather than raise an arm by means of apology, Soderling let out a full throated roar. It is a safe to say that no win, certainly not one which read 6-4, 6-4, 6-7, 4-6, 7-5 had given Nadal greater satisfaction – not even that mind-bending fifth set finale to the Italian Open in Rome 14 months earlier when he had beaten Roger Federer having been match point down twice.

Robin Soderling

The trouble was that, to reach the final, it was now beholden on Nadal to play matches on successive days, without rest, and the weather forecast still left a lot to be desired. This one, though, was out of the way, a thorn had been picked from the sole of his shoe, for Soderling was by nature a prickly customer, so much so that Sweden's leading tennis writer paused at my desk and wondered, tape recorder running, what I had thought of his behaviour. My belief was that it had left a bitter taste which was very unfortunate.

It was a viewpoint shared by James Lawton, the avuncular columnist for *The Independent*, who wrote: "Soderling's reaction was pretty much in line with his approach to the most important match of his life: hard, deeply unsentimental and utterly detached from any ambition other than stealing an edge, any kind, anyhow. Nadal says he will try his best; yes, one match over five days and now possibly four in four; finishing with arguably the greatest player in the game is a bizarre, potentially draining challenge. But it could be worse. He may just have to spend another minute in the company of Soderling."

Nadal would have agreed with every word. "He is not one of the best in the locker room," he said. "In the end we will see what is happening in the end of the life, no?" Which was Nadal's way of suggesting that when the great game was over, the rackets had been laid down, the last sock had been tugged at, and everyone could start to count their medals, he might have a few more pinned to his chest than the Swede. It was a safe presumption. ➤

The tournament seemed to be running on parallel shifts. Nadal was into the fourth round, as was Serbia's Novak Djokovic, courtesy of a four set win over Nicolas Kiefer, and how re-assuring it was to see the German back in the groove after the best part of year on the sidelines with wrist problems. In the opposite half of the draw, where the French threatened a take-over, Richard Gasquet was joined a stride further down the track by Andy Roddick and the

pair would meet in the quarter-final. Roddick was there, courtesy of a 6-2, 7-5, 7-6 victory over France's Paul-Henri Mathieu, while Gasquet doused the fire of his compatriot, Jo-Wilfried Tsonga, a wild card, 6-4, 6-3, 6-4, in the fifth all-French meeting in the men's singles.

What pleased Roddick as much as anything was that, once more, he had proved redoubtable in tie-breaks, recovering from 5-0 down in the sudden death of the third set

Clockwise from above: Richard Gasquet, Novak Djokovic, Andy Roddick and Jo-Wilfried Tsonga

QUOTE of the Day
IAN RITCHIE, CHIEF EXECUTIVE OF THE ALL ENGLAND
CLUB AND LIFELONG LEEDS UNITED FAN:

*"It's a bit like football where everyone
fancies their chances of being a referee and
the only people who really know what
goes on are those in the referee's office. It is
a fantastically complicated balancing act.
There were two reasons why we didn't
play on Sunday, the tournament was on
schedule and the weather looked awful. It
turned out to be a sunny afternoon and I
wish I was Nostradamus and had known
that would happen."*

to secure victory. The American's good
natured wish that he hoped Gasquet and
Tsonga would play 'for about 12 hours' was
not granted, however, as Gasquet, the 12th
seed, required merely an hour and 42
minutes to see off a foe who, though a few
months his elder, he had never met at tour
level. Tsonga's cause was not helped by 40
unforced errors but he had played a huge part
in The Championship and was worthy of
consideration as a future contender.

**Sir Tim Rice enjoying
Wimbledon in the sun**

Justine Henin

Tsonga had definitely brightened up a Championship that had, up to now, been dull in only that the weather had been so unhelpful. So had Serena Williams, in her own contrary way. It was time for her to depart as well, after a quarter-final against Justine Henin, the top seed, which, if it did not have the feistiness we had come to expect from the pair, was compelling in its way. And it was completed without a single rain delay.

Prior to the match, Richard Williams, Serena's father insisted that the advice of both himself, and a doctor, was that she risked further damaged to her left calf if she chose to play. Quitting, though, especially before a ball had been hit, was not in the Williams DNA, especially given how disgusted she had been with her efforts against the Belgian at the same stage of the recent French Open and, in the Sony Ericsson final in Miami in April, had recovered from 6-0, 5-4, 40-15 down to win. That may have had something to with the fact that Henin came over all-a-tizzy when she led 5-1 in the final set.

There was noticeable quickening of her pace, too many slapdash shots and Williams

Serena Williams

was sneaking back into the match. It took a moment of genuine audacity for the Henin cobwebs to disperse when, at 5-3, 15-30 the Belgian conjured a drop shot that fell within a few inches of the scampering Williams's outstretched racket. Imagine how the match may have turned out had Williams made up the ground and fashioned a winner.

On her first match point, Henin came charging in behind a first serve but dumped her backhand volley into the net. There was a good deal more circumspection on the second when she wisely chose to stay back,

rallied for a few shots and then watched, relieved, as a Williams backhand drifted over the baseline.

It was a pity that, later, Williams felt the need to bemoan her lack of fitness, as if trying to take the gloss from Henin's victory. She said she sprained her thumb against Hantuchova in the previous round on top of the injuries we had known about – she and Venus later withdrew from the doubles. "I should be proud of myself because I've come a really long way," Williams said. "I was pretty much out of it (the sport) last year, I was 140 in the world and everyone had written me off. I'm in the top ten now which is pretty awesome. And I still have another Grand Slam this year. I was probably only 40 to 50 per cent max today. Had I been 100 per cent, I reckon I would have won." Henin did not give a fig for such assumptions. ➤

Marion Bartoli

Maria Sharapova

Andre Sa and
Marcelo Melo

COURT NO. 16

PREVIOUS SETS	PLAYER	SETS	GAMES
7 6 6 6	P. HANLEY ⑥ K. ULLYETT	2	2 6
5 7 4 7	M. MELO A. SA	2	2 8

Slazenger

Her opponent in the semi-finals would be the girl who was becoming the surprise package of the championships. Marion Bartoli defeated Michaella Krajicek of the Netherlands 3-6, 6-3, 6-2 – once more saving her best tennis for the final set. And she did so with two hours less sleep than she said she normally needed to function properly. Perhaps that was the cause for her sluggish start as Krajicek, urged on by Richard, her half-brother and Guus Hiddink, the famed Holland football coach, who was now masterminding the fortunes of the Russian national side, took control and had it not been for a break in the second set for rain (a two hour sojourn during which Bartoli slept soundly) it may have been a very different outcome.

Henin and Bartoli were a round ahead – the bottom half of the women's draw was as congested as the men's but another former champion had been summarily dismissed – Maria Sharapova. The US Open champion had taken pummellings in her time – when she was good she was very, very good but when she was bad, she was appalling – and this was to be another one of those distressing reverses when the harder she tried, the worse it became. The beneficiary was Venus Williams, who won 6-1, 6-3 – a result and performance reminiscent of the Australian Open final in January when it was Serena's turn to run amok.

This match was remarkable mostly for a single game that spanned the one rain break and contained 13 deuces. It was a titanic collision of power-crazed, hollering women,

lashing the ball at each other in endless rallies, peppering the lines and screaming at the tops of their voices. The last point was a howling drive volley from Williams, a lob escape from Sharapova and a soaring overhead from Williams that plunged into the net. The crowd roared their approval of such a rally but it was only to suspend the outcome for a few minutes as Williams then broke to love and, in one bound, was free.

A piece of history was made on Court No.5 by an unlikely pair, Andre Sa and Marcelo Melo, of Brazil. In the first round, the pair had almost come to blows with Frenchmen, Nicolas Mahut and Julien Benneteau – the latter was fined for his part in the contretemps. The fracas had served to sharpen their edge for, a round later, they were to encounter Paul Hanley, of Australia, and Zimbabwe's Kevin Ullyett, who make their fortune travelling the world playing nothing but doubles and who were The Championships' No.6 seeds.

This was another match that took five days to complete, lasting five hours and 58 minutes of court time, the second longest match in the annals of Wimbledon doubles; however, the boys from Brazil penned themselves into championships' folklore as their 5-7, 7-6, 4-6, 7-6, 28-26 victory (after which they rolled around like a pair of puppies) set a record for the most games for a fifth set in any match at Wimbledon. Its 102 games in total was ten short of the overall record, set in the 1969 classic between Pancho Gonzalez and Charlie Pasarell. ●

Above: Venus Williams
Winner of The Rolex Wimbledon Picture of the Year Competition 2007

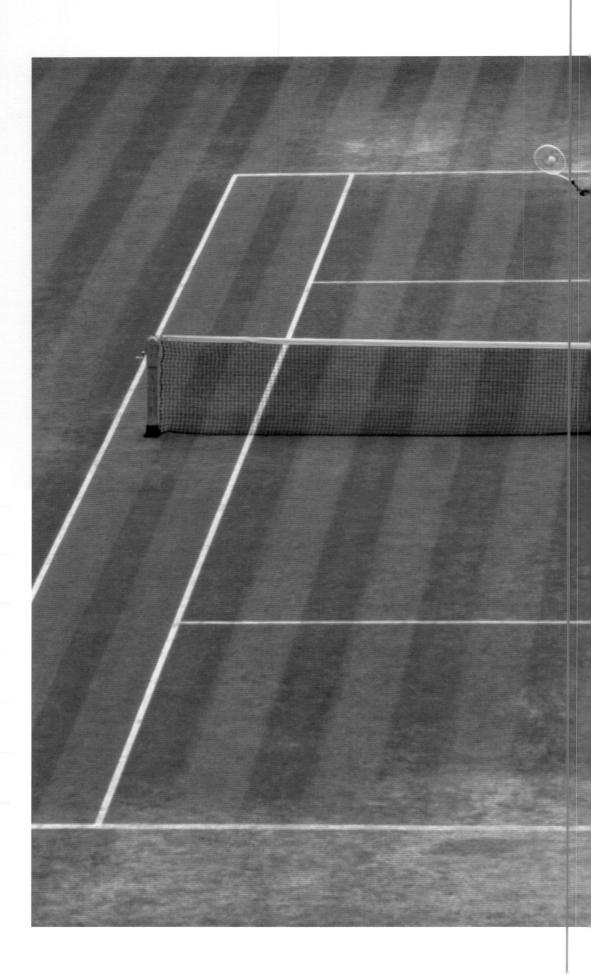

Day **TEN**
5.07.2007

FEDERER
VS
FERRERO

BJORKMAN
VS
BERDYCH

NADAL
VS
YOUZHNY

BAGHDATIS
VS
DAVYDENKO

DJOKOVIC
VS
HEWITT

IVANOVIC
VS
VAIDISOVA

V. WILLIAMS
VS
KUZNETSOVA

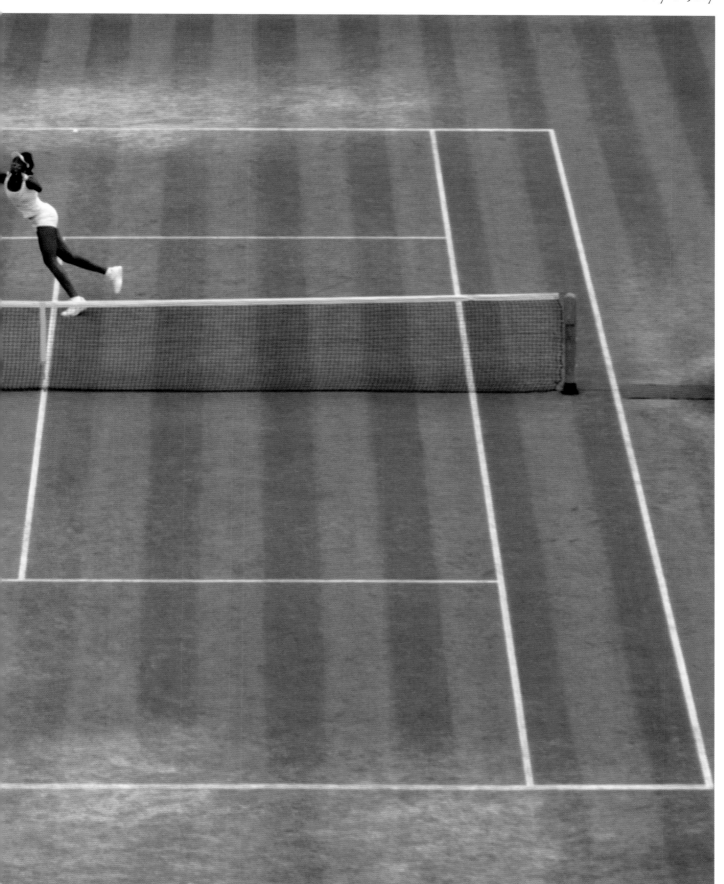

Thursday 5 July…

Who was that fellow in the long pants? The face was familiar, outfit rang a bell, played a bit didn't he, seen him around the place a few times, spent a lot of time holding a cup in the air as I seem to recall. Hadn't he been on a bit of a busman's holiday? After all, that Andy Roddick had intimated there was a probability that whatsisname had spent his time off 'on one of those red bus tours of London.'

Roger Federer – that's him! – had actually shown up at Wimbledon every day since the previous Friday. It is just that he had not been able to do what he did best – play. A combination of weather, the schedule and opponents who had gone lame, contrived to keep the Swiss out of the performance frame until he stepped back as dusk approached to face Juan Carlos Ferrero of Spain in the quarter-finals.

By heck, we had missed him, if not he us. But we only saw him for ten games, not enough to warm the cockles of anyone's heart and, when he was forced off by rain, he had allowed a 5-2 lead to be pegged back to 5-all. Not only that, serving for the set at 5-3, he had been broken to love, a game which included three errant forehands. Obviously, this once imperious shot needed time to warm up after five days in hibernation. Still, it was good to know that the fellow existed and we hoped he would be back the next day to see us again.

For once, those in the bottom half of the men's draw had something of a leg-up. The four quarter-finalists from that section would be Rafael Nadal, Tomas Berydch, Novak Djokovic and Marcos Baghdatis as Wimbledon prepared to host one of the youngest last eight line-ups in living memory. The average age was 21 – the meeting of Federer and Ferrero pitted the two oldest men left, at 27 and 25, while Andy Roddick (24) and Richard Gasquet (21) completed the youthful octet.

The average had been brought down significantly with the departure of Jonas Bjorkman, of Sweden, who chose not to go quietly. One newspaper described his explosion of temper as X-rated. That didn't sound like Bjorkman at all but on examining the circumstances of his outburst, one discovered he had the right to be a bit peeved. Already trailing by two sets to Berdych, he had carved out his first break points of the match at 3-2 in the third, when a Czech serve was called out on the far side from the umpire's chair.

Usually, these were the overrules umpires avoid like the plague and when James Keothavong, the British official, decided that he would interject and rule it a 133 mph ace,

Roger Federer

112

Bjorkman could not believe it. Cue Swedish outburst. He lost the next point and erupted once more. An English/Swedish; Swedish/English dictionary at hand, one was able to discover that he said: "You bloody fool. I'm so tired of you. It's not the first time you've ruined it for me. You're lucky I'm not John McEnroe." Or words to that effect.

Actually, Bjorkman managed to snaffle the third set despite the steam coming out of his ears but was overpowered in the fourth as Berdych – who had won the title in Halle two weeks before The Championships – reached the quarter-finals of a Grand Slam tournament for the first time.

There, he would play Nadal, whose exploits were becoming the stuff of legend. There were those of a conspiratorial nature who thought that, as the No.2 seed had had the temerity to criticise The Championships for not playing on the middle Sunday, they had decided to teach him a lesson and schedule him on Court No.2, a venue famed for the cutting down to size of the big stars.

Joining the Spanish writing contingent on a cool early afternoon, it was clear they feared for their man on the cramped confines of the court, against a player like Mikhail Youzhny, the Russian who was slightly more used to these surroundings. One of the club's finest honorary stewards made an impassioned speech to those in our vicinity, thanking us for coming, reminding us that this was 'an iconic match' and that if we left our seats, we could not presume to have them back because there was a queue of people waiting and this was a first come, first served court. None of your royalty here, chum.

Behind him, Nadal had emerged to a thunderous roar. It was soon clear that Spanish apprehension was not misplaced as he struggled to come to terms with the fact that he had exhausted himself the previous day and too many of Youzhny's shots were of the highest order. The first game, in which Youzhny did not miss a first serve, was a significant warning shot across Nadal's bows.

The Spaniard required two aces to extricate himself from trouble in the fourth game, another to bring him level in the eighth, and was hanging on for much of the set until Youzhny pounced, in the tenth, forcing Nadal into a backhand error that unnerved him to the extent that he double-faulted to bring up a set point for the Russian. With that, Youzhny won the equivalent of a fencing joust at the net and the advantage was his.

Youzhny did not take long to double that advantage; Nadal was, it seemed, in deep trouble. What turned the story around happened in the time it takes to flick a switch. Youzhny from two sets up, began not to ➤

MATCH of the Day
NOVAK DJOKOVIC BEAT LLEYTON HEWITT 7-6, 7-6, 4-6, 7-6.

Djokovic ripped off his shirt and stood, Goran Ivanisevic like, in the middle of No.1 Court, drinking in the ovation that greeted his victory over the former champion, a man who had given his all. The tennis was pulsating, 90 per cent of it played from the back of the court where some of Djokovic's recovery shots – he was sliding on the brown patches as if they were Parisien clay – defied belief. Hewitt had his opportunities – at 5-5, 15-40 on Djokovic's serve in the first set, and at 6-4 in the ensuing tie-break, a couple of forehand errors on its final two points handing Djokovic the advantage.

The second tie-break was much more clear cut at 7-2. Hewitt snagged the third set and broke twice in the fourth, only for Djokovic to break back immediately, the second when Hewitt served at 5-4. A successful Hawk-Eye challenge saw Djokovic take an advantage in the tie-break which he won 7-5 after Hewitt had saved two match points.

believe; Nadal believed. Nadal saw his opponent was grimacing and sensed that his back was starting to play up, a back whose weakness that had forced the 25-year-old to withdraw from his previous tournament. He had been able only to last this long, he explained later, as Wimbledon's rain breaks gave him sufficient time to be massaged into playing condition.

As the pain began to impede his movement, Youzhny look to the skies – yes, they were overcast – and hoped for a spot more of the wet stuff. He thought about calling for a medical time out "but I knew if I asked for the doctors against Nadal it's very difficult because if he sees you have problems, he has a lot of emotion, power and motivation." At the end of the third set, though, all that did not seem to matter as much. Three times, Youzhny required manipulation on his back and, with each one, the stretching increased in intensity and the Russian's brow furrowed accordingly. It was not a surprise, then, that Nadal should go on to win 4-6, 3-6, 6-1, 6-2, 6-2.

"After the first two sets, in the next three, maybe I play the best grass court tennis of my life today, no?" Nadal said. "If I am not motivated to play well here, at Wimbledon, where am I going to be motivated? I love the competition." ➢

Cherie Blair

STATISTIC of the Day

Wimbledon has the best line-judges in the world. To date, there had been 135 challenges using the Hawk-Eye review, and only 40 had been called incorrectly. That worked out at around 70% in favour of the officials. At last year's US Open, the success rate was 68% and at this year's Australian Open, a miserable 46%.

Mikhail Youzhny

Novak Djokovic

Of all the quarter-finals, the prospect of Djokovic against Baghdatis really did sweeten the taste buds. Australian guts were busted, for Lleyton Hewitt, who had begun to find his stride, was undone in four sets by Djokovic; whereas there was much less sadness at the demise of Nikolay Davydenko, the world no.4, who had not made it onto either of the tournament's two major show courts. He never really liked it here anyway – "Wimbledon is the world's most boring tournament," he is alleged to have told a Russian reporter. "There's hardly anything to do apart from tennis."

"Blimey," Giles Smith wrote in *The Times* "more boring than S'hertogenbosch? Duller than Halle? You've got to feel sorry for these players though. They come to a big tennis tournament and what do they find? Tennis."

Not for long in Davydenko's case as Baghdatis, as eager a retriever of a ball as there is ran his socks off and played some spellbindingly effective tennis to record a 7-6, 7-6, 6-3 victory much to the delight of his Cypriot contingent of supporters – six of whom spelt the name M-A-R-C-O-S on their t-shirts, so long as they stayed in the same seats! A single moment that summarised the Baghdatis commitment came on ➤

Lleyton Hewitt

Marcos Baghdatis

117

Nikolay Davydenko

Davydenko's serve in what would prove the final game of the match, when the Cypriot fell over behind the baseline but still made it back up to reach the drop shot with which the Russian had sought to capitalise.

Not only did Baghdatis reach it, but he pushed the ball across Davydenko for an outright winner. It was true that subduing his hair beneath his bandana was, for Baghdatis, almost a full time job, yet he somehow juggled it with producing tennis of a powerful and astonishingly elastic order.

In his four previous rounds, Andy Roddick had won each on a tie-break but Djokovic was threatening to take his mantle of the king of sudden death tennis. Djokovic beat Hewitt 7-6, 7-6, 4-6, 7-6, which meant of the 23 tie-breaks he had played this year, the Serb had won 17. He had lost one of seven of his Wimbledon allotment thus far this year. (See Match of the Day).

The reviews of Ana Ivanovic's 4-6, 6-2, 7-5 victory over Nicola Vaidisova, which earned the 19-year-old Serb a place in consecutive Grand Slam semi-finals were decidedly mixed. The match was Vaidisova's for the taking but the statuesque teenager from the Czech Republic could not take her opportunities, wasting three match points, the last of which, on an Ivanovic second serve, she netted a return.

In *The Telegraph*, Robert Philip did not mince words. "The highlight of this error-strewn muddle of a match was an all-too-brief rain delay in the first set. At one point amid the stream of fluffed forehands, vapid volleys, laughable lobs, shocking smashes, successive scrawls in my notebook read: ugly, ugly, ugly. The Spanish cheers for Nadal, wafting over from Court No.2, were like listening to a wonderful party, to which you haven't been invited, raging next door."

There was little for Venus Williams to rage at in her 6-3, 6-4 victory over Svetlana Kuznetsova, of Russia. Her progress on a blustery Centre Court contained the hallmark accomplishments that had proved too much for Maria Sharapova in the previous round – drilled serves, athletic returns and occasional paroxyisms of weakness. Serving for the match at 5-4 and 40-0 up, she missed the first two match points and, on the third, having netted her first serve, she took stock before doing exactly the same with a dreadful second. Indeed, a missed forehand on the next point meant she was a break point down, only to pull herself together and bulldoze the Russian aside.

What if the forecast, for more rain, came good? "Rain is good for me," Venus said. "The longer I have to sit around, the clearer my game becomes. I achieve clarity when it rains."

Hmmmmm.

Ana Ivanovic

119

Day **ELEVEN**
6.07.2007

NADAL
VS
BERDYCH

DJOKOVIC
VS
BAGHDATIS

RODDICK
VS
GASQUET

V. WILLIAMS
VS
IVANOVIC

BARTOLI
VS
HENIN

Rafael Nadal

Friday 6 July…

An 11 am start on all 19 courts had been determined as a means of getting the schedule roughly to where it ought to be and the forecast from the Meteorological Office indicated high hopes for 'an uninterrupted days' play'. They had been as rare as hen's teeth. There were still six matches in the main draws that could not be given a court and plenty of juniors mooching around waiting for the call to arms.

Given this continuing logjam, how would it be, after all his grievances, if Rafael Nadal should be the first man to reach the semi-finals? Tomas Berdych, his opponent, had not been this far in the Grand Slam before, Centre Court was beckoning, the wind was getting up, as was the Spaniard's dander. He recalled that in Madrid, last October, when Berdych had beaten him in straight sets in the Masters quarter-final, he had circled the stadium with a finger to his lips, showing how he had hushed the crowd. Spain did not take too kindly to such a gesture.

They had played subsequently, in the semi-finals of the Monte Carlo Masters in April, which Nadal won decisively but Berdych still had a 3-2 advantage over his opponent and the Spaniard knew it. As it turned out, this match turned out to be the day's only damp squib, a three set 7-6, 6-4, 6-2 stroll but it

Marcos Baghdatis

Tomas Berdych

showed that Nadal was into his stride – he had had his 'horrible' match, against Robin Soderling in the third round and was into a decisive roll, which was a worrisome thought for the rest as the weekend approached.

Against Berdych, it was clearer that his serve had become a genuine grass court weapon, whereas previously it had been a means of starting a point. In every aspect of the game, indeed, he was a touch ahead of the Czech who, unsurprisingly, did not take long to get down on himself – an element of his character which has to be improved if he is to seriously challenge for the game's major prizes. How someone so tall, so physically strong, so young (21) and possessed of all the shots could fall away so poorly was something his coach, Jaroslav Navratil, needed to work on. It would surely help him, too, if he developed a personality.

He only had to look at Novak Djokovic and Marcos Baghdatis to see where he might improve in that regard. They were involved in what was to become the best match of the tournament – and only 24 hours after Djokovic had needed more than four hours to see off a player of Lleyton Hewitt's ferocious commitment. It was astonishing to see this 20–year-old Serbian still have the energy to play four hours and 59 minutes further, to defeat the Cypriot, 7-6, 7-6, 6-7, 4-6, 7-5.

It was a purist's delight. Richard Eaton wrote in *The Guardian*: "the rallies were long and

colourfully patterned, both men moved like the wind until the latter stages and when Djokovic slowed noticeably in the fourth set, the energy count was almost as important as the score. Baghdatis once tried to eat his racket, he grinned and gesticulated, but he also fretted and chastised himself for his flaws, too much, perhaps, for his own good. Djokovic closed out the match slowly, relentlessly, despite his aching muscles and leaned back with a slightly drunken smile on his face as the job was completed."

Baghdatis, having clawed his way back so improbably, would no doubt rue the drop shot he netted when he dropped serve in the 11th game of the final set, for any such gifts were usually seized on by a player of the Serb's resolve. It was remarkable, though, that Baghdatis was still around at all for, after he had lost the first two sets, he had required plenty of shoulder massage to keep his racket arm strong. His revival was amazing.

"It was nothing special," Baghdatis said of his shoulder concerns, "just a bit heavy with the balls and the wind. I am a human being, I

accept losing. I accept a lot of things in life. You have to accept it and continue. I lost today, I'm a bit disappointed but I'm happy for Novak. Maybe he can win here. He's jumping around all the time in the locker room, acting like a small kid. But he's a funny guy, a great guy."

That was everyone's view of Roger Federer as well (save the 'leaping around in the locker room acting like a small kid' bit). The Swiss returned to attempt to see off Juan Carlos Ferrero, another Spaniard who had begun to thoroughly enjoyed himself in these peculiarly English surroundings. The pair had withdrawn from sight the previous evening at 5-5 in the first set and, though the No.1 seed secured a foothold in the tie-break, he lost the second set 6-3, the first he had dropped this year.

He managed to shake off the ring-rustiness in the third set, when he came out full of aggressive intent and broke twice. The second break contained two sumptuous backhand winners that came with Federer's signature on them. The going got a bit tougher in the fourth, with Federer frustrated and niggled by the tricky conditions and the problems he had

Michael and Mary Parkinson watch the action between Rafael Nadal and Tomas Berdych

Roger Federer takes on Juan Carlos Ferrero

in dealing with them (he was not, by nature, considered one of the better 'wind' players). But he was still dominant, controlling the majority of the longer exchanges with deep, powerful strokes and subtle changes of speed and angle. He was finding his stride and his range again.

Once all his thoughts had been re-gathered, Federer went on to win 7-6, 3-6, 6-1, 6-3. "I knew that it was going to be very difficult to beat him in any conditions," Ferrero said. "But today, it was the worst conditions to feel the ball good, to hit the ball strong all the time. It was impossible to play three times nice. Was very difficult out there." At least, we could put those all-Spanish final dreams to bed.

The previous weekend, when everyone was picking through the debris of the first week and look forward with renewed vim to the second, my newspaper asked if I would come up with a couple of completed draw sheets, to anticipate the upcoming results and give those souls on railway journeys and aircraft flights something to have a good laugh at. We shall not dwell on my prognostications for the ➤

Richard Gasquet

women's finale but I was pretty proud of how I saw the men's competition ending up. My two semi-final picks were Nadal v. Djokovic and Federer v. Richard Gasquet.

Now before Andy Roddick sues for defamation of character, it should be said that I had had a gut feeling from seeing the Frenchman play at Nottingham, from listening to Eric Deblicker, his coach, over a baguette on the player's lawn at the All England Club, midway through The Championships, and sensing the young man's mood, that Gasquet was ready for his Grand Slam breakthrough.

When he was two sets down to Roddick on Court No.1, of course, those senses had begun to feel a little blurry but even then, Gasquet did not seem completely out of the match. A break down in the third, which should have been his end, was not compelling evidence of certain Roddick success. Gasquet had failed to come to terms with the punishing speed and depth of the Roddick serve but then, out of the blue, the first time he had break points, he pounced on the second when a loose backhand volley from the American gave him the chance to pass.

What followed was quite astonishing, for Gasquet began to serve beautifully and go for absolute broke with his single-handed backhand, which is the finest of its kind in the men's game. Time and again, Roddick was left stranded, almost mesmerised, as if he knew that to come in on any approach played to Gasquet's backhand was tantamount to suicide yet he could not stop himself. The tide had inexorably turned, the Frenchman was inspired to a 4-6, 4-6, 7-6, 7-6, 8-6 victory and – though he was going through agony inside – Roddick actually climbed the net and patted Gasquet on the cheek. If there was a more stirring display of sportsmanship in the entire Championships I had not seen it.

The completion of the men's quarter-finals allowed the two women's semi-finals to take centre stage. Venus Williams loved that. She performed in a champions' manner, from the word go against Ana Ivanovic – how daunting for the Serb to bounce the ball in her first service game, look up and see the tall, imposing figure of Williams standing inside the baseline and inching ever closer. The American led 4-0 in just 12 minutes,

Venus Williams after beating Ana Ivanovic

including a change-over. The fifth game lasted a further 12 minutes, Ivanovic surviving six deuces and saving two further break points before holding serve. Thereafter, the teenager performed creditably without putting Williams under real pressure.

Richard Williams had described his elder daughter 'running like the south wind' through The Championships, only a month after her defeat to Jelena Jankovic, in the third round of the French Open, had led him to suggest that if she could not hit the ball any better, she might as well pack the game in.

Logic was being tossed to the four winds by the Williamses again for, two years earlier, Venus had arrived in London without form or match hardness and swept all before her to win the title. Now Ivanovic was well and truly trapped in the tail wind as Williams won 6-2, 6-4. The Serb could point, though, to the exertions of reaching the semi-finals in Paris and said she had surprised herself by reaching the semi-finals here.

Incidentally, that was not Marion Bartoli's viewpoint. But who would have believed that someone so out of the loop, so unconsidered, would reach her first Grand Slam final and, in doing so, dump the No.1 player in the world out of the event after she had been so overwhelmed in the first set? That was the way it worked out as Bartoli defeated Justine Henin, of Belgium, 1-6, 7-5, 6-1, the player to whom she had lost in Eastbourne and collected only four games. And she achieved it demonstrating not a shred of fear.

"I know her personality," Henin said. "I knew she wouldn't be afraid to win the match. I wasn't really surprised. I couldn't expect her to make mistakes. I had to try to win more points and do more winners, but she took her chances more than I did. I don't make this tournament an obsession. It's normal to be disappointed." ●

QUOTE(S) of the Day

"I'm sitting here feeling pretty crappy, but I promise you I'm aware in the grand scheme of things that I'm pretty blessed, very lucky and very fortunate – that being said, when you put your blood, sweat and tears, everything you have into something, you can almost taste it, envision it, it's not easy. I'd love to make you try to understand what it feels like in the pit of my stomach right now."

"This is just incredible. It's a great day for me, maybe the beginning of my career. In my head I played maybe 10 times against Roddick because we were waiting two days in the locker room. In France, everybody is waiting I play good, like this. Now, I have a lot of texts on my phone. Everybody is crazy with me. I like that a lot."

Pierce Brosnan and Keely Shaye Smith

"Well, I looked up and saw Pierce Brosnan in the stands, he's one of my favourite actors. I guess he gave me some luck – so, Pierce, maybe if you could come back tomorrow, it would be good. I was focusing on Pierce Brosnan because he is so beautiful, I saw he was cheering for me, so I said, 'Oh, maybe it's good.' I have to play better for him." *Marion Bartoli*

Marion Bartoli (below) goes through to the final after beating Justin Henin (left)

Day **TWELVE**
7.07.2007

V. WILLIAMS
VS
BARTOLI

NADAL
VS
DJOKOVIC

GASQUET
VS
FEDERER

Saturday 7 July…

It was the 73rd anniversary of the first of Fred Perry's three Wimbledon triumphs in succession, a 6-3, 6-0, 7-5 victory over Australia's Jack Crawford in the 1934 final, the conclusion of which was reported thus in the *Manchester Guardian* "Perry led 6-5, and Crawford was 40-love on his service when his forehand went and with it, his hopes. The last point was tragic; Crawford served and was foot-faulted, his second serve was another fault. Crawford turned, bowed to the foot-fault judge and slowly walked to meet his conqueror. In their shouts for Perry, there was a sob in the throat of the crowd, they felt so very sorry for Crawford."

The piece evoked so many powerful images, not least the thought of a player bowing to a foot-fault judge who had called him for stepping onto the line on match point. They were sticklers in those days. It was hard to imagine any one of the four protagonists in the men's semi-finals, or the ladies competing in their singles final reacting in such a spirited way but that was no slight on their character, just a sign of the times.

And there was an English crowd feeling bad for an Australian – where did that one come from? One wondered who they favoured today, for this was ladies' final day – America's

Venus Williams against Marion Bartoli, from France, a match few would have contemplated ten days (it seemed more like ten months) earlier when the event had begun. It was also men's semi-finals day, the matches beginning concurrently at midday on the two show courts; a bumper prize for Saturday ticket holders.

Stretching one's legs before the off, I bumped into Srdjan and Dijana Djokovic, Novak's parents, who did not look as contented as they ought with their son about to play Rafael Nadal for a place in the Wimbledon final for the first time. Mr and Mrs Djokovic were puffing on their cigarettes as normal but anxiety was writ large on their faces. Dijana said she did not think Novak was going to be able to play, he had not practised at all – the little toe on his left foot had bled during the night and he had barely slept. It looked to be all too much for her. I said I was sure everything would be all right.

Having been tempted to cross to No.1 Court to watch Nadal and Djokovic, the prospect of there not being too much of a match made up my mind to see how Richard Gasquet would fare against Roger Federer, the oldest of the four by more than four years and the first time in his 15 Grand Slam semi-final ➤

appearances that he had been the oldest of the semi-finalists.

Gasquet had expressed the fear that a noon start, having completed his five set quarter-final victory over Andy Roddick as late as he had, was 'not good'. He seemed sprightly enough at the outset, surviving a break point in the fourth game when Federer missed an attempted backhand pass and stepping up in the next with a break opportunity of his own, that required an ace to obliterate. In the eleventh game of the set, too, Gasquet had a couple of sniffs, the first again saved with an ace and the second, when he skied a forehand service return.

This first set was, surely, to be all important to the Frenchman's chances because the longer the match went on, the more the tiredness of the previous day would seep into his mind. Trust Federer then to pounce in the next game as Gasquet allowed a 40-15 lead (two chances for a tie-break) to slip, eventually netting a backhand volley on the first set point that surrendered the initiative.

From here, it would require a superhuman effort to win and Gasquet was not feeling the least bit superhuman. Federer pulled away as one suspected he might, winning 7-5, 6-3,

6-4. "I wasn't far away because I had two breakpoints at 5-all," Gasquet said. "If I did this breakpoint, everything can happen if I win the first set. He served too well today for me in the second and third set. I was tired. It was Roger. It was maybe impossible."

Remarkably, within two minutes of the match ending there, before there was time to skip across to Court No.1, that semi-final had also reached a rather more subdued conclusion. Though their initial doubts as to whether their son would make it to play at all, proved not to be true, it was clear that the concerns of his parents were well founded. Djokovic had been forced to retire when trailing 3-6, 6-1, 4-1 when it was evident that he could not push away off his left side. And being able to run only one way against Nadal meant that you were severely handicapped.

Djokovic had spent the period before the match desperately attempting not to make eye contact with his foe. "There were a lot of people around me, I was trying to avoid him and his sight," he said. "My intentions before the match were not to show him that I am weak, whatever, so he can be an advantage. Like I said, it was in question should I play or not, but I decided to go on the court. The first set I played really, really good, I served especially well which helped me to make the points shorter, and I was really aggressive. But as soon as I dropped a little bit with the serve, he used it."

Coming across him later on the competitors' lawn, one could only sympathise with a player who had proved to be a lion-hearted young man who did not deserve to lose in this way. He felt he would win The Championships this year and, given Federer's draw, such a belief could well have been confirmed. He grabbed my right hand and thumped it into his chest; there were tears in his eyes, he was emotionally drained. He would deserve his upcoming holiday in Capri. He would return a stronger player.

After all that, all the heartache, all the interruptions, all the cut and thrust, all the to-ing and fro-ing, we would have a repeat of last year's men's final, just the way it probably would have worked out had there been no rain at all. What a prospect.

The ladies' final was more difficult to pick. There was no No.1 v. No.2 here. Williams (ranked No.31 on the Sony Ericsson WTA Tour and seeded No.23) and Bartoli (ranked No.19 and seeded No.18) had the lowest combined ranking and seeding of any Grand Slam event final since the inception of computer rankings in 1975, with the exception of a few Australian Opens in the 1970s, when few of the leading players attended. Indeed, not since the 1979 Australian final between Barbara Jordan and Sharon Walsh, of the United States, had two non-top ten players reached this stage of a Grand Slam.

Bartoli was only the second woman who struck the ball double-handed on both sides to reach a Grand Slam final after Monica Seles (who reached 13), and whose technique had inspired Bartoli's father, Walter, a doctor by profession but also his daughter's coach, to persuade a young Marion that it could well work for her. She had beaten the world's No.1 and No.3 players to make it, so the No.23 – although a three-time former Wimbledon champion – was unlikely to hold too many fears.

There was a distinct commonality between the two players. When they were young girls both their fathers brought them to the game, reckoned that anyone could do it, taught themselves how to coach, and inspired their girls to an uncommon level of self-belief. Richard Williams brought up Venus and her sisters in Los Angeles; Walter Bartoli brought up Marion near Le Puy in the Massif Central, a region of volcanoes. Neither had wanted to know about the tennis systems in their countries, or about classic styles.

Finding a way, any way, to get the ball in ➤

Richard Gasquet

court again and again was their purpose. As a way of winning, it worked. Bartoli's *pere* gave up his practice in St Etienne to devote himself to his daughter's tennis career and had been her only coach. "My dad always believed in me," Bartoli said. "To see in the eyes of your parents that you can be one of the best gives you so much confidence, you're able to take on the world."

Unorthodox methods were used, such as sticking tennis balls to the arches of Marion's feet so that she would always be on her toes. In the winter, she trained indoors in a small hall. There was a wall just behind the baseline which meant that she had to stand inside the court to receive service. She did that today, unsettling opponents who found the ball coming back a lot faster than they expected.

Ambidextrous, signing her autograph with her left hand, serving with the right and hitting groundstrokes with both, Bartoli was certainly peculiar. And although she had much to offer in fortitude and guile, it had to be said that she did not much look like a tennis player at all, at least not a modern one. And it was her service action and the strange antics that preceded it that really raised one's eyebrows.

First, she jumped on the spot like a nervous squirrel. Then she walked to the baseline and stepped up to it as though she was approaching the end of the high diving board. She gripped the end of the racket as if attempting to perfect a sequence not properly learnt; held the ball close – again like a squirrel, but with a nut – and then launched it before awkwardly reaching up to give it a good biff. Then there was her stroke rehearsal when, especially before important points, she retired to the back of the court, faced the stop-netting and swished madly, trying to remember what to do next. And they said Venus was strange.

From 3-0 down in the opening set, she recovered to 3-all and was giving as good as she received until the tenth game when nerves overcame her, she double-faulted to offer the former champion one set point and on the second, when she could only manage a 72 mph second serve and her attempt at a lob was cut off by a superb high backhand crosscourt volleyed winner by the American.

Once she had fallen 2-0 behind after an arduous first service game in the second set, it was clear that Bartoli had met her match – this time there would be no third set heroics as in her three previous matches. The title would go to Venus for the fourth time and the 27-year-old would return to the top 20, at No.17, for the first time in a year. As runner up, Bartoli would reach a career-high No.11. ●

FINAL Day
8.07.2007

FEDERER
VS
NADAL

Sunday 8 July…

Who said it would not be done and dusted in time for the Champions' Dinner, 9.30 pm for 10.00 on the second Sunday at the Savoy Hotel, as per the original booking? Where were the purveyors of the third Wednesday finish? Whatever became of those contingency plans of which we heard so much but were never allowed to know what they were?

Smugness is not the way of it at the All England Club but a bit of chest thrusting would not have gone amiss as The Championships, which had had to endure drear weather and dire portents until the second weekend, squeaked through and everyone who ought to have been there for the final fling made it.

For the second time in three years, Roger Federer was seated alongside Venus Williams at the Chairman's table. And yet, so nearly did Wimbledon embrace its 19th different men's champion of the Open Era – it is the most difficult of the Grand Slam tournaments to win if you go by the statistics – in Rafael Nadal. As glasses were raised, and the best of the best were toasted, the overriding celebration was of the best men's final for a quarter of a century.

Federer defeated Nadal 7-6, 4-6, 7-6, 2-6, 6-2, a match of constant brilliance, mesmeric and unexpected shifts of emphasis, stunning bravado, and, ultimately, of that little edge on grass that Federer brings to the party as opposed to the subservience he feels to Nadal on clay. The difference was that Nadal looked ready to win a Wimbledon final, whereas Federer still appeared petrified of Paris.

There were a plethora of former champions on Centre Court to see it, from Jack Kramer from the 40s, through Dick Savitt from the 50s, Manuel Santana of the 60s, Stan Smith, Jimmy Connors and Bjorn Borg from the 70s, John McEnroe, Boris Becker and Pat Cash from the 80s, Michael Stich from the 90s and Goran Ivanisevic from this century. Of course, it was Borg's arrival that caused the greatest stir for, the 2000 Millenium Champions' Parade besides, the Swede had not set foot on Centre Court since 1981.

His hair was silver and shorter than we remembered, he was clean shaven, which was a first for men's finals day, his gait had not changed a bit, with its round shouldered, slightly pigeon-toed rolling shuffle. He made his way onto the court with Connors and McEnroe, who were heading in their different directions later, one to commentate for British and one for American viewers. They made for a stunning sight. Something had to give for Borg, either Federer equalled his record of five successive Wimbledon titles or Nadal became the first man since 1980 to win the French Open and Wimbledon within the space of a month. He sat back in his wicker chair and waited.

It was time to banish the bad images, forget about the damp, the cold, the drizzle, harken not to those who departed Wimbledon muttering darkly under their breath about the unfairness of it all and celebrate instead the brilliance of the two best players in the world, who sparkled and shone on a day that was just perfect for the kind of sport they provided.

We spared a thought for Nadal because he came perilously close to upsetting the Swiss bandwagon – four times in the fifth set he had break points and on two of those he ought to have kept the ball in play. The last momentum shift, however, was in Federer's favour, two of his favoured forehand passes skipping off the turf in the sixth game of the final set to engineer the crucial break of serve, one backed by three aces, his 22nd, 23rd and 24th of an afternoon when that component of his game proved the critical difference.

The Swiss had the better of the breaks, there was no arguing about that. When all else were losing their heads, he won three matches with limited toil, learned that Tommy Haas, his fourth round opponent, had

withdrawn with a stomach muscle tear, returned after a five-day hiatus and was disconcerted for all of just one set, against Juan Carlos Ferrero in the quarter-finals. His arrival at this juncture was in marked contrast to Nadal, who lived on the premises for the best part of a week, came perilously close to losing in the third round to Robin Soderling, a feisty Swede, before needing five sets the next day to close out Russia's Mikhail Youzhny.

Given that, though, Federer knew that Nadal would not give an inch, for it was simply not the Spaniard's style. The Swiss burst to a 3-0 lead and one re-visited last year's final when he breezed the first set to love but Nadal was not about to let him rush away with it this time and recovered; a crunching double fisted backhand winner which took the Federer serve the first indication that this would be a seismic scrap.

It took Federer five set points, and the first duel with his second opponent of the afternoon – the Hawk-Eye line-calling technology – to get his nose in front. The timing of Nadal's use of the machine could get under an opponent's skin – he often waited until the opponent was walking around to serve before pointing to the sky – almost as much as the trustworthiness of the system. ➤

Bjorn Borg applaudes Roger Federer

The longer the final went on, the more intense became Federer's exasperation; indeed, it was further testament to his temperament that he was able to keep body and soul in harness.

That temperament was sorely tested when Nadal claimed the one break in the second set, winning one point in that game when seated on his backside on the baseline and managing to conjure a winning backhand pass. If Becker had a copyright on the full length dive, the winner-while-seated patent was one for the Spaniard.

A third set without a break of serve might have been Nadal's to claim when, at 5-6, 15-30, he had sight of a forehand in mid-court, the like of which he usually drills into the corner but he snatched at this one and netted. The reprieve offered Federer a second wind and he played a tie-break of consummate concentration. Then, he answered a call of nature which is an unusual occurence for him – during a match, that is.

Perhaps Federer sneaked a look at the champions' roll of honour because he returned

in an agitated state. The ball was bouncing from the frame at crazy angles, Hawk-Eye was giving him more bad calls and Nadal was suddenly 4-0 ahead. At the 4-1 changeover, Federer let rip. "This system is s***," he stormed at Carlos Ramos, the umpire. "Look at the score, look what it's doing, it's killing me." He asked for the umpire to throw the off switch but Ramos declined.

And so to a fifth set, the first time Federer had been in such territory in a Grand Slam final. He held serve to love, Nadal hung in and, within a flash, the champion was a couple of break points down – but Nadal missed another of his whipped forehands on the second. 2-1 to Federer. In his subsequent service game, he was break points down – Nadal got a second service sighter but pushed a backhand return long and Federer's next serve was akin to a thunderbolt. 3-2 to Federer.

It became 4-2 in the blink of an eye, Nadal's forehand on the first point clipping the top of the net and falling wide, a slice of fortune that Federer followed with two of his finest forehands of the afternoon. The final game lasted 12 points, Nadal kept flashing his biceps but this was not Roland Garros. He got very close but not close enough again for Federer to stumble within sight of glory.

Nadal was questioned about one break point when an American – wouldn't you know it? – suggested he had not put enough bite on a backhand volley. According to my notes, there was not a volley on any of the break points. Nadal looked confused. "I remember all the break points if you want," he said. "My best opportunity was at 30-40 at 1-1, I hit a good return, he came back, I touch very good close backhand, he return the ball very good and I miss the forehand for go to the other side. The winning forehand. That was the best chance." So very near.

If we thought that was the end of the high drama, though, another think was coming. Jamie Murray, of Scotland, and Jelena Jankovic, of Serbia, had teamed up to play mixed doubles on a kind of tennis blind date, arranged by Jamie's mother, Judy, and his agent, Patricio Apey. Not only that, they had earned a place in the final by winning both quarter-final and semi-final on Saturday evening, a 68-game marathon.

To win the title, their opponents, Jonas Bjorkman, of Sweden, and Australia's Alicia Molik would also require back-to-back victories and they managed the first part of the bargain, defeating Fabrice Santoro and Severine Bremond of France on No.13 Court. Bjorkman had more experience of big time doubles than the other three put together.

But there was something about Jelena and Jamie – Beauty and Stretch as they were dubbed as a contrast to Murray's partnership with Eric Butorac, of the United States, which was known in the tennis world as Booty and Stretch. It was the way they played, the way they smiled, the way they cranked up their levels at critical moments, the tremendous shot-making both perpetrated – not least Jankovic's returning during the critical break of Bjorkman's serve in the third set of the final.

There was a tear in many eyes when the pair won the final 6-4, 3-6, 6-1 and the roar that greeted their ascent to the Royal Box induced an outbreak of goose pimples. Murray, whose brother, Andy, had been summarising for BBC Radio, became the first British victor in The Championships since Jeremy Bates and Jo Durie won the mixed 20 years earlier.

➢ **Arnaud Clement (left) and Michael Llodra**

Liezel Huber and
Cara Black

Anastasia Pavlyuchenkova and Urszula
Radwanska

On Court No.1, there were scenes of delirium almost as intense, when Arnaud Clement and Michael Llodra, of France, won the men's doubles title, defeating the No.1 seeds and defending champions, Mike and Bob Bryan of the United States 6-7, 6-3, 6-4, 6-4. Sources in the French press disclosed that the preparation for their pair was, how shall we say this… 'unconventional' by normal standards. After every win, in true French style, they went to the best wine cellar in Wimbledon Village and bought a fine, vintage wine – one magnum they purchased cost £600 – and polished it off after dinner. The pair stripped to the waist after their victory and tossed their shirts to the crowd – Llodra needing to borrow one for the presentation because he had run out.

France had had to wait even longer for doubles success, Jean Borotra and Jacques Brugnon the last to win the title in 1933. Clement, formerly an Australian Open singles runner up, said: "The first thing is that it is not about 74 years, it's about us. For me, it's very special because it's my first Grand Slam title in doubles. For Michael, it's the third one. But for me it's a very special feeling. Winning a Grand Slam with one of my best friends, it's more special."

Cara Black, of Zimbabwe, and Liezel Huber, from South Africa, the No.2 seeds, won the ladies doubles for the second time in three years, defeating Katerina Srebotnik, of Slovakia and Japan's Ai Sugiyama 3-6, 6-3, 6-2.

Donald Young, of the United States, prevented Vladimir Ignatic, of Belarus, completing a classic sweep of the French Open boys' title, the Artois junior championship and Wimbledon, when he won the boys' event, 7-5, 6-1. It might have been a one-two for America in the junior event, but the girls' title went to Urszula Radwanska, of Poland, a 6-2, 6-3, 6-0 victor over Madison Brengle.

There were few people happier to be clutching a dinner jacket than Vittorio Selmi, the highly popular ATP Tour manager, who had never been to the Champions' Dinner before and was asked to chaperone his Italian compatriots, Daniel Lopez and Matteo Trevisan, winners of the boys' doubles. They had defeated Roman Jebavy, of the Czech Republic, and his Slovak partner, Martin Klizan, 7-6, 4-6, 10-8 on a champion's tie-break. The girls' doubles final was equally close, a tie-break needed to separate Urszula Radwanska (who completed the girls' singles and doubles 'double') and Anastasia Pavlyuchenkova, who won the final 6-4, 2-6, 10-7 over Japan's Misaki Doi and Kurumi Nara.

The ladies' invitation doubles was won by the Czech pair, Jana Novotna, the 1998 singles champion and Helena Sukova, who defeated Ros Nideffer (nee Fairbank) and Ilana Kloss, from South Africa, 6-3, 6-3.

There was healthy representation for Britain at that end of the age range. Jeremy Bates, the former No.1 and Davis Cup captain, and Anders Jarryd, of Sweden, defeated Johan Kriek and Kevin Curren, defending champions from the USA, 6-3, 6-3 in the senior gentlemen's invitation doubles, while Mark Petchey, once Andy Murray's coach and men's manager at the LTA, and Chris Wikinson reached the climax of the (not so senior) gentleman's invitation doubles, only to be beaten 6-2, 6-2 by Jacco Eltingh and Paul Haarhuis, of Holland.

There was further cause for a celebration of Dutch courage when Ronald Vink and Robin Ammerlaan, the No.2 seeds, defeated Japan's Shingo Kunieda and Satoshi Saida, the reigning champions and No.1 seeds 4-6, 7-5, 6-2 in the increasingly popular wheelchair doubles final. ●

Helena Sukova, Jana Novotna, Ilana Kloss and Ros Nideffer

Kevin Curren, Johan Kriek, Anders Jarryd and Jeremy Bates

Roger Federer
The Gentlemen's Singles

Venus Williams
The Ladies' Singles

Arnaud Clement & Michael Llodra
The Gentlemen's Doubles

Cara Black & Liezel Huber
The Ladies' Doubles

Jamie Murray & Jelena Jankovic
The Mixed Doubles

Robin Ammerlaan & Ronald Vink
The Wheelchair Gentlemen's Invitation Doubles

**Anastasia Pavlyuchenkova &
Urszula Radwanska**
The Girls' Doubles

Daniel Lopez & Matteo Trevisan
The Boys' Doubles

Photo by Getty Images

Jacco Eltingh & Paul Haarhuis
The Gentlemen's Invitation Doubles

Helena Sukova & Jana Novotna
The Ladies' Invitation Doubles

Urszula Radwanska
The Girls' Singles

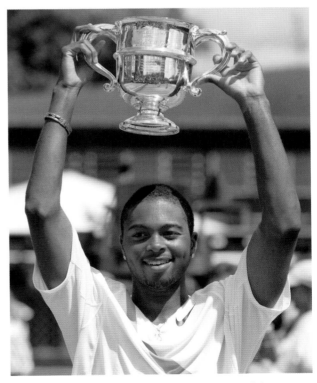

Donald Young
The Boys' Singles

145

CHAMPIONSHIP
RECORDS
2007

EVENT I – THE GENTLEMEN'S SINGLES CHAMPIONSHIP 2007
HOLDER: R. FEDERER

The Winner became the holder, for the year only, of the CHALLENGE CUP presented by The All England Lawn Tennis and Croquet Club in 1887. The Winner received a silver replica of the Challenge Cup. A Silver Salver was presented to the Runner-up and a Bronze Medal to each defeated Semi-finalist. The matches were the best of five sets.

First Round

1. Federer, Roger [1] (1) (SUI)
2. Gabashvili, Teimuraz (86) (RUS)
3. Del Potro, Juan Martin (56) (ARG)
4. Sanguinetti, Davide (105) (ITA)
5. (Q) Qureshi, Aisam-Ul-Haq (279) (PAK)
6. (Q) Childs, Lee (408) (GBR)
7. (Q) De Voest, Rik (124) (RSA)
8. Safin, Marat [26] (24) (RUS)
9. Tursunov, Dmitry [21] (23) (RUS)
10. Almagro, Nicolas (40) (ESP)
11. Berrer, Michael (94) (GER)
12. Montanes, Albert (48) (ESP)
13. (Q) Zib, Tomas (133) (CZE)
14. Hartfield, Diego (88) (ARG)
15. (Q) Fleishman, Zack (172) (USA)
16. Haas, Tommy [13] (10) (GER)
17. Blake, James [9] (9) (USA)
18. Andreev, Igor (27) (RUS)
19. Guzman, Juan-Pablo (100) (ARG)
20. Pavel, Andrei (122) (ROU)
21. (Q) Muller, Gilles (156) (LUX)
22. Hernandez, Oscar (50) (ESP)
23. Hajek, Jan (139) (CZE)
24. Ferrero, Juan Carlos [20] (18) (ESP)
25. Kohlschreiber, Philipp [27] (30) (GER)
26. Serra, Florent (90) (FRA)
27. Peya, Alexander (103) (AUT)
28. Tipsarevic, Janko (64) (SRB)
29. (Q) Falla, Alejandro (119) (COL)
30. Querrey, Sam (81) (USA)
31. Ginepri, Robby (46) (USA)
32. Gonzalez, Fernando [5] (6) (CHI)
33. Roddick, Andy [3] (3) (USA)
34. Gimelstob, Justin (73) (USA)
35. Udomchoke, Danai (114) (THA)
36. Berlocq, Carlos (92) (ARG)
37. Verdasco, Fernando (41) (ESP)
38. (Q) Reynolds, Bobby (141) (USA)
39. Seppi, Andreas (112) (ITA)
40. Hrbaty, Dominik [31] (33) (SVK)
41. Ferrer, David [17] (15) (ESP)
42. Roitman, Sergio (71) (ARG)
43. Mathieu, Paul-Henri (39) (FRA)
44. Stepanek, Radek (61) (CZE)
45. Gicquel, Marc (42) (FRA)
46. Hernych, Jan (130) (CZE)
47. Spadea, Vincent (66) (USA)
48. Ljubicic, Ivan [15] (12) (CRO)
49. Gasquet, Richard [12] (14) (FRA)
50. Ulihrach, Bohdan (145) (CZE)
51. (Q) Clement, Arnaud (34) (FRA)
52. (Q) Mahut, Nicolas (77) (FRA)
53. (WC) Baker, Jamie (238) (GBR)
54. (Q) Roger-Vasselin, Edouard (109) (FRA)
55. Becker, Benjamin (44) (GER)
56. Chela, Juan Ignacio [24] (20) (ARG)
57. Moya, Carlos [25] (22) (ESP)
58. Henman, Tim (74) (GBR)
59. (WC) Goodall, Joshua (226) (GBR)
60. Lopez, Feliciano (78) (ESP)
61. (WC) Tsonga, Jo-Wilfried (110) (FRA)
62. Benneteau, Julien (54) (FRA)
63. Lapentti, Nicolas (63) (ECU)
64. (LL) Kim, Kevin (117) (USA)
65. Davydenko, Nikolay [6] (4) (RUS)
66. Korolev, Evgeny (79) (RUS)
67. (WC) Bogdanovic, Alex (108) (GBR)
68. Guccione, Chris (96) (AUS)
69. Monfils, Gael (73) (FRA)
70. Johansson, Thomas (75) (SWE)
71. Vliegen, Kristof (76) (BEL)
72. Monaco, Juan [32] (32) (ARG)
73. Nalbandian, David [23] (25) (ARG)
74. (Q) Zverev, Mischa (134) (GER)
75. (LL) Dancevic, Frank (113) (CAN)
76. Koubek, Stefan (60) (AUT)
77. Devilder, Nicolas (102) (FRA)
78. Zabaleta, Mariano (83) (ARG)
79. Gulbis, Ernests (82) (LAT)
80. Baghdatis, Marcos [10] (16) (CYP)
81. Hewitt, Lleyton [16] (19) (AUS)
82. (WC) Bloomfield, Richard (194) (GBR)
83. Garcia-Lopez, Guillermo (58) (ESP)
84. Bolelli, Simone (65) (ITA)
85. Mirnyi, Max (57) (BLR)
86. Lu, Yen-Hsun (106) (TPE)
87. Navarro Pastor, Ivan (93) (ESP)
88. Canas, Guillermo [22] (17) (ARG)
89. Volandri, Filippo [30] (27) (ITA)
90. Kiefer, Nicolas (17) (GER)
91. Santoro, Fabrice (70) (FRA)
92. Karlovic, Ivo (45) (CRO)
93. Delic, Amer (67) (USA)
94. Dlouhy, Lukas (107) (CZE)
95. Starace, Potito (47) (ITA)
96. Djokovic, Novak [4] (5) (SRB)
97. Berdych, Tomas [7] (11) (CZE)
98. Massu, Nicolas (52) (CHI)
99. Wawrinka, Stanislas (43) (SUI)
100. Llodra, Michael (68) (FRA)
101. Lee, Hyung-Taik (51) (KOR)
102. Vassallo-Arguello, Martin (89) (ARG)
103. Horna, Luis (85) (PER)
104. Calleri, Agustin [29] (29) (ARG)
105. Bjorkman, Jonas [19] (35) (SWE)
106. (Q) Vicente, Fernando (165) (ESP)
107. (Q) Kunitsyn, Igor (91) (RUS)
108. (Q) Wang, Yeu-Tzuoo (168) (TPE)
109. (Q) Arthurs, Wayne (195) (AUS)
110. (WC) De Bakker, Thiemo (391) (NED)
111. Kendrick, Robert (87) (USA)
112. Robredo, Tommy [11] (7) (ESP)
113. Youzhny, Mikhail [14] (13) (RUS)
114. Pless, Kristian (80) (DEN)
115. (WC) Cilic, Marin (101) (CRO)
116. Simon, Gilles (55) (FRA)
117. Mayer, Florian (37) (GER)
118. (Q) Warburg, Sam (208) (USA)
119. Russell, Michael (69) (USA)
120. Nieminen, Jarkko [18] (21) (FIN)
121. Soderling, Robin [28] (28) (SWE)
122. Rochus, Olivier (53) (BEL)
123. (WC) Marray, Jonathan (263) (GBR)
124. Grosjean, Sebastien (62) (FRA)
125. Eschauer, Werner (72) (AUT)
126. Ramirez Hidalgo, Ruben (95) (ESP)
127. Fish, Mardy (38) (USA)
128. Nadal, Rafael [2] (2) (ESP)

Second Round

- R.Federer [1] 6/3 6/2 6/4
- J.Del Potro 3/6 6/3 6/4 6/4
- A-U-H.Qureshi 6/3 6/4 7/6(6)
- M.Safin [26] 7/6(5) 6/4 7/5
- D.Tursunov [21] 7/6(2) 6/4 6/7(7) 6/3
- M.Berrer 6/3 6/3 6/2
- T.Zib 4/6 7/6(4) 3/6 6/3 6/4
- T.Haas [13] 6/3 6/4 6/2
- J.Blake [9] 6/3 6/4 6/4
- A.Pavel 6/4 6/4 6/1
- G.Muller 6/2 6/7(6) 4/3 Ret'd
- J.C.Ferrero [20] 6/7(5) 4/6 6/3 6/2 7/5
- F.Serra 7/6(4) 6/4 6/4
- J.Tipsarevic 4/6 3/6 6/4 6/4 6/3
- A.Falla 7/6(5) 6/1 6/4
- F.Gonzalez [5] 3/6 7/6(4) 6/2 6/2
- A.Roddick [3] 6/1 7/5 7/6(3)
- D.Udomchoke 6/4 7/5 6/3
- F.Verdasco 6/4 6/4 6/3
- A.Seppi 7/6(8) 6/1 6/2
- D.Ferrer [17] 6/3 6/3 6/1
- P-H.Mathieu 7/6(4) 6/2 6/2
- J.Hernych 0/6 6/4 6/4 6/4
- I.Ljubicic [15] 6/4 4/6 7/6(4) 6/4
- R.Gasquet [12] 6/3 6/4 6/4
- N.Mahut 6/3 3/6 7/6(5) 6/4
- E.Roger-Vasselin 7/6(2) 6/2 6/3
- J.I.Chela [24] 3/6 4/6 6/4 6/4 10/8
- T.Henman 6/3 1/6 5/7 6/2 13/11
- F.Lopez 6/1 6/4 6/4
- J-W.Tsonga 7/6(4) 7/5 6/4
- N.Lapentti 2/6 6/2 4/6 6/3 6/4
- N.Davydenko [6] 7/6(12) 7/4 7/6(5)
- C.Guccione 7/6(2) 6/4 6/4
- G.Monfils 6/4 7/6(5) 6/2
- K.Vliegen 6/4 6/3 7/6(3)
- D.Nalbandian [23] 6/3 6/4 6/2
- F.Dancevic 6/2 6/4 6/2
- N.Devilder 6/7(3) 6/4 7/5 6/4
- M.Baghdatis [10] 3/6 6/4 6/3 6/2
- L.Hewitt [16] 7/5 6/3 7/5
- S.Bolelli 4/6 7/6(5) 6/4 6/4
- M.Mirnyi 6/3 6/4 2/1 Ret'd
- G.Canas [22] 7/6(3) 6/3 6/4
- N.Kiefer 6/3 7/6(6) 6/1
- F.Santoro 4/6 7/6(4) 7/6(3) 3/6 6/4
- A.Delic 6/3 6/4 5/7 6/4
- N.Djokovic [4] 6/0 6/3 6/4
- T.Berdych [7] 7/6(5) 6/4 6/2
- M.Llodra 6/4 6/4 6/1
- H-T.Lee 6/4 6/2 6/3
- A.Calleri [29] 6/2 7/6(4) 7/5
- J.Bjorkman [19] 6/3 6/1 6/2
- Y-T.Wang 6/3 6/4 6/7(5) 6/7(8) 6/2
- W.Arthurs 6/7(7) 6/7(7) 7/6(4) 6/4 6/2
- T.Robredo [11] 6/2 3/6 6/3 6/7(5) 6/3
- M.Youzhny [14] 6/4 6/2 6/4
- G.Simon 3/6 7/5 6/4 4/6 6/3
- F.Mayer 6/4 6/2 6/2
- J.Nieminen [18] 6/3 6/2 7/5
- R.Soderling [28] 6/3 6/2 6/2
- S.Grosjean 6/2 7/6(0) 7/5
- W.Eschauer 6/2 3/6 6/4 6/3
- R.Nadal [2] 6/3 7/6(4) 6/3

Third Round

- R.Federer [1] 6/2 7/5 6/1
- M.Safin [26] 6/4 6/2 7/6(4)
- D.Tursunov [21] 4/6 6/4 6/4 6/4
- T.Haas [13] 6/3 7/6(5) 6/4
- J.Blake [9] 6/4 6/3 6/3
- J.C.Ferrero [20] 6/4 6/4 6/7(2) 7/6(8)
- J.Tipsarevic 6/3 6/2 6/7(3) 3/6 6/2
- F.Gonzalez [5] 4/6 6/3 6/4 7/6(1)
- A.Roddick [3] 6/3 6/4 7/6(3)
- F.Verdasco 6/3 6/2 6/4
- P-H.Mathieu 6/3 4/6 6/3
- I.Ljubicic [15] 6/4 6/3 6/4
- R.Gasquet [12] 6/4 6/3 6/4
- E.Roger-Vasselin 7/6(3) 6/4 7/5
- F.Lopez 7/6(3) 7/6(5) 3/6 2/6 6/1
- J-W.Tsonga 6/4 6/2 6/3
- N.Davydenko [6] 3/6 5/7 7/6(5) 6/4 6/2
- G.Monfils 7/5 7/6(4) 7/6(1)
- D.Nalbandian [23] 6/2 6/3 5/7 6/3
- M.Baghdatis [10] 6/0 7/6(5) 6/7(4) 6/2
- L.Hewitt [16] 6/2 6/2 6/1
- G.Canas [22] 6/7(4) 6/1 7/6(4) 7/6(4)
- N.Kiefer 6/4 6/3 6/4
- N.Djokovic [4] 6/3 3/6 6/3 7/6(4)
- T.Berdych [7] 7/6(4) 7/6(2) 3/6 7/6(4)
- H-T.Lee 7/6(6) 6/4 6/7(3) 6/3
- J.Bjorkman [19] 6/0 6/3 6/7(8) 6/4
- W.Arthurs 6/3 7/6(5) 6/3
- M.Youzhny [14] 6/4 4/6 3/6 7/5 6/4
- J.Nieminen [18] 3/6 6/3 7/6(2) 2/6 6/3
- R.Soderling [28] 6/3 3/6 6/3 6/2
- R.Nadal [2] 6/2 6/4 6/1

Fourth Round

- R.Federer [1] 6/1 6/4 7/6(4)
- T.Haas [13] 1/6 6/4 7/6(5) 6/4
- J.C.Ferrero [20] 3/6 6/3 6/3 7/6(4)
- J.Tipsarevic 6/3 3/6 6/3 4/6 8/6
- A.Roddick [3] 6/3 6/4 7/6(2)
- P-H.Mathieu 4/6 7/5 6/2 6/3
- R.Gasquet [12] 6/3 6/4 6/2
- J-W.Tsonga 6/4 6/2 6/3
- N.Davydenko [6] 6/3 7/5 6/3
- M.Baghdatis [10] 6/2 7/5 6/0
- L.Hewitt [16] 6/4 3/6 6/3 6/4
- N.Djokovic [4] 7/6(4) 6/7(6) 6/2 7/6(5)
- T.Berdych [7] 4/6 7/6(2) 7/6(3) 6/3
- J.Bjorkman [19] 6/2 6/1 6/4
- M.Youzhny [14] 7/5 7/6(5) 6/3
- R.Nadal [2] 6/4 6/4 6/7(7) 4/6 7/5

Quarter-Finals

- R.Federer [1] w/o
- J.C.Ferrero [20] 7/5 6/3 7/6(5)
- A.Roddick [3] 6/2 7/5 7/6(6)
- R.Gasquet [12] 6/4 6/3 6/4
- M.Baghdatis [10] 7/6(5) 7/6(5) 6/3
- N.Djokovic [4] 7/6(8) 7/6(2) 4/6 7/6(5)
- T.Berdych [7] 6/4 6/0 6/7(5) 6/0
- R.Nadal [2] 4/6 3/6 6/1 6/2 6/2

Semi-Finals

- R.Federer [1] 7/6(2) 3/6 6/1 6/3
- R.Gasquet [12] 4/6 4/6 7/6(2) 7/6(3) 8/6
- N.Djokovic [4] 7/6(4) 7/6(9) 6/7(3) 4/6 7/5
- R.Nadal [2] 7/6(1) 6/4 6/2

Final

- R.Federer [1] 7/5 6/3 6/4
- R.Nadal [2] 3/6 6/1 4/1 Ret'd

Winner

- R.Federer [1] 7/6(7) 4/6 7/6(3) 2/6 6/2

HOLDERS: B. BRYAN & M. BRYAN

The Winners became the holders, for the year only, of the CHALLENGE CUPS presented by the OXFORD UNIVERSITY LAWN TENNIS CLUB in 1884 and the late SIR HERBERT WILBERFORCE in 1937. The Winners received a silver replica of the Challenge Cup. A Silver Salver was presented to each of the Runners-up, and a Bronze Medal to each defeated Semi-finalist. The matches were the best of five sets.

	First Round	Second Round	Third Round	Quarter-Finals	Semi-Finals	Final	Winners
	1. **B.Bryan** (USA) & **M.Bryan** (USA) [1]	**B.Bryan & M.Bryan** [1]					
	2. G.Garcia-Lopez (ESP) & F.Verdasco (ESP)	6/1 6/3 6/3	**B.Bryan & M.Bryan** [1]				
(LL)	3. O.Rochus (BEL) & K.Vliegen (BEL)	**O.Rochus & K.Vliegen**	6/0 7/6(4) 6/1	**B.Bryan & M.Bryan** [1]			
(LL)	4. L.Burgsmuller (GER) & O.Tereshchuk (UKR)	7/6(7) 6/4 6/2		6/2 6/2 7/6(4)			
(LL)	5. S.Ratiwatana (THA) & S.Ratiwatana (THA)	**R.Bloomfield & J.Marray**	R.Bloomfield & J.Marray				
(WC)	6. R.Bloomfield (GBR) & J.Marray (GBR)	7/6(4) 6/4 6/4	6/3 3/6 6/4 7/5				
(WC)	7. J.Baker (GBR) & A.Bogdanovic (GBR)	**M.Fyrstenberg & L.Kubot** [16]			**B.Bryan & M.Bryan** [1]		
	8. **M.Fyrstenberg** (POL) & **L.Kubot** (POL) [16]	6/4 6/7(3) 6/2 6/4			6/3 6/2 6/4		
	9. **L.Dlouhy** (CZE) & **P.Vizner** (CZE) [9]	**L.Dlouhy & P.Vizner** [9]					
	10. T.Cibulec (CZE) & J.Kerr (AUS)	6/4 6/4 6/2	**L.Dlouhy & P.Vizner** [9]				
	11. F.Cermak (CZE) & L.Friedl (CZE)	F.Cermak & L.Friedl	6/4 3/6 2/6 7/6(5) 7/5	**L.Dlouhy & P.Vizner** [9]			
	12. H-T.Lee (KOR) & J.Tipsarevic (SRB)	6/3 6/7(7) 6/4 6/3		7/6(5) 6/3 3/6 6/2			
	13. O.Hernandez (ESP) & P.Starace (ITA)	E.Butorac & J.Murray	E.Butorac & J.Murray				
	14. E.Butorac (USA) & J.Murray (GBR)	6/3 6/3 6/3	3/6 6/4 6/3 6/4				
(Q)	15. A.Kuznetsov (USA) & M.Zverev (GER)	**J.Erlich & A.Ram** [7]					
	16. **J.Erlich** (ISR) & **A.Ram** (ISR) [7]	7/6(2) 3/6 6/2 6/3					
	17. **F.Santoro** (FRA) & **N.Zimonjic** (SRB) [4]	**F.Santoro & N.Zimonjic** [4]					
(WC)	18. L.Childs (GBR) & J.Delgado (GBR)	6/2 6/7(4) 7/6(4) 7/6(5)	**F.Santoro & N.Zimonjic** [4]				
(WC)	19. N.Bamford (GBR) & J.May (GBR)	R.Ginepri & T.Parrott	6/1 6/4 6/2	**F.Santoro & N.Zimonjic** [4]			
	20. R.Ginepri (USA) & T.Parrott (USA)	7/6(12) 6/3 6/2		6/1 6/2 6/4			
(LL)	21. K.Kim (USA) & R.Smeets (AUS)	K.Kim & R.Smeets	**J.Levinsky & D.Skoch** [13]				
	22. E.Gulbis (LAT) & I.Ljubicic (CRO)	6/7(5) 7/6(6) 6/4 7/5	7/6(2) 5/7 7/6(4) 7/6(8)				
	23. M.Granollers-Pujol (ESP) & T.Robredo (ESP)	**J.Levinsky & D.Skoch** [13]			**F.Santoro & N.Zimonjic** [4]		
	24. **J.Levinsky** (CZE) & **D.Skoch** (CZE) [13]	6/4 7/6(4) 6/2			7/6(6) 6/7(5) 6/4 6/3		
	25. **A.Fisher** (AUS) & **T.Phillips** (USA) [12]	M.Berrer & M.Kohlmann	S.Lipsky & D.Martin				
	26. M.Berrer (GER) & M.Kohlmann (GER)	7/6(4) 6/2 7/5	6/7(3) 7/5 7/6(5) 7/6(9)				
(Q)	27. S.Lipsky (USA) & D.Martin (USA)	S.Lipsky & D.Martin		**M.Damm & L.Paes** [5]			
	28. A.Montanes (ESP) & R.Ramirez Hidalgo (ESP)	6/3 6/3 6/0		6/2 6/4 6/2			
	29. J.Auckland (GBR) & S.Huss (AUS)	J.Auckland & S.Huss	**M.Damm & L.Paes** [5]				
(Q)	30. I.Bozoljac (SRB) & D.Norman (BEL)	4/6 6/4 7/5 7/5	7/6(4) 7/6(4) 3/6 7/6(3)				
	31. C.Haggard (RSA) & M.Matkowski (POL)	**M.Damm & L.Paes** [5]					
	32. **M.Damm** (CZE) & **L.Paes** (IND) [5]	7/6(4) 6/3 7/5					
	33. **P.Hanley** (AUS) & **K.Ullyett** (ZIM) [6]	**P.Hanley & K.Ullyett** [6]					
	34. N.Devilder (FRA) & P-H.Mathieu (FRA)	6/1 6/3 6/3	M.Melo & A.Sa				
	35. M.Melo (BRA) & A.Sa (BRA)	M.Melo & A.Sa	5/7 7/6(4) 4/6 7/6(7)				
	36. J.Benneteau (FRA) & N.Mahut (FRA)	6/7(4) 6/3 7/6(6) 2/6 6/3	28/26	M.Melo & A.Sa			
	37. W.Arthurs (AUS) & J.Gimelstob (USA)	W.Arthurs & J.Gimelstob		6/4 6/7(6) 7/6(2) 6/7(9)			
	38. S.Bolelli (ITA) & J.Del Potro (ARG)	6/4 6/3 6/2	C.Kas & A.Peya	6/4			
	39. C.Kas (GER) & A.Peya (AUT)	C.Kas & A.Peya	6/2 6/4 7/5				
	40. Y.Allegro (SUI) & **J.Thomas** (USA) [17]	7/6(4) 3/6 6/4 6/4			M.Melo & A.Sa		
	41. **J.Coetzee** (RSA) & **R.Wassen** (NED) [14]	W.Moodie & T.Perry	W.Moodie & T.Perry		6/4 6/3 6/4		
	42. W.Moodie (RSA) & T.Perry (AUS)	2/6 6/2 7/6(5) 6/4	7/4 6/1 3/6 6/3				
	43. T.Behrend (GER) & F.Mayer (GER)	T.Behrend & F.Mayer		**M.Knowles & D.Nestor** [3]			
	44. K.Pless (DEN) & M.Verkerk (NED)	6/0 7/6(1) 6/3		6/3 5/7 5/7 6/4 6/4			
	45. M.Gicquel (FRA) & F.Serra (FRA)	M.Gicquel & F.Serra	**M.Knowles & D.Nestor** [3]				
	46. I.Andreev (RUS) & T.Gabashvili (RUS)	3/6 7/6(4) 6/4 6/2	7/6(2) 6/4 4/6 6/0				
	47. N.Almagro (ESP) & I.Navarro Pastor (ESP)	**M.Knowles & D.Nestor** [3]					
	48. **M.Knowles** (BAH) & **D.Nestor** (CAN) [3]	7/6(2) 6/3 6/1					
	49. **S.Aspelin** (SWE) & **J.Knowle** (AUT) [8]	T.Johansson & A.Pavel	T.Johansson & A.Pavel		**A.Clement & M.Llodra** [10]		
	50. T.Johansson (SWE) & A.Pavel (ROU)	6/4 5/7 6/4 6/4	7/6(3) 1/6 6/4 6/4		7/6(8) 6/3 6/3		
	51. I.Kunitsyn (RUS) & D.Tursunov (RUS)	I.Kunitsyn & D.Tursunov		**A.Clement & M.Llodra** [10]			
(WC)	52. J.Goodall (GBR) & R.Hutchins (GBR)	6/2 3/6 7/6(6) 6/4		7/5 6/3 1/0 Ret'd			
	53. A.Delic (USA) & B.Reynolds (USA)	A.Delic & B.Reynolds	**A.Clement & M.Llodra** [10]				
	54. M.Baghdatis (CYP) & S.Wawrinka (SUI)	6/3 6/7(3) 7/5 6/4	6/3 6/4 6/7(5) 6/7(9)				
	55. M.Russell (USA) & G.Simon (FRA)	**A.Clement & M.Llodra** [10]	14/12			**A.Clement & M.Llodra** [10]	**A.Clement & M.Llodra** [10]
	56. **A.Clement** (FRA) & **M.Llodra** (FRA) [10]	6/2 6/1 6/3				6/7(5) 6/3 6/4 6/4	
	57. **M.Garcia** (ARG) & **S.Prieto** (ARG) [15]	**M.Garcia & S.Prieto** [15]	H.Levy & R.Ram				
	58. A.Calleri (ARG) & N.Lapentti (ECU)	6/4 4/1 Ret'd	7/6(0) 6/7(4) 7/6(4)				
	59. D.Hrbaty (SVK) & M.Mertinak (SVK)	H.Levy & R.Ram	6/7(3) 10/8	H.Levy & R.Ram			
(Q)	60. **H.Levy** (ISR) & **R.Ram** (USA)	6/4 6/4 6/4		6/3 5/7 6/2 3/6 6/2			
	61. B.Becker (GER) & P.Pala (CZE)	B.Becker & P.Pala	B.Becker & P.Pala				
	62. C.Suk (CZE) & R.Vik (CZE)	7/6(5) 7/6(6) 2/6 6/3	4/6 3/6 6/4 6/4 8/6				
	63. R.Lindstedt (SWE) & J.Nieminen (FIN)	R.Lindstedt & J.Nieminen					
	64. **J.Bjorkman** (SWE) & **M.Mirnyi** (BLR) [2]	2/6 7/6(4) 7/5 6/3					

Heavy type denotes seeded players. The figure in brackets against names denotes the order in which they have been seeded. (WC)=Wild card. (Q)=Qualifier. (LL)=Lucky loser.

EVENT III – THE LADIES' SINGLES CHAMPIONSHIP 2007
HOLDER: MISS A. MAURESMO

The Winner became the holder, for the year only, of the CHALLENGE TROPHY presented by The All England Lawn Tennis and Croquet Club in 1886. The Winner received a silver replica of the Trophy. A Silver Salver was presented to the Runner-up and a Bronze Medal to each defeated Semi-finalist. The matches were the best of three sets.

First Round

1. Henin, Justine [1] *(1)* (BEL)
2. Cravero, Jorgelina *(117)* (ARG) (Q)
3. Bacsinszky, Timea *(91)* (SUI)
4. Dushevina, Vera *(83)* (RUS)
5. Sun, Tiantian *(107)* (CHN)
6. Loit, Emilie *(43)* (FRA)
7. Vesnina, Elena *(67)* (RUS)
8. Poutchkova, Olga [30] *(32)* (RUS)
9. Bondarenko, Alona [24] *(24)* (UKR)
10. Craybas, Jill *(64)* (USA)
11. Szavay, Agnes *(72)* (HUN) (Q)
12. Birnerova, Eva *(97)* (CZE)
13. Harkleroad, Ashley *(79)* (USA)
14. Vinci, Roberta *(49)* (ITA)
15. Pin, Camille *(78)* (FRA)
16. Schnyder, Patty [15] *(15)* (SUI)
17. Hantuchova, Daniela [10] *(12)* (SVK)
18. Pavlyuchenkova, Anastasia *(311)* (RUS) (WC)
19. Likhovtseva, Elena *(50)* (RUS)
20. Camerin, Maria Elena *(70)* (ITA)
21. Ozegovic, Nika *(186)* (CRO) (Q)
22. Groenefeld, Anna-Lena *(135)* (GER)
23. Baltacha, Elena *(274)* (GBR) (WC)
24. Srebotnik, Katarina [19] *(22)* (SLO)
25. Stosur, Samantha [27] *(28)* (AUS)
26. Brandi, Kristina *(204)* (PUR) (Q)
27. Sequera, Milagros *(56)* (VEN)
28. Schruff, Julia *(110)* (GER)
29. Molik, Alicia *(75)* (AUS)
30. Rodionova, Anastasia *(69)* (RUS)
31. Dominguez Lino, Lourdes *(57)* (ESP)
32. Williams, Serena [7] *(8)* (USA)
33. Jankovic, Jelena [3] *(3)* (SRB)
34. Keothavong, Anne *(178)* (GBR) (WC)
35. Shaughnessy, Meghann *(33)* (USA)
36. Gajdosova, Jarmila *(105)* (SVK)
37. Dulko, Gisela *(36)* (ARG)
38. Daniilidou, Eleni *(47)* (GRE)
39. Ondraskova, Zuzana *(120)* (CZE)
40. Safarova, Lucie [25] *(25)* (CZE)
41. Bartoli, Marion [18] *(19)* (FRA)
42. Pennetta, Flavia *(63)* (ITA)
43. Govortsova, Olga *(156)* (BLR) (Q)
44. Arn, Greta *(95)* (GER)
45. Kanepi, Kaia *(58)* (EST)
46. Malek, Tatjana *(87)* (GER)
47. Tanasugarn, Tamarine *(55)* (THA)
48. Peer, Shahar [16] *(16)* (ISR)
49. Hingis, Martina [9] *(11)* (SUI)
50. Cavaday, Naomi *(232)* (GBR) (WC)
51. Nakamura, Aiko *(68)* (JPN)
52. Sucha, Martina *(132)* (SVK)
53. Wozniak, Aleksandra *(90)* (CAN)
54. Granville, Laura *(77)* (USA)
55. Lepchenko, Varvara *(102)* (UZB)
56. Bammer, Sybille [20] *(21)* (AUT)
57. Krajicek, Michaella [31] *(45)* (NED)
58. Obziler, Tzipora *(81)* (ISR)
59. Kloesel, Sandra *(104)* (GER)
60. O'Brien, Katie *(154)* (GBR) (WC)
61. Kutuzova, Viktoriya *(159)* (UKR) (WC)
62. Poutchek, Tatiana *(85)* (BLR)
63. Kerber, Angelique *(76)* (GER)
64. Chakvetadze, Anna [8] *(7)* (RUS)
65. Ivanovic, Ana [6] *(6)* (SRB)
66. Czink, Melinda *(133)* (HUN)
67. Gallovits, Edina *(73)* (ROU)
68. Tu, Meilen *(38)* (USA)
69. Perry, Shenay *(88)* (USA)
70. Rezai, Aravane *(60)* (FRA)
71. Kremer, Anne *(118)* (LUX)
72. Schiavone, Francesca [29] *(30)* (ITA)
73. Medina Garrigues, Anabel [22] *(26)* (ESP)
74. Ruano Pascual, Virginia *(96)* (ESP)
75. Perebiynis, Tatiana *(201)* (UKR) (Q)
76. Gagliardi, Emmanuelle *(129)* (SUI)
77. Mirza, Sania *(44)* (IND)
78. Shvedova, Yaroslava *(80)* (RUS)
79. King, Vania *(74)* (USA)
80. Petrova, Nadia [11] *(9)* (RUS)
81. Vaidisova, Nicole [14] *(10)* (CZE)
82. Knapp, Karin *(65)* (ITA)
83. Pratt, Nicole *(40)* (AUS)
84. Dell'Acqua, Casey *(111)* (AUS) (Q)
85. Azarenka, Victoria *(53)* (BLR)
86. Kostanic Tosic, Jelena *(86)* (CRO)
87. Yan, Zi *(197)* (CHN) (Q)
88. Garbin, Tathiana [21] *(23)* (ITA)
89. Santangelo, Mara [28] *(29)* (ITA)
90. Morita, Ayumi *(174)* (JPN) (Q)
91. Wozniacki, Caroline *(103)* (DEN) (WC)
92. Yakimova, Anastasiya *(130)* (BLR)
93. Razzano, Virginie *(52)* (FRA)
94. Meusburger, Yvonne *(98)* (AUT)
95. Jackson, Jamea *(158)* (USA)
96. Mauresmo, Amelie [4] *(4)* (FRA)
97. Kuznetsova, Svetlana [5] *(5)* (RUS)
98. Vakulenko, Julia *(41)* (UKR)
99. Mattek, Bethanie *(116)* (USA)
100. Bardina, Vasilisa *(62)* (RUS)
101. Pironkova, Tsvetana *(109)* (BUL)
102. Radwanska, Agnieszka *(35)* (POL)
103. Smashnova, Anna *(166)* (ISR)
104. Muller, Martina [32] *(34)* (GER)
105. Golovin, Tatiana [17] *(17)* (FRA)
106. Hsieh, Su-Wei *(125)* (TPE) (Q)
107. Zahlavova Strycova, Barbora *(152)* (CZE) (Q)
108. Paszek, Tamira *(54)* (AUT)
109. Castano, Catalina *(92)* (COL)
110. Benesova, Iveta *(100)* (CZE)
111. Dechy, Nathalie *(48)* (FRA)
112. Dementieva, Elena [12] *(13)* (RUS)
113. Safina, Dinara [13] *(14)* (RUS)
114. Bondarenko, Kateryna *(39)* (UKR)
115. Brianti, Alberta *(101)* (ITA)
116. Morigami, Akiko *(71)* (JPN)
117. Peng, Shuai *(46)* (CHN)
118. Sromova, Hana *(170)* (CZE) (Q)
119. Kudryavtseva, Alla *(59)* (RUS)
120. Williams, Venus [23] *(31)* (USA)
121. Sugiyama, Ai [26] *(27)* (JPN)
122. South, Melanie *(169)* (GBR) (WC)
123. Kirilenko, Maria *(42)* (RUS)
124. Cornet, Alize *(139)* (FRA) (LL)
125. Bremond, Severine *(37)* (FRA)
126. Bychkova, Ekaterina *(93)* (RUS)
127. Chan, Yung-Jan *(51)* (TPE)
128. Sharapova, Maria [2] *(2)* (RUS)

Second Round

- Miss J.Henin [1] 6/3 6/0
- Miss V.Dushevina 6/4 7/5
- Miss E.Loit 6/3 6/1
- Miss E.Vesnina 6/1 6/3
- Miss A.Bondarenko [24] 6/1 6/2
- Miss A.Szavay 6/4 6/1
- Miss R.Vinci 6/2 6/1
- Miss P.Schnyder [15] 6/1 4/6 8/6
- Miss D.Hantuchova [10] 6/0 6/1
- Mrs E.Likhovtseva 3/6 6/1 7/5
- Miss N.Ozegovic 6/3 6/2
- Miss K.Srebotnik [19] 7/6(4) 3/6 6/2
- Miss S.Stosur [27] 4/6 6/2 6/2
- Miss M.Sequera 6/3 6/2
- Miss A.Molik 6/3 6/2
- Miss S.Williams [7] 7/5 6/0
- Miss J.Jankovic [3] 6/2 6/0
- Miss J.Gajdosova 6/2 6/4
- Miss E.Daniilidou 5/7 6/3 8/6
- Miss L.Safarova [25] 7/5 6/2
- Miss M.Bartoli [18] 6/3 6/1
- Miss O.Govortsova 6/7(5) 7/6(4) 6/1
- Miss K.Kanepi 6/1 6/4
- Miss S.Peer [16] 7/5 6/2
- Miss M.Hingis [9] 6/7(1) 7/5 6/0
- Miss A.Nakamura 7/5 6/2
- Miss L.Granville 7/6(4) 6/3
- Miss S.Bammer [20] 6/2 6/2
- Miss M.Krajicek [31] 6/2 6/7(6) 6/1
- Miss K.O'Brien 6/3 7/5
- Miss T.Poutchek 6/4 6/2
- Miss A.Chakvetadze [8] 7/5 6/3
- Miss A.Ivanovic [6] 6/0 7/6(3)
- Miss M.Tu 4/6 6/2 6/2
- Miss A.Rezai 6/2 7/6(4)
- Miss F.Schiavone [29] 5/7 6/4 6/3
- Miss V.Ruano Pascual 6/3 2/6 6/2
- Miss T.Perebiynis 6/3 6/3
- Miss S.Mirza 6/0 6/3
- Miss N.Petrova [11] 6/0 6/1
- Miss N.Vaidisova [14] 7/6(6) 6/2
- Miss N.J.Pratt 6/3 6/4
- Miss V.Azarenka 6/3 6/1
- Miss T.Garbin [21] 3/6 6/2 6/3
- Miss M.Santangelo [28] 6/1 3/6 6/3
- Miss C.Wozniacki 7/5 6/2
- Miss Y.Meusburger 6/4 7/5
- Miss A.Mauresmo [4] 6/1 6/3
- Miss S.Kuznetsova [5] 4/6 6/4 6/3
- Miss B.Mattek 6/1 6/0
- Miss A.Radwanska 6/2 6/1
- Miss M.Muller [32] 6/0 6/0
- Miss T.Golovin [17] 5/7 6/3 8/6
- Miss T.Paszek 6/4 7/6(3)
- Miss I.Benesova 6/0 7/5
- Miss E.Dementieva [12] 6/2 7/6(7)
- Miss D.Safina [13] 7/5 7/6(7)
- Miss A.Morigami 6/4 6/0
- Miss H.Sromova 6/4 6/4
- Miss V.Williams [23] 2/6 6/3 7/5
- Miss A.Sugiyama [26] 6/3 6/2
- Miss A.Cornet 6/4 6/4
- Mrs S.Bremond 6/4 6/4
- Miss M.Sharapova [2] 6/1 7/5

Third Round

- Miss J.Henin [1] 6/0 6/4
- Miss E.Vesnina 6/1 6/2
- Miss A.Bondarenko [24] 6/2 6/3
- Miss P.Schnyder [15] 2/6 6/2
- Miss D.Hantuchova [10] 7/5 7/6(3)
- Miss K.Srebotnik [19] 6/1 6/1
- Miss M.Sequera 6/2 5/7 6/4
- Miss S.Williams [7] 6/1 6/0
- Miss J.Jankovic [3] 6/1 6/1
- Miss L.Safarova [25] 6/4 3/6 6/3
- Miss M.Bartoli [18] 7/5 6/2
- Miss S.Peer [16] 6/4 7/5
- Miss M.Hingis [9] 6/1 6/2
- Miss L.Granville 6/1 6/4
- Miss M.Krajicek [31] 6/0 6/1
- Miss A.Chakvetadze [8] 6/2 6/1
- Miss A.Ivanovic [6] 6/4 6/3
- Miss V.Ruano Pascual 7/5 6/2
- Miss N.Petrova [11] 6/2 6/2
- Miss N.Vaidisova [14] 6/3 6/2
- Miss M.Santangelo [28] 6/0 7/6(4)
- Miss A.Mauresmo [4] 6/1 6/2
- Miss S.Kuznetsova [5] 7/6(2) 6/4
- Miss A.Radwanska 6/1 4/0 Ret'd
- Miss T.Paszek 6/2 3/6 6/1
- Miss E.Dementieva [12] 6/2 6/2
- Miss A.Morigami 6/4 7/5
- Miss V.Williams [23] 6/2 6/2
- Miss A.Sugiyama [26] 4/6 6/0 6/3
- Miss M.Sharapova [2] 6/0 6/3

Fourth Round

- Miss J.Henin [1] 6/1 6/3
- Miss A.Bondarenko [24] 6/2 6/3
- Miss P.Schnyder [15] 6/4 3/6 8/6
- Miss D.Hantuchova [10] 2/6 6/3 6/4
- Miss S.Williams [7] 6/1 6/0
- Miss J.Jankovic [3] 5/7 7/6(4) 6/2
- Miss M.Bartoli [18] 6/3 6/2
- Miss M.Hingis [9] Miss L.Granville 6/4 6/2
- Miss M.Krajicek [31] 7/6(8) 6/7(5) 6/2
- Miss A.Ivanovic [6] 6/3 6/2
- Miss N.Petrova [11] 6/3 7/6(3)
- Miss N.Vaidisova [14] 6/4 6/2
- Miss A.Mauresmo [4] 6/1 6/2
- Miss S.Kuznetsova [5] 6/2 6/3
- Miss T.Paszek 3/6 6/2 6/3
- Miss V.Williams [23] 6/2 3/6 7/5

Quarter-Finals

- Miss J.Henin [1] 6/2 6/2
- Miss D.Hantuchova [10]
- Miss S.Williams [7] 6/2 6/7(2) 6/2
- Miss M.Bartoli [18] 3/6 7/5 6/3
- Miss M.Krajicek [31] 6/3 6/4
- Miss A.Ivanovic [6] 6/1 2/6 6/4
- Miss N.Vaidisova [14] 7/6(6) 4/6 6/1
- Miss V.Williams [23] 6/1 6/3

Semi-Finals

- Miss J.Henin [1] 6/4 3/6 6/3
- Miss M.Bartoli [18] 3/6 6/3 6/2
- Miss A.Ivanovic [6] 4/6 6/2 7/5
- Miss V.Williams [23] 6/4 6/1

Final

- Miss M.Bartoli [18] 1/6 7/5 6/1
- Miss V.Williams [23] 6/3 6/4

EVENT IV – THE LADIES' DOUBLES CHAMPIONSHIP 2007
HOLDERS: MISS Z.YAN & MISS J.ZHENG

The Winners became the holders, for the year only, of THE CHALLENGE CUPS presented by H.R.H. PRINCESS MARINA, DUCHESS OF KENT, the late President of The All England Lawn Tennis and Croquet Club in 1949 and The All England Lawn Tennis and Croquet Club in 2001. The Winners received a silver replica of the Challenge Cup. A Silver Salver was presented to each of the Runners-up and a Bronze Medal to each defeated Semi-finalist. The matches were the best of three sets.

	First Round	Second Round	Third Round	Quarter-Finals	Semi-Finals	Final	Winners
	1. Miss L.M.Raymond (USA) & Miss S.Stosur (AUS) [1]	Miss L.M.Raymond & Miss S.Stosur [1]					
	2. Miss L.Hradecka (CZE) & Miss R.Voracova (CZE)	6/2 3/6 6/3	Miss L.M.Raymond & Miss S.Stosur [1]				
(WC)	3. Miss E.Baltacha (GBR) & Miss N.Cavaday (GBR)	Miss S.Foretz & Miss S.Sfar	6/2 6/4	Miss L.M.Raymond & Miss S.Stosur [1]			
(Q)	4. Miss S.Foretz (FRA) & Miss S.Sfar (TUN)	6/0 7/6(7)					
	5. Miss A.Szavay (HUN) & Miss V.Uhlirova (CZE)	Miss A.Szavay & Miss V.Uhlirova		6/0 6/7(4) 6/1			
	6. Miss I.Benesova (CZE) & Miss G.Voskoboeva (RUS)	6/4 6/7(2) 8/6	Miss S.Mirza & Miss S.Peer [16]				
(Q)	7. Miss S.Arvidsson (SWE) & Miss L.Osterloh (USA)	Miss S.Mirza & Miss S.Peer [16]	6/4 6/3				
	8. Miss S.Mirza (IND) & Miss S.Peer (ISR) [16]	7/5 6/3			Miss L.M.Raymond & Miss S.Stosur [1]		
	9. Miss M.E.Camerin (ITA) & Miss G.Dulko (ARG) [11]	Miss M.Krajicek & Miss A.Radwanska			7/5 6/2		
	10. Miss M.Krajicek (NED) & Miss A.Radwanska (POL)	6/3 6/7(7) 8/6	Miss M.Krajicek & Miss A.Radwanska				
(LL)	11. Miss A.Hlavackova (CZE) & Miss S.Kloesel (GER)	Miss A.Hlavackova & Miss S.Kloesel	6/3 6/3				
	12. Miss K.Jans (POL) & Miss A.Rosolska (POL)	6/2 6/4		Mrs K.Peschke & Miss R.P.Stubbs [5]			
	13. Miss L.Dominguez Lino (ESP) & Miss A.Parra Santonja (ESP)	Miss L.Dominguez Lino & Miss A.Parra Santonja		6/2 5/7 6/2			
	14. Miss P.Cetkovska (CZE) & Miss L.Safarova (CZE)	6/1 6/2	Mrs K.Peschke & Miss R.P.Stubbs [5]				
	15. Miss C.Ji (CHN) & Miss S-N.Sun (CHN)	Mrs K.Peschke & Miss R.P.Stubbs [5]	6/1 6/0				
	16. Mrs K.Peschke (CZE) & Miss R.P.Stubbs (AUS) [5]	6/0 6/4					Miss L.M.Raymond & Miss S.Stosur [1]
	17. Miss K.Srebotnik (SLO) & Miss A.Sugiyama (JPN) [4]	Miss K.Srebotnik & Miss A.Sugiyama [4]					1/6 6/3 6/2
	18. Mrs A.Ehritt-Vanc (ROU) & Miss A.Rodionova (RUS)	4/6 6/2 6/3	Miss K.Srebotnik & Miss A.Sugiyama [4]				
	19. Miss E.Loit (FRA) & Miss N.J.Pratt (AUS)	Miss E.Loit & Miss N.J.Pratt	6/0 6/3				
	20. Miss Y.Fedak (UKR) & Miss K.Kanepi (EST)	6/2 2/6 7/5		Miss K.Srebotnik & Miss A.Sugiyama [4]			
(WC)	21. Miss S.Borwell (GBR) & Miss J.Curtis (GBR)	Miss M.Bartoli & Miss M.Tu		w/o			
	22. Miss M.Bartoli (FRA) & Miss M.Tu (USA)	6/0 6/2	Miss M.Bartoli & Miss M.Tu				
	23. Miss N.Vaidisova (CZE) & Mrs B.Zahlavova Strycova (CZE)	Miss N.Vaidisova & Mrs B.Zahlavova Strycova	7/5 7/6(6)				
	24. Miss V.Dushevina (RUS) & Miss T.Perebiynis (UKR) [14]	6/2 6/2			Miss K.Srebotnik & Miss A.Sugiyama [4]		
	25. Mrs E.Likhovtseva (RUS) & Miss T.Sun (CHN) [10]	Mrs E.Likhovtseva & Miss T.Sun [10]			6/4 7/6(5)		
	26. Miss O.Poutchkova (RUS) & Miss M.Sequera (VEN)	6/4 6/2	Mrs E.Likhovtseva & Miss T.Sun [10]				
(LL)	27. Miss A.Fitzpatrick (GBR) & Miss E.Webley-Smith (GBR)	Miss A.Nakamura & Miss T.Tanasugarn	6/4 0/6 9/7				
	28. Miss A.Nakamura (JPN) & Miss T.Tanasugarn (THA)	6/1 6/4		Mrs E.Likhovtseva & Miss T.Sun [10]			
(WC)	29. Miss C.Curran (GBR) & Miss A.Keothavong (GBR)	Miss S.Williams & Miss V.Williams		4/6 6/1 6/4			
(WC)	30. Miss S.Williams (USA) & Miss V.Williams (USA)	6/1 6/3	Miss A.Medina Garrigues & Miss V.Ruano Pascual [8]				
	31. Miss N.Grandin (RSA) & Miss C.Pin (FRA)	Miss A.Medina Garrigues & Miss V.Ruano Pascual [8] 6/4 6/4	w/o				
	32. Miss A.Medina Garrigues (ESP) & Miss V.Ruano Pascual (ESP) [8]						
	33. Miss A.Molik (AUS) & Miss M.Santangelo (ITA) [6]	Miss A.Molik & Miss M.Santangelo [6]					
	34. Miss C.Morariu (USA) & Miss P.Schnyder (SUI)	6/1 6/3	Miss A.Molik & Miss M.Santangelo [6]				
	35. Miss S.Cohen-Aloro (FRA) & Miss V.Razzano (FRA)	Miss A.Bondarenko & Miss K.Bondarenko	6/2 6/0				
	36. Miss A.Bondarenko (UKR) & Miss K.Bondarenko (UKR)	6/1 6/2		Miss A.Molik & Miss M.Santangelo [6]			
(Q)	37. Miss S-W.Hsieh (TPE) & Miss A.Kudryavtseva (RUS)	Miss V.Azarenka & Miss A.Chakvetadze		4/6 6/3 6/3			
	38. Miss V.Azarenka (BLR) & Miss A.Chakvetadze (RUS)	6/3 7/5	Miss M.Kirilenko & Miss E.Vesnina [12]				
	39. Miss A.Rezai (FRA) & Miss J.Vakulenko (UKR)	Miss M.Kirilenko & Miss E.Vesnina [12]	6/7(3) 6/1 8/6				
	40. Miss M.Kirilenko (RUS) & Miss E.Vesnina (RUS) [12]	5/0 Ret'd			Miss A.Molik & Miss M.Santangelo [6]		
	41. Miss D.Safina (RUS) & Miss R.Vinci (ITA) [13]	Miss E.Daniilidou & Miss J.Woehr			6/4 6/1		
	42. Miss E.Daniilidou (GRE) & Miss J.Woehr (GER)	3/6 7/5 6/3	Miss S.Peng & Miss Z.Yan				
	43. Miss A.Harkleroad (USA) & Miss T.Obziler (ISR)	Miss S.Peng & Miss Z.Yan	6/0 6/3				
	44. Miss S.Peng (CHN) & Miss Z.Yan (CHN)	4/6 6/4 6/2		Miss S.Peng & Miss Z.Yan			
(Q)	45. Miss J.Ditty (USA) & Miss R.Kops-Jones (USA)	Miss E.Laine & Miss M.Martinez Sanchez		6/3 6/2			
	46. Miss E.Laine (FIN) & Miss M.Martinez Sanchez (ESP)	7/6(5) 0/6 6/2	Miss Y-J.Chan & Miss C.Chuang [3]				
	47. Miss D.Hantuchova (SVK) & Miss A.Ivanovic (SRB)	Miss Y-J.Chan & Miss C.Chuang [3]	6/4 6/2				
	48. Miss Y-J.Chan (TPE) & Miss C.Chuang (TPE) [3]	7/6(4) 6/4			Miss A.Molik & Miss M.Santangelo [6]		
	49. Miss J.Husarova (SVK) & Miss M.Shaughnessy (USA) [7]	Miss J.Husarova & Miss M.Shaughnessy [7]			6/4 6/1		
(WC)	50. Miss K.Paterson (GBR) & Miss M.South (GBR)	6/1 7/5	Miss J.Husarova & Miss M.Shaughnessy [7]				
	51. Miss J.Gajdosova (SVK) & Miss A.Morigami (JPN)	Miss J.Gajdosova & Miss A.Morigami	7/5 4/6 8/6				
	52. Miss E.Gagliardi (SUI) & Miss F.Schiavone (ITA)	6/4 6/2		Miss S.Kuznetsova & Miss N.Petrova			
	53. Miss A-L.Groenefeld (GER) & Miss T.Malek (GER)	Miss A-L.Groenefeld & Miss T.Malek		6/3 6/4			
(LL)	54. Miss H.Sromova (CZE) & Mrs K.Zakopalova (CZE)	6/3 1/6 6/2	Miss S.Kuznetsova & Miss N.Petrova				
	55. Miss S.Kuznetsova (RUS) & Miss N.Petrova (RUS)	Miss S.Kuznetsova & Miss N.Petrova	6/2 6/0				
	56. Miss T.Garbin (ITA) & Miss P.Suarez (ARG) [9]	/6(4) 6/3			Miss C.Black & Mrs L.Huber [2]		
	57. Miss V.King (USA) & Mrs J.Kostanic Tosic (CRO) [15]	Miss J.Craybas & Miss L.Granville			6/4 7/6(6)		
	58. Miss J.Craybas (USA) & Miss L.Granville (USA)	6/3 6/4	Miss J.Craybas & Miss L.Granville 6/3 6/3				
	59. Miss E.Dementieva (RUS) & Miss F.Pennetta (ITA)	Miss E.Dementieva & Miss F.Pennetta					
	60. Miss S.Bammer (AUT) & Miss T.Paszek (AUT)	6/1 6/0		Miss C.Black & Mrs L.Huber [2]			
	61. Miss B.Mattek (USA) & Miss B.Stewart (AUS)	Miss B.Mattek & Miss B.Stewart		6/1 6/1			
	62. Miss M.Muller (GER) & Miss G.Navratilova (CZE)	7/6(1) 7/5	Miss C.Black & Mrs L.Huber [2]				
	63. Mrs S.Bremond (FRA) & Miss N.Dechy (FRA)	Miss C.Black & Mrs L.Huber [2]	6/3 6/3				
	64. Miss C.Black (ZIM) & Mrs L.Huber (RSA) [2]	7/6(4) 6/3					

Semi-Finals:
Miss L.M.Raymond & Miss S.Stosur [1] / Miss K.Srebotnik & Miss A.Sugiyama [4] — Miss K.Srebotnik & Miss A.Sugiyama [4] 6/4 7/6(5)

Miss A.Molik & Miss M.Santangelo [6] / Miss C.Black & Mrs L.Huber [2] — Miss C.Black & Mrs L.Huber [2] 6/4 4/6 6/1

Final:
Miss K.Srebotnik & Miss A.Sugiyama [4] / Miss C.Black & Mrs L.Huber [2] — Miss C.Black & Mrs L.Huber [2] 3/6 6/3 6/2

Heavy type denotes seeded players. The figure in brackets against names denotes the order in which they were seeded. (WC)=Wild card. (Q)=Qualifier. (LL)=Lucky loser.

EVENT V – THE MIXED DOUBLES CHAMPIONSHIP 2007
HOLDERS: A. RAM & MISS V. ZVONREVA

The Winners became the holders, for the year only, of the CHALLENGE CUPS presented by members of the family of the late Mr. S. H. SMITH in 1949 and The All England Lawn Tennis and Croquet Club in 2001. The Winners received a silver replica of the Challenge Cup. A Silver Salver was presented to each of the Runners-up and a Bronze Medal to each defeated Semi-finalist. The matches were the best of three sets.

First Round

1. **M.Bryan** (USA) & **Miss L.M.Raymond** (USA) [1]
2. Bye
(WC) 3. A.Bogdanovic (GBR) & Miss M.South (GBR)
4. B.Becker (GER) & Miss A-L.Groenefeld (GER)

5. A.Fisher (AUS) & Miss B.Stewart (AUS)
6. J.Coetzee (RSA) & Mrs J.Kostanic Tosic (CRO)

7. Bye
8. **R.Wassen** (NED) & **Miss Y-J.Chan** (TPE) [13]

9. **D.Nestor** (CAN) & **Mrs E.Likhovtseva** (RUS) [11]
10. Bye

11. T.Phillips (USA) & Miss V.Uhlirova (CZE)
12. S.Prieto (ARG) & Miss A.Medina Garrigues (ESP)

13. W.Moodie (RSA) & Miss V.Dushevina (RUS)
14. M.Mirnyi (BLR) & Miss V.Azarenka (BLR)

15. Bye
16. **S.Aspelin** (SWE) & **Miss M.Santangelo** (ITA) [6]

17. **M.Knowles** (BAH) & **Miss Z.Yan** (CHN) [3]
18. Bye

19. J.Murray (GBR) & J.Jankovic (SRB)
(WC) 20. R.Bloomfield (GBR) & Miss S.Borwell (GBR)

21. M.Fyrstenberg (POL) & Miss A.Radwanska (POL)
22. J.Nieminen (FIN) & Miss E.Laine (FIN)

23. Bye
24. **J.Knowle** (AUT) & **Miss T.Sun** (CHN) [14]

25. **M.Matkowski** (POL) & **Miss C.Black** (ZIM) [9]
26. Bye

27. D.Skoch (CZE) & Miss J.Husarova (SVK)
28. M.Bhupathi (IND) & Miss S.Mirza (IND)

29. Y.Allegro (SUI) & Miss E.Daniilidou (GRE)
30. L.Kubot (POL) & Miss S.Bammer (AUT)

31. Bye
32. **A.Ram** (ISR) & **Miss N.Dechy** (FRA) [7]

33. **J.Bjorkman** (SWE) & **Miss A.Molik** (AUS) [5]
34. Bye

(A) 35. V.Spadea (USA) & Miss V.King (USA)
36. F.Cermak (CZE) & Miss R.Vinci (ITA)

37. M.Damm (CZE) & Miss M.Krajicek (NED)
(A) 38. M.Melo (BRA) & Miss T.Paszek (AUT)

39. Bye
40. **P.Vizner** (CZE) & **Mrs K.Peschke** (CZE) [10]

41. **P.Hanley** (AUS) & **Miss T.Perebiynis** (UKR) [16]
42. Bye

43. L.Friedl (CZE) & Miss R.P.Stubbs (AUS)
44. E.Butorac (USA) & Miss C.Morariu (USA)

45. J.Thomas (USA) & Miss M.Tu (USA)
46. J.Kerr (AUS) & Miss K.Bondarenko (UKR)

47. Bye
48. **K.Ullyett** (ZIM) & **Mrs L.Huber** (RSA) [4]

49. **L.Paes** (IND) & **Miss M.Shaughnessy** (USA) [8]
50. Bye

51. J.Levinsky (CZE) & Miss R.Voracova (CZE)
52. C.Kas (GER) & Miss M.Muller (GER)

(WC) 53. L.Childs (GBR) & Miss K.O'Brien (GBR)
(WC) 54. J.Auckland (GBR) & Miss C.Curran (GBR)

55. Bye
56. **T.Perry** (AUS) & **Miss C.Chuang** (TPE) [12]

57. **J.Erlich** (ISR) & **Miss E.Vesnina** (RUS) [15]
58. Bye

(WC) 59. J.Delgado (GBR) & Miss A.Keothavong (GBR)
60. F.Santoro (FRA) & Mrs S.Bremond (FRA)

61. N.Zimonjic (SRB) & Miss F.Pennetta (ITA)
62. M.Garcia (ARG) & Miss P.Suarez (ARG)

63. Bye
64. **B.Bryan** (USA) & **Miss S.Stosur** (AUS) [2]

Second Round

M.Bryan & Miss L.M.Raymond [1]

A.Bogdanovic & Miss M.South
6/4 7/6(0)

J.Coetzee & Mrs J.Kostanic Tosic
6/3 6/1

R.Wassen & Miss Y-J.Chan [13]

D.Nestor & Mrs E.Likhovtseva [11]

S.Prieto & Miss A.Medina Garrigues
6/1 6/4

W.Moodie & Miss V.Dushevina
7/6(3) 6/3

S.Aspelin & Miss M.Santangelo [6]

M.Knowles & Miss Z.Yan [3]

J.Murray & Miss J.Jankovic
3/6 7/6(4) 6/2

J.Nieminen & Miss E.Laine
3/6 6/3 6/2

J.Knowle & Miss T.Sun [14]

M.Matkowski & Miss C.Black [9]

M.Bhupathi & Miss S.Mirza
6/3 6/4

L.Kubot & Miss S.Bammer
3/6 6/4 6/2

A.Ram & Miss N.Dechy [7]

J.Bjorkman & Miss A.Molik [5]

V.Spadea & Miss V.King
4/6 6/1 6/2

M.Melo & Miss T.Paszek
6/2 6/7(7) 6/4

P.Vizner & Mrs K.Peschke [10]

P.Hanley & Miss T.Perebiynis [16]

L.Friedl & Miss R.P.Stubbs
6/2 Ret'd

J.Kerr & Miss K.Bondarenko
7/6(3) 6/2

K.Ullyett & Mrs L.Huber [4]

L.Paes & Miss M.Shaughnessy [8]

J.Levinsky & Miss R.Voracova
6/3 3/6 11/9

J.Auckland & Miss C.Curran
6/2 6/1

T.Perry & Miss C.Chuang [12]

J.Erlich & Miss E.Vesnina [15]

F.Santoro & Mrs S.Bremond
6/1 6/3

M.Garcia & Miss P.Suarez
6/4 6/4

B.Bryan & Miss S.Stosur [2]

Third Round

A.Bogdanovic & Miss M.South
6/4 3/6 6/3

R.Wassen & Miss Y-J.Chan [13]
4/6 6/4 6/2

D.Nestor & Mrs E.Likhovtseva [11]
6/1 6/2

S.Aspelin & Miss M.Santangelo [6]
6/3 7/5

J.Murray & Miss J.Jankovic
7/6(4) 6/7(5) 6/3

J.Knowle & Miss T.Sun [14]
7/6(5) 6/3

M.Matkowski & Miss C.Black [9]
6/4 6/4

A.Ram & Miss N.Dechy [7]
6/4 6/4

J.Bjorkman & Miss A.Molik [5]
1/6 6/4 6/4

P.Vizner & Mrs K.Peschke [10]
6/3 6/2

P.Hanley & Miss T.Perebiynis [16]
6/4 6/4

J.Kerr & Miss K.Bondarenko
7/6(0) 4/6 6/4

L.Paes & Miss M.Shaughnessy [8]
6/0 6/0

T.Perry & Miss C.Chuang [12]
7/5 6/2

F.Santoro & Mrs S.Bremond
6/3 6/4

B.Bryan & Miss S.Stosur [2]
6/1 6/4

Quarter-Finals

A.Bogdanovic & Miss M.South
6/4 6/3

D.Nestor & Mrs E.Likhovtseva [11]
6/4 3/6 13/11

J.Murray & Miss J.Jankovic
6/3 7/6(1)

M.Matkowski & Miss C.Black [9]
6/3 6/4

J.Bjorkman & Miss A.Molik [5]
6/4 6/4

J.Kerr & Miss K.Bondarenko
4/6 6/4 6/4

L.Paes & Miss M.Shaughnessy [8]
7/5 7/5

F.Santoro & Mrs S.Bremond
w/o

Semi-Finals

D.Nestor & Mrs E.Likhovtseva [11]
6/3 7/6(4)

J.Murray & Miss J.Jankovic
7/6(1) 6/7(4) 7/5

J.Bjorkman & Miss A.Molik [5]
4/6 6/3 6/4

F.Santoro & Mrs S.Bremond
2/6 6/3 6/4

Final

J.Murray & Miss J.Jankovic
6/4 4/6 6/4

J.Bjorkman & Miss A.Molik [5]
6/3 3/6 6/3

Winners

J.Murray & Miss J.Jankovic
6/4 3/6 6/1

Heavy type denotes seeded players. The figure in brackets against names denotes the order in which they were seeded. (WC)=Wild card. (A)=Alternates.

EVENT VI – THE GENTLEMEN'S INVITATION DOUBLES 2007
HOLDERS: T.A. WOODBRIDGE & M. WOODFORDE

The Winners became the holders, for the year only, of a cup presented by The All England Lawn Tennis and Croquet Club. The Winners received miniature silver salvers. A silver medal was presented to each of the Runners-up. The matches were the best of three sets. If a match reached one set all a 10 point tie-break replaced the third set.

GROUP A	P. Cash (AUS) & R. Krajicek (NED)	G. Ivanisevic (CRO) & C. Pioline (FRA)	M. Petchey (GBR) & C. Wilkinson (GBR)	T.A. Woodbridge (AUS) & M. Woodforde (AUS)	WINS	LOSSES
P. Cash (AUS) & R. Krajicek (NED)		3-6 6-3 (8-10) L	6-7(5) 4-6 L	4-6 6-3(6-10) L	0	3
G. Ivanisevic (CRO) & C. Pioline (FRA)	6-3 3-6 (10-8) W		4-6 3-6 L	7-6(4) 7-6(10) W	2	1
M. Petchey (GBR) & C. Wilkinson (GBR)	7-6(5) 6-4 W	6-4 6-3 W		3-6 6-7(3) L	2	1
T.A. Woodbridge (AUS) & M. Woodforde (AUS)	6-4 3-6 (10-6) W	6-7(4) 6-7(10) L	6-3 7-6(3) W		2	1

FINAL: M. Petchey (GBR) & C. Wilkinson (GBR) vs J. Eltingh (NED) & P. Haarhuis (NED) — J. Eltingh (NED) & P. Haarhuis (NED) 6/2 6/2

GROUP B	M. Chang (USA) & T.J. Middleton (USA)	J. Eltingh (NED) & P. Haarhuis (NED)	W. Ferreira (RSA) & H. Leconte (FRA)	L. Jensen (USA) & M. Jenson (USA)	WINS	LOSSES
M. Chang (USA) & T.J. Middleton (USA)		7-6(4) 0-6 (4-10) L	W/O W	3-6 6-3 (10-6) W	2	1
J. Eltingh (NED) & P. Haarhuis (NED)	6-7(4)6-0 (10-4) W		W/O W	6-3 6-3 W	3	0
W. Ferreira (RSA) & H. Leconte (FRA)	W/O L	W/O L		7-6(1) 6-4 W	1	2
L. Jensen (USA) & M. Jenson (USA)	6-3 3-6 (6-10) L	3-6 3-6 L	6-7(1) 4-6 L		0	3

FINAL winner: J. Eltingh (NED) & P. Haarhuis (NED)

This event was played on a 'round robin' basis. 8 invited pairs were divided into 2 groups and each pair in each group played one another.
The pairs winning most matches were the winners of their respective groups and played a final round as indicated above.
If matches were equal in any group, the head to head result between the two pairs with the same number of wins, determined the winning pair of the group.
If that did not split the ties, then the percentage of sets won to sets played decided.

EVENT VII – THE GENTLEMEN'S SENIOR INVITATION DOUBLES 2007
HOLDERS: K. CURREN & J. KRIEK

The Winners became the holders, for the year only, of a Cup presented by The All England Lawn Tennis and Croquet Club. The Winners received miniature silver salvers. A Silver Medal was presented to each of the Runners-up. The matches were the best of three sets. If a match reached one set all a 10 point tie-break replaced the third set.

GROUP A	A. Amritraj (IND) & V. Amritraj (IND)	M.J. Bates (GBR) & A. Jarryd (SWE)	P. McNamara (AUS) & P. McNamee (AUS)	I. Nastase (ROU) & S.R. Smith (USA)	WINS	LOSSES
A. Amritraj (IND) & V. Amritraj (IND)		0-6 2-6 L	3-6 3-6 L	7-6(4) 6-1 W	1	2
M.J. Bates (GBR) & A. Jarryd (SWE)	6-0 6-2 W		6-1 7-6(4) W	6-4 6-2 W	3	0
P. McNamara (AUS) & P. McNamee (AUS)	6-3 6-3 W	1-6 6-7(4) L		6-1 6-1 W	2	1
I. Nastase (ROU) & S.R. Smith (USA)	6-7(4) 1-6 L	4-6 2-6 L	1-6 1-6 L		0	3

FINAL: M.J. Bates (GBR) & A. Jarryd (SWE) vs K. Curren (USA) & J. Kriek (USA) — M.J. Bates (GBR) & A. Jarryd (SWE) 6/3 6/3

GROUP B	M. Bahrami (IRI) & G. Mayer (USA)	K. Curren (USA) & J. Kriek (USA)	P. Fleming (USA) & G. Vilas (ARG)	H. Guenthardt (SUI) & B. Taroczy (HUN)	WINS	LOSSES
M. Bahrami (IRI) & G. Mayer (USA)		1-6 2-6 L	6-7(0) 6-4 (10-8) W	6-1 6-2 W	2	1
K. Curren (USA) & J. Kriek (USA)	6-1 6-1 W		6-3 6-2 W	6-3 3-6 (10-3) W	3	0
P. Fleming (USA) & G. Vilas (ARG)	7-6(0) 4-6 (8-10) L	3-6 2-6 L		7-5 7-5 W	1	2
H. Guenthardt (SUI) & B. Taroczy (HUN)	1-6 2-6 L	3-6 6-3 (3-10) L	5-7 5-7 L		0	3

FINAL winner: K. Curren (USA) & J. Kriek (USA)

This event was played on a 'round robin' basis. 8 invited pairs were divided into 2 groups and each pair in each group played one another.
The pairs winning most matches were the winners of their respective groups and played a final round as indicated above.
If matches were equal in any group, the head to head result between the two pairs with the same number of wins, determined the winning pair of the group.
If that did not split the ties, then the percentage of sets won to sets played decided.

EVENT VII – THE LADIES' INVITATION DOUBLES 2007
HOLDERS: MRS R.D. NIDEFFER & MISS J. NOVOTNA

The Winners became the holders, for the year only, of a Cup presented by The All England Lawn Tennis and Croquet Club. The Winners received miniature Cups. A Silver Medal was presented to each of the Runners-up. The matches were the best of three sets. If a match reached one set all a 10 point tie-break replaced the third set.

GROUP A	Miss G. Fernandez (USA) & Miss N. Zvereva (BLR)	Miss I. Kloss (RSA) & Mrs R.D. Nideffer (USA)	Miss H. Mandlikova (AUS) & Miss L. McNeil (USA)	Mrs E.M. Smylie (AUS) & Miss N. Tauziat (FRA)	WINS	LOSSES	FINAL
Miss G. Fernandez (USA) & Miss N. Zvereva (BLR)		6-7(4) 6-2(4-10) L	6-1 6-3 W	6-2 3-6 (4-10) L	1	2	
Miss I. Kloss (RSA) & Mrs R.D. Nideffer (USA)	7-6(4) 2-6(10-4) W		6-1 6-2 W	7-6(7) 3-6(10-5) W	3	0	Miss I. Kloss (RSA) & Mrs R.D. Nideffer (USA)
Miss H. Mandlikova (AUS) & Miss L. McNeil (USA)	1-6 3-6 L	1-6 2-6 L		3-6 6-7(4) L	0	3	
Mrs E.M. Smylie (AUS) & Miss N. Tauziat (FRA)	2-6 6-3 (10-4) W	6-7(7) 6-3 (5-10) L	6-3 7-6(4) W		2	1	

GROUP B	Miss M.M. Bollegraf (NED) & Miss C. Lindqvist (SWE)	Miss A. Croft (GBR) & Miss J.M. Durie (GBR)	Mrs G. Magers (USA) & Miss C. Martinez (ESP)	Miss J. Novotna (CZE) & Miss H. Sukova (CZE)	WINS	LOSSES	FINAL
Miss M.M. Bollegraf (NED) & Miss C. Lindqvist (SWE)		6-0 7-6(4) W	2-6 1-6 L	6-7(3) 2-6 L	1	2	
Miss A. Croft (GBR) & Miss J.M. Durie (GBR)	0-6 6-7(4) L		W/O L	1-6 2-6 L	0	3	
Mrs G. Magers (USA) & Miss C. Martinez (ESP)	6-2 6-1 W	W/O W		4-6 6-7(3) L	2	1	Miss J. Novotna (CZE) & Miss H. Sukova (CZE)
Miss J. Novotna (CZE) & Miss H. Sukova (CZE)	7-6(3) 6-2 W	6-1 6-2 W	6-4 7-6(3) W		3	0	

Final: Miss J. Novotna (CZE) & Miss H. Sukova (CZE) beat Miss I. Kloss (RSA) & Mrs R.D. Nideffer (USA) 6/3 6/3

This event was played on a 'round robin' basis. 8 invited pairs were divided into 2 groups of 4 and each pair in each group played one another.
The pairs winning most matches were the winners of their respective groups and played a final round as indicated above.
If matches were equal in any group, the head to head result between the two pairs with the same number of wins, determined the winning pair of the group.
If that did not split the ties, then the percentage of sets won to sets played decided.

EVENT IX – THE WHEELCHAIR GENTLEMEN'S DOUBLES 2007
HOLDERS: S. KUNIEDA & S. SAIDA

The Winners received Silver Salvers. The matches were the best of three tie-break sets.

Third & Fourth Place Play-off

M. Legner (NED) & M Scheffers (NED)

M. Brychta (CZE) & T. Kruszelnicki (POL)

M. Legner (NED) & M Scheffers (NED) 6-3 6-2

First Round
1. S.Kunieda (JPN) & S.Saida (JPN) [1]
2. M.Legner (NED) & M Scheffers (NED)
3. M.Brychta (FRA) & T.Kruszelnicki (POL)
4. R.Ammerlaan (NED) & R.Vink (NED) [2]

Final
S.Kunieda (JPN) & S.Saida (JPN) [1] 7-6(6) 6-3
R.Ammerlaan (NED) & R.Vink (NED) [2] 6-3 6-4

R.Ammerlaan (NED) & R.Vink (NED) [2] 4-6 7-5 6-2

Heavy type denoted seeded players. The figure in brackets against names denoted the order in which they were seeded.

ALPHABETICAL LIST – INVITATION DOUBLES EVENTS
GENTLEMEN

Cash P. *(Australia)*
Chang M. *(USA)*
Eltingh J. *(Netherlands)*
Ferreira W. *(South Africa)*

Haarhuis P. *(Netherlands)*
Ivanisevic G. *(Croatia)*
Jensen L. *(USA)*
Jensen M. *(USA)*

Krajicek R. *(Netherlands)*
Leconte H. *(France)*
Middleton T-J. *(USA)*
Petchey M. *(Great Britain)*

Pioline C. *(France)*
Wilkinson C. *(Great Britain)*
Woodbridge T.A. *(Australia)*
Woodforde M. *(Australia)*

LADIES

Bollegraf Miss M.M. *(Netherlands)*
Croft Miss A. *(Great Britain)*
Durie Miss J.M. *(Great Britain)*
Fernandez Miss G. *(USA)*

Kloss Miss I. *(South Africa)*
Lindqvist Miss C. *(Sweden)*
Magers Mrs G. *(USA)*
Mandlikova Miss H. *(Australia)*

Martinez Miss C. *(Spain)*
McNeil Miss L. *(USA)*
Nideffer Mrs R.D. *(USA)*
Novotna Miss J. *(Czech Republic)*

Smylie Mrs E.M. *(Australia)*
Sukova Miss H. *(Czech Republic)*
Tauziat Miss N. *(France)*
Zvereva Miss N. *(Belarus)*

ALPHABETICAL LIST – GENTLEMEN'S SENIOR INVITATION DOUBLES EVENT

Amritraj A. *(India)*
Amritraj V. *(India)*
Bahrami M. *(Iran)*
Bates M.J. *(Great Britain)*

Curren K. *(USA)*
Fleming P. *(USA)*
Guenthardt H. *(Switzerland)*
Jarryd A. *(Sweden)*

Kriek J. *(USA)*
Mayer G. *(USA)*
McNamara P. *(Australia)*
McNamee P. *(Australia)*

Nastase I. *(Romania)*
Smith S.R. *(USA)*
Taroczy B. *(Hungary)*
Vilas G. *(Argentina)*

EVENT X – THE BOYS' SINGLES CHAMPIONSHIP 2007
HOLDER: T. DE BAKKER

The Winner became the holder, for the year only, of a Cup presented by The All England Lawn Tennis and Croquet Club. The Winner received a miniature Cup and the Runner-up received a memento. The matches were best of three sets.

First Round	Second Round	Third Round	Quarter-Finals	Semi-Finals	Final	Winner
1. **Ignatic, Vladimir [1]** (BLR)	V.Ignatic [1] 6/3 6/1	V.Ignatic [1] 6/2 6/2				
2. Schoorel, Thomas (NED)			V.Ignatic [1] 5/7 6/3 [10-8]			
(Q) 3. Kecki, Mateusz (USA)	M.Kecki 6/2 7/6(6)			V.Ignatic [1] 6/3 1/6 [10-3]		
(Q) 4. Dimov, Valentin (BUL)						
5. Rice, David (GBR)	D.Rice 6/4 7/5	T.Fabbiano [15] 6/2 6/2				
6. Maytin, Roberto (VEN)						
(Q) 7. Angus, Niall (GBR)	T.Fabbiano [15] 6/3 6/1					
8. **Fabbiano, Thomas [15]** (ITA)						
9. **Smith, John-Patrick [12]** (AUS)	J-P.Smith [12] 6/2 6/0	M.Willis 6/4 7/6(6)				V.Ignatic [1] 7/5 3/6 6/1
10. Wachiramanowong, Kittipong (THA)						
(WC) 11. Willis, Marcus (GBR)	M.Willis 7/5 2/6 [10-6]		G.Elias 7/6(5) 7/6(6)			
12. Peng, Hsien-Yin (TPE)						
13. Elias, Gastao (POR)	G.Elias 6/3 6/4	G.Elias 7/6(3) 6/1				
(Q) 14. Szmigiel, Mateusz (POL)						
15. Arsenov, Danila (RUS)	D.Arsenov 6/3 6/2					
16. **Piro, Stephane [7]** (FRA)				R.Berankis 6/2 6/2		
17. **Romboli, Fernando [4]** (BRA)	R.Berankis 6/4 6/3	R.Berankis 6/1 6/2				
18. Berankis, Ricardas (LTU)						
19. Ramiaramanan, Lofo (MAD)	L.Ramiaramanan 7/6(4) 6/3		R.Berankis 7/6(0) 6/2			
20. Cho, Sung Jae (KOR)						
(WC) 21. Dyce, Graeme (GBR)	G.Dyce 7/5 6/4	G.Dyce 7/5 6/4				
22. Lopez, Daniel (ITA)						
23. Semrajc, Janez (SLO)	J.Semrajc 7/6(2) 6/3					
24. **Rivera, Guillermo [16]** (CHI)				B.Klein [9] 1/6 6/3 [10-7]		
25. **Klein, Brydan [9]** (AUS)	B.Klein [9] 6/3 6/2	B.Klein [9] 6/1 3/6 [10-5]				
26. Alvarado, Patricio (ECU)						
(Q) 27. Martin, Andrei (SVK)	J.Milton 6/2 1/6 [11-9]		K.Damico [8] 6/3 3/6 [10-6]			
(WC) 28. Milton, Joshua (GBR)						
(WC) 29. Thornley, Sean (GBR)	R.Roy 5/7 7/6(4) [10-7]	K.Damico [8] 6/3 6/2				
30. Roy, Rupesh (IND)						
31. Hume, Damian (RSA)	K.Damico [8] 6/3 6/2					D.Young [3] 7/5 6/1
(WC) 32. **Damico, Kellen [8]** (USA)						
33. **Eysseric, Jonathan [5]** (FRA)	J.Eysseric [5] 6/4 6/1	J.Eysseric [5] 6/3 6/4				
34. Thomas, Andrew (AUS)						
35. Cox, Glen (GBR)	D.Cox 7/5 6/1		D.Kleftakos 6/4 2/6 [11-9]			
36. Ramirez, Cesar (MEX)						
(WC) 37. Krajicek, Austin (USA)	D.Smethurst 6/7(6) 6/3 [11-9]	D.Kleftakos 6/4 6/1				
(WC) 38. Smethurst, Daniel (GBR)						
(Q) 39. Kleftakos, Dimitris (GER)	D.Kleftakos 6/4 3/6 [10-7]		D.Young [3] 6/1 6/1			
40. **Klizan, Martin [10]** (SVK)						
41. **Donald, Stephen [13]** (AUS)	C.Rungkat 6/2 6/3	C.Rungkat 6/0 7/6(9)				
42. Rungkat, Christopher (INA)						
43. Albot, Radu (MDA)	R.Albot 7/6(0) 7/6(8)			D.Young [3] 3/6 6/1 [10-8]		
44. Siriluthaiwattana, Peerakiet (THA)						
45. Donskoy, Evgeny (RUS)	A.Karatchenia 6/3 0/6 [10-6]	D.Young [3] 6/7(6) 6/1 [10-4]				
(Q) 46. Karatchenia, Andrei (BLR)						
(WC) 47. Pauffley, Neil (GBR)	D.Young [3] 6/2 6/3					
48. **Young, Donald [3]** (USA)						
49. **Jones, Greg [6]** (AUS)	G.Jones [6] 6/4 6/3	G.Jones [6] 6/2 6/1				
50. De Fays, Frederic (BEL)						
(WC) 51. James, Mathew (GBR)	M.James 4/6 6/2 [10-5]		G.Jones [6] 6/1 6/2			
52. Cunha, Henrique (BRA)						
(Q) 53. Trombetta, Ty D (USA)	T.Van Terheijden 4/6 6/2 [10-6]	T.Van Terheijden 1/6 7/6(5) [10-3]				
54. Van Terheijden, Tim (NED)						
55. Gonzalez, Alejandro (COL)	A.Gonzalez 6/1 6/4			G.Jones [6] 7/6(7) 6/2		
56. **Jebavy, Roman [11]** (CZE)						
57. **Urzua, Ricardo [14]** (CHI)	R.Urzua [14] 6/1 6/3	R.Urzua [14] 6/1 6/3				D.Young [3] 6/4 7/5
58. Martinoski, Ilija (MKD)						
59. Hamui, Johnny (USA)	D.Mirtea 6/2 7/5		M.Trevisan [2] 2/6 6/3 [10-3]			
60. Mirtea, Dragos Cristian (ROU)						
61. Evans, Daniel (GBR)	M.Verryth 2/6 7/6(6) [10-8]	M.Trevisan [2] 7/5 6/2				
(Q) 62. Verryth, Mark (AUS)						
63. Bedene, Aljaz (SLO)	M.Trevisan [2] 6/2 4/6 [10-4]					
64. **Trevisan, Matteo [2]** (ITA)						

Heavy type denotes seeded players. The figure in brackets against names denotes the order in which they were seeded.
(WC)=Wild card. (Q)=Qualifier.

EVENT XI – THE BOYS' DOUBLES CHAMPIONSHIP 2007
HOLDERS: K. DAMICO & N. SCHNUGG

The Winners became the holders, for the year only, of a Cup presented by The All England Lawn Tennis and Croquet Club.
The Winners received miniature Cups and the Runners-up received mementos. The matches were best of three sets.

First Round	Second Round	Quarter-Finals	Semi-Finals	Final	Winners
1. **K.Damico** (USA) & **J.Eysseric** (FRA) **[1]**	K.Damico & J.Eysseric [1] 6/3 6/2	R.Jebavy & M.Klizan 4/6 6/0 [10-7]			
2. V.Ignatic (BLR) & N.Zotov (RUS)					
3. H.Cunha (BRA) & A.Gonzalez (COL)	R.Jebavy & M.Klizan 6/1 6/3				
4. R.Jebavy (CZE) & M.Klizan (SVK)			R.Jebavy & M.Klizan 7/6(5) 3/6 [10-4]		
5. J.Kosler (CZE) & K.Wachiramanowong (THA)	J.Kosler & K.Wachiramanowong 7/5 5/7 [10-4]	T.Fabbiano & A.Karatchenia [6] 6/4 7/6(5)			
6. E.Donskoy (RUS) & M.Szmigiel (POL)				R.Jebavy & M.Klizan 7/5 6/2	
7. F.De Fays (BEL) & S.Piro (FRA)	T.Fabbiano & A.Karatchenia [6] 6/4 4/6 [10-8]				
8. **T.Fabbiano** (ITA) & **A.Karatchenia** (BLR) **[6]**					
9. **P.Alvarado** (ECU) & **F.Romboli** (BRA) **[4]**	D.Kleftakos & M.Verryth 7/6(2) 6/3	R.Maytin & A.Thomas w/o			
10. D.Kleftakos (GER) & M.Verryth (AUS)					
11. R.Maytin (VEN) & A.Thomas (AUS)	R.Maytin & A.Thomas 6/4 6/2		T.Schoorel & T.Van Terheijden 6/4 6/2		
12. G.Elias (POR) & C.Ramirez (MEX)					
(WC) 13. N.Angus (GBR) & T.Knights (GBR)	N.Angus & T.Knights 6/2 6/4	T.Schoorel & T.Van Terheijden 6/2 6/3			
14. L.Ramiaramanan (MAD) & P.Siriluthaiwattana (THA)					
15. T.Schoorel (NED) & T.Van Terheijden (NED)	T.Schoorel & T.Van Terheijden 6/2 6/3				D.Lopez & M.Trevisan [7] 7/6(5) 4/6 [10-8]
16. **G.Rivera** (CHI) & **R.Urzua** (CHI) **[5]**					
17. **R.Albot** (MDA) & **D.Mirtea** (ROU) **[8]**	J.Hamui & D.Young 6/3 6/4	J.Hamui & D.Young 7/6(3) 6/3			
18. J.Hamui (USA) & D.Young (USA)					
19. D.Hume (RSA) & R.Roy (IND)	D.Britton & A.Krajicek 6/1 3/6 [10-5]		J.Hamui & D.Young 7/6(4) 6/3		
(A) 20. D.Britton (USA) & A.Krajicek (USA)					
21. D.Arsenov (RUS) & M.Kecki (USA)	D.Arsenov & M.Kecki 6/3 6/3	D.Arsenov & M.Kecki 6/3 5/7 [10-6]			
22. G.Gigounon (BEL) & H-Y.Peng (TPE)				J.Hamui & D.Young 7/6(4) 6/3	
(WC) 23. N.Pauffley (GBR) & M.Willis (GBR)	N.Pauffley & M.Willis 3/6 6/3 [10-8]				
24. **S.Donald** (AUS) & **J-P.Smith** (AUS) **[3]**					
25. **D.Lopez** (ITA) & **M.Trevisan** (ITA) **[7]**	D.Lopez & M.Trevisan [7] 4/6 6/3 [10-8]	D.Lopez & M.Trevisan [7] 6/4 4/6 [10-7]			
(WC) 26. M.James (GBR) & S.Thornley (GBR)					
27. R.Berankis (LTU) & C.Rungkat (INA)	R.Berankis & C.Rungkat 6/3 3/6 [10-4]		D.Lopez & M.Trevisan [7] 3/6 6/4 [10-2]		
28. G.Dyce (GBR) & D.Evans (GBR)					
29. D.Cox (GBR) & D.Rice (GBR)	G.Coupland & D.Smethurst 7/6(1) 5/7 [10-4]	G.Coupland & D.Smethurst 4/6 6/3 [10-5]			
(WC) 30. G.Coupland (GBR) & D.Smethurst (GBR)				D.Lopez & M.Trevisan [7] 6/3 2/6 [10-4]	
31. I.Martinoski (MKD) & J.Semrajc (SLO)	G.Jones & B.Klein [2] 6/7(6) 6/4 [10-4]				
32. **G.Jones** (AUS) & **B.Klein** (AUS) **[2]**					

Heavy type denotes seeded players. The figure in brackets against names denotes the order in which they were seeded.
(WC)=Wild card. (A)=Alternates

EVENT XII – THE GIRLS' SINGLES CHAMPIONSHIP 2007
HOLDER: MISS C. WOZNIACKI

The Winner became the holder, for the year only, of a Cup presented by The All England Lawn Tennis and Croquet Club.
The Winner received a miniature Cup and the Runner-up received a memento. The matches were best of three sets.

First Round	Second Round	Third Round	Quarter-Finals	Semi-Finals	Final	Winner
1. **Pavlyuchenkova, Anastasia [1]** (RUS)	Miss A.Pavlyuchenkova [1] 4/6 7/5 [10-5]	Miss A.Pavlyuchenkova [1] 6/4 6/1	Miss A.Pavlyuchenkova [1] 6/3 6/2	Miss U.Radwanska [6] 7/5 6/1		
2. Larcher De Brito, Michelle (POR)						
3. Begu, Irina (ROU)	Miss A.Rus 6/1 6/0					
4. Rus, Arantxa (NED)						
5. Bua, Tatiana (ARG)	Miss T.Bua 1/6 6/3 [10-8]					
6. Moore, Jessica (AUS)		Miss R.Zsilinszka [14] 6/4 4/6 [10-3]				
(Q) 7. Jackson, Jessica (AUS)	Miss R.Zsilinszka [14] 6/4 6/2					
8. **Zsilinszka, Reka [14]** (USA)						
9. **Cavaday, Naomi [9]** (GBR)	Miss N.Cavaday 6/2 6/1	Miss N.Cavaday [9] 6/2 6/1	Miss O.Kalashnikova 6/3 6/4		Miss U.Radwanska [6] 7/6(3) 6/3	
10. Tinjic, Jasmina (CRO)						
11. Kalashnikova, Oxana (GEO)	Miss O.Kalashnikova 6/1 6/4					
12. Rodionova, Arina (RUS)						
(Q) 13. Boserup, Julia (USA)	Miss K.Kucova 6/4 7/5	Miss U.Radwanska [6] 6/2 6/2	Miss U.Radwanska [6] 7/5 6/1			
14. Kucova, Kristina (SVK)						
15. Hendler, Tamaryn (BEL)	Miss U.Radwanska [6] 6/1 6/1					
16. **Radwanska, Urszula [6]** (POL)						
17. **Milevskaya, Ksenia [4]** (BLR)	Miss K.Milevskaya [4] 6/3 5/7 [10-2]	Miss A.Fitzpatrick 6/4 6/4	Miss A.Fitzpatrick 6/2 0/6 [10-8]	Miss A.Fitzpatrick 6/2 7/5		
18. Zhou, Yi-Miao (CHN)						
19. Oudin, Melanie (USA)	Miss A.Fitzpatrick 7/5 6/4					
(WC) 20. Fitzpatrick, Anna (GBR)						
21. Nara, Kurumi (JPN)	Miss K.Nara 6/3 6/1					
(Q) 22. Peers, Sally (AUS)		Miss K.Lykina [13] 7/5 4/6 [11-9]				
23. Ciolkowski, Nelly (FRA)	Miss K.Lykina [13] 6/2 6/4					
24. **Lykina, Ksenia [13]** (RUS)						
25. **Pervak, Ksenia [10]** (RUS)	Miss K.Pervak [10] 6/2 6/2	Miss G.Brodsky 6/4 5/7 [10-6]	Miss G.Brodsky 4/6 7/5 [12-10]			
26. Lertcheewakarn, Noppawan (THA)						
(WC) 27. Moore, Tara (GBR)	Miss G.Brodsky 6/4 6/2					
28. Brodsky, Gail (USA)						
29. Kayser, Syna (GER)	Miss K.Vankova 6/3 6/2	Miss K.Vankova 6/1 6/7(4) [10-6]				
30. Vankova, Katerina (CZE)						
31. Gorny, Monica (RSA)	Miss N.Hofmanova [5] 6/3 6/1					
32. **Hofmanova, Nikola [5]** (AUT)						
33. Kvitova, Petra (CZE)	Miss P.Kvitova [8] 6/4 6/2	Miss P.Kvitova [8] 6/2 6/1	Miss K.Piter 7/6(4) 6/2	Miss K.Piter 6/3 6/1		
(WC) 34. Rae, Jocelyn (GBR)						
35. Gordo, Malena (ARG)	Miss M.Gordo 6/3 2/6 [10-5]					
36. Chernyakova, Elena (RUS)						
(Q) 37. Frilling, Kristy(USA)	Miss K.Piter 6/0 6/1					
38. Piter, Katarzyna (POL)		Miss K.Piter 6/2 6/2				
39. Doi, Misaki (JPN)	Miss M.Doi 6/7(1) 6/4 [10-7]					
40. **Glushko, Julia [12]** (ISR)						
(WC) 41. **Duque Marino, Mariana [16]** (COL)	Miss M.Duque Marino [16] 6/3 6/1	Miss S.Halep 7/5 7/5			Miss M.Brengle [7] 7/5 7/6(3)	
42. Tabakova, Romana (SVK)						
43. Halep, Simona (ROU)	Miss S.Halep 6/2 6/1					
44. Cecil, Mallory (USA)						
45. Calderwood, Tyra (AUS)	Miss J.Windley 6/1 3/6 [10-6]	Miss E.Rodina [3] 6/2 6/3	Miss E.Rodina [3] 6/4 5/7 [10-4]	Miss K.Piter 6/3 6/1		
(WC) 46. Windley, Jade (GBR)						
47. Martic, Petra (CRO)	Miss E.Rodina [3] 6/1 6/3					
48. **Rodina, Evgeniya [3]** (RUS)						
49. **Brengle, Madison [7]** (USA)	Miss M.Brengle [7] 6/1 7/5	Miss M.Brengle [7] 6/1 6/7(3) [10-5]	Miss M.Brengle [7] 6/3 7/5	Miss M.Brengle [7] 5/7 6/3 [10-5]		
(WC) 50. Curtis, Jade (GBR)						
51. Chala, Cindy (FRA)	Miss C.Chala 2/6 6/2 [11-9]					
(Q) 52. Roma, Sandra (SWE)						
53. Akita, Shiho (JPN)	Miss A.Bai 6/2 6/2					
(Q) 54. Bai, Alison (AUS)		Miss A.Bai 7/6(3) 7/6(3)				
(Q) 55. Mosolova, Maria (RUS)	Miss K-C.Chang [11] 6/3 6/4					
56. **Chang, Kai-Chen [11]** (TPE)						
57. **Jovanovski, Bojana [15]** (SRB)	Miss B.Jovanovski [15] 3/6 6/3 [10-6]	Miss B.Jovanovski [15] 6/4 5/7 [10-5]	Miss B.Jovanovski [15] 6/4 6/3			
(LL) 58. Ripoll, Dominice (GER)						
(Q) 59. Gavenko, Julia (RUS)	Miss V.Li 7/6(2) 6/4					
60. Li, Veronica (USA)						
61. Jurikova, Lenka (SVK)	Miss L.Jurikova 6/4 6/2					
62. Berkova, Andrea (CZE)		Miss A.Pivovarova [2] 6/1 6/2				
(WC) 63. Broady, Naomi (GBR)	Miss A.Pivovarova [2] 6/3 6/3					
(WC) 64. **Pivovarova, Anastasia [2]** (RUS)						

Heavy type denotes seeded players. The figure in brackets against names denotes the order in which they were seeded.
(WC)=Wild card. (Q)=Qualifier. (LL)=Lucky Loser.

Winner: **Miss U.Radwanska [6]** 2/6 6/3 6/0

EVENT XIII – THE GIRLS' DOUBLES CHAMPIONSHIP 2007
HOLDERS: MISS A. KLEYBANOVA & MISS A. PAVLYUCHENKOVA

The Winners became the holders, for the year only, of a Cup presented by The All England Lawn Tennis and Croquet Club.
The Winners received miniature Cups and the Runners-up received mementoes. The matches were best of three sets.

First Round	Second Round	Quarter-Finals	Semi-Finals	Final	Winners
1. **Miss A.Pavlyuchenkova** (RUS) & **Miss U.Radwanska** (POL) [1]	Miss A.Pavlyuchenkova & Miss U.Radwanska [1] 6/4 6/3	Miss A.Pavlyuchenkova & Miss U.Radwanska [1] 6/3 6/1	Miss A.Pavlyuchenkova & Miss U.Radwanska [1] 6/2 6/2	Miss A.Pavlyuchenkova & Miss U.Radwanska [1] 4/6 6/4 [10-5]	
2. Miss A.Bai (AUS) & Miss M.Gorny (RSA)					
(WC) 3. Miss S.Cornish (GBR) & Miss J.Rae (GBR)	Miss M.Brengle & Miss C.Gullickson 6/4 6/4				
4. Miss M.Brengle (USA) & Miss C.Gullickson (USA)					
5. Miss P.Kvitova (CZE) & Miss K.Vankova (CZE)	Miss M.Duque Marino & Miss M.Larcher De Brito 3/6 6/4 [10-6]	Miss M.Duque Marino & Miss M.Larcher De Brito w/o			
6. Miss M.Duque Marino (COL) & Miss M.Larcher De Brito (POR)					
7. Miss Y.Buchina (RUS) & Miss A.Rodionova (RUS)	Miss Y.Buchina & Miss A.Rodionova w/o				
8. **Miss J.Glushko** (ISR) & **Miss D.Ripoll** (GER) [5]					
9. **Miss K.Lykina** (RUS) & **Miss A.Pivovarova** (RUS) [3]	Miss N.Hofmanova & Miss S.Roma w/o	Miss N.Hofmanova & Miss S.Roma 6/3 6/1	Miss N.Hofmanova & Miss S.Roma 7/6(1) 6/2		
10. Miss N.Hofmanova (AUT) & Miss S.Roma (SWE)					
(WC) 11. Miss N.Broady (GBR) & Miss T.Moore (GBR)	Miss N.Broady & Miss T.Moore 6/3 4/6 [10-7]				
12. Miss M.Cecil (USA) & Miss K.Frilling (USA)					
13. Miss B.Jovanovski (SRB) & Miss S.Kayser (GER)	Miss J.Curtis & Miss A.Fitzpatrick 6/7(2) 7/5 [10-1]	Miss J.Curtis & Miss A.Fitzpatrick 6/1 6/3			
(WC) 14. Miss J.Curtis (GBR) & Miss A.Fitzpatrick (GBR)					
15. Miss G.Brodsky (USA) & Miss T.Hendler (BEL)	Miss T.Calderwood & Miss E.Chernyakova [6] 6/2 1/6 [10-2]				
16. **Miss T.Calderwood** (AUS) & **Miss E.Chernyakova** (RUS) [6]					
17. **Miss J.Moore** (AUS) & **Miss Y-M.Zhou** (CHN) [8]	Miss J.Moore & Miss Y-M.Zhou [8] 4/6 6/2 [11-9]	Miss J.Moore & Miss Y-M.Zhou [8] 6/1 6/3	Miss I.Begu & Miss O.Kalashnikova [4] 6/4 6/4	Miss M.Doi & Miss K.Nara 6/3 6/4	
(WC) 18. Miss K.Brown (GBR) & Miss J.Windley (GBR)					
19. Miss J.Gavenko (RUS) & Miss M.Mosolova (RUS)	Miss J.Jackson & Miss A.Voicu w/o				
(A) 20. Miss J.Jackson (GBR) & Miss A.Voicu (CAN)					
21. Miss S.Akita (JPN) & Miss S.Peers (AUS)	Miss T.Bua & Miss M.Gordo 6/4 6/4				
22. Miss T.Bua (ARG) & Miss M.Gordo (ARG)					
23. Miss S.Halep (ROU) & Miss A.Rus (NED)	Miss I.Begu & Miss O.Kalashnikova [4] w/o	Miss I.Begu & Miss O.Kalashnikova [4] 6/3 6/3			
24. **Miss I.Begu** (ROU) & **Miss O.Kalashnikova** (GEO) [4]					
25. Miss L.Jurikova (SVK) & Miss K.Kucova (SVK) [7]	Miss L.Jurikova & Miss K.Kucova [7] 7/6(2) 6/2	Miss L.Jurikova & Miss K.Kucova [7] 3/6 7/5 [10-6]	Miss M.Doi & Miss K.Nara 7/5 6/3		
26. Miss A.Berkova (CZE) & Miss R.Zsilinszka (USA)					
(A) 27. Miss A.Hubacek (AUS) & Miss Y.Tanaka (JPN)	Miss K.Piter & Miss R.Tabakova 6/4 6/4				
28. Miss K.Piter (POL) & Miss R.Tabakova (SVK)					
29. Miss C.Chala (FRA) & Miss N.Ciolkowski (FRA)	Miss M.Doi & Miss K.Nara 6/4 7/6(2)	Miss M.Doi & Miss K.Nara 7/6(2) 6/2			
30. Miss M.Doi (JPN) & Miss K.Nara (JPN)					
31. Miss K-C.Chang (TPE) & Miss V.Li (USA)	Miss K-C.Chang & Miss V.Li 6/7(3) 6/0 [10-5]				
32. **Miss K.Milevskaya** (BLR) & **Miss K.Pervak** (RUS) [2]					

Winners: **Miss A.Pavlyuchenkova & Miss U.Radwanska [1]** 6/4 2/6 [10-7]

Heavy type denotes seeded players. The figure in brackets against names denotes the order in which they were seeded.
(A)=Alternates. (WC)=Wild card.

155

THE CHAMPIONSHIP ROLL

GENTLEMEN'S SINGLES — CHAMPIONS & RUNNERS UP

1877 S. W. Gore *W. C. Marshall*	1901 A. W. Gore *R. F. Doherty*	* 1929 H. Cochet *J. Borotra*	* 1959 A. Olmedo *R. Laver*
1878 P. F. Hadow *S. W. Gore*	1902 H. L. Doherty *A. W. Gore*	1930 W. T. Tilden *W. Allison*	* 1960 N. A. Fraser *R. Laver*
* 1879 J. T. Hartley *V. St. L. Goold*	1903 H. L. Doherty *F. L. Riseley*	* 1931 S. B. Wood *F. X. Shields*	1961 R. Laver *C. R. McKinley*
1880 J. T. Hartley *H. F. Lawford*	1904 H. L. Doherty *F. L. Riseley*	1932 H. E. Vines *H. W. Austin*	1962 R. Laver *M. F. Mulligan*
1881 W. Renshaw *J. T. Hartley*	1905 H. L. Doherty *N. E. Brookes*	1933 J. H. Crawford *H. E. Vines*	* 1963 C. R. McKinley *F. S. Stolle*
1882 W. Renshaw *E. Renshaw*	1906 H. L. Doherty *F. L. Riseley*	1934 F. J. Perry *J. H. Crawford*	1964 R. Emerson *F. S. Stolle*
1883 W. Renshaw *E. Renshaw*	* 1907 N. E. Brookes *A. W. Gore*	1935 F. J. Perry *G. von Cramm*	1965 R. Emerson *F. S. Stolle*
1884 W. Renshaw *H. F. Lawford*	* 1908 A. W. Gore *H. Roper Barrett*	1936 F. J. Perry *G. von Cramm*	1966 M. Santana *R. D. Ralston*
1885 W. Renshaw *H. F. Lawford*	1909 A. W. Gore *M. J. G. Ritchie*	* 1937 J. D. Budge *G. von Cramm*	1967 J. D. Newcombe *W. P. Bungert*
1886 W. Renshaw *H. F. Lawford*	1910 A. F. Wilding *A. W. Gore*	1938 J. D. Budge *H. W. Austin*	1968 R. Laver *A. D. Roche*
* 1887 H. F. Lawford *E. Renshaw*	1911 A. F. Wilding *H. Roper Barrett*	* 1939 R. L. Riggs *E. T. Cooke*	1969 R. Laver *J. D. Newcombe*
1888 E. Renshaw *H. F. Lawford*	1912 A. F. Wilding *A. W. Gore*	* 1946 Y. Petra *G. E. Brown*	1970 J. D. Newcombe *K. R. Rosewall*
1889 W. Renshaw *E. Renshaw*	1913 A. F. Wilding *M. E. McLoughlin*	1947 J. Kramer *T. Brown*	1971 J. D. Newcombe *S. R. Smith*
1890 W. J. Hamilton *W. Renshaw*	1914 N. E. Brookes *A. F. Wilding*	* 1948 R. Falkenburg *J. E. Bromwich*	* 1972 S. R. Smith *I. Nastase*
* 1891 W. Baddeley *J. Pim*	1919 G. L. Patterson *N. E. Brookes*	1949 F. R. Schroeder *J. Drobny*	* 1973 J. Kodes *A. Metreveli*
1892 W. Baddeley *J. Pim*	1920 W. T. Tilden *G. L. Patterson*	* 1950 B. Patty *F. A. Sedgman*	1974 J. S. Connors *K. R. Rosewall*
1893 J. Pim *W. Baddeley*	1921 W. T. Tilden *B. I. C. Norton*	1951 R. Savitt *K. McGregor*	1975 A. R. Ashe *J. S. Connors*
1894 J. Pim *W. Baddeley*	*† 1922 G. L. Patterson *R. Lycett*	1952 F. A. Sedgman *J. Drobny*	1976 B. Borg *I. Nastase*
* 1895 W. Baddeley *W. V. Eaves*	* 1923 W. M. Johnston *F. T. Hunter*	* 1953 V. Seixas *K. Nielsen*	1977 B. Borg *J. S. Connors*
1896 H. S. Mahony *W. Baddeley*	* 1924 J. Borotra *R. Lacoste*	1954 J. Drobny *K. R. Rosewall*	1978 B. Borg *J. S.Connors*
1897 R. F. Doherty *H. S. Mahony*	1925 R. Lacoste *J. Borotra*	1955 T. Trabert *K. Nielsen*	1979 B. Borg *R. Tanner*
1898 R. F. Doherty *H. L . Doherty*	* 1926 J. Borotra *H. Kinsey*	* 1956 L. A. Hoad *K. R. Rosewall*	1980 B. Borg *J. P. McEnroe*
1899 R. F. Doherty *A. W. Gore*	1927 H. Cochet *J. Borotra*	1957 L. A. Hoad *A. J. Cooper*	1981 J. P. McEnroe *B. Borg*
1900 R. F. Doherty *S. H. Smith*	1928 R. Lacoste *H. Cochet*	* 1958 A. J. Cooper *N. A. Fraser*	1982 J. S. Connors *J. P. McEnroe*

1983 J. P. McEnroe *C. J. Lewis*
1984 J. P. McEnroe *J. S. Connors*
1985 B. Becker *K. Curren*
1986 B.Becker *I. Lendl*
1987 P. Cash *I. Lendl*
1988 S. Edberg *B. Becker*
1989 B. Becker *S. Edberg*
1990 S. Edberg *B. Becker*
1991 M. Stich *B. Becker*
1992 A. Agassi *G. Ivanisevic*
1993 P. Sampras *J. Courier*
1994 P. Sampras *G. Ivanisevic*
1995 P. Sampras *B. Becker*
1996 R. Krajicek *M. Washington*
1997 P. Sampras *C. Pioline*
1998 P. Sampras *G. Ivanisevic*
1999 P. Sampras *A. Agassi*
2000 P. Sampras *P. Rafter*
2001 G. Ivanisevic *P. Rafter*
2002 L. Hewitt *D. Nalbandian*
2003 R. Federer *M. Philippoussis*
2004 R. Federer *A. Roddick*
2005 R. Federer *A. Roddick*
2006 R. Federer *R. Nadal*
2007 R. Federer *R. Nadal*

For the years 1913, 1914 and 1919-1923 inclusive the above records include the "World's Championships on Grass" granted to The Lawn Tennis Association by The International Lawn Tennis Federation.
This title was then abolished and commencing in 1924 they became The OYcial Lawn Tennis Championships recognised by The International Lawn Tennis Federation.
Prior to 1922 the holders in the Singles Events and Gentlemen's Doubles did not compete in the Championships but met the winners of these events in the Challenge Rounds.
*† Challenge Round abolished: holders subsequently played through. * The holder did not defend the title.*

THE CHAMPIONSHIP ROLL
LADIES' SINGLES—CHAMPIONS & RUNNERS UP

1884 Miss M. Watson *Miss L. Watson*	1907 Miss M. Sutton *Mrs. Lambert Chambers*	* 1934 Miss D. E. Round *Miss H. H. Jacobs*	* 1963 Miss M. Smith *Miss B. J. Moffitt*	1986 Miss M. Navratilova *Miss H. Mandlikova*	
1885 Miss M. Watson *Miss B. Bingley*	* 1908 Mrs. A. Sterry *Miss A. M. Morton*	1935 Mrs. F. S. Moody *Miss H. H. Jacobs*	1964 Miss M. E. Bueno *Miss M. Smith*	1987 Miss M. Navratilova *Miss S. Graf*	
1886 Miss B. Bingley *Miss M. Watson*	* 1909 Miss D. P. Boothby *Miss A. M. Morton*	* 1936 Miss H. H. Jacobs *Frau. S. Sperling*	1965 Miss M. Smith *Miss M. E. Bueno*	1988 Miss S. Graf *Miss M. Navratilova*	
1887 Miss L. Dod *Miss B. Bingley*	1910 Mrs. Lambert Chambers *Miss D. P. Boothby*	1937 Miss D. E. Round *Miss J. Jedrzejowska*	1966 Mrs. L. W. King *Miss M. E. Bueno*	1989 Miss S. Graf *Miss M. Navratilova*	
1888 Miss L. Dod *Mrs. G. W. Hillyard*	1911 Mrs. Lambert Chambers *Miss D. P. Boothby*	* 1938 Mrs. F. S. Moody *Miss H. H. Jacobs*	1967 Mrs. L. W. King *Mrs. P. F. Jones*	1990 Miss M. Navratilova *Miss Z. Garrison*	
* 1889 Mrs. G. W. Hillyard *Miss L. Rice*	* 1912 Mrs. D. R. Larcombe *Mrs. A. Sterry*	* 1939 Miss A. Marble *Miss K. E. Stammers*	1968 Mrs. L. W. King *Miss J. A. M. Tegart*	1991 Miss S. Graf *Miss G. Sabatini*	
* 1890 Miss L. Rice *Miss M. Jacks*	* 1913 Mrs. Lambert Chambers *Mrs. R. J. McNair*	* 1946 Miss P. Betz *Miss L. Brough*	1969 Mrs. P. F. Jones *Mrs. L. W. King*	1992 Miss S. Graf *Miss M. Seles*	
* 1891 Miss L. Dod *Mrs. G. W. Hillyard*	1914 Mrs. Lambert Chambers *Mrs. D. R. Larcombe*	* 1947 Miss M. Osborne *Miss D. Hart*	* 1970 Mrs. B. M. Court *Mrs. L. W. King*	1993 Miss S. Graf *Miss J. Novotna*	
1892 Miss L. Dod *Mrs. G. W. Hillyard*	1919 Mlle. S. Lenglen *Mrs. Lambert Chambers*	1948 Miss L. Brough *Miss D. Hart*	1971 Miss E. F. Goolagong *Mrs. B. M. Court*	1994 Miss C. Martinez *Miss M. Navratilova*	
1893 Miss L. Dod *Mrs. G. W. Hillyard*	1920 Mlle. S. Lenglen *Mrs. Lambert Chambers*	1949 Miss L. Brough *Mrs. W. du Pont*	1972 Mrs. L. W. King *Miss E. F. Goolagong*	1995 Miss S. Graf *Miss A. Sanchez Vicario*	
* 1894 Mrs. G. W. Hillyard *Miss E. L. Austin*	1921 Mlle. S. Lenglen *Miss E. Ryan*	1950 Miss L. Brough *Mrs. W. du Pont*	1973 Mrs. L. W. King *Miss C. M. Evert*	1996 Miss S. Graf *Miss A. Sanchez Vicario*	
* 1895 Miss C. Cooper *Miss H. Jackson*	† 1922 Mlle. S. Lenglen *Mrs. F. Mallory*	1951 Miss D. Hart *Miss S. Fry*	1974 Miss C. M. Evert *Mrs. O. Morozova*	* 1997 Miss M. Hingis *Miss J. Novotna*	
1896 Miss C. Cooper *Mrs. W. H.Pickering*	1923 Mlle. S. Lenglen *Miss K. McKane*	1952 Miss M. Connolly *Miss L. Brough*	1975 Mrs. L. W. King *Mrs. R. Cawley*	1998 Miss J. Novotna *Miss N. Tauziat*	
1897 Mrs. G. W. Hillyard *Miss C. Cooper*	1924 Miss K. McKane *Miss H. Wills*	1953 Miss M. Connolly *Miss D. Hart*	* 1976 Miss C. M. Evert *Mrs. R. Cawley*	1999 Miss L.A. Davenport *Miss S. Graf*	
* 1898 Miss C. Cooper *Miss L Martin*	1925 Mlle. S. Lenglen *Miss J. Fry*	1954 Miss M. Connolly *Miss L. Brough*	1977 Miss S. V. Wade *Miss B. F. Stove*	2000 Miss V. Williams *Miss L.A. Davenport*	
1899 Mrs. G. W. Hillyard *Miss C. Cooper*	1926 Mrs. L. A. Godfree *Sta. L. de Alvarez*	* 1955 Miss L. Brough *Mrs. J. G. Fleitz*	1978 Miss M. Navratilova *Miss C. M. Evert*	2001 Miss V. Williams *Miss J. Henin*	
1900 Mrs. G. W. Hillyard *Miss C. Cooper*	1927 Miss H. Wills *Sta. L. de Alvarez*	1956 Miss S. Fry *Miss A. Buxton*	1979 Miss M. Navratilova *Mrs. J. M. Lloyd*	2002 Miss S. Williams *Miss V. Williams*	
1901 Mrs. A. Sterry *Mrs. G. W. Hillyard*	1928 Miss H. Wills *Sta. L. de Alvarez*	* 1957 Miss A. Gibson *Miss D. R. Hard*	1980 Mrs. R. Cawley *Mrs. J. M. Lloyd*	2003 Miss S. Williams *Miss V. Williams*	
1902 Miss M. E. Robb *Mrs. A. Sterry*	1929 Miss H. Wills *Miss H. H. Jacobs*	1958 Miss A. Gibson *Miss A. Mortimer*	* 1981 Mrs. J. M. Lloyd *Miss H. Mandlikova*	2004 Miss M. Sharapova *Miss S. Williams*	
* 1903 Miss D. K. Douglass *Miss E. W. Thomson*	1930 Mrs. F. S. Moody *Miss E. Ryan*	* 1959 Miss M. E. Bueno *Miss D. R. Hard*	1982 Miss M. Navratilova *Mrs. J. M. Lloyd*	2005 Miss V. Williams *Miss L. Davenport*	
1904 Miss D. K. Douglass *Mrs. A. Sterry*	* 1931 Fraulein C. Aussem *Fraulein H. Krahwinkel*	1960 Miss M. E. Bueno *Miss S. Reynolds*	1983 Miss M. Navratilova *Miss A. Jaeger*	2006 Miss A. Mauresmo *Mrs J. Henin-Hardenne*	
1905 Miss M. Sutton *Miss D. K. Douglass*	* 1932 Mrs. F. S. Moody *Miss H. H. Jacobs*	* 1961 Miss A. Mortimer *Miss C. C. Truman*	1984 Miss M. Navratilova *Mrs. J. M. Lloyd*	2007 Miss V. Williams *Miss M. Bartoli*	
1906 Miss D. K. Douglass *Miss M. Sutton*	1933 Mrs. F. S. Moody *Miss D. E. Round*	1962 Mrs. J. R. Susman *Mrs. V. Sukova*	1985 Miss M. Navratilova *Mrs. J. M. Lloyd*		

MAIDEN NAMES OF LADY CHAMPIONS (*In the tables the following have been recorded in both married and single identities*)

Mrs. R. Cawley ....Miss E. F. Goolagong Mrs. Lambert Chambers.............Miss D. K. Douglass Mrs. B. M. Court ....Miss M. Smith Mrs. B. C. Covell....................Miss P. L. Howkins Mrs. D. E. Dalton....................Miss J. A. M. Tegart Mrs. W. du Pont ....Miss M. Osborne Mrs. L. A. Godfree...................Miss K. McKane Mrs. H. F. Gourlay Cawley..........Miss H. F. Gourlay	Mrs J. Henin-Hardenne ....Miss J. Henin Mrs. G. W. Hillyard....................Miss B. Bingley Mrs. P. F. Jones.........................Miss A. S. Haydon Mrs. L. W. King ....Miss B. J. Moffitt Mrs. M. R. King ....Miss P. E. Mudford Mrs. D. R. Larcombe..................Miss E. W. Thomson Mrs. J. M. Lloyd ....Miss C. M. Evert Mrs. F. S. Moody ....Miss H. Wills	Mrs. O. Morozova ....Miss O. Morozova Mrs. L. E. G. Price ....Miss S. Reynolds Mrs. G. E. Reid ....Miss M. Melville Mrs. P. D. Smylie ....Miss E. M. Sayers Frau. S. Sperling ....Fraulein H. Krahwinkel Mrs. A. Sterry ....Miss C. Cooper Mrs. J. R. Susman ....Miss K. Hantze

THE CHAMPIONSHIP ROLL

GENTLEMEN'S DOUBLES—CHAMPIONS & RUNNERS UP

1879 L. R. Erskine & H. F. Lawford
F. Durant & G. E. Tabor

1880 W. Renshaw & E. Renshaw
O. E. Woodhouse & C. J. Cole

1881 W. Renshaw & E. Renshaw
W. J. Down & H. Vaughan

1882 J. T. Hartley & R. T. Richardson
J. G. Horn & C. B. Russell

1883 C. W. Grinstead & C. E. Welldon
C. B. Russell & R. T. Milford

1884 W. Renshaw & E. Renshaw
E. W. Lewis & E. L Williams

1885 W. Renshaw & E. Renshaw
C. E. Farrer & A. J. Stanley

1886 W. Renshaw & E. Renshaw
C. E. Farrer & A. J. Stanley

1887 P. Bowes-Lyon & H. W. W. Wilberforce
J. H. Crispe & E. Barratt Smith

1888 W. Renshaw & E. Renshaw
P Bowes-Lyon & H. W. W. Wilberforce

1889 W. Renshaw & E. Renshaw
E. W. Lewis & G. W. Hillyard

1890 J. Pim & F. O. Stoker
E. W. Lewis & G. W. Hillyard

1891 W. Baddeley & H. Baddeley
J. Pim & F. O. Stoker

1892 H. S. Barlow & E. W. Lewis
W. Baddeley & H. Baddeley

1893 J. Pim & F. O. Stoker
E. W. Lewis & H. S. Barlow

1894 W. Baddeley & H. Baddeley
H. S. Barlow & C. H. Martin

1895 W. Baddeley & H. Baddeley
E. W. Lewis & W. V. Eaves

1896 W. Baddeley & H. Baddeley
R. F. Doherty & H. A. Nisbet

1897 R. F. Doherty & H. L. Doherty
W. Baddeley & H. Baddeley

1898 R. F. Doherty & H. L . Doherty
H. A. Nisbet & C. Hobart

1899 R. F. Doherty & H. L. Doherty
H. A. Nisbet & C. Hobart

1900 R. F. Doherty & H. L. Doherty
H. Roper Barrett & H. A. Nisbet

1901 R. F. Doherty & H. L. Doherty
Dwight Davis & Holcombe Ward

1902 S. H. Smith & F. L. Riseley
R. F. Doherty & H. L. Doherty

1903 R. F. Doherty & H. L. Doherty
S. H. Smith & F. L. Riseley

1904 R. F. Doherty & H. L. Doherty
S. H. Smith & F. L. Riseley

1905 R. F. Doherty & H. L. Doherty
S. H. Smith & F. L. Riseley

1906 S. H. Smith & F. L. Riseley
R. F. Doherty & H. L. Doherty

1907 N. E. Brookes & A. F. Wilding
B. C. Wright & K. H. Behr

1908 A. F. Wilding & M. J. G. Ritchie
A. W. Gore & H. Roper Barrett

1909 A. W. Gore & H. Roper Barrett
S. N. Doust & H. A. Parker

1910 A. F. Wilding & M. J. G. Ritchie
A. W. Gore & H. Roper Barrett

1911 M. Decugis & A. H. Gobert
M. J. G. Ritchie & A. F. Wilding

1912 H. Roper Barrett & C. P. Dixon
M. Decugis & A. H. Gobert

1913 H. Roper Barrett & C. P. Dixon
F. W. Rahe & H. Kleinschroth

1914 N. E. Brookes & A. F. Wilding
H. Roper Barrett & C. P. Dixon

1919 R. V. Thomas & P. O'Hara-Wood
R. Lycett & R. W. Heath

1920 R. N. Williams & C. S. Garland
A. R. F. Kingscote & J. C. Parke

1921 R. Lycett & M. Woosnam
F. G. Lowe & A. H. Lowe

1922 R. Lycett & J. O. Anderson
G. L. Patterson & P. O'Hara-Wood

1923 R. Lycett & L. A. Godfree
Count de Gomar & E. Flaquer

1924 F. T. Hunter & V. Richards
R. N. Williams & W. M. Washburn

1925 J. Borotra & R. Lacoste
J. Hennessey & R. Casey

1926 H. Cochet & J. Brugnon
V. Richards & H. Kinsey

1927 F. T. Hunter & W. T. Tilden
J. Brugnon & H. Cochet

1928 H. Cochet & J. Brugnon
G. L. Patterson & J. B. Hawkes

1929 W. Allison & J. Van Ryn
J. C. Gregory & I. G. Collins

1930 W. Allison & J. Van Ryn
J. H. Doeg & G. M. Lott

1931 G. M Lott & J. Van Ryn
H. Cochet & J. Brugnon

1932 J. Borotra & J. Brugnon
G. P. Hughes & F. J. Perry

1933 J. Borotra & J. Brugnon
R. Nunoi & J. Satoh

1934 G. M. Lott & L. R. Stoefen
J. Borotra & J. Brugnon

1935 J. H. Crawford & A. K. Quist
W. Allison & J. Van Ryn

1936 G. P. Hughes & C. R. D. Tuckey
C. E. Hare & F. H. D. Wilde

1937 J. D. Budge & G. Mako
G. P. Hughes & C. R. D. Tuckey

1938 J. D. Budge & G. Mako
H. Henkel & G. von Metaxa

1939 R. L. Riggs & E. T. Cooke
C. E. Hare & F. H. D. Wilde

1946 T. Brown & J. Kramer
G. E. Brown & D. Pails

1947 R. Falkenburg & J. Kramer
A. J. Mottram & O. W. Sidwell

1948 J. E. Bromwich & F. A. Sedgman
T. Brown & G. Mulloy

1949 R. Gonzales & F. Parker
G. Mulloy & F. R. Schroeder

1950 J. E. Bromwich & A. K. Quist
G. E. Brown & O. W Sidwell

1951 K. McGregor & F. A. Sedgman
J. Drobny & E. W. Sturgess

1952 K. McGregor & F. A. Sedgman
V. Seixas & E. W. Sturgess

1953 L. A. Hoad & K. R. Rosewall
R. N. Hartwig & M. G. Rose

1954 R. N. Hartwig & M. G. Rose
V. Seixas & T. Trabert

1955 R. N. Hartwig & L. A. Hoad
N. A. Fraser & K. R. Rosewall

1956 L. A. Hoad & K. R. Rosewall
N. Pietrangeli & O. Sirola

1957 G. Mulloy & B. Patty
N. A. Fraser & L. A. Hoad

1958 S. Davidson & U. Schmidt
A. J. Cooper & N. A. Fraser

1959 R. Emerson & N. A. Fraser
R. Laver & R. Mark

1960 R. H. Osuna & R. D. Ralston
M. G. Davies & R. K. Wilson

1961 R. Emerson & N. A. Fraser
R. A. J. Hewitt & F. S. Stolle

1962 R. A. J. Hewitt & F. S. Stolle
B. Jovanovic & N. Pilic

1963 R. H. Osuna & A. Palafox
J. C. Barclay & P. Darmon

1964 R. A. J. Hewitt & F. S. Stolle
R. Emerson & K. N. Fletcher

1965 J. D. Newcombe & A. D. Roche
K. N. Fletcher & R. A. J. Hewitt

1966 K. N. Fletcher & J. D. Newcombe
W. W. Bowrey & O. K. Davidson

1967 R. A. J. Hewitt & F. D. McMillan
R. Emerson & K. N. Fletcher

1968 J. D. Newcombe & A. D. Roche
K. R. Rosewall & F. S. Stolle

1969 J. D. Newcombe & A. D. Roche
T. S. Okker & M. C. Reissen

1970 J. D. Newcombe & A. D. Roche
K. R. Rosewall & F. S. Stolle

1971 R. S. Emerson & R. G. Laver
A. R. Ashe & R. D. Ralston

1972 R. A. J. Hewitt & F. D. McMillan
S. R. Smith & E. J. van Dillen

1973 J. S. Connors & I. Nastase
J. R. Cooper & N. A. Fraser

1974 J. D. Newcombe & A. D. Roche
R. C. Lutz & S. R. Smith

1975 V. Gerulaitis & A. Mayer
C. Dowdeswell & A. J. Stone

1976 B. E. Gottfried & R. Ramirez
R. L. Case & G. Masters

1977 R. L. Case & G. Masters
J. G. Alexander & P. C. Dent

1978 R. A. J. Hewitt & F. D. McMillan
P. Fleming & J. P. McEnroe

1979 P. Fleming & J. P . McEnroe
B. E. Gottfried & R. Ramirez

1980 P. McNamara & P. McNamee
R. C. Lutz & S. R. Smith

1981 P. Fleming & J. P. McEnroe
R. C. Lutz & S. R. Smith

1982 P. McNamara & P. McNamee
P. Fleming & J. P. McEnroe

1983 P. Fleming & J. P McEnroe
T. E. Gullikson & T. R. Gullikson

1984 P. Fleming & J. P. McEnroe
P. Cash & P. McNamee

1985 H. P. Guenthardt & B. Taroczy
P. Cash & J. B. Fitzgerald

1986 J. Nystrom & M. Wilander
G. Donnelly & P. Fleming

1987 K. Flach & R. Seguso
S. Casal & E. Sanchez

1988 K. Flach & R. Seguso
J. B. Fitzgerald & A. Jarryd

1989 J. B. Fitzgerald & A. Jarryd
R. Leach & J. Pugh

1990 R. Leach & J. Pugh
P. Aldrich & D. T. Visser

1991 J. B. Fitzgerald & A. Jarryd
J. Frana & L. Lavalle

1992 J. P. McEnroe & M. Stich
J. Grabb & R. A. Reneberg

1993 T. A. Woodbridge & M. Woodforde
G. Connell & P. Galbraith

1994 T. A. Woodbridge & M. Woodforde
G. Connell & P. Galbraith

1995 T. A. Woodbridge & M. Woodforde
R. Leach & S. Melville

1996 T. A. Woodbridge & M. Woodforde
B. Black & G. Connell

1997 T. A. Woodbridge & M. Woodforde
J. Eltingh & P. Haarhuis

1998 J. Eltingh & P. Haarhuis
T. A. Woodbridge & M. Woodforde

1999 M. Bhupathi & L. Paes
P. Haarhuis & J. Palmer

2000 T. A. Woodbridge & M. Woodforde
P. Haarhuis & S. Stolle

2001 D. Johnson & J. Palmer
J. Novak & D. Rikl

2002 J. Bjorkman & T. A Woodbridge
M. Knowles & D. Nestor

2003 J. Bjorkman & T. A Woodbridge
M. Bhupathi & M. Mirnyi

2004 J. Bjorkman & T. A Woodbridge
J. Knowle & N. Zimonjic

2005 S. Huss & W. Moodie
B. Bryan & M. Bryan

2006 B. Bryan & M. Bryan
F. Santoro & N. Zimonjic

2007 A. Clement & M. Llodra
B. Bryan & M. Bryan

LADIES' DOUBLES—CHAMPIONS & RUNNERS UP

1913 Mrs. R. J. McNair & Miss D. P. Boothby
Mrs. A. Sterry & Mrs. Lambert Chambers

1914 Miss E. Ryan & Miss A. M. Morton
Mrs. D. R. Larcombe & Mrs. F. J. Hannam

1919 Mlle. S. Lenglen & Miss E. Ryan
Mrs. Lambert Chambers & Mrs. D. R. Larcombe

1920 Mlle. S. Lenglen & Miss E. Ryan
Mrs. Lambert Chambers & Mrs. D. R. Larcombe

1921 Mlle. S. Lenglen & Miss E. Ryan
Mrs. A. E. Beamish & Mrs. G. E. Peacock

1922 Mlle. S. Lenglen & Miss E. Ryan
Mrs. A. D. Stocks & Miss K. McKane

1923 Mlle. S. Lenglen & Miss E. Ryan
Miss J. Austin & Miss E. L. Colyer

1924 Mrs. H. Wightman & Miss H. Wills
Mrs. B. C. Covell & Miss K. McKane

1925 Mlle. S. Lenglen & Miss E. Ryan
Mrs. A. V. Bridge & Mrs. C. G. McIlquham

1926 Miss E. Ryan & Miss M. K. Browne
Mrs. L. A. Godfree & Miss E. L. Colyer

1927 Miss H. Wills & Miss E. Ryan
Miss E. L. Heine & Mrs. G. E. Peacock

1928 Mrs. Holcroft-Watson & Miss P. Saunders
Miss E. H. Harvey & Miss E. Bennett

1929 Mrs. Holcroft-Watson & Mrs. L.R.C. Michell
Mrs. B. C. Covell & Mrs. D. C. Shepherd-Barron

1930 Mrs. F. S. Moody & Miss E. Ryan
Miss E. Cross & Miss S. Palfrey

1931 Mrs.D.C. Shepherd-Barron & MissP.E. Mudford
Mlle. D. Metaxa & Mlle. J. Sigart

1932 Mlle. D. Metaxa & Mlle. J. Sigart
Miss E. Ryan & Miss H. H. Jacobs

1933 Mme. R. Mathieu & Miss E. Ryan
Miss F. James & Miss A. M. Yorke

1934 Mme. R. Mathieu & Miss E. Ryan
Mrs. D. Andrus & Mme. S. Henrotin

1935 Miss F. James & Miss K. E. Stammers
Mme. R. Mathieu & Frau. S. Sperling

1936 Miss F. James & Miss K. E. Stammers
Mrs. S. P. Fabyan & Miss H. H. Jacobs

1937 Mme. R. Mathieu & Miss A. M. Yorke
Mrs. M. R. King & Mrs. J. B. Pittman

1938 Mrs. S. P. Fabyan & Miss A. Marble
Mme. R. Mathieu & Miss A. M. Yorke

1939 Mrs S. P. Fabyan & Miss A. Marble
Miss H. H. Jacobs & Miss A. M. Yorke

1946 Miss L. Brough & Miss M. Osborne
Miss P. Betz & Miss D. Hart

1947 Miss D. Hart & Mrs. P. C. Todd
Miss L. Brough & Miss M. Osborne

1948 Miss L. Brough & Mrs. W. du Pont
Miss D. Hart & Mrs. P. C. Todd

1949 Miss L. Brough & Mrs. W. du Pont
Miss G. Moran & Mrs. P. C. Todd

1950 Miss L. Brough & Mrs. W. du Pont
Miss S. Fry & Miss D. Hart

1951 Miss S. Fry & Miss D. Hart
Miss L. Brough & Mrs. W. du Pont

1952 Miss S. Fry & Miss D. Hart
Miss L. Brough & Miss M. Connolly

1953 Miss S. Fry & Miss D. Hart
Miss M. Connolly & Miss J. Sampson

1954 Miss L. Brough & Mrs. W. du Pont
Miss S. Fry & Miss D. Hart

1955 Miss A. Mortimer & Miss J. A. Shilcock
Miss S. J. Bloomer & Miss P. E. Ward

1956 Miss A. Buxton & Miss A. Gibson
Miss F. Muller & Miss D. G. Seeney

1957 Miss A. Gibson & Miss D. R. Hard
Mrs. K. Hawton & Mrs. T. D. Long

1958 Miss M. E. Bueno & Miss A. Gibson
Mrs. W. du Pont & Miss M. Varner

1959 Miss J. Arth & Miss D. R. Hard
Mrs. J. G. Fleitz & Miss C. C. Truman

1960 Miss M. E. Bueno & Miss D. R. Hard
Miss S. Reynolds & Miss R. Schuurman

1961 Miss K. Hantze & Miss B. J. Moffitt
Miss J. Lehane & Miss M. Smith

1962 Miss B. J. Moffitt & Mrs. J. R. Susman
Mrs. L. E. G. Price & Miss R. Schuurman

1963 Miss M. E. Bueno & Miss D. R. Hard
Miss R. A. Ebbern & Miss M. Smith

1964 Miss M. Smith & Miss L. R. Turner
Miss B. J. Moffitt & Mrs. J. R. Susman

1965 Miss M. E. Bueno & Miss B. J. Moffitt
Miss F. Durr & Miss J. LieVrig

1966 Miss M. E. Bueno & Miss N. Richey
Miss M. Smith & Miss J. A. M. Tegart

1967 Miss R. Casals & Mrs. L. W. King
Miss M. E. Bueno & Miss N. Richey

1968 Miss R. Casals & Mrs. L. W. King
Miss F. Durr & Mrs. P. F. Jones

1969 Mrs. B. M. Court & Miss J. A. M. Tegart
Miss P. S. A. Hogan & Miss M. Michel

1970 Miss R. Casals & Mrs. L. W. King
Miss F. Durr & Miss S. V. Wade

1971 Miss R. Casals & Mrs. L. W. King
Mrs. B. M. Court & Miss E. F. Goolagong

1972 Mrs. L. W. King & Miss B. F. Stove
Mrs. D. E. Dalton & Miss F. Durr

1973 Miss R. Casals & Mrs. L. W. King
Miss F. Durr & Miss B. F. Stove

1974 Miss E. F. Goolagong & Miss M. Michel
Miss H. F. Gourlay & Miss K. M. Krantzcke

1975 Miss A. Kiyomura & Miss K. Sawamatsu
Miss F. Durr & Miss B. F. Stove

1976 Miss C. M. Evert & Miss M. Navratilova
Mrs. L. W. King & Miss B. F. Stove

1977 Mrs. H. F. Gourlay Cawley & Miss J. C. Russell
Miss M. Navratilova & Miss B. F . Stove

1978 Mrs. G. E. Reid & Miss. W. M. Turnbull
Miss M. Jausovec & Miss V. Ruzici

1979 Mrs. L. W. King & Miss M. Navratilova
Miss B. F. Stove & Miss W. M. Turnbull

1980 Miss K. Jordan & Miss A. E. Smith
Miss R. Casals & Miss W. M. Turnbull

1981 Miss M. Navratilova & Miss P. H. Shriver
Miss K. Jordan & Miss A. E. Smith

1982 Miss M. Navratilova & Miss P. H. Shriver
Miss K. Jordan & Miss A. E. Smith

1983 Miss M. Navratilova & Miss P. H. Shriver
Miss R. Casals & Miss W. M. Turnbull

1984 Miss M. Navratilova & Miss P. H. Shriver
Miss K. Jordan & Miss A. E. Smith

1985 Miss K. Jordan & Mrs. P. D. Smylie
Miss M. Navratilova & Miss P. H. Shriver

1986 Miss M. Navratilova & Miss P. H. Shriver
Miss H. Mandlikova & Miss W. M. Turnbull

1987 Miss C. Kohde-Kilsch & Miss H. Sukova
Miss B. Nagelsen & Mrs. P. D. Smylie

1988 Miss S. Graf & Miss G. Sabatini
Miss L. Savchenko & Miss N. Zvereva

1989 Miss J. Novotna & Miss H. Sukova
Miss L. Savchenko & Miss N. Zvereva

1990 Miss J. Novotna & Miss H. Sukova
Miss K. Jordan & Mrs. P. D. Smylie

1991 Miss L. Savchenko & Miss N. Zvereva
Miss G. Fernandez & Miss J. Novotna

1992 Miss G. Fernandez & Miss N. Zvereva
Miss J. Novotna & Mrs. L. Savchenko-Neiland

1993 Miss G. Fernandez & Miss N. Zvereva
Mrs. L. Neiland & Miss J. Novotna

1994 Miss G. Fernandez & Miss N. Zvereva
Miss J. Novotna & Miss A. Sanchez Vicario

1995 Miss J. Novotna & Miss A. Sanchez Vicario
Miss G. Fernandez & Miss N. Zvereva

1996 Miss M. Hingis & Miss H. Sukova
Miss M.J. McGrath & Mrs. L. Neiland

1997 Miss G. Fernandez & Miss N. Zvereva
Miss N.J. Arendt & Miss M.M. Bollegraf

1998 Miss M. Hingis & Miss J. Novotna
Miss L.A. Davenport & Miss N. Zvereva

1999 Miss L.A. Davenport & Miss C. Morariu
Miss M. de Swardt & Miss E. Tatarkova

2000 Miss S. Williams & Miss V. Williams
Mrs J. Halard–Decugis & Miss A. Sugiyama

2001 Miss L.M. Raymond & Miss R.P. Stubbs
Miss K. Clijsters & Miss A. Sugiyama

2002 Miss S. Williams & Miss V. Williams
Miss V. Ruano Pascual & Miss P. Suarez

2003 Miss K. Clijsters & Miss A. Sugiyama
Miss V. Ruano Pascual & Miss P. Suarez

2004 Miss C. Black & Miss R.P. Stubbs
Mrs L. Huber & Miss A. Sugiyama

2005 Miss C. Black & Mrs L. Huber
Miss S. Kuznetsova & Miss A. Muresmo

2006 Miss Z. Yan & Miss J. Zheng
Miss V. Ruano Pascual & Miss P. Suarez

2007 Miss C. Black & Mrs L. Huber
Miss K. Srebotnik & Miss A. Sugiyama

THE CHAMPIONSHIP ROLL
MIXED DOUBLES—CHAMPIONS & RUNNERS UP

1913 H. Crisp and Mrs. C. O. Tuckey
J. C. Parke and Mrs. D. R. Larcombe

1914 J. C. Parke and Mrs. D.R. Larcombe
A. F. Wilding and Mlle. M. Broquedis

1919 R. Lycett and Miss E. Ryan
A. D. Prebble and Mrs. Lambert Chambers

1920 G. L. Patterson and Mlle. S. Lenglen
R. Lycett and Miss E. Ryan

1921 R. Lycett and Miss E. Ryan
M. Woosnam and Miss P. L. Howkins

1922 P. O'Hara-Wood and Mlle. S. Lenglen
R. Lycett and Miss E. Ryan

1923 R. Lycett and Miss E. Ryan
L. S. Deane and Mrs. D. C. Shepherd-Barron

1924 J. B. Gilbert and Miss K. McKane
L. A. Godfree and Mrs. D. C. Shepherd-Barron

1925 J. Borotra and Mlle. S. Lenglen
H. L. de Morpurgo and Miss E. Ryan

1926 L. A. Godfree and Mrs. L. A. Godfree
H. Kinsey and Miss M. K. Browne

1927 F. T. Hunter and Miss E. Ryan
L. A. Godfree and Mrs. L. A. Godfree

1928 P. D. B. Spence and Miss E. Ryan
J. Crawford and Miss D. Akhurst

1929 F. T. Hunter and Miss H. Wills
I. G. Collins and Miss J. Fry

1930 J. H. Crawford and Miss E. Ryan
D. Prenn and Fraulein H. Krahwinkel

1931 G. M. Lott and Mrs L. A. Harper
I. G. Collins and Miss J. C. Ridley

1932 E. Maier and Miss E. Ryan
H. C. Hopman and Mlle. J. Sigart

1933 G. von Cramm and Fraulein H. Krahwinkel
N. G. Farquharson and Miss M. Heeley

1934 R. Miki and Miss D. E. Round
H. W. Austin and Mrs D. C. Shepherd-Barron

1935 F. J. Perry and Miss D. E. Round
H. C. Hopman and Mrs. H. C. Hopman

1936 F. J. Perry and Miss D. E. Round
J. D. Budge and Mrs. S. P. Fabyan

1937 J. D. Budge and Miss A. Marble
Y. Petra and Mme. R. Mathieu

1938 J. D. Budge and Miss A. Marble
H. Henkel and Mrs. S. P. Fabyan

1939 R. L. Riggs and Miss A. Marble
F. H. D. Wilde and Miss N. B. Brown

1946 T. Brown and Miss L. Brough
G. E. Brown and Miss D. Bundy

1947 J. E. Bromwich and Miss L. Brough
C. F. Long and Mrs. N. M. Bolton

1948 J. E. Bromwich and Miss L. Brough
F. A. Sedgman and Miss D. Hart

1949 E. W. Sturgess and Mrs. S. P. Summers
J. E. Bromwich and Miss L. Brough

1950 E. W. Sturgess and Miss L. Brough
G. E. Brown and Mrs. P. C. Todd

1951 F. A. Sedgman and Miss D. Hart
M. G. Rose and Mrs. N. M. Bolton

1952 F. A. Sedgman and Miss D. Hart
E. Morea and Mrs. T. D. Long

1953 V. Seixas and Miss D. Hart
E. Morea and Miss S. Fry

1954 V. Seixas and Miss D. Hart
K. R. Rosewall and Mrs. W. du Pont

1955 V. Seixas and Miss D. Hart
E. Morea and Miss L. Brough

1956 V. Seixas and Miss S. Fry
G. Mulloy and Miss A. Gibson

1957 M. G. Rose and Miss D. R. Hard
N. A. Fraser and Miss A. Gibson

1958 R. N. Howe and Miss L. Coghlan
K. Nielsen and Miss A. Gibson

1959 R. Laver and Miss D. R. Hard
N. A. Fraser and Miss M. E. Bueno

1960 R. Laver and Miss D. R. Hard
R. N. Howe and Miss M. E. Bueno

1961 F. S. Stolle and Miss L. R. Turner
R. N. Howe and Miss E. Buding

1962 N. A. Fraser and Mrs. W. du Pont
R. D. Ralston and Miss A. S. Haydon

1963 K. N. Fletcher and Miss M. Smith
R. A. J. Hewitt and Miss D. R. Hard

1964 F. S. Stolle and Miss L. R. Turner
K. N. Fletcher and Miss M. Smith

1965 K. N. Fletcher and Miss M. Smith
A. D. Roche and Miss J. A. M. Tegart

1966 K. N. Fletcher and Miss M. Smith
R. D. Ralston amd Mrs. L. W. King

1967 O. K. Davidson and Mrs. L. W. King
K. N. Fletcher and Miss M. E. Bueno

1968 K. N. Fletcher and Mrs. B. M. Court
A. Metreveli and Miss O. Morozova

1969 F. S. Stolle and Mrs. P. F. Jones
A. D. Roche and Miss J. A. M. Tegart

1970 I. Nastase and Miss R. Casals
A. Metreveli and Miss O. Morozova

1971 O. K. Davidson and Mrs. L. W. King
M. C. Riessen and Mrs. B. M. Court

1972 I. Nastase and Miss R. Casals
K.G. Warwick and Miss E. F. Goolagong

1973 O. K. Davidson and Mrs. L. W. King
R. Ramirez and Miss J. S. Newberry

1974 O. K. Davidson and Mrs. L. W. King
M. J. Farrell and Miss L. J. Charles

1975 M. C. Riessen and Mrs. B. M. Court
A. J. Stone and Miss B. F. Stove

1976 A. D. Roche and Miss F. Durr
R. L. Stockton and Miss R. Casals

1977 R. A. J. Hewitt and Miss G. R. Stevens
F. D. McMillan and Miss B. F. Stove

1978 F. D. McMillan and Miss B. F. Stove
R. O. Ruffels and Mrs. L. W. King

1979 R. A. J. Hewitt and Miss G. R. Stevens
F. D. McMillan and Miss B. F. Stove

1980 J. R. Austin and Miss T. Austin
M. R. Edmondson and Miss D. L. Fromholtz

1981 F. D. McMillan and Miss B. F. Stove
J. R. Austin and Miss T. Austin

1982 K. Curren and Miss A. E. Smith
J. M. Lloyd and Miss W. M. Turnbull

1983 J. M. Lloyd and Miss W. M. Turnbull
S. Denton and Mrs. L. W. King

1984 J. M. Lloyd and Miss W. M. Turnbull
S. Denton and Miss K. Jordan

1985 P. McNamee and Miss M. Navratilova
J. B. Fitzgerald and Mrs. P. D. Smylie

1986 K. Flach and Miss K. Jordan
H. P. Guenthardt and Miss M. Navratilova

1987 M. J. Bates and Miss J. M. Durie
D. Cahill and Miss N. Provis

1988 S. E. Stewart and Miss Z. L. Garrison
K. Jones and Mrs. S. W. Magers

1989 J. Pugh and Miss J. Novotna
M. Kratzmann and Miss J. M. Byrne

1990 R. Leach and Miss Z. L. Garrison
J. B. Fitzgerald and Mrs P. D. Smylie

1991 J. B. Fitzgerald and Mrs. P. D. Smylie
J. Pugh and Miss N. Zvereva

1992 C. Suk and Mrs L. Savchenko-Neiland
J. Eltingh and Miss M. Oremans

1993 M. Woodforde and Miss M. Navratilova
T. Nijssen and Miss M. M. Bollegraf

1994 T. A. Woodbridge and Miss H. Sukova
T. J. Middleton and Miss L. M. McNeil

1995 J. Stark and Miss M. Navratilova
C. Suk and Miss G. Fernandez

1996 C. Suk and Miss H. Sukova
M. Woodforde and Mrs. L. Neiland

1997 C. Suk and Miss H. Sukova
A. Olhovskiy and Mrs L. Neiland

1998 M. Mirnyi and Miss S. Williams
M. Bhupathi and Miss M. Lucic

1999 L. Paes and Miss L.M. Raymond
J. Bjorkman and Miss A. Kournikova

2000 D. Johnson and Miss K. Po
L. Hewitt and Miss K. Clijsters

2001 L. Friedl and Miss D. Hantuchova
M. Bryan and Mrs L. Huber

2002 M. Bhupathi and Miss E. Likhovtseva
K. Ullyett and Miss D. Hantuchova

2003 L. Paes and Miss M. Navratilova
A. Ram and Miss A. Rodionova

2004 W. Black and Miss C. Black
T.A. Woodbridge and Miss A. Molik

2005 M. Bhupathi and Miss M. Pierce
P. Hanley and Miss T. Perebiynis

2006 A. Ram and Miss V. Zvonareva
B. Bryan and Miss V. Williams

2007 J. Murray & Miss J. Jankovic
J. Bjorkman & Miss A. Molik

THE CHAMPIONSHIP ROLL

BOYS' SINGLES

1947 K. Nielsen (Denmark)
S. V. Davidson (Sweden)
1948 S. Stockenberg (Sweden)
D. Vad (Hungary)
1949 S. Stockenberg (Sweden)
J. A.T. Horn (G.B.)
1950 J. A.T. Horn (G.B.)
K. Mobarek (Egypt)
1951 J. Kupferburger (S.A.)
K. Mobarek (Egypt)
1952 R. K. Wilson (G.B.)
T. T. Fancutt (S.A.)
1953 W. A. Knight (G.B.)
R. Krishnan (India)
1954 R. Krishnan (India)
A. J. Cooper (Australia)
1955 M. P. Hann (G.B.)
J. E. Lundquist (Sweden)
1956 R. Holmberg (U.S.A.)
R. G. Laver (Australia)
1957 J. I. Tattersall (G.B.)
I. Ribeiro (Brazil)
1958 E. Buchholz (U.S.A.)
P. J. Lall (India)
1959 T. Lejus (U.S.S.R.)
R. W. Barnes (Brazil)
1960 A. R. Mandelstam (S.A.)
J. Mukerjea (India)
1961 C. E. Graebner (U.S.A.)
E. Blanke (Austria)
1962 S. Matthews (G.B.)
A. Metreveli (U.S.S.R.)
1963 N. Kalogeropoulos (Greece)
I. El Shafei (U.A.R.)
1964 I. El Shafei (U.A.R.)
V. Korotkov (U.S.S.R.)
1965 V. Korotkov (U.S.S.R.)
G. Goven (France)
1966 V. Korotkov (U.S.S.R.)
B. E. Fairlie (N.Z.)
1967 M. Orantes (Spain)
M. S. Estep (U.S.A.)
1968 J. G. Alexander (Australia)
J. Thamin (France)
1969 B. Bertram (S.A.)
J. G. Alexander (Australia)
1970 B. Bertram (S.A.)
F. Gebert (Germany)
1971 R. Kreiss (U.S.A.)
S. A. Warboys (G.B.)
1972 B. Borg (Sweden)
C. J. Mottram (G.B.)
1973 W. Martin (U.S.A.)
C. S. Dowdeswell (Rhodesia)
1974 W. Martin (U.S.A.)
Ash Amritraj (India)
1975 C. J. Lewis (N.Z.)
R. Ycaza (Ecuador)
1976 H. Guenthardt (Switzerland)
P. Elter (Germany)
1977 V. A. Winitsky (U.S.A.)
T. E. Teltscher (U.S.A.)
1978 I. Lendl (Czechoslovakia)
J. Turpin (U.S.A.)
1979 R. Krishnan (India)
D. Siegler (U.S.A.)
1980 T. Tulasne (France)
H. D. Beutel (Germany)
1981 M. W. Anger (U.S.A.)
P. Cash (Australia)
1982 P. Cash (Australia)
H. Sundstrom (Sweden)
1983 S. Edberg (Sweden)
J. Frawley (Australia)
1984 M.Kratzmann (Australia)
S. Kruger (S.A.)
1985 L. Lavalle (Mexico)
E. Velez (Mexico)
1986 E. Velez (Mexico)
J. Sanchez (Spain)
1987 D. Nargiso (Italy)
J. R. Stoltenberg (Australia)
1988 N. Pereira (Venezuela)
G. Raoux (France)
1989 N. Kulti (Sweden)
T. A. Woodbridge (Australia)
1990 L. Paes (India)
M. Ondruska (S.A.)
1991 T. Enquist (Sweden)
M. Joyce (U.S.A.)
1992 D. Skoch (Czechoslovakia)
B. Dunn (U.S.A.)
1993 R. Sabau (Romania)
J. Szymanski (Venezuela)
1994 S. Humphries (U.S.A.)
M. A. Philippoussis (Australia)
1995 O. Mutis (France)
N. Kiefer (Germany)
1996 V. Voltchkov (Belarus)
I. Ljubicic (Croatia)
1997 W. Whitehouse (South Africa)
D. Elsner (Germany)
1998 R. Federer (Switzerland)
I. Labadze (Georgia)
1999 J. Melzer (Austria)
K. Pless (Denmark)
2000 N. Mahut (France)
M. Ancic (Croatia)
2001 R. Valent (Switzerland)
G. Muller (Luxembourg)
2002 T. Reid (Australia)
L. Quahab (Algeria)
2003 F. Mergea (Romania)
C. Guccione (Australia)
2004 G. Monfils (France)
M. Kasiri (G.B.)
2005 J. Chardy (France)
R. Haase (Netherlands)
2006 T. De Bakker (Netherlands)
M. Gawron (Poland)
2007 D. Young (U.S.A)
V. Ignatic (Belarus)

BOYS' DOUBLES

1982 P. Cash & J. Frawley
R. D. Leach & J. J. Ross
1983 M. Kratzmann & S. Youl
M. Nastase & O. Rahnasto
1984 R. Brown & R. Weiss
M. Kratzmann & J. Svensson
1985 A. Moreno & J. Yzaga
P. Korda & C. Suk
1986 T. Carbonell & P. Korda
S. Barr & H. Karrasch
1987 J. Stoltenberg & T. Woodbridge
D. Nargiso & E. Rossi
1988 J. Stoltenberg & T. Woodbridge
D. Rikl & T. Zdrazila
1989 J. Palmer & J. Stark
J-L. De Jager & W. R. Ferreira
1990 S. Lareau & S. Leblanc
C. Marsh & M. Ondruska
1991 K. Alami & G. Rusedski
J-L. De Jager & A. Medvedev
1992 S. Baldas & S. Draper
M. S. Bhupathi & N. Kirtane
1993 S. Downs & J. Greenhalgh
N. Godwin & G. Williams
1994 B. Ellwood & M. Philippoussis
V. Platenik & R. Schlachter
1995 M. Lee & J.M. Trotman
A. Hernandez & M. Puerta
1996 D. Bracciali & J. Robichaud
D. Roberts & W. Whitehouse
1997 L. Horna & N. Massu
J. Van de Westhuizen & W. Whitehouse
1998 R. Federer & O. Rochus
M. Llodra & A. Ram
1999 G. Coria & D. Nalbandian
T. Enev & J. Nieminem
2000 D. Coene & K. Vliegen
A. Banks & B. Riby
2001 F. Dancevic & G. Lapentti
B. Echagaray & S. Gonzales
2002 F. Mergea & H. Tecau
B. Baker & B. Ram
2003 F. Mergea & H. Tecau
A. Feeney & C. Guccione
2004 B. Evans & S. Oudsema
R. Haase & V. Troicki
2005 J. Levine & M. Shabaz
S. Groth & A. Kennaugh
2006 K. Damico & N. Schnugg
M. Klizan & A. Martin
2007 D. Lopez & M. Trevisan
R. Jebavy & M. Klizan

GIRLS' SINGLES

1947 Miss G. Domken (Belgium)
Miss B. Wallen (Sweden)
1948 Miss O. Miskova (Czechoslovakia)
Miss V. Rigollet (Switzerland)
1949 Miss C. Mercelis (Belgium)
Miss J. S. V. Partridge (G.B.)
1950 Miss L. Cornell (G.B.)
Miss A. Winter (Norway)
1951 Miss L. Cornell (G.B.)
Miss S. Lazzarino (Italy)
1952 Miss F. J. I. ten Bosch (Netherlands)
Miss R. Davar (India)
1953 Miss D. Kilian (S.A.)
Miss V. A. Pitt (G.B.)
1954 Miss V. A. Pitt (G.B.)
Miss C. Monnot (France)
1955 Miss S. M. Armstrong (G.B.)
Miss B. de Chambure (France)
1956 Miss A. S. Haydon (G.B.)
Miss I. Buding (Germany)
1957 Miss M. Arnold (U.S.A.)
Miss E. Reyes (Mexico)
1958 Miss S. M. Moore (U.S.A)
Miss A. Dmitrieva (U.S.S.R.)
1959 Miss J. Cross (S.A.)
Miss D. Schuster (Austria)
1960 Miss K. Hantze (U.S.A)
Miss L. M Hutchings (S.A.)
1961 Miss G. Baksheeva (U.S.S.R.)
Miss K. D. Chabot (U.S.A.)
1962 Miss G. Baksheeva (U.S.S.R.)
Miss E. P. Terry (N.Z.)
1963 Miss D. M. Salfati (France)
Miss K. Dening (Australia)
1964 Miss P. Bartkowicz (U.S.A)
Miss E. Subirats (Mexico)
1965 Miss O. Morozova (U.S.S.R.)
Miss R. Giscarfe (Argentina)
1966 Miss B. Lindstrom (Finland)
Miss J. A. Congdon (g.b)
1967 Miss J. Salome (Netherlands)
Miss E. M. Strandberg (Sweden)
1968 Miss K. Pigeon (U.S.A)
Miss L. E. Hunt (Australia)
1969 Miss K. Sawamatsu (Japan)
Miss B. I. Kirk (S.A.)
1970 Miss S. Walsh (U.S.A)
Miss M. V. Kroshina (U.S.S.R.)
1971 Miss M.V. Kroschina (U.S.S.R.)
Miss S. H. Minford (G.B.)
1972 Miss I. Kloss (S.A.)
Miss G. L. Coles (g.b)
1973 Miss A. Kiyomura (U.S.A)
Miss M. Navratilova (Czechoslovakia)
1974 Miss M. Jausovec (Yugoslavia)
Miss M. Simionescu (Romania)
1975 Miss N. Y. Chmyreva (U.S.S.R.)
Miss R. Marsikova (Czechoslovakia)
1976 Miss N. Y. Chmyreva (U.S.S.R.)
Miss M. Kruger (S.A.)
1977 Miss L. Antonoplis (U.S.A)
Miss Mareen Louie (U.S.A.)
1978 Miss T. Austin (U.S.A)
Miss H. Mandlikova (Czechoslovakia)
1979 Miss M. L. Piatek (U.S.A)
Miss A. A. Moulton (U.S.A.)
1980 Miss D. Freeman (Australia)
Miss S. J. Leo (Australia)
1981 Miss Z. Garrison (U.S.A)
Miss R. R. Uys (S.A.)
1982 Miss C. Tanvier (France)
Miss H. Sukova (Czechoslovakia)
1983 Miss P. Paradis (France)
Miss P. Hy (Hong Kong)
1984 Miss A. N. Croft (G.B.)
Miss E. Reinach (S.A.)
1985 Miss A. Holikova (Czechoslovakia)
Miss J. M. Byrne (Australia)
1986 Miss N.M. Zvereva (U.S.S.R.)
Miss L. Meskhi (U.S.S.R.)
1987 Miss N.M. Zvereva (U.S.S.R.)
Miss J. Halard (France)
1988 Miss B. Schultz (Netherlands)
Miss E. Derly (France)
1989 Miss A. Strnadova (Czechoslavakia)
Miss M. J. McGrath (U.S.A.)
1990 Miss A. Strnadova (Czechoslavakia)
Miss K. Sharpe (Australia)
1991 Miss B. Rittner (Germany)
Miss E. Makarova (U.S.S.R.)
1992 Miss C. Rubin (U.S.A)
Miss L. Courtois (Belgium)
1993 Miss N. Feber (Belgium)
Miss R. Grande (Italy)
1994 Miss M. Hingis (Switzerland)
Miss M-R. Jeon (Korea)
1995 Miss A. Olsza (Poland)
Miss T. Tanasugarn (Thailand)
1996 Miss A. Mauresmo (France)
Miss M. L. Serna (Spain)
1997 Miss C. Black (Zimbabwe)
Miss A. Rippner (U.S.A.)
1998 Miss K. Srebotnik (Slovenia)
Miss K. Clijsters (Belgium)
1999 Miss I. Tulyagnova (Uzbekhistan)
Miss L. Krasnoroutskaya (U.S.S.R.)
2000 Miss M. E. Salerni (Argentina)
Miss T. Perebiynis (Ukraine)
2001 Miss A. Widjaja (Indonesia)
Miss D. Safina (U.S.S.R.)
2002 Miss V. Douchevina (Russia)
Miss M. Sharapova (U.S.S.R.)
2003 Miss K. Flipkens (Belgium)
Miss A. Tchakvetadze (U.S.S.R.)
2004 Miss K. Bondarenko (Ukraine)
Miss A. Ivanovic (Serbia and Montenegro)
2005 Miss A. Radwanska (Poland)
Miss T. Paszek (Austria)
2006 Miss C. Wozniacki (Denmark)
Miss M. Rybarikova (Slovakia)
2007 Miss U. Radwanska (Poland)
Miss M. Brengle (U.S.A)

GIRLS' DOUBLES

1982 Miss B. Herr & Miss P. Barg
Miss B. S. Gerken & Miss G. A. Rush
1983 Miss P. Fendick & Miss P. Hy
Miss C. Anderholm & Miss H. Olsson
1984 Miss C. Kuhlman & Miss S. Rehe
Miss V. Milvidskaya & Miss L.I. Savchenko
1985 Miss L. Field & Miss J. Thompson
Miss E. Reinach & Miss J. A. Richardson
1986 Miss M. Jaggard & Miss L. O'Neill
Miss L. Meskhi & Miss N. M. Zvereva
1987 Miss N. Medvedeva & Miss N.M. Zvereva
Miss I. S. Kim & Miss P. M. Moreno
1988 Miss J. A. Faull & Miss R. McQuillan
Miss A. Dechaume & Miss E. Derly
1989 Miss J. Capriati & Miss M. McGrath
Miss A. Strnadova & Miss E. Sviglerova
1990 Miss K. Habsudova & Miss A. Strnadova
Miss N. J. Pratt & Miss K. Sharpe
1991 Miss C. Barclay & Miss L. Zaltz
Miss J. Limmer & Miss A. Woolcock
1992 Miss M. Avotins & Miss L. McShea
Miss P. Nelson & Miss J. Steven
1993 Miss L. Courtois & Miss N. Feber
Miss H. Mochizuki & Miss Y. Yoshida
1994 Miss E. De Villiers & Miss E. E. Jelfs
Miss C. M. Morariu & Miss L. Varmuzova
1995 Miss C. Black & Miss A. Olsza
Miss T. Musgrove & Miss J Richardson
1996 Miss O. Barabanschikova &
Miss A. Mauresmo
Miss L. Osterloh & Miss S. Reeves
1997 Miss C. Black & Miss I. Selyutina
Miss M. Matevzic & Miss K. Srebotnik
1998 Miss E. Dyrberg & Miss J. Kostanic
Miss P. Rampre & Miss I. Tulyaganova
1999 Miss D. Bedanova & Miss M.E. Salerni
Miss T. Perebiynis & Miss I. Tulyaganova
2000 Miss I. Gaspar & Miss T. Perebiynis
Miss D. Bedanova & Miss M. E. Salerni
2001 Miss G. Dulko & Miss A. Harkleroad
Miss C. Horiatopoulos & Miss B. Mattek
2002 Miss E. Clijsters & Miss B. Strycova
Miss A. Baker & Miss A-L. Groenfeld
2003 Miss A. Kleybanova & Miss S. Mirza
Miss K. Bohmova & Miss M. Krajicek
2004 Miss V. Azarenka & Miss V. Havartsova
Miss M. Erakovic & Miss M. Niculescu
2005 Miss V. Azarenka & Miss A. Szavay
Miss M. Erakovic & Miss M. Niculescu
2006 Miss A. Kleybanova & Miss A. Pavlyuchenkova
Miss A. Antoniychuk & Miss A. Dulgheru
2007 Miss A. Pavlyuchenkova & Miss U. Radwanska
Miss M. Doi & Miss K. Nara